CONTEMPORARY PERSPECTIVES on RHETORIC

Second Edition

Sonja K. Foss

Karen A. Foss

Robert Trapp

WAVELAND
PRESS, INC.
Prospect Heights, Illinois

For information about this book, write or call:
    Waveland Press, Inc.
    P.O. Box 400
    Prospect Heights, Illinois 60070
    (708) 634-0081

Contents

Preface

Through this book, we hope to add to the conversation about rhetoric that has been continuing since the days of ancient Greece. Our contribution is to present the perspectives on rhetoric of eight contemporary thinkers—I.A. Richards, Richard Weaver, Stephen Toulmin, Chaim Perelman, Ernesto Grassi, Kenneth Burke, Michel Foucault, and Jürgen Habermas.

We believe our presentation of their ideas here is useful in several ways. First, we have included three scholars—Grassi, Foucault, and Habermas—whose contributions to rhetoric only recently have begun to be studied within the discipline of speech communication. We hope our inclusion of these three will make them accessible to larger numbers of people and will open up new possibilities for the study of rhetoric based on their works.

Second, rather than providing excerpts from the works of these eight scholars, we have chosen to summarize their ideas about rhetoric. While we believe that reading at least the major works of these scholars is important for anyone seriously interested in their perspectives on rhetoric, we believe that reading an overview of their ideas will make tackling the various writings in their original form easier.

In addition, we have included biographical information on the eight individuals because, more often than not, their life experiences were influential in shaping the perspectives they take on rhetorical thought. We hope to offer, then, a holistic view of their lives and works in order to provide a more complete understanding of their notions about rhetoric.

Furthermore, because we are not interested in advocating any single approach to the study of rhetoric, we do not suggest categories for or groupings of the eight individuals around certain themes or areas of emphasis. We believe such an approach tends to restrict unnecessarily the scope and applicability of their ideas. This does not mean we avoid any mention of particular perspectives or the uses to which they might be put. On the contrary, we begin, in Chapter One, by summarizing the perspectives important to the rhetorical paradigm from ancient times to the contemporary period. We arrange the chapters about the individual thinkers not according to pre-established perspectives but in the order of the appearance of each rhetorician's first major work relevant to rhetoric. Readers thus should gain a sense of how the contemporary conversation about rhetoric emerged and developed. In Chapter Ten, we provide summaries of the feminist, Afrocentric, and Asian challenges to this conversation. In our last chapter, we pull out some common threads that seem to emerge from the works of the eight writers and the various challenges to the rhetorical tradition that suggest directions in which current rhetorical thinking is moving.

Finally, we have included an extensive bibliography at the end of the book that lists works by and about all eight individuals. We hope this list will serve as a useful resource for readers interested in pursuing the conversation on rhetoric of which the eight writers are a part.

We see this book as useful primarily as a resource about rhetoric and as a textbook in courses in rhetorical theory. It also has value for a variety of other disciplines, including English and philosophy, since many of these scholars' works bear on these fields as well as on rhetoric. It also may serve as the foundation for a rhetorical criticism course, since most critical methods are grounded in many of the ideas presented by these eight scholars.

Just as the development of rhetorical thought is an ongoing conversation, the process of writing this book was as well, and many people were involved in it. We are indebted, first of all, to the scholars included in this book— I.A. Richards, Richard Weaver, Stephen Toulmin, Chaim Perelman, Ernesto Grassi, Kenneth Burke, Michel Foucault, and Jürgen Habermas—whose writings, of course, enabled this book to be. Special thanks to Grassi and to members of Perelman's family—Mme. F. Perelman and Noemi Mattis— who helped in varying ways by supplying biographical material, unpublished sources, photographs and, in Grassi's case, by granting an interview and reading drafts of the chapter about him. Others contributed by commenting on various chapters: Molefi Asante, Lewis Bright, Wayne Brockriede, Brant Burleson, George Cheney, Martha Cooper, Robert Martin, and Karen Massetti-Miller. We are particularly grateful to Mary Garrett for her contribution of the section on Asian rhetoric in Chapter Ten.

We also would like to thank those who helped in various stages of the preparation of this book. The following individuals helped us locate sources: Eric Berson, Wayne Brockriede, Meryl Anne Fingrutd, Walter Fisher, Peg Ingolia, Richard Johannesen, Marla Kanengieter, Niki Lilienthal, Noemi Mattis, Richard Rieke, John Paul Russo, Craig Schultz, Giorgio Tagliacozzo, Donald Phillip Verene, David Werling and Daniel Wildeson. Belle Edson, Brad Golphenee, Dorothy Mettee, Kathaleen Reid, and Nancy Reist helped check the accuracy of the sources included in the bibliography. Polly Weaver Beaton, Noemi Mattis, Mme. F. Perelman, John Paul Russo, Julie Yingling, Beacon Press, the Intercollegiate Studies Institute, Random House, and the University of California Press were helpful in securing photographs of the eight scholars. Stephen Littlejohn, Bonnie Mesinger, Marianne Pennekamp, and Roswitha Kima Smale helped translate correspondence from Grassi, and Susan Stakel translated correspondence to Foucault. We also are indebted to David Baker for his drawing of the dog in Chapter Two and Sharon Bracci Blinn, for her preparation of the index.

Our institutions also provided support in various forms for this project. At Humboldt State University, the HSU Foundation funded a visit to Germany to interview Grassi, several Affirmative Action Faculty Development grants provided release time from teaching as well as money for supplies, and the Department of Speech Communication provided temporary help funds for a research assistant. The University of Denver provided an Arts and Sciences Faculty Development Grant for release time from teaching and funds for research assistants. Mary Rogers and a very cooperative staff at the Interlibrary Loan Office of Penrose Library at the University of Denver and David Shocklee at the Interlibrary Loan Office of Pius XII Library at St. Louis University also were very helpful; without them, we would have been unable to check many of the bibliographic citations for accuracy.

Special thanks to our publishers, Neil Rowe and Carol Rowe, for their support and confidence; and to our reviewer, Richard L. Johannesen, for his insightful comments, dedication to the project, and continual encouragement. Above all, we are grateful for the love, encouragement, and support of our families, Hazel M. Foss, Anthony J. Radich, Stephen W. Littlejohn, Raye Trapp and Robert W. Trapp, Erin Trapp, Judy Bowker, Hilary Jones, and Parker Jones.

1

Perspectives
on the
Study of Rhetoric

When we hear the word "rhetoric" used today, the meaning frequently is pejorative. More often than not, it refers to talk without action, empty words with no substance, or flowery, ornamental speech. A typical use of the term is the headline of a newspaper article describing the first few months of George Bush's Presidency: "The President is Long on Rhetoric and Short on Cash."[1] The writer argues that Bush has offered Americans "soaring rhetoric" without the resources to implement the ambitious new plans and programs.

Rhetoric, however, should not engender only negative connotations for us. In the Western tradition, rhetoric has a long and distinguished history as an art dating back to classical Greece and Rome. Although our focus in this book is on contemporary treatments of rhetoric, we will begin with a general overview of the rhetorical tradition. We have chosen to organize this review around individuals or groups of thinkers who have made important contributions to rhetoric throughout various historical eras. This approach is in keeping with the chapters that follow, in which we examine contemporary ideas about rhetoric through the works of eight individuals. We are aware that there are a variety of ways to write the history of rhetoric, with each construction leading to a different set of insights about the nature and function of rhetoric.[2]

A Brief History of Rhetorical Thought

The art of rhetoric is said to have originated in the fifth century B.C. with Corax of Syracuse. A revolution on Syracuse, a Greek colony on the island of Sicily, in about 465 B.C., was the catalyst for the formal study of rhetoric. When the tyrannical dictators on the island were overthrown and a democracy was established, the courts were deluged with conflicting property claims: was the rightful owner of a piece of land its original owner or the one who had been given the land during the dictator's reign? The Greek legal system

1

required that citizens represent themselves in court—they could not hire attorneys to speak on their behalf as we can today. The burden, then, was on the claimants in these land disputes to make the best possible case and to present it persuasively to the jury.

Corax realized the need for systematic instruction in the art of speaking in the law courts and wrote a treatise called the "Art of Rhetoric." Although no copies of this work survive, we know from later writers that the notion of probability was central to his rhetorical system. He believed that a speaker must argue from general probabilities or establish probable conclusions when matters of fact cannot be established with absolute certainty. He also showed that probability can be used regardless of the side argued. For instance, to argue that someone convicted of driving under the influence of alcohol probably is guilty if arrested for a second time on the same charge is an argument from probability. But so is the opposing argument—that the person convicted once will be especially cautious and probably will not get into that same situation again. In addition to the principle of probability, Corax contributed the first formal treatment of the organization of speeches. He argued that speeches consist of three major parts—an introduction, an argument or proof, and a conclusion—an arrangement that was elaborated on by later writers about rhetoric.[3]

Corax's pupil, Tisias, is credited with introducing Corax's rhetorical system to mainland Greece. With the coming of rhetorical instruction to Athens and the emerging belief that eloquence was an art that could be taught, the rise of a class of teachers of rhetoric, called sophists, was only natural. The word *sophos* means knowledge or wisdom, so a sophist was essentially a teacher of wisdom. Sophistry, not unlike rhetoric, has a tarnished reputation, so that today we associate the sophists with fallacious or devious reasoning.

The Greeks' distrust of the sophists was due to several factors. First, the sophists were itinerant professors and often foreigners to Athens, and some distrust existed simply because of their foreign status. They also professed to teach wisdom or excellence, a virtue that traditionally the Greeks believed could not be taught. In addition, the sophists charged for their services, a practice not only at odds with tradition, but one that made sophistic education a luxury that could not be afforded by all. This in itself may have generated some ill feelings. In large part, however, the continuing condemnation accorded the sophists can be attributed to an accident of history—the survival of Plato's dialogues. Plato, to whom we will return shortly, stood in adamant opposition to the sophists, and several of his dialogues make the sophists look silly indeed.[4] While Plato's views now are considered unjustified in large part, an anti-sophistic sentiment nevertheless was perpetuated in his dialogues that has continued to the present day.[5]

Protagoras of Abdera (c. 480-411 B.C.) is called the initiator of the sophistic movement. He is remembered for the statement, "Man is the measure of all things," which indicates the interest the sophists as a group placed on the study of humanity as the perspective from which to approach the world. This phrase also suggests the relative position many of the sophists accorded to truth: absolute truth was unknowable and perhaps nonexistent and had to be established in each individual case.[6] A second sophist deserving of mention is Gorgias, who was the subject of one of Plato's disparaging dialogues on the sophists and their brand of rhetoric. Originally from Sicily, Gorgias established a school of rhetoric in Athens and became known for his emphasis on the poetic dimensions of language. He also is called the father of impromptu speaking because this was a favored technique at his school.[7]

Another sophist whose work is significant in the history of rhetorical thought is Isocrates (436-338 B.C.). He began his career as a speechwriter for those involved in state affairs because he lacked the voice and nerve to speak in public. In 392 B.C., he established a school of rhetoric in Athens and advocated as an ideal the orator active in public life. He believed that politics and rhetoric could not be separated; both disciplines were needed for participation in the life of the state. In addition, unlike many other teachers of his day, Isocrates encouraged his students to learn from other teachers — to take instruction with those best qualified to teach them.[8]

The sophists envisioned an incomplete, ambiguous, and uncertain world, interpreted and understood by means of language. According to the sophists, truth and reality do not exist prior to language but are creations of it. In his encomium on Helen of Troy, Gorgias captured the sophists' view of language: "Speech is a powerful lord, . . . it can stop fear and banish grief and create joy and nurture pity."[9] The sophists valued figurative and poetic language in particular because of its capacity to appeal directly to the senses through images, thus providing alternative possibilities for seeing and doing.

While the sophists offered the beginnings of a philosophical position on rhetoric, the codification of rhetoric was left to those who followed them. The work of the Greek philosopher, Plato (427-347 B.C.), provided the foundation for such developments, although paradoxically, he also is remembered as one of the great opponents of rhetoric. Plato was a wealthy Athenian who rejected the ideal of political involvement in favor of philosophy after the death of his teacher and mentor, Socrates. At his school, the Academy, he espoused a belief in philosophical thought and knowledge, or dialectic, and rejected any form of relative knowledge or opinions as unreal. Thus, he opposed the practical and relative nature of rhetoric advocated by the sophists.

The two dialogues in which Plato's views on rhetoric emerge most clearly are the *Gorgias* and the *Phaedrus*. In the *Gorgias*, Plato set Gorgias and others against Socrates in order to distinguish true from false rhetoric, or the rhetoric as practiced by the sophists from an ideal rhetoric grounded in philosophy.

Plato faulted rhetoric for ignoring true knowledge; for failing to work toward the good, which for Plato was the end toward which all human pursuits should be directed; and because it was a technique or knack rather than an art: "[R]hetoric seems not to be an artistic pursuit at all, but that of a shrewd, courageous spirit which is naturally clever at dealing with men; and I call the chief part of it flattery. It seems to me to have many branches and one of them is cookery, which is thought to be an art, but according to my notion is no art at all, but a knack and a routine."[10]

In Plato's later dialogue, the *Phaedrus*, he used three speeches on love as analogies for his ideas about rhetoric. The first two speeches illustrate the faults of rhetoric as practiced in contemporary Athens: either it fails to move listeners at all or it appeals to evil or base motives. With the third speech, however, which Plato had Socrates deliver, he articulated an ideal rhetoric. It is based first and foremost on knowing the truth and the nature of the human soul: "any man who does not know the truth, but has only gone about chasing after opinions, will produce an art of speech which will seem not only ridiculous, but no art at all."[11] In addition to his concern for content, Plato also commented on organization, style, and delivery in the *Phaedrus*, thus paving the way for a comprehensive treatment of all areas of rhetoric.

Plato's student, Aristotle (384-322 B.C.), was responsible for first systematizing rhetoric into a unified body of thought. In fact, his *Rhetoric* often is considered the foundation of the discipline of speech communication. While Aristotle could not avoid the influence of Plato's ideas, he diverged significantly from his teacher in his treatise on rhetoric.

Aristotle was a scientist trained in classification, and this orientation emerges in the *Rhetoric*. Rather than attempting a moral treatise on the subject, as did Plato, Aristotle sought to categorize objectively the various facets of rhetoric, which he defined as "the faculty of discovering in the particular case what are the available means of persuasion."[12] The result was a philosophic and pragmatic treatise that drew upon Plato's ideas as well as on the sophistic tradition.

Aristotle devoted a large portion of the *Rhetoric* to invention, or the finding of materials and modes of proof to use in presenting those materials to an audience. He dealt as well, however, with style, organization, and delivery, or the pragmatic processes of presentation. Thus, he incorporated what now are considered to be the major canons of rhetoric that have formed the parameters of its study for centuries. The canons consist of invention, or the discovery of ideas and arguments; organization, or the arrangement of the ideas discovered by means of invention; elocution or style, which involves the linguistic choices a speaker must make; and delivery, or the presentation of the speech. Memory is the fifth canon, although Aristotle made no mention of it.

No major rhetorical treatises survived in the two hundred years after Aristotle's *Rhetoric*. This was a time of increasing Roman power in the Mediterranean, and not surprisingly, the next extant work on rhetoric was a Latin text, the *Ad Herennium*, written about 100 B.C. The Romans were borrowers and, as with most other aspects of Greek culture, they adopted the basic principles of rhetoric developed by the Greeks. The Romans were practical people, however, and the more pragmatic aspects of rhetoric were the ones that appealed most to them. They added little that was new to the study of rhetoric but rather organized and refined it as a practical art.

The *Ad Herennium* appears to be a representative Roman text in that it is essentially Greek in content and Roman in form. A discussion of the five canons constitutes the essence of this schoolboys' manual, but the practical aspects, not their theoretical underpinnings, are featured. The systematization and categorization that characterized the *Ad Herennium*'s approach to rhetoric were typical of the Roman treatises that followed.[13]

Cicero (106-43 B.C.) represents the epitome of Roman rhetoric, since in addition to writing on the art of rhetoric, he was himself a great orator. His earliest treatise on the subject was *De Inventione* (87 B.C.), which he wrote when only twenty years old. Although he considered it an immature piece in comparison to his later thinking on the subject, it offers another model of the highly prescriptive nature of most Roman rhetorical treatises.

Cicero's major work on rhetoric was *De Oratore* (55 B.C.), in which he attempted to restore the union of rhetoric and philosophy by advocating that rhetoric be taught as the single art useful for dealing with all practical affairs. He drew heavily on Isocrates' ideas in advocating an integration of natural ability, comprehensive knowledge of all the liberal arts, and extensive practice in writing. As a practicing orator, Cicero developed the notion of style more fully than did his predecessors and devoted virtually an entire treatise, *Orator* (46 B.C.), to distinguishing three types of style—the plain, the moderate, and the grand.[14]

A final Roman rhetorician deserving of mention is the Roman lawyer and educator, M. Fabius Quintilian (35-95 A.D.). In his *Institutes of Oratory* (93 A.D.), Quintilian described the ideal training of the citizen-orator from birth through retirement. He defined the orator as "the good man speaking well," and his approach was not rule bound as were many Roman rhetorics.[15] He was eclectic and flexible, drawing from Plato, Aristotle, Isocrates, and Cicero and also integrating his own teaching experiences into traditional theory. His work was so systematic that it not only serves as an excellent synthesis of Greek and Roman rhetorical thought, but it was an important source of ideas on education throughout the Middle Ages.

With the decline of democracy in Rome, rhetoric entered an era when it essentially was divorced from civic affairs. A series of emperors were in power, and anyone who spoke publicly in opposition to them was likely to be punished. Rhetoric, then, was relegated to a back seat and became an art concerned with style and delivery rather than with content. This period, from about 150 to 400 A.D., often is referred to as the Second Sophistic because of the excesses of delivery and style similar to those for which the early sophists were criticized.

The Middle Ages (400-1400 A.D.) followed the Second Sophistic, and during this period, rhetoric became aligned with preaching, letter writing, and education. The concern with preaching as an oratorical form might be said to have begun with St. Augustine (354-430 A.D.). Many call Augustine a bridge between the classical and medieval periods; nevertheless, he is the only major thinker on rhetoric associated with the Middle Ages. As Christianity became increasingly powerful, rhetoric was condemned as a pagan art; many Christians believed that the rhetorical ideas formulated by the pagans of classical Greece and Rome should not be studied and that possession of Christian truth was accompanied by an automatic ability to communicate that truth effectively. St. Augustine, however, had been a teacher of rhetoric before converting to Christianity in 386. Thus, in his *On Christian Doctrine* (426), he argued that preachers need to be able to teach, to delight, and to move— Cicero's notion of the duties of the orator—and that to accomplish the aims of Christianity, attention to the rules of effective expression was necessary.[16] Because St. Augustine believed such rules were to be used only in the expression of truth, he revitalized the philosophic basis of rhetoric that largely had been ignored since Quintilian.

Letter writing was another form in which rhetoric found expression during the Middle Ages. Many political decisions were made privately through letters and decrees; in addition, letter writing became a method of record keeping for both secular and religious organizations as they increased in size and complexity. Letter writing, too, was necessary in order to bridge the distances of the medieval world, which no longer consisted of a single center of culture and power as was the case with the classical period.[17] Thus, principles of letter writing, including the conscious adaptation of salutation, language, and format to a particular addressee, were studied as rhetoric.

Finally, rhetoric played a role in education in the Middle Ages as one of the three great liberal arts. Along with logic and grammar, rhetoric was considered part of the *trivium* of learning, much as our three Rs of reading, writing, and arithmetic function today.[18] While the emphasis shifted among these arts from time to time, each was treated in a highly practical rather than a theoretic manner.

The Renaissance, from 1400 to 1600, signalled the end of the Middle Ages and gave rise to Humanism, a movement that encompassed a diverse group of thinkers and writers. While the term ''humanism'' today has a broad meaning—concern for and interest in humans and their activities—during the Renaissance, it referred to a scholarly interest in the learning and languages of classical antiquity, especially in the fields of history, moral philosophy, poetry, and rhetoric. The movement began and reached its height in Italy, so we will focus here on the Italian Humanists.

For the most part, the Italian Humanists were the professional successors of the medieval monks who had served as letter writers and secretaries— copying rediscovered texts from antiquity and recording the deeds of the present. But unlike the monks who lived and worked in seclusion, the Humanists were active participants in civic life; they were lawyers, historians, grammarians, and teachers as well as intellectuals and scholars. Thus, while required to perform technical writing as part of their professions, they pursued philosophical and literary interests in their leisure time and developed a theory of rhetoric not unlike that of the sophists.[19]

While both the Middle Ages and the Renaissance rhetorics have as a foundation the rediscovery of classical texts—in particular those of Cicero— each epoch selected different themes and forms of discourse for study and emulation. The medievalists concentrated on Cicero's formal speeches as examples of the judicial rhetoric that dominated Roman rhetorical theory, while the Italian Humanists of the Renaissance chose to attend to Cicero's letters and dialogues.[20] Consistent with this emphasis, the Humanists adopted informal rhetorical modes such as letters and dialogues for the expression of their philosophical ideas. These formats allowed them to present critical or controversial ideas ambiguously—not necessarily claiming responsibility for the point of view expressed—thus avoiding censure from authorities and other possible recriminations.

Interested in the human world as constructed through language, rather than in the natural world, the Humanists gave the human as knower a central position. They highlighted the world of human culture and language, believing and delighting in the power of the word not only because it gives those with a command of it special advantage in practical affairs but because of its inherent capacity to disclose the world to humans.[21] The Italian Humanists believed rhetoric, not philosophy, to be the primary discipline because it is through language that humans gain access to the world. Poetry, not the rational proofs of logic, was considered the original source of intelligibility and inspiration, capable of transforming the world.

Francesco Petrarcha (1304-1374), the Italian poet and essayist, is perhaps the best known member of the Italian Humanists. Particularly interested in ancient Roman literature, he revived the style of great Roman writers in his own works. Coluccio Salutati (1331-1374) was a prominent disciple of Petrarch; among his works is *De laboribus Herculis*, in which he argued that only through poetry does human history emerge. Lorenzo Valla (1407-1457) scholar, polemicist, and pamphleteer—is another representative of Italian Humanism. In his *De ver falsoque bono*, he argued for privileging everyday language over formal, arcane usage, suggesting values of rhetorical accessibility, flexibility, and responsiveness. The work of Giambattista Vico (1668-1774) often is seen as the culmination of Italian Humanist thought, although he was separated from the mainstream of Humanism by almost a century. We will see Vico's influence, in particular, on Ernesto Grassi in Chapter Six, when we discuss his efforts to revitalize the ideas of the Italian Humanists.

A second trend in rhetoric also began during the Renaissance—a trend that dominated the theories of rhetoric to follow. Rationalism, represented by the work of Peter Ramus (1515-1572) and René Descartes (1596-1650), sought objective, scientific truths that would exist for all time. Not surprisingly, the rationalists had little patience for rhetoric: while poetry and oratory might be aesthetically pleasing, they were seen as having no connection to science and truth.

Ramus was a French scholar who made rhetoric subordinate to logic by placing invention and organization under the rubric of logic and leaving rhetoric with only style and delivery.[22] This dichotomizing and departmentalizing of knowledge made for easy teaching, and Ramus' taxonomy was perpetuated for generations through the educational system. Descartes believed that in order to reach certain knowledge, the foundations of thought provided by others had to be abandoned.[23] He was willing to accept only that which would withstand all doubt. Thus, he rejected truths established in speech or in the course of social or political action. Language became only a means of communicating the truth once it was discovered, not a powerful sphere in which human life emerges.

Dominated by the rationalism instituted by Descartes and Ramus, modern rhetoric continued to promote the importance of science and philosophy over rhetoric. Francis Bacon (1561-1626) was a prominent figure of the modern period. He was concerned with the lack of scholarly progress during the Middle Ages and sought to promote a revival of secular knowledge through an empirical examination of the world. He introduced ideas about the nature of sensory perception, arguing that our sensory interpretations are highly inaccurate and should be subjected to reasoned, empirical investigation. Likewise, he rejected narratives, myths, and fables as highly inaccurate tales of the past from which a rational humanity should be freed. His definition of rhetoric suggests his effort to bring the power of language under rational control: "the duty of rhetoric is to apply Reason to Imagination for the better moving of the will."[24] Bacon, then, furthered the scientific approach to the study of rhetoric that would undergird the three strands of modern rhetorical thought.

Three trends in rhetoric characterized the modern period—epistemological, belletristic, and elocutionist. Epistemology is the study of the origin, nature, methods, and limits of human knowledge. Epistemological thinkers sought to recast classical approaches in terms of modern developments in psychology. They attempted to understand rhetoric in relation to underlying mental processes and contributed to the development of a rhetoric firmly grounded in a study of human nature.

George Campbell (1719-1796) and Richard Whately (1758-1859) exemplify the best of the epistemological tradition. Campbell was a Scottish minister, teacher, and author of *The Philosophy of Rhetoric* (1776). He drew on Aristotle, Cicero, and Quintilian as well as the faculty psychology and empiricism of his times. Faculty psychology attempted to explain human behavior in terms of five powers or faculties of the mind—understanding, memory, imagination, passion, and will—and Campbell's definition of rhetoric was directed to these faculties: "to enlighten the understanding, to please the imagination, to move the passions, or to influence the will."[25] Campbell's approach to evidence suggests his ties to the rational, empirical approach to knowledge gaining prominence in his day. He distinguished three types of evidence—mathematical axioms, derived through reasoning; consciousness, or the result of sensory stimulation; and common sense, an intuitive sense shared by virtually all humans.

Richard Whately, like Campbell, was a preacher, and his *Elements of Rhetoric*, published in 1828, often is considered the logical culmination of Campbell's thought.[26] His view of rhetoric was similar to Campbell's in its dependence on faculty psychology, but he deviated in making argumentation the focus of the art of rhetoric: "The *finding* of suitable arguments to prove a given point, and the skilful [sic] *arrangement* of them, may be considered as the immediate and proper province of Rhetoric, and of that alone."[27] He also is remembered for his analysis of presumption and burden of proof, which paved the way for modern argumentation and debate practices. The epistemologists, then, combined their knowledge of classical rhetoric and contemporary psychology to create rhetorics based on an understanding of human nature. In this, they offered audience-centered approaches to rhetoric and paved the way for contemporary concerns with audience analysis.

The second direction rhetoric took in the modern period is known as the belles lettres movement; the term, in French, literally means "fine or beautiful letters." It referred to literature valued primarily for its aesthetic qualities more than for its informative value. Belletristic rhetorics were distinguished by their breadth—rhetoric was considered to consist not only of spoken discourse but of writing and criticism as well. In addition, the scholars of this school believed that all the fine arts, including rhetoric, poetry, drama, music, and even gardening and architecture, could be subjected to the same critical standards.[28] Thus, the critical component to rhetoric gained an importance not seen in earlier approaches.

Hugh Blair (1718-1800) stands as a representative figure of the belletristic period. In his *Lectures on Rhetoric and Belles Lettres*, based on a series of lectures he delivered at the University of Edinburgh, he presented an overview of the relationship among rhetoric, literature, and criticism. One of his most innovative contributions was his discussion of taste, or the faculty that is capable of deriving pleasure from contact with the beautiful. Taste, according to Blair, is perfected when a sensory pleasure is coupled with reason—when reason can explain the source of that pleasure.[29] Blair's ideas on rhetoric proved extremely popular and laid the foundations for contemporary literary and rhetorical criticism.

The elocutionary movement, the third rhetorical trend of the modern period, reached its height in the mid-eighteenth century. It developed in response to the poor delivery styles of contemporary preachers, lawyers, and other public figures and because the canon of delivery had been neglected, for the most part, since classical times. Like the epistemologists, the elocutionists were concerned about contributing to a more scientific understanding of the human being and believed that their observations on voice and gesture—characteristics unique to humans—constituted one such contribution.[30] The elocutionists also sought to determine the effects of delivery on the various faculties of the mind, thus continuing the link with modern psychology. Despite a stated concern for invention, however, many elocutionary treatises were not much more than prescriptive and often highly mechanical techniques for the management of voice and gestures.

Gilbert Austin's guidelines are representative of the highly stylized approach of the elocutionists. He offered this advice to the speaker, for instance, about eye contact and volume: "He should not stare about, but cast down his eyes, and compose his countenance: nor should he at once discharge the whole volume of his voice, but begin almost at the lowest pitch, and issue the smallest quantity; if he desire to silence every murmur, and to arrest all attention."[31] As another example, James Burgh believed each emotion could be linked to a specific, external expression; he categorized seventy-one emotions and their particular manifestations. Thomas Sheridan (1719-1788), who wrote *A Course of Lectures on Elocution* in 1762, was perhaps the most famous elocutionist. Sheridan not only was in the forefront in terms of criticizing the speakers of his day, but he sought to establish a universal standard of pronunciation for the English language in addition to offering the usual techniques for delivery.[32]

The elocutionists have been criticized for their excesses in terms of style and delivery and for the inflexibility of their techniques. Their efforts to derive an empirical science of delivery based on observation, however, foreshadowed the use of the scientific method to study all aspects of human communication.

So far, we have been describing the development of rhetoric in Europe and Great Britain. Each of the trends had its counterparts in the approaches taken toward rhetoric in the United States. The earliest rhetorical instruction in the United States, offered at Harvard in the seventeenth century, was based on the work of Ramus. This emphasis on style and delivery persisted until the revival, in the next century, of a classical conception of rhetoric.

A System of Oratory, published by John Ward in 1759, did much to generate a renewed interest in the United States in the rhetorics of antiquity. Widely used as a text until the late eighteenth century, this book dealt with all of the classical canons—invention, organization, style, delivery, and memory— thus restoring invention to a place of primacy in rhetorical education.[33] The rediscovery of the classics prompted an increased attention to rhetoric in American colleges that lasted into the early years of the nineteenth century. Seen as a broad art of communication, rhetoric integrated ideas from a variety of areas and flourished in a curriculum that lacked rigid boundaries. Chairs of rhetoric were common and were held by some of the most respected American scholars. Among them was future President John Quincy Adams, who served as the first Boylston Professor of Rhetoric at Harvard in 1806 and published *Lectures on Rhetoric and Oratory* in 1810.

With the rise of the belles lettres and elocutionary movements, however, rhetoric again began to decline as a subject of study and a teaching area. Both of these movements emphasized style and aesthetic appreciation over issues of substance. Simultaneously, the college curriculum became more specialized. Separate departments formed, including departments of English, and there no longer was a place for rhetoric as a multidisciplinary art. A third factor also contributed to rhetoric's decline: colleges shifted from testing students orally to giving written examinations, thus making written skills more important than competence in public speaking.[34] All of these developments furthered the image of rhetoric as associated primarily with composition, style, and standards of usage. By the beginning of the twentieth century, then, the teaching of speech was provided in departments of English and clearly was seen as having a secondary role to the teaching of written composition.

A major shift again occurred in the development of rhetoric in the United States in 1910, when a small group of public speaking teachers, housed in English departments, broke away from the National Council of Teachers of English. Interested in restoring the richness and breadth of the study of rhetoric to their classrooms, these teachers established, in 1914, a new association called the National Association of Academic Teachers of Public Speaking.[35] This organization remains the national association for speech communication, although its name has undergone several changes since its inception. Today, it is called the Speech Communication Association.

The development of the new field of speech essentially followed the division in approach that first appeared in the Renaissance in the humanistic versus scientific debate. On one hand, there was what came to be called the Cornell school of rhetoric, whose beginnings can be traced to a graduate seminar dealing with classical texts offered by Everett Hunt in 1920. Proponents of this school believed the discipline should focus on public speaking or oratory, with an emphasis on classical principles and models from a humanistic perspective.

The Midwestern school of speech, associated with James O'Neill at the University of Wisconsin and Charles Woolbert at the University of Illinois, was influenced by the research methods of behavioral psychologists. Members of this school advocated specialized and scientific studies of the process or act of speaking, thus following in the footsteps of the rationalists in the Renaissance who sought scientific principles as the way to understand the world.[36] Both schools were concerned with recapturing the substance of communication for the discipline but disagreed on what that substance should be. The Midwestern and Cornell schools initiated a split between rhetoric and communication that survives today in some department names — Rhetoric and Communication, for example — as well as in departmental ideologies.

Yet another set of issues for the emerging discipline was prompted by World War II. An international concern with persuasion and propaganda arose during the War, with scholars from journalism, political science, sociology, and information institutes directing their attention to all aspects of rhetorical processes as part of the war effort. This multidisciplinary effort eventually resulted in the emergence of the field of mass communications.[37] As a new source of material about the communication process, the field of mass communications was bolstered by European critical theory, the result of the emigration of the Frankfurt School to New York during the War. Jürgen Habermas, the subject of Chapter Nine, is a member of the Frankfurt School, so we will return later to the contributions of critical theory to rhetoric.

A history of the recent developments in rhetoric would not be complete without returning to departments of English, from which speech departments first emerged. Not surprisingly, English scholars have moved away from a primary emphasis on the finished product of a composition to the composing process and the transaction between writer and audience involved in the process. English scholars, like those in speech, draw on a variety of disciplines for theoretical input about rhetoric, including linguistics, semiotics, semantics, psycholinguistics, anthropology, and biology. They formulate conceptual theories of rhetoric that investigate the possible relationships between thought and discourse as well as pragmatic ones that explore what humans do with discourse.[38] Whatever aspect of the rhetorical process receives attention, there is recognition that rhetoric is a "mode of approaching the phenomena of discourse''[39] and thus must deal with motives and substance as well as with forms and processes. I.A. Richards and Kenneth Burke, in different ways, sought to develop ''new rhetorics'' that would encompass the totality of the discursive process; we will follow the directions of their thought in later chapters.

The rapprochement of rhetorical, philosophical, literary, psychological, and mass communication studies, then, suggests yet another revival of interest in the study of rhetorical processes. Whether or not the scholars in these disciplines use the term ''rhetoric'' to define their interests, there is widespread concern for how symbols function—personally, socially, and epistemologically—in the human world. The eight individuals who follow represent the disciplinary diversity among those who study human symbols. The contemporary study of rhetoric is an eclectic one that has been and can be approached from an almost infinite number of starting points. Our next task, then, is to offer a definition of rhetoric that can serve as a common starting point from which to approach the ideas offered in the remainder of this text.

A Definition of Rhetoric

Because definitions are so commonplace and familiar, we tend to forget they are not a part of the natural world—that they are, in fact, human inventions. We fail to realize, for example, that the category ''mammal'' is a division that was invented by humans and that its definition, ''a warm-blooded animal with hair covering all or most of its body, the female of which produces milk to nurse the young,'' is an arbitrary human creation. When the biological taxonomy was invented, the categories could have been defined more broadly (so as to include more animals) or more narrowly (so as to include fewer animals). To create such definitions, some human being arbitrarily determines the characteristics of a category or a concept; those characteristics, then, determine whether particular cases legitimately fall within that category or concept.

Defining a concept is an arbitrary, human process that includes some cases while simultaneously excluding others. Still, the process of definition is an important one because our definitions determine which cases are legitimate examples of a concept and which are not. A narrow definition is advantageous because it leads us to focus on clear-cut examples of the concept but is disadvantageous because it leads us to exclude other important, if less clear-cut, cases. A broad definition is advantageous because it leads us to include important cases that a narrow definition might exclude but is disadvantageous because it leads us to include cases that are, at best, marginally legitimate cases of the concept. Wayne Booth's metaphor of fish and nets reminds us that just as too large a net will catch some fish we want to throw out, too small a net will cause us to miss some fish we might want to keep.[40] Thus, the breadth of the definition directly influences which cases are included and excluded in the concept.

One way to choose a definition of appropriate range is to consider the purposes of a definition. While the primary purpose of a definition is to tell us what the concept is, it also must tell us what it is not. Just as a biologist wants a definition of "animal" that distinguishes animals from plants, we need a definition of rhetoric that allows us to contrast rhetoric with things that are non-rhetorical. Thus, our goal ought to be to select a definition that meets two criteria: first, it should be broad enough to include all of the interesting and important examples; and second, it should be narrow enough to distinguish the rhetorical from the non-rhetorical.[41]

We have decided that our definition must recognize two senses of the term "rhetoric." In one sense, rhetoric is an action human beings perform, and in a second sense, it is a perspective humans take. As an action, rhetoric involves humans' use of symbols for the purpose of communicating with one another. As a perspective humans take, rhetoric involves focusing on symbolic processes. The ways we have defined both senses of the term "rhetoric" are fraught with difficulties, so let us begin by unpacking and explaining each of the two major parts of our definition.

Rhetoric as an Action Humans Perform

When we say rhetoric is an action humans perform when they use symbols for the purpose of communicating with one another, we are saying four things: (1) rhetoric is an *action*; (2) rhetoric is a *purposive* action; (3) rhetoric is a *symbolic* action; and (4) rhetoric is a *human* action. Although these four ideas are overlapping, for the sake of clarity, we will discuss each of them separately.

Action. Action is the key term because it subsumes the other three. In Chapter Seven, we will discuss Kenneth Burke's distinction between action and motion; the other three elements we have included here (human, purpose, symbol) are all a part of Burke's distinction between action and motion. When we engage in action, we are not being passive; we are making conscious decisions about what to do. When we engage in rhetorical action, not only do we make a conscious decision to communicate, but we also make conscious choices about the strategies we will employ.

Let's take a couple of examples to see whether or not the concept of action can help us distinguish between the rhetorical and the non-rhetorical. In the first case, let's say that someone goes to a doctor because she is suffering from pain in her chest and arm. After she explains the nature and location of the pain, the doctor diagnoses her condition as a heart attack. In the second case, the woman is awakened in the middle of the night by a severe pain in her arm and chest. An ambulance takes her to the hospital, where she is examined by a doctor. The doctor examines her heart rate and rhythm and concludes that she has suffered a heart attack. In the first example, she chose to explain her condition to the doctor, selecting strategies in an effort to make the nature and location of her pain clear to the doctor. This is an example of rhetorical action. In the second example, the woman communicated to her doctor through symptoms (heart rate and rhythm) that were directly connected to her illness. But the changes in the rate and rhythm of her heart beat were not conscious choices. They were directly connected to her physical condition. This is not an example of action and thus is not rhetorical.

Purposive Action. Some communication is purposive, and some is not. Rhetorical action has occurred when someone does something for the purpose of communicating to another person. When the United States deploys an aircraft carrier off the coast of a Central American nation to warn its government not to install a weapons system that could endanger North America, the United States has performed a rhetorical action. We have taken action designed to communicate our intentions to the government of another nation. If a United States reconnaissance plane *accidentally* strays over the Soviet Union without the purpose of communicating anything to the Soviet Union, the pilot is not engaged in rhetorical action.[42]

Symbolic Action. Communication is a system of signs. In the simplest sense, a sign communicates when it is connected to another object. A distorted heart rhythm is connected to a heart attack. The changing of the leaves in autumn is connected to the change in temperature. The word "kitchen" is connected to the place where we prepare our meals. Some signs are symbolic; others are not. A non-symbolic sign is inherently connected to its physical referent in the way that changes in heart rate and rhythm are connected to a heart attack and the changing leaves are connected to temperature. All of these events are communication, but none is rhetorical. A symbolic sign, in contrast, is only indirectly connected to its referent and is a human creation. The word "kitchen" has no natural relationship to the place where we prepare our meals; it was invented by someone who needed to refer to the place where meals were being prepared. Thus, rhetoric involves symbolic action or the use of arbitrary symbols to communicate with other people.

But how does the concept of symbolic action help us to distinguish the rhetorical from the non-rhetorical? All sorts of non-rhetorical ways of communicating exist. When a patient communicates his condition to his doctor with a cry of pain, his communication is symptomatic not symbolic. In a similar fashion, a barometer communicates the barometric pressure, the clouds in the sky warn us of rain, and a word processor beeps when an error is committed. All of these events are communication, but none is rhetorical.[43]

Human Action. As far as we know, humans are the only animals who create a substantial part of their reality through the use of symbols. Some people debate whether or not symbol use is a characteristic that distinguishes humans from all other species of animals, pointing to recent research with chimpanzees and gorillas in which these animals have been taught to communicate using American Sign Language or other kinds of signs. Although many of the people whose ideas we will discuss in this book argue that symbols are uniquely human, we believe that this debate is unresolved and perhaps unresolvable.

Fortunately, we can avoid much of the debate by reducing the scope of our claim. We claim that the difference between humans and other animals with regard to symbol usage involves such a *difference in degree* that whether or not it is also a *difference in kind* is largely irrelevant to the position that the human is the symbol-using animal. Even if certain primates can be taught signs that operate in some fundamentally symbolic ways, these species do not create any substantial part of their reality through their use of symbols. Accordingly, humans are animals who engage in action and who use rhetoric. Birds, bees, flowers, and trees communicate, but they do not communicate rhetorically.

How does the question of whether symbol use is uniquely human help us distinguish the rhetorical from the non-rhetorical? Quite simply, rhetoric is not found in nature. It is a human invention. Trees cannot use rhetoric, and trees are not rhetoric; however, people can use trees as a part of rhetorical action. For instance, Christmas trees are used in symbolic ways. Simply the act of bringing a tree into the house and decorating it symbolizes certain aspects of the Christmas holiday. But Christmas trees can be used to symbolize other meanings, as well. Some people choose real rather than artificial Christmas trees to symbolize their disdain for anything counterfeit. Some people keep a live Christmas tree in a pot that can be reused year after year to symbolize their respect for nature and their disdain for killing trees. Humans use all sorts of non-rhetorical objects in rhetorical ways, but only humans can use rhetoric. Rhetoric, then, is a *human* action.

In summary, people engage in rhetorical action when they use symbols for the purpose of communicating with one another. Another important sense of the term "rhetoric" exists as well.

Rhetoric as a Perspective Humans Take

Although rhetoric as an action humans perform is the most common meaning attributed to "rhetoric," another important sense involves rhetoric as a perspective humans take. To say that someone takes a "perspective" on something is to say that person has a particular way of viewing that object or concept.[44] A perspective is a set of conceptual lenses through which a person views the world. Just as a real set of lenses can color our world, a set of conceptual lenses can color the way we interpret a phenomenon. A person's religion, race, educational background, or personal philosophy are just a few examples of things that can become perspectives through which we view other objects and concepts. Say that two persons are examining fossil records for the purpose of understanding them. A person whose educational background is in anthropology will see the fossil record as a trace of the process of human evolution. A person whose religious background is in line with some types of Christian fundamentalism may see the remnants of animal species that were biologically similar to each other because they were created by the same God.

When we analyze the process of symbolism, we are taking a rhetorical perspective. The two key terms involved in this definition of rhetoric are "process" and "symbolism."

Process. We take a rhetorical perspective when we focus on the process rather than on the content of symbolism. Examples of how we take rhetorical perspectives are many and varied. Common examples include attempting to understand how a world view is created by the communication strategies of an anti-abortion group, attempting to understand the argumentative strategies of social scientists, analyzing the persuasive strategies of an evangelist, or even attempting to understand how an artist or an architect creates a symbolic message. Thus, adoption of a rhetorical perspective involves an interest in the analysis of the symbolic processes. We focus on the process of symbolism rather than the content when we analyze how the symbols work rather than what the symbols communicate.

The notion that a person focuses on the process of symbolism rather than on the content does not mean that content and process are separate and unrelated. We cannot analyze process without content because the process cannot be seen without its content. Similarly, since all content is produced by a process and that process is always a part of the content, we cannot understand content apart from form. Process and content are like the parts of a two-color mosaic; if either of them is taken away, the entire structure crumbles. Still, we can focus on one color in the mosaic and then switch our focus to the other color. For example, Donald N. McCloskey argues that the science of economics is a rhetorical process.[45] When he studies articles reporting the results of economic studies, he focuses on the rhetorical processes that economists use to persuade their audiences (other economists) instead of on the content as it relates to the field of economics. For McCloskey, the rhetorical process is in the foreground, while economics is in the background. A different economist, say Lawrence Summers, may read the same econometric study not because of interest in its rhetorical processes but because of interest in its content. Both persons read the same econometric study, but McCloskey takes a rhetorical perspective, while Summers takes an economic perspective.

Symbolism. We can focus on the process of symbolism in at least two ways: (1) by analyzing how people perform rhetorical action; or (2) by analyzing how people interpret symbols. The first way of taking a rhetorical perspective overlaps almost entirely with the first sense of rhetoric (performing a rhetorical action). If someone is performing a rhetorical action by telling a story about a small Midwestern town, I can take a rhetorical perspective on that action by analyzing the narrative strategies used. In this case, the two senses are overlapping. One person is performing a rhetorical action, while another person is using a rhetorical perspective to analyze that action.

The second way of taking a rhetorical perspective may not overlap with the first. We can analyze the symbolic interpretations of a deed that is non-symbolic from the perspective of the sender. In this case, the first person is taking a rhetorical perspective by analyzing a situation for its symbolic interpretation, even though the other person's action may have been committed for non-symbolic purposes. Let's return to the example we discussed earlier where a United States reconnaissance plane accidentally strayed over the territory of an unfriendly government. If the situation were truly accidental, the pilot was not performing a symbolic action. At the same time, a rhetorical critic might take a rhetorical perspective by analyzing how military movements can be used as warnings against certain actions. In this case, the critic has taken a rhetorical perspective by focusing on the symbolic interpretation of the U.S. action, even though that action was not committed for symbolic purposes.

This example of the reconnaissance plane illustrates how the two parts of our definition are different by showing how someone can take a rhetorical perspective on a non-rhetorical action. This and other examples of taking a rhetorical perspective on non-rhetorical objects raise the question of how we fulfill the second criterion for an adequate definition—how we distinguish the rhetorical from the non-rhetorical. According to our definition, no objects are inherently rhetorical. Rhetoric has a symbolic but not a material existence. Objects such as copies of speeches, billboards, songs, paintings, and trees are not rhetoric. They may be rhetorical artifacts—remnants or traces of rhetorical actions—but they are not rhetoric. Rhetoric is an action people perform or a perspective people take, but it is not an object.

We have attempted to define rhetoric as broadly as we can while still maintaining clear lines of demarcation between the rhetorical and the non-rhetorical. However, we realize that these lines of demarcation are clearer in the examples we have invented than they are in the real-world examples that students of rhetoric encounter every day. Regardless of how we try to provide guidelines to separate the rhetorical from the non-rhetorical, trying to decide whether the term "rhetoric" legitimately applies to this or that action occasionally will be problematic. In cases when we have difficulty distinguishing between the rhetorical and the non-rhetorical, we are still able to distinguish between "paradigm cases" and "peripheral cases" of rhetoric. Paradigm cases of rhetoric are those clear-cut examples that most obviously fit the criteria in our definition.[46] Peripheral cases are those that fit the definition ambiguously.

Paradigm cases of rhetoric include, for example, the use of the spoken word to persuade an audience. Examples include a lawyer arguing before a jury, a legislator attempting to persuade the legislative body to pass a major bill, a minister addressing a congregation, or a politician attempting to persuade the populace to vote for her. These paradigm cases can be contrasted with more peripheral cases of rhetoric, such as the songwriter whose work intentionally or unintentionally leads others to construct a particular view of the world or the artist's attempt to depict particular images that elicit certain responses by viewers.

We want to be careful not to imply that we believe our interest should be directed primarily to the paradigm cases rather than to the peripheral ones. The study of paradigm cases is preferable in certain circumstances, while the study of peripheral ones is appropriate in others. For instance, students of rhetoric interested in the use of argumentation and persuasion might profit from an examination of paradigm cases of rhetoric. They might examine public debates on important issues or study rhetoric in the courtroom. Others who are interested in some specific aspect of rhetoric might profit from the examination of peripheral cases that better illuminate those aspects of rhetoric. For instance, a scholar interested in the rationality of rhetoric might decide to examine a peripheral case of rhetoric such as scientific discourse, or a scholar interested in the use of metaphor might do well to examine the rhetoric of poetry. Peripheral cases of rhetoric, then, are not necessarily less important or less deserving of our attention than are paradigm ones—both offer significant information to the scholar of rhetoric, and both have their place.

We have defined rhetoric in two ways—as a particular type of action that humans perform and as a particular type of perspective that they take. While these two senses of rhetoric are neither exhaustive nor mutually exclusive, they are both important to the study of rhetoric. Although we have chosen to emphasize one of these senses (perspective) instead of the other (action) in the title of this book, we will deal with both senses of rhetoric. The eight scholars whose contributions to rhetoric we discuss here take a rhetorical perspective; at the same time, their ideas explain how people perform rhetorical action.

Contemporary Perspectives on Rhetoric

We have chosen to use the term "perspectives" rather than "theories" or "philosophies" to describe the contemporary views of rhetoric included in the chapters that follow. We prefer to see them as "perspectives" for two reasons. First, that term is consistent with our definition of rhetoric. Second, "theory" is frequently interpreted according to its use in the physical, biological, and social sciences. Used in this sense, "theory" implies a coherent body of knowledge that attempts to organize, explain, and predict some aspect of the world. Since rhetorical theories are aimed more at explanation than prediction, we decided to avoid confusion by using the term "perspective" instead.[47] Similarly, while some of the ideas we discuss clearly are "philosophies" in that they deal with questions about the nature of reality, knowledge, or values, others do not. Thus, "perspective" is the most descriptive term we could find to organize and present the work of these eight thinkers.

Rationale for Selection of Perspectives

Each of the writers discussed in the following chapters—I.A. Richards, Richard Weaver, Stephen Toulmin, Chaim Perelman, Ernesto Grassi, Kenneth Burke, Michel Foucault, and Jürgen Habermas—offers a different perspective on rhetoric. Richards and Burke, for instance, focus on the study of language as central to rhetoric. For Weaver and Perelman, however, values are a starting point for their examinations of rhetoric. The approaches to or perspectives on rhetoric provided by Toulmin, Grassi, Foucault, and Habermas might be described best as epistemological; for them, how we know and communicate based on that knowledge is of central concern. One also could see Toulmin, Weaver, and Perelman as taking an "argumentative" perspective on rhetoric, since they are concerned with the development of arguments as a means of persuasion. Our notion that people take different perspectives on rhetoric does not imply, then, that they are studying different subjects. Rather, because we believe that rhetoric is the study of how humans use symbols to communicate with one another, we find that many of the differences that appear to exist among the ideas of various scholars are differences in perspective rather than real disagreements.

Our decision to include the particular eight writers we did was not based simply on their illustrating a variety of perspectives on rhetoric. Neither was it based on a belief that they comprise a "necessary" or "best" list of rhetorical scholars. Our position is somewhere between these two. We do not believe there is anything sacred about our list of authors, and we realize that others well might have included different writers on rhetoric. The best way we know to justify our choices is to articulate the three standards we used in making our choices.

First, we agreed that each individual included should not only have some important things to say about rhetoric but should have developed a somewhat coherent body of knowledge relevant to the study of discourse. Because we could not include everyone who falls into this category, of course, additional criteria were needed for the selection process. The individuals we included here met one or both of two additional standards: they intended to develop a perspective (or theory or philosophy) on rhetoric, and people in our discipline see their thinking as contributing in important ways to the subject of rhetoric. The works of Richards, Weaver, Burke, Perelman, and Grassi are directed intentionally toward the development of perspectives on rhetoric; thus, they met the former standard. Toulmin, Foucault, and Habermas did not intend to write about rhetoric, but their works have been interpreted as relevant to its study by those in the discipline of speech communication. Thus, these writers met our last criterion.

In deciding on the order in which to place the eight writers in this book, we chose a chronological arrangement by date of major work dealing with rhetoric. In this way, the reader is able to gain a sense of the development and evolution of the various perspectives that constitute the study of contemporary rhetoric. A progression from a focus on specific aspects of rhetoric to a broad conception of rhetoric also emerges from this order. The earlier writers tended to single out a particular aspect for attention, while later writers, such as Burke, Foucault, and Habermas, have developed broader conceptions of rhetoric.

We begin with I. A. Richards, whose *The Meaning of Meaning*, co-authored with C. K. Ogden in 1923, focused on symbols and their meanings. Richard Weaver wrote *The Ethics of Rhetoric* in 1953, bringing a values perspective to the forefront. Toulmin published *The Uses of Argument* in 1958 and provided the discipline of speech communication with a new approach to the study of everyday argumentation. The next author is Chaim Perelman. His *The New Rhetoric*, co-authored with L. Olbrechts-Tyteca, was published in French in 1958 and translated into English in 1969. In it, he reconceptualized the rhetoric of classical times. Ernesto Grassi's work only recently has begun to be translated into English, and a pivotal work for English readers of Grassi is *Rhetoric as Philosophy*, a collection of essays by Grassi published in 1980. A more accurate dating of Grassi's ideas, however, is 1970, when he published *Macht des Bildes, Ohnmacht der rationale Sprache: zur Rettung d. Rhetorischen [The Authority of Form and the Demise of Rational Speech: The Rescue of Rhetoric]*. This book outlined the beliefs that are reiterated in all of his recent works.

Kenneth Burke, a prolific writer, could fit virtually anywhere in this grouping. We have placed him next, although his two major treatises on rhetoric—*A Grammar of Motives* and *A Rhetoric of Motives*—were published in 1945 and 1950 respectively. Not only is he a writer on rhetoric who presents an encompassing treatment of the topic, but his works are perhaps valued even more today than they were when they first were published. Probably the strongest evidence of this are the Burke conferences, which bring together scholars from a variety of disciplines to discuss Burke's work and to honor his contributions to those disciplines.[48] Burke, then, remains an extremely current and vital figure in the study of contemporary rhetoric. Our next chapter deals with Foucault. While ideas about rhetoric are implicit in virtually all of his works, the first dating to 1954, two of his major works were made available in English in the 1970s—*The Order of Things* (1970) and *The Archaeology of Knowledge* (1972). We have placed Jürgen Habermas last because he published three important works dealing with rhetoric during the 1970s: *Knowledge and Human Interests* (1971), *Theory and Practice* (1973), and *Communication and the Evolution of Society* (1979). In addition, Habermas published four books in the 1980s, including his two volumes of *The Theory of Communicative Action*, evidence that he will continue his research in the area of communication in the years to come. The book ends with two chapters designed to encourage the exploration and synthesis of rhetorical perspectives. In Chapter Ten, we summarize three challenges to the Western rhetorical tradition offered by feminist, Afrocentric, and Asian perspectives. In Chapter Eleven, we suggest some general questions for exploring the rhetorical process and summarize directions to the study of rhetoric in the speech communication field.

We are excited by the contributions the following eight writers have made and are making to the study of rhetoric. While they have their roots in the classical tradition of the ancient Greeks and Romans, they clearly are moving rhetorical scholarship in new directions. We hope that the summaries of their ideas that follow will intrigue you and motivate you to work with and to apply their ideas. Ultimately, we hope you, too, will contribute to the conversations about the nature and function of rhetoric begun by the classical rhetoricians and carried on by these writers.

Notes

[1] David Hoffman, "The President is Long on Rhetoric and Short on Cash," *San Francisco Chronicle*, July 26, 1989, p. 20.

[2] For a discussion of history as a process of composing discourse or constructing a narrative about rhetoric rather than simply recording facts that exist outside the human knower, see John Schilb, "The History of Rhetoric and the Rhetoric of History," *Pre/Text*, 7 (Spring/Summer 1986), 11-34.

[3] George Kennedy, *The Art of Persuasion in Greece* (Princeton, NJ: Princeton University Press, 1963), pp. 58-61; and Bromley Smith, "Corax and Probability," *Quarterly Journal of Speech*, 7 (February 1921), 13-42.

[4] Kennedy, *The Art of Persuasion in Greece*, pp. 13-15; and Lester Thonssen and A. Craig Baird, *Speech Criticism: The Development of Standards for Rhetorical Appraisal* (New York: Ronald, 1948), pp. 36-37.

[5] That Plato's negative view of the sophists was unjustified has been asserted by numerous scholars. His views in the *Gorgias*, in particular, have come under frequent re-examination. See, for example, Bruce E. Gronbeck, "Gorgias on Rhetoric and Poetic: A Rehabilitation," *Southern Speech Communication Journal*, 38 (Fall 1972), 27-38; and Richard Leo Enos, "The Epistemology of Gorgias' Rhetoric: A Re-examination," *Southern Speech Communication Journal*, 42 (Fall 1976), 35-51.

[6] Kennedy, *The Art of Persuasion in Greece*, p. 13; and Philip Wheelwright, *The Presocratics* (Indianapolis: Odyssey, 1966), pp. 238-40.

[7] Thonssen and Baird, p. 38.

[8] Russell H. Wagner, "The Rhetorical Theory of Isocrates," *Quarterly Journal of Speech*, 8 (November 1922), 323-37; and William L. Benoit, "Isocrates on Rhetorical Education," *Communication Education*, 33 (April 1984), 109-20.

[9] Gorgias, *Encomium on Helen*, trans. George Kennedy, in *The Older Sophists*, ed. R. K. Sprague (Columbia: University of South Carolina Press, 1972), p. 52.

[10] Plato *Gorgias* 463.

[11] Plato *Phaedrus* 262.

[12] Aristotle *Rhetoric* 1.2 1355b. For a comparison of the rhetorics of Aristotle and Plato, see Everett Lee Hunt, "Plato and Aristotle on Rhetoric and Rhetoricians," in *Studies in Rhetoric and Public Speaking* (New York: Russell & Russell, 1962), pp. 3-60.

[13] George Kennedy, *The Art of Rhetoric in the Roman World* (Princeton, NJ: Princeton University Press, 1972), pp. 106-08.

[14] For a summary of Cicero's style, see Thomas R. King, "The Perfect Orator in *Brutus*," *Southern Speech Journal*, 33 (Winter 1967), 124-28.

[15] Thonssen and Baird, p. 92.

[16] James J. Murphy, "Saint Augustine and the Debate About a Christian Rhetoric," *Quarterly Journal of Speech*, 56 (December 1960), 400-10; and Saint Augustine *On Christian Doctrine* xvii, 34.

[17] Nancy L. Harper, *Human Communication Theory: The History of a Paradigm* (Rochelle Park, NJ: Hayden, 1979), p. 71; and James Murphy, *Rhetoric in the Middle Ages: A History of Rhetorical Theory from Saint Augustine to the Renaissance* (Berkeley: University of California Press, 1974).

[18] Donald Lemen Clark, *Rhetoric in Greco-Roman Education* (Westport, CT: Greenwood, 1957), p. 12.

[19] John F. Tinkler, "Renaissance Humanism and the *genera* eloquentiae," *Rhetorica*, 5 (Summer 1987), 279-309.

[20] Tinkler, p. 283.

[21] Samuel Ijsseling, *Rhetoric and Philosophy in Conflict: An Historical Survey* (The Hague: Martinus Nijhoff, 1976), p. 55.

[22] Wilbur Samuel Howell, *Logic and Rhetoric in England, 1500-1700* (New York: Russell & Russell, 1956), p. 148.

[23] Ijsseling, p. 64.

[24] Hugh C. Dick, ed., *Selected Writings of Francis Bacon* (New York: Modern Library, 1955), p. x; and Harper, pp. 100, 109.

[25] George Campbell, *The Philosophy of Rhetoric*, ed. Lloyd F. Bitzer (1776; rpt. Carbondale: Southern Illinois University Press, 1963), p. 1.

[26] Douglas Ehninger, "Introduction," in Richard Whately, *Elements of Rhetoric*, ed. Douglas Ehninger (1828; rpt. Carbondale: Southern Illinois University Press, 1963), p. xv.

[27] Whately, p. 39.

[28] James L. Golden, Goodwin F. Berquist, and William E. Coleman, *The Rhetoric of Western Thought*, 3rd ed. (1976; rpt. Dubuque: Kendall/Hunt, 1983), pp. 107-08.

[29] Hugh Blair, *Lectures on Rhetoric and Belles Lettres* (London: William Baynes, 1825), p. 24.

[30] Golden, Berquist, and Coleman, pp. 175-76.

[31] Gilbert Austin, *Chironomia or a Treatise on Rhetorical Delivery*, ed. Mary Margaret Robb and Lester Thonssen (1806; rpt. Carbondale: Southern Illinois University Press, 1966), p. 94.

[32] Thomas Sheridan, *A Course of Lectures on Elocution* (London: W. Strahan, 1762).

[33] Robert J. Connors, Lisa S. Ede, and Andrea A. Lunsford, "The Revival of Rhetoric in America," in *Essays on Classical Rhetoric and Modern Discourse*, ed. Robert J. Connors, Lisa S. Ede, and Andrea A. Lunsford (Carbondale: Southern Illinois University Press, 1984), p. 1.

[34] Connors, Ede, and Lunsford, pp. 3-4.

[35] George Gerbner and Wilbur Schramm, "Communications, Study of," *International Encyclopedia of Communications*, I, ed. Erik Barnouw (New York: Oxford University Press, 1989), 360.

[36] For descriptions of the Cornell and Midwestern schools, see W. Barnett Pearce, "Scientific Research Methods in Communication Studies and Their Implications for Theory and Research," in *Speech Communication in the Twentieth Century*, ed. Thomas W. Benson (Carbondale: Southern Illinois University Press, 1985), pp. 260-64.

[37] The emergence of the field of mass communications is described by James Carey, "Graduate Education in Mass Communication," *Communication Education*, 28 (1979), 282-93.

[38] For examples of three contemporary approaches to rhetoric within the field of English, see Walter H. Beale, *A Pragmatic Theory of Rhetoric* (Carbondale: Southern Illinois University Press, 1987); Frank J. D'Angelo, *A Conceptual Theory of Rhetoric* (Cambridge, MA: Winthrop, 1975); and James L. Kinneavy, *A Theory of Discourse: The Aims of Discourse* (New York: W.W. Norton, 1971).

[39] Donald C. Bryant, "Literature and Politics," in *Rhetoric, Philosophy, and Literature: An Exploration*, ed. Don M. Burks (West Lafayette, IN: Purdue University Press, 1978), p. 107.

[40] Wayne Booth, "The Scope of Rhetoric Today: A Polemical Excursion," in *The Prospect of Rhetoric*, ed. Lloyd F. Bitzer and Edwin Black (Englewood Cliffs, NJ: Prentice-Hall, 1971), pp. 93-114.

[41] Our readers may wonder why we chose to use the term "rhetoric" rather than "communication." Although in a very literal sense, the term "communication" is so broad that it can even include such non-rhetorical processes as slime growing on a rock (Frank Dance, "The 'Concept' of Communication," *Journal of Communication*, 20 (June 1970), 201-10), we believe that the terms as they are used by scholars in communication and speech communication departments are essentially synonymous terms. Gerald R. Miller, in *Speech Communication: A Behavioral Approach* (Indianapolis: Bobbs-Merrill, 1966), considers the terms interchangeable, as does Wayne E. Brockriede in "Dimensions of the Concept of Rhetoric," *Quarterly Journal of Speech*, 54 (February 1968), 1-18. For more contemporary examples, see Harper, p. 11; and Walter R. Fisher, "Narration as a Human Communication Paradigm: The Case of Public Moral Argument," *Communication Monographs*, 51 (March 1984), 1-22. The choice of the term—"rhetoric" or "communication"—seems to be a personal one, often stemming from the tradition of inquiry in which one is grounded. Scholars trained in the social-scientific areas of communication, for example, may prefer the term "communication," while those who gravitate toward more qualitative or critical methods of inquiry or who are rooted in the humanities and philosophy may tend to select the term "rhetoric."

[42] In contrast, the second part of our definition will show how others might take a rhetorical perspective on that and other non-rhetorical action.

[43] Because humans have highly developed symbol systems, our symbolic processes are even brought to bear on these symptomatic signs. For instance, while the height of a column of mercury in a barometer is a symptom (not a symbol) of the weight of the air in a column extending from the barometer to the highest point in the atmosphere, some human being invented the barometer and placed symbols (numbers corresponding to the height of the column of mercury) on it in order to allow us to talk symbolically about air pressure. Even though symptoms of the weather such as clouds and barometers are not inherently rhetorical, they are interpreted symbolically (thus rhetorically) by humans communicating with one another.

[44] We are using the term "perspective" in the same way that Brockriede and Fisher do. See Wayne Brockriede, "Arguing About Human Understanding," *Communication Monographs*, 49 (September 1982), 137-47; and B. Aubrey Fisher, *Perspectives on Human Communication* (New York: Macmillan, 1978), especially p. 51.

[45] Donald N. McClosky, *The Rhetoric of Economics* (Madison: University of Wisconsin Press, 1985).

[46] Our use of this term is consistent with the distinction offered by Daniel J. O'Keefe, "The Concepts of Argument and Arguing," in *Advances in Argumentation Theory and Research*, ed. J. Robert Cox and Charles Arthur Willard (Carbondale: Southern Illinois University Press, 1982), pp. 8-23.

[47] Barry Brummett, in "Rhetorical Theory as Heuristic and Moral: A Pedagogical Justification," *Communication Education*, 33 (April 1984), 97-107, proposes an interesting distinction between social-scientific and rhetorical theories of communication. His definition of rhetorical theory implies intent and actual application to experience: "a rhetorical theory is a form, pattern, or recipe, a statement in the abstract of how a person might experience a rhetorical transaction" (p. 103). A social-science theory, on the other hand, must consist of a set of systematic propositions that assert that some regularities exist in the world" (p. 98). His distinction, although quite specific, seems to confirm the distinction we are proposing between a theory as regarded in the social sciences and the notion of perspectives.

[48] The first Burke conference, sponsored by Temple University and the Speech Communication Association, was held in Philadelphia, March 6-8, 1984. The goals of the conference, as stated in the conference program, included "exploring affinities between Burke's writings and those of other contemporary theorists; examining the ways in which Burkean theory has been applied in the various disciplines; assessing the potential and the limitations of Burkean theory as a unifying force across disciplines; and celebrating 60 + years of scholarship and creative works." A second such conference, sponsored by The Kenneth Burke Society, was held May 4-7, 1990, in New Harmony, Indiana.

2

I. A. Richards

"What I feel is that if there is a way of doing things which is obviously much better than what anyone else has to offer then, in a bad enough emergency, everyone will jump at it. I've been only concerned to produce something really better than anyone else has."[1] This statement by I. A. Richards might be considered the motive for much of his work in the areas of rhetoric, linguistics, and literature. His concern was to help solve the problems he saw facing people, many of which seemed directly related to an inability to communicate effectively.

Ivor Armstrong Richards was born in Sandbach, Cheshire, in England, on February 26, 1893. An early interest in language developed when he became ill with tuberculosis in his early teens and read poetry for amusement during the period of recuperation. He pursued a college education at Magdalene College at Cambridge, intending to specialize in history. He turned from history, however, at the end of his first year, when he went to his advisor "one morning in a grim mood" and said he "didn't think History ought to have happened" and "didn't see why we should study it." His advisor then introduced him to C. K. Ogden, a senior, and as a result of their discussion, Richards decided to specialize instead in moral sciences or philosophy.

At Cambridge, Richards was supervised in his studies by the idealist philosopher J. M. E. McTaggart and the logician W. E. Johnson. But the most powerful influence on him was G. E. Moore, whose lectures on the philosophy of mind were not understood, for the most part, by the students in the class, including Richards. Moore re-awakened Richards' interest in language because Richards felt "something must be done to stop the leakage of information" or the lack of understanding in the classroom. Moore's questioning contributed as well to the development of his interest in language; Moore incessantly asked, "What do we mean?" and was convinced that few people possibly could *mean* what they *said*. Richards silently disagreed with him, believing that people could not possibly *say* what they *meant*.

Richards obtained a First Class in the Moral Science Tripos (the equivalent of a bachelor's degree) in 1915, left Cambridge, and suffered another bout with tuberculosis. While recovering in northern Wales, he became interested in mountaineering and found that he was "fairly good at floating up difficult rocks." When he had regained his health, he returned to Cambridge and studied biology, chemistry, psychology, and physiology with the intention of pursuing a medical career as a psychoanalyst.

In 1918, Richards met C. K. Ogden again, and they began to discuss language and meaning, outlining one of the books they were to co-author, *The Meaning of Meaning*. Ogden had been publishing a penny weekly digest of world news as an aid to the war, but he turned it into a quarterly journal, which he used as a means of publishing *The Meaning of Meaning*. Each issue of the quarterly contained a portion of the work; thus, Richards and Ogden wrote the book "in bits and pieces quarter by quarter."

Tired of living in poverty, or suffering from what Ogden called "Hand to Mouth Disease," Richards dropped his medical studies in 1919 and asked Mansfield Forbes, a professor at Clare College, to write some letters recommending him for a position as a professional mountaineering guide at Skye, an island of Scotland. After the letters were written, Forbes and Richards began to discuss literature. Two hours later, Forbes tore up the letters and invited Richards to lecture on the contemporary novel and the theory of criticism in the English School of Clare College, enabling him to "collect fifteen shillings a head from anyone who came six times to the course." He was appointed Lecturer in English and Moral Science in 1922 by his own college, Magdalene, and he became a Fellow of the College four years later.

Richards became interested in aesthetics as a result of an experience in the summer of 1920. He usually spent his summers in the Alps, but he suffered a fall on an early expedition and returned to Cambridge. There he ran into James Wood, a painter and a close friend of Ogden, and the three of them decided to form a triumvirate, sorting "out this art talk." The result was the co-authorship of *The Foundations of Aesthetics*, published in 1922.

Richards and Ogden's next project together was Basic English, a language composed of 850 English words that cover the needs of everyday life. While writing *The Meaning of Meaning*, they decided that everything could be said with under a thousand words simply by substituting descriptive phrases for specific words: if "a word can be defined in a descriptive phrase of not more than ten words, you can substitute the descriptive ten words for the word and get rid of it." Ogden spent a great deal of time talking to people who were experts in a variety of fields, finding out which words were essential and which could be dropped from the vocabulary. The result was his *General Basic English Dictionary*, in which more than 20,000 words are defined using the 850 words of Basic English.

Richards became interested in promoting Basic English as an international auxiliary language and a method for teaching English as a second language. He spent several years in China trying to establish Basic English as the method for teaching English there; he served as a visiting professor at Tsing Hua University in Peking in 1929-1930 and as director of the Orthological Institute of China from 1937 to 1938.

In 1939, Richards received an invitation from Harvard to direct the Commission of English Language Studies (later called Language Research) and to produce Basic English textbooks and train teachers in the method of Basic English. While working on these projects under a three-year endowment, he decided that television might be an important part of the teaching method because the eye and ear would be cooperating in the learning process. He received a grant from the Rockefeller Foundation to study cartooning and animation at Walt Disney's studios, where he worked on developing a universal simplified script in which various situations can be expressed. With his collaborator, Christine M. Gibson, Richards turned out a number of textbooks over the years for teaching Basic English in a variety of languages. Despite its promising beginnings, however, Basic English never was accepted as the standard method of teaching English in any country.

At the age of sixty, Richards added another dimension to his career when he began to write poetry. He was writing a play, *A Leak in the Universe*, and "it seemed definitely to require a lyrical component." He went on to write several volumes of poetry, including *Goodbye Earth and Other Poems* and *The Screens and Other Poems.*

Richards made his home in Cambridge, England, until his death on September 7, 1979. Mountaineering was a strong interest throughout his life, and with his wife, Dorothea Pilley Richards, he climbed the Matterhorn; Mont Blanc; Adam's Peak in Ceylon; Mount Hermon in Lebanon; Mt. Hood in Oregon; the Japanese Alps; the Canadian Rockies; the Andes; and mountains in China, Greece, and Alaska.[2] Richards' climbing has been called a metaphor for his intellectual life: " 'Poking about corners for something new' was said of him on Welsh rocks, but seems as true of the corners of his mind. . . . As he delighted in crossing a ridge to come down into a new valley, so we can see him in his critical works raiding across the ridges that divide one academic discipline from another, adventuring into new country."[3] This interdisciplinary approach can be seen clearly in Richards' ideas about rhetoric.

Objections to Traditional Rhetoric

Richards objects to the traditional view of rhetoric, a position evident in his statement that so "low has Rhetoric sunk that we would do better just to dismiss it to Limbo than to trouble ourselves with it."[4] Richards rejects the work of such traditional rhetorical theorists as Aristotle and Richard Whately, which provides the basis for much of the contemporary study of rhetoric, primarily because he believes it is largely irrelevant for the study of how rhetoric functions in the twentieth century. The "old" study of rhetoric revolved around learning a collection of rules about how to speak and write effectively, such as, "be clear, yet don't be dry; be vivacious, use metaphors when they will be understood not otherwise; respect usage; don't be long-winded, on the other hand don't be gaspy." The study of such rules, however, is not what the study of rhetoric should be: a "philosophic inquiry into how words work in discourse."[5]

A second major objection Richards makes to the old rhetoric is that its central theme is persuasion; it is "the theory of the battle of words and has always been itself dominated by the combative impulse." But persuasion is only one of many aims of rhetoric, among them exposition, and to narrow the study of rhetoric to only one function does not encourage scholars of rhetoric to study the larger problem of how language works.[6]

Proposal for a New Rhetoric

The traditional study of rhetoric, Richards believes, should be replaced by a view of rhetoric as "a philosophic discipline aiming at a mastery of the fundamental laws of the use of language."[7] Echoing the nineteenth-century rhetorical theorist, George Campbell, Richards defines rhetoric as " 'the art by which discourse is adapted to its end' " and sees its task to be "to distinguish the different sorts of ends, or aims, for which we use language, to teach how to pursue them separately and how to reconcile their diverse claims."[8] In short, rhetoric should be "a study of misunderstanding and its remedies." Such a rhetoric would offer explanations for questions such as how losses in communication can be measured, how good communication differs from bad communication, and how much of communication is distorted by habitual attitudes toward and outdated assumptions about words.[9]

Richards suggests that three major requirements must be met if a new rhetoric is to discover answers to these questions and truly to provide explanations for how discourse works. First, scholars must question and evaluate the assumptions of rhetoric and not simply accept as valid the assumptions it has inherited from other disciplines. Without such questioning, the study of rhetoric will rely on terminology, data, and presuppositions that may prevent the much-needed innovative and comprehensive examination of how discourse operates.

Second, Richards advocates that the study of rhetoric begin with an analysis of the smallest units for conveying meaning—words. This focus on words makes Richards' perspective very different from that of traditional scholars of rhetoric, whose focus was on arguments, speeches, and how such compositions of words function as a whole. Richards believes, however, that if we first understand how words function, we will be able to put together larger messages for whatever end we desire—whether to persuade, to explain, to create a particular relationship with an audience, or to write poetry.

Finally, a new rhetoric must be viewed and studied as holding a central place in the order of knowledge; it should not be seen as a discipline that is peripheral or irrelevant to other studies. Consequently, rhetoric could provide the core of the sound educational curriculum that Richards believes is missing today. Nothing is central and primary in the educational curriculum; nothing holds it together or provides a center around which all subjects studied can be grouped. The study of rhetoric—the "systematic study of *the inherent and necessary opportunities for misunderstanding* which language offers"— well might constitute this center. Such a study would involve a knowledge of how central intellectual terms such as "being," "have," "cause," and "same" can shift their meanings and thus give rise to varied misunderstandings and how misinterpretations in one field illuminate misinterpretations in others. The same problems in interpretation exist in all fields, and a discovery of patterns of meaning and misunderstanding in different areas of study would provide a unifying theme for education.[10]

Meaning

Much of Richards' perspective on rhetoric is concerned with how words come to mean what they do. Richards sees meanings of words as central to a theory of rhetoric not only because they are the essential components in the function of language but also because of the ways in which meanings serve us. Meanings mediate or serve as a screen for us in our thinking, feeling, and willing — between all cognitive, affective, and volitional activities and the actuality with which these activities are concerned. Meanings are what we think of and think with when we think of a horse, what we feel when we dread an exam, and what we want when we envy a wealthy individual. In each case, we think of, feel, or want a representative of actuality; thus, meanings are those portions of actuality through which we deal with the rest. Our meanings, of course, are themselves part of actuality, as we are, but our dealings with the rest of actuality occur only through our meanings.

In addition to mediating for us in our thinking, feeling, and wanting, meanings mediate among individuals. They constitute the common world for people because they serve as common representatives of actuality. Although we all never will have exactly the same meanings for words, there are words — such as "president," "post office," and "stove" — whose meanings we use to create and maintain a somewhat common world.[11]

Richards begins his exploration of meaning with a discussion of other theories about how words come to have meaning. These theories usually involve some type of association, whereby ideas or images become associated with words. For example, we learn what the word "cat" means by seeing an actual cat at the same time that we hear the word, and thus a link is formed between the sight of the cat and the particular sound of the word, "cat." The next time we hear the word, an image of a cat comes to mind. Because we are likely to come into contact with different kinds of cats, however, this type of theory next suggests that actual images eventually are relegated to the background, and something imprecise, such as the idea of a cat, becomes associated with the word.

Richards objects to such theories because to say that images and ideas cluster around a word in the mind does not really answer the question of how a word comes to have meaning; such a theory only leads to the question of how an image or an idea comes to mean what it does.[12] Richards sets out to answer these questions and to develop a more satisfactory theory of meaning as a result.

Richards' explanation of meaning begins with the process of perception. As human beings, we are responsive to incoming sensory data from our perceived environment, and every stimulus that is received through the senses leaves an imprint, a trace, or what Richards calls an engram on the mind that is capable of being revived later.[13] To explain how sensory perceptions are developed into meanings, Richards introduces the notion of context. Context is a "cluster of events that recur together" or "a set of entities (things or events) related in a certain way." In every perception, a context is formed composed of the sensations being experienced.[14]

Whenever any part of a context appears, the possibility exists that the entire context will be called up and remembered; this is possible, of course, because the various perceptions of the context left residual traces in the mind. When part of the context appears, that part affects us as though the whole context were present; it serves the function of a sign. A sign, for Richards, is a thing that is understood to refer to something else. For example, dark skies, thunder, lightning, and rain once may have constituted a context for us. After that, when we hear thunder, that one sensation that comes to us through sound becomes a sign of rain, and thus we carry an umbrella or make plans to stay indoors. Signs come to have meaning, then, because they previously have been members of a context that once affected us as a whole.[15]

Words function in the same way that signs do. Since words are used as instruments of thought and for purposes of communication by humans, Richards calls them "symbols" rather than "signs." Like signs, words derive meaning through belonging to a context and serve as substitutes for the part of the context that currently is not present. A word, then, means the missing parts of the context. For example, suppose you hear the word, "scissors." The word causes you to focus on and sort back through your category of scissors and draws up past contexts in which you had experience with scissors. To you, then, the word means the missing parts of those contexts—all that is not currently present from those experiences with scissors but that provides the meaning of the symbol for you.[16]

Semantic Triangle

Richards illustrates his theory of meaning in a device called the "semantic triangle." At each of the three corners of a triangle are the three major components in the process of meaning—symbol, reference or thought, and referent or the object of thought. At the top of the triangle, "reference" indicates the realm of memory where recollections of past experiences and contexts occur. "Referents" are the objects that are perceived and that create the impressions stored in the thought area, and "symbol" is the word that calls up the referent through the mental processes of the reference.[17]

Different kinds of relationships exist between the three components of the triangle. Between the reference and the symbol, a causal relationship exists. When we speak, the symbol we choose to use is caused partly by the reference we are making and partly by social and psychological factors in the present, such as the purpose of the reference, the proposed effect of the symbol on

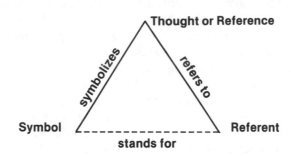

the audience, and our attitude. Similarly, when we hear something that is said, the symbol causes us to perform an act of reference and to assume an attitude that will be more or less similar to the act and attitude of the speaker.

The relation between the reference and the referent can be either direct or indirect. It is direct when we think about something that we are perceiving — for example, the color of a house. It is indirect when we think about something that is not immediately present — such as the opening of the Berlin wall — and that may require a long chain of interpretations of signs or symbols that lead to other signs or symbols, among them "Communism," "East Germany," "West Germany," "freedom," "prosperity," and "reunification."

Between the symbol and the referent, however, only an indirect relation is possible because these two entities are not connected directly; thus, the relation is indicated by the dotted line at the base of the triangle. The exceptional case is when the symbol essentially is equivalent to the referent for which it is used — for example, an onomatopoeic word such as "buzz," an explicit gesture, or a drawing. In these instances, the triangle is completed because its base is solid.[18] But in the usual situation, no such direct relation holds between the symbol and the referent.

Not only does the semantic triangle summarize the process of meaning, but it reminds us that no direct connection exists between a word and the object it symbolizes. For example, there is no particular relation between the word "plate" and the object from which we eat at the dinner table; it could be called as well a "fish" or a "book." What makes us believe a connection exists is that this particular symbol occurs in a context with the flat, round object that holds food.

In addition, the semantic triangle serves to warn us not to assume that the person to whom we are talking has identical thought processes around a symbol and referent as we do. For example, assume a man was bitten by a dog as a child. He avoids dogs, rarely pets them, and is uncomfortable in their

presence. The meaning of the word "dog," for him, may be represented in
the semantic triangle in this way:

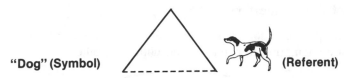

**Dangerous animal;
avoid any contact (Thought/Reference)**

"Dog" (Symbol)   (Referent)

Another person, however, has a very different reference for "dog." She grew
up among dogs, her family owned several dogs while she was a child—all
of them friendly—and she generally enjoys dogs. For her, the meaning of
the word "dog" may be expressed in the semantic triangle in this way:

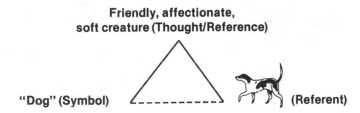

**Friendly, affectionate,
soft creature (Thought/Reference)**

"Dog" (Symbol)   (Referent)

When these two people are discussing dogs, they are using the identical
symbol, "dog," and they are reacting to a similar referent—an animal that
barks and has four legs and a tail. But their thoughts or references about that
animal, based on their individual experiences with dogs, are very different.
If they assume that the other person has the same meaning as they do for
"dog," there will be many opportunities for misunderstanding in their
conversation about dogs.

Richards gives the name "proper meaning superstition" to the belief that
a word has a meaning all its own about which everyone should agree. This
belief is not uncommon; generally, when we hear a word, we assume that
the speaker is referring to what we would be referring to were we speaking
the word ourselves. The semantic triangle is a practical tool for refuting the
proper meaning superstition because it makes clear that meanings exist in

people rather than in the symbols themselves. Only when a thinker makes use of a word does it "stand for anything, or . . . have 'meaning.'" Contexts determine and shape the meanings of words, and since every human being is a unique entity who has had different experiences, each person will attach somewhat different meanings to the same words.[19]

Model of Communication

Richards presents another diagram to illustrate how meaning operates when people are attempting to communicate with each other:

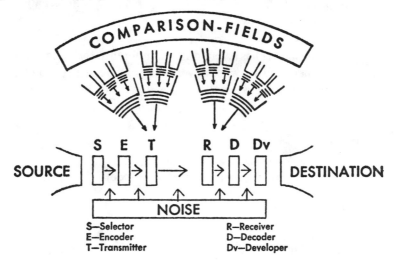

This model includes a source — the communicator — who selects mental images and encodes or translates them into words that can be transmitted to people who receive them. These receivers then decode or translate the words into mental images in accordance with their past experiences. In short, the process can be viewed in this way: Source Experience ——► Source Mind ——► Environment ——► Destination Mind ——► Destination Experience. Noise, in the model, refers to foreign elements that may interfere with the intended meaning — for example, a cough, illegible handwriting, or static in the electronic signal.[20]

All of these elements are common in communication models; what makes Richards' model different from many is the addition of "comparison-fields."

Comparison-fields are the various experiences of the people involved in the communicative effort—the contexts from which the symbols derive their meaning. The units of the comparison-fields consist of "utterances-within-situations," represented by the open boxes and lines in the model. Richards defines utterances-within-situations in this way: "The comprehending of any utterance is guided by any number of partially similar situations in which partially similar utterances have occurred." This model shows how the similar utterances in similar situations are brought together (represented in the synthesis of boxes and lines) to represent a more or less similar experience and thus to assist in the interpretation of the message. This process, of course, may not be a conscious one: "The past utterances-within-situations need not have been consciously remarked or wittingly analysed; still less need they be explicitly remembered when the comprehending occurs."[21]

The source's experience may be similar to or very different from the destination's experience, but the closer the comparison-fields or experiences of a source and a receiver, the more similar their interpretations of meaning are likely to be and thus the greater probability of successful communication. Communication, if defined as strict transference of or participation in identical experiences, does not occur. Communication is a use of symbols in such a way that acts of reference occur in a hearer that are similar to those symbolized by them in the speaker; an experience occurs in the hearer's mind that is like the experience in the speaker's mind. Communication results in misunderstanding, then, when there is a lack of common experience. If people are to communicate effectively, "long and varied acquaintanceship, close familiarity, lives whose circumstances have often corresponded, in short an exceptional fund of common experience" is needed.[22]

Feedforward

Although not explicitly included in his model of communication, Richards' concept of "feedforward" is an integral part of his theory of meaning and perspective on communication. Feedforward is the process in which we as receivers affect ourselves, in contrast to feedback, which is the effect of receivers on a source. Feedforward is a readiness, a preparation, or a design arrangement for one sort of outcome rather than another; it is the getting ready to act in one way or another. Feedforward can be seen when you walk downstairs, for example, and expect and ready your advanced leg to meet the stair under your toe. Usually, this feedforward is fulfilled, and there is confirmatory feedback at the end of each step you take—your foot finds the expected step of the stair. Sometimes, however, the expected feedback does not come; it does not conform to the feedforward, and you encounter feedback different from that for which you were prepared. For example, when you believe there is one more stair at the bottom of a dark staircase when there is not, your foot hits the floor with a thud. In this case, your feedforward or plan for feedback was not accurate.

Meaning in a communicative exchange functions, in part, on the principle of feedforward. As we hear the words spoken by the source of a message, we are led to consider certain choices for meanings from our past experiences and contexts as more salient and relevant than others. Our ability to select meanings similar to those envisioned by the source is dependent on our past experiences and choices of meanings from those experiences; feedforward prepares us to attribute particular meanings to words rather than others. When the word's meaning for us seems roughly equivalent to that expected by the speaker or writer, we receive confirmatory feedback and are more likely to symbolize that meaning with that word again in the future.[23]

"The entirety of activity . . . seems to consist of *choices*," Richards asserts. "Initial choices would be free; but, when choice has been made, the subsequent choices are bound thereby while the choice is held."[24] The pattern of choices made with regard to meaning thus constitutes feedforward as it creates plans for the attribution of particular meanings to the words that we encounter.

Functions of Discourse

The process of comprehending meaning becomes more complex as Richards introduces various functions that discourse serves for the source and the receiver. To explain how words work from both perspectives, Richards suggests that language performs a variety of tasks so that whether "we know and intend it or not, we are all jugglers when we converse, keeping the billiard-balls in the air while we balance the cue on our nose. . . . Language . . . has not one but several tasks to perform simultaneously." The four functions of language from the point of view of the speaker are:

(1) Sense: Words function to direct the listeners' attention to some state of affairs and to cause them to think about selected events or items.

(2) Feeling: Words express feelings or attitudes toward the referent; only in exceptional cases—as in the language of mathematics—is no feeling conveyed through an utterance. Feeling also involves the degree of certainty or confidence the speaker has in the soundness of the statement being made.

(3) Tone: Words convey the attitude of the speaker toward the audience.

(4) Intention: Words express the aim or outcome desired by the speaker or writer—whether this is conscious or unconscious.[25]

Just as words may function in various ways for the speaker, they also have various functions for the audience. Richards suggests that if comprehension is to occur, an audience must distinguish among seven[26] functions or activities of language:

(1) Indicating: A message points to or selects which items are to be the focus of attention.

(2) Characterizing: The utterance says something about the items on which attention is being focused; it begins to sort from among various characteristics and qualities.

(3) Realizing: Realizing concerns the degree and vividness to which the utterance makes the audience sense the particular item; "what is in question is the nearness and fulness [sic] with which something is to be present to us." This activity deals with the nature of the presentation, whether the subject is presented "vividly or plainly, excitingly or quieteningly, close up or remotely."

(4) Valuing: Valuing is the raising of the question, "Should this be so?" Valuing functions to assign a positive or negative value to the item being discussed.

(5) Influencing: At issue in this function is whether the audience would like to maintain or change the status quo. Encouraging an audience to change a situation and persuading it to become adjusted to a set of circumstances are major activities of this function.

(6) Controlling: Controlling is the management and administration of the other activities or functions so that they do not interfere too much with one another.

(7) Purposing: In this function, the end, aim, or intention that is being pursued in the discourse is revealed to the audience.

Any full utterance, Richards asserts, does all seven of these activities at once and invites all of them in the listener. But in some types of discourse, some aspects will be emphasized more than others. In mathematics, for example, the activities of indicating, controlling, and purposing will be predominant functions, while in the act of swearing, the functions of valuing, influencing, and purposing will be the focus.[27]

These seven constituent parts of the process of comprehending help to explain why communication often goes awry. Misunderstanding may occur, for example, if the communicators do not agree about the subject of their interaction (indicating), if they do not realize the implications of what is being said (realizing), if they do not accept the proposals that are offered (influencing), if they do not understand or will not agree about the way in which a proposal should be carried forward (controlling), or if they do not agree about the purpose of their interaction (purposing).[28]

A complete model of how Richards sees the process of communication, then, might look like this:[29]

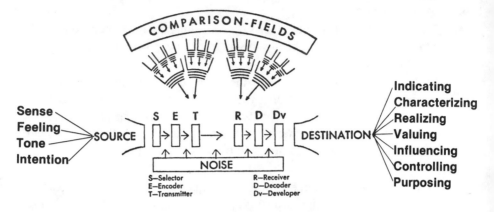

UTTERANCES-in-SITUATIONS

Emotive Versus Referential Language

The process by which communicators come to comprehend is further affected by the type of discourse involved. Richards distinguishes between two uses of language, the referential and the emotive, which correspond roughly to the discourse of science and poetry.[30] Each of these involves the seven comprehending activities to varying degrees. Although the referential and emotive uses may occur together in an utterance, they function in very different ways.

The referential function of language is the scientific use of language or the simple statement of references, where words are used "for the sake of the references they promote." In contrast, the emotive use of language is language that is used to express or excite feelings and attitudes.[31] "The house has seven rooms" is an example of referential use, while "sisterhood is powerful!" is largely emotive. Most language, of course, is mixed or rhetorical as opposed to the purely referential or emotive. "The majestic mountains sparkled against the blue sky" exemplifies the rhetorical use of language, which is the type used in most discourse.

The distinction among the three types of language perhaps can be seen more clearly in these sentences:

1. The Mississippi River is 3,960 feet wide at Baton Rouge where the ferry crosses.

2. The lovely Mississippi glides smoothly into the Gulf.

3. Old Man River, that old man river, he just keeps rolling along.

Referential language can be tested by reference to objective reality. The depth and width of the Mississippi River, for example, can be measured to determine the truth of the first statement; thus, it is referential. The second statement is rhetorical; it contains some words with specific referents—"gulf," for instance—and some without. "Lovely," for example, does not have a referent in the environment that can be assessed objectively. A rhetorical statement, then, contains some referential and some emotive words. The third sentence, in contrast, has no objective "truth"; it simply is a representation of someone's experience, attitude, and feeling.[32]

The differences between emotive and referential language are important particularly in terms of the mental processes of meaning and comprehension. We fail to comprehend referential language when the references differ in the minds of the communicators, when the primary aim of the discourse—the communication of specific references—has not been attained. Moreover, in referential language, the connections and relations of references to one another must be logical and must not interfere with each other. For emotive language, however, wide differences in reference are of little importance as long as it produces the required attitude and emotion; the essential consideration is the character of the attitude aroused. Thus, for referential language, comprehension consists of factual accuracy, while agreement or comprehension in emotive language is accomplished by what Richards calls engagement of the will.[33]

There are, of course, greater opportunities for misunderstanding in language in which the emotive use is emphasized because of the likelihood that the symbols may not lead the communicators to precisely the same emotional responses. Each use of language also focuses on different activities of comprehension. In referential language, the functions of indicating, characterizing, realizing, appraising, and influencing are predominant, while emotive language emphasizes the functions of appraising, influencing, indicating, characterizing, and realizing.[34]

Elimination of Misunderstanding

Richards' recognition of the many ways in which communication may be ineffective leads him to suggest some means by which communicators may work to prevent such misunderstandings. Among these means are the use of metaphor, definitions, literary context, and specialized quotation marks.

Metaphor

For Richards, metaphor is more than a figure of speech that is used for stylistic effect in a speech or an essay. It holds a central place in his theory of meaning and is a major technique for facilitating comprehension. An examination of his view of metaphor is best begun with his objections to traditional conceptions of metaphor; in particular, he disagrees with Aristotle's view of metaphor in the *Poetics*. In this work, Aristotle says that the use of metaphor is a gift that some people have and some do not; in other words, it cannot be imparted or taught. In addition, Aristotle calls the metaphor something special and exceptional in the use of language, a deviation from its normal mode of working.[35]

Richards refutes these notions in his definition of metaphor, which he sees as the use of one reference to a group of things that are related in a particular way in order to discover a similar relation in another group. Our thought process, then, is metaphoric. When we attribute meaning, we are simply seeing in one context an aspect similar to that encountered in an earlier context. Thus, two thoughts of different things are supported by a single word or phrase and derive meaning from their interaction. In this process, we are employing the principles of sorting, categorization, comparison, and abstraction.[36]

When we encounter a moving vehicle with four wheels and an engine, for example, we sort back through our contexts to discover when we have encountered similar objects and come up with the word "car" to stand for our various thoughts about cars. The meaning for "car" is derived, then, from "the attraction of likes" or from our recognition of the similar characteristics that both things have in common.[37] The symbol pulls together our thoughts about various cars, and the meaning of "car" is the result of the interaction among the thoughts.

Not only is metaphor the means by which meaning is developed, but it is a method by which a communicator may provide listeners with the experience needed to elicit similar references for a particular symbol. In cases where "the speaker must himself supply and control a large part of the causes of the listener's experience," metaphor is used to supply the experience: "But what is needed for the wholeness of an experience is not always naturally present, and metaphor supplies an excuse by which what is needed may be smuggled in."[38] For example, suppose a professor is attempting to communicate with graduate students about the process of writing a doctoral dissertation. These students never have written a dissertation and never have had experience with any aspects of the process. The professor might use a metaphor to supply some of the needed experience and thus to assist in the development of a meaning for "dissertation" in their minds that is similar to the meaning she holds: "Writing a dissertation is writing a series of term papers."

Richards proposes two terms to enable metaphor to be analyzed and discussed easily. "Tenor" is the term he uses to refer to the underlying idea or principal subject of the metaphor—what is meant. "Vehicle" is the means of conveying the underlying idea, the borrowed idea, or what the tenor resembles. "Metaphor" refers to the double unit as a whole. In the metaphor, "the sun is a red balloon," the tenor is the sun and the vehicle is the balloon, which attributes the characteristics of redness and roundness to the sun.

In the analysis of metaphor, Richards cautions that metaphor does not depend for its operation only on resemblances or correspondence between the tenor and vehicle. A metaphor works through disparity or dissimilarity, as well. While the action of the vehicle certainly invites us to regard the tenor as like it in some respects, it also invites us to consider its differences. In the metaphor of the sun and the balloon, the balloon invites the reader to note similarities between a balloon and the sun, but it also warns us implicitly not to take the resemblances too strictly or not to ignore the differences. We do not see, for example, the sun as something that holds air and can be popped with a pin, something that can be attached to a string, or something that is a toy. We must play, then, "an incessant game with the discrepancies" in metaphor.[39]

In addition to resemblance and discrepancy, the relationship of a metaphor may be based on a common attitude held toward the tenor and vehicle. For example, if we call someone a "duck" in an endearing manner, to use Richards' example, we do not mean "to imply that she has a bill and paddles or is good to eat." What is being suggested instead is that the speaker views ducks and the person in a similar way—as, perhaps, with a "'tender and amused regard.'"[40]

Definition of Words

For Richards, the definition of words is another means for eliminating misunderstanding. Clear definitions of references can make discussion more profitable by bringing individuals into open agreement or disagreement with one another. Some words such as "beauty" or "truth," for example, actually are not single words at all but rather sets of discrepant symbols. Yet, if people use them as if only one meaning is possible for them, misunderstanding is likely to result. Similarly, whenever we want to examine and analyze a concept seriously, we should begin with as complete a list as possible of the different uses of the word. Without a map of the separate fields covered by the term, it "is liable to be confused with another, to their common detriment, or to yield an apparent contradiction of purely verbal origin."[41]

Definition involves finding the referent for a symbol through the substitution of a symbol or symbols that are better understood than the one being defined. It involves the selection of referents with which the listener is familiar and their connection to the word being defined. Richards suggests several methods of definition or possible routes to reach an unclear or unknown referent:

Symbolization is the simplest, most fundamental means of definition. Using this route to define "apple," for example, you could take an actual apple, point to it, and say, "'Apple' is a symbol that stands for this."

In definition by *similarity*, a relation of likeness is used to connect the concept to be defined to the familiar referent. If you are asked to define "purple," for example, you could do so by pointing to something that is purple and saying, "Anything that is like this object in color is purple."

Spatial relations also may be used to define terms. Words such as "in," "on," "above," "between," "beside," "to the right of," "near," "bigger than," or "part of" are used in such definitions to connect a symbol by spatial relations to another referent. "The library is the building to the east of the student union" is a definition of "library" using spatial relations.

Similarly, *temporal relations* can be used to connect unknown referents to known ones. Using this method of definition, "yesterday," for example, could be defined as "the day before today," and "Sunday" could be defined as "the first day of the week."

Causation is a route of definition that includes physical causation, psychological causation, and psycho-physical causation. Physical causation is used to define by indicating a physical cause-and-effect relationship between referents. For example, "thunder" could be defined as "what is caused by certain electrical disturbances," and "sunburn" could be defined as "a burn on the skin caused by overexposure to the sun." Psychological causation as a definition indicates a psychological cause-and-effect relationship between referents; thus, the term "pleasure" might be defined as "the conscious accompaniment of successful psychic activity." Some definitions involve both psychological and physical causation; using this method of definition, "sight" could be defined as "the effect in consciousness (psychological effect) of certain vibrations falling on the retina (physical cause)."

Another type of definition Richards suggests is that in which the *object of a mental state* is described. Examples of this type of relation are referring, desiring, willing, and feeling. Using such a definition, "piteous things" could be defined as "those things toward which we feel sympathy," and "good things" might be defined as "those things of which we approve."

Legal relations provide the basis for definitions that frequently are employed in courts of law. They are subject to the test of satisfying the judge and generally involve terms such as "belonging to," "subject of," "liable to," and "evidence of." A definition of "abandonment" in a lease agreement for the rental of an apartment, for example, would use legal relations: "The premises shall be conclusively presumed to be abandoned permanently by the tenant if the same are apparently unoccupied for a period of fifteen (15) days or more."

Aware that some concepts may not be able to be defined easily using only one of these methods, Richards suggests that definitions also can be formed from combinations of the various methods in a form he calls *common complex relations*. "Imitation," for example, could be defined as "the act of modeling or copying," which implicitly relies on the methods of similarity (doing an act that is like another act) and psycho-physical causation (a desire to repeat an observed behavior causes the behavior in the observer).[42]

In summary, Richards suggests that unclear references be symbolized by means of various routes of definition, where the starting points are familiar things that occur freely in ordinary experience and then are linked to the unclear or new word in order to understand its meaning. The list he suggests is not exhaustive, he admonishes, and other relations could be used to define, including shape, function, purpose, and opposition.

Literary Context

Using literary context is another way to eliminate misunderstanding in communication. Words never appear in isolation but instead occur in literary contexts, in which sentences, phrases, or paragraphs are dependent upon one another to provide clues to possible meanings of the words. This mutual dependency or interaction, which Richards calls the interinanimation of words, constitutes their literary context.

The process of paying attention to literary context is one in which we engage unconsciously; Richards hopes to bring it to our attention as a device to aid us in the comprehension of meaning. The process operates in this manner: We come to a word in a sentence that has a disputable or unclear meaning for us—as nearly all words do. At this point, we note a reservation about it, leaving unsettled for the time what the meaning is going to be. Richards calls this use of a word—the creating of a gap to be filled later—the "Mesopotamian" use. This term comes from a story "about an old woman who told her pastor that she found great support in that blessed word 'Mesopotamia.'" Just as the reader of this story waits to see what meaning the woman gives to "Mesopotamia" (and Richards does not say!), so we as readers wait to discover what meanings words have until we become acquainted with their literary context. A word generally keeps to a Mesopotamian use for only a brief moment; it soon has its immense field of possible meanings narrowed down by the influence of the other words that accompany it.

Richards' concept of literary context reinforces his notion that a word does not have a meaning of its own or a fixed correct usage (what he earlier called the proper meaning superstition). The meaning we find for a word comes to it only with respect to the meanings of the other words that surround it; a word is always a cooperative member of a group of words. Just as a note in a musical phrase takes its character from and makes its contribution only with the other notes about it and a color is what it is only with respect to other colors present with it in the visual field, so meanings of words must be considered only in literary context. This means that words cannot be judged correct or appropriate in isolation; they may be viewed as such only in some literary context.[43]

The principle of literary context holds not only for the meaning of words but for other elements of communication as well—for example, a speaker's attitude and tone. As with the meanings of words, the attitude and tone conveyed in the opening words of a speech are likely to be ambiguous. Only when the speaker has continued to speak and more context is revealed can the audience tell if the tone of the speech is sarcastic or serious, confident or hesitant.[44]

The mutual dependence of words, of course, varies with the type of discourse. At one end of the scale, with discourse that is technical and scientific—the referential use of language—a large part of the words are independent. They tend to mean the same regardless of the words with which they are combined, and if they fluctuate, they move only into a small number of stable positions. At the opposite end of the scale, in poetic discourse—the emotive use of language—words are likely to have no fixed and settled meanings separable from those of the words with which they occur.[45]

Specialized Quotation Marks

To assist the reader further in discovering the intended meaning of a word, phrase, or sentence, Richards devised a set of special symbols to take the place of usual quotation marks. "Metasemantic markers" are small letters placed, as quotation marks are, around the words, phrases, and sentences they single out. Believing that quotation marks must perform a great number of functions, Richards advocates the following set of marks "as a technical notation by which we could better keep track of the uses we are making of our words." He used the system in much of his own writing and was "persuaded of the usefulness of this device."

[w]. . .[w] indicates that the word itself is being talked about; these marks are equivalent to "the word." For example, [w]table[w] may mean an article of furniture or a list.

[r]. . .[r] indicates that the author is referring to some special use of the word or phrase. For example, [r]nature[r] for Whitehead is not Wordsworth's [r]nature.[r]

[nb]. . .[nb] indicates that how the word is understood is a turning point in the discussion and that it easily may be read in more than one way or without an adequate perception of its importance. It is short for *nota*

bene, or "note well." American automobile companies, we might say, have lost a share of the American market to the Japanese because they have failed in the [nb]art[nb] of automobile manufacture.

[i]. . .[i]   indicates that other meanings the word may have in other occurrences may intervene in the meaning the writer is attempting to convey. The marks are equivalent to "intervention likely." In writing about Kenneth Burke's concept of piety, for example, which he defines as conformity to the sources of one's being,[46] these marks could indicate that religious meanings of [i]piety[i] could intervene that are not Burke's meaning of the term.

[hi]. . .[hi]   means "helpful intervention." It signals that other meanings the word is likely to have in other occurrences may intervene, and such intervention is likely to help in understanding the meaning of the word in this situation. For example, in "the organization implemented a [hi]democratic[hi] system of decisionmaking," the marks would indicate that the usual meanings of the word should be utilized here in determining its meaning.

[t]. . .[t]   means "technical term" and is used to show that the word or phrase is being used as a technical term and is fixed in this meaning. In the sentence, "she has formulated several notions about politics but has not devised a [t]theory,[t]" for example, these marks indicate that the word is being used in a specialized, technical way.

[!]. . .[!]   indicates surprise or astonishment that people can write or talk so. It signals an attitude of "Good heavens! What a way to talk!" It may be read [!]shriek[!] if one has occasion to read the word or phrase aloud. The marks could be used to indicate astonishment at an idea, as in: "He claimed that his theory was [!]the only legitimate theory that had been developed in the discipline.[!]"[47]

For Richards, the goal of communication — for communicators to attribute similar meanings to symbols — is difficult to attain. An awareness of and use of metaphor, definition, literary context, and specialized quotation marks can be used not to guarantee that communication will be effective but as beginning steps to aid in the elimination of misunderstandings that inevitably occur.

Responses to Richards

An assessment of I. A. Richards' contributions to contemporary rhetoric must begin with an examination of how his ideas fit into scholarship in rhetoric in general. Such study traditionally examines rhetoric macroscopically — in terms of patterns, characteristics, and functions of composite discourse such as debates, speeches, and rhetorical acts. Richards, however, approaches rhetoric from a microscopic perspective; his focus is on how the pieces that make up these composites function.[48] He created and put into circulation a number of terms to study these microscopic functions, including "tenor," "vehicle," and "emotive and referential language." By providing a much-needed microscopic supplement to the study of rhetoric, Richards encouraged rhetorical theorists to study rhetoric in a more holistic fashion, examining, in essence, both the pieces of the puzzle and the completed puzzle itself.

Yet another characteristic of Richards' contributions to rhetoric is his use of a variety of disciplines and fields to develop his perspective on rhetoric. As Hyman has noted, "Perhaps more than any man since Bacon, Richards has taken all knowledge as his province, and his field is the entire mind of man." He continues: "Not only is he thoroughly familiar with the dozen fields . . . that he has staked out as his own, but he has invaded almost every other area of knowledge. To make a minor point, he is apt not only to quote theoretical physics with authority, but to quote Lenin's *Materialism and Empirico-Criticism* against it with equal authority." This willingness and ability to use the knowledge of a variety of fields should not suggest, however, a lack of focus in Richards' work. His writings are consistently concerned with the study of words and meanings, how communication works, and how it can be made to work better.[49]

Richards' ideas, however, are not without their detractors. One criticism that has been leveled against his works concerns the "looseness" of his writings.[50] In some instances, his understanding of a particular subject seems superficial or even incorrect. His attack on traditional rhetoricians, for example, has been described as "more dogmatic than accurate," since ancient and modern rhetoricians consider rhetoric and the use of language in terms that are as functional as those that Richards provides.[51] In many cases, Richards provides little evidence or support for his assertions. They well might be true and much evidence might be available to support them, but Richards often does not provide it. Another complaint about Richards' writing is that many of the crucial terms in his theory "are so vague as to be virtually undefined."[52]

Another problem concerning "looseness" that the reader of Richards is likely to note is that his works sometimes contain incongruities. As Fisher explains, what he asserts in one work will be different from his assertions in another. Hyman describes this tendency as a "curiously dilettantish irresponsibility toward ideas" and "an inability to hold to a consistent point of view at any given time." This problem is evident, for example, when Richards cites different numbers of functions of comprehending. There are seven listed in *Practical Criticism* and only four in *Interpretation in Teaching*, and he does not address the discrepancy or explain the change. Incongruities also are evident in Richards' "frequent changes in vocabulary," which, according to Russo, produce "a confused effect."[53] These incongruities, however, may be less a problem with clarity of thought and writing than they are evidence of Richards' own "healthy growth."[54] Richards' views on aspects of his ideas appeared to change over time, and these discrepancies can be viewed simply as evidence of the evolution of his thought.

Richards also has been criticized for an overemphasis on science in his ideas and for his apparent desire for a "science" of symbolism and criticism. That he weighted his ideas—particularly his early ideas—in favor of science is reflected in his psychological approach to the problem of meaning, which drew on a variety of psychological theories, including "physiological and neurological psychology, behaviorism, Pavlov's conditioned-reflex psychology, psychoanalysis, Gestalt, and snips and snatches from every other psychological theorizer or experimenter." This scientific focus well may have been due to the influence on Richards of his early collaborator, C. K. Ogden, a renowned psychologist.[55]

Richards' scientific bias was lessened, to some degree, in his later works, although he never explicitly renounced his early theory of the science of symbolism and continued sporadically to adapt pieces of scientific models in his later writings. He seemed to retire his psychological model of meaning from active duty, however, after the middle 1930s, suggesting a shift away from a behavioristic theory with mechanical metaphors of stimulus and response to notions more influenced by humanism.[56]

Richards' expressed goals concerning rhetoric—to solve the problem of understanding and misunderstanding and to launch a new rhetoric—have been attacked as pretentious and as failing to yield the results he promised. "But the general effect . . . is . . . of a largeness of promise and an impressiveness of operation quite disproportionate to anything that emerges," suggested Leavis. "Moreover, this effect is such as to impose the regretful conviction that had the ambition been less the profit might very well have been greater." One example of this "largeness of promise" is Richards' assertion that no "revolution in human affairs would be greater than that" initiated by observance of the distinction between prose and poetry. To attribute such results to this distinction seems an exaggeration, Black notes, when what Richards actually has done is simply to recognize "that scientific discourse is not the sole significant mode of human communication."[57]

The unrealistic, idealistic, and unattainable social goal Richards established for his work has been the subject of even stronger attacks. His primary aim was to furnish a means to improve social life or civilization in general through the improvement of communication.[58] He viewed the ailments of the world primarily as verbal ones with verbal remedies.

Richards proposed to accomplish his goal through education, thus joining "the ranks of those who would save mankind from its verbal frailties by pedagogical dogma." He had "faith in education, and particularly the humanities, as *the* way of improving verbal understanding, both in the metaphoric or dialectic shaping of messages and in the dialogical or balanced reception of them."[59] Richards summarized this position as "while you're teaching beginning English, you might as well teach everything else." He elaborated: "That is to say, a world position, what's needed for living, a philosophy of religion, how to find things out, and the whole works — mental and moral seed for the planet. In this way the two-thirds of the planet that doesn't yet know how to read and write would learn in learning how to read and write English, the things that would help them in their answers to 'Where should man go?'"[60]

Richards believed his goal of improving civilization could be accomplished specifically through the educational tools of world literacy programs and Basic English, the 850-word language he developed with C. K. Ogden. Yet, these techniques were not of the magnitude of the problems he set out to solve. Hyman suggests, for example, that rather than solving the problem of the breakdown of civilization through educational means, Richards actually formulated a method for teaching reading more effectively in the schools — a considerably lower achievement than the one for which he aimed. Neither was Richards concerned with the pragmatics of education that would have to be addressed were education to serve the vital role he suggested — pragmatics such as variations in instructors' abilities to teach the breadth in content he required, varying levels of students' abilities, and the like. As Enholm explains, "None of these problems is necessarily insolvable, but they are problems not dealt with by Richards, and they should indicate that between his proposals for improving verbal understanding and our hopes for realizing them, lies considerable distance, most of it uphill."[61]

Richards' transition from a commitment to theory of criticism and meaning to a preoccupation with education — particularly Basic English — which took place gradually from 1929 to 1939, is difficult to explain. Russo suggests his motive might have been "the need to be challenged and to be creative in response to challenge," as well as a desire to investigate the lower levels of education, since his career until then had focused on the upper levels.[62] His background as a literary critic, however, seemed opposed in many ways to the very concept of Basic English. As Hyman explained in a 1948 essay:

> To put it bluntly, there seems to be no way of reconciling the two, and to the extent that he continues working with Basic he renounces criticism and abdicates his position as our foremost living critic. The concept of Basic in Criticism, . . . seems to be at its best superfluous and at its worst

a fraud, and even in the hands of Richards . . . it has produced no critical insights particularly worth having.[63]

Richards appeared to solve the conflict between Basic English and his more theoretical work in rhetoric and criticism by giving up the writing of literary criticism and his theorizing about rhetoric.[64] His failure to continue to develop his notions in these areas well might be a reason why Richards' ideas, which seemed initially to constitute original and significant starting points for a new rhetoric, did not, in the end, have the impact on contemporary rhetoric many had believed they would. Other scholars of rhetoric simply passed him by and developed his contributions into more sophisticated notions when he, himself, did not.

That Richards did not continue to develop his perspective on rhetoric in his later works does not denigrate, however, his earlier achievements in this area. As Hyman asserted, "we shall still have, in his early books, work to rank with the finest of our time, as well as a whole dazzling body of work stemming out of it. Those are in no danger."[65]

Notes

[1] I. A. Richards, *Complementarities: Uncollected Essays*, ed. John Paul Russo (Cambridge, Mass.: Harvard University Press, 1976), p. 268.

[2] Biographical information on Richards was obtained from the following sources: Reuben Brower, "Beginnings and Transitions: I. A. Richards Interviewed by Reuben Brower," in *I. A. Richards: Essays in His Honor*, ed. Reuben Brower, Helen Vendler, and John Hollander (New York: Oxford University Press, 1973), pp. 19, 20, 23, 24, 34, 37; and Janet Adam Smith, "Fare Forward, Voyagers!" in *I. A. Richards: Essays in His Honor*, pp. 307-10.

[3] Smith, p. 316.

[4] I. A. Richards, *The Philosophy of Rhetoric* (1936; rpt. New York: Oxford University Press, 1965), p. 3.

[5] Richards, *The Philosophy of Rhetoric*, p. 8.

[6] Richards, *The Philosophy of Rhetoric*, p. 24.

[7] Richards, *The Philosophy of Rhetoric*, p. 7.

[8] I. A. Richards, *Interpretation in Teaching* (New York: Harcourt, Brace, 1938), pp. 12, 13.

[9] Richards' views of the new rhetoric and what it would involve are discussed in Richards, *The Philosophy of Rhetoric*, pp. 3, 4; and C. K. Ogden and I. A. Richards, *The Meaning of Meaning: A Study of the Influence of Language Upon Thought and of the Science of Symbolism* (1923; rpt. New York: Harcourt, Brace, 1930), p. 243.

[10] Richards discusses requirements for the new rhetoric in *The Philosophy of Rhetoric*, pp. 10, 23; and *Speculative Instruments* (Chicago: University of Chicago Press, 1955), pp. 74, 76.

[11] The functions of meanings are discussed in I. A. Richards, *So Much Nearer: Essays Toward a World English* (New York: Harcourt, Brace & World, 1960), pp. 130-32.

[12] Richards, *The Philosophy of Rhetoric*, pp. 14-15.

[13] Richards' view of the process of perception is discussed in Ogden and Richards, *The Meaning of Meaning*, p. 53; and I. A. Richards, *Principles of Literary Criticism* (New York: Harcourt, Brace, 1924), p. 103.

[14] See Richards, *The Philosophy of Rhetoric*, p. 34; and Ogden and Richards, *The Meaning of Meaning*, p. 58, for a discussion of Richards' notion of context.

[15] Sign is defined in Ogden and Richards, *The Meaning of Meaning*, pp. 21, 50.

16 The meaning of words as missing parts of context is discussed in Ogden and Richards, *The Meaning of Meaning*, pp. 23, 174; and Richards, *The Philosophy of Rhetoric*, p. 34.

17 Richards discusses the semantic triangle in *The Meaning of Meaning*, pp. 10-11.

18 Ogden and Richards, *The Meaning of Meaning*, p. 12.

19 Richards' notion of the proper meaning superstition is discussed in *The Philosophy of Rhetoric*, p. 11; and Ogden and Richards, *The Meaning of Meaning*, pp. 10, 15.

20 This model is described in Richards, *Speculative Instruments*, pp. 22, 23; and Paul R. Corts, "I. A. Richards on Rhetoric and Criticism," *Southern Speech Journal*, 36 (Winter 1970), 119.

21 For a discussion of the notion of comparison-fields, see Richards, *Speculative Instruments*, pp. 23, 24.

22 Richards discusses the need for common experience in communication in *Principles of Literary Criticism*, pp. 177-78; and *The Meaning of Meaning*, pp. 205-06.

23 Feedforward is discussed in Richards, *Complementarities*, pp. 246-53.

24 Richards, *Speculative Instruments*, p. 19.

25 For discussions of the functions of discourse for the speaker, see I. A. Richards, *Practical Criticism: A Study of Literary Judgment* (New York: Harcourt, Brace, 1939), pp. 180-82; and Ogden and Richards, *The Meaning of Meaning*, pp. 226-27.

26 Richards proposes four functions of comprehending — to point to or name things, to express our feelings about them, to represent our acts, and to indicate directions — in *Interpretation in Teaching*, p. 196.

27 The functions of discourse for the audience are discussed in Richards, *Speculative Instruments*, pp. 26-38; and Richards, *Complementarities*, pp. 100-01.

28 Keith Jensen, "I. A. Richards and his Models," *Southern Speech Communication Journal*, 37 (Spring 1972), 312.

29 Corts, p. 122.

30 Richards discusses referential and emotive language in *Complementarities*, pp. 88-97; *The Meaning of Meaning*, pp. 234-35; and *Principles of Literary Criticism*, pp. 261-71.

31 Richards sometimes seems to use the term, "emotive language," simply to mean language that is used "non-referentially." For a discussion of Richards' various uses of "emotive," see Jerome P. Schiller, *I. A. Richards' Theory of Literature* (New Haven: Yale University Press, 1969), pp. 50-61.

32 Marie Hochmuth Nichols, *Rhetoric and Criticism* (Baton Rouge: Louisiana State University Press, 1963), p. 101.

33 For a discussion of comprehension in referential and emotive language, see Richards, *Principles of Literary Criticism*, pp. 268-69; and Richards, *Complementarities*, pp. 93-94.

34 Richards, *Complementarities*, pp. 92-93.

35 Aristotle *Poetics* 22; and Richards, *The Philosophy of Rhetoric*, pp. 89-90.

36 Metaphor is discussed in Ogden and Richards, *The Meaning of Meaning*, p. 213; and Richards, *The Philosophy of Rhetoric*, p. 93.

37 Richards, *Interpretation in Teaching,* p. 49.

38 Richards discusses the use of metaphor to supply experience in *Principles of Literary Criticism*, pp. 178, 240.

39 Richards discusses dissimilarity in metaphor in *Interpretation in Teaching*, p. 133.

40 For a discussion of metaphor based on common attitude, see Richards, *The Philosophy of Rhetoric*, pp. 117-18.

41 See Ogden and Richards, *The Meaning of Meaning*, pp. 132, 246-47, for a discussion of the notion of definition.

42 Various means of definition are discussed in Ogden and Richards, *The Meaning of Meaning*, pp. 117-21.

43 Richards discusses literary context in *The Philosophy of Rhetoric*, pp. 47, 53-55, 69; and *Interpretation in Teaching*, p. 248.

44 Richards, *The Philosophy of Rhetoric,* p. 50.

45 Richards, *The Philosophy of Rhetoric*, p. 49.

46 Kenneth Burke, *Permanence and Change: An Anatomy of Purpose* (1954; rpt. Indianapolis: Bobbs-Merrill, 1965), pp. 71-79.

[47] Richards explains his system of specialized quotation marks in *Speculative Instruments*, pp. 29-30; *So Much Nearer,* pp. x-xi; and *Complementarities*, p. 98.

[48] "Marie Hochmuth [Nichols], "I. A. Richards and the 'New Rhetoric,'" *Quarterly Journal of Speech*, 44 (February 1958), 16.

[49] Stanley Edgar Hyman, *The Armed Vision: A Study in the Methods of Modern Literary Criticism* (New York: Alfred A. Knopf, 1948), pp. 308, 315, 344.

[50] Schiller, p. 68.

[51] William G. Hardy, *Language, Thought, and Experience: A Tapestry of the Dimensions of Meaning* (Baltimore: University Park Press, 1978), p. 95.

[52] Max Black, "Some Objections to Ogden and Richards' Theory of Interpretation," *Journal of Philosophy*, 39 (May 21, 1942), 287; and Max Black, *Language and Philosophy: Studies in Method* (Ithaca, NY: Cornell University Press, 1959), p. 196.

[53] B. Aubrey Fisher, "I. A. Richards' Context of Language: An Overlooked Contribution to Rhetorico-Communication Theory," *Western Speech*, 35 (Spring 1971), 111; Hyman, p. 344; and John Paul Russo, "I. A. Richards in Retrospect," *Critical Inquiry*, 8 (Summer 1982), 745.

[54] Hardy, p. 96.

[55] Black, *Language and Philosophy*, p. 211; and Hyman, p. 315. For a summary of Ogden's work in psychology, see Hyman, pp. 335-36.

[56] Russo, p. 749; Black, *Language and Philosophy*, pp. 192, 213; and Hardy, p. 90.

[57] Hardy, p. 62; F. R. Leavis, "Advanced Verbal Education," rev. of *The Philosophy of Rhetoric*, by I. A. Richards, *Scrutiny*, 6 (September 1937), 212; Richards, *Principles of Literary Criticism*, p. 274; and Black, *Language and Philosophy*, p. 203.

[58] Hardy, p. 62.

[59] Hardy, p. 67; and Donald K. Enholm, "Rhetoric as an Instrument for Understanding and Improving Human Relations," *Southern Speech Communication Journal*, 41 (Spring 1976), 232.

[60] Richards, *Complementarities*, pp. 268-69.

[61] Hyman, p. 313; and Enholm, p. 233.

[62] Russo, p. 755.

[63] Hyman, p. 343.

[64] Hyman, p. 343.

[65] Hyman, p. 346.

3

Richard M. Weaver

Rhetoric could be called the key to Richard Weaver's life work: "The word *rhetoric* was often on his lips. For him it had a rich and vital meaning." He "taught rhetoric, he wrote about rhetoric, and he used rhetoric to present the truths in which he believed."[1]

Richard Malcolm Weaver, Jr., was born on March 3, 1910, to Richard Malcolm Weaver and Carolyn Embry Weaver in Asheville, North Carolina, where his father owned a livery stable and raised thoroughbred horses. When his father died of a heart attack in 1915, his mother was pregnant with her fourth child, Embry; she took Richard and his sisters, Polly and Betty, to live with relatives in Weaverville, North Carolina. Two years later, the family moved to Lexington, Kentucky, his mother's home town, where she resumed her career as a milliner.

Weaver attended the public schools of Lexington through the eighth grade and then was sent to Lincoln Memorial Academy in Harrogate, Tennessee, a college preparatory school. He paid his way through his three years there working in the school's kitchens. At the age of seventeen, Weaver returned to Lexington and enrolled in the University of Kentucky, describing himself at the beginning of his schooling as "gloomy, ardent, and stupid." He was prominent in literary, debate, and political circles and was initiated into Phi Beta Kappa in his senior year. After "many wayward choices," he emerged from his course of study, in 1932, with a bachelor's degree in English and a minor in philosophy.

In the year of his graduation, Weaver joined the American Socialist Party. He was unemployed during the 1932-1933 school year and was "bitter" about the experience, which may have made the Socialist Party particularly attractive to him. But he also had been influenced by his professors at the university, most of whom were social democrats or liberals. "I had no defenses whatever against their doctrine," Weaver later explained. Weaver was an active member of the Socialist Party, serving for a time as secretary of the "local." He discovered, however, that while the socialist program had "a certain intellectual appeal" for him, he "could not like the members of the movement as *persons*. They seemed dry, insistent people, of shallow objectives; seeing them often and sharing a common endeavor, moreover, did nothing to remove the disliking." He performed his duties as secretary with decreasing enthusiasm and began to feel that socialism was not a movement in which he could find "permanent satisfaction"; he quit the party in 1934.

In 1933, Weaver was awarded a scholarship to Vanderbilt University in Nashville, Tennessee. At that time, Vanderbilt was the chief seat of the Southern Agrarians, a group of scholars and writers that included John Crowe Ransom, Robert Penn Warren, Donald Davidson, and Allen Tate. Their position opposed the doctrines of socialism in almost every way. They sought to resist the ills of industrialism by a return to the agricultural economy of the Old South and argued against progress, science, and rationalism as supreme values.[2] Weaver discovered that while he disagreed with the Agrarians on social and political doctrine, he "liked them all as persons." He found the "intellectual maturity and personal charm of the Agrarians" unsettling to his allegiance to socialism.

The professor who influenced him the most at Vanderbilt was John Crowe Ransom, who taught literature and psychology, and under whom Weaver wrote his master's thesis. Ransom had the "gift of dropping living seeds into minds," and one idea of Ransom's that particularly intrigued Weaver was his notion of the "unorthodox defense of orthodoxy." Weaver began to perceive, after listening to Ransom discuss this idea, that many traditional positions suffered not so much because of inherent defect but because of the inept defense of those positions. Perhaps, he thought, he had been turned away from older, more traditional solutions to problems simply because they had been poorly defended.

Weaver received his master's degree from Vanderbilt in 1934 and remained as a teaching fellow and doctoral student until 1936, when he took a position as instructor of English at Alabama Polytechnic Institute. He then accepted a position as assistant professor at the Agricultural and Mechanical College of Texas in 1937. Weaver dates his conversion to the "poetic and ethical vision of life" from his contact "with its sterile opposite" at Texas A&M: "I encountered a rampant philistinism, abetted by technology, large-scale organization, and a complacent acceptance of success as the goal of life. Moreover, I was here forced to see that the lion of applied science and the lamb of the humanities were not going to lie down together in peace, but that the lion was going to devour the lamb unless there was a very stern keeper of order."

In the fall of 1939, as he was driving across Texas to begin his third year of teaching there, Weaver realized he "did not *have* to go back to this job, which had become distasteful," and that he "did not *have* to go on professing the clichés of liberalism, which were becoming meaningless." At the age of thirty, Weaver switched his allegiance from socialism to conservatism, "chucked the uncongenial job," and enrolled as a teaching assistant in the doctoral program at Louisiana State University. His dissertation was an inquiry into the Southern mind, "The Confederate South, 1865-1910: A Study in the Survival of a Mind and a Culture." He was awarded the doctoral degree in 1943.[3]

In the 1943-1944 school year, Weaver served as a special instructor at North Carolina State College. He then joined the faculty at the University of Chicago, beginning as an instructor and working his way up to the rank of professor in 1957. At Chicago, he taught courses in the humanities sequence dealing with the interpretation of history, philosophy, and rhetoric and with the analysis and criticism of fiction, drama, and poetry. But he gave most of his time to the teaching of lower level, required writing courses such as freshman composition; he was dedicated "to helping students increase their skill in using the English language." That he was successful was evidenced in 1949, when he received a $1,000 award for best undergraduate teaching at the university. Two of Weaver's works reflect his dedication to the study and teaching of rhetoric and English as well — *The Ethics of Rhetoric*, published in 1953, and *Composition: A Course in Reading and Writing*, which appeared in 1957.

Weaver's life in Chicago was characterized by order, routine, and simplicity.

He lived in an apartment hotel located some distance from campus in order to give himself the pleasure of the daily walk back and forth. He taught his classes early in the morning, left his office for lunch at the same time every day—eating most of his meals in the university cafeteria—and returned to devote his afternoons to grading papers or taking care of the administrative details of the basic English courses. He then went home to pursue his own scholarly writing. During the summers, which he spent with his mother in the home he had bought for her in Weaverville, a town founded by his ancestors, he followed a precise schedule as well. The purpose of Weaver's routine was clear to those who knew him: it freed his energies for the reading and writing that mattered to him as a scholar.

Weaver would interrupt his work schedule to practice the sport of rifle marksmanship or to gather with friends and family, an opportunity, he felt, to be "a practicing humanist." His sister, Polly, described his enjoyment at such gatherings during his visits to North Carolina:

> He enjoyed good food and liked beer. He and my late husband [Kendall Beaton]. . . used to sit up until the early hours talking and drinking beer. They both loved H.L. Menken [sic] and I have seen them exchanging Menkian [sic] barbs at the foibles of mankind in almost helpless glee. They got into politics and the state of the world, too, and after a number of beers my brother would raise his favorite battle cry: "keep the barbarians out!"

Yet, Weaver lived apart much of the time and remained a bachelor throughout his life; privacy and reserve were predominant characteristics of him, as one colleague described: "He did not put you off, he did not hold you at arm's length, as some people do; but somehow you did not breach the reserve that kept his inwardness inviolate and inviolable."

As will be evidenced in his ideas on rhetoric and his critique of culture, Weaver preferred those things that are connected historically to a culture and that embody noble ideals; he did not see all new things and all progress as positive advances. He traveled by train rather than plane, and he flew only once in his life—from California to Chicago—when he had to meet a schedule. He said he enjoyed the trip and admired the Grand Canyon from the air, but he did not fly again. "You have to draw the line somewhere," he would say. The train, he felt, had been around for a century and had become part of the landscape and language, and its continuity was important to him. Similarly, he plowed his land in Weaverville with a horse-drawn plow rather than a tractor. The horse had lived with humans for centuries, and Weaver took such relationships seriously.

Weaver was regarded highly not only as a professor of English and rhetoric but also as a political conservative. Leading conservatives held him in esteem, and he is known as one of the founders of the "new conservatism." He saw the movement as the effort "to conserve the great structural reality which has been given us and which is on the whole beneficent,"[4] and he proudly accepted the label of conservative. Recognizing, however, that the conservative cause was "not getting across to the market in sufficient force and volume," he worked to achieve intellectual and political legitimacy for it by providing it with the strongest rhetorical defense possible.[5]

In this effort, he made numerous speeches defending the conservative cause before a variety of groups; served as a trustee of the Intercollegiate Society of Individualists, a conservative youth action group; and helped found the *National Review* and *Modern Age*, both conservative periodicals. He won a citation from the Freedom Foundation for his pamphlet, *Education and the Individual*, and he was honored by the Young Americans for Freedom at Madison Square Garden on March 7, 1962. His books, *Ideas Have Consequences* (1948) and *Visions of Order* (1964), were major efforts by Weaver to address the state of our culture and to suggest conservative solutions for its regeneration.

Weaver had just accepted a one-year appointment as a visiting professor at Vanderbilt University when he died of a heart attack on April 3, 1963.[6] His life perhaps best can be summarized as one that focused on the art of rhetoric: "In an age when most lives are divided and compartmentalized, his life had an enviable unity. In an age when words are cheap and the use of words is a skill cheaply held, he believed and taught and demonstrated that rhetoric is the most civilized and civilizing of the arts."[7]

Nature of the Human Being

Weaver's perspective on rhetoric rests on a view of the human being as composed of body, mind, and soul.[8] The body is the physical being that houses the mind and soul during life. It is self-centered and attempts to pull the individual downward toward excessive satisfaction of sensory pleasure.

The second aspect of the human being, the mind, is composed of four faculties or modes of apprehension. The emotional or aesthetic faculty, which is largely contemplative, allows experiences of pleasure, pain, and beauty. The ethical capacity determines orders of goods and judges between right and wrong, while the religious capacity, which is essentially intuitive, involves a yearning for something infinite and provides individuals with a glimpse of their destiny and ultimate nature. The rational or cognitive capacity provides human beings with knowledge because it allows them to define concepts, order ideas, and the like.[9]

The soul or spirit, the third part of the human, is "an integrative power binding the individual into an intellectual, emotional, and spiritual unity which is his highest self." It is composed "of wishes and hopes, of things transfigured, of imaginations and value ascriptions." It guides the mind and the body either toward good or evil, depending on whether it has been trained well or ill; essentially, it is degree of spiritual insight.[10]

Two additional characteristics complete Weaver's conception of the human being. First, as human beings, we are symbol using, which allows us to rise above the sensate level of knowledge to communicate feelings and values and thus to create a culture or civilization. Second, we are creatures of choice or free agents, and our dignity arises from our power of choice. Yet, for Weaver, freedom does not mean license to do whatever we please. Rather, it means freedom to act according to criteria for choice making implicit in the notion of truth held by a culture; we are free to actualize that truth.[11]

Knowledge and Truth

Within Weaver's tripartite division of the human being, he further divides the rational capacity into three kinds of knowledge or levels of conscious reflection: ideas, beliefs, and a metaphysical dream. The first level deals with specific ideas about things. These are the thoughts we employ in the activity of daily living or facts about existing physical entities. The measurements of a room or the amount of rainfall an area receives constitute knowledge at this level. These data direct our "disposition of immediate matters and, so, constitute [our] worldliness." At this level, we respond to impinging circumstances in a habitual manner and with little deliberation. The act of turning on a faucet, accomplished by taking physical entities and facts into account, is the result of knowledge at this level.

The second level is that of beliefs, convictions, theories, laws, generalizations, or concepts that order the world of facts. A generalization about average amount of rainfall in an area or the scientific law that water freezes at zero degrees centigrade are examples of this level of knowledge. We may inherit these beliefs from others, or we may formulate them from our own observations and reflection.

The third level of knowledge is the metaphysical dream, which is "an intuitive feeling about the immanent nature of reality." This is the level of philosophical opinion, statements about the statements on the second level, or ideals. Because it concerns values and ideals, this is the level to which both ideas or facts and beliefs ultimately are referred for verification; it provides judgmental standards for the evaluation of all other knowledge. A statement about the implications of a theory concerning amount of rainfall or the value of various amounts of rain would constitute knowledge of the third order.

With each of these three levels of knowledge, human beings impose something on the raw data of the world — we order, shape, and evaluate our experiences of those raw data. Without such an ordering, reason is impossible, for rational activities begin only after an appropriate perspective is gained that orders and shapes phenomena into a meaningful whole.[12]

Following Plato, Weaver depicts truth as residing at the third level of knowledge, in the ideal. Truth is the degree to which things and ideas in the material world conform to their ideals, archetypes, and essences. He contends that "the thing is not true and the act is not just unless these conform to a conceptual ideal." Truth, then, resides at the level of the metaphysical dream, not at the level of individual facts. The enumeration of facts at the first level of knowledge will not lead to truth, for "we do not find the secret of man's life in the study of things."[13]

Instead, facts gain meaning only by reference to a higher conceptual scheme of reality: "Before we can have the idea of relative evaluation at all, we must have a *tertium quid*, a third essence, an ideal ideal, as it were."[14] Weaver agrees with the remark attributed to Einstein, "If the facts do not fit the theory, so much the worse for the facts." If the facts used by someone appear to be incorrect, that has no necessary bearing on the truth. Such "wrong" facts simply suggest imperfect skill on the part of the rhetor in finding instances of the truth. In an unpublished essay about Mason Locke Weems, the first biographer of George Washington, Weaver explains this relationship between fact and truth in his discussion of whether or not Weems' biographies are true:

> If they are not true in the sense of fidelity to fact, neither are they false in the sense of presenting a misleading picture. . . .Weems was very shrewd at guessing the integrating principle of man's character; and it is doubtful whether the most plodding scrutiny of the career of Washington, aided by all the apparatus of modern scholarship, has changed the impression of ingrained honesty which Weems sought to convey with his pretty tales and invented speeches.[15]

The empirical level of facts, then, is interpreted in terms of the ideals of the third level, so that a connection always is made between the fact and the ideal.

Nature of Culture

Weaver's notion of the metaphysical dream, or the third level of knowledge at which truth resides, cannot be understood apart from his conception of culture. Culture, for Weaver, does not consist of material goods such as "armrests and soft beds and extravagant bathing facilities," for these cater to sensation. Rather, culture is of the imagination, the spirit, and inward tendencies: "A culture defines itself by crystallizing around. . . feelings which determine a common attitude toward large phases of experience; . . . They originate in our world view, in our ultimate vision of what is proper for men as higher beings."[16]

At the heart of every culture is a center of authority, which Weaver calls the "tyrannizing image." This center represents the cultural ideal or vision of excellence for which a society strives and sees as perfection: "There is a center which commands all things, and this center is open to imaginative but not logical discovery. It is a focus of value, a law of relationships, an inspiriting vision. By its nature it sets up rankings and orders." The tyrannizing image may be discerned in part through the "uncontested terms" of a culture. These are terms that embody beliefs and values that are "fixed by universal enlightened consensus." A term such as "freedom," for example, was uncontested in America in the nineteenth century and simply was accepted without argument as representing the highest ideals of the culture. The tyrannizing image also may be embodied in a religious ritual, a sacred scripture, a literary work everyone is expected to know, codes of conduct, or the like, but it is always an "inward facing toward some high representation."

The tyrannizing image of a culture contributes to our metaphysical dream because it inserts itself between us and our empirical experiences: "a developed culture is a way of looking at the world through an aggregation of symbols, so that empirical facts take on significance." It exerts subtle, pervasive pressures upon us to conform and to reject that which does not conform to the ideal. Thus, it exerts control over our actions, serving as the "sacred well of the culture from which inspiring waters like magnetic lines of force flow out and hold the various activities in a subservience of acknowledgement."

The tyrannizing image serves another function in a culture as well. Because it provides a structure for ordering and ranking, it also establishes hierarchy in the culture:

> Civilization is measured by its power to create and enforce distinctions. Consequently there must be some source of discrimination, from which we bring ideas of order to bear on a fortuitous world. Knowledge and virtue constitute this source, and these two things, it must be said to the vexation of the sentimental optimists, are in their nature aristocracies. Participation in them is open to all: this much of the doctrine of equality is sound; but the participation will never occur in equal manner or degree, so that however we allow men to start in the world, we may be sure that as long as standards of quality exist, there will be a sorting out.

Because a tyrannizing image represents an ideal of excellence, it necessarily creates societal distinctions of all kinds according to degree of conformity to that ideal.[17]

Despite the pressure exerted by our cultural ideal, we always have freedom of choice in our actions with regard to it. We may uphold the conception of truth of our culture, or we may place our own viewpoint above the expression of the ideal and the welfare of the culture. Proper motivation for action will lead us to select the former option and to work to resolve the discrepancy between what is and what should be in our culture. Weaver recognizes, of course, that individuals never can comprehend the cultural ideal perfectly and often will fall short of enacting it. Yet, if the truth in the ideal is recognized and the individuals of a culture work toward its actualization, they will be united in a strong, vigorous culture.

Rhetoric and Dialectic

Language is the process through which the ultimate truth of the metaphysical dream is conveyed to the individuals of a culture. Two means are available for revealing truth through language—dialectic and rhetoric—although they both are imperfect vehicles for the demonstration of truth. Language, of course, cannot fully express truth, for if it did, truth would be reduced from its ultimate essence to a lesser form.

For Weaver, dialectic is the means for attaining knowledge of universals and essences at the third level of knowledge; it is a "method of investigation whose object is the establishment of truth about doubtful propositions." It is "abstract reasoning" through such processes as the analysis of fundamental terms, categorization, definition, the drawing out of implications, and the exposure of contradictions.

Weaver's notion of dialectic is limited in its application to dealings with dialectical rather than positive terms. Positive terms stand for observable objects capable of physical identification and measurement. They are terms whose referents are things that exist in the world and whose existence supposedly everyone can be brought to acknowledge. "Rock," "tree," and "dog," for example, are positive terms. Arguments over such terms are not really arguments, since the point of dispute can be resolved by accurate observation and reporting.

Dialectical terms, in contrast, are words for "essences and principles, and their meaning is reached not through sensory perception, but through the logical processes of definition, inclusion, exclusion, and implication." "Justice" and "goodness" are examples of dialectical terms. Dialectic, then, aims to determine what belongs in the category of the "just," for example, rather than what belongs in the genus of "dog"; the terms with which it deals concern values. The standard by which to judge competing value positions in dialectic is the ideal or the truth at the third level of knowledge. If the dialectician's soul "has its impulse in the right direction, its definitions will agree with the true nature of intelligible things."[18]

The capacity of dialectic to deal with universals and essences has appeal for Weaver; however, he realizes that limitations to the process exist. First, dialectic cannot move individuals. It lacks the ability to obtain commitment to a position or action. For instance, the speaker who has arrived at the position, through dialectic, that generosity is a virtue and argues for that position wins our intellectual assent but has not produced in us a resolve to practice generosity.[19] As Weaver explains: "In sum, dialectic is epistemological and logical; it is concerned with discriminating into categories and knowing definitions. . . . That would be sufficient if the whole destiny of man were to know. But we are reminded that the end of living is activity and not mere cognition."[20]

A second problem with pure dialectic is that it is not involved with the actual world. The "dialectician knows, but he knows in a vacuum." In other words, the dialectician's deliberations occur independently of the facts of a situation and with no necessary reference to reality. In addition, the process occurs apart from the culture in which the dialectician resides. The dialectician need not share the sentiments of the culture and thus is asocial because discriminations are made apart from the organic feeling of the community. If the dialectician shows no sympathy for or allegiance to the culture's institutions and values, the logic produced breeds distrust in the worth of any of the forms created by the culture because they are judged solely on whether they meet the requirements for logical perfection.

Weaver cites Socrates as an example of a dialectician who was removed from his culture. While he was a great dialectician and an ethical teacher, he was charged with and put to death for being a subverter and a corrupter when his dialectic offended the culture. Thus, Weaver asserts, those who believe that dialectic by itself should be practiced "are among the most subversive enemies of society and culture. They are attacking an ultimate source of cohesion in the interest of a doctrine which can issue only in nullity." To trust all to dialectic, then, "is a fast road to social subversion."[21]

Weaver's solution to the subversive nature of extreme dialecticism is rhetoric. He believes that the limitations of dialectic can be overcome and its advantages maintained through the use of rhetoric as a complement to dialectic. Weaver defines rhetoric as "truth plus its artful presentation," which means that rhetoric takes a "dialectically secured position. . . and shows its relationship to the world of prudential conduct." It instills belief and action and cannot be separated from a concern with values. Weaver explains that "it is the nature of the conscious life of man to revolve around some concept of value," which he sees as "the ultimate sanction of rhetoric." The conception of value, of course, is derived from the tyrannizing image of the culture, and rhetoric ideally moves individuals in the direction of that image.[22]

Rhetoric is able to move individuals to act because it goes beyond mere scientific demonstration and relates to the world. It is directed to a particular audience in its particular situation. In summary, rhetoric adds a consideration of the character and situation of the audience to the knowledge gained through dialectic: "The honest rhetorician therefore has two things in mind: a vision of how matters should go ideally and ethically and a consideration of the special circumstances of his auditors."[23]

Because rhetoric deals with action in real situations at the same time that it concerns ideals, it "is an essential ingredient of social cohesion"; it has an inevitable connection to culture. Because rhetoric emanates from a group's "imaginative picture" of the world or its tyrannizing image, it functions as a bond for the members of a culture. It conveys the permanent values of the culture and thus serves as a "common denominator of truth" for its members. Rhetoric, then, urges the individuals of a culture to move toward the tyrannizing image by acting in ways that bring them closer to that image; it also enables the members of a culture to talk together because they share basic premises.[24]

Rhetoric is able to serve as a bond for members of a culture because it is a storehouse of universal memory for a culture. The uses of words in a culture acquire a significance greater than the meanings individuals have for them and greater than their application to single situations. By embodying the experiences and meanings of words of all individuals, rhetoric is suprapersonal; it operates beyond the single individual to unite all the minds of the culture in their quest for the attainment of the tyrannizing image.[25]

Although rhetoric should be used to move people toward the ideal, Weaver realizes it is not always used in this fashion. It also can be neutral — not moving its audience at all — or it can be perverted to the use of base techniques and to serve evil ends. The evil or base speaker conveys attitudes of exploitation, domination, selfishness, superiority, and deception and frequently blocks clear definition and an honest examination of alternatives by discussing only one side of an issue. To lead an audience toward the good, however, requires a noble speaker who exalts the intrinsic worth of the audience and reflects such attitudes as respect, concern, unselfishness, and a desire to help the audience actualize its ideals.[26] Rhetoric, for Weaver, is not a value-free tool. It rests on fundamental assumptions that either accord or not with the good, the true, and the ideal. Thus, the particular value positions to which rhetors are committed determine whether the rhetoric they employ is good and ethical or evil and base.[27]

Because rhetoric inevitably promotes values by reflecting choices among goods, Weaver sees all rhetoric as sermonic. It always is "a carrier of tendency"; it "is never innocent of intention, but always has as its object the exerting of some kind of compulsion." As rhetors, then, we "are all of us preachers in private or public capacities. We have no sooner uttered words than we have given impulse to other people to look at the world, or some small part of it, in our way.'' If our basic vision of the truth is good, our messages will urge others to virtuous action; if it is evil, we will encourage vice.

Weaver thus asserts that being objective about anything is impossible. A rhetorical or persuasive dimension is present even in a statement that says a straight line is the shortest distance between two points: "The scientist has some interest in setting forth the formulation of some recurrent feature of the physical world, although his own sense of motive may be lost in a general feeling that science is a good thing because it helps progress along.'' [28]

We've seen that Weaver views dialectic as abstract reasoning that seeks to establish understanding but does not engage the issues of the actual world. Rhetoric, in contrast, takes a position secured through dialectic and asks us to believe it and to act on it. To separate the two is dangerous, for rhetoric alone does not have knowledge of the truth, and an isolated dialectic does not engage the issues of the empirical world. Weaver explains:

> A failure to appreciate this distinction is responsible for many lame performances in our public controversies. The effects are, in outline, that the dialectician cannot understand why his demonstration does not win converts; and the rhetorician cannot understand why his appeal is rejected as specious. The answer, . . . is that the dialectician has not made reference to reality, which men confronted with problems of conduct require; and the rhetorician has not searched the grounds of the position on which he has perhaps spent much eloquence. [29]

A sound rhetoric, then, presupposes dialectic, bringing together understanding and action. Weaver thus affirms an essential connection between dialectic and rhetoric.

Rhetorical Embodiment of World View

Weaver's belief that rhetoric expresses the ultimate values of its users is developed explicitly in his system of sources of arguments, grammatical categories, and ultimate terms.

Sources of Argument

Weaver believes that the type of argument a person habitually uses reveals much about that person and "is a surprisingly effective means of reading the character and intentions of the man behind the argument. Once this truth is appreciated you find that you can judge a man not wholly by the specific thing he asks for but also by the way he asks for it.'' The type of argument used, in fact, may be a better source of judgment about or "truer index in his beliefs than his explicit profession of principles."

A connection can be made between the source of an argument and the philosophical position of the rhetor, Weaver believes, because sources of content for rhetoric lie in how we interpret and classify our experiences of reality. Sources for arguments are means for interpreting the universe or frames through which the world is viewed, and when speakers use particular arguments, they are asking their listeners not simply to follow a valid reasoning form but to agree with the particular view of reality being presented. Through the use of certain argumentative sources, rhetors say that they believe in and urge acceptance of a particular construction of the universe—whatever one is necessary for the statements to make sense. They try to persuade the audience to read the world as they do.[30] Weaver also asserts that these sources or types of argument can be ranked or ordered according to their ethical worth. Certain ways of arriving at conclusions and of arguing are better, in an ethical sense, than others."[31] The most ethical type of argument is that of genus and definition.

Genus and Definition. One way of thinking about reality or interpreting experience is expressed in the language of philosophy as "being," where the world is viewed in terms of things belonging to certain classes and having certain essences. This can be translated into argument by genus or definition. This type of argument relies on the presupposition "that there exist classes which are determinate and therefore predictable." In presenting this type of argument, the rhetor refers the subject of deliberation to its class, and if the audience is sufficiently impressed with the actuality of that class, it grants that whatever is true of the class is true of the subject under consideration.[32]

Suppose you are accosted by a robber, who threatens you with a gun and demands your money. Assuming you could get him to listen to argument, you might argue by genus or definition that what he is attempting is a crime, which is illegal."[33] Weaver also includes argumentation from example in this category of argument. An example, he feels, always implies a general class.

Although they function in the same way and reveal similar world views, Weaver distinguishes between genus and definition in this type of argument. In argument by genus, a classification already is established and accepted in the mind of the audience. When a minister before a fundamentalist congregation categorizes an action as a "sin," for example, the argument is one of genus; the genus of "sin" is so well established that support for it is not necessary. Support probably would not be necessary for the definition of crime in our argument to the robber; thus, it also is argument by genus. Argument by definition, in contrast, requires that the classification be established in the course of the argument. The rhetor must define the characteristics of a class and then may use the defined term as a genus. For example, the speaker who wishes to argue that women deserve equal rights with men first would have to establish that all human beings deserve certain rights.[34]

Argument based on definition or genus is most ethical, according to Weaver, because it involves the interpretation of a subject by defining the fundamental and unchanging properties of its nature or being; it deals with permanent universals and essences: "That which is perfect does not change; that which has to change is less perfect. Therefore, if it is possible to determine unchanging essences or qualities and to speak in terms of these, one is appealing to what is most real in so doing. . . . The realm of essence is the realm above the flux of phenomena, and definitions are of essences and genera."[35] Those who habitually argue from genus are, in their personal philosophies, idealists; they are committed to the assumption that things have a nature. Use of this type of argument, according to Weaver, indicates that arguers have used dialectic, tempered by rhetoric, as a means of analyzing the situation and thus that they hold knowledge at the level of universals.

Similitude. A second way of thinking about reality is through "relationship," where we see that something has a significant resemblance to something else. This translates into argument by similitude, which involves the interpretation of a subject in relationships of similarity and dissimilarity. Here a rhetor draws a conclusion by suggesting that a subject "is like something which we know in fuller detail, or that it is unlike that thing in important respects." This type of argument includes analogy, metaphor, figuration, comparison, and contrast.

Argument from similitude could be employed when confronted with the robber by telling him that this is the sort of thing he would dislike if he were the victim of it. That marijuana should be legalized because alcohol is constitutes argumentation by similitude as well.

Similitude ranks second in terms of ethics. Although rhetors using this argument search for the underlying essence or ideal that must be present if it is to have the capacity to prove, they are less confident about the ability to know the truth fully and thus to produce that essence or ideal for the audience. Because it is based ultimately on essence, however, argument by similitude still is an ethical argument to use; it simply does not reveal the essence at its core as explicitly as does argument by genus or definition.[36]

Cause and Effect. A third way of thinking about reality is through "cause," where something is the known cause of a certain effect. Argument by cause and effect, or consequence, then, involves the interpretation of experience in a causal relationship. This type of argument attempts to predict the results of a particular action, and the anticipated results are used to determine whether or not that action should be undertaken. As with arguments from definition, these arguments may involve self-evident and widely accepted causal linkages, or the rhetor may have to establish them. A cause-to-effect argument would be the type used by a politician who argues that war causes inflation. In the case of the robber, you could tell him that the act of robbery will result in his having to spend years in the penitentiary.

Although Weaver recognizes that "we all have to use it because we are historical" people, he sees argument by cause and effect as less ethical than the first two types because it asks the audience to respond to a lower order of reality—"the realm of becoming." This realm, where things are in flux, is a lower state of being than that of essence, the ideal, and the unchanging.[37]

Argument from circumstance is a kind of causal argument that Weaver believes is the least ethical type that can be used. It reads surrounding circumstances, accepts them as coercive, and says, "step lively." The key consideration in such an argument is not what a thing is but in what directions the forces are piling up. Thus, it is the nearest of all the arguments to pure expediency. "I must quit school because I have no money" is argument from circumstance, as is a reply to the robber of "I must surrender all of my money to you because you have a gun, are bigger than I am, and cannot be persuaded by reason." Present circumstances are the overbearing consideration, and even the bond of cause and effect is not discussed.

Argument by circumstance is least ethical, Weaver believes, because it indicates that a subject has been analyzed at the level of perception of fact; the rhetor views facts as having philosophical primacy. Use of this type of argument amounts to a surrender of reason, and the arguer expresses an instinctive feeling that in this situation, reason is powerless.[38]

Authority and Testimony. While being, relationship, and cause are internal ways of interpreting the world, the fourth mode of interpretation—"authority"—is an external one. Here, statements made by observers and experts take the place of the direct interpretation of evidence, and individuals we respect vouch for the truth. The force of argument by authority and testimony is not derived from the immediate subject matter of the discourse but from consideration of the competence and integrity of the witness: "If a proposition is backed by some weighty authority, like the Bible, or can be associated with a great name, people may be expected to respond to it in accordance with the veneration they have for these sources." "The Bible says that stealing is wrong" might be an argument by authority you could present to the robber; to argue that the Declaration of Independence says that all human beings are created equal is another example of such argument. This type of argument is different from the other three sources not only in its reliance on external proof; it also differs in that it seldom stands alone as the primary source of an extensive argument.

Arguments based on testimony and authority have to be judged in a different way from arguments of definition, similitude, and cause and effect. An argument of this type is as good as the authority on which it is based. Such testimony, however, often embodies arguments from genus, similitude, and cause and effect; thus, arguments from authority can be judged as well by the standards appropriate to such arguments.[39]

Rhetorical-Historical. Toward the end of his life, Weaver identified another category of argument—the rhetorical-historical argument. This mode of argument exemplified his view of the essential connection between dialectic and rhetoric and synthesized the arguments by genus, similitude, and cause and effect. Rhetorical-historical argument is a composite argument that requires a definition of genus or principle and a reference to historical circumstances. In his study of the debate between Robert Hayne and Daniel Webster in 1830, Weaver cites as an example of this kind of argument Hayne's assertion that South Carolina was patriotic to the Union. Hayne first offered a definition of the Union and then turned to the historical record to show South Carolina's loyalty to it. In the case of our robber, we might use rhetorical-historical argument by pointing out that robbery is legally defined as a crime and that the court's criminal records in the county reveal that numerous individuals like him were convicted and sent to prison for performing actions of the type he is attempting.[40]

In his discussion of rhetoric and dialectic, Weaver advocates that the rhetor hold a vision of the ideal but consider as well the special circumstances of the audience and its particular situation. The rhetorical-historical argument, which involves a synthesis of principle with cause and circumstance and the ideal with the concrete, explicitly points to Weaver's concern both for principle and the circumstances of a particular situation. Thus, it clearly keeps rhetoric and dialectic in their proper relationship as counterparts.

Grammatical Categories

The sources of argument used by a rhetor are not the only indication of philosophical position; grammatical choices also can reveal a rhetor's world view. Different patterns of expression denote different interests in saying something.

Knowledge of the ways in which various grammatical categories function also can help a speaker "prevent a loss of force through friction," which "occurs whenever a given unit of the system of grammar is tending to say one thing while the semantic meaning and the general organization are tending to say another." A knowledge of what various grammatical categories suggest in terms of philosophy, then, also enables a rhetor to achieve congruence between grammatical form and message content. There "is a kind of use of language which goes against the grain as that grain is constituted by the categories, and there is a kind which facilitates the speaker's projection by going with it. Our task is an exploration of the congruence between well understood rhetorical objectives and the inherent character of major elements in modern English.''[41]

Among the grammatical categories that Weaver discusses as indicative of a rhetor's world view are kinds of sentences. When the mind frames a sentence, it performs intellectual operations of analysis and re-synthesis—taking two or more classes and uniting them in some way. The manner in which this unification is accomplished is revealing.

A simple sentence, for example, "tends to emphasize the discreteness of phenomena within the structural unity," for its pattern is that of subject, verb, object or complement, with no major competing elements. Such a sentence leaves our attention focused on the classes involved, as in "Catharine is a professor" or "The children played." These types of sentences are often the style, Weaver asserts, "of one who sees the world as a conglomerate of things" or "who seeks to present certain things as eminent against a background of matter uniform or flat." Weaver also sees such sentences as indicating "an elementary level of perception" or an "unclouded perspective."[42]

A complex sentence contains one or more dependent clauses and one independent clause; it is "the branching sentence." In contrast to the simple sentence, it "does not stop with seeing discrete classes as co-existing, but distinguishes them according to rank or value, or places them in an order of cause and effect." The complex sentence, "The students failed the exam because they did not study," for example, goes beyond simple perception; it perceives causal principle and grades elements according to a standard of interest. By the very structure of the sentence, the reader understands which point is primary. In other words, those who use the complex sentence have performed a second act of analysis, in which the objects of perception, after being seen, are given an ordering.[43]

The compound sentence, which consists of two or more simple sentences joined in some way, simply may reflect artlessness—the uncritical pouring together of simple sentences. But it also may be a mature sentence in which a writer or speaker wishes to show a particularly close relationship between points." Such a sentence often gives a complete statement by offering two views of a subject—a view with an explanation, or a qualifying view that seems to finish off the assertion. A sentence such as, "Last July was hot, but August was even hotter," for example, shows a settled view of the world; the world is seen as a compensatory system in balance. In such a sentence, an abstract statement often will be balanced by a more concrete expression of the same thing—a fact balanced by its causal explanation or a description of one part balanced by a description of a contrasting part. Such sentences convey the completion and symmetry that the world ought to have.[44]

Just as types of sentences selected are revealing of the rhetor, so are the types of words or parts of speech selected. A noun or name word is a word for a material or conceptual substance whose being is complete rather than in process. Nouns deal with essences, which have a higher degree of being than actions or qualities.[45] Adjectives, in contrast, are words of secondary force and status; they are added to nouns and are attributes conceptually dispensable to the substance to which they are joined. If a thing to be expressed is real, it is expressed through a noun; if it is expressed mainly through adjectives, we feel something is defective in its reality because it requires secondary support. For example, the statement, "Have some white milk," would make most of us curious, and we would suspect some defect in the original image that must be corrected. Of course, in some situations, modifiers do make a useful contribution, but for Weaver, a style that relies heavily on adjectives suggests a lack of confidence about essences and reality on the part of the rhetor.[46]

Verbs—words that describe actions or states of being—rank with nouns in force. They represent a process of going on, a state of becoming, whereby things change while still maintaining the essence of their identities. Weaver uses an example of the political state to demonstrate the "paradox of both being and becoming":

> The same process is visible even when we look at the political state. It persists under one name, and it may even affirm in its organic law that it is indestructible. But its old leaders pass on or are removed, and new ones appear. After a twenty-year absence, one would come back and find the leaders looking different in almost any country. But while these individual particles are being shuffled and replaced, "the state" goes on, maintaining some character and identity through all the changes.

A style that uses verbs, then, typically is a vigorous one because it reflects the rhetor's ability to label the quality of an action while at the same time recognizing the essence of a state of being.[47]

While we will not discuss them here, Weaver also examines adverbs, conjunctions, prepositions, and phrases and sees each as serving a rhetor in various ways. A rhetor's use of the various parts of speech and types of sentences allows the creation of rhetoric that functions formally and substantively to create the force desired. At the same time, an audience can use these grammatical categories to assess the world view of the rhetor.

Ultimate Terms

Yet another way by which rhetors' world views can be revealed is through the ultimate terms on which they rely. Ultimate terms are terms to which the highest respect is paid in a culture and to which the populace appears to attribute the greatest sanction. Such terms are rhetorical absolutes in that they generally are uncontested and are widely accepted by members of a culture. These terms, because they represent the ideal or tyrannizing image of a culture, are a primary rhetorical means for motivating individuals to push forward toward that ideal: "We have shown that rhetorical force must be conceived as a power transmitted through the links of a chain that extends upward toward some ultimate source. The higher links of that chain must always be of unique interest to the student of rhetoric, pointing, as they do, to some prime mover of human impulse."[48]

Weaver divides ultimate terms into three major categories: "god," "devil," and "charismatic" terms. A god term is a term "about which all other expressions are ranked as subordinate. . . . Its force imparts to the others their lesser degree of force, and fixes the scale by which degrees of comparison are understood." In other words, a god term carries the greatest blessing in a culture and has the capacity to demand sacrifice.[49]

Several terms may compete for the ultimate position if a strong religion is not present in a culture. In the 1950s, when Weaver was writing, "progress" was a god term in our culture. "Fact" also was a god term; "it is a fact" meant it was the kind of knowledge to which all other knowledge must defer. "American" was another god term—one that still seems to have maintained its god status for us today. We tend to see "American" as identified with that which is destined to be or the goal toward which all creation moves. In fact, we tend to judge a country's civilization by its resemblance to the American model.[50]

Devil terms, the counterpart of god terms, are terms of repulsion—whatever is perceived as the enemy or greatest evil in a culture. In our society, "Communism" is a devil term, as political enemies generally are; "Tory," "Nazi," and "Fascist" all have been devil terms for us in the past. "Poverty" and "nuclear war" also are current devil terms in our culture. These are not "ultimate" in the way that god terms are, of course, because they are the counterfeit of the good and do not represent what is ultimate, unconditional, and true.[51]

Charismatic terms function somewhat differently from god and devil terms. We are able to understand the appeal of god and devil terms through their connection with something we apprehend—something derived from observable aspects of the world. But charismatic terms seem to operate independently of referential connections. They have "a power which is not derived, but which is in some mysterious way given"; their meaning seems to come from "a popular will that they *shall* mean something. In effect, they are rhetorical by common consent, or by 'charisma.'" As in the case with charismatic leaders, where the populace gives them a power that cannot be explained through their personal attributes alone, the charismatic term is given its load of impulsion without reference and functions by convention. "Freedom" and "democracy" are charismatic terms in our culture. We demand sacrifice in the name of these terms, yet the referents most of us attach to them are obscure and often contradictory. In fact, Weaver says, we may resist the attempt to define such terms, perhaps fearing that a term defined explicitly will have its charisma taken away.[52]

An examination of the ultimate terms used in a culture, then, reveals the ideals held by the members of that culture. Similarly, the ultimate terms used by a particular rhetor reflect a particular vision of the world and the degree to which it contributes to or detracts from the effort to move the culture closer toward the truth and perfection embodied in its tyrannizing image. To discover that the god and devil terms of a culture or rhetor are inappropriate, reflecting values out of line with the tyrannizing image, encourages the attempt to persuade others to see the error, as Weaver himself attempted to do in his critique of culture.

Decline of Rhetoric

Weaver did not write about culture and the role rhetoric plays in it only on a theoretical level; he applied his ideas to our own culture to evaluate and assess it. In this role, he saw himself as "a kind of doctor of culture" — an individual "who may entertain hope of doing something about a culture that is weakening."[53] He explained his concern:

> Those who argue that our civilization is advancing are safe as long as they stick to what is above the surface, and they can usually smother you with statistics. But as soon as one peers beneath the surface and looks at what is happening to the only sources of order man has, one sees that those are being seriously weakened if not destroyed, in which case the great superstructure is in danger of collapse.[54]

Weaver pointed to many signs that our culture is degenerating, among them scientism; nominalism; semantic positivism; uncritical homage to the theory of evolution; radical egalitarianism; pragmatism; cultural relativism; materialism; emphasis on techniques at the expense of goals; idolization of youth; progressive education; disparagement of historical consciousness; deleterious effects of the mass media; and degenerate literature, music, and art.[55]

For Weaver, one of the most alarming signs of our culture's degeneration is the decline of rhetoric. Weaver saw our public rhetoric as reflecting the corrupt and unsound foundations of our thought; in all likelihood, he would have found it even more so today. A century ago, rhetoric was regarded as the most important humanistic discipline taught in our colleges. That position of status and value no longer exists: "the wheel of fortune would seem to have turned for rhetoric; what was once at the top is now at the bottom, and because of its low estate, people begin to wonder on what terms it can survive at all." [56]

The decline of rhetoric is evident in who currently is considered qualified to teach it. In the nineteenth century, "to be a professor of rhetoric, one had to be *somebody*. . . a person of gifts and imagination." Now, however, the teaching of rhetoric is left to almost anyone who is willing to teach it: "Beginners, part-time teachers, graduate students, . . . and various fringe people, are now the instructional staff of an art which was once supposed to require outstanding gifts and mature experience." [57]

The degeneration of rhetoric further is evidenced in the view that language is relative, "that language, like every other phenomenon, has to be viewed as part of a changing world." Fixed significations for words or an absolutist position from which the application of words can be judged "right" or "wrong," as was the case in earlier times when cultures were more stable, no longer exist. Rather, Weaver points out, meanings now depend on the time and place in which the words are used, the perspective of the user, and estimates as to what the majority of individuals will accept. [58]

Weaver is not arguing here that the meanings of words never can change. Such change is essential when unsatisfactory terms in a culture are clarified through dialectic. But such changes occur according to two constraints. The first is the convention in effect in the culture. Because we are part of a community of language users, a change in language should not be made unless it is endorsed by the linguistic group to which we belong. Words are tied to objects via our minds; thus, a language—if it is to be shared by individuals—cannot exist unless a "oneness of mind" lies behind it. Language rests on a consensus or common point of view of things; it serves as a covenant:

> It is in the nature of a covenant to be more than a matter of simple convenience, to be departed from for light and transient causes. A covenant. . . binds us at deeper levels and involves some kind of confrontation of reality. When we covenant with one another that a word shall stand for a certain thing, we signify that it is the best available word for that thing in the present state of general understanding.

Weaver provides an example of this notion of a covenant as agreement that a certain symbol shall be attached to a certain object or idea: "It has been agreed that 'sweet' stands for one kind of sensory response and 'sour' for a very different one, and nobody can singly on his own volition switch these two around, anymore than he could tell the clerk in a store that in his lexicon five is more than ten and that therefore he ought to have change for his five dollar bill when he has made a ten dollar purchase." Language, then, cannot be changed by a single individual as a matter of whim but is subject to the convention of the culture concerning language.[59]

A second constraint on changes in our language is linked to the ultimate and universal truth embodied in our words. From a dialectical perspective, our words hold meanings that theoretically are absolutely "right." Our meanings for words include an awareness of a meaning beyond our everyday, obtuse understanding of a word; this meaning is the one that reflects the high ideals of the culture and that individual members as yet may not fully understand. Thus, words function not as a description of experience at the level of sensation but as a window to glimpse ultimate truth. We cannot change our meanings for words without effecting change at the level of universals and essences. Our meanings, Weaver believes, therefore should not change without careful consideration of the consequences.[60]

Finally, the decline of rhetoric is evidenced in the fact that while it once was taught as the art of speaking truthfully, it now has become the art of speaking usefully. According to Weaver, students previously were taught a conception of the true and the ideal through rhetoric; now they are taught how to use language to better their position in the world, to get whatever they want, or to prevail with verbal deception. Today, teachers of rhetoric generally teach sophistry or etiquette rather than the terms that constitute a standard for truth in the culture, and this view is a major enemy of true rhetoric.[61]

In spite of his pessimism about the degeneration of culture, evidenced in part, in the decline of rhetoric, Weaver sees hope for the restoration of culture. Such a process would involve the revitalization of memory or the recreation of the value of history, as well as a restoration of respect for the right to exist of things not of one's own creation, including nature, other people, and the past. Another essential ingredient would be a renewed emphasis on the right of private property, which Weaver sees as a relationship or identification between individuals and their substance. Property helps individuals express their being, encourages virtues such as providence in the maintenance of the property, and insures quality in many areas of life as individuals assume responsibility for the products they create and with which their names are connected.[62]

Also essential to the revitalization of culture is the restoration of rhetoric because it is a vehicle of order that enables individuals to understand one another. To restore rhetoric to its proper place in a culture, rhetorical training is needed that features the study of a number of subject areas. Poetry should be studied since great poets are the quickest to apprehend necessary truth. The study of dialectic is important because "it involves the science of naming" or definition. This enables the student to see limitation and contradiction — to learn, in effect, how to think. Foreign languages also should be studied, including Latin and Greek, for such study discourages slovenliness in the use of language: "Focusing upon what a word means and then finding its just equivalent in another language compels one to look and to think before he commits himself to any expression."[63]

Not only must the subject matter taught under the rubric of rhetoric be changed, but teachers of rhetoric also must assume responsibilities they currently do not. While most teachers of rhetoric probably would agree that the objective of courses in rhetoric is to make students more articulate, Weaver asserts, their duty should not stop simply with making students articulate or eloquent. About what, Weaver asks, do we wish to make them articulate? Those who instruct in the art of speech "are turning loose upon the world a power. Where do we expect the wielders of that power to learn the proper use of it?"[64]

The teacher of rhetoric, then, must be a definer, a namer, and an orderer of the universe of meanings: "The world has to be named for the benefit of each oncoming generation, and who teaches more names than the arbiter of the use of language?" This means that the teacher must discover and show essential values, as well as deal with the subject matter of essences or the structure of reality. If a teacher, for example, assigns an essay or speech on the topic of "democracy," that teacher must be able to tell students what "democracy" names or means. For Weaver, a teacher of rhetoric is one who names well — someone who gives the proper names for things and reflects the tyrannizing image of the culture. If teachers are going to participate in the redemption of culture, they must "desert certain primrose paths of dalliance and begin the difficult, the dangerous, work of teaching men to speak and to write the truth."[65] Weaver's view of this role of the teacher leads him to see the teacher as determining the fate of each student: "I sometimes say to classes: when a teacher walks into a room, part of your fate walks into the room. Because that teacher is going to determine something for you — an attitude, a conviction, or an evaluation. . . . But his personality and what he communicates to the class are going to leave their mark or their residue.[66]

Those who oppose Weaver's view of education may argue that the teacher must be very arrogant to know what things really are and to name them. Weaver expects the teacher to approach knowledge with an attitude of humility, realizing that "there are a number of things that man will never fully understand." Yet, the teacher must "transmit respect for that hard won knowledge which has served to construct a providential social order," and this act is an arrogant one, to some degree: "By what act of arrogance do we set ourselves up as teachers? There are two postulates basic to our profession: the first is that one man can know more than another, and the second is that such knowledge can be imparted. Whoever cannot accept both should retire from the profession and renounce the intention of teaching anyone anything."[67]

Still others would argue, in opposition to Weaver's position, that teachers should present all sides of a question, giving all possible names previously and currently applied to a thing and allowing students to choose among the names. Weaver's reply is that this position assumes "that there are sources closer to the truth than are the schools and that the schools merely act as their agents. It would be interesting," Weaver muses, "to hear what these sources are."[68]

Weaver's program for teachers of rhetoric, he admits, requires courage; it "is an invitation to lead the dangerous life. Whoso comes to define comes bearing the sword of division." The consequences of these actions, however, are ultimately beneficial: "The teacher will find himself not excluded from the world but related to it in ways that may become trying. But he will regain something that has been lost in the long dilution of education, the standing of one with a mission. He will be able, as he has not been for a long while, to take his pay partly in honor."[69]

Another consequence of such a role for the teacher is that it is incompatible with student-centered education, where everything is adapted to children according to their limitations; no ideals are set by which they are to measure themselves. Knowledge, as a result, "will take on an authority which some mistake for arrogance." The student will learn, however, "that the world is not wholly contingent, but partly predictable, and that, if he will use his mind rightly, it will not lie to him about the world."[70]

Responses to Weaver

Weaver has been described as a "Socialist Party member who became a conservative crusader, a Southern Agrarian who exiled himself to a northern megalopolis and an academic rhetor who dialectically dissected contemporary culture."[71] This description of Weaver, with its paradoxes, explains why the student of Weaver "appears to be hard put to it to 'classify' Richard Weaver, or to say what he was up to without, pretty soon, sticking his foot in his mouth."[72]

A number of different frameworks have been suggested by which to interpret and understand Weaver's thinking and writing. He has been labeled a Platonist by many; others have said he only was oriented toward Platonism and held an appreciation for it. Some of his ideas—such as his belief in the reality of transcendentals and the primacy of ideas—clearly were in line with Plato's thinking.[73]

Others argue that Weaver's work best is interpreted in a framework of

Christian theology. Some interpreters, such as East, believe that Weaver's thinking reveals a religious foundation and character to his mind, so that while he never explicitly stated he was a Christian, his position is markedly Christian. Another view, exemplified by Hariman, is that Christian language and terminology are important in Weaver's work but that his use of that language is doctrinally empty. In other words, he appropriates religious terms to transpose or secularize them in order to generate rhetorical power. Still others, including Follette, have argued that Weaver's thinking does more than simply appropriate religious terms for his purposes; Follette believes he takes God seriously and assumes a God-based theological stance that affects his entire perspective on rhetoric.[74]

Christianity and Platonism may not be incompatible as frameworks for interpreting Weaver. The Platonic transcendent ideals on which Weaver focuses may originate, in Christian terms, in God. In fact, Weaver aligned himself with both the traditions of Platonism and Christianity in a letter responding to a review of *Ideas Have Consequences* and appeared to see them as quite compatible: "I am quite willing to be identified with the not inconsiderable number of thinkers in the Platonic-Christian tradition who have taken the same stand."[75]

Weaver's capacity to relate his work to a number of conceptual frameworks and to deal with a variety of disciplines has been a point of criticism of his work. He "spent the major part of his working day. . . swimming far from the safe shores of his own competence towards high seas that were beyond his depth," commented one critic. "A rhetor doing the work of a philosopher, he tackled problems for which he was not equipped."[76] This was evident, his critics have asserted, in that he seemed to be unaware of, to ignore, or to misinterpret relevant material. He has been questioned, for example, by Johannesen for misinterpreting the General Semanticists' position. Similarly, his use of predominant types of argument to discover a rhetor's philosophical position has been criticized by respondents such as Johannesen and Kirk because he seems to ignore the possibility that the form an argument assumes simply may be a rhetorical choice by a rhetor and because the evidence he uses to support his position is weak. When he attacks science, with its materialistic, mechanistic, and deterministic concepts, Muller points out, he is "seemingly unaware that physicists themselves have scrapped such concepts." Even in his works on rhetoric, he sometimes exhibits a disregard for the rhetorical scholarship of the past; "the result sometimes is a quite needless tone of ingenuousness." For example, in his essay on the *Phaedrus*, Vivas asserts, he discovers what long has been known—that it is a dialogue on rhetoric. Most critics, however, are not willing to dismiss Weaver's entire system of thought because of such problems, for "he nearly always returned from his adventures with something worthwhile to show for them."[77]

Others fault Weaver for the provincialism and ethnocentrism of his thinking—deriving in part from his strong allegiance to his Southern identity. Goodnight, for example, asserts that his provincialism limits his thinking and fails to provide a legitimate interpretation for the total American experience and the rest of the world. "Given any knowledge of the history of civilization," echoes Muller, Weaver's certitudes "look arrogantly provincial." He ignores the great civilizations of the East, and his universal, eternal truths are those of Westerners or Americans or Southerners. He does not think, as a result of his provincialism, in truly universal terms of other forms of idealism and systems of truth other than our own.[78]

Despite the citation of such problems with Weaver's work, critics recognize his influence on conservatism as substantial. He has been called a "powerful intellectual force in the American conservative movement of the post-World War II period," and his book, *Ideas Have Consequences*, has been called the informing principle of the contemporary American conservative movement.[79] *Visions of Order* also has been cited as highly influential for conservatives in that "it and it alone among American Conservative books, is the one that they must place on their shelves beside *The Federalist*, and confer on it, as on *The Federalist*, the political equivalent of biblical status." It will prepare the reader "as no other book, *not even The Federalist* will prepare you, for your future encounters with the protagonists of the Liberal Revolution, above all by teaching you how to drive the debate to a deeper level than that on which our present spokesmen are engaging the Liberals."[80]

Weaver, in fact, has been called the founding father of the American conservative movement in that he brought conservatives together into a cohesive movement:

> That movement had, of course, its roots in the scattered remnants of opposition which remained after Roosevelt's revolution of 1932. But the groups that stood against that tidal wave were diverse, often unidimensional, without cohering principle to hold them together and make a single movement of them. . . .
> There did not exist anything in the nature of a broadly principled coherent conservative movement. In the last fifteen or twenty years such a movement has been welded in thought and action. What is remarkable is the extent to which the attitudes and principles that characterize that movement are prefigured in *Ideas Have Consequences*.[81]

More important for our purposes, of course, are Weaver's contributions to rhetorical thought. While he may be criticized for his normative approach to rhetoric in which he seems to begin by attaching his own values to and evaluating various concepts rather than by describing them, he is considered to have made a solid contribution to the re-establishment of rhetoric in a central position among the arts of thought and language. His concepts of god and devil terms, the tyrannizing image, hierarchy of modes of argument, and the sermonic nature of language continue to be widely used in contemporary rhetorical criticism. His writings on rhetoric, of course, were enhanced by his own powerful use of rhetoric; "rhetoric. . . in Weaver's hands was a gleaming, powerful instrument. He used it on the problems of English scholarship, on language, on politics, and when he was through something new had been established; outlines and interior relationships came into the light."[82]

What characterizes Weaver's thought across all of the spheres in which he worked, however, was the authenticity and consistency of his thought, which came from his coherent and fully examined attitudes; behind his judgments is something that might be called "instinct." While his arguments were not always the best, Vivas explains, "the attitudes from which his rejections and acceptances were issued were for the most part unerring. Weaver was authentic in the original sense of the term."[83]

Weaver had the courage to stick to his core of values and his own vision, even when they were unpopular: "What he wrote was designed to please no one's fancy but only . . . to make what he thought of as his own modest contribution to the disclosing of a portion of the truth in which a system of values is embedded."[84] He had the talent that would have enabled him to have had an easy and successful career as a popular writer and professor promoted by the academic community for his contributions. But he "chose the harder path. And he paid the price in slow academic recognition and in the size of the audiences he reached. But in the end he won. He earned promotion in the field, into the leadership of a band of rebels . . . who have been teaching us to value truth."[85] Perhaps Davidson best captured this aspect of Weaver:

> Weaver's light may at first seem only exploratory and instructive. [The reader] may be tempted to think that it is merely picking out a devious way among heaps of ancient rubbish. But that reader may not realize how deeply his own thought is being engaged—how he is being persuaded to look and look again at what he may have taken for granted or ignored or assumed, in some vain way, that he understood. Presently he is "seeing" (in the sense of understanding or knowing) as never before. He may also feel that he is in the company of a vision that is high and generous and very brave, and that this vision—the vision of Richard Weaver—is making irresistible claims upon his attention, indeed upon his life.[86]

Notes

[1] Wilma R. Ebbitt, "Two Tributes to Richard M. Weaver: Richard M. Weaver, Teacher of Rhetoric," *Georgia Review*, 17 (Winter 1963), 417, 418.

[2] For a description of the philosophy and ideals of the Southern Agrarians, see: Richard M. Weaver, "The Tennessee Agrarians," *Shenandoah*, 3 (Summer 1952), 3-10; and M.E. Bradford, "The Agrarianism of Richard Weaver: Beginnings and Completions," *Modern Age*, 14 (Summer-Fall 1970), 249-56.

[3] After Weaver's death, his dissertation was published, with new material added as an introduction and epilogue, as *The Southern Tradition at Bay: A History of Postbellum Thought*, ed. George Core and M.E. Bradford (New Rochelle, NY: Arlington, 1968).

[4] Richard M. Weaver, *Life Without Prejudice and Other Essays* (Chicago: Henry Regnery, 1965), p. 159.

[5] For a discussion of the techniques Weaver used to defend conservatism, see: Gerald Thomas Goodnight, "Rhetoric and Culture: A Critical Edition of Richard M. Weaver's Unpublished Works," Diss. University of Kansas 1978, pp. 434-37, 460-62, 787-89; Richard M. Weaver, "Rhetorical Strategies of the Conservative Cause," speech delivered at the University of Wisconsin, Madison, April 26, 1959, in Goodnight, pp. 574-608; and Charles Kellogg Follette, "A Weaverian Interpretation of Richard Weaver," Diss. University of Illinois 1981, pp. 32-34, 407.

[6] Biographical information of Weaver was obtained from the following sources: Charles Kellogg Follette, "A Weaverian Interpretation of Richard Weaver," Diss. University of Illinois 1981, pp. 53-55, 65-68, 117, 123, 130-33; Gerald Thomas Goodnight, "Rhetoric and Culture: A Critical Edition of Richard M. Weaver's Unpublished Works," Diss. University of Kansas 1978, pp. 431, 674-75; Richard M. Weaver, "Up From Liberalism," *Modern Age*, 3 (Winter 1958-59), 21-24; Ralph T. Eubanks, "Two Tributes to Richard M. Weaver: Richard M. Weaver: In Memoriam," *Georgia Review*, 17 (Winter 1963), 413-15; Ebbitt, p. 416; Eugene Davidson, "Richard Malcolm Weaver—Conservative," *Modern Age*, 7 (Summer 1963), 227; Russell Kirk, "Richard Weaver, RIP," *National Review*, 14 (April 23, 1963), 308; and Henry Regnery, *Memoirs of a Dissident Publisher* (New York: Harcourt Brace Jovanovich, 1979), p. 191.

[7] Ebbitt, p. 418.

[8] The nature of the human being is discussed in Richard M. Weaver, *Visions of Order: The Cultural Crisis of Our Time* (Baton Rouge: Louisiana State University Press, 1964), pp. 9, 144; and Weaver, *Life Without Prejudice*, pp. 146-47.

[9] Weaver discusses the nature of the mind in *Visions of Order*, p. 85.

[10] For a discussion of Weaver's notion of the soul, see *Visions of Order*, pp. 9, 43, 144.

[11] Symbol use and choice as features of the human being are discussed in Weaver, *Visions of Order*, p. 135; and Richard M. Weaver, "Contemporary Southern Literature," *Texas Quarterly*, 2 (Summer 1959), 143. A summary of these concepts is provided in Follette, pp. 384-98.

[12] For a discussion of the three levels of knowledge, see Richard M. Weaver, *Ideas Have Consequences* (Chicago: University of Chicago Press, 1948), p. 18; and Richard M. Weaver, *The Ethics of Rhetoric* (South Bend, IN: Regnery/Gateway, 1953), pp. 30-31.

[13] Weaver's notion of truth is discussed in Weaver, *Ideas Have Consequences*, p. 130; and Richard M. Weaver, "Humanism in an Age of Science," ed. Robert Hamlin, *Intercollegiate Review*, 7 (Fall 1970), 13.

[14] Weaver, "Humanism in an Age of Science," p. 17. This view led Weaver to reject empiricism and nominalism. Empiricism is an attitude expressed by two basic doctrines: (1) words or concepts can be grasped only if connected with actual or possible experiences; and (2) beliefs depend for their justification ultimately and necessarily on experience—particularly on that of the sense organs. Nominalism denies the existence of universals—words that can be applied to individual things that have something in common. It denies their existence on the ground that the use of a general word such as "humanity" does not imply the existence of a general thing named by it.

[15] Richard M. Weaver, "'Parson' Weems: A Study in Early American Rhetoric," in Goodnight, p. 295.

[16] Culture is defined in Weaver, *Ideas Have Consequences*, p. 117; and Weaver, *The Southern Tradition at Bay*, pp. 39-40.

[17] The tyrannizing image is discussed in: Weaver, "Contemporary Southern Literature," p. 133; Weaver, *Visions of Order*, pp. 11-12, 117; Weaver, *Ideas Have Consequences*, pp. 19, 117; Weaver, *The Southern Tradition at Bay*, pp. 32, 36; and Weaver, *The Ethics of Rhetoric*, pp. 166, 170.

18 Dialectic is discussed in Richard M. Weaver, *Language is Sermonic: Richard M. Weaver on the Nature of Rhetoric*, ed. Richard L. Johannesen, Rennard Strickland, and Ralph T. Eubanks (Baton Rouge: Louisiana State University Press, 1970), pp. 71-73, 145.

19 Weaver, *The Ethics of Rhetoric*, p. 28.

20 Weaver, *Visions of Order*, p. 64.

21 Socrates as a dialectician is discussed in Weaver, *Visions of Order*, p. 65; and Weaver, *Language is Sermonic*, pp. 164-70, 181.

22 Rhetoric is defined in: Weaver, *The Ethics if Rhetoric*, pp. 15, 25, 27-28, 115, 213; Weaver, *Ideas Have Consequences*, pp. 19-20; and Weaver, *Language is Sermonic*, p. 225.

23 Weaver discusses the relation of rhetoric to the audience and reality in *Language is Sermonic*, pp. 206-08, 211.

24 The connection of rhetoric to culture is discussed in Weaver, *Language is Sermonic*, pp. 46, 138; and Richard M. Weaver, "The Strategy of Words," speech delivered at the Lake Bluff Woman's Club, Lake Bluff, Illinois, February 13, 1962, in Goodnight, pp. 556-59. A summary of the connection is provided in Goodnight, pp. 37, 75-92.

25 Weaver, *Language is Sermonic*, p. 35.

26 Weaver, *The Ethics of Rhetoric*, pp. 3-26. A summary of the notion of the noble rhetor is provided in Richard L. Johannesen, "Richard M. Weaver on Standards for Ethical Rhetoric," *Central States Speech Journal*, 29 (Summer 1978), 134-35.

27 For a more comprehensive discussion of Weaver's view of the connection between values and rhetoric, see Follette, pp. 47, 149-206.

28 Language as sermonic is discussed in Weaver, *Visions of Order*, p. 69; and Weaver, *Language is Sermonic*, pp. 140, 221-25.

29 Weaver, *The Ethics of Rhetoric*, p. 28. For a summary of examples cited by Weaver of the separation of rhetoric and dialectic in argumentation, see Johannesen, "Richard M. Weaver on Standards for Ethical Rhetoric," pp. 133-34.

30 The link between type of argument and principles is discussed in Weaver, *The Ethics of Rhetoric*, p. 58; and Richard M. Weaver, "Responsible Rhetoric," ed. Thomas D. Clark and Richard L. Johannesen, *Intercollegiate Review*, 12 (Winter 1976-77), 87.

31 Weaver, *Language is Sermonic*, pp. 210-11. While Weaver ranks the sources of argument here, he does not order them in his descriptions in: Weaver, "A Responsible Rhetoric," p. 87.; Manuel Bilsky et al., "Looking for an Argument," *College English*, 14 (January 1953), 211-14; and Richard M. Weaver and Richard S. Beal, *A Rhetoric and Handbook* (New York: Holt, Rinehart, and Winston, 1967), pp. 136-46.

32 Argument by genus or definition is discussed in: Weaver, *The Ethics of Rhetoric*, p. 86; Weaver, *Language is Sermonic*, p. 209; and Bilsky et al., pp. 212-13.

33 This example is cited by Bilsky et al., pp. 211-12.

34 The distinction between genus and definition is discussed in Bilsky et al., p. 213; and Weaver, *Language is Sermonic*, p. 213.

35 Weaver, *Language is Sermonic*, p. 212.

36 For a discussion of argument by similitude, see Weaver, *Language is Sermonic*, p. 209; and Bilsky et al., pp. 212, 214.

37 Argument by cause and effect is discussed in Weaver, *Language is Sermonic*, pp. 209, 214; and Bilsky et al., p. 212.

38 Weaver discusses argument by circumstance in *Language is Sermonic*, p. 215; and *The Ethics of Rhetoric*, p. 57.

39 Argument by authority and testimony is discussed in Weaver, *Language is Sermonic*, pp. 209-10; and Bilsky et al., p. 214.

40 Richard M. Weaver, "Two Orators," ed. George Core and M.E. Bradford, *Modern Age*, 14 (Summer-Fall 1970), 232, 240. Weaver's connection of genus to history is discussed in Richard L. Johannesen, "Conflicting Philosophies of Rhetoric/Communication: Richard M. Weaver Versus S.I. Hayakawa," *Communication*, 7 (1983), 297.

41 For a discussion of the function of grammatical categories, see Weaver, *The Ethics of Rhetoric*, pp. 115-17.

[42] The simple sentence is discussed in Weaver, *The Ethics of Rhetoric*, pp. 117, 119-20; and Weaver and Beal, p. 169.

[43] The complex sentence is discussed in Weaver, *The Ethics of Rhetoric*, pp. 120-24; and Weaver and Beal, pp. 171-73.

[44] Weaver discusses the compound sentence in *The Ethics of Rhetoric*, pp. 124-27; and Weaver and Beal, pp. 170-71.

[45] See *The Ethics of Rhetoric*, pp. 127-28, for Weaver's discussion of nouns.

[46] Weaver's discussion of adjectives can be found in *The Ethics of Rhetoric*, pp. 129-33.

[47] Verbs are discussed in Weaver, *The Ethics of Rhetoric*, pp. 135-36; and Weaver, *Visions of Order*, pp. 23-24. For Weaver's discussion of the other parts of speech, see Weaver, *The Ethics of Rhetoric*, pp. 133-41.

[48] Ultimate terms are discussed in Weaver, *The Ethics of Rhetoric*, p. 211.

[49] Weaver defines god terms in *The Ethics of Rhetoric*, p. 212.

[50] Weaver provides examples of god terms in *The Ethics of Rhetoric*, pp. 212-22.

[51] Devil terms are discussed in Weaver, *The Ethics of Rhetoric*, pp. 222-24. A summary of the concept of the devil term is provided in Follette, p. 225.

[52] Weaver discusses charismatic terms in *The Ethics of Rhetoric*, pp. 227-32.

[53] Weaver, *Visions of Order*, p. 7.

[54] Richard M. Weaver, "Making the Most of Two Worlds," commencement address, Gilmour Academy, June 1956, in Goodnight, p. 513.

[55] This summary is provided in Richard L. Johannesen, Rennard Strickland, and Ralph T. Eubanks, "Richard M. Weaver on the Nature of Rhetoric: An Interpretation," in Weaver, *Language is Sermonic*, p. 15. Weaver discusses these ideas in detail in *Visions of Order* and *Ideas Have Consequences*.

[56] Weaver, *Language is Sermonic*, p. 203.

[57] Weaver discusses teachers of rhetoric in *Language is Sermonic*, pp. 201-03.

[58] Weaver discusses language as relative in *Language is Sermonic*, p. 117.

[59] Changes in language are discussed in Weaver, *Language is Sermonic*, pp. 129-36; and Weaver, "The Strategy of Words," in Goodnight, p. 548.

[60] For Weaver's discussion of the link between language and truth, see *Language is Sermonic*, pp. 123, 136.

[61] Current practices in the teaching of rhetoric are discussed in Weaver, *Language is Sermonic*, pp. 190, 196.

[62] Weaver, *Ideas Have Consequences*, pp. 129-47, 170-87; and Weaver, *Visions of Order*, pp. 40-54.

[63] See *Language is Sermonic*, pp. 48, 52-55, for Weaver's discussion of proper rhetorical training.

[64] Weaver, *Language is Sermonic*, pp. 187-88.

[65] The proper role for the teacher of rhetoric is discussed in Weaver, *Language is Sermonic*, pp. 193-94, 198.

[66] Richard M. Weaver, "The Role of Education in Shaping Our Society," speech delivered at the Metropolitan Area Industrial Conference, Chicago, October 25, 1961, in Goodnight, p. 625.

[67] Weaver, *Language is Sermonic*, p. 194.

[68] Weaver, *Language is Sermonic*, pp. 195-96.

[69] Weaver, *Language is Sermonic*, p. 197.

[70] Weaver, *Language is Sermonic*, p. 197.

[71] Bruce A. White, "Richard M. Weaver: Dialectic Rhetorician," *Modern Age*, 26 (Summer-Fall 1982), 256.

[72] Willmoore Kendall, "How to Read Richard Weaver: Philosopher of 'We the (Virtuous) People,'" *Intercollegiate Review*, 2 (September 1965), 81.

[73] Among those who classify Weaver as a Platonist or as having an orientation toward Platonic idealism are: James Powell, "The Conservatism of Richard M. Weaver," *New Individualist Review*, 3 (1964), 3; John Bliese, "Richard M. Weaver: Conservative Rhetorician," *Modern Age*, 21 (Fall 1977), 378; John P. East, "Richard M. Weaver: The Conservatism of Affirmation," *Modern Age*, 19 (Fall 1975), 339-42; Robert E. Haskell and Gerard A. Hauser, "Rhetorical Structure: Truth and Method in Weaver's Epistemology," *Quarterly Journal of Speech*, 64 (October 1978), 236; and Johannesen, "Conflicting Philosophies of Rhetoric/Communication."

[74] East, pp. 342-44; Robert Hariman, "Evidence of Things Unseen: Holy Order and the Conservative Mind of Richard Weaver," paper presented at the Speech Communication Association convention, Washington, D.C., November 1983; and Follette, pp. 362-431.

[75] Letter to Sonja K. Foss from Richard L. Johannesen, October 17, 1983; and Richard M. Weaver, Letter, *New York Times Book Review*, March 21, 1948, p. 29.

[76] Eliseo Vivas, "The Mind of Richard Weaver," *Modern Age*, 8 (Summer 1964), 309.

[77] Johannesen, "Conflicting Philosophies of Rhetoric/Communication," pp. 289-305; Johannesen, Strickland, and Eubanks, pp. 26-27; Russell Kirk, "Ethical Labor," rev. of *The Ethics of Rhetoric*, by Richard M. Weaver, *Sewanee Review*, 62 (Summer 1954), 490-91; Herbert J. Muller, "The Revival of the Absolute," *Antioch Review, 9* (March 1949), 104-05; and Vivas, p. 309.

[78] Goodnight, pp. 780, 784-85; and Muller, pp. 101-03.

[79] East, p. 338; and Frank S. Meyer, "Richard M. Weaver: An Appreciation," *Modern Age*, 14 (Summer-Fall 1970), 243.

[80] Kendall, pp. 81, 85.

[81] Meyer, p. 243.

[82] Eugene Davidson, p. 228.

[83] Vivas, p. 310.

[84] Eugene Davidson, p. 227; and Kirk, p. 487.

[85] Vivas, p. 310.

[86] Donald Davidson, "The Vision of Richard Weaver: A Foreword," in Weaver, *The Southern Tradition at Bay*, p. 13.

4

Stephen Toulmin

In Stephen Toulmin's early works, the term "rhetoric" appeared rarely and when it did, it was never a central feature of his writing.[1] In fact, as late as 1975, Richard D. Rieke and Malcolm O. Sillars claimed that "Toulmin has no expressed interest in the process of communication or with the development of ways to construct claims and reasons to win adherence."[2] Nevertheless, because his work had so many implications for the field of rhetoric, many communication scholars began to view Toulmin as an influential thinker in the field of rhetoric. His more recent work is beginning to take a more rhetorical bent, probably due to his association with people like Rieke and others in the field of communication. In his most recent work, Toulmin writes,

> Since the mid-1960s, rhetoric has begun to regain its respectability as a topic of literary and linguistic analysis. . . . Many American colleges and universities have departments devoted to "communication studies," or "speech." These departments are responsible for college debating teams, but their faculty members do serious research on different aspects of oral communication and argumentation.[3]

Thus, Toulmin is a professional philosopher who began his career without an interest in the field of rhetoric but who, as his career has progressed, has come to see the importance of rhetoric for his ideas about philosophy.

Stephen Edelson Toulmin was born in London, England, on March 25, 1922 to Geoffrey Edelson Toulmin and Doris Holman Toulmin.[4] He received a Bachelor of Arts degree in mathematics and physics from King's College in 1942. From 1942 to 1945, he was a junior scientific officer for the Ministry of Aircraft Production. He first was employed at the Malvern Radar Research and Development Station and later at the Supreme Headquarters of the Allied Expeditionary Force in Germany, where he did technical intelligence work. At the end of World War II, he returned to England to earn a Master of Arts degree in 1947 and a Doctorate of Philosophy degree in 1948 from Cambridge University. "From the start," he wrote, "my couriosity drew me toward the subject of 'rationality.'" Wondering if knowledge really were certain and enduring, he asked himself if "intelligent fish learned to do science, . . . must they in the long run end up with the same body of ideas as human beings?"[5] His first major attempt to deal with this issue was his doctoral thesis, "Reason in Ethics,"[6] in which he compared and contrasted the ways humans reason about moral and scientific issues.

Toulmin's career as an educator and philosopher began when he was appointed University Lecturer in Philosophy of Science at Oxford University in 1949. He published *The Philosophy of Science: An Introduction*[7] in 1953 and remained at Oxford until 1954. He then was appointed to the position of Visiting Professor of History and Philosophy of Science at Melbourne University in Australia from 1954-55. He served as Professor and Chair of the Department of Philosophy at the University of Leeds in England from 1955 to 1959.

Pursuing his belief that traditional logic is incomplete as a tool of rationality, Toulmin published *Uses of Argument* in 1958.[8] His "chief purpose in writing *The Uses of Argument* in the late 1950s was to relate traditional philosophical paradoxes to the standing contrast between 'substantive' and 'formal' aspects of reasoning and argument." Because philosophers were so entrenched in the study of formal logic, the book was received poorly in England. Toulmin lamented that Richard Braithwaite, his graduate advisor at Cambridge, "was deeply pained by the book, and barely spoke to me for twenty years; while one of my colleagues at Leeds, Peter Alexander described it as 'Toulmin's *anti*-logic book.'" In fact, wrote Toulmin, "a great hush fell upon my colleagues in England. After that, I assumed that the book would (in Hume's words) 'fall stillborn from the press,' so I was a little surprised when it continued to sell in worthwhile numbers: it took me some time to find out why."[9]

In 1959, Toulmin came to the United States, where he was a visiting professor at New York, Stanford, and Columbia Universities. At approximately this time, Wayne Brockriede and Douglas Ehninger introduced Toulmin's work to communication scholars in this country.[10] They interpreted his work as being useful to scholars of rhetoric and argumentation because it provided "an appropriate structural model by means of which rhetorical arguments may be laid out for analysis and criticism . . .[and provided]. . . a system for classifying artistic proofs which employs arguments as a central and unifying construct."[11]

Since the introduction of Toulmin's work into the United States, rhetoricians have found his ideas about rationality relevant to their own thinking about rhetoric. The successes of *The Uses of Argument* was due not to professional philosophers but to rhetoricians. In fact, Toulmin learned that the people in the United States who had been purchasing his book were the same people who had been keeping the study of practical argumentation and rhetoric alive at the time he was lamenting its death. While in his early writings, he claimed that the study of practical argumentation was dead, he later admitted: "I met people from Departments of Speech and Communication up and down the country, who told me that they used it as a text on rhetoric and argumentation. So, the study of practical reasoning was kept alive after all; but this was done only *outside* the Departments of Philosophy, under the wing of Speech or English, or at Schools of Law."[12]

In 1960, Toulmin briefly returned to London, where he was the director of the Unit for History of Ideas of the Nuffield Foundation. He returned to the United States again in 1965 to become a Professor of the History of Ideas and Philosophy at Brandeis University (1965-69) and later a Professor of Philosophy at Michigan State University (1969-72). Seven years later, he accepted a position as Professor of Humanities at the University of California at Santa Cruz (1972-73) and published the first of what is to be a three-volume set entitled *Human Understanding: The Collective Use and Evolution of Concepts.*

The next year, in 1973, he published *Wittgenstein's Vienna* with Alan Janik[13] and became Professor in the Committee on Social Thought at the University of Chicago (1973-86). From 1975 until 1978, he worked with the National Commission for the Protection of Human Subjects of Biomedical and Behavioral Research, established by the United States Congress. During this time, he collaborated with Albert R. Jonsen to write *The Abuse of Casuistry: A History of Moral Reasoning*.[14] When he left the University of Chicago, he moved to Northwestern University as the Avalon Foundation Professor of the Humanities, where he remains today. His latest work, *Cosmopolis: The Hidden Agenda of Modernity* (1990), proposes a radical revision of our ideas about modernity.

While in the United States, Toulmin held visiting professorships and lectureships at schools such as Dartmouth College, Southern Methodist University, and Bryn Mawr College. He also has been a Phi Beta Kappa national lecturer, a senior visiting scholar at the Hastings Center, and a Guggenheim Fellow. Throughout his entire career, Toulmin's primary interest was and continues to be in questions concerning the rationality of human enterprises.

Theoretical and Practical Argument

Throughout many of his works, Toulmin has contrasted two types of arguments. In *Uses of Argument*, he distinguishes between "substantial and analytic arguments." A substantial argument involves an inference from some data or evidence to the conclusion of the argument; the conclusion of an analytic argument, in contrast, goes no farther than the material contained in its premises. Individuals using analytic arguments attempt to base their claims on unchanging and universal principles. Those who use substantial arguments, on the other hand, ground their claims in the context of a particular situation rather than in abstract, universal principles. Jonsen and Toulmin describe a similar distinction between what they call theoretical and practical arguments; "theoretical" is their term for analytic argument and "practical" is their term for substantive argument. They claim that the distinction between these two types of argument lies at the base of "two very different accounts of ethics and morality: one that seeks eternal, invariable principles, the practical implications of which can be free of exception or qualifications, and another which pays closest attention to the specific details of particular moral cases and circumstances." Thus, an argument that "seeks eternal, invariable principles" is an analytic one, while an argument that "pays closest attention to the specific details of particular moral cases and circumstances" is a substantial argument.[15]

In summary, these types of argument represent idealized formal logic on the one hand and practical, everyday reasoning on the other. Theoretical or analytic argument is consistent with Plato's ideal of formal deductive logic. It leads to universal truths regardless of context; in other words, it is decontextualized. Practical or substantial argument, on the other hand, conforms more closely to the ideas that Aristotle developed in the *Topics* and the *Rhetoric*. It is judged not by its correspondence to deductive form but by its substance. It deals with matters of probability rather than with universal truths, and it varies according to context; it is contextualized.

Toulmin offers both a critical and an historical account of theoretical and practical argument. The critical account shows the irrelevance of theoretical argument to human affairs, and the historical account shows why the dominance of the universalist approach to argument was not broken from classical Greece throughout modernity.

A Critical Account of Theoretical and Practical Argument

Toulmin's starting point involves the irrelevance of theoretical argument to the assessment of practical argument. During much of the history of the Western world, particularly the Modern Period (approximately 1650-1950), philosophers presupposed the existence of prior and immutable standards to judge the adequacy of concepts, especially scientific ones. According to Toulmin, these presuppositions "imposed on philosophy a certain epistemic picture of Man the Rational Knower facing Nature the Unchanging Object of Knowledge."[16] At various times throughout history, philosophers have rebelled against this notion of immutable standards but have been unable to provide standards that are not completely relativistic.

Responses to this problem have been either to develop standards that can distinguish "correct" arguments from "incorrect" ones or to admit that such standards are relative to the people, times, and places in which the arguments are developed. The works of two scholars in the later part of the Modern Period, Gottlob Frege and R. G. Collingwood, represent two major attempts to come to grips with the question of how the worth of scientific concepts is to be judged. Frege is described by Toulmin as an absolutist who argues that adequacy of concepts ought to be modeled on mathematics. Collingwood, on the other hand, is forced into relativism in his attempts to avoid the problems of absolute standards. Toulmin criticizes these approaches because although Frege may have succeeded in explaining mathematics in absolutist terms, absolutist notions such as his are more difficult to sustain when we leave the discipline of mathematics for, say, political theory. In Toulmin's words:

> The absolutist reaction to the diversity of our concepts, thus emancipates
> itself from the complexities of history and anthropology only at the price
> of irrelevance. . . . [while the relativistic reaction of Collingwood]. . . takes
> good care to avoid the defects of historical irrelevance, but in doing so

(as we shall see) it ends in equal difficulties by denying itself any impartial standpoint for rational judgement.[17]

The choice, then, is seen as between a completely absolutist and a completely relativistic position — a choice which Toulmin views as untenable. In *Human Understanding*, and, for that matter, in his entire line of work, Toulmin attempts to develop standards for assessing the worth of ideas that are neither absolutist nor relativistic. His purpose is to form a "new 'epistemic self-portrait': that is, a fresh account of the capacities, processes, and activities, in virtue of which Man acquires an understanding of Nature, and Nature in turn becomes intelligible to Man."[18]

In summary, Toulmin contrasts theoretical and practical argumentation in order to cast light on his claim that theoretical arguments are irrelevant to most of the important aspects of human affairs. At the same time, he is unwilling to go to the other extreme, which trades the completely absolute for the completely relative. He sees the idea of practical argument as one of the ways to find a middle ground between absolutism and relativism. In order to understand this middle ground, we first must understand Toulmin's specific objections to absolutism and relativism.

Objections to Absolutism. Jonsen and Toulmin claim that theoretical or analytic arguments are not relevant to the world of practical affairs because too many situations are not covered by appeals to a single universal principle. The problems we face in everyday life are not simple because they vary according to the details of the situation. For example:

> If I go next door and borrow a silver soup tureen, it goes without saying that I am expected to return it as soon as my immediate need for it is over: that is not an issue and gives rise to no problem.
>
> If, however, it is a pistol that I borrow and if, while it is in my possession, the owner becomes violently enraged and threatens to kill one of his neighbors as soon as he gets back the pistol, I shall find myself in a genuinely problematic situation. I cannot escape from it by lamely invoking the general maxim that borrowed property ought to be returned promptly.[19]

An analytic argument will not solve this problem because no universal, absolute principle exists that will allow us to resolve it.

Jonsen and Toulmin use the abortion issue as an example of a controversy that cannot be resolved by an analytic argument. They claim that the activists in the abortion controversy have focused their public rhetoric on "*universal laws and principles, which they could then nail to their respective masts.*"[20] By focusing on analytic argument and absolutism, Jonsen and Toulmin argue, these activists have made the abortion debate unresolvable.

The absolutist position is seen in the belief that the syllogism is the only appropriate way to substantiate claims to knowledge. The syllogism is a method of reasoning that produces absolute knowledge from the combination of two premises. A classic syllogism is the one that combines the major premise, "All people are mortal," with the minor premise, "Socrates is a person," to arrive at the conclusion "Socrates is bound to die." In addition to Toulmin's objections to the absolutist nature of this type of logic, he is able to point to several technical confusions in syllogistic logic. Although many of his objections to the syllogism are beyond the scope of our interest, through a complex analysis of logic, he shows how what formal logicians call "premises" actually serve different functions and thus cannot satisfactorily be grouped together.[21]

One of the most fundamental concepts in Toulmin's perspective is that of argument fields. Practical argument, he asserts, is a tool that is used in a variety of different fields, and some aspects of arguments vary from field to field. These he calls "field-dependent" aspects of argument. Other elements of argument are the same from one field to another; Toulmin calls these elements "field invariant." Toulmin believes that the ideal of formal logic assumes that all aspects of argument are field invariant. Formal logic assumes that mathematics (particularly geometry) is *the* standard by which arguments in all fields can be judged:

> These special characteristics of their first chosen class of arguments [mathematics] have been interpreted by logicians as signs of special merit; other classes of argument, they have felt, are deficient in so far as they fail to display all the characteristic merits of the paradigm class. . . . Many of the current problems in the logical tradition spring from adopting the analytic paradigm—argument as a standard by comparison with which all other arguments can be criticized.[22]

But since all fields of human activity are not based on assumptions identical to those of mathematics and geometry, logical arguments are largely irrelevant to the practical world of rationality.

Because they are derived from mathematical fields, analytic arguments are highly impersonal. The person "doing" logic is no more important to formal logic than the person "doing" mathematics is to the formula for determining the circumference of a circle, for example. In contrast, the person engaging in argument is extremely important in rational assessment in the practical world. Rational procedures, according to Toulmin, "do not exist in the air, apart from actual reasoners: they are things which are learned, employed, sometimes modified, on occasion even abandoned, by the people doing the reasoning."[23]

Toulmin does not conclude that analytic logic needs to be abandoned completely; he simply sees its range of applicability as much narrower than many philosophers have claimed: "This is not to say that the elaborate mathematical systems which constitute 'symbolic logic' must now be thrown away; but only that people with intellectual capital invested in them should retain no illusions about the extent of their relevance to practical arguments."[24]

Another reason Toulmin considers formal logic to be largely irrelevant to practical argument is that formal logic assumes concepts do not change with time. For an argument to be considered valid in formal logic, "it must surely be good once and for all."[25] Toulmin believes, however, that most argument fields cannot accommodate "timeless" claims to knowledge. He phrases this claim in a question to which he provides the answer: "Can one cast into a timeless mathematical mould the relations upon which the soundness and acceptability of our arguments depend, without distorting them beyond recognition? I shall argue that this cannot be done."[26] Even in a highly specialized science such as astronomy, the requirement that analytic arguments be "timeless" is problematic:

> Consider the confident predictions of astronomers. What grounds have they for making them? A vast collection of records of telescopic observations and dynamical theories tested, refined and found reliable over the last 250 years. This answer may sound impressive, and indeed from the practical point of view, it should do so; but the moment a philosopher begins to demand entailments, the situation changes. For, in the nature of the case, the astronomers' records can be no more up-to-date than the present hour; and, as for their theories, these will be worth no more to the epistemologist than the experiments and observations used to test their adequacy—experiments and observations which, needless to say, will also have been made in the past.[27]

One difficulty with the application of absolutism to practical problems is that answers are either "correct" or "incorrect" instead of "probably correct" or "probably incorrect." Many of the questions that rational procedures are designed to answer cannot be answered with certainty. Did Lyndon Johnson lie to the American public when he claimed the United States was winning the war in Vietnam? Did George Bush lie to the American public when he said, "Read my lips—no new taxes"? These answers are probably, but not certainly, yes.

But the difficulty goes beyond philosophical speculation about truth and falsity or right and wrong. Because analytic arguments are used to analyze situations that are properly the domain of substantial arguments, many of our social debates, such as the abortion controversy, are not resolvable. Jonsen and Toulmin claim that "the zealot's concentration on universal and invariable principles" has condemned us to a "practical deadlock" from which we cannot escape.[28]

Since Toulmin considers absolutism to be in the mainstream of modern thinking, he voices greater objections to it than he does to relativism. Before reviewing an historical account of the theoretical and practical arguments, however, we will look briefly at Toulmin's objections to relativism.

Objections to Relativism. Toulmin's general objection to absolute standards of argument is that they are so strict that they are irrelevant to the practice of rational criticism. On the other hand, his objection to relativistic standards of argument is that they are so relative that they constitute no standards at all. The field of anthropology is one that has been tempted to go in the direction of relativism since anthropologists noticed that rational arguments vary from culture to culture. According to Toulmin, these relativistic standards preclude anthropologists from developing adequate standards of judgment:

> If a tribe with a long tradition of sympathetic magic insists on using homeopathic medicines in preference to antidotes, must the anthropologist necessarily accept this as "rational" behavior? No doubt, the members of the tribe will give their own reasons for doing so—reasons which seem to them good and sufficient—yet in judging the adequacy of those procedures, what attitude should the anthropologist himself adopt? Confronted by this question, anthropologists were for a long time tempted to change the subject. It was easier to take the relativist way out: of considering only what was regarded as rational by any particular tribe, and avoiding the question whether that attitude was sound or unsound, well-founded or groundless.[29]

Toulmin's concern, then, is that a completely relativist point of view provides no basis for distinguishing between a good or a poor argument. Toulmin's historical account of argument helps clarify his positions and consequent perspectives.

A Historical Account of Theoretical and Practical Argument

If the absolutist position out of which the ideal of theoretical argument flows is irrelevant to humanity, as Toulmin suggests, why has it survived from the classical age of Greece? This is one of the questions that Toulmin pursues in *Cosmopolis: The Hidden Agenda of Modernity.*

An absolutist position was held by Plato, who argued that an absolute truth could be produced by dialectic and that the rhetoric of probability as taught by the sophists was wrong. But prior to 1600, "no one questioned the right of rhetoric to stand alongside logic in the canon of philosophy; nor was rhetoric treated as a second-class—and necessarily inferior field."[30] During the Renaissance period, the realm of the theoretical and the practical both were regarded as legitimate. According to Toulmin, "theoretical inquiries were balanced against discussions of concrete practical issues, such as the specific conditions on which it is morally acceptable for a sovereign to launch a war, or for a subject to kill a tyrant.''[31] The context in which these discussions were held legitimated the place of rhetoric in human affairs.

Since the end of the Renaissance, most philosophers have been committed to abstract, universal theory to the exclusion of practical issues. A shift occurred ''from a style of philosophy that keeps equally in view issues of local, timebound practice, and universal, timeless theory, to one that accepts matters of universal, timeless theory as being entitled to an exclusive place in the agenda of 'philosophy.' ''[32] Toulmin's thesis is that the doctrine of absolutism that persisted throughout the entirety of the Modern Period resulted from the '' 'theory-centered' style of philosophizing—i.e. one that poses problems, and seeks solutions stated in timeless, universal terms''[33] advocated by René Descartes.

The story of the dominance of absolutism begins with an assassination. Assassinations of public figures frequently have affected the course of history, and the assassination of Henri IV of France in 1610 was no exception. During the reign of Henri IV, the conflict between the French Catholics and Protestants was becoming intolerable. Because Henri IV wanted to build a kingdom that balanced Catholicism and Protestantism, he was perceived as the only person who had any chance of resolving the situation. Toulmin suggests that ''Henri's murder came as the final confirmation of people's worst fears. His disappearance from the scene dashed the last hope of escaping from irresoluble conflicts.''[34] After his murder, the tide turned against religious pluralism, and the Thirty Years' War ensued.

The Thirty Years' War created so much uncertainty in Europe that an escape was needed. Toulmin noted that ''if uncertainty, ambiguity, and the acceptance of pluralism led, in practice, only to an intensification of the religious war, the time had come to discover some *rational method* for demonstrating the essential correctness or incorrectness of philosophical, scientific, or theological doctrines.''[35] Descartes, a young student at La Fleche, was to be the one who would provide that method.

Descartes' ideas resulted from the historical context in which he lived, which included both the assassination of Henri IV and the Thirty Years' War. The latter was a major catastrophic event that lasted most of Descartes' adult life, beginning when he was in his early twenties and ending only two years before his death. Descartes' attempt to avoid relativism and skepticism involved finding a ''single certain thing,'' the *cognito*, that made certainty possible. Toulmin notes that ''fifty years later, for a generation whose central experience was the Thirty Years' War, and a social destruction that had apparently become entirely out of hand, the joint appeal of geometric certainty and 'clear and distinct' ideas helped Descartes' program to carry a new conviction.''[36] Descartes' position had such influence on intellectual thought in Europe that it lasted well into the twentieth century.

In the twentieth century, almost as quickly as the Renaissance was transformed into modernity, the scaffolding of modernity was dismantled and foundation for the Post-Modern Period was begun. In Toulmin's words,

> The intellectual and cultural situation in Europe and North America was just as deeply transformed, between the 1920s and the 1970s, as it was from the 1590s to the 1640s, but *in reverse*. . . . By 1910 . . . [the authority of the Modern Period] was weakening, but its grip outlasted another thirty years of warfare among the nations of Europe, and people were ready to suspend the Quest for Certainty, acknowledge the demolition of modern cosmopolis, and returned belatedly to the humane and liberal standpoint of the late Renaissance, only when the Second World War was well behind them.[37]

Toulmin draws numerous interesting parallels between the beginning and ending of the Modern Period. In fact, as the assassination of Henri IV ushered in modernity, Toulmin claims that the undoing of modernity "was framed by a new emblematic assassination"[38] — the assassination of John F. Kennedy.

One result of the ideas that dominated the Modern Period, according to Toulmin, was that philosophy made very little progress during these 300 years. He claimed that:

> the formal doctrines that underpinned human thought were practiced from 1700 on followed a trajectory with the shape of an Omega, i.e. Ω . After 300 years we are back close to our starting point. Natural scientists no longer separate the "observer" from the "world observed", as they did in the heyday of classical physics; sovereign nation-states find their independence circumscribed; and Descartes' *foundations* ambitions are discredited, taking philosophy back to the skepticism of Montaigne.[39]

In summary, an approach to philosophy was born that had no place for a rhetoric based in probability rather than certainty; this philosophy continued for three hundred years, ending only mid-way through this century. Such is Toulmin's historical account of why the philosophical community settled on an absolutist, theoretical approach to philosophizing that was to last until approximately the 1950s. Since we have accepted universalist rules and principles as central to all aspects of human knowledge and values, "no middle way can be found between absolutism and relativism."[40] Of course, Toulmin's job is not complete until he provides just such a middle ground, and that is the topic we will consider in the next section.

In order to avoid the dilemma of absolutism versus relativism, Toulmin proposes to study how concepts change and how those conceptual changes are judged to be worthy or not worthy in particular fields. Thus, Toulmin analyzes practical arguments in various disciplines, ranging from the physical sciences to ethics, in order to develop a position between the extremes of absolutism and relativism.

Elements of Practical Argument

As we saw in the previous section, Toulmin believes that the contest between absolutism and relativism was decided in favor of absolutism, a situation that he finds less than desirable. The solution, he believes, is not to return to complete relativism but to find a middle road between these two extremes. Between the years of 1958 and 1990, Toulmin has authored or co-authored four books, each of which has something to say about this goal. All four are connected in their concern for practical rather than theoretical argument and in their concern for contextualized rather than decontextualized analysis. In this section, we will discuss Toulmin's layout of argument, his evolutionary model of conceptual change, his analysis of modern casuistry, and his hope for humanizing modernity.

Layout of Argument

The element of Toulmin's theory that is most well known is his layout of practical argument, which he believes avoids formal logic without resorting to relativism.[41] This layout of argument was developed from his concern for the justificatory function of substantive argumentation.[42] The primary use of substantive arguments is to justify claims rather than to infer claims from evidence. Justification is a retrospective activity, while inference is a prospective one. In other words, justification of a claim involves producing reasons for a claim after the fact of arriving mentally at that claim. Inference, on the other hand, refers to the uses of reasons to arrive at a claim and is the province of analytic argumentation. From the perspective of justification,

> reasoning is less a way of *hitting on new ideas* — for that we have to use our imaginations — than it is a way of *testing and sifting ideas critically*. It is concerned with how people share their ideas and thoughts in situations that raise the question of whether those ideas are worth sharing. It is a collective and continuing human transaction.[43]

Even in the sciences, where one of argument's functions is discovery (or inference), justification plays an important role in argument. "The making of discoveries," Toulmin claims, "may be one facet of the scientist's professional work, but the justifying of his discoveries — by the presentation of 'acceptable' supporting arguments — is another, complementary facet of this same work."[44]

The idea that the function of argument is justification leads Toulmin to discuss the standards by which arguments succeed or fail to provide justification for claims. An argument is sound if it is able to survive the criticism offered by those who participate in the rational enterprises of various fields. In his words, a "sound argument, a well-grounded or firmly-backed claim, is one which will stand up to criticism, one for which a case can be presented coming up to the standard required if it is to deserve a favourable verdict."[45]

Because Toulmin perceives justification as critical in argument, a prerequisite to comprehending Toulmin's approach to the layout of argument is his consideration of modal terms. Modal terms are terms that frequently occur in arguments, such as "possible," "probable," "impossible," "certainly," "presumably," "as far as the evidence goes," or "necessarily." Toulmin claims that modal terms are characterized by two different aspects—"force" and "criteria." The force of an argument refers to the strength or power of the claim. The claim that a person who jumps from a tall building certainly will hit the ground has a greater degree of force than the claim that a person taking an airline trip from New York to Los Angeles probably will survive the trip or that a person reading this book possibly will find it interesting. The first claim has a higher degree of certainty than the last two claims. Criteria for an argument refer to the standards used to justify the claim. As we have indicated, the standards used to judge the adequacy of a work of abstract art are not the same standards as those used to judge the adequacy of a scientific theory or the wisdom of the President's speech. According to Toulmin, a modal term's force is "field invariant," while its criteria are "field dependent."[46] Arguments from various fields may carry similar force, but the criteria for assessing them differ greatly.

To better explain "field variant" and "field dependent," we will examine Toulmin's notion of "argument fields."[47] While other perspectives assume that arguments are the same regardless of the field, Toulmin argues that some elements of argument differ from one field to another. One of the questions Toulmin pursues is which aspects of arguments are field dependent and which are field invariant. In what ways, for example, is an argument designed to justify the conclusion that Picasso was a great artist similar to an argument designed to justify the claim that liberty is a more important value than life, or that Darwin's theory of evolution is a useful explanation for the existence of human life on the planet Earth? In other words, Toulmin is searching for ways to explain how some portions of arguments remain the same, regardless of field, while other portions of arguments vary from field to field. While formal logicians believe the criteria for judging the adequacy of arguments should be the same, regardless of field, Toulmin disagrees:

> As we move from the lunch counter to the executive conference table, from the science laboratory to the law courts, the "forum" of discussion changes profoundly. This kind of involvement that the participants have with the outcome of the reasoning is entirely different in the different situations and so also will be the ways in which possible outcomes of the argument are tested and judged.[48]

Arguments vary from field to field in a variety of ways.[49] Some arguments vary according to the degree of *formality* required in different fields. The degree of formality in an argument between film critics such as Gene Siskel and Roger Ebert about the quality of *My Left Foot* is much less than that of an argument between defense attorney F. Lee Bailey and the prosecutor about the admissability of lie-detector evidence. Arguments also differ according to the degree of *precision* required in different fields. The amount of precision in an argument about theoretical physics is much greater than that in an argument concerning which applicant for a job is more qualified. Fields of arguments also differ with regard to the *modes of resolution* that are required. The United States judicial system, for example, functions with an adversarial mode of resolution, where one party wins and the other loses. Negotiation between labor and management, on the other hand, uses a compromise or consensus mode of resolution. These are a few of the ways in which practical argument differs from one field to another.

According to Toulmin, one of the ways that arguments do not vary from field to field is that they all may be analyzed according to his layout of argument.[50] This layout is based on an analog of motion: "an argument is *movement* from accepted *data*, through a *warrant*, to a *claim*."[51] Making an argument is, therefore, analogous to taking a trip. One is trying to "get someplace" from "someplace else." We will pursue this analogy further as we explore the different parts of his layout.

Toulmin's layout of an argument involves six interrelated components. The first three components, the most basic elements, are claim, grounds, and warrant. The next three components—backing, modal qualifier, and rebuttal—modify the first three.

The first component is called a "claim." The claim is the conclusion of the argument that a person is seeking to justify. It is the answer to the question, "Where are we going?" The claim is the destination of the trip. Toulmin calls the second component of an argument "grounds." The grounds of an argument are the facts or other information on which the argument is based. Grounds provide the answer to the question, "What do we have to go on?" The grounds constitute the vehicle by which we reach the destination. The third component of an argument is called the "warrant." This portion of the argument authorizes our movement from the grounds to the claim. It answers the question, "How do you justify the move from these grounds to that claim? What road do you take to get from this starting point to that destination?"[52] The warrant assesses whether or not our "trip" from grounds to claim is a legitimate one. These three components are the primary elements of an argument, and in simple arguments, they may be the only components visible.

The three elements of Toulmin's layout can be depicted spatially as follows:

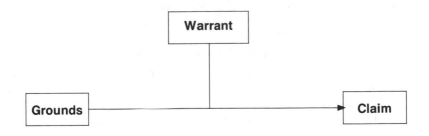

One of the examples Toulmin uses to illustrate his layout concerns a man named Harry and a claim that Harry is a British citizen:[53]

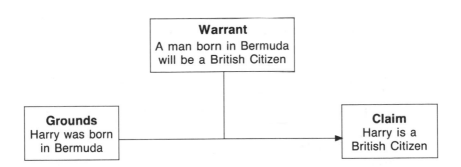

Alone, these three primary elements fail to distinguish analytic from practical arguments. We could transform, for instance, Toulmin's example into a formal syllogism:

Major Premise: A man born in Bermuda will be a British citizen.
Minor Premise: Harry was born in Bermuda.
Conclusion: Harry is a British citizen.

Three additional elements complete the layout of an argument by showing how practical arguments are contextualized and, thus, are different from analytic arguments. The first of these is called "backing." In formal logic, the major premise requires no support because it is seen as a universal principle. In practical argument, sometimes the movement called for in the warrant is not obvious; backing or additional support for a warrant may be required. While the warrant answers the question, "What road do you take?" the backing answers the question, "Why is this road a safe one?"

The next element in Toulmin's layout of an argument is called a "modal qualifier." Modal qualifiers indicate the strength of the step taken from data to warrant. Analytic arguments do not require modal qualifiers because the conclusion drawn from an analytic argument is structurally certain. Some arguments include qualifiers like "probably" or "certainly," indicating the strength of the relationship between the data and the warrant. Strength also is indicated when, for example, we hear the weather reporter give a prediction that the chances of rain are seventy percent or a scientist claim results that are significant at the .05 level of confidence. Modal qualifiers answer the question, "How certain are we of arriving at our destination?"

The final element of an argument is called the "rebuttal," which refers to specific circumstances when the warrant does not justify the claim. When using rebuttal, an arguer is presenting claims with a degree of caution. For example, the weather reporter might say that tomorrow will bring rain *unless* the Pacific front gets stalled over the Rocky Mountains. The rebuttal answers the question, "Under what circumstances should we decide against taking this trip?" This element emphasizes how practical argument, as opposed to analytic argument, is contextualized—how it is grounded in the specifics of the situation.

The complete diagram of Toulmin's layout of argument is as follows:

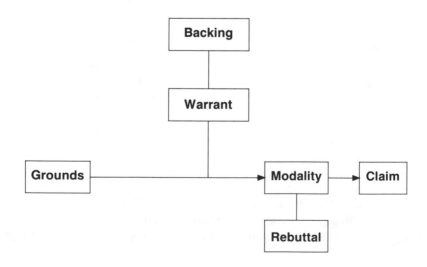

Toulmin's example of Harry, presented earlier, is completed in the following layout:

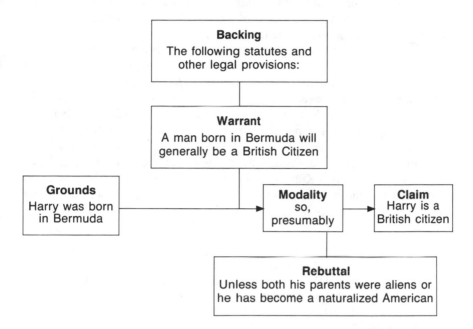

Thus, these six elements, considered as parts of an interdependent whole, constitute Toulmin's layout of an argument. Toulmin claims his layout is based on legal argument rather than formal logic. His layout is modeled on the kind of arguments that typically occur in the courtroom.

When Toulmin first described the layout in *Uses of Argument*, he did not emphasize and, in fact, did not realize, the implications this layout had for the field of rhetoric. He did not recognize, for example, that his layout could be adapted to provide a model of how people *communicate* arguments. Only after he was introduced to rhetoricians by Brockriede and Ehninger, after he moved to the United States, and after he published *Introduction to Reasoning* with Rieke and Janik were the rhetorical implications of his layout of argument stated explicitly.

Evolutionary Model of Conceptual Change

The publication of *Uses of Argument* was followed in 1972 by Toulmin's book, *Human Understanding*, which presents an evolutionary model of conceptual change. *Human Understanding*, like *Uses of Argument*, shows how argument in science is conducted by practical, contextualized argument rather than by formal, analytic argument. Concepts in all fields, Toulmin claims, are constantly in a process of evolution, and argument is a part of the process of evolutionary change.

Prior to discussing his own perspective on conceptual change, Toulmin criticizes the approach of Thomas S. Kuhn, who attempts to account for conceptual change in his seminal work, *The Structure of Scientific Revolutions*.[54] Kuhn's thesis is that concepts change when the current scientific paradigm no longer is able to provide a useful answer to questions that confront them. At such a time, Kuhn claims, a scientific revolution occurs, and new paradigms compete to replace the old. The actors in the competing paradigms are so different that they are unable to communicate clearly with one another.

Toulmin believes that Kuhn's notion of the scientific revolution continues to suffer from the earlier problems of relativism since concepts are not comparable from one paradigm to another. In contrast to Kuhn, Toulmin claims:

> The merits of intellectual "revolutions" cannot be discussed or justified in rational terms — since no common set of procedures for judging this rationality are acceptable, or even intelligible, to both sides in the dispute. So the considerations operative within a revolutionary change must apparently be interpreted as causes or motives, rather than as reasons or justifications.[55]

As opposed to Kuhn, Toulmin believes that conceptual change is *evolutionary*, not *revolutionary*, and that scientists from competing paradigms are able to — and, in fact, do — argue about the merits of the competing ideas:

> The so-called "Copernican Revolution" took a century and a half to complete and was argued out every step of the way. The world-view that emerged at the end of this debate had — it is true — little in common with earlier pre-Copernican conceptions. Yet, however radical the resulting change in physical and astronomical *ideas and theories*, it was the outcome of a continuing rational discussion.[56]

Toulmin believes that concepts develop according to a pattern of evolution in much the same way that organisms evolve biologically. In fact, he uses Darwin's model of biological evolution to explain conceptual evolution. The development of concepts involves two processes: innovation and selection. Innovative factors account for the appearance of variations in populations of plants and animals as well as for the appearance of variations in scientific theories, while selective factors account for the perpetuation of the healthiest plants and animals and the soundest scientific theories.

Innovation occurs when professionals in a particular discipline come to view their concepts in ways that differ from those in which concepts traditionally have been viewed. These innovative concepts then are subjected to a process of debate and inquiry in what Toulmin calls a "forum of competition." This "forum of competition" involves the process of selection. The ideas that survive the competition are selected as replacements for or revisions of the traditional concepts. As Toulmin explains, "suitable 'forums of competition' . . .[must exist]. . . within which intellectual novelties can survive for long enough to show their merits or defects; but in which they are also criticized and weeded out with enough severity to maintain the coherence of the discipline."[57]

In science, the selection process includes both disciplinary and professional aspects. The disciplinary aspects of a science—the ideas and objects of the science—insure evolution as old theories no longer are able to offer adequate explanations for those objects of that science. These disciplinary concerns do not comprise, however, all of the factors involved in the evolution of ideas. Professional factors that influence evolution include such things as the political nature of professional organizations, the needs of society for the "products" of the particular science, and the organization and editorship of journals for publishing scholarly work. Toulmin explains these professional factors:

> Individuals and organizations in fact exercise as real a power and influence over the development of science as they do in any other sphere of human life. Correspondingly, the roles, offices, and positions of influence within a scientific profession are worth fighting for—and are, in practice fought for—as singlemindedly, methodologically, and even deviously, as in any other sphere.[58]

Thus, an event like the nature of the person elected to office in a professional organization can affect the development of concepts in that scientific discipline.

Toulmin claims that these selection processes are rational when "rational enterprises" provide forums of criticism for ideas that are neither absolute nor relative. In the court of rationality, clear-headed people

> with suitable experience are qualified to act as judges or jurors. Within different cultures and epochs, reasoning may operate according to different methods and principles, so that different milieus represent (so to say) the parallel "jurisdictions" of rationality. But they do so out of a shared concern with common "rational enterprises," just as parallel legal jurisdictions do with their common judicial enterprises.[59]

As concepts change from one period of time to another or from one culture to another, they are either "valid" or "invalid" from an absolutist point of view. From a relativistic approach, one concept is neither better nor worse than a competitive concept from a different culture or milieu. From Toulmin's perspective, such "evaluations are always a matter of comparison. The operative questions are never of the form, 'Is this concept uniquely "valid" or "invalid"?'. . . Instead, the operative form is 'Given the current repertory of concepts and available variants, would this particular conceptual variant *improve* our explanatory power *more than* its rivals?'"[60]

The fact that Toulmin's approach to argumentation does not distinguish absolutely between the "valid" and "invalid" might lead some to the conclusion that he believes that the rational evaluation of ideas is purely subjective and thus not rational at all. Toulmin disputes this view by introducing a concept he calls the "impartial rational standpoint." The impartial rational standpoint is a significant part of Toulmin's attempt to explain how concept evaluation can be objective without falling prey to the criticisms of absolutism. The impartial rational standpoint is, in his words, "an 'objective one,' in the sense of being neutral as between the local and temporary views of different historico-cultural milieus; but its conclusions are always subject to reconsideration, and it does not divorce itself from the actual testimony of history and anthropology."[61] It is, thus, simultaneously objective and contextual; it is objective in the sense of being neutral and contextual in the sense of considering the relevant facets of history and anthropology. The evolutionary model of argument, then, is Toulmin's attempt to explain how "rational enterprises" evaluate concepts through a process of criticism and evaluation of those concepts. Toulmin claims that through such a process, persons are able to achieve an "impartial standpoint of rationality."

The Revival of Casuistry

By reviving casuistry, or case ethics, Toulmin believes we will find a path between the extremes of absolutism and relativism. Casuistry, widely used in the medieval and Renaissance times, fell into disrepute during the Modern Period but is being revived in the Post-Modern Period.[62] In *The Abuse of Casuistry*, Jonsen and Toulmin show how the process of casuistry was an effective form of practical argumentation in Medieval and Renaissance times: "Human experience long ago developed a reasonable and effective set of practical procedures for resolving the moral problems that arise in particular real-life situations. These procedures came to be known as 'casuistry' and those who employed these procedures were 'casuists.'"[63]

Casuistry is a procedure used to resolve moral problems without resorting to analytic argument. An analytic approach to moral problems begins by specifying absolute moral principles and then applying a specific case to the principle. If the sanctity of life is an absolute moral principle and if abortion involves the taking of a life, then abortion is immoral. The approach of casuistry is different. Casuistry begins by using what Jonsen and Toulmin call "type cases" or "paradigm cases" as objects of reference in moral arguments. These type cases create an initial presumption of moral action for cases which do not contain exceptional circumstances. An individual case is then compared and contrasted with the type case in an attempt to determine whether the specifics of the individual case are comparable to the type case.

Type cases serve as the final objects of reference. For instance, "willfully using violence against innocent and defenseless human beings, taking unfair advantage of other people's misfortunes, deceiving others by lying to them, damaging the community by your disloyalty, and acting—in general—inconsiderately toward your fellows" were type cases in the classical period of Greece and Rome and continue to be so today. In casuistry, "these type cases are the markers or boundary stones that delimit the territory of 'moral' considerations in practice."[64] Using the type case of willful violence against the innocent, we can see how willful violence against a child is easily called into question on moral grounds. Thus, the type case is the starting point for a moral discussion.

In some cases, additional facts surrounding the context may refute the presumption of the rules embedded in the type case. Jonsen and Toulmin discuss three problematic examples: first, the situation when the type case fits the individual case ambiguously; second, the situation when two or more type cases apply to the same individual case in conflicting ways; and third, the situation when an individual case is so unprecedented that it defies resolution in terms of existing type cases. In each of these cases, analytic argument is inappropriate because the universal moral principle, like the type case, fits the situation only ambiguously, clashes with another universal moral principle, or does not apply at all to the situation. We will present one case that illustrates both the first and second examples and then will present a second case to illustrate the third.

The first and second situation that Jonsen and Toulmin discuss can be illustrated by their example of a specific situation occasionally faced by a doctor in a neonatal intensive care unit. Medical science has developed to the point that we now have the technical capacity to maintain the breathing of very small, premature infants who, a few years ago, certainly would have died. This doctor is faced with deciding whether Nancy, a very premature infant, should be treated or should be allowed to die without treatment. The procedures that the doctor will have to follow will have certain serious side effects; even if Nancy survives, she may live a lifetime of physical pain, or she may be seriously handicapped.

We will choose as a type case that of terminally ill patients who have asked to have their treatments discontinued. The comparison of this type case to the specific case of Nancy illustrates Jonsen and Toulmin's first example of a problematic moral case because Nancy's case fits the type case ambiguously.

Certainly, the question faced in Nancy's case is similar to the one doctors face in the cases of these terminally ill patients. Should Nancy be treated, or should she be allowed to die? Should these terminally ill patients be forced to endure weeks of pain and suffering associated with being tied to mechanical life-support systems, or should they be allowed to die?

Since the type case selected to resolve this dispute involves the presumptive rule that a physician should "mercifully refrain" from saving the life of a terminally ill patient who has asked to die, the type case fits Nancy's case ambiguously—the primary difference being that Nancy, unlike terminally ill patients, has no way of telling us whether she would prefer to have her life prolonged or would prefer to be allowed to die. Many other ambiguities exist, such as the fact that as an infant, Nancy cannot reflect on her physical pain nor can she anticipate the duration of suffering ahead of her. Terminally ill patients, on the other hand, may be fully cognizant and reflective about their painful physical circumstances.

Nancy's case also can be used to illustrate Jonsen and Toulmin's second example of a problematic moral case. This second example occurs when two different type cases apply to the specific case in conflicting ways. The first type case—the type case we have just discussed—involves the presumptive rule that a doctor should not take extraordinary measures to save the lives of those patients who choose death over further pain and suffering. The second type case involves a contrary presumptive rule stated in the doctor's oath to "act to preserve life." These two paradigms or type cases apply to Nancy's example in competing ways. The first suggests that the doctor let Nancy die; the second suggests that the doctor attempt to save Nancy's life. To make the situation even more difficult, Congress recently has passed legislation that categorizes "withholding care from the newborn" as "child abuse." Thus, a third paradigm is introduced into Nancy's situation. The dilemma posed when two or more type cases apply to a specific case in conflicting ways is solved not by analytic argument but by personal decision: which type case best fits the specific situation and under what circumstances should the rules of the type case be set aside?

The third problematic situation involves a moral discussion that is so unprecedented that no paradigm exists to resolve it. Jonsen and Toulmin's example concerns a man married for eight years with three children. He decides to have hormone therapy and a sex-change operation. This case raises many interesting and unprecedented issues, not the least of which is whether or not this man and his wife still have mutual sexual obligations.

Each of these problematic situations must be resolved by practical argument rather than by analytic argument. In Jonsen and Toulmin's words:

> The heart of moral experience does not lie in a mastery of general rules
> and theoretical principles, however sound and well reasoned those

principles may appear. It is located rather, in the wisdom that comes from seeing how the ideas behind those rules work out in the course of people's lives: in particular, seeing more exactly what is involved in insisting on (or waiving) this or that rule in one or another set of circumstances.[65]

Jonsen and Toulmin offer a model of practical argument that explains the procedures of casuistry.[66] This model, similar to the one developed in *Uses of Argument*, is presented below:

Practical Reasoning

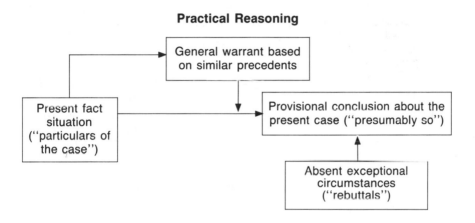

This model is similar to Toulmin's original layout of argument in many respects. This model has four elements rather than the original six; backing and modality are incorporated into other elements. In this model, the authors have eliminated backing by making grounds apply to the general warrant as well as to the claim. Modality, or the degree of certainty, has been incorporated into the claim, as we can see by the phrase, "presumably so." One of Jonsen and Toulmin's examples involves whether or not a person has a moral obligation to return a borrowed pistol to a man who claims that he will shoot his wife as soon as he gets the pistol back. The grounds in this case involve data from the context of the particular situation. In this example, the warrant is a general maxim (one should return borrowed property) developed from type cases or paradigm cases. The warrant developed from these type cases is that borrowed property ought to be returned. The claim, a provisional conclusion about the present case, is that he ought to return the pistol. But this argument hinges on the rebuttal, where the differences in the specific case and the paradigm case are considered. Thus, the procedures of casuistry involve the interaction of a general warrant developed from a paradigm case, data based on the particulars of the present case, and rebuttals concerning exceptional circumstances that exist in the present case. The conclusion of the argument serves as a guide to future action. Jonsen and Toulmin show how the example of the borrowed pistol is analyzed using the model of practical argument:[67]

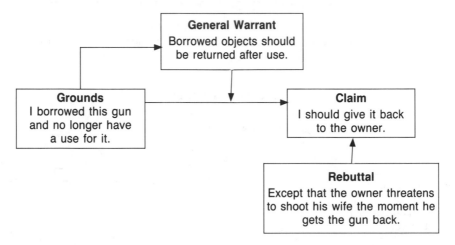

Jonsen and Toulmin claim that since the 1960s, casuistry has been revived:

> [I]n the practical quandaries of everyday life, the use of case analysis continues uninterrupted. Friends and colleagues, psychotherapists and agony columnists, parents and children, priests and ministers: anyone who has occasion to consider moral issues in actual detail knows that morally significant *differences* between cases are as vital as their *likenesses*.[68]

Since the 1960s, they claim, discussion of issues of professional ethics in fields such as medicine, business, and law has begun using the methods and principles of casuistry. In addition, "the 1960s and 1970s saw people enter the moral debates about medicine, legal practice, social policy, nuclear war, and a half a dozen such problems." These debates, they maintain, always return to the particular situation in which a person faces a moral problem, rather than returning to universal moral principles. In summary, their claim is that "our inquiry confirms what Aristotle taught long ago: that ethical arguments have less in common with formal analytic arguments than they do with topical or rhetorical ones."[69]

Humanizing Modernity

In order to humanize modernity, Toulmin believes that we need to "balance the hope for certainty and clarity in theory with the impossibility of avoiding uncertainty and ambiguity in practice."[70] This process, already well underway in science and beginning in philosophy, does not involve tossing out all of the progress that was made during the Modern Period; it involves reconciling these advances with humanism. As Toulmin states: "We are not compelled to *choose between* 16th-century humanism and 17th-century exact science: rather, we need to hang on to the positive achievements of them both." The task, therefore, is neither to reject modernity nor to cling to it in its historic form: it is "rather, to reform, and even reclaim, our inherited modernity, by *humanizing* it."[71]

Toulmin believes that the process of humanizing modernity is well underway in the sciences. Today's sciences, Toulmin believes, "are deeply grounded in experience; while, increasingly, their practical use is subject to criticism, in terms of their human impact."[72] The lines dividing the moral from the technical and the applied from the pure have become less and less distinct. As evidence, he cites the changing in the consciousness of the physicists who worked to produce the atom bomb at White Sands Missile base in New Mexico: "The immediate consequence of this change was the founding of *The Bulletin of the Atomic Scientists*, which still gives a monthly, transnational nongovernmental commentary on the politics of nuclear weapons and related topics."[73] The humanization of the sciences is, he suggests, responsible for bringing questions about ecology to center stage.

If science can be humanized, then so can philosophy. Today, matters of life and death challenge philosophers — specifically, problems of nuclear war, medical technology, and the claims of environment that cannot "be addressed without bringing to the surface questions about the value of human life, and our responsibility for protecting the world of nature, as well as that of 'humanity.'"[74]

Toulmin claims that modernity will focus on four elements that were elements of focus prior to the seventeenth century's turn from humanism to rationalism. These elements, which largely were considered unimportant during the Modern Period, are the oral, the particular, the local, and the timely. For our purposes, the oral is the most important of these four elements, so we will discuss it more fully than the other three.

The oral was rejected by modern philosophers; the scholarly focus was on the printed page. This came from the desire of literary critics "to isolate literary works, as products, from facts about historical situations and personal lives of their authors, as producers — i.e., to decontextualize the text." Prior to the 1950s, philosophical analysis rejected the oral for the written because logical propositions, and hence rationality, were analyzed more easily in written form. But since the 1950s, Toulmin claims, "questions about oral *utterances* have displaced questions about written *propositions*."[75] The return to the oral is, according to Toulmin, one of the reasons for the resurgence of rhetoric as an academic field since the 1950s.

In addition to the return to the oral, we are also returning to the particular, the local, and the timely. The return to the particular is signaled by the revival of casuistry, which we discussed earlier. The return to the local has caused us to reject "Descartes' belief that factual realms of human study like history and ethnography lack intellectual depth, and can teach us nothing of intellectual importance."[76] The return to the timely has meant that, in addition to addressing questions that are timeless, philosophers are concerned with questions of the here and now. In addition, the humanization of modernity brings with it "a renewed acceptance of practice, which requires us to *adapt* action to the special demands of particular occasions."[77]

Toulmin's perspective, then, is that during the Modern Period, analytic argument replaced practical argument and absolutism replaced relativism. Toulmin argues that we need to find a path that rejects complete absolutism while avoiding total relativism. Between 1958 and 1990, he has pursued the goal of describing such a path. To date, he has argued that practical argument, an evolutionary view of science, the revival of casuistry, and the humanization of modernity demonstrate the possibility of such a path.

Responses to Toulmin

Initially, Toulmin's perspective was not well accepted by philosophers.[78] The specific responses of philosophers are beyond the scope of our discussion here since many of them deal with arguments concerning the nature of formal logic rather than rhetoric or practical logic. In general, however, philosophers believe that Toulmin has defined logic too narrowly and that if defined more broadly, it is more relevant to everyday discourse than Toulmin claims. Lewis summarizes this response: "(1) Toulmin erred in his interpretation of traditional logic, (2) his logic was not new since previous logicians had dealt with the problem and, (3) some of the concepts of his 'new logic' were erroneous."[79]

Despite the negative reading of *Uses of Argument* by philosophers, the book generally is applauded by scholars of rhetoric. One sign of Toulmin's wide acceptance among rhetoricians in the United States is the number of argumentation textbooks that have adopted the Toulmin layout in part or in whole.[80] In addition to persons interested in argumentation and debate, Toulmin's layout has gained approval from those who teach communication. For example, McCroskey shows how the Toulmin layout can be used in the basic speech course as an aid to audience analysis and speech organization.[81] Bettinghaus, searching for an adequate model for argumentative speeches, claims that Toulmin is the "most adequate available model."[82]

Others have used the Toulmin layout of argument as a way to explain the process of persuasion and attitude change. D'Angelo demonstrates that attitude theories, particularly the theory of Sherif, Sherif, and Nebergall,[83] can be incorporated within the Toulmin layout of argument in order to provide a more adequate approach to the study of persuasion.[84] Another attempt to integrate the Toulmin layout of argument into a theory of attitude change can be seen in Cronkhite's paradigm of persuasion.[85] Even more recently, Toulmin's approach has been shown to be relevant to argumentation in interpersonal communication. For instance, Burleson extends Toulmin's conception of warrants to show how they are applicable to social reasoning processes evident in argumentation in interpersonal interaction.[86]

Not all communication scholars are equally enamored of Toulmin's ideas. Just as he has critics among philosophers, he has them among communication professionals. Trent, for example, asserts that logic still has some relevance to argument and that Toulmin's ideas should not be allowed to divorce formal logic and practical argument completely.[87] Burleson, in an article comparing Toulmin's approach to rationality with that of Habermas, finds Toulmin's "impartial standpoint of rationality" unable to accomplish the goal of avoiding the perils of both absolutism and relativism. In Burleson's analysis, Toulmin's system lapses into the relativism it was intended to avoid.[88] Anderson and Mortensen, on the other hand, applaud and extend Toulmin's idea that context-invariant forms of logic are not relevant to argument in the "marketplace."[89]

Toulmin's most vocal critic in the field of rhetoric is Willard, who claims that Toulmin's approach to the analysis of argument is inadequate for building a descriptive model of argument. Willard claims that the layout contains three sources of distortion: "(1) the process of translation—translating the message into analytic premises; (2) the linguistic bias of argument models; and (3) the model's intrinsic isolation of context—both linguistic and sociopolitical."[90]

Willard's claim started a debate among Kneupper, Burleson, and Willard. This debate, which extended over a series of convention papers and articles,[91] has enabled Willard to create a credible attack on Toulmin's approach to argumentation as outlined in *Uses of Argument*. Willard claims that the study of argument ought to begin with a description of argument as a social phenomenon rather than as a prescription of ways to produce "good arguments." Without denying that prescriptions have their place, he argues that they should flow from carefully constructed descriptions of arguments. Willard believes that a substantial error in Toulmin's entire project may be that he begins with an attempt to distinguish good reasons from bad ones without first describing the nature of reason giving as a social process.[92]

Another area of criticism of Toulmin's perspective on rhetoric concerns his concept of argument fields.[93] Some writers praise the concept, insisting that it "offers considerable promise for empirical and critical studies of argumentation,"[94] while others, who claim that it is of little value, retort that its "most attractive feature . . . is owed to the fact that it can be made to say virtually anything."[95]

Toulmin's work has been an important aspect of rhetoric in the last quarter of a century. Despite his initial lack of awareness of the relationship of his ideas to rhetoric and lack of consensus on the validity of all aspects of his program of practical argumentation, many rhetoricians have found his ideas instrumental in allowing them to break away from the grip of formal logic. Toulmin's work, particularly his most recent ideas about casuistry and modernity, may be useful in pointing the direction to a path between absolutism and relativism.

Notes

[1] See, for example, Stephen Toulmin, *Human Understanding: Volume 1: The Collective Use and Evolution of Concepts* (Princeton: Princeton University Press, 1972), pp. 111, 313.

[2] Richard D. Rieke and Malcolm O. Sillars, *Argumentation and the Decision Making Process* (New York: John Wiley, 1975), p. 19. The fact that this statement is not included in later editions of Rieke and Sillars may be taken to indicate that they believe Toulmin's later work has taken a more direct interest in the process of communication.

[3] Stephen Toulmin, *Cosmopolis: The Hidden Agenda of Modernity* (New York: Free, 1990). p. 187.

[4] Unless otherwise noted, biographic information on Toulmin was obtained from the following sources: Ann Avory, ed., *Contemporary Authors* (Detroit: Gale Research, 1982), p. 533; *Who's Who in America*, 42nd ed. (Chicago: Marquis Who's Who, 1982), II, 3354; and Jacques Cattel Pres, ed., *Directory of American Scholars*, 8th ed. (New York: R. R. Bowker, 1982), IV, 541.

[5] Stephen Toulmin, "Logic and the Criticism of Arguments," in James L. Golden, Goodwin F. Berquist, William E. Coleman, *The Rhetoric of Western Thought*, 4th ed. (1976; rpt. Dubuque: Kendall-Hunt, 1989), p. 374.

[6] Stephen Toulmin, *An Examination of the Place of Reason in Ethics* (Cambridge: Cambridge University Press, 1950).

[7] Stephen Toulmin, *The Philosophy of Science: An Introduction* (London: Hutchison University Library, 1953).

[8] Stephen Toulmin, *The Uses of Argument* (Cambridge: Cambridge University Press, 1958).

[9] Toulmin, "Logic and the Criticism of Arguments," p. 375.

[10] Wayne Brockriede and Douglas Ehninger, "Toulmin on Argument: An Interpretation and Application," *Quarterly Journal of Speech*, 46 (February 1960), 44-53; and Douglas Ehninger and Wayne Brockriede, *Decision by Debate* (New York: Dodd, Mead, 1963), especially chpt. 8.

[11] Brockriede and Ehninger, p. 44.

[12] Toulmin, "Logic and the Criticism of Arguments," p. 395.

[13] Stephen Toulmin and Allan Janik, *Wittgenstein's Vienna* (New York: Simon and Schuster, 1973).

[14] Albert R. Jonsen and Stephen Toulmin, *The Abuse of Casuistry: A History of Moral Reasoning* (Berkeley: University of California Press, 1988).

[15] Jonsen and Toulmin, p. 2.

[16] Toulmin, *Human Understanding*, p. 23.

[17] Toulmin, *Human Understanding*, pp. 65-66.

[18] Toulmin, *Human Understanding*, p. 25.

[19] Jonsen and Toulmin, p. 7.

[20] Jonsen and Toulmin, p. 3.

[21] Toulmin, *Uses of Argument*, pp. 107-22.

[22] Toulmin, *Uses of Argument*, p. 145.

[23] Toulmin, *Uses of Argument*, p. 212.

[24] Toulmin, *Uses of Argument*, p. 185.

25 Toulmin, *Uses of Argument*, p. 184.
26 Toulmin, *Uses of Argument*, p. 182.
27 Toulmin, *Uses of Argument*, p. 220.
28 Jonsen and Toulmin, p. 5.
29 Toulmin, *Human Understanding*, p. 92.
30 Toulmin, *Cosmopolis*, p. 30.
31 Toulmin, *Cosmopolis*, p. 24.
32 Toulmin, *Cosmopolis*, p. 24.
33 Toulmin, *Cosmopolis*, p. 11.
34 Toulmin, *Cosmopolis*, p. 48.
35 Toulmin, *Cosmopolis*, p. 55.
36 Toulmin, *Cosmopolis*, p. 62.
37 Toulmin, *Cosmopolis*, p. 160-61.
38 Toulmin, *Cosmopolis*, p. 161.
39 Toulmin, *Cosmopolis*, p. 167.
40 Jonsen and Toulmin, p. 6.
41 The information for this section is taken from: Toulmin, *Uses of Argument*, chpt. 3; and Stephen Toulmin, Richard Rieke, and Alan Janik, *An Introduction to Reasoning* (1979; rpt. New York: Macmillan, 1984), chpts. 2-7. The information in both sources is similar, although a few terms have been changed. For example, the term "data" in *Uses of Argument* is "grounds" in *Introduction to Reasoning*. Since *Introduction to Reasoning* is the most recent of Toulmin's writings on the subject, we have used the language of *Introduction to Reasoning*. This decision was not an easy one since the older source, *Uses of Argument*, was authored by Toulmin alone, while the more recent source was co-authored with Rieke and Janik. To determine exactly how much the thinking of Rieke has influenced the difference in these two sources is impossible, but the increased emphasis on communication in *Introduction to Reasoning* is probably more than coincidental.
42 Toulmin, *Uses of Argument*, p. 6.
43 Toulmin, Rieke, and Janik, p. 10.
44 Toulmin, *Human Understanding*, p. 313.
45 Toulmin, *Uses of Argument*, p. 8.
46 Toulmin, *Uses of Argument*, p. 36.
47 Toulmin, *Uses of Argument*, chpt. 1.
48 Toulmin, Rieke, and Janik, p. 8.
49 Toulmin, Rieke, and Janik, chpt. 25.
50 Toulmin, *Uses of Argument*, p. 175.
51 Brockriede and Ehninger, p. 544.
52 Toulmin, Rieke, and Janik, p. 26.
53 The content of this and all other examples of the layout of argument are from *Uses of Argument*, while the form is consistent with *Introduction to Reasoning*.
54 Thomas S. Kuhn, *The Structure of Scientific Revolutions* (Chicago: University of Chicago Press, 1962); and Thomas S. Kuhn, *The Structure of Scientific Revolutions*, 2nd ed. (1962; rpt. Chicago: University of Chicago Press, 1970).
55 Toulmin, *Human Understanding*, p. 102.
56 Toulmin, *Human Understanding*, p. 105.
57 Toulmin, *Human Understanding*, p. 140.
58 Toulmin, *Human Understanding*, p. 267.
59 Toulmin, *Human Understanding*, p. 95.
60 Toulmin, *Human Understanding*, p. 225.
61 Toulmin, *Human Understanding*, p. 50.
62 The revival of casuistry is discussed in Jonsen and Toulmin, *The Abuse of Casuistry*, pp. 304-32.
63 Jonsen and Toulmin, p. 10.
64 Jonsen and Toulmin, p. 307.
65 Jonsen and Toulmin, p. 314.
66 Jonsen and Toulmin, p. 35.

[67] Jonsen and Toulmin, p. 324.

[68] Jonsen and Toulmin, p. 14.

[69] Jonsen and Toulmin, p. 327.

[70] Toulmin, *Cosmopolis*, p. 175.

[71] Toulmin, *Cosmopolis*, p. 180.

[72] Toulmin, *Cosmopolis*, p. 181.

[73] Toulmin, *Cosmopolis*, p. 182.

[74] Toulmin, *Cosmopolis*, p. 186.

[75] Toulmin, *Cosmopolis*, p. 187.

[76] Toulmin, *Cosmopolis*, p. 188.

[77] Toulmin, *Cosmopolis*, p. 192.

[78] For a summary of the responses of logicians, see Albert L. Lewis, "Stephen Toulmin: A Reappraisal," *Central States Speech Journal*, 23 (Spring 1972), 48-55.

[79] Lewis, p. 50.

[80] For instance, see Ehninger and Brockriede, chpts. 8-15; Austin J. Freeley, *Argumentation and Debate: Rational Decision Making* (Belmont, CA: Wadsworth, 1976), pp. 138-42; Halbert E. Gulley, *Discussion, Conference and Group Process* (New York: Holt, Rinehart and Winston, 1960), pp. 146-54; Gerald R. Miller and Thomas R. Nilsen, *Perspectives on Argumentation* (Chicago: Scott, Foresman, 1966); Glen E. Mills, *Reason in Controversy: On General Argumentation* (Boston: Allyn and Bacon, 1968), pp. 110-111; John F. Wilson and Carroll C. Arnold, *Public Speaking as a Liberal Art* (Boston: Allyn and Bacon, 1964), pp. 139-42; Russell R. Windes and Arthur Hastings, *Argumentation and Advocacy* (New York: Random, 1965), pp. 157-86; Richard D. Rieke and Malcolm O. Sillars, *Argumentation and the Decision-Making Process* (New York: John Wiley, 1975), pp. 16-19; and Richard E. Crable, *Argumentation as Communication: Reasoning with Receivers* (Columbus, OH: Merrill, 1976).

[81] James C. McCroskey, "Toulmin and the Basic Course," *Speech Teacher*, 14 (March 1965), 91-100.

[82] Erwin P. Bettinghaus, "Structure and Argument," in Miller and Nilsen, pp. 130-55.

[83] Carolyn W. Sherif, Muzafer Sherif, and Roger E. Nebergall, *Attitude and Attitude Change: The Social Judgement-Involvement Approach* (Philadelphia: W. B. Saunders, 1965).

[84] Gary D'Angelo, "A Schema for the Utilization of Attitude Theory within the Toulmin Model of Argument," *Central States Speech Journal*, 22 (Summer 1971), 100-09.

[85] Gary Cronkhite, *Persuasion: Speech and Behavioral Change* (Indianapolis: Bobbs-Merrill, 1969).

[86] Brant R. Burleson, "A Cognitive-Developmental Perspective on Social Reasoning Processes," *Western Journal of Speech Communication*, 45 (Spring 1981), 133-47. See also Marcus L. Ambrester and Glynis Holm Strause, *A Rhetoric of Interpersonal Communication* (Prospect Heights, IL: Waveland, 1984), pp. 310-15.

[87] Jimmie D. Trent, "Toulmin's Model of and Argument: An Examination and Extension," *Quarterly Journal of Speech*, 54 (October 1968), 252-59.

[88] Brant R. Burleson, "On the Foundations of Rationality: Toulmin, Habermas, and the *a Priori* of Reason," *Journal of the American Forensic Association*, 16 (Fall 1979), 112-27.

[89] Ray Lynn Anderson and C. David Mortensen, "Logic and Marketplace Argumentation," *Quarterly Journal of Speech*, 53 (April 1967), 143-50.

[90] Charles Arthur Willard, "On the Utility of Descriptive Diagrams for the Analysis and Criticism of Arguments," *Communication Monographs*, 43 (November 1976), 314.

[91] See for instance, Charles W. Kneupper, "On Argument and Diagrams," *Journal of the American Forensic Association*, 14 (Spring 1978), 181-86; Brant R. Burleson, "On the Analysis and Criticism of Arguments: Some Theoretical and Methodological Considerations," *Journal of the American Forensic Association*, 15 (Winter 1979), 137-47; and Charles Arthur Willard, "The Status of the Non-Discursiveness Thesis," *Journal of the American Forensic Association*, 17 (Spring 1981), 190-214.

[92] Charles Arthur Willard, *Argumentation and the Social Grounds of Knowledge* (University, AL: University of Alabama Press, 1983), especially chpt. 3; and Charles Arthur Willard, *A Theory of Argumentation* (University, AL: University of Alabama Press, 1989).

93 See, for example, Robert Rowland, "Argument Fields," in *Dimensions of Argument: Proceedings of the Second Summer Conference on Argumentation*, ed. George Ziegelmueller and Jack Rhodes (Annandale, VA: Speech Communication Association, 1982), pp. 56-79.

94 David Zarefsky, "Persistent Questions in the Theory of Argument Fields," *Journal of the American Forensic Association*, 18 (Spring 1982), 191.

95 Charles Arthur Willard, "Field Theory: Cartesian Mediation," in *Dimensions of Argument: Proceedings of the Second Summer Conference on Argumentation.* ed. George Ziegelmueller and Jack Rhodes (Annandale, VA: Speech Communication Association, 1982), pp. 21-43.

5

Chaim Perelman

Chaim Perelman and Kenneth Burke are "two writers whom historians of twentieth-century rhetorical theory are sure to feature," asserts Wayne Brockriede. He believes that "they may dominate an account of rhetorical theory in this century as Adam Smith and George Campbell dominate Wilbur Samuel Howell's characterization of eighteenth-century rhetoric."[1] We will examine Burke's contributions to contemporary rhetoric in Chapter Seven; the focus here will be on those of Perelman.

Chaim Perelman was born in Warsaw, Poland, on May 20, 1912;[2] his family moved to Belgium in 1925. Perelman was exposed to the study of rhetoric in secondary school, where he was introduced to Richard Whately's *Elements of Rhetoric* (1828), among other works, and he studied such diverse topics as the syllogism and figures of style. These topics later seemed to Perelman to be conspicuously unrelated to one another: "Since then I have often wondered what link a professor of rhetoric could possibly discover between the syllogism and the figures of style with their exotic names that are so difficult to remember."[3] Perelman completed his education at the Free University of Brussels, where he earned a doctorate in law in 1934 and a doctorate in philosophy in 1938.

Perelman was an individual of action as well as of ideas. During the second World War, he was a leader of the resistance movement in Belgium and, at the conclusion of the war, was offered a number of medals for heroism. He refused them, saying, "My heart was on fire. I simply picked up a pail of water to douse the flames. I want no medals." After the war, he returned to the Free University as a professor of logic, ethics, and metaphysics. Later, he served as director of the Center for the Philosophy of Law and the National Center for Logical Research. He also received honorary degrees from the University of Florence and the Hebrew University of Jerusalem.

Because of his interest in law, Perelman studied the nature of justice early in his professional career; these studies led him to develop a concept he calls "formal justice." He defines formal justice as *"a principle of action in accordance with which beings of one and the same essential category must be treated in the same way."*[4] Perelman soon discovered that application of this principle to particular cases led immediately to questions of values and to the question, "How do we reason about values?"

Perelman found the answers provided by the philosophical literature about values and reason to be highly unsatisfactory. He himself could think of no way to resolve questions of value on rational grounds: "Indeed, as I entirely accepted the principle that one cannot draw an 'ought' from an 'is'—a judgment of value from a judgment of fact—I was led inevitably to the conclusion that if justice consists in the systematic implementation of certain value judgments, it does not rest on any rational foundation." Thus, the student of law and rhetoric found questions regarding how one rationally or logically compares one value to another to be ones that could be answered by neither of his fields of study: "I found myself in a situation similar to Kant's. If Hume is right in maintaining that empiricism cannot provide a basis for either science or morals, must we not then look to other empirical methods to justify them?" Perelman then set out to discover what those methods might be.

Perelman and his colleague, Lucie Olbrechts-Tyteca, decided to follow the method used by German logician Gottlob Frege, who studied examples of reasoning used by mathematicians to cast new light on logic. Perelman and Olbrechts-Tyteca similarly decided to investigate the ways authors in diverse fields use argument to reason about values. These methods included a study of specific examples of argumentation texts concerning questions of value; they also studied specific examples of political discourse, philosophical discourse, reasons given by judges to justify their decisions, and other daily discussions involving deliberations about matters of value. "For almost ten years, Mme. L. Olbrechts-Tyteca and I conducted such an inquiry and analysis," Perelman explained. He summarized their results:

> We obtained results that neither of us had ever expected. Without either knowing or wishing it, we had rediscovered a part of Aristotelian logic that had been long forgotten or, at any rate, ignored and despised. It was the part dealing with dialectical reasoning, as distinguished from demonstrative reasoning—called by Aristotle *analytics*—which is analyzed at length in the *Rhetoric, Topics*, and *On Sophistical Refutations*. We called this new, or revived, branch of study, devoted to the analysis of informal reasoning, *the new rhetoric*.[5]

Their study was presented in 1958 in a two-volume work entitled *The New Rhetoric: A Treatise on Argumentation*, which was translated into English in 1969. According to the editors of *The Great Ideas Today*, "more than any single item, this work aroused a renewed interest in the idea [of rhetoric]."[6]

After the French edition of *The New Rhetoric* was published, but before the English translation had been completed, Perelman came to the United States as a distinguished visiting professor at Pennsylvania State University. He came at the joint invitation of Henry W. Johnstone, chair of the Department of Philosophy, and Robert Oliver, chair of the Department of Speech. "I was very perplexed," noted Perelman, "for I knew nothing of 'speech,' a discipline entirely unknown in European universities. . . . I chose as the title of my course, 'The Philosophical Foundations of Rhetoric,' but I could not prepare my lessons, because I did not know what the preoccupations of the members of the Department of *Speech* were."[7]

Prior to his visit to the United States, Perelman assumed that rhetoric and argumentation were subjects that had been neglected or had been studied by non-humanistic methods. Out of his ignorance, "which lasted until 1962," Perelman concluded, he knew nothing "of the very existence of a university profession in the United States devoted to the study and teaching of rhetoric (Speech Communication)."[8] Later, he explained his earlier conclusion as one "which we find ridiculous today."[9] Perelman maintained close association with his friends in the speech communication field until his death. His last "official" visit with the profession was marked by his attendance at the annual convention of the Speech Communication Association in Louisville in 1982.

On December 5, 1983, a law was passed in Belgium making Perelman a Baron in recognition of his work in philosophy and of the renown he had brought to Belgium. Following a dinner to celebrate the honor with some of his close friends, on January 22, 1984, Perelman died of a heart attack in his home.

Need for a New Rhetoric

Perelman felt that a new approach to rhetoric was needed because rhetoric stressed matters of style at the expense of matters of rationality.[10] The contemporary state of disrepute of rhetoric is due to this emphasis, which Perelman traces to attitudes about rhetoric in classical Greece: "Among the ancients, rhetoric appeared as the study of a technique for use by the common man impatient to arrive rapidly at conclusions, or to form an opinion, without first of all taking the trouble of a preliminary serious investigation."[11] Thus, because rhetoric seemed to be concerned more with matters of style than with matters of rationality, the subject has not been one that historically has commanded respect, particularly among philosophers.

Perelman traces the connection of rhetoric to style (and thus its current disrepute) largely to Aristotle's "misleading analysis . . . of the epideictic or ceremonial form of oratory."[12] Aristotle divided rhetoric into three forms of oratory. Forensic oratory or judicial speaking is speaking in a court of law; it is concerned with matters of the past, such as whether or not a certain act has or has not occurred. Deliberative oratory, or speaking in a legislative assembly, is concerned with matters of the future, such as what courses of action are advisable. Epideictic oratory, or ceremonial speaking such as a Fourth of July address, concerns speaking about matters of praise and blame.

The audiences of both forensic and deliberative oratory were expected to judge the speech on the merits of its content. "Was it or was it not true that a certain person committed an act of murder?" was a question that might concern the forensic speaker. "Is it or is it not advisable for the state to enact this policy or that policy?" might be the question a deliberative speaker must answer. In epideictic oratory, however, the audience was expected to judge on the basis of the orator's skill: "Such set speeches were often delivered before large assemblies, as at the Olympic Games, where competition between orators provided a welcome complement to the athletic contests. On such occasions, the only decision that the audience was called upon to make concerned the talent of the orator, by awarding the crown to the victor." While deliberative and forensic speaking were concerned with matters of policy and fact, epideictic oratory was concerned with matters of value. Since it was concerned with values, no standards for judging the content of the speech supposedly existed; thus, audiences had to be instructed to judge on matters of skill.

This classical treatment of rhetoric seemed to indicate that audiences, although capable of judging matters of fact and policy on their merits, were incapable of judging matters of value in the same way. Because epideictic oratory, the form of speaking most closely associated with values, was judged on style instead of content, Perelman felt the need for a theory of argument in which values could be assessed rationally — in the same way as facts and policies. He believes that questions of value are especially important to rhetoric: "The epideictic genre is not only important but essential from an educational point of view, since it too has an effective and distinctive part to play — that, namely, of bringing about a consensus in the minds of the audience regarding the values that are celebrated in the speech." How a speaker achieves assent with an audience became of particular interest to Perelman, and the topic was one he felt best could be dealt with by rhetoric — rather than law or philosophy.

Argumentation and Logic

Perelman's theory of rhetoric is a theory of argumentation. Argumentation, however, is not the same as logic; Perelman believes that argumentation is separate and distinct from demonstration or formal logic. "Demonstration," according to Perelman, "is a calculation made in accordance with the rules that have been laid down before hand,"[13] while "argumentation is the study of the discursive techniques that "induce or increase the mind's adherence to the theses presented for its assent."[14] Demonstration uses mathematical language such as that contained in the mathematical formula $a/b = c/d$, while argumentation uses the naturally ambiguous language of humans. Thus, demonstration allows us to produce a conclusion (or a claim) by reasoning from premises, while argumentation attempts to produce adherence to that claim.

The primary difference between argumentation and demonstration, according to Perelman, is that demonstration is impersonal, while argumentation is personal. Demonstration or formal logic is conducted according to a system that largely is unrelated to people, but argumentation is a person-centered activity. The aim of demonstration is calculation — the deduction of formally valid conclusions by conforming to a particular set of rules — while the aim of argumentation is not calculation but seeking adherence to a thesis, which presupposes a "meeting of minds."[15] The conclusion of demonstration is assumed to be certain, while the conclusion of an argument is a probable one. Demonstration begins with axioms that are assumed to be true regardless of an audience's agreement with them. Argumentation, on the other hand, is personal because it begins with premises that the audience accepts. The conclusion of demonstration, then, is a self-evident one, while the conclusion of an argument is one that is more or less strong, more or less convincing.

Audience

Perelman's concern with argumentation as opposed to demonstration led him to focus on the audience.[16] All argumentation must be planned in relation to an audience: "a speech must be heard, as a book must be read."[17] Sometimes, groups such as scientists pretend they do not address an audience and that they merely report the facts. Perelman rejects such an attitude since it "rests on the illusion, widespread in certain rationalistic and scientific circles, that facts speak for themselves."[18] Perelman insists that facts do not "speak"; "facts" only become facts when an audience consents to call them facts.

Perelman believes that, in order for argumentation to occur, a contact of the minds or, in Perelman's words, a "formulation of an effective community of minds" must exist. This meeting of the minds is an intellectual contact that requires people engaged in argumentation to share some frame of reference. In some cases, of course, contact of minds can be inadequate. Perelman uses the example of Alice in *Alice in Wonderland* to show how failure to have this contact of minds results in ineffective or non-existent argumentation. Alice was unable to communicate effectively with the characters in Wonderland because the rules of conversation there were so different from those in Alice's natural environment; a shared frame of reference between speaker and audience did not exist.[19]

How is "audience" to be defined? Is it to be limited to the audience to whom the speaker physically is speaking? Perelman does not impose this limitation on his definition, explaining that "a member of Parliament in England must address himself to the Speaker, but he may try to persuade those listening throughout the country." At the same time, however, situations exist where the speaker may choose to ignore certain persons to whom argumentation is actually addressed because they are beyond appeal. For example, a politician may realize the futility of attempting to persuade a certain group of people actually present for a speech. Thus, Perelman defines the audience "for the purposes of rhetoric, as *the ensemble of those whom the speaker wishes to influence by his argumentation.*"[20] His concept of audience refers to the speaker's mental conception of the audience rather than to the physical presence of a group of people assembled to hear a speech.

Perelman divides the audience into two types—particular and universal. The *universal* audience is composed of all reasonable and competent people; a *particular* audience is any group of people whether or not they are reasonable or competent. The particular audience may range from people who are physically present and who are addressed at a particular time to a specific group of persons whom the speaker is attempting to influence. The particular audience for a politician, for example, may include all of the voters of the precinct, although the speech is presented only to an assembly of the League of Women Voters. For a doctor, a particular audience may be the patient, although the entire family is present.

In contrast to the particular audience, the universal audience "may be all of humanity, or at least all those who are competent and reasonable . . . which may itself be made up of an infinite variety of particular audiences."[21] The universal audience is a mental concept that the speaker constructs; thus, every culture and perhaps every speaker has a different universal audience. The universal audience generally is not an elite audience or even an audience of experts in a subject area. Those who wish to appeal to elite audiences well may consider elite audiences to be above common people: "The elite audience embodies the universal audience only for those who acknowledge this role of vanguard and model. For the rest it will be no more than a particular audience. The status of an audience varies with the concepts one has of it."[22] An elite audience may or may not conceptualize the universal audience, depending on the attitude of the speaker.

The universal audience does not have to be composed of many people; it can be one person or one's own self. Argumentation before a single hearer might include one philosopher attempting to convince another to accept her position on the question of ethics. Similarly, we all probably are familiar with instances when we argue with ourselves. These constitute argumentation before the universal audience only when the speaker chooses arguments and appeals that merit consideration beyond the particular audience. In these cases, "the interlocutor in a dialogue and the man debating with himself are regarded as an incarnation of the universal audience."[23] The distinguishing feature of the universal audience, then, "does not depend upon the number of persons who hear the speaker but upon the speaker's intention: does he want the adherence of some or of every reasonable being?"[24] The speaker may envision those to whom the speech is delivered—even in an instance of private deliberation—as the universal audience.

The concept of the universal audience serves two purposes for the speaker. First, it serves as an aid in the choice of arguments and appeals or as a "metaphor which functions as an inventional tool."[25] The speaker begins with a conception of the universal audience and from that conception makes decisions regarding the types of appeals that seem most appropriate for that audience. In selecting appeals and arguments, the speaker actually is selecting the audience, universal or particular, toward whom the argumentation is directed. The conception of the audience, then, aids the speaker in selection of appeals and thus is a tool used in the invention of the speech.

A second purpose of the universal audience is that it serves as a norm or a standard for differentiating "good arguments" from "bad arguments." This purpose seems to be more relevant to philosophical argument than everyday argument. For philosophical arguments, the universal audience provides a sense of rationality since the universal audience gives its assent to good arguments and withholds it from those it considers bad. Perelman does not consider truth and validity in argumentation to be absolute; argumentation must provide for a variety of interpretations of reality: "To reconcile philosophic claims to rationality with the plurality of philosophic systems, we must recognize that the appeal to reason must be identified not as an appeal to a single truth but instead as an appeal for adherence of an audience";[26] various audiences and various members of the audience will have, of course, varying conceptions of what must be provided before assent will be given.

The concept of the universal audience implies that the quality of argument depends on the quality of the audience that accepts the thesis of the speaker. While adherence of a particular audience may not be indicative of a strong argument, adherence of the universal audience is the ultimate in rationality in Perelman' s theory. Thus, an argument addressed to a particular audience may be persuasive to that audience but not to the universal audience. An argument that would persuade members of the National Rifle Association, for example, to write their legislators opposing gun control might not be one that would convince all reasonable and competent people that gun control is unwise.

The Starting Points of Argumentation

The purpose of argumentation is to move an audience from agreement about premises to agreement about some conclusion. Thus, the process of argumentation is different from that of demonstration, where the purpose is to produce "Truth" by reasoning from premises to a conclusion. In Perelman's words, "the aim of argumentation is not, like demonstration, to prove the truth of the conclusion from premises, but to transfer to the conclusion the *adherence* accorded to the premises." [27]

Although the conclusions of argumentation may be uncertain, contingent, and unacceptable to an audience, the argumentation process begins with premises the audience accepts. For example, a speaker may seek assent for a controversial thesis such as the value of a nuclear freeze by appealing to agreed-upon premises concerning the value of peace. Once the speaker has identified premises that the audience accepts, the next step is to cause the members of the audience to adhere to the speaker's conclusion in the same way that they agree with the premises. This is accomplished by "the establishment of a bond between the premises and the theses whose acceptance the speaker wants to achieve." [28]

A variety of points of agreement are available as starting points of argument.[29] Perelman distinguishes between starting points that deal with reality (facts, truths, and presumptions) and those that concern the preferable (values, hierarchies, and the *loci* of the preferable).

Starting Points Dealing with Reality

Facts, truths, and presumptions are among the starting points of argumentation that deal with reality. Facts and truths are "characterized by objects that already are agreed to by the universal audience."[30] Since something's status as a fact depends on agreement by the universal audience, no way exists "to define 'fact' in such a manner that would allow us, at any time, to classify this or that concrete datum as a fact." A fact is a fact due to the agreement accorded it by the universal audience. While its "actual" correspondence to the structures of reality is not the issue, universal agreement is achieved when persons perceive data to be rooted in those structures of reality. "From the standpoint of argumentation," Perelman asserts, "we are confronted with a fact only if we can postulate uncontroverted, universal agreement with respect to it."[31]

Because facts are given universal agreement, they are not subject to argumentation. Adherence to a fact requires no justification, and an audience expects no reinforcement. Facts have a privileged status in argumentation that easily can be lost; if justification is called for, the datum loses its status as a fact. Simply questioning a statement is sufficient to cause that statement to lose its privileged status as a fact that enjoys universal agreement. The speaker, in this case, no longer can use that statement as a fact unless the speaker shows "that the person who opposes him is mistaken or, at least, shows that there is no reason to take the latter's opinion into account—that is, by disqualifying him, by denying him the status of a competent and reasonable interlocutor."[32]

To summarize, a fact loses its privileged status as a fact when it is the conclusion rather than the starting point of argument. While argumentative conclusions are uncertain and contingent, the starting points of argumentation require agreement; thus, agreement is precisely the criterion that defines a fact. In the days prior to Christopher Columbus, for example, a well-accepted "fact" was that the earth was flat. This idea was granted the status of fact not because of its enduring truth but because of the agreement accorded to it.

Truths are similar to facts because both enjoy universal agreement. Perelman uses the term "fact" to refer to a particular datum and the term "truth" to refer to some broader principle connecting facts to one another. They are different in that truths involve "more complex systems relating to connections between facts. They may be scientific theories or philosophical or religious conceptions."[33] Both facts and truths serve as starting points of argument that concern the nature of reality.

Presumptions are the third starting point of argument bearing on the nature of reality. Presumptions, like facts and truths, enjoy universal agreement: ''We habitually associate presumptions with what happens and with what can reasonably be counted upon.'' Unlike facts and truths, however, the audience's adherence to presumptions falls short of being maximum; thus, presumptions can be reinforced by argumentation. Speakers engage in preliminary argumentation to establish certain presumptions or to reinforce those presumptions in the minds of the audience. According to Perelman, audiences expect that which is normal and likely, and presumptions are based on these expectations. For example, audiences expect good people to commit good deeds, evil people to commit evil deeds, truthful people to tell the truth, liars to lie, and reasonable people to act in sensible ways.

Facts, truths, and presumptions are alike in that they deal with reality and enjoy agreement of the universal audience. Presumptions differ from facts and truths because presumptions can be violated, whereas facts and truths cannot. We presume that good people will commit good deeds, but we often encounter exceptions.

One of the important advantages associated with the use of presumption in argumentation is that it ''imposes the burden of proof upon the person who wants to oppose its application.''[34] One example of this advantage is the presumption of innocence followed in our legal system, whereby juries are supposed to accept the presumption of innocence on the part of the defendant. Of course, a presumption such as this does not last forever, and although jury members are informed of the presumption of innocence, they also are informed that it can be overturned by proof beyond a reasonable doubt. Presumptions, then, are overturned when they are shown to be contrary to facts.

In summary, the starting points of argument concerned with reality involve facts, truths, and presumptions, all of which enjoy agreement by the universal audience. Facts and truths are accorded a higher status, however, because, unlike presumptions, they do not require reinforcement in the minds of the audience.

Starting Points Dealing with the Preferable

While facts, truths, and presumptions are starting points of argument dealing with reality, the next group of starting points — values, hierarchies, and *loci* of the preferable — bear on the preferable.[35] The statement that ''Denver is a large city,'' for example, is classified as a fact in Perelman's schema. In contrast, the statement that ''large cities are undesirable places'' is classified as a value judgment. Both sets of ideas are starting points for argumentation; the primary difference between them is that facts, truths, and presumptions deal with matters of reality, while values, hierarchies, and *loci* deal with matters of preference.

Although facts, truths, and presumptions hold the adherence of the universal audience, values, hierarchies, and *loci* hold only the adherence of particular audiences. Some values, such as truth or beauty, seem to be ones that might secure the adherence of the universal audience. But Perelman contends this is true only to the extent that these values are not made specific. As soon as one applies the value to a particular case, the adherence of particular audiences is all that one reasonably can expect. He maintains that their "claim to universal agreement . . . seems to us to be due solely to their generality. They can be regarded as valid for a universal audience only on condition that their content not be specified; as soon as we try to go into details, we meet only the adherence of particular audiences."[36] While honesty, for example, may be a universal value in general, most people would not expect someone to tell a thief where the family jewels are hidden.

Perelman divides values into two types—the abstract and the concrete. Values are called abstract when they are not attached to a particular person or institution. "Truth," "justice," and the "American way" are examples of abstract values. Values are considered concrete when they are attached to some person, institution, or object. For example, in general, "truth" is an abstract value that becomes concrete when we attach it to a particular person in a claim that "Superman is a good person because he fights for 'truth,' 'justice,' and the 'American way.'"

People who argue for the status quo, according to Perelman, are more likely to begin their arguments with concrete values because concrete values are more persuasive when "one wishes to preserve than when one wishes to renovate." On the other hand, those who argue for change are more likely to begin their argumentation with abstract values: "Abstract values can readily be used for criticism, because they are no respectors of persons and seem to provide criteria for one wishing to change the established order."[37]

Hierarchies are even more important than values. Hierarchies refer to the way values are arranged in terms of importance, as in the "superiority of men over animals, of gods over men" or in the importance of a fair trial over freedom of the press. Selecting values that audiences accept usually is a simple matter; determining how that audience compares one value to another is much more difficult: "Most values are indeed shared by a great number of audiences, and a particular audience is characterized less by which values it accepts than by the way it grades them. Values may be admitted by many different audiences, but the degree of their acceptance will vary from one audience to another."[38]

Value hierarchies help to clarify the interrelationship between abstract and concrete values because an abstract value can be used to establish a hierarchy among concrete values. The abstract value that the individual is more important than society can be used to argue that the American judicial system is preferable to systems that do not offer a presumption of innocence. In this case, the abstract value of individualism is related to two or more persons or institutions in a concrete manner.

As in the case of values, hierarchies also can be classified as abstract or concrete. The superiority of humans over animals is a concrete hierarchy because it is related to specific objects. The superiority of the just over the useful is an example of an abstract hierarchy because these values are not applied to particular objects.

Hierarchies also are classified by Perelman as homogeneous and heterogeneous. A homogeneous hierarchy is one that compares similar values—for example, the danger of a mild illness compared to a severe illness. Since the values are different only in degree, these hierarchies are relatively easy to determine. More of a good thing is usually better, just as less of a bad thing is preferred.

A heterogeneous hierarchy is more difficult to determine since the values are different and often may come into conflict. The values of honesty and truth may come into conflict, for example, when you are approached by a friend who is wearing a positively ugly dress; she asks, "What do you think of my dress?" The answer to this question illustrates your heterogeneous value hierarchy relative to the values of honesty and kindness. The need for consideration of value hierarchies, particularly heterogeneous ones, is apparent since simultaneous pursuit of certain values leads to incompatibilities that force us to make choices among them. For instance, while most Americans value both fair trial and free press, these values come into conflict when a newspaper reporter reports evidence that ordinarily would be suppressed by a judge.

In addition to values and hierarchies, Perelman isolates a third starting point of argument related to the preferable that he calls "*loci*." *Loci*, also called "topics" or "*topoi*," are general headings corresponding to the ways that value hierarchies can be organized. As values are arranged according to hierarchies, hierarchies are arranged according to *loci*. Perelman points to two types of *loci*—the general and the special. General *loci* "are affirmations about what is presumed to be of higher value in any circumstances whatsoever while special *loci* concern what is preferable in specific situations."[39]

Perelman describes six *loci* of the preferable: quantity, quality, order, existent, essence, and person. We will use the *loci* of quantity and quality to explain how value hierarchies are arranged according to *loci*. If a person's value hierarchies are founded on the *locus* of quantity, that person probably will argue for the greatest good for the greatest number. On the other hand, a person whose value hierarchies are organized according to the *locus* of quality probably will argue for something based on its uniqueness or its irreplacibility. Gregg B. Walker and Malcolm O. Sillars use the example of the forestry dispute over the spotted owl in the Pacific Northwest to illustrate this type of argumentation. Environmentalists want the spotted owl to be designated an endangered species, an act the logging industry opposes because it would endanger jobs in the region. Walker and Sillars explain:

> The environmentalists' views correspond with a locus of quality. They believe that the spotted owl's ecological value is unique and irreplaceable. Consequently, they value protection, beauty, ecological balance, and the sanctity of each species.
> The loggers base their position on the locus of quantity and order. They see protection of a small number of spotted owls as a threat to their livelihood and the economy of the region.[40]

Perelman's system, then, includes starting points of argument that bear on the preferable as well as those that deal with reality. He concludes that, in order to address any audience properly, a speaker should consider the values, hierarchies, and *loci* of the preferable that are acceptable to that audience.

Presence and Communion

Because Perelman's perspective includes a variety of starting points and a focus on the audience, choice is an important factor in his conception of argumentation. Unlike the mathematician or the computer engaging in analytical reasoning, the speaker engaging in argumentation must choose from among the available starting points to decide how to create presence and communion.

An important element in Perelman's perspective on rhetoric is the concept of presence.[41] When a speaker has a variety of elements of argumentation from which to choose, "the orator must select certain elements on which he focuses attention by endowing them, as it were, with a 'presence.'"[42] Certain elements in our perception, depending upon the situation, can seem more important or special than other elements. The elements that are present in our mind are the most important, of course, while those that are absent are less important. Presence, then, is "the displaying of certain elements on which the speaker wishes to center attention in order that they may occupy the foreground of the hearer's consciousness."[43]

One way to explain the notion of presence is by using the metaphor of figure and ground. A person standing on a mountain top looking into a valley may see trees, a lake, and a stream, along with other objects. When that person focuses on, for instance, a tree, the tree becomes the figure and the rest of the objects become the ground. Perelman might say that, in this case, the tree has achieved "presence" in that person's perception.

One role of argumentation is to create presence and thus importance. To illustrate this concept, Perelman tells a Chinese story in which a "king sees an ox on its way to sacrifice. He is moved to pity for it and orders that a sheep be used in its place. He confesses he did so because he could see the ox, but not the sheep." [44] Other examples of the function of presence can be seen in real objects, such as "Caesar's bloody tunic as brandished by Antony, . . .[or]. . .the children of the victim of the accused." [45] These objects can be presented to an audience to establish presence. In these cases, the speaker is acting on the senses of the audience in order to move that audience.

Establishing the presence of what is absent, however, is a more difficult but often more important task. Through the use of argumentation, a lawyer can cause a jury to "live" a situation that occurred in the past, a legislator can assist an audience in imagining how much better the world would be if a bill were enacted, and a minister can bring audience members to distant places and times that existed before their birth or will exist after their death. The concept of presence implies that a speaker has the ability "to make present, by verbal magic alone, what is actually absent but what he considers important to his argument. [46]

Some would argue that the elements of argumentation that are physically present are more important to argument since they are the most persuasive, but Perelman warns us against this belief. Often, he claims, the most persuasive ideas are more abstract and are not represented by physically present objects; in these cases, the techniques of presentation aimed at the creation of presence can cause those ideas to hold importance for the audience. Perelman's perspective on rhetoric, then, does not restrict us to the use of concrete starting points but allows us to expand the variety of appropriate starting points to include those that are intangible and abstract.

In addition to creating presence, argumentation also strives to establish communion with an audience. "Communion" is Perelman's term for establishing commonalities or identifying with the audience, and he believes that a speaker who establishes such communion is more likely to be persuasive than a speaker who does not. For example, a speaker might establish communion with a group of members of the Veterans of Foreign Wars by referring to his own experiences in World War II. This notion of communion reasserts Perelman's notion that the starting point of argument is agreement.

Techniques of Presentation

Perelman introduces various techniques of presentation—or stylistic aspects of argument—that are used to establish presence and communion. He recognizes that these techniques have been developed to the point that their "study came to form the whole material of rhetoric," [47] but he views them in a substantially different way from how they were viewed in the traditional study of rhetoric. He does not consider the techniques of presentation from their stylistic aspect; rather, he offers an in-depth consideration of the techniques of presentation as they function to argue and to assist in the attainment of communion, presence, and adherence.

For Perelman, the style or form of an argument cannot be separated from its content: "The presentation of data is necessarily connected with problems of language. Choice of terms to express the speaker's thought is rarely without significance in the argumentation." He claims that the argumentative intent of a speaker often is conveyed by the choice of one word over another. For example, when a person is described as "having a tendency to mislead," the meaning communicated is different from when that same person is described as a "liar."[48]

For the speaker, argumentation involves the choice of data and techniques of presentation to insure presence and communion. For the listener, it involves choices among various interpretations that might be assigned to the speaker's data. In this respect, argumentation stands in stark contrast to formal logic. In logic, no choice exists because the language of logic is unambiguous, while in argumentation, many choices exist because human language is symbolic and thus inherently ambiguous. The study of argumentation, then, must take into account the study of human language and the matter of interpretation. In Perelman's words, "the study of argumentation compels us to take into account not only the choice of data but also the way in which they are interpreted, the meaning attributed to them."[49]

The speaker's presentational techniques and the listener's interpretive choices, of course, are interrelated. A speaker's presentational techniques may be aimed at securing a particular interpretation from among several potential interpretations on the part of the listener; this is done by choosing certain techniques to establish the presence of the favored interpretation. The speaker creates presence for a particular interpretation by "setting it in the foreground of consciousness. . .[and pushing]. . . the others into the shadow. The core of many arguments is formed of this play of innumerable interpretations and of the struggle to impose some of them and get rid of others."[50] Argumentation may succeed or fail depending on whether or not the speaker is successful in choosing techniques that achieve presence or communion.

Techniques of Argumentation

A substantial portion of Perelman's perspective on rhetoric is concerned with techniques of argumentation.[51] The two main categories of techniques are called liaison and dissociation. Argumentation in the form of a liaison "allows for the transference to the conclusion of the adherence accorded the premises," while argumentation in the form of dissociation "aims at separating elements which language or a recognized tradition have previously tied together."[52]

Techniques of Liaison

Techniques of liaison seek to establish a bond between an arguer's starting point and thesis. For example, a speaker might take the value of life as a starting point and attempt to create a liaison or bond between life and the act of abortion in order to convince an audience that abortion is immoral. Perelman shows how liaison can be created by quasi-logical arguments, arguments based on the structure of reality, and arguments that attempt to establish the structure of reality.

Quasi-Logical Arguments. Quasi-logical arguments are similar to formal logic and, in fact, much of their persuasive force is achieved because of their similarity to logic.[53] Since people are inclined to accept claims based on "logic," this type of argument seems particularly persuasive. Still, they differ from formal logic because they seek audience adherence rather than demonstration. We will examine quasi-logical arguments that are analogous to syllogisms and those that are analogous to the law of non-contradiction.

A common type of quasi-logical argument is similar in form to the syllogism. Participants in the public debate on abortion frequently use this type of quasi-logical argument when they make statements such as "abortion violates the sanctity of life" or "laws prohibiting abortion violate freedom of choice." In each of these cases, "sanctity of life" or "freedom of choice" is analogous to one term in a syllogism, while "abortion" or "laws prohibiting abortion" is analogous to the other term. In syllogistic form, these arguments might appear as follows:

Major premise: The sanctity of life is an absolute value.
Minor premise: Abortion violates the sanctity of life.
Conclusion: Abortion violates an absolute value.

Major premise: Freedom of choice is an absolute value.
Minor premise: Laws prohibiting abortion violate freedom of choice.
Conclusion: Laws prohibiting abortion violate an absolute value.

Although this kind of argument is similar in form to formal logic, it is different from formal logic in that it is used to gain audience adherence, while formal logic is a system of calculus that is unconcerned with audience adherence.

Another quasi-logical argument is argument from incompatibility. A charge of incompatibility in argumentation is similar to a charge of violating the law of non-contradiction in formal logic. In formal logic, a contradiction consists of two statements that are inconsistent with one another. Incompatibility in argumentation occurs when we find ourselves faced with a position that appears to be in conflict with a previously held one. A child, for instance, is faced with an incompatibility when instructed by a teacher, "Never tell a lie," and when ordered by a parent, "Tell the clerk at the movie you are eleven so you can pay half price." The person who says to another, "How can you be against legal abortion and in favor of capital punishment?" is using an argument of incompatibility.

A major difference between incompatibility and contradiction is that we can escape from an incompatibility, but we cannot break the law of non-contradiction. The child who lies about her age to the movie clerk can rationalize the lie as only a "little white lie"; the anti-abortion advocate can say, "But, you see, I'm only in favor of protecting *innocent* life." One can escape from an incompatibility but not from a contradiction; "X" never can be "not X."

Arguments Based on the Structure of Reality. After quasi-logical arguments, Perelman considers arguments based on the structure of reality. These arguments are based on associations of succession and coexistence. Perelman claims that these are two different ways of structuring reality. Arguments based on an association of succession involve the relationship between phenomena on the same level, such as cause and effect, while arguments based on an association of coexistence involve the relationship between phenomena on different levels, such as act and essence.

An example of an association of succession is the "pragmatic argument," which exemplifies argumentation relevant to consequences. Such an argument presumes that the value of an act can be determined by its consequences. To produce a good reason for an action using the pragmatic argument, a speaker would argue that the action will lead to good consequences. For example, a speaker might argue that capital punishment is desirable because it is successful as a deterrent to crime.

The second type of association based on the structure of reality involves associations of coexistence. These involve the relationships among phenomena on different levels, such as the relationship between a person and an act. The relationship between person and act is less direct than the relationship between cause and effect, which are on the same level. Associations of coexistence "are based on the link that unites a person and his actions. When generalized, this argument establishes the relation between the essence and the act." [54] Perelman calls the argument about person and act the "prototype case of such a liaison," [55] for these are ordinarily developed by claiming that a person can be judged by the quality of the acts the person commits. An argument claiming that Manuel Noriega was an evil person because he committed evil deeds is such an argument.

Argument from authority is another association of coexistence that depends on the relationship between person and act. This argument claims that some proposition should be accepted because it is accepted by important and well-qualified people. For example, someone might claim that abortion is immoral because George Bush said it was so. According to Perelman, argument from authority is only acceptable in the absence of better types of arguments.

Arguments that Establish the Structure of Reality. Associations of succession and coexistence are arguments based on the structure of reality; the next categories include arguments that attempt to establish the structure of reality. These arguments fall into two broad types: (1) argumentation by example, illustration, and model; and (2) argumentation by analogy.

Argumentation by example consists of using examples to create a generalization. It presumes the existence of regularities among cases, and by presentation of several cases, a rhetor aims at convincing an audience of those regularities. For example, the argument that professors are absent minded can be developed by showing an audience that Professor Powell constantly loses his keys, Professor Riley constantly misplaces her briefcase, and Professor Hollihan never can find a pen when he needs one. Aside from moving from a particular case to a general statement, argument from example can be used to move from particular cases to other particular cases. For example, a speaker argues in this way when asserting that since capital punishment did not reduce the incidence of murder in Texas, it could not be expected to do so in Colorado.

While argumentation by example serves to establish a prediction or a rule, argumentation by illustration serves simply to illustrate that rule. Thus, illustration is used to clarify or make salient a rule that has been established through example. Perelman explains that the "transition from example to illustration occurs almost imperceptibly in cases in which a rule is justified before being illustrated. The first examples need to be generally accepted, since their role is to give the rule credibility; the others, once the rule is accepted, will in turn be supported by it." [56]

Argumentation by model aims at presentation of a specific case to be imitated. If, for example, you make the argument that the qualities of a superior teacher are exemplified in Professor Davis, you are not establishing a generalization that all teachers are like Professor Davis; rather, you give the audience a model of a teacher that it profitably could imitate. Another example of argumentation by model concerns the ideal of legal precedent, which implies that previous court opinions are worth imitating. Argumentation by anti-model also can be used; such an argument consists of showing examples not to be imitated but to be avoided.

The second broad category of arguments designed to establish the structure of reality consists of argumentation by analogy and metaphor. An analogy is an argument that attempts to gain adherence about the relationship that exists in one pair (called the "theme" of the analogy) because of its similarity to the relationship that exists in another pair (called the "phoros" of the analogy). A metaphor, also important in argumentation, is a condensed analogy in which the theme and phoros are fused. In the phrase, "the lion charged," used in reference to a courageous warrior, we understand metaphorically that the "lion" actually is a "warrior." The metaphor is made explicit in the following analogy: "This warrior in relation to other people is as a lion in relation to other animals." Sometimes, metaphorical expressions become so commonplace that we actually forget we are dealing with metaphors. The "foot" of a mountain or the "arm" of a chair both are metaphors that are so commonly used that we tend to forget they are metaphorical.[57]

Techniques of Dissociation

While quasi-logical arguments, arguments based on the structure of reality, and arguments that establish the structure of reality are created through liaison, other arguments are established by the process of dissociation. Perelman's development of argument by dissociation is important to his perspective on rhetoric since this type of argumentation is one that often is ignored in other perspectives. Argumentation by the process of dissociation occurs when one idea is split into two in order to avoid an incompatibility. When one is faced with an incompatibility caused by the belief that to take the life of another human is wrong and the simultaneous belief that abortion is acceptable, one uses argumentation to dissociate the concept of "life" into two concepts: "life in general" and "human life." In such an instance, "life in general" may be defined to include all organismic growth ranging from an amoeba to plant life to the life of an appendix, while "human life" is defined as consisting only of those life forms that possess certain qualities of humanity such as free will. With such a dissociation, the incompatibility described above can be avoided because abortion can be viewed as destroying "life in general" (in the same way one destroys life when picking a head of cabbage or removing an appendix from a human), rather than as destroying "human life."

Making an argument based on the process of dissociation consists of the presentation of philosophical pairs, a presentation that takes the form of what Perelman calls "term I" and "term II." Term I corresponds to appearance, while term II corresponds to reality. In the above example, "life in general" corresponds to term I and is dissociated from "human life" or term II. Thus, term II is understood only in comparison to term I and aims at "getting rid of the incompatibilities that may appear between different aspects of term I."[58]

Perelman's chief contribution to rhetorical thought is his presentation of a coherent theory of argumentation. He claims that argumentation is different from demonstration and formal logic in that the former is more personal, and the latter is more impersonal. Argumentation requires an audience, and the aim of argumentation is to secure its adherence. In some cases, the audience is a particular one; in other cases, it is the universal audience. The universal audience, in Perelman's schema, constitutes the highest aim of argumentation.

In order to secure audience adherence, speakers start with points of agreement. Certain starting points such as facts, truths, and presumptions are relevant to the nature of the real, while other starting points—such as values, hierarchies, and *loci* of the preferred—concern the nature of the preferable. A rhetor, then, attempts to transfer the agreement accorded these starting points to a thesis that may be contingent or controversial. This is accomplished by attempting to establish presence and secure communion with the audience.

Perelman then discusses a variety of techniques aimed at accomplishing these argumentative aims. Three techniques of argumentation—quasi-logical arguments, arguments based on the structure of reality, and arguments establishing the structure of reality—involve the creation of a bond or liaison between the starting points of argument and the speaker's thesis. The technique of dissociation involves dividing concepts that otherwise would produce a conclusion incompatible with the speaker's thesis.

Responses to Perelman

While most scholars find Perelman and Olbrechts-Tyteca's work useful, others have soundly criticized it. A comprehensive critique is offered by Dutch scholars van Eemeren, Grootendorst, and Kruiger.[59] One of the primary difficulties with Perelman's conception of a new rhetoric, they suggest, is that it fails to work out the details of the relationship between the audience and the techniques of argumentation. Are particular argumentative techniques more persuasive to certain audiences or to audiences in general?[60] Van Eemeren, Grootendorst, and Kruiger also fault the new rhetoric for identifying argumentation techniques that are neither mutually exclusive nor exhaustive.[61] Alone, this is not a particularly serious criticism, but they argue that Perelman used two different criteria to distinguish among various techniques. For instance, form was used to distinguish quasi-logical arguments, while arguments based on the structure of reality and arguments establishing the structure of reality are distinguished by their content.

Another important criticism is directed toward Perelman's universal audience. Some have found this notion to be so ambiguous that it is almost useless.[62] Johnstone has argued that Perelman's theory would be no worse if the notion of the universal audience (in fact, the entire notion of audience) were ignored completely: "All these ambiguities and perplexities in the concept of the *universal audience* make me wonder whether the concept is after all really necessary to the project that the authors of *The New Rhetoric* have undertaken. What would the book be like without it?"[63] Ray argues that the "universal audience follows in the philosophical tradition of Rousseau's and Diderot's general will and Kant's ethical theory, particularly Kant's emphasis on the categorical imperative. . . . The concept of the universal audience is open to many of the same criticisms leveled against the general will and the categorical imperative."[64] Ray notes that the "Categorical Imperative" and the "General Will" are too formal to be useful in providing standards for ethical theory; likewise, the "universal audience is excessively formal and abstract— too formal and abstract to provide a standard for rhetorical theory."[65]

Perelman published an essay in the *Quarterly Journal of Speech* that was designed to respond to some of his critics. In that article, he defended his notion of the universal audience against criticisms such as those of Ray, claiming that Ray and others have misinterpreted his position. Perelman noted that a formalist point of view to which he was opposed "was described in *The New Rhetoric* in such a sufficiently convincing manner as to lead certain rhetorical readers to consider it as expressing my own ideas." He claims that Ray's criticisms "would certainly be justified if they were not a result of a false interpretation" of *The New Rhetoric*.[66]

Despite these criticisms, the work of Perelman and Olbrechts-Tyteca has been particularly useful and influential to scholars interested in rhetorical thought. Walker and Sillars provide an especially readable account of how Perelman and Olbrechts-Tyteca's perspective on rhetoric contributes to our understanding of argumentation and values. Perelman's perspective allows us, they claim, to understand "how the arguer develops arguments and the critic of argumentation analyzes argument from this value-centered perspective."[67] Many scholars have been able to extend Perelman's work in ways that are consistent with Perelman's view of rhetoric. "I am happy to state that certain rhetoricians have been able to utilize and extend my works. I think of the texts that I know of Karl A. Wallace, of Louise A. Karon, and of J. Robert Cox, which have certainly enriched the theory of rhetoric. I am convinced that there are works of which I am unaware, but, above all, that there is a great deal more to do in this field."[68]

Notes

[1] Wayne Brockriede, rev. of *The New Rhetoric and the Humanities: Essays on Rhetoric and Its Applications,* by Chaim Perelman, *Philosophy and Rhetoric*, 15 (Winter 1982), 76.

[2] Biographical information on Perelman was obtained from the following sources: Carroll Arnold,

"Introduction," in Chaim Perelman, *The Realm of Rhetoric*, trans. William Kluback (Notre Dame, IN: University of Notre Dame Press, 1982); Chaim Perelman, "The New Rhetoric: A Theory of Practical Reasoning," in *The Great Ideas Today* (Chicago: Encyclopedia Brittanica, 1970), p. 272; *Who's Who in World Jewry* (New York: Pittman, 1972), p. 681; Editor's note, Chaim Perelman, "The New Rhetoric and the Rhetoricians: Remembrances and Comments," *Quarterly Journal of Speech*, 70 (May 1984), 196; and Telephone conversation with Perelman's daughter, Noemi Mattis, May, 1984.

3 Perelman, "The New Rhetoric," p. 273.
4 Chaim Perelman, *The Idea of Justice and the Problem of Argument*, trans. John Petrie (New York: Humanities, 1963), p. 16.
5 Perelman, "The New Rhetoric," p. 281.
6 Perelman, "The New Rhetoric," p. 272.
7 Perelman, "Remembrances and Comments," pp. 188-89.
8 Perelman, "Remembrances and Comments," p. 188.
9 Perelman, "Remembrances and Comments," p. 189.
10 Perelman, "The New Rhetoric," pp. 273-77.
11 Chaim Perelman and L. Olbrechts-Tyteca, *The New Rhetoric: A Treatise on Argumentation*, trans. John Wilkinson and Purcell Weaver (Notre Dame, IN: University of Notre Dame Press, 1968), p. 7.
12 Aristotle's analysis of epideictic, deliberative, and forensic oratory is discussed in Perelman and Olbrechts-Tyteca, *The New Rhetoric*, pp. 47-51; and Perelman, "The New Rhetoric," pp. 277-78.
13 For discussions of the differences between demonstration and formal logic, see: Perelman and Olbrechts-Tyteca, *The New Rhetoric*, pp. 13-17; Perelman, *The Realm of Rhetoric*, pp. 1-10; and Perelman, "The New Rhetoric," p. 281.
14 Perelman and Olbrechts-Tyteca, *The New Rhetoric*, p. 4.
15 Perelman, *The Realm of Rhetoric*, p. 9.
16 References relevant to Perelman's concept of audience include: John W. Ray, "Perelman's Universal Audience," *Quarterly Journal of Speech*, 64 (December 1978), 361-75; Allen Scult, "Perelman's Universal Audience: One Perspective," *Central States Speech Journal*, 27 (Fall 1976), 176-80; John R. Anderson, "The Audience as a Concept in the Philosophic Rhetoric of Perelman, Johnstone, and Natanson," *Southern Speech Communication Journal*, 38 (Fall 1972), 39-50; Perelman and Olbrechts-Tyteca, *The New Rhetoric*, pp. 11-62; Perelman, *The Realm of Rhetoric*, pp. 9-20; and Perelman, "The New Rhetoric," pp. 285-86.
17 Perelman, *The Realm of Rhetoric*, p. 10.
18 Perelman and Olbrechts-Tyteca, *The New Rhetoric*, p. 17.
19 Perelman and Olbrechts-Tyteca, *The New Rhetoric*, pp. 14-15.
20 Perelman and Olbrechts-Tyteca, *The New Rhetoric*, p. 19.
21 Perelman, *The Realm of Rhetoric*, p. 14.
22 Perelman and Olbrechts-Tyteca, *The New Rhetoric*, p. 34.
23 Perelman and Olbrechts-Tyteca, *The New Rhetoric*, p. 30.
24 Perelman, *The Realm of Rhetoric*, p. 18.
25 Scult, p.177.
26 Perelman, "The New Rhetoric," p. 285.
27 Perelman, *The Realm of Rhetoric*, p. 21.
28 Perelman, *The Realm of Rhetoric*, p. 21.
29 The starting points of argumentation are discussed in: Karl R. Wallace, "'Topoi' and the Problem of Invention," *Quarterly Journal of Speech*, 58 (December 1972), 387-96; Perelman, *The Realm of Rhetoric*, pp. 21-47; Perelman and Olbrechts-Tyteca, *The New Rhetoric*, pp. 65-183; and Perelman, "The New Rhetoric," pp. 287-89.
30 Perelman, "The New Rhetoric," p. 287.
31 Perelman and Olbrechts-Tyteca, *The New Rhetoric*, p. 67.
32 Perelman, *The Realm of Rhetoric*, pp. 23-24.
33 Perelman and Olbrechts-Tyteca, *The New Rhetoric*, p. 69.
34 Perelman, *The Realm of Rhetoric*, pp. 24-25.

35 Values, hierarchies, and *loci* of the preferable are discussed in Perelman and Olbrechts-Tyteca, *The New Rhetoric*, pp. 74-99; and Perelman, *The Realm of Rhetoric*, pp. 76. For an excellent discussion of Perelman's approach to the values, hierarchies, and *loci* of the preferable, see Gregg B. Walker and Malcolm O. Sillars. "Where is Argument?" in *Perspectives on Argumentation: Essays in Honor of Wayne Brockriede*, ed. Robert Trapp and Janice Schuetz (Prospect Heights, IL: Waveland, 1990), pp. 134-50.

36 Perelman and Olbrechts-Tyteca, *The New Rhetoric*, p. 76.

37 Perelman and Olbrechts-Tyteca, *The New Rhetoric*, p. 79.

38 Perelman and Olbrechts-Tyteca, *The New Rhetoric*, p. 81.

39 Perelman, *The Realm of Rhetoric*, pp. 29-30.

40 Walker and Sillars, "Where is Argument?" p. 145.

41 The concept of presence is discussed in: Louise A. Karon, "Presence in *The New Rhetoric*," *Philosophy and Rhetoric*, 9 (Spring 1976), 96-111; Perelman and Olbrechts-Tyteca, *The New Rhetoric*, pp. 115-42; and Perelman, *The Realm of Rhetoric*, pp. 33-40.

42 Perelman, "The New Rhetoric," p. 289.

43 Perelman and Olbrechts-Tyteca, *The New Rhetoric*, p. 142.

44 Perelman, *The Realm of Rhetoric*, p. 34; Perelman and Olbrechts-Tyteca, *The New Rhetoric*, p. 116; and Perelman, "The New Rhetoric," p. 289.

45 Perelman, *The Realm of Rhetoric*, p. 35.

46 Perelman and Olbrechts-Tyteca, *The New Rhetoric*, p. 117.

47 Perelman and Olbrechts-Tyteca, *The New Rhetoric*, p. 142.

48 Perelman and Olbrechts-Tyteca, *The New Rhetoric*, p. 149.

49 Perelman and Olbrechts-Tyteca, *The New Rhetoric*, pp. 120-21.

50 Perelman and Olbrechts-Tyteca, *The New Rhetoric*, pp. 121-22.

51 Perelman and Olbrechts-Tyteca, *The New Rhetoric*, pp. 187-508.

52 Perelman, *The Realm of Rhetoric*, p. 49.

53 For an excellent discussion of quasi-logical argument, see Ray D. Dearin, "Perelman's 'Quasi-Logical Argument': A Critical Elaboration," in J. Robert Cox and Charles Arthur Willard, *Advances in Argumentation Theory* (Carbondale: Southern Illinois Press, 1982), pp. 78-94.

54 Perelman, "The New Rhetoric," p. 293.

55 Perelman, *The Realm of Rhetoric*, p. 90.

56 Perelman, *The Realm of Rhetoric*, p. 108.

57 Perelman, *The Realm of Rhetoric*. pp. 120-22.

58 Perelman, *The Realm of Rhetoric*, p. 127.

59 Frans H. van Eemeren, Rob Grootendorst, and Tjark Kruiger, *Handbook of Argumentation Theory: A Critical Survey of Classical Backgrounds and Modern Studies* (Dordrecht, The Netherlands: Foris, 1987)

60 van Eemeren, Grootendorst, and Kruiger, p. 254.

61 van Eemeren, Grootendorst, and Kruiger, pp. 254-55.

62 See, for instance, Thomas H. Olbricht, rev. of *The Idea of Justice and the Problem of Argument*, by Chaim Perelman, *Quarterly Journal of Speech*, 50 (October 1964), 323-24.

63 Henry W. Johnstone, Jr., "The Idea of a Universal Audience," in his *Validity and Rhetoric in Philosophical Argument: An Outlook in Transition* (University Park, PA: Dialogue Press of Man & World, 1978), p. 105.

64 Ray, p. 361.

65 Ray, p. 372.

66 Perelman, "Remembrances and Comments," pp. 190-91.

67 Walker and Sillars, p. 135.

68 Perelman, "Remembrances and Comments," p. 195.

6

Ernesto Grassi

When we look at today's scientific panorama, philosophy hardly appears still to play a role, and rhetorical speech is recognized only outside the framework of scientific discourse as the superficial art of persuasion. . . . But let it be remembered that it is only within the limits of human communication and the tasks that arise from it that the problems of philosophy and the function of rhetoric can be discussed.[1]

This statement captures the core of Ernesto Grassi's conception of rhetoric. The continuing intent of his writings has been to return to and re-emphasize the definition of rhetoric espoused by the Italian Humanists in order to give rhetoric more relevance for contemporary times.

Ernesto Grassi was born in Milan, Italy, on May 2,1902, the son of Giovanni Battista Grassi and Caterina Luce Grassi. His interest in philosophy developed as a result of a serious illness as a youth; thinking he might die led him to ponder questions about the nature of reality and the place of humans within the world. He decided to pursue his interest in philosophy outside of Italy in order to broaden his perspective on the discipline and studied at the University of Freiburg in Germany. He went on to earn his doctorate from the University of Milan in 1925 and married Elena Stigler in the same year.

Grassi became a lecturer in Italian literature at the University of Freiburg in 1929 and an honorary professor there in 1935. In 1939, he was named director of the Italian Institute for Humanist Studies in Berlin. During World War II, however, he was advised by a colleague to leave Germany immediately because he was in danger of persecution from the Nazi regime. He went first to Florence, Italy, and then to the University of Zurich, where he was a visiting professor in philosophy from 1943 to 1946.

In 1948, he returned to Germany to become a professor at the University of Munich and director of the Center for the Study of Philosophy and Humanism. He since has served as the president of the International Center for the Study of Humanism in Rome and as director of a series of philosophical seminars that served as the foundation for a set of volumes called *Zurcher Gespräche* [*Conversations in Zurich*]. Grassi served as visiting professor at the University of Valparaiso, Chile, during the winters of 1950, 1951, and 1952, teaching at the University of Munich during the summers. He also studied at the University of Buenos Aires, the University of San Paolo, and the University of Caracas. He has published prolifically since 1939; one of his major works is *Macht des Bildes. Ohnmacht der rationale Sprache: zur Rettung d. Rhetorischen* [*The Primacy of Image and the Powerlessness of Rational Speech*], published in 1970.

Grassi is now an emeritus professor at the University of Munich. He spends winters in Munich, where he continues to write and lecture, and summers at his home on the island of Ischia, Italy. Since his retirement, he has published three books in English: *Rhetoric as Philosophy: The Humanist Tradition* (1980); *Heidegger and the Question of Renaissance Humanism* (1983); and *Folly and Insanity in Renaissance Literature* (1986), coauthored with Maristella Lorch. A fourth book, *Vico and Humanism: Essays on Vico, Heidegger, and Rhetoric* (1990) is a collection of essays previously published elsewhere. He also has presented several lecture series at various universities, including Columbia University, Pennsylvania State University, and Mount Allison University in Canada. In addition, he has edited several book series, including *Rowohlts Deutsche Enzyklopadie* [*Rowohlts German Encyclopedia*], *ro-ro Studium* [pocket editions of Greek and Roman classics], and *Humanistische Bibliothek* [*Humanistic Library*].[2]

Origins of Interest in Rhetoric

Grassi did not set out deliberately to formulate a perspective on rhetoric. Rather, circumstances of birth and education brought together for him two opposing philosophical traditions—German Idealism and Italian Humanism. The tension between the two led him to explore his intellectual roots and eventually to conceive of rhetoric not simply as persuasion or expression but as constituting the foundation of human thought.

Grassi's exploration of Italian and German thought had its beginnings in his early years as a lecturer of Italian literature at the University of Freiburg. At this time, philosophy was dominated by the thinking of German philosophers—especially Georg Hegel—and it was rooted in the rational tradition formulated by Descartes. Grassi describes the prevalence of this approach to philosophy: "Neither when Descartes calls upon the 'cogito' as an original axiom for the definition of knowledge, nor when Kant deduces knowledge from original forms of experience and thought, nor when Hegel gives his *a priori* dialectical deduction of the real do we ever leave this model of rational deductive thought."[3]

The assumption of the superiority of German thought brought into focus for Grassi the contrast between his philosophical heritage as an Italian and his German educational background. He singles out two experiences that heightened this contrast. The first occurred when he read a statement by Bertrando Spaventa, an Italian philosopher of the late nineteenth century, which succinctly captured the prevailing sentiments about the differences between the German and Italian philosophical traditions: " 'The development of German thought is natural, free, and independent, in a word, it is critical. The development of Italian thought is unsteady, hindered, and dogmatic. This is the great difference.' "[4]

Grassi's work with Martin Heidegger, another German philosopher, provided an additional opportunity for him to consider his intellectual identity. Grassi encountered Heidegger at Marburg in 1928; at this time, Heidegger still was largely unknown as a philosopher. After attending a few of his lectures and courses, Grassi decided to work with Heidegger, which he did for a period of ten years while Heidegger was at Freiburg. Heidegger rejected Italian thought as without philosophical importance, and this largely negative attitude toward the intellectual heritage of his homeland caused Grassi to ponder the significance of the Italian philosophical tradition.[5]

Humanism Versus the Scientific Tradition

Because Grassi's philosophical and rhetorical contributions have emerged from the tension between Italian Humanism and the scientific tradition that culminated in German Idealism, more precise definitions of these two positions are necessary in order to understand Grassi's approach to rhetoric.

Scientific thought, as represented by the German tradition, is based on the presumption that we can know objectively and that reason is the tool for comprehending the objects in the world around us. Also referred to as "logical," "analytic," "modern," or "critical" thought, it is characterized by the use of the scientific method.

At the core of the scientific method is rational deduction. When reasoning deductively, we start from premises and derive the inferences already inherent in them. The purpose is to go back to first principles or to discover self-evident axioms that are universally valid: "statements are scientifically valid only if they can be strictly deduced from an unquestionable, ultimate axiom in a necessary and universally valid manner." René Descartes' thinking often is considered the starting point for the scientific tradition; he considered his statement, *cogito ergo sum* [I think; therefore I am], to be one such self-evident axiom. The human power to apprehend reality by means of reason was, for him, the key to understanding the world.[6]

Grassi discusses three characteristics of the scientific paradigm, all of which he considers to be limitations. First, the scientific method seeks to discover first principles; it does not examine the source of those principles. In other words, knowledge exists within the boundaries of the system under examination, and no attempt is made to understand the origins of the system itself.[7] As we will see, this characteristic is, for Grassi, a serious shortcoming of the scientific tradition.

Another constraint of scientific thought is its focus on quantification. According to Grassi, deduction forces processes and phenomena of the world to be reduced to measurable principles; "the axioms of geometry refer only to being *as* magnitude; the axioms of physics only to being *as* movement, and so on."[8] This quantification results in the belief that all reality is rational; what cannot be empirically observed, tested, and verified is not considered real, knowable, or worth studying: "The concrete reality underlying our forms of cognition is regarded as being beyond cognizance, and nothing is concrete but the *a priori* forms of understanding from which reality is to be deduced."[9] Grassi believes such an approach ignores an entire realm of reality—the realm of contradiction, paradox, silence, and hiddenness—that cannot be captured in logical terms.

Finally, scientific thought is concerned only with universals and not with individual cases or situations. It deals with claims that are valid for all times and places and thus ignores the particulars or concrete details of the human situation:

> [Scientific knowledge] must be compelling to all, in the sense that its necessity and universal validity must make it convincing for all; it must, because of its claim to necessity and universal validity, be timeless and spaceless; it must be unemotive, because the *ratio* can only be impaired by emotions; it can have no connection with common sense or with everyday forms of speech, which are mainly obtuse forms of rational thought.[10]

Grassi suggests that the limitations embedded in the scientific paradigm, in turn, constrain what is studied as philosophy, since any discipline that does not have its source in logical processes is denigrated:

> This approach leads to a repudiation of *history*, for the latter is not in a position to contribute to knowledge or truth, since all discussions as to how events have taken place or how they are described by historians remain merely within the framework of "possibility." Nor can *philology* be attributed any philosophical significance; it can at most serve as a useful means for the understanding of ancient or foreign texts. . . . Still more dangerous is the inclusion of *art* and *poetry*, because they represent possibility rather than truth; *rhetoric*, a discipline which acquired great significance in Humanism, fares no better, because the passions impair the clarity of thought and consequently are not to be taken into account. So all branches of humanism are systematically excluded from the framework of philosophy.[11]

Grassi sees Humanism as in direct opposition to the modern, scientific tradition. When Grassi speaks of "Humanism," he does not mean the broad and rather ambiguous meaning given the word today—the study of human experiences and capabilities from the viewpoint of the human being. Nor does he mean the Renaissance rediscovery of the literature, art, and civilization of ancient Greece and Rome and the corresponding renewal of interest in the study of the human being. While this definition frequently is associated with Humanism, to Grassi, it characterizes later Humanism and is Platonic and Aristotelian in orientation. Humanism, according to Grassi, refers to the philosophical movement that occurred in Italy from the second half of the fourteenth century to the final third of the fifteenth century; it was concerned not with the problem of existence and being but with "the problem of words, of metaphorical thought, and of the knowledge of the philosophical function of rhetorical thinking and speaking that was perfected as a new way of philosophizing in the fifteenth century."[12]

The Humanists' interest in and philosophical observations about language stemmed from their experience with translating and interpreting texts: "They experienced how the same word in the writings of one author has a particular specific meaning but receives a different meaning in the context of another author's works."[13] In their analysis of texts, the Humanists sought to understand the ways in which humans respond to a set of claims or demands made on them by the world and the kind of world revealed to them as a result of their linguistic choices. They labeled such language "rhetorical" because it sought to manage strategically the "essential concerns of existence, . . . matters of life and death."[14] Thus, they came to value literature as a means of knowing about the human condition: "literature is a way of forming a meaning without losing the details of an event. The fable, the tale, the narration has a universal meaning, but this meaning is achieved through the relating of particular events and qualities."[15] The Humanists' emphasis on literature is, in part, responsible for the belief that their contributions primarily were literary in nature rather than philosophical; because they did not write in traditional philosophical terms, their ideas tended to be devalued or ignored.

The Humanists' attention to language as a way of knowing the world was in direct contrast to rational approaches. Rational philosophy, articulated powerfully by Descartes, privileges scientific objectivity, universality, and rational deduction over other ways of knowing the world.[16] Grassi describes the rational paradigm as a "desperate effort of freeing oneself from relativity, from the subjectivity of what appears through the senses."[17] With the Humanists, he considers rational knowledge incomplete and misleading because it fails to take into account the particular contexts and needs of life situations; objectivity and abstraction cannot handle the contextual variations always present in human experience. Grassi offers a simple example to illustrate his point: "The color *red* has one meaning in the traffic code, another in the political code, a third in optics, another in the set of rules regulating human relations. A lover offers a red rose to his beloved."[18] The objectivity and generalizability demanded by the rational paradigm simply are unable to deal with such distinctions, which are, in fact, crucial to human life.

The rational approach, however, came to dominate philosophy, and the work of the Humanists was considered to be only the confused anticipation of Descartes' approach. In other words, the Humanist philosophers were believed to be searching for and moving toward the position advocated by Descartes; he was seen as clarifying their thought and presenting it as a coherent system.[19]

While Descartes and the entire scientific tradition rejected Humanism, Grassi did not. He came to terms with his intellectual heritage by breaking with his mentors and embracing Italian Humanism as the way in which he wished to conceptualize the world. The essence of what became Grassi's philosophical position first was outlined in a 1940 essay, "Der Beginn des modernen Denkens" ["The Beginning of Modern Thought"], which he sees as still containing the core of his philosophical beliefs.[20] The scientific method is only one tool for understanding the world, and for Grassi, it is a limited and partial approach compared to that of Humanism.

Grassi's career has been devoted in large part, then, to a reflection on and advocacy of the ideals of Italian Humanism. The question he has pursued is whether the Humanist tradition is important to study philosophically or whether it has—as many rationalists believe—only historical and literary value. In other words, can the ideas of the Humanist philosophers help us better understand the contemporary situation, or are they significant only because they brought to our attention the great ideas, art, and literature of ancient Greece and Rome?

Grassi's interest in Italian Humanism unavoidably led him to a study of rhetoric because the Italian Humanists did not separate rhetoric and philosophy. Grassi could not consider the philosophic importance of the tradition without exploring its view of rhetoric as well.

Giambattista Vico: A Source for Grassi's Rhetoric

Grassi's views of philosophy and rhetoric are based largely on the work of Giambattista Vico, an eighteenth-century Italian philosopher, who Grassi believes represents the thought of Italian Humanism most fully. Vico, born in 1668, was professor of rhetoric at the University of Naples from 1699 to 1741.[21] His major philosophical works are *De nostri tempori studiorum ratione* [*On the Study Methods of Our Time*] (1709), *De antiquissima Italorum Sapienta* [*On Ancient Italian Knowledge*] (1710), and *Scienza Nuova Prima* [*New Science*] (1725). Grassi describes Vico's role and influence on philosophy this way:

> At the end of the humanist period Vico—in whose theories the whole humanistic tradition reached its highest philosophical consciousness—is in radical opposition to Descartes and tries to reestablish the connection between philosophy and rhetoric and, at the same time, to reinstate the humanistic branches of knowledge . . . by rendering their philosophical significance.[22]

Vico was concerned with the essence and form in which human history appeared. For Vico, the rise of human history was the basic problem of philosophy; he saw history as the realm of human action, in contrast to nature, which is the domain of other biological creatures: "The fundamentally human element consists in the fact that the forms of human behavior must continually be sought and defined anew and are therefore to be discovered in the historical role of man and in the elucidation of that role; it is history which differentiates the human being from the animal."[23]

The Humanization of Nature

Since Grassi builds on Vico's foundation, an elaboration of Vico's conception of human society is necessary in order to understand why Grassi advocates a return to Humanist thought. For Vico, human society is the result of the awareness that humans are not part of but rather separate and distinct from nature.

Both humans and other animals are grounded in their senses—both experience the world through seeing, hearing, touching, smelling, or tasting it. All living beings also cope with and organize their environment in order to have certain needs met—needs of nutrition, reproduction, and the like. Grassi refers to this as meeting the claim or demands of life; in fact, Grassi sees life as a "continuous transition from one demand to another."[24]

In the process of coping with various life situations, living creatures essentially create a reality in which they can function. For animals, this process takes place instinctively—they use their senses to cope with the world they encounter. A bird, for example, does not have to think about *how* to catch a worm or *why* it catches worms; it must only rely on instinct in order to catch a worm.

For humans, however, the process is more complex for two reasons: (1) they can make choices about how to act—that is, they are not limited to instinctual responses; and (2) they have the ability to define or name sensory images via language and thus can interpret their world in a variety of ways. Humans, to continue with our example, catch worms as birds do, but for a variety of purposes and in a variety of ways. Moreover, they have a different relationship to worms than birds because they can name them, talk about them, and therefore give a variety of meanings or interpretations to them. The capacity to make choices—both in terms of what actions to undertake and the linguistic options available for talking about or interpreting those actions—is what distinguishes and separates humans from animals: "Animals live *in* nature; but we human beings live over and against it, because whoever knows he is not 'bound' by nature does not recognize it as his home and thus sees it as something foreign and strange to him."[25]

Once humans become conscious of their intellectual powers and their abilities to make choices, to express themselves through a language, and therefore to direct their own destinies, they begin to make adjustments in nature. Vico terms this process the "humanization" or "historicization" of nature: "We can only attain a 'humanization' and 'historicization' of nature by giving meaning to the phenomena that our sensory tools offer to us."[26] Humans, in other words, must develop ways of coping with what they perceive through their senses in order to translate it into human terms. They must transfer meaning from the sensory level to the level of the intellect in order to realize their humanness.

Vico describes the first awakening or unfolding of human consciousness as beginning when humans cleared forests and cultivated fields in their place. These cleared places represent the first human places in history because they demonstrate the human control of nature. Grassi cites Vico's explanation of this process:

> In the terror that seizes man in the experience of his own alienation from nature, he creates and establishes the first human place in his historicity. . . . As Vico asserts: ". . . the first cities, which were all founded on cultivated fields, arose as a result of families being for a long time quite withdrawn and hidden among the sacred terrors of the religious forests. These [cultivated fields] are found among all the ancient gentile nations and, by an idea common to all, were called by the Latin peoples *luci*, meaning burnt lands within the enclosure of the woods."[27]

Vico's use of the term *luci*, or light, and the notion of clearing are significant. For Vico and the other Humanists, "light" suggests the basic problem of philosophy or the unconcealing or unveiling to humans of what they need to know to meet the demands of life. The notion of light, conceptualized as a clearing in the woods, signifies human control over the natural environment.

While the clearing of land epitomizes the human control of nature, this process of clearing was by no means sudden. Vico suggests that human development occurred gradually and was distinguished by three major phases. First, in the cultural age, humans did not see themselves as separate from the natural world or capable of action apart from the influence of that world. Rather, they attributed all events that occurred to divine beings. The second stage, which Vico calls the age of heroes, was characterized by superhuman benefactors—combinations of humans and gods—who were seen as helping humans by introducing social institutions and laws. Finally, in the age of humanity, the third stage, humans realized that they could control nature on their own without assistance from superhuman or divine powers of any kind. Here is the awakening or revelation of free will and choice, of confronting nature and imposing control over it.[28]

Ingenium: **The Process of Humanization**

The basic process by which humans gain control over nature and thus historicize or humanize it involves the transfer of meaning from the sensory world to a higher human one. This is accomplished through the faculty of *ingenium*, defined as nonrational insight into similarities; it is a practical knowing, an intuition that exists apart from formal reasoning processes. *Ingenium* refers to a basic capacity to grasp what is common or similar in objects, ideas, or experiences—to see relationships and make connections. Verene summarizes Grassi's view of *ingenium*: It "allows us to 'see' with the word, to make connections in experience we have not before made and which we need in order to think new thoughts."[29] It frees humans to create and order their own lives, choosing how to respond to life's changing demands because individuals always can make choices about how to respond to any particular experience: "History in its continuous novelty is rooted in the necessity of finding always new correspondences to the essential calls which vary according to time and place. Finding the correspondence to each of these calls is the task of *ingenium*."[30]

Manifestations of *Ingenium*

There are three basic ways in which *ingenium* is manifest to create the human world—in imagination, work, and language. By imagination, Grassi does not simply mean the ability to form mental images of things not present or the capacity for creativity. Rather, imagination is fundamentally and uniquely a human process that embodies *ingenium* and depends on the creation of new images and relationships. Grassi cites Vico to make his point: " 'Imagination collects from the senses the sensory effects of natural phenomena and combines and magnifies them to the point of exaggeration, turning them into luminous images to suddenly dazzle the mind with their lightning and stir up human passions in the thunder and roar of their wonder.' "[31]

According to Vico, imagination functions in two basic ways to foster the emergence of human history. First, only through imagination do humans realize they are not bound to nature in the same way that animals are: "It is shown in and through imagination that the human being, unlike the animal, does not stand under the dominion of ruling patterns which give sense perceptions an unequivocal meaning. He therefore can, and does, give sensory phenomena the most varied interpretations."[32]

Furthermore, imagination allows humans to explain the world around them. The basic human response in the face of things not understood is fear: Humans break "out of nature through startling fear at the experience of . . . alienation from nature—the primordial forest—in order to create the first place of . . . historicity, the 'new' world and its institutions, which arise from . . . ingenious and fantastic activity."[33] The fear inspired by the human imagination caused humans to begin making adjustments in nature or constructing an order by which to understand the world: "Thus it was fear which created gods in the world"—not fear awakened in humans by others but fear awakened in them by themselves. Imagination, then, allows humans to select certain interpretations of sensory experiences and to use these to define or order the world in certain ways. The ultimate result of this interpretation process is an entire system of reality, or history, that is uniquely human.[34]

Work is the second manifestation of *ingenium* or means by which humans make connections among or interpretations of sensory phenomena. Imagination allows humans to conceptualize needs apart from those of animals; work allows for the fulfillment of these needs: "By establishing relationships (similitudes) between what man needs (e.g., to quench a thirst) and what his senses report to him in each specific concrete situation in nature (e.g., the availability of water), man works out the transfer of meanings leading him to the appropriate action (e.g., looking for water and making it available to himself)."[35] Work, then, is another way of conveying a meaning to natural things or of making connections between the world of the senses and a higher, human level. When we plant a garden or cultivate an apple tree, for example, we are giving the earth and the tree an interpretation or meaning that did not exist before we engaged in those tasks.

Vico chooses the figure of Hercules as a symbol for how work functions to allow humans to step out of or transform nature.[36] Hercules, who performed twelve feats for Eurystheus, king of Mycenae, in return for immortality, is referred to by Vico as the founder of human society. In the performance of the twelve tasks, Hercules subjugated nature to human purposes: "The myth of Hercules lies at the base of the making of history, because that mythical figure always has been, according to Vico, the first to carry out the humanization of nature."[37] Work, like imagination, is for Vico and Grassi a form of self-assertion and control over the natural realm.

Language was the third manifestation of *ingenium* for the Humanists; it is another way of elucidating human history because it is another way of assigning meaning to the world. When we name an object a "cat," for example, we can talk about that object even when it is not present. Before we gave it a name, we existed at its level and were able to deal with the cat only by pointing to it or interacting with it when it was around. By naming it, we create a symbolic, abstract reality that exists apart from the object—in this case, the cat. Language does more than simply create a symbolic world, however. For the Humanists, meaning could not be understood without a simultaneous examination of the words used, the person using those words, and the context in which the object or situation arises: "the meaning of things arises in their concrete relationship to people and their human endeavour to come to grips with them."[38]

Just as the Humanists did not separate language from context, neither did they separate philosophical knowledge from human action in the world. Thus, *praxis*, which literally translates to "practice," "doing," or "action," was important to the Humanists because it embodies the realities of the particular situation—it is not just an abstract philosophical stance: "reality, constantly changing, manifests itself as something not ever fixed but rather revealed only in concrete situations."[39]

The Humanists, then, constantly sought to understand something in the context of practical human action. This pragmatic emphasis led many Humanists to call themselves "grammarians" rather than philosophers.[40] To them, traditional philosophers dealt with the abstract human condition and ignored the realm of individual action. They preferred to see the study of philology or grammar as the new form of philosophizing because grammar requires, at its most basic level, attention to subject (content) and verb (form). The subject of a sentence is not understood unless the action involved also is considered: "To be a *grammaticus* means to elucidate the essence of . . . humanity. . . . in . . . development, in the process of . . . coming to terms with things by means of studying the word."[41]

Metaphor: Linguistic Manifestation of *Ingenium*

Although the Humanists studied imagination, work, and language as they contributed to the development of human history, their focus clearly was on the latter: how does *ingenium*, the basic human faculty for seeing relationships, operate linguistically? For the Humanists, the operation of *ingenium* in language best is captured by the metaphor. The metaphor is the most important figure of speech because it embodies the notion of transfer and movement from inward personal space to external domain that is at the heart of *ingenium*. Grassi turns to the ancients—who recognized the special importance of metaphor—for definitions of this figure. He draws extensively on Aristotle's definition:

> In order to be effective, the metaphor must be so constructed that by uncovering relationships, something peculiar and unique . . . becomes visible. The metaphor uncovers something that has not previously been seen; it leads to light because it stems from the need to see: that which is not obvious . . . is to be transferred. It permits us, "to see the similarity between what is actually the most widely separated". . . . Finally the metaphor is characterized by the fact that it shows us something unusual . . . , something unexpected.[42]

Grassi also points to Cicero's definition of metaphor: "the metaphor acts like a 'light' because it presupposes an insight into 'relationship.'"[43] Cicero's definition seems especially appropriate since it is itself a metaphor and captures as well the notion of light and clearing central to the Humanists' world view.

According to Grassi, the metaphor is powerful because it allows for the transfer of insights on several levels. At the most fundamental level, metaphor is the basic process of human thinking: it is a grasping of similarities between two unrelated things. When we call frost "mother nature's paintbrush" or the sky a "blue ceiling," we are pointing out commonalities between things of the human world and things in nature. Thus, metaphor operationalizes *ingenium*, the primary means by which humans grapple with the world of nature, because it enables them to make connections between the world of the senses and the human realm: "But what is metaphorical speaking? It is the transference of meaning of beings to a new level, i.e., to the level of human being." [44] Vico reinforces this point nicely when he notes that humans tend to describe the inanimate aspects of the world through metaphoric references to the human body; they give their special human interpretation to nature:

> It is noteworthy that in all languages the greater part of the expressions relating to inanimate things are formed by metaphor from the human body and its parts. . . . Thus, head for top or beginning; the brow and shoulders of a hill; the eyes of needles and potatoes; mouth for any opening; the lip of a cup or pitcher; the teeth of rake, a saw, a comb; the beard of wheat; the tongue of a shoe; the gorge of a river; a neck of land; an arm of the sea. . . . Innumerable other examples could be collected from all languages. All of which is a consequence of our axiom that man in his ignorance makes himself the rule of the universe, for in the examples cited he has made of himself an entire world. [45]

Metaphor is important at yet another level: it is the basic process embedded in the nature of language. Using language is a process of connecting a symbol to an experience; thus, language is one way of interpreting or addressing a situation that the world presents to us: "existence becomes known to us only in the need for expression." [46] The process of interpreting the world via language is metaphoric because the word refers to something beyond itself—an event or situation that we perceive a certain way because of the language we have chosen to use to address it.

A third level of metaphoric activity occurs in the process of philosophizing. The act of imagination at the heart of metaphor is basic to the philosophical enterprise. No philosophical argument can be made without grasping the fundamental or original principles upon which the argument is based. First principles always are nonrational and nondeductive, understood "pathetically" through an emotional connection with them. Grassi says we must "experience" first principles as an "urge" and not as the content of thought. [47] The fear of death, for example, may be such an original, emotional urge. Humans may be the only animals who have foreknowledge of death; this fear results in a belief in the value of human life. This belief functions as a first principle upon which entire philosophical systems are constructed. The leap from the original urge by which we become interested in a philosophical problem in the first place to the process of searching for understanding through logical reasoning is metaphoric. We are required to make connections and see similarities between the original impulse and the arguments we use to extend that impulse into a formal system of reasoning.

Metaphor, then, is the essence of human life. It is the basic process by which humans understand their worlds—they make connections among experiences. This process also operates in language; the choice of a word always is a metaphor for the object or experience for which the word stands. Finally, the process of philosophizing itself is metaphoric. Every system of philosophy ultimately is grounded in a nonrational, ingenious grasp of first principles. That original impulse is transferred to a logical system in order to express it to the world, but that process of connecting the urge to rational forms of expression is metaphoric.

Types of Speech

After establishing the primacy of the metaphor in human thought and speech, Grassi proceeds to discuss the primacy of rhetorical language—grounded in the metaphoric function—over rational speech. As we have seen, the Humanists turned to language and literature in order to understand both the particulars and the universals of the human condition. Rhetorical speech—whether a poem, story, or other narration—embodies *ingenium* and accounts for why humans are attracted to and excited by an image and move to translate it into terms applicable to their own lives. Grassi uses the story of Iris in Greek mythology to explain the power of rhetorical language. Iris, a word meaning "to speak or announce," was personified as the rainbow, with her colors spanning the sky between the heavens and earth. Her role was that of mediator between the divine or inexplicable realm and the human one. As "the word," Iris shows the way between the inexplicable, original, wondrous images that humans encounter and the way they make sense of them in the concrete realities of human life.[48] Imagistic or rhetorical language allows humans to capture those original images and to interpret them using language, thus giving an order or structure to the human world.

Their view of the role of *ingenium* in rhetorical language explains why the Humanists made such extensive use of literature such as myths, fables, and narrations. They saw these not simply as charming tales of earlier times but as embodying the ways humans respond to new situations, experience their humanness, and create a history. Grassi argues that poets and historians, in fact, have a common aim: to clarify how humans have managed their world in different times and places. They also share a rhetorical foundation because, in recounting a historical event, the historian must attend not only to the causal relationships involved but also to the language proper to it. Grassi suggests, for example, that a historian might describe the siege of a city as the result of a temporal chain of causes and effects. But this alone is not sufficient. She also must adapt "adjectives, verbs, [and] the rhythm of . . . narration . . .

to the concrete situation." [49] In the process of expressing historical insights, she is aware of the range of interpretations possible of human behavior; her interpretation is only one explanation. Each interpretation serves as a way humans can respond and thus becomes a model for humans to turn to as a guide to future action. Rhetorical language, then, illuminates historical fact, making the situation concrete, memorable, relevant, and understandable. The rhetorical process is crucial if humans are to learn from history: "The Poets are named . . . seers, because they see new possible human relationships in an original underived manner and give birth to these possibilities." [50]

In reviving the Humanist tradition, Grassi asserts the primacy of rhetorical language over rational language and thus over the entire scientific tradition. Unlike the imagistic foundations of rhetorical speech, rational speech is deductive in nature and achieves its effect through logical demonstration. It is, by design, a closed system in which the starting premises are not questioned: "The deductive process is completely closed within itself and as such cannot admit other forms of persuasion which do not derive from the logical process." [51] Thus, rational language can explain the sequence of events by which something came to be but not the impulse or idea that gave rise to that process. A sound, for example, might be explained causally—it was produced by the human voice, by hitting two sticks together, or by ringing a bell. These explanations offer no clue, however, as to the reason for producing the sound—is it an expression of fear or excitement or joy? [52]

Not only does rhetorical speech precede rational speech, but it is superior because it deals with the concrete particulars of life. Rational speech is universal and abstract—it transcends differences in interpretation and nuance to provide a single way of talking about the world. While useful at times, rational speech is not the primary way humans cope with the ever-changing world in which they find themselves.

Grassi demonstrates the differences between rhetorical and rational speech by drawing an analogy between monologue and dialogue. He considers rational speech monologic because it has no need to interact with circumstances of situation in order to proceed, just as a person delivering a monologue can proceed without concern for or input from the others present and without regard for situational factors. [53] Grassi cites definition via the scientific classification system as an example of how scientific speech seeks universal meanings. For instance, to define a Canadian dogwood, a scientist would refer to it as a *Cornus canadensis*. *Cornus* is the genus or category of all dogwoods, while the species is *canadensis*, which is a particular type of dogwood. By defining it in this way, the dogwood is considered in its universality; we are not asked to think of a particular dogwood that blooms profusely along a favorite hiking trail.

Rhetorical speech, on the other hand, is likened to dialogue because it must take the world—in this case, the particular, profusely blooming dogwood—into account. For Grassi, dialogue (and thus rhetorical speech) deals with objects as they exist in time and space, while monologue, which represents scientific speech, treats them as abstract, universally definable phenomena. Rhetorical speech achieves an emotional identification with specific images that simply does not occur with rational speech.

Grassi also uses the legend of Cassandra as it is presented in Aeschylus' drama, *Agamemnon*, to illustrate the relationship between rhetorical and rational speech. Cassandra, the daughter of Priam, the king of Troy, was chosen by Apollo to be his mistress. She agreed to this arrangement given that he would grant her the gift of prophecy. Upon receipt of prophetic vision, however, Cassandra refused to submit to Apollo, whereby he punished her by willing that no one would understand her prophecies.

In *Agamemnon*, Aeschylus has a chorus attempt to engage Cassandra in a conversation. She does not hear the chorus, however, and neither can the chorus understand her senseless babble. In this scene, Cassandra's expressions represent rhetorical speech. As a prophet, she speaks only in images, symbols, and metaphors; she describes death as a net and Agamemnon as a bull. Hers is neither a logical nor an explanatory language. The chorus, in contrast, signifies rational speech. It attempts to deal with events logically by understanding them in chronological sequence. Thus, a dialogue between Cassandra and the chorus is impossible until Cassandra asks the god *why* she has been brought to this place. By asking for a reason or explanation, she abandons the world of allusion, insight, and metaphor and moves into the sphere of reason and logic.

What is significant for Grassi about this episode is that Cassandra's transition into the realm of reason is accomplished by means of metaphor. Metaphor is a crucial way by which humans know and understand their world; it is the foundation for rationality:

> This conversational passage becomes a sign of her departure from the world of the inexplicable, the original, the purely semantic. The change is brought about through a *metaphor*, as though this were the only possible bridge between the rational and semantic realms. The Chorus compares her complaints with those of Prokne, the nightingale (v. 1140). This *image* touches Cassandra in her longing for the human world to which she originally belonged. . . . *For the first time*, stimulated by this *image*, Cassandra hears the words of the Chorus and reacts to them (v. 1146).[54]

Metaphor, then allows humans to connect the purely semantic sphere of images and the human world of explanation and sequence.

Another way that Grassi distinguishes between rational and rhetorical speech and suggests the role of metaphor in their relationship is through an extended example of the concept of a "code." A code is a "system of signs whose elements receive their meanings within this system." The dots and dashes of a call for help are decoded, for instance, by means of the Morse code; the code provides the means by which to interpret the message. Similarly, any language is a code in which things come to have meaning within that framework. Grassi likens a code to rational speech: it "establishes the governing system of relations that are already given and on the basis of which something is interpreted. No existing code can lead to a *new* code because its essence consists in 'fixing' certain things into place so that they appear in this light as beings. This way the real is 'read' on the basis of a previously given code."[55]

Both a code and rational speech lack an inventive function. The metaphor supplies such invention because it does not simply move between the levels of an established code to determine meaning but finds new codes and structures:

> The function of a metaphor, unlike that of a code, does not consist merely in applying an interpretation but also in "finding" the new code on the basis of which reality is rendered. It gives us a new perspective of relationships between beings. Metaphor's function is that of invention – the seeing of new relationships. It is metaphor that produces each new code.[56]

Thus, rhetorical or poetic language goes beyond the boundaries of the formal system that is scientific thought to get at the origins or sources of that thought.

In addition to identifying rhetorical and rational forms of speech, Grassi adds a third form to his conceptual scheme: "external, rhetorical speech."[57] This refers to the superficial and mistaken definition of rhetoric as a technical art of persuasion that acts on the emotions to form beliefs. This is a "false" kind of speech, according to Grassi, because the images by which we are persuaded stem not from metaphoric insight or a genuine grasp of the nature of something but from a limited and often superficial understanding of it.

A contemporary example illustrates the difference between genuine rhetorical speech and external rhetorical speech. A student in a public speaking class gave a persuasive speech on the topic of hit-and-run drivers. To begin, he placed a pair of bloody baby shoes on the podium, stating that they had belonged to his baby sister, who had been killed by a hit-and-run driver. He then proceeded to deliver a highly emotional speech that left most of the class in tears. When the professor expressed regret over his sister's death, the student's casual response was, "Oh, don't worry. I never had a baby sister. I made that part up for effect."[58] External, rhetorical speech, then, depends on images for its impact, as does genuine rhetorical speech, but these images are not grounded in a genuine grasp of the subject matter; experience with the basic sensory image is lacking.

For Grassi, then, rhetorical speech is the primary and original form of speech. It is not the superficial play on emotions that commonly but mistakenly has been associated with rhetoric. Based on the act of metaphor, it leads us from the sensory images of our biological roots to a realization of our humanness. Rational speech, on the other hand, always must be grounded in rhetorical speech since it is based on the acceptance of certain premises that are not knowable in rational terms. Grassi summarizes:

> The metaphor lies at the root of our human world. Insofar as metaphor has its roots in the analogy between different things and makes this analogy immediately spring into "sight," it makes a fundamental contribution to the structure of our world. Empirical observation itself takes place through the "reduction" of sensory phenomena to types of meanings existing in the living being; and this "reduction" consists in the "transferring" of a meaning to sensory phenomena. It is only through this "transference" that phenomena can be recognized as similar or dissimilar, useful or useless, for our human realization. In order to make "sensory" observations we are forced to "reach back" for a transposition, for a metaphor. Man can manifest himself only through his own "transpositions," and this is the essence of his work in every field of human activity.[59]

The Significance of Rhetoric

The Humanists' world view offers a positive view of rhetoric, in contrast to many negative definitions of this art. Grassi suggests that, for many, rhetoric is considered only the art of expression or a technical doctrine "to be appreciated primarily from outside, for *pedagogical reasons*, that is, as aids to 'alleviate' the 'severity' and 'dryness' of rational language."[60] Rhetoric, in other words, often is seen as supplying the form of a message, while philosophy—a system of rational knowledge—supplies the factual content.

The primacy of rhetoric, as conceptualized by the Italian Humanists, reverses the commonly held view of rhetoric that gives logic precedence, subordinates the passions to reason, and presents rhetoric as merely a way of making logical reasons palatable to an audience. For Grassi, there is no separation of content from form, of passion from logic. The power of any message derives from its starting point in images that inspire wonder, admiration, engagement, and passion. Rhetoric, rather than logical deduction, then, is the true philosophy since it grapples with the fundamental questions of human existence—questions grounded in basic processes by which humans know, interpret, and create their world: "Philosophy itself becomes possible only on the basis of metaphors, on the basis of the ingenuity which supplies the foundation of every rational, derivative process."[61]

For Grassi, the Humanist world view is in direct contrast to the prevailing thrust of contemporary Western thought. The emphasis on science has resulted in a separation of content from form: science is believed to provide the true content of human action, and a thing is not to be believed or trusted if scientific proof for it cannot be offered. As a result, we have forgotten the need to examine the insights upon which such calculations are based:

> Today we glory in science and in cybernetic instruments, entrusting our future to them, forgetting that we still have the problem of finding "data," of "inventing them," since the cybernetic process can only elaborate them and draw consequences from them. The problem of the essence of the human genius and of its creativity cannot be reduced to that of rational deduction, which modern technology is developing to improbable depths.[62]

For Grassi, an understanding of the true function of rhetoric is needed to give science its philosophical underpinnings.

Grassi suggests some of the consequences for society of the over-valuation of the rational paradigm. One such manifestation is an attitude of superiority on the part of those who believe in the primacy of logic and in the capability of technology to deal with all human problems. Rather than allowing the essence of the world to reveal itself through beings, humans see their rationality as giving them dominance over all others. The assumption is that once a being can be explained rationally, its meaning is established. In actuality, what results is a fixed and limited interpretation of that thing. Since cats have been a frequent source of examples in this chapter, let's take the case of a member of the cat family — the mountain lion. The premise of rationality has allowed humans to hunt mountain lions, to make decorative use of their pelts, to stuff their heads as trophies, and to put them in zoos so that they can be viewed at human convenience. Were the paradigm of rationality not operating, however, the mountain lion would be allowed to exist in its natural environment, without human interference.

The attitude of rational superiority is inherent, too, in our dealings with non-Western cultures that do not share this attitude. Grassi makes this suggestion: "If this calculating and purely rational attitude, about which Western culture is so proud, were called into question, then a new inroad to understanding foreign cultures that do not have this basic attitude would result. Here I am thinking of Far Eastern cultures whose relationship to things is imagistic and metaphorical."[63] We presume that technology is beneficial and that countries that do not have our technological competence are "behind" or "underdeveloped." Thus, the attitude of calculating rationality makes nearly impossible our genuine understanding of other cultures and hinders our interactions with them.

Furthermore, the dominance of the rational paradigm results in the widespread consumption ethic characteristic of Western society. When we consider ourselves rationally superior and thus dominant over all other beings — animals, objects, and other nonrational peoples — the consumption of such beings is likely. We act as if we have the right, in other words, to take over or encroach upon the environment, whether this means putting all plants and animals in nature to human use; taking territory inhabited by other peoples and creatures and making it our own; or polluting oceans, rivers, streams, and even outer space with the waste products of technology. As long as an action furthers human ends, we tend not to consider it ill conceived or detrimental. For Grassi, then, logical thought becomes linked with the availability and domination of beings and ultimately with their consumption.

The attitude of the primacy of technology also has led us to the atomic age, characterized by the discovery, technological applications, and sociopolitical consequences of atomic energy. Grassi acknowledges that the attitude of rational calculation has assumed different forms throughout the history of Western thought; yet, he sees the present atomic epoch as its ultimate manifestation.[64] The discovery of how to apply or make use of the atom is indeed an almost perfect expression of the desire for domination over nature, for whoever has atomic control has the power not only to dominate other beings but to destroy the entire world. Grassi contrasts this stance with that of the Italian Humanists:

> Any society which fails to raise and answer the question as to the meaning of man's intervention in nature, thus establishing a theory of the essence of man — a philosophical question — must degenerate into an alien form of community, despite or even through whatever social improvements it accomplishes. This alienation arises out of the fact that man ceases to concern himself with a question which is essential to him. The question regarding the nature of man was the question continually raised by the Italian Humanists in their polemics against any science seeking its own ends.[65]

For Grassi, the rational approach to the world that has dominated Western philosophy has been detrimental: "we have lost and we are still losing the 'match' of the Western world."[66]

The Problem of Folly

An appropriate concluding point for a study of Grassi's perspective on rhetoric is the notion of folly because this concept summarizes and embodies the content and method of his rhetorical approach. In his approach to folly, Grassi analyzes the concept of folly philosophically as the Humanists would have done—through searching literature—and uses his findings to offer an interpretation of folly that differs from traditional understandings of it. Grassi suggests that the notion of folly in the literature of Renaissance Humanism offers an alternative approach to the concept of folly, which traditionally has been viewed as "thinking, speaking or acting without well-grounded reasons"—acting irrationally.[67]

Grassi offers a definition that is just the opposite. Folly is the ability, through language, to choose what perspective to take on a situation; it is *"reality in the unveiling of its essence."*[68] Verene elaborates: "To see human affairs as folly is to have an ontological insight into what is possible in any situation; that is, to see all as folly is to realize that things are never what they seem."[69] Folly is not a loss of contact with reality but an engagement, at the most fundamental level, with the process of *ingenium*, which distinguishes humans from other animals; thus, it is an ever-present capacity of language. Not only do we choose a word and therefore structure our interpretation of the world, but we can envision entirely different alternatives to that world because of language. For Grassi, this process of envisioning alternatives is folly.

Folly also functions as a metaphor for the process of *ingenium. Ingenium* allows humans to see opposite possibilities and to make connections between images and events: "Animal mentality reacts only to what is before it. But the human mentality can see this reality as reversed."[70] The capacity to see what might be as well as what is depends not on a logical deduction but on a metaphoric grasp or insight into similarities between dissimilar things. Folly, then, embodies the fundamental process by which humans move from the nonhuman to the human realm. *Ingenium*—and, by extension, folly—allows humans to imagine themselves in new situations and to deal with those situations effectively: "It is folly which allows the projection of . . . one's own desires, hopes, worries, expectations, fears . . . on the stage of life, the stage where our own interactions with the environment take place. Folly creates life as a theatre" in that an individual projects the self into "the concrete situation in a different time and place, and in this process the individual builds...[a personal] structure."[71] Folly is grounded in the essential human capacity for *ingenium* or metaphoric insight; thus, it epitomizes the means by which humans approach and construct the world in which they live.

The notion of folly also summarizes Grassi's perspective on rhetoric by providing an example of the analysis of literature to discover philosophical insights. The Humanists repeatedly turned to literary texts as a way to understand universal meanings without leaving the particulars of human life that are present in any story or fable. Similarly, in presenting his views on the concept of folly, Grassi analyzes a variety of literary works, including

Erasmus' *Praise of Folly*, Alberti's *Momus*, and Cervantes' *Don Quixote*, for insights about the philosophical significance of folly. Through this process, Grassi suggests that the fundamental questions of interest to the Humanists emerge—questions about the nature, structure, and function of rhetorical language and about the insufficiency of rational processes to capture the human world adequately. Grassi concludes, along with the writers on folly whom he studies, that folly is the appropriate stance with which to approach the world: "To live in folly is the profound reason for existence."[72]

Grassi turns to the Humanists to suggest an alternative to the rational paradigm for contemporary society. For him, the Humanists' realization of the rhetorical nature of first premises is a lesson contemporary society needs to relearn. Grassi, then, does not so much take rhetorical theory in new directions as he revitalizes a conceptualization of rhetoric from the past. As a result, rhetoric becomes not only relevant to but crucial for redirecting the course of modern times.

Responses to Grassi

Grassi's ideas about rhetoric have not yet had widespread impact on the field of speech communication; he is best known to scholars interested in Vico and in Renaissance Humanism. Of the journals read most frequently by communication scholars, Grassi has published only in *Philosophy and Rhetoric*, and relatively few critical discussions of his work exist. His four books that have been translated into English have increased his familiarity in the discipline, but to date, no essays elaborating on Grassi's ideas or using them methodologically have appeared in the field at large. Part of the reason for this limited attention to Grassi simply may be that he, himself, is more concerned with asserting the contributions of Italian Humanism to rhetoric and philosophy than with fully developing the contemporary implications of this philosophical perspective. Furthermore, because he is a philosopher, largely unfamiliar with the speech communication field in the United States, he cannot be expected to make connections to other contemporary thinkers in that field, which might stimulate additional interest in his work.

Yet, Grassi's writings do provide access to a largely neglected rhetorical tradition—Renaissance Humanism. One of Grassi's most important contributions from this perspective is the assertion that rhetoric and philosophy are necessarily connected. Verene, a personal friend of Grassi's and a major commentator on his work, summarizes this contribution: "Ernesto Grassi has brought into contemporary rhetoric an absolutely new understanding of the relation between rhetoric and philosophy." More specifically, Grassi makes rhetoric the basis of philosophy by asserting that rhetorical speech is the starting point for philosophy and not the reverse. Rhetorical speech is primary because it relies on the human "power of *ingenium* to create metaphors from which we can produce reasoning." Thus, rhetoric "is not something added on to philosophical truth; it is the genesis of this truth."[73]

As a result of this thesis, Grassi contributes a new perspective for understanding the contemporary world. First, with his emphasis on *ingenium*, or the process of making connections between the human and natural domains, Grassi reasserts the need to ground our thought, speech, and action in an understanding of our nature as human beings. Grassi argues that with logical thought, so highly prized in modern society, we cannot see beyond the system itself to the premises or assumptions of the system. Such thought is not grounded; it is unconnected with reality, and in it, all "existence becomes a throw of the dice, a game in which the rules have no ground."[74] Grassi's rejection of objective, logical thought in favor of a subjective, rhetorical one is in line with much of what is being referred to as the "new paradigm" in research. New-paradigm approaches are concerned with the human being's role in constructing knowledge rather than with the possibility of objective knowledge.[75]

Krois, one of Grassi's translators, also points out the high priority Grassi gives to the theme that our lives currently are divorced from our basic nature as humans: "contemporary men feel the need for values that can unify their lives. But the source of this need lies in man's original nature as a human being and not in his momentary situation."[76] Grassi's work on folly is an extension of this theme; he believes that the notion of folly, rather than being a kind of insanity, is, in fact, an original grounding in the essential human condition—a linguistic capacity to see things as they are and the opposite possibilities simultaneously. This singularly human ability allows humans to create the world in which they live by making choices about how to perceive and live in it.

By giving renewed significance to rhetorical speech, Grassi also asks us to reconceptualize our definition of rhetoric. For him, it is not a "language of the emotions" or an "art of persuasion or of communicating truth that is independently established by means of logical and philosophical thought." Rather, rhetoric "is identified with the power of language and human speech to generate a basis for human thought."[77] Grassi returns, then, to the ancients, who valued rhetoric as an art fundamental to the nature of human existence.

Grassi's work also is important because it generates renewed interest in the Renaissance Humanists. Grassi reinterprets these authors, seeking to recover themes generally ignored in their works—"*ingenium*, imagination, memory, the idea of folly, the role of metaphor, the primacy of human speech that forms a particular event of our social world."[78] Grassi takes these concepts and from them constructs a perspective useful for contemporary times:

Grassi's thesis asks us to choose Vico over Descartes, the humanities over science as our master key to understanding the power of language. In an age in which philosophy is dominated by conceptual analysis Grassi's view calls us back to remember what has been denied in the modern basing of philosophy and knowledge on logic and not on the imagination. He brings forth from his account of antiquity, the Renaissance, and Vico a whole world that has been lost.[79]

Notes

[1] Ernesto Grassi, *Rhetoric as Philosophy: The Humanist Tradition* (University Park: Pennsylvania State University Press, 1980), p. 68.

[2] Biographical information on Grassi was obtained from the following sources: *Who's Who in the World* (Chicago: Marquis Who's Who, 1976), p. 308; Ernesto Grassi, *Rhetoric as Philosophy*, acknowledgments and p. 2; Ernesto Grassi, letter to Karen A. Foss, October 17, 1983; and personal interview with Grassi in Munich, West Germany, conducted by Karen A. Foss, August 21, 1983.

[3] Ernesto Grassi, "Italian Humanism and Heidegger's Thesis of the End of Philosophy," *Philosophy and Rhetoric*, 13 (Spring 1980), 83.

[4] Bertrando Spaventa, *La filosofia italiana nelle sue relazioni colla filosofia europa* (Bari, 1908), as quoted in Grassi, *Rhetoric as Philosophy*, p. 2.

[5] Grassi, *Rhetoric as Philosophy*, p. 4.

[6] See Ernesto Grassi, "The Priority of Common Sense and Imagination: Vico's Philosophical Relevance Today," trans. Azizeh Azodi, in *Vico and Contemporary Thought*, ed. Giorgio Tagliacozzo, Michael Mooney, and Donald P. Verene (Atlantic Highlands, NJ: Humanities, 1979), p. 164; and René Descartes, *Meditations on First Philosophy*, trans. Laurence J. Lafleur (Indianapolis: Bobbs-Merrill, 1951), p. 26.

[7] Grassi, "The Priority of Common Sense and Imagination," p. 166.

[8] Ernesto Grassi, "Critical Philosophy or Topical Philosophy: Meditations on the *De nostri temporis studiorum ratione*," trans. Hayden V. White, in *Giambattista Vico: An International Symposium*, ed. Giorgio Tagliacozzo and Hayden V. White (Baltimore: Johns Hopkins University Press, 1969), p. 43.

[9] Ernesto Grassi, "Marxism, Humanism, and the Problem of Imagination in Vico's Works," trans. Azizeh Azodi, in *Giambattista Vico's Science of Humanity*, ed. Giorgio Tagliacozzo and Donald Verene (Baltimore: Johns Hopkins University Press, 1976), p. 276.

[10] Grassi, "Marxism, Humanism, and the Problem of Imagination in Vico's Works," p. 278.

[11] Grassi, "Marxism, Humanism, and the Problem of Imagination in Vico's Works," p. 276.

[12] Ernesto Grassi, "Remarks on German Idealism, Humanism, and the Philosophical Function of Rhetoric," *Philosophy and Rhetoric*, 19 (1986), 125.

[13] Grassi, "Remarks on German Idealism," p. 128.

[14] Grassi, "Remarks on German Idealism," p. 128.

[15] Donald Phillip Verene, "Preface," in Ernesto Grassi and Maristella Lorch, *Folly and Insanity in Renaissance Literature* (Binghamton, NY: Medieval & Renaissance Texts & Studies, 1986), p. 10.

[16] Descartes.

[17] Ernesto Grassi, "The Ordinary Quality of the Poetic and Rhetorical Word: Heidegger, Ungaretti, and Neruda," *Philosophy and Rhetoric*, 20 (1987), 248.

[18] Grassi, "The Ordinary Quality of the Poetic," p. 249.

[19] Grassi, *Rhetoric as Philosophy*, pp. 35-36.

[20] Ernesto Grassi, "Der Beginn des Modernen Denkens," in *Jahrbuch des geistigen Uberlieferung*, 1 (Berlin, 1940). See also Grassi, *Rhetoric as Philosophy*, p. 4.

21 Henry Thomas, *Biographical Encyclopedia of Philosophy* (Garden City, NY: Doubleday, 1965), p. 248.

22 Grassi, *Rhetoric as Philosophy*, p. 37.

23 Grassi, "Marxism, Humanism, and the Problem of Imagination in Vico's Works," p. 283.

24 Grassi and Lorch, p. 35.

25 Grassi, "The Priority of Common Sense and Imagination," p. 189.

26 Ernesto Grassi, "Vico *Versus* Freud: Creativity and the Unconscious," in *Vico: Past and Present*, ed. Giorgio Tagliacozzo (Atlantic Highlands, NJ: Humanities, 1981), p. 147.

27 Ernesto Grassi, "Vico, Marx, and Heidegger," trans. Joseph Vincenzo, in *Vico and Marx: Affinities and Contrasts* (Atlantic Highlands, NJ: Humanities, 1983), pp. 240-41. See also Giambattista Vico, *The New Science*, trans. Thomas Bergin and Max Fisch (Ithaca, NY: Cornell University Press, 1968), par. 16.

28 Vico, *The New Science*, par. 374-84.

29 Donald Phillip Verene, "Response to Grassi," *Philosophy and Rhetoric*, 19 (1986), 135.

30 Grassi, "The Ordinary Quality of the Poetic," p. 250.

31 Giambattista Vico, "*Orazione in morte di donn'Angela Cimmino marchesa della Petrella*, in *Opere di G.B. Vico*, 4, ed. Fausto Nicolini, 7:170, as quoted in Grassi, "The Priority of Common Sense and Imagination," p. 173.

32 Grassi, "Marxism, Humanism, and the Problem of Imagination in Vico's Works," p. 290.

33 Grassi, *Heidegger and the Question of Renaissance Humanism*, p. 26.

34 Vico, *The New Science*, par. 382, 405.

35 Grassi, "The Priority of Common Sense and Imagination," p. 175.

36 Grassi, "The Priority of Common Sense and Imagination," p. 174.

37 Grassi, "The Priority of Common Sense and Imagination," p. 174. The twelve feats performed by Hercules were: to kill the Nemean lion; to destroy the Lernaean Hydra, a monster reared by Hera as a menace to Hercules; to capture the Ceryneian Hind, a creature with golden horns like a stag; to capture alive the Erymanthian Boar, a beast that haunted Mt. Erymanthus; to clean King Augeia's filthy cattle yard in one day; to remove the man-eating Stymphalian birds; to capture the Cretan bull; to capture the four savage mares of King Diomedes; to fetch the golden girdle worn by the Amazon queen, Hippolyte; to fetch the cattle of Geryon from Erytheia; to fetch fruit from the golden apple tree in Hera's garden; and finally, to bring the dog Cerberus up from Tarturus. See Robert Graves, *Greek Myths* (London: Cassell, 1955), pp. 462-520.

38 Ernesto Grassi, *Die Macht des Bildes*, 221, cited in Walter Veit, "The Potency of Imagery — the Impotence of Rational Language: Ernesto Grassi's Contribution to Modern Epistemology," *Philosophy and Rhetoric*, 17 (1984), 235.

39 Grassi and Lorch, p. 116.

40 Grassi, "Marxism, Humanism, and the Problem of Imagination in Vico's Works," p. 284.

41 Grassi, "Marxism, Humanism, and the Problem of Imagination in Vico's Works," p. 284.

42 Aristotle *Rhetoric* 1412a, paraphrased by Grassi in *Heidegger and the Question of Renaissance Humanism*, p. 65.

43 Grassi, *Rhetoric as Philosophy*, p. 96.

44 Ernesto Grassi, "The Denial of the Rational and the Priority of Metaphoric Thinking," paper available from Ernesto Grassi.

45 Vico, *The New Science*, par. 405; also cited by Grassi in "Marxism, Humanism, and the Problem of Imagination in Vico's Works," p. 292.

46 Grassi, "Remarks on German Idealism," p. 132.

47 Veit, "The Potency of Imagery," p. 230.

48 Ernesto Grassi, "Humanistic Rhetorical Philosophizing: Giovanni Pontano's Theory of the Unity of Poetry, Rhetoric, and History," *Philosophy and Rhetoric*, 17 (1984), 146.

49 Grassi, "Humanistic Rhetorical Philosophizing," p. 150.

50 Grassi, *Rhetoric as Philosophy*, p. 75.

51 Grassi, "Critical Philosophy or Topical Philosophy?," p. 39.

52 Grassi and Lorch, p. 40.

53 Grassi, *Rhetoric as Philosophy*, p. 113.

54 Grassi, *Rhetoric as Philosophy*, p. 23.

[55] Grassi, *Heidegger and the Question of Renaissance Humanism*, pp. 68-69.

[56] Grassi, *Heidegger and the Question of Renaissance Humanism*, p. 70.

[57] Grassi, *Rhetoric as Philosophy*, p. 32.

[58] David M. Jabusch and Stephen W. Littlejohn, *Elements of Speech Communication* (Boston: Houghton Mifflin, 1981), p. 108.

[59] Grassi, *Rhetoric as Philosophy*, p. 33.

[60] Grassi, *Rhetoric as Philosophy*, p. 26.

[61] Grassi, *Rhetoric as Philosophy*, p. 34.

[62] Grassi, "Critical Philosophy or Topical Philosophy?" p. 50.

[63] Grassi, *Heidegger and the Question of Renaissance Humanism*, p. 44.

[64] Grassi, *Heidegger and the Question of Renaissance Humanism*, p. 43.

[65] Grassi, "Marxism, Humanism, and the Problem of Imagination in Vico's Works," p. 294.

[66] Ernesto Grassi, "Why Rhetoric is Philosophy," *Philosophy and Rhetoric*, 20 (1987), 75.

[67] Grassi and Lorch, p. 37.

[68] Grassi and Lorch, p. 92.

[69] Verene, "Preface," p. 11.

[70] Verene, "Preface," p. 11.

[71] Grassi and Lorch, p. 89.

[72] Grassi and Lorch, p. 113.

[73] Donald Phillip Verene, "Remarks on Ernesto Grassi's Work," December 9, 1983, unpublished paper available from Karen A. Foss, pp. 1-2.

[74] Donald Phillip Verene, rev. of *Die Macht der Phantasie* and *Rhetoric as Philosophy*, by Ernesto Grassi, *Philosophy and Rhetoric*, 13 (Fall 1980), 281.

[75] For other characteristics of the new paradigm, see Fritjof Capra, "New Paradigm Thinking in Science," *Revision*, 9 (Summer/Fall 1986), 11-12.

[76] John Michael Krois, "Comment on Professor Grassi's Paper," *Social Research*, 43 (1976), 577.

[77] Verene, rev., p. 279

[78] Verene, "Remarks," p. 2.

[79] Verene, rev., p. 282.

7

Kenneth Burke

"The reason reviewers and editors have had such trouble fastening on Burke's field is that he has no field, unless it be Burkology."[1] This statement by Stanley Hyman, one of Kenneth Burke's interpreters, captures well the difficulty of characterizing the field to which Burke belongs. In his works, he demonstrates mastery of concepts from numerous disciplines, including philosophy, literature, linguistics, sociology, and economics. His primary perspective, however, could be considered a rhetorical one. His object of study is the communicative medium itself—language—and he seeks to discover its nature, its ends, and what it does to us. He is "a specialist in symbol-systems and symbolic action";[2] as he characterizes himself, "What am I but a *word* man?"[3]

Kenneth Duva Burke was born on May 5, 1897, in Pittsburgh, Pennsylvania. He attributes his love of literature to his father who, while working intermittently for Westinghouse in a clerical job, continually submitted short stories to the *Saturday Evening Post*, although without success. At Peabody High School in Pittsburgh, Burke was an "unpopular high school intellectual" and member of the literary crowd. Also a member of this group was Malcolm Cowley, a childhood friend from the age of three; Cowley's father was the Burke family's physician. Burke spent one summer working "in one of those damn factories" in Pittsburgh and attributes his anti-technological attitude to the experience. It also convinced him that he "wanted out."

Following graduation from high school in 1916, Burke went to stay with relatives in New Jersey and secured a job in New York as a bank runner. He worked there for only three months, quitting to study at Ohio State University, where he stayed only one semester. He then attended Columbia University for a year but was frustrated at having "to take so many prerequisite courses" before he could enroll in the ones he wanted to take. Despite hints that he would be asked to join the faculty at Columbia, he dropped out of college a second time: "I didn't want to go into academics, because in those days teachers only taught—I wanted to *write*." As he explained in a letter to Cowley:

> Suddenly becoming horrified at the realization of what college can do to a man of promise. . . . I don't want to be a virtuoso; I want to be a— a—oh hell, why not? I want to be a—yes—a genius. I want to learn to work, to work like a Sisyphus—that is my only chance. I am afraid, I confess it, but I am going to try hard. This is my final showdown. I am in it for life and death this time. Words, words—mountains of words—If I can do that I am saved.

He made a deal with his father: "Let me save you some money. Put me up in the Village [Greenwich Village] with just enough to pull through on, and I'll go on with my studies." His father agreed, and Burke became part of the bohemian subculture of the Village, living in a dingy garret and eating oatmeal and milk twice a day. As a member of an informal group of writers that included Malcolm Cowley, Matthew Josephson, Hart Crane, Allen Tate, e.e. cummings, and Edna St. Vincent Millay, Burke settled down to "very serious devotion to study and carousing." The group was dispersed somewhat during World War I; Burke himself was not drafted because he failed to pass the army medical examination. He spent the war working in a shipyard and in a factory "making gauges to check gauges."

In 1919, Burke married Lillian Batterham. When his three daughters began arriving, he and his family moved to a house on seventy acres in Andover, in the hills of western New Jersey. He always has kept the farm rustic; he did not install electricity there until 1949, and running water was not added until nearly twenty years later.

Throughout the 1920s, Burke supported himself and his family with various translating, editing, and writing jobs. In 1921, he was given a steady job at *The Dial*, a literary magazine. He worked there for several years in various capacities—as a reviewer, contributor, translator, music critic, and editor. In 1924, during his tenure at *The Dial*, his first book, a collection of short fiction called *The White Oxen and Other Stories*, was published. He also published numerous essays, poems, and book reviews in various outlets during that time. In 1929, Burke was presented the Dial Award for distinguished services to American letters.

In that same year, *The Dial* ceased publication: "I was lost," Burke recalls. "*The Dial* and the whole feeling behind it—that was magic to me, it was my life." Burke then did research and writing on drug addiction at the Laura Spelman Rockefeller Foundation. This work equipped Burke for his later studies of Samuel Taylor Coleridge, in which he analyzed images in the work relating to Coleridge's addiction to opium. Burke also did editorial work for the Bureau of Social Hygiene and was a reviewer and music critic for the *Nation* and the *New Republic*. In 1931, Burke's first book of literary criticism, *Counter-Statement*, was published, a work in which he views literature not only as an end in itself but also as a piece of rhetoric and of self-revelation about the author. He recommends an attitude of critical openness toward literature that permits numerous angles of vision.

In the early 1930s, Burke's personal life was beset by what he calls "the trouble." He fell in love with his wife's sister, Elizabeth "Libbie" Batterham. He divorced his first wife and married Libbie in 1933; two sons were born from this marriage. He worked out "the trouble" in his novel, *Towards a Better Life*, published in 1932: "I couldn't go to a psychoanalyst because I was too pigheaded. So I used my novel."

At the time of the Depression, Burke was increasingly attracted, as were many American writers, to Communism, although he never became a member of the Communist Party. His writing took on an ideological cast as he incorporated some of the ideas of cooperation from Communist doctrine; this was particularly evident in his book, *Permanence and Change*, published in 1935. In this work, Burke applies his interest in poetry and critical techniques to human relations in general; he believes that artists can provide insights into the problems confronting society—problems that are inseparable from problems of language. He introduces the concept of perspective by incongruity, in which categories are merged that once were believed to be mutually exclusive — such as "Arabian Puritanism" — reversing the normal order of things in order to generate new perspectives.

Burke's disillusionment with Communism began with the first Writers' Congress in 1935, a Communist-sponsored convocation of prominent "committed" literary figures in America. Burke presented a paper on propaganda called "Revolutionary Symbolism in America," and he argued for the substitution of the term "the people" for "the worker" because it was "more accurately attuned to us" and "more of an ideal incentive"; it would broaden the appeal of the movement. Some in the audience wanted their ideology confirmed and felt Burke's proposal would transform the revolution into a middle-class movement and weaken its economic thrust. The reaction to his paper was strong and negative: "But when the time came for criticism, — O my god! It was a slaughter! Mike Gold and Joe Freeman — they just tore me apart: 'We have a snob among us' — and so on. And when I was going out of the hall I heard a girl in front of me say: 'And yet he seemed so honest!'" Burke was devastated: "I went home and lay down, but just as I was about to fall asleep, I'd hear 'Burke!' — and I'd awake with a start. Then I'd doze off again, and suddenly again: 'Burke!' My name had become a kind of charge against me — a dirty word." Ironically, Burke discovered the next day that he had been elected a member of the Executive Committee of the newly founded League of American Writers — a position he accepted.

Burke read a paper at the second Writers' Congress in 1937, but he no longer held any office. At the third Congress, he also presented a paper. By then, events such as the Stalinist purges, the Moscow trials of 1936-1938, Soviet participation in Nazi Germany's attack on Poland, and the Russian invasion of Finland in 1939 were turning him away from Communism. He remained anti-Fascist and might be called an Agrarian liberal, but he generally is independent of any political affiliation.

Burke began his teaching career as a lecturer in criticism at the New School of Social Research in New York in 1937. In the same year, he published *Attitudes Toward History*, a study of literary attitudes as symbolic action. He divides these attitudes into those of acceptance and those of rejection, with both leading to the development of a comic theory of human relations or an attitude of irony. From 1943 to 1961, with some interruptions, he held a teaching position at Bennington College in Vermont. Most of his life has been spent as a "gypsy scholar"; he has served as a visiting professor at a number of schools, including the University of Chicago, Harvard University, Northwestern University, and Princeton University. He was granted an honorary doctorate degree in 1966 from Bennington College.[4]

Burke dropped out of college to write, and he has spent his life doing just that. *The Philosophy of Literary Form*, published in 1941, is a collection of critical essays and reviews written between 1933 and 1940; they are united by their common concern with speculation on the nature of symbolic action. In 1945, Burke published *A Grammar of Motives*, the first volume of what was to be a trilogy of works based on a three-fold division of language into grammar, rhetoric, and poetics. This volume deals with the intrinsic nature of a work, focusing on dramatism as the key metaphor and the pentad as the method for discovering motivation. The second work of the trilogy, *A Rhetoric of Motives*, published in 1950, deals with the strategies people use for persuasion. Burke discusses traditional principles of rhetoric and then suggests that the key term for rhetoric is "identification." The planned third book of the trilogy, *A Symbolic of Motives*, has not been released for publication.[5] Burke's next major work, *The Rhetoric of Religion*, published in 1961, exemplifies his shift from poetry to theology as the model for logology, or the study of language. *Language as Symbolic Action* appeared in 1966 and has been described as a "Burkean grab bag." It collects works by Burke from 1950 to 1966 and demonstrates the enormous range of Burke's writings. Burke's dedication to his writing and the contribution it has made were recognized in 1981, when he was awarded the National Medal for Literature, a $15,000 award that honors a living American writer for a contribution to American letters.

Burke continues to live on his farm in Andover. Although his wife died in 1969, he is surrounded by his family, for many of his children and grandchildren have vacation homes that border his farm. One of his grandsons is the late singer, Harry Chapin; he recorded Burke's song, "One Light in a Dark Valley," on one of his albums. Burke continues to work with undiminished vigor and has no plans to stop: "Basically, I'm still terribly interested in what I'm doing, and I want to get it cleared up."

Perhaps Burke himself provides as good a description as any of what he is trying "to get cleared up." In a poem written in response to Hyman's comment that Burke's field is Burkology, Burke explains: "When I itch/ It's not from fleas,/ But from a bad case/ of Burke's Disease." He concludes the poem with an announcement of his motive in his work: "What then in sum/ Bedevils me?/ I'm flunking my Required Course/ In Advanced Burkology."[6]

Nature of Rhetoric

Burke defines rhetoric as "the use of words by human agents to form attitudes or to induce actions in other human agents." Whatever form rhetoric takes, it is *"rooted in an essential function of language itself, . . . the use of language as a symbolic means of inducing cooperation in beings that by nature respond to symbols."*[7]

Burke sees rhetoric as a subset of a larger category, symbolic action, which will be discussed in more detail in connection with his notion of dramatism. Included in symbolic action are rhetoric, poetics, science, and philosophy. Rhetoric is concerned with persuasion and identification, poetics is concerned with symbolic action in and for itself, science is concerned with symbolic action in relation to the ends of factual knowledge, and philosophy is concerned with symbolic action in relation to discussions of first principles.[8]

Burke's definition of rhetoric, centered in persuasion, appears to be very similar to traditional definitions of rhetoric. Yet, Burke introduces other characteristics of rhetoric that expand his definition beyond that of the traditional ones.

Identification

Burke's major addition to definitions of rhetoric begins with his concept of identification, rooted in the notion of substance. We form selves or identities through various properties or substances, including physical objects, occupations, friends, activities, beliefs, and values. As we ally ourselves with various properties or substances, we share substance with whatever or whomever we associate. Burke uses the term ''consubstantial'' to describe this association. As two entities are united in substance through common ideas, attitudes, material possessions, or other properties, they are consubstantial. Men and women, for example, while different, are consubstantial in that they share the substance of humanness. Two artists are consubstantial in that they share the substance of being artists.[9]

Burke uses the term ''identification'' synonymously with ''consubstantiality.'' Shared substance constitutes an identification between an individual and some property or person: ''To identify A with B is to make A 'consubstantial' with B.'' Burke also equates ''persuasion'' with ''consubstantiality'' and ''identification,'' seeing ''no chance of our keeping apart the meanings,'' for persuasion is the result of identification: ''You persuade a man only insofar as you can talk his language by speech, gesture, tonality, order, image, attitude, idea, *identifying* your ways with his.'' Burke thus has expanded the notion of rhetoric so that it is change in attitude or action through identification. In this expansion, Burke does not mean to make ''identification'' the key term for rhetoric in place of the traditional term ''persuasion''; rather, he sees identification as a supplement to the traditional view of rhetoric as persuasion.[10]

Identification functions in three basic ways. First, it may be used as a means to an end. A candidate for office, for instance, may attempt to win votes simply by telling an audience of anti-abortion advocates that he holds the same position they do on the issue of abortion. Or a Presidential candidate may tell a group of farmers that she was raised on a farm. If she can convince the farmers that they thus share substance, she may win their votes. In these cases, "insofar as their interests are joined, A is *identified* with B," and persuasion concerning a desired end occurs.

The second kind of identification involves the operation of antithesis, when identification is created among opposing entities on the basis of a common enemy. The United States and Russia, for example, joined forces against Germany in World War II—uniting two countries that were ideologically opposed on the basis of an enemy of both. Similarly, two faculty members in a university department who oppose each other on a number of issues may become identified with one another when financial difficulties at the university indicate that their department will be eliminated. They unite against the common enemy of the threatened elimination of the department.

The third type of identification—and often the most powerful—"derives from situations in which it goes unnoticed"; in this case, identification is used to persuade at an unconscious level. The person who buys Marlboro cigarettes, for example, may be identifying unconsciously with the image of the "Marlboro man" in the advertisements. Or, to use Burke's example, to say "that 'we' are at war includes under the same head soldiers who are getting killed and speculators who hope to make a killing in war stocks." In this case, again, identification subtly and unconsciously is being created among individuals.[11]

An understanding of identification is not complete without an understanding of the notion of division, or what Burke sometimes calls "alienation" or "dissociation." Human beings are inevitably isolated and divided from each other as a result of their separate physical bodies. The "*individual centrality of the nervous system*" requires that what "the body eats and drinks becomes its special private property; the body's pleasures and pains are exclusively its own pleasures and pains." "In being identified with B," then, "A is 'substantially one' with a person other than himself. Yet at the same time he remains unique, an individual locus of motives. Thus he is both joined and separate, at once a distinct substance and consubstantial with another."

In division, then, we find a basic motive for rhetoric: People communicate in an attempt to eliminate division. Burke asserts that if individuals were not apart from each other, "there would be no need for the rhetorician to proclaim their unity." Only because of their separateness do individuals communicate with one another and try to resolve their differences. Paradoxically, then, identification is rooted in division. Rhetoric is an attempt to bridge the conditions of estrangement that are natural and inevitable and is a means for transcending, to some degree, these conditions.[12]

Unconscious Motivation

Burke's notion of rhetoric as identification suggests yet another distinction between his view of rhetoric and traditional views. While classical definitions of rhetoric focus on "the speaker's explicit designs with regard to the confronting of an audience," identification includes the possibility of unconscious persuasion, for we may not be consciously aware of the identifications we are making. Thus, while citing her farm background to an audience of farmers certainly would involve conscious intent on the part of the candidate, which usually is the case when identification is used as a means to an end, dressing in a manner similar to a respected professor might be unconscious. In this case, identification is the end, which is achieved through action taken on the self.[13]

Self as Audience

Persuasion implies an audience, and in accord with traditional views of rhetoric, Burke includes as a condition of rhetoric its "nature as *addressed*." Rhetoric is concerned with an appeal either to a real or an ideal audience. Burke, however, believes that rhetoric also can involve the self as the audience: "A man can be his own audience, insofar as he, even in his secret thoughts, cultivates certain ideas or images for the effect he hopes they may have upon him; he is here what Mead would call 'an "I" addressing its "me"'"; and in this respect he is being rhetorical quite as though he were using pleasant imagery to influence an outside audience rather than one within." While many definitions of rhetoric certainly do not preclude the self as audience, Burke's notion of the self as an audience for rhetoric means that processes such as socialization would fall under the rubric of rhetoric.[14]

Scope of Rhetoric

Although rhetoric includes, in Burke's view, spoken and written discourse, it also includes less traditional forms of discourse such as sales promotion, courtship, social etiquette, education, hysteria, and witchcraft. It includes, as well, works of art such as literature and painting. Art is "a means of communication" that is "designed to elicit a 'response' of some sort"; it is symbolic action—action that symbolizes something.[15]

Despite Burke's use of the term, "language," in his definition of rhetoric, he see rhetoric as including nonverbal elements or nonsymbolic conditions that "can themselves be viewed as a kind of symbolism having persuasive effects." While a nonverbal element in itself is not rhetoric, rhetoric is apparent in its meaning. For example, food, "eaten and digested, is not rhetorical," but rhetoric exists "in the *meaning* of food . . . the meaning being persuasive enough for the idea of food to be used, like the ideas of religion, as a rhetorical device." Such "nonverbal conditions or objects can be considered as signs by reason of persuasive ingredients inherent in the 'meaning' they have for the audience to which they are 'addressed.'" The broad scope Burke sees for rhetoric is summarized in his statement, "Wherever there is persuasion, there is rhetoric. And wherever there is 'meaning,' there is 'persuasion.'"[16]

Function of Rhetoric

While Burke sees rhetoric as having a number of functions, one function it always performs is the naming or defining of situations for individuals. A speech or a poem, for example, is *"a strategy for encompassing a situation*, "an answer to the question "posed by the situation." It sizes up the situation and names its structure and outstanding ingredients. The Constitution of the United States, for example, names a situation concerned with political governance, just as calling a person a "friend" or naming certain admission standards to a school "rigorous" tells the qualities of the situation that are deemed important by the rhetor and suggests the action that will be taken in that situation.

But rhetoric does not simply provide a name for a situation. It also represents a creative strategy for dealing with that situation or for solving the problems inherent in the situation. It gives us commands or instructions of some kind. Rhetoric, in other words, helps us maneuver through life, directs the movements and operations of life, and helps us feel more at home in the chaos of the modern world.

Because rhetoric is one rhetor's solution to problems faced in the search for the self and the better life, it may be considered a chart, formula, manual, or map that the audience may consult in trying to decide on various courses of action. Just as the rhetor uses the strategy selected to adjust to life and help determine what attitude and thus action to take toward it, so the audience that finds itself in the same situation is able to use the rhetor's work as stylistic medicine.[17]

A rhetorical work provides assistance in a number of ways. It may provide a vocabulary of thoughts, actions, emotions, and attitudes for codifying and thus interpreting the situation. It may encourage the acceptance of a situation that cannot be changed, or it may serve as a guide for how to correct a situation. In other instances, it may help us justify our conduct, turning actions that seem to be wicked or absurd into ones considered virtuous or accurate. Rhetoric, then, helps us orient ourselves in some way to a situation and to adjust to it.[18]

Each rhetorical act is not only a strategic answer to a situation, but it is a stylized answer as well. The rhetor not only names the situation but names it in a particular fashion; the manner used to do the naming Burke calls "style." There "is a difference," Burke explains, "in style or strategy, if one says 'yes' in tonalities that imply 'thank God' or in tonalities that imply 'alas!'" The situation has been named with the same response or label, but the style is different. While the same facts may be communicated about a situation, many styles are available for the communication of the facts of the situation.[19]

Rhetorical Form

Our discussion of Burke's definition of rhetoric thus far has focused on the content of rhetoric. But because "form and content cannot be separated" and a rhetor "can't possibly make a statement without its falling into some sort of pattern," any consideration of the subject or content of rhetoric also must include a consideration of its form.[20]

For Burke, how an idea is developed through form is inextricably linked to the effects of rhetoric on an audience. Seeking "a system of judging *how effects are produced*, Burke came to realize that "form is the *process of producing the effect*." An impact is produced on an audience, Burke asserts, in that the development of an idea involves the creation and satisfaction of expectations. Burke realized the significance of expectation in the process of achieving desired effects when he recognized that reality itself is "a structure of expectations." In fact, life is structured by expectations: "life itself has form only insofar as you get a sense of expectancy, and life becomes unreal, and puzzling, and disarrayed when we do not have any way of expecting the next event."[21]

Burke defines form as "an arousing and fulfillment of desires" or "the creation of an appetite in the mind of the auditor, and the adequate satisfying of that appetite." "A work has form," he suggests, "in so far as one part of it leads a reader to anticipate another part, to be gratified by the sequence." If, for example, in a novel, an author says something "about a meeting, writes in such a way that we desire to observe that meeting, and then, if he places that meeting before us—that is form." Identification or persuasion results from an interaction of form and content. Through involvement in its form, a rhetorical work induces tensions or expectations with which the audience identifies. When the rhetor resolves the tension and creates some sort of resolution in the work, the audience views the work's resolution as its own. Form "is 'correct,'" in Burke's view, when "it gratifies the needs which it creates." Impact is produced because an idea has been developed in such a way as to excite and satisfy audience expectations.[22]

Burke sees form as reduced to "three primary principles" or types: conventional, repetitive, and progressive; each type relies on the arousing and fulfilling of expectations managed through different patterns. *Conventional form* is the expectation of a particular form prior to encountering a work. It involves "the kind of 'built-in' expectations that audiences bring with them" to the form. A sonnet, for example, must follow a certain form, and someone who reads a sonnet brings to the work the expectation of this form. Similarly, the audience at an Athenian tragedy expected to see a chorus and attended the play with this form in mind, just as the Roman audience at the gladiatorial games expected the form of the games to include live victims.

Repetitive form is "the consistent maintaining of a principle under new guises. It is restatement of the same thing in different ways." This type of form "involves the ways in which a work embodies a fixed character or identity" or "manifests some kinds of internal self-consistency." A succession of images in a poem, each regiving the same joyous mood, for example, is repetitive form. Another example is a town in which numerous signs—boarded-up buildings, blowing trash, vacant streets, and weeds growing in the cracks of sidewalks—point to the same conclusion: the town is not flourishing.

Progressive form involves the use of situations that lead the audience "to anticipate or desire certain developments." One type of progressive form is syllogistic progression, "the form of a perfectly conducted argument" that advances step by step. It is called syllogistic because, just as with a syllogism, given certain starting points, certain things must follow. Upon acquaintance with the premises, in other words, the audience is fairly certain as to where the work is going to end up: "The arrows of our desires are turned in a certain direction, and the plot follows the direction of the arrows." In many traditional gangster movies, for example, the audience knows from the opening scenes what the ending of the movie will be—that the hero will win the love of the woman and will conquer the villain. Similarly, in a fast-food restaurant such as McDonald's, the observations the audience makes upon entering—of plastic surroundings, a limited menu, and low prices—suggest the conclusion that this is not a place where gourmet dining will take place. Given such premises, the audience cannot help but draw certain conclusions.

A second type of progressive form is qualitative progression. This is a more subtle kind of form than syllogistic progression, for rather than "one incident in the plot preparing us for some other possible incident of plot . . . the presence of one quality prepares us for the introduction of another." The tone of scenes or events, rather than the action of the scenes themselves, is involved in this form, so that we "are put into a state of mind which another state of mind can appropriately follow." The grotesque seriousness of a murder scene in a play, for example, might prepare us for the grotesque buffoonery of the scene that follows—although the action differs, the quality characterizing the scenes is the same.

A second difference between qualitative and syllogistic progressive form is that in qualitative progression, the structure of the form is recognized as appropriate only after the work has been experienced—it is not anticipated at the outset. It lacks the pronounced anticipatory nature of syllogistic progression, and we "are prepared less to demand a certain qualitative progression than to recognize its rightness after the event." In Alfred

Hitchcock's film, *Vertigo*, for example, the audience has no idea at the beginning of the film that the woman with whom Scottie Ferguson [James Stewart] falls in love, Madeleine/Judy [Kim Novak] will be involved in murder and deception and be killed at the end of the film. After her death, however, the audience realizes how appropriate the ending is. Ferguson cannot continue to love her because of her involvement in murder and deception, but he cannot stop loving her. Thus, her death is the only appropriate solution to the emotions involved in the situation and constitutes a correct end to the film's qualitative progression.

In addition to the three major types of form, Burke discusses minor or incidental forms. Among these are metaphor, paradox, reversal, contraction, expansion, and series. The effect of these kinds of forms partially depends on their function in the work as a whole, and they often serve as parts of the three complex types of form. In some instances, however, these minor forms may appeal and play a major role on their own in the development of tensions and resolution concerning content.

Identification may result, in large part, from the form of a rhetorical act. In this case, consubstantiality is based on the form in which the claim or proposition being argued is presented. The goal with this type of identification is to induce ''the auditor to participation in the form'' and then to transfer that participation over to agreement with the content. While an audience initially may disagree with the proposition being presented, it often will yield to the symmetry of the form in which the proposition is being presented. This attitude of assent then may be transferred to the argument associated with the form.[23] Burke provides an example of this type of identification:

> ''Who controls Berlin, controls Germany; who controls Germany controls Europe; who controls Europe controls the world.'' As a proposition it may or may not be true. And even if it is true, unless people are thoroughly imperialistic, they may not want to control the world. But regardless of these doubts about it as a proposition, by the time you arrive at the second of its three stages, you feel how it is destined to develop—and on the level of purely formal assent you would collaborate to round out its symmetry by spontaneously willing its completion and perfection as an utterance. Add, now, the psychosis of nationalism, and assent on the formal level invites assent to the proposition as doctrine.[24]

While Burke's definition of rhetoric is centered in persuasion, as are most definitions, the uniqueness of his view lies in his equation of identification with persuasion and the expansion of persuasion to include unconscious intent, the self as audience, and nonverbal elements that have meaning for an audience. With the addition of his notion that rhetoric provides equipment for living and generally assumes one of three major forms, the result is a comprehensive examination of rhetoric on which Burke builds his elaborate rhetorical system.

Dramatism

Dramatism is the approach Burke uses to study human motivation through the analysis of drama. It is "a technique of analysis of language and of thought as basically modes of action rather than a means of conveying information." In this "philosophy of language," language is seen not just as a means for naming or defining but is a form of action. It is designed to discover human motives for acts via inquiry into words.

The dramatistic view of language as action makes explicit the idea that our thoughts and ideas are never free from the language we use to frame them. Our words create orientations or attitudes, shaping our views of reality and thus generating different motives for our actions. If parents define their young child's behavior as "expressive," for example, they will tend to look upon the child's transgressions as healthy self-disclosure and as signs of the child's intelligence. Consequently, they will put up with the child's interruptions, antics, and screams. If, however, they define that child's same behavior as "obnoxious," those behaviors will be seen as signs of rudeness and lack of respect and will not be tolerated. The parents' actions toward the child and the child's actions, then, are dependent on the terminology used to describe that behavior. The language we select makes all of us act in particular ways rather than others, making language serve an important function of generating motives for action.

Burke selects dramatism as his representative or informative anecdote because it meets the criteria he feels are necessary for an adequate description of human motivation: "A given calculus must be supple and complex enough to be representative of the subject-matter it is designed to calculate. It must have scope. Yet it must also possess simplicity, in that it is broadly a reduction of the subject-matter." For Burke, the dramatistic model fulfills all of these criteria.[25]

Action Versus Motion

The key term in Burke's dramatistic approach to the study of motivation is "act." Dramatism is a study of "action" as opposed to "motion." The major distinction between action and motion lies in the difference between animality — the biological aspect of the human being that corresponds to motion, and symbolicity — the neurological aspect of the human being that corresponds to action.

Animality is that part of the human concerned with bodily processes: "growth, metabolism, digestion, peristaltic 'action,' respiration, functions of the various organs, secretion of the endocrine glands, ways in which elements in the bloodstream reinforce or check one another, and so on."

Certain motives arise out of our animality—"the desires for food, shelter, mates, rest," for example, in their most basic forms. Animality "is in the realm of sheer matter, sheer motion"; we are in motion, rather than acting, at this level. As Burke explains, because motion "encompasses the realm of entities that do not respond to words as such," he labels this realm the "nonsymbolic."

In addition to their biological nature, humans have a neurological aspect, which is the ability of an organism to acquire language or a symbol system. With a symbol system, we transcend animality and become human. This is the realm of action, the "symbolic," or "symbolic action." While the "material conditions in which the space program takes place, for instance, are in the realm of motion," the "theorizing, planning, and human coordination involved are in the realm of action" because a symbol system is necessary for these kinds of activities to occur. Just as some of our motives are derived from our animality, others originate in our symbolicity. These motives include the numerous goals toward which we strive in such areas as "education, political systems, moral codes, religions, commerce, money, and so on." To be motivated in these areas requires a symbol system that creates the possibility for such desires in the first place.[26]

Three conditions are required for action. First, freedom must be involved; "if an act weren't 'free,' it wouldn't be an 'act.'" Implicit in the idea of action is choice: "If one cannot make a choice, one is not acting, one is but being moved, like a billiard ball tapped with a cue and behaving mechanically in conformity with the resistances it encounters." Freedom to choose, however, requires adequate knowledge of the act's consequences; a person must know the consequences involved in making a particular choice. Thus, we never can be completely free because we never know the full consequences of our acts.

A second condition necessary for an act is purpose or will. A person must will a choice. Burke provides an example of the difference between action and motion regarding will, showing how something that begins as motion may be converted to action through the addition of purpose: "If one happened to stumble over an obstruction, that would be not an act, but a mere motion. However, one could convert even this sheer accident into something of an act if, in the course of falling, one suddenly *willed* this fall (as a rebuke, for instance, to the negligence of the person who had left the obstruction in the way)."

The third necessary condition for action is motion. Although motion can exist without action (as when balls roll down an inclined plane), action cannot exist without motion. We may use the symbol "bread," for example, but we "cannot live by the *word* for bread alone." Symbolic action, then, ultimately is grounded in the realm of the nonsymbolic—the word "bread" is grounded in the loaf of bread. While motion is necessary for action, action cannot be reduced to motion. The " 'essence' or 'meaning' of a sentence is not reducible," for example, "to its sheer physical existence as sound in the air or marks on the page, although material motions of some sort are necessary for the production, transmission, and reception of the sentence."

Once organisms acquire a symbol system, for them to do something purely in the realm of motion without the mediation of this system or symbolic action is virtually impossible. Building a house, for example, might be considered motion since it involves the biological need for shelter. Yet, to build a house without our symbolic conceptions of house entering into that process, turning it into an act, is not likely. Similarly, two people might be performing the same motion—running an elevator, for example. But they would be "performing different *acts*, in proportion as they differed in their attitudes toward their work. We might realistically call it one kind of act to run an elevator under a system of private ownership, and another kind of act to run that same elevator, by exactly the same routines, under a system of communal ownership." [27]

Burke's focus on action leads him to suggest that dramatism should be taken literally and not as a metaphor. Dramatism is not just a metaphor or perspective for discussing reality; it provides a literal statement about the nature of reality. Burke's term, "linguistic realism," summarizes this notion that language is as real as physical objects.

Words are important in their own right and not merely as names that convey information or stand for their counterparts in reality. In fact, not only does Burke assert that words are not only terms used to name things, but he reverses the equation and asserts that things are "signs" of words. We cannot look to reality to know what a word means; instead, we must look at language to see what reality means. Words impose knowledge on us—they create a reality for us. For example, calling a police officer a "pig" is not as much a literal definition of the person as it is the placing of a person in a category that emphasizes certain attributes and attitudes that then serve as motivation for our actions toward the officer. We also can see the literal nature of words in the fact that we often learn words for and thus create realities surrounding objects, places, or situations before we "actually" encounter them or that we never will encounter. An American citizen who has not traveled outside of the country, for example, develops a version—or reality—of what Australia is that is as real as the actual continent for her. The words connected with Australia literally have created her knowledge, in this case. Implicit in Burke's notion of dramatism, then, is the literal function of language to produce reality for us.[28]

Pentad

We have seen that Burke's dramatistic perspective studies language as action rooted in motion and characterized by freedom and purpose. Because language use is characterized by freedom and purpose, a rhetor's language can be used to discover motive. Motives and language are so closely associated that by analyzing a rhetorical artifact, we can discover a rhetor's underlying motives. Burke asserts that by inspecting a rhetor's work, "we or he may disclose by objective citation the structure of motivation operating here. There is no need to 'supply' motives. The interrelationships themselves *are* his motives. For they are his *situation*; and *situation* is but another word for *motives*. The motivation out of which he writes is synonymous with the structural way in which he puts events and values together when he writes; . . ."[29]

Burke has developed a tool or method of analysis, called the "pentad," to discover the motivation in symbolic action. It is a critical instrument designed to reduce statements of motives to the most fundamental level, which Burke argues consists of five terms that constitute the pentad: "act," "agent," "agency," "scene," and "purpose." These five terms are the principles or "grammar" for the discovery of motive, and motive is seen as the product of interrelationships or tensions among the terms. Burke explains his rationale for the selection of these five terms: "In a rounded statement about motives, you must have some word that names the *act* (names what took place, in thought or deed), and another that names the *scene* (the background of the act, the situation in which it occurred); also, you must indicate what person or kind of person (*agent*) performed the act, what means or instruments he used (*agency*), and the *purpose*." In a study of motivation, we might find, for example, these elements designated at the outset of the study as follows: "The hero (agent) with the help of a friend (co-agent) outwits the villain (counter-agent) by using a file (agency) that enables him to break his bonds (act) in order to escape (purpose) from the room where he has been confined (scene)."

Burke intended the pentad to be used internally—within a rhetorical transaction such as a speech—so that the pentadic elements are selected from the actual content of the discourse. The act, then, would be the act discussed by the rhetor, the scene would be where the rhetor says the act occurs, and the agent would be the person or persons the rhetor sees as engaging in the act. The pentad has been extended, however, to apply as well to the larger context in which the rhetoric studied is seen as the act, with the other elements selected to correspond to it. In this case, a speech would be viewed as the act, the scene would be the place where the speech was delivered, the agent would be the rhetor delivering the speech, and so on.[30]

By "act," as we've seen, Burke means any conscious or purposive action. Thus, "any verb, no matter how specific or how general, that has connotations of consciousness or purpose" constitutes an act. Giving a speech, running in a marathon, or painting an image on canvas, for example, are symbolic acts that can be studied in terms of their rhetors' motivations.[31]

"Scene" is the ground, location, or situation in which the act takes place. Terms for scene include such labels as, "it is 12:20 p.m.," historical epochs such as the "Elizabethan period" or the "Depression," or "in Florida in January." A scenic statement might even be as broad as "in a period following the invention of the atomic bomb but prior to a soft landing of electronic instruments on the surface of the moon."

How the scene is designated is important because this label indicates the scope of the analysis. A variety of circumstances are available to select as characterizations of a scene: "For a man is not only in the situation peculiar to his era or to his particular place in that era (even if we could agree on the traits that characterize his era). He is also in a situation extending through centuries; he is in a 'generically human' situation; and he is in a 'universal' situation." The scene in which the artist is painting, then, could be described as "a studio," "New York City," "midnight on February 3, 1990," "the United States," "the post-modern era in art," or "the planet earth." The scene selected has an impact on the selection of the other terms in the pentad and establishes the circumference of the analysis. No particular description of setting is the correct one; Burke simply points out that how scene is labeled affects the scope of the critic's interpretation of motivation.[32]

The "agent" is the group or individual who performs the act. It includes general or specific words for person such as "actor," "character," "hero," "villain," "mother," "doctor," or "artist" as well as words for the motivational properties of agents such as "drives," "instincts," and "states of mind." An agent also may be a collective term such as "nation," "race," or "church."[33]

"Agency" is the means used to perform the act or the instruments used to accomplish it. For example, a paintbrush and canvas or a particular use of color might be the agencies used by the visual artist. For the politician presenting a speech, the agencies might be the particular language style and communication strategies used. For the runner, self-discipline, training, self-image as an athlete, and even leg muscles might be considered instruments used to accomplish the act.

The "purpose" of the act is the agent's private purpose for performing the act. It may be overt, but it more often is covert and thus unknown to an outside observer. Thus, when Marc Lepine shot and killed fourteen women at the University of Montreal's engineering school while shouting diatribes against feminists in 1989, his purpose might have been to gain self-recognition or affirmation.[34] Purpose is not synonymous with "motive." Motive is the much broader, often unconscious reason for the performance of the act; it might be thought of as a "rough, shorthand description" of a situation or the terminology we use to interpret a situation. An examination of all five elements of the pentad is needed to discover the motive for a particular rhetorical act.[35]

In addition to terms for act, scene, agent, agency, and purpose, Burke sometimes includes "attitude" as an element to be considered in the analysis of motivation. While agency denotes the means employed in an act, attitude designates the manner: "To build something with a hammer would involve an instrument, or 'agency'; to build with diligence would involve an 'attitude,' a 'how.'" Burke states that "on later occasions I have regretted that I had not turned the pentad into a hexad, with 'attitude' as the sixth term," but he continues to analyze motivation through a pentad, seeing attitude as subsumed under agent: "Where would attitude fall within our pattern? Often it is the *preparation* for an act, which would make it a kind of symbolic act, or incipient act. But in its character as a state of *mind* that may or may not lead to an act, it is quite clearly to be classed under the head of *agent*." In other cases, an attitude may serve as a substitute for an act—as when, for example, "the sympathetic person can let the intent do service for the deed." Simply expressing the "correct" attitude may be enough—performance of acts of sympathy thus may not be needed.[36]

Burke introduces the term "ratio" to describe the relationships among the elements of the pentad. All of the terms are consubstantial in that they share in the substance of the act. An act inevitably implies, for example, the idea of an agent, and the idea of an agent acting implies the idea of a scene in which the act takes place. Burke formulates ten ratios that allow a more detailed examination of the various relationships among the terms: scene-act, scene-agent, scene-agency, scene-purpose, act-purpose, act-agent, act-agency, agent-purpose, agent-agency, and agency-purpose; reversal of the order of the terms in each pair creates an additional ten ratios.

Ratios suggest a relationship of propriety, suitability, or requirement among the elements. A scene-act ratio, for example, deals with the kind of act called for by the scene or the modes of response that are required by the situation in which the act occurs. A church scene, for example, determines that only certain acts with certain characteristics will be performed there. Praying, for example, would be proper in the scene, while doing cartwheels would not. Or, in a scene of a shipwreck, everyone on the ship responds in some way to the situation; the scene, then, determines or creates acts in accordance with it. In examining such relationships, the scene would be analyzed as "a fit 'container' for the act, expressing in fixed properties the same quality that the act expresses."

The act-agent ratio focuses on a different relationship. It is used to examine how acts can remake individuals in accordance with their nature. The act of betraying a friend, for example, forms the individual, to some degree, into a traitor. By reversing the terms to create an agent-act ratio, the analysis focuses on how a person's character requires the performance of certain acts. A staid professor, for example, would be expected to perform acts that exemplify intelligence and seriousness; such a professor would not be likely to perform a comedy routine as a part of a local talent night at a bar. We also see evidence of the act-agent ratio in how the donning of clerical garments, judicial robes, or a police uniform may transform the character of the agent.

According to the relationship of the agency-act ratio, the means selected for carrying out an act confine and restrict it in particular ways. To express thoughts in the form of a sonnet, for example, necessarily constrains the act of expression by forming it into a particular scheme of rhythm and rhyme. On the other hand, the act-agency ratio suggests that if a particular act is to be accomplished, certain means must be used. An act of forgiveness by one individual toward another, for example, requires agencies that embody love and gentleness, not hate and violence.[37]

An examination of all of the ratios aids the critic in discovering which term in the pentad receives the greatest attention by the rhetor and thus suggests in what term to look for the motivation of the act. In the debate on the Equal Rights Amendment, for example, an examination of various ratios leads to the conclusion that the proponents featured the scene in their arguments. The scene—a discriminatory, exclusionary setting for women—required that the characters or agents be women willing and able to challenge the system, that their acts be struggles for equality using agencies such as lobbying and marching, and that their purpose be the attainment of justice and equality for women. In contrast, the opponents featured the term of agent in their discourse, or "real" women who are housewives and mothers. This required a scene of the home, acts of caring for home and family, and a purpose of adequately performing the housewife role. The motivation differed greatly, then, between the two groups—one wanting to change the scene into one of justice and equality, the other wanting women to remain true to their characters and natures.

Thus, Burke's pentad, rooted in a dramatistic perspective, enables the critic first to name the elements involved in the act and then to investigate the relationships among those elements. As a result, an interpretation of the motivation of the rhetor whose act is the object of study can be formulated. This information then can be used to understand the rhetor's particular orientation and the kinds of interpretations she is likely to apply to her current and future actions. It also can be used to discover alternative perspectives for viewing an act—by featuring a different term in the framing of a topic or perspective, the critic can see it from a different viewpoint. The pentad thus can provide a way to detect and correct for bias in an interpretation, serving as the basis for efforts to overcome the limitations of a single critical vocabulary.[38]

Logology

With Burke's notion of dramatism, he applies literary criticism to the study of human action in general, seeing drama as a model for human relations. From dramatism, he has moved to the analysis of language through logology. "Logology" is a rare word for philology or historical linguistics. For Burke, it refers to his effort to discover how language works—in particular, to discover motivational systems and orientations through the examination of words. The source for this study of words is theology; in logology, Burke studies theological terms for the insight they provide into the operation of language. Logology, then, is an approach to the study of symbol systems using a neutralized Christian theology as its model.[39]

Rather than seeing literature or drama as representative of symbol use in general, as Burke does in dramatism, theology is representative in logology. Burke wants to discover the fundamental truths about the nature and forms of language as a motive, and he is seeking the perfect model of the use of words. He selects theology as this model because he sees it as one field where the resources of language as language have been worked out exhaustively: "religious cosmogonies are designed, in the last analysis, as exceptionally thoroughgoing modes of persuasion. . . . And in order to plead . . . as persuasively as possible, the religious always ground their exhortations (to themselves and others) in statements of the widest and deepest possible scope, concerning the authorship of men's motives." The "close study of theology and its forms," Burke believes, "will provide us with good insight into the nature of language itself as a motive." His interest, then, is not to argue whether religious doctrine is true; instead, he sees in theology many examples that help us understand the basic principles of language. He also sees theology as an appropriate model for the study of language because language creates theology; "you couldn't have theology without language." Faith, doctrine, and the notion of an ultimate supernatural being—all are possible only through language. Theology thus models a basic function of language—the creation of reality through symbol use.

Burke develops the notion of logology by drawing six analogies between language and the supernatural. These reveal principles of language and how those principles underpin ideological and motivational systems, including religion. Among the analogies he suggests is the analogy that words are to non-verbal nature as spirit is to matter. Words transcend things as spirit transcends matter; the realm of matter is pervaded by the realm of the symbolic. Another analogy suggests that the relation between the thing and its name is like the relationships among the components of the Trinity. There is a correspondence or communion between the symbolized and the symbol, for example, just as there is between the Father and the Son.

With the development of his notion of logology, Burke has not abandoned dramatism. The shift from dramatism to logology, explains Rueckert, is "the shift from the smaller category (literature or drama) to the larger category (words) from which the smaller one derives." Logology, then, might be seen as a theory and methodology about words at a higher level of generalization than that of dramatism. Another way to understand the difference between dramatism and logology is to view dramatism as concerned more with ontology or being and logology with epistemology or knowledge. Burke sees the nature of the human being in dramatistic terms and answers questions about how we know reality in logological terms. As Burke explains: "My 'Dramatism' . . . is ontological. It stresses what we *are*: the symbol-using animal. I call logology epistemological because it relates to the initial *duplication* that came into the world when we could go from *sensations* to *words* for sensations. . . . The discriminations that we make by language constitute our realm of *knowledge*, thus being epistemological." [40]

The Negative and its Consequences

Choice, which we saw earlier is essential for action, is made possible only through the concept of the negative, which provides for distinctions among acts. Burke begins the development of his notion of the negative by examining the world of motion or nature. In this world, he finds, no negatives exist; "everything simply is what it is and as it is." A tree, for example, is a tree; in no way can it be "not a tree." The only way in which something can "not be" something in nature is for it to "be" something else. As Burke explains, "To look for negatives in nature would be as absurd as though you were to go out hunting for the square root of minus-one. The negative is a function peculiar to symbol-systems, quite as the square root of minus-one is an implication of a certain mathematical symbol system." There is no image of nothing in nature.

The negative is a concept that has no referent in reality; it is purely a creation of language. The notion of the negative was added to the natural world as a product of our language; with language, humans invented the negative. The negative is the essence of language, according to Burke, and "the ultimate test of symbolicity."

The principle of the negative developed inevitably out of language because, in using language, we must recognize that a word for a thing is not that thing: "Quite as the *word* "tree" is verbal and the *thing* tree is non-verbal, so all words for the non-verbal must, by the very nature of the case, discuss the realm of the non-verbal in terms of *what it is not*." In using language, we "must have a *spontaneous feeling* for the negative"—we "must know when something is *not* quite what language, taken literally, states it to be.""[41]

Moral action arises only as a consequence of the hortatory, judgmental uses of the negative that are possible in language; moral action is not possible apart from language. Burke reaches this conclusion by examining the relationship between the negative and his starting point for dramatism, action. The negative allows the establishment of commands or admonitions that govern the actions of individuals, which Burke refers to as "thou shalt nots," or "do not do thats." The Ten Commandments are examples of such "thou shalt nots." The ability to distinguish between right and wrong thus is a consequence of the concept of the negative. Without the negative implicit in language, moral action, or action based on conceptions of right and wrong behavior (such as law, moral and social rules, and rights), would not exist.[42]

Hierarchy

The concept of the negative inherent in language necessarily leads to the establishment of hierarchies constructed on the basis of numerous negatives and commandments and the degree to which they are followed. Hierarchy might be called as well "bureaucracy," "the ladder," "a sense of order," or, as Rueckert describes it, "any kind of graded, value-charged structure in terms of which things, words, people, acts, and ideas are ranked." It deals with "the relation of higher to lower, or lower to higher, or before to after, or after to before" and concerns the "arrangement whereby each rank is overlord to its underlings and underling to its overlords."

Hierarchies may be built around any number of elements—a division of labor, possession of different properties, differentiation by ages, status positions, stages of learning, or levels of skill. No one hierarchy is inevitable, and hierarchies are crumbling and forming constantly. What is important, Burke emphasizes, is the inevitability of the hierarchic principle—the human impulse to build society around ambition or hierarchy on the basis of commandments derived from the concept of the negative.

The hierarchic principle motivates individuals to perform a variety of actions. Some seek to attain positions above them on the hierarchy. Others do not have to reach higher positions in actuality to be satisfied—they may rise vicariously by being used in some way by those higher than they. A graduate research assistant, for example, may endure verbal abuse and attack by a professor in order to assume vicariously the professor's status. Those at or near the top of the hierarchy, on the other hand, are motivated to act in certain ways by the threat of descending the hierarchy, evidenced, for example, in a family's effort to "keep up with the Joneses" lest that family slip on the hierarchy through insufficient purchase of material goods. Individuals also might allow themselves to be used by or grant favors to those below them in order to reaffirm their own positions; they might reject those lower than they for the same reason. The consequences of such actions—guilt—will be discussed as part of the pollution-purification-redemption ritual.[43]

Perfection

In any hierarchical arrangement of increasing worth or value, each class of being in the hierarchy strives to achieve the perfection that the top of the hierarchy represents. Thus, the hierarchy sets in motion a drive for perfection. Burke's notion of perfection is based on Aristotle's concept of entelechy, whereby each being aims at the perfection natural to its kind, and things are seen according to the "'perfection' or 'finishedness'" of which they are capable. The seed, for example, "'implicitly contains' a future conforming to its nature." Everything, according to Burke, is trying to perfect or complete itself—to bring to completion the kind of thing it is.

The principle of perfection operates regardless of the ends we conceive as ultimate; our ends may be positive or negative, beneficial or destructive. Thus, we may strive to be the perfect criminal, the perfect villain, or the perfect fool, just as we may seek to become the perfect teacher or the perfect husband. We attempt to live out the implications of our selected terms, whatever they are. As Burke explains, "Let a man have a gun; and if he shoots it, not because it gives him a sense of power, or because it might prepare him to defend himself, or because it has secret analogies with sexual prowess, etc., but simply because *there is a certain range of things that can be done with guns qua guns*—there you have 'perfection' as a motive."[44] The universe thus is filled with entities in various stages of progress toward perfection or completion. Whether in physics, Christianity, poetry, swimming, or growing vegetables, we drive uncontrollably and irreversibly toward the end of whatever line we are on. We attempt to perfect whatever we do so that nothing is free of this entelechial motive; thus, we are always, to an extent, rotten with or corrupted by a drive toward perfection.

This principle of perfection is derived, as is the concept of the negative, from the nature of language. According to Burke, "symbolicity, for all its imperfection, contains in itself a principle of perfection by which the symbol-using animals are always being driven, or rather, towards which they are always striving, as with a lost man trying to answer a call in a stormy night." This principle of perfection is derived from our language in that the "mere desire to name something by its 'proper' name, or to speak a language in its distinctive ways is intrinsically 'perfectionist.'" Because language is part of the essence of humans, this perfectionist quality of language becomes an essential part of humans, as well, since we have a tendency to make ourselves over "in the image of" the "distinctive trait, language." As we desire to use our language correctly, we strive toward perfection in all of our symbolic action — driving toward unattainable ideals and "given to excess" in our attempts to attain those ideals.[45]

Together, the principles of hierarchy and perfection explain how unification occurs among those who are involved in a hierarchy. All ranks share in the principle of hierarchy, accepting the upward and downward movement, regardless of the positions they hold on it. While the culminating or top stage of the hierarchy best represents the ideal of the hierarchy, every member of the hierarchy represents the order or is "infused with the spirit of the Ultimate Stage" as well. "For if any point, or 'movement,' in a hierarchic series can be said to represent, in its limited way, the principle of 'perfection' of the ultimate design," Burke explains, "then each tiny act shares in the absolute meaning of the total act."[46]

Mystery

Hierarchy, while unifying its members through the perfection embodied in its ideal, also is characterized by division. As an ordering of classes, hierarchy results inevitably in estrangement and divisiveness. The differences among members of a hierarchy arise not only from the separateness of their physical bodies but also from their different modes of life.[47] Three concepts used by Burke help explain the existence of such differences among beings — occupational psychosis, terministic screen, and trained incapacity.

"Occupational psychosis," a term Burke borrows from John Dewey, is a pronounced character of mind relating to one's occupation or "a certain way of thinking that went with a certain way of living." It reinforces particular life patterns: "To equip themselves for their kinds of work, people develop emphases, discriminations, attitudes, etc. Special preferences, dislikes, fears, hopes, apprehensions, idealizations are brought to the fore." By "occupation," Burke is not limiting his meaning to a trade or career; he means anything with which we are occupied. An occupation, for example, might be to have a hunchback, to be religious, or to be divorced.[48]

The development of a particular perspective on life results in a framework for seeing, a "terministic screen." The terms or vocabulary we use as a result of our occupations constitute a kind of screen that directs our attention to particular aspects of reality rather than others. A person trained in medicine, for example, will see life from a medical point of view or through a terministic screen of medicine. Such terminologies, then, by directing the attention differently, lead to different kinds and qualities of observations.[49]

The result of occupational psychosis and its accompanying terministic screens is "trained incapacity," the condition in which our abilities "function as blindnesses." As we adopt measures in keeping with our past training, the very soundness of that training may lead us to misjudge situations and adopt the wrong measures for the achievement of our goals; thus, our training becomes an incapacity. A person trained to work in the competitive business world of the United States, for example, may be unable to cooperate with other businesspersons because of that training, even when cooperative action alone will prevent the failure of the business.[50]

Given different occupations, terministic screens, and the consequent trained incapacity, some differences among members of a hierarchy are likely to be significant—as with a king and peasant, for example, an accountant and a musician, or a Sunday painter and a renowned professional artist. In other cases, the differences among beings are imaginary; members of different racial groups, for example, may see differences where none exist. In either case, members lack knowledge about other beings and see different modes of living in other classes as implying different modes of thought. In these differences, there is the unknown, the unexplained, the secret—or what Burke calls mystery.[51]

Mystery performs two important functions in a hierarchical system. First, it encourages the maintenance and preservation of the hierarchy because it encourages obedience:

> For, once a believer is brought to accept mysteries, he will be better minded to take orders without question from those persons whom he considers authoritative. In brief, mysteries are a good grounding for obedience, insofar as the acceptance of a mystery involves a person in the abnegation of his own personal judgment. . . . So, if a man, in accepting a "mystery," accepts someone else's judgment in place of his own, by that same token he becomes subject willingly. That is, subjection is implicit in his act of belief.[52]

Mystery, then, is used as an instrument of governance, cohesion, and preservation of the particular nature of a hierarchy.

A second function of mystery, however, is perhaps more important: it enables the members of the hierarchy to communicate with and persuade each other. Mystery allows for the transcending of the differences among members—whether real or imagined—by hiding some of the differences that do exist and allowing them to believe that they share some substance with one another. Fans of a rock star, for example, generally have little in common with their idol in terms of life style, values, wealth, or prestige—the musician is substantially higher on a number of hierarchies than they are. But to the degree that mystery cloaks their differences, the fans will be able to identify with her and be persuaded in many ways by her—whether to adopt her style of dress, to buy her albums, to attend her concerts, to buy the products she advertises, or even to take singing or dancing lessons. Burke summarizes this phenomenon:

> Rhetorically considered, Mystery is a major resource of persuasion. Endow a person, an institution, a thing with the glow or resonance of the Mystical, and you have set up a motivational appeal to which people spontaneously ("instinctively," "intuitively") respond. In this respect, an ounce of "Mystery" is worth a ton of "argument." Indeed, where Mystery is, we can be assured that the arguments will profusely follow."[53]

For Burke, the concept of the negative, derived from language, is crucial in the understanding of the communication process. It leads to the establishment of hierarchies in which we strive to perfect ourselves according to the ideal at the top. While divided from each other in numerous ways, members of a hierarchy are able to identify and communicate with each other through the mystery that hides our differences.

Pollution-Purification-Redemption: The Rhetoric of Rebirth

Rhetoric performs a number of functions for the rhetor and audience, according to Burke, but a major function is its capacity to effect redemption, rebirth, or a new identity for the individual involved.[54] The rhetoric of rebirth, which accomplishes this function, involves movement through three steps— pollution, purification, and redemption. Pollution is the initial state of guilt, an unclean condition of sins and burdens; purification is the step of cleansing or catharsis, where the guilt is sloughed off; and redemption is the stage of cleanliness in which a new state—whether physical, spiritual, or psychological—is achieved. The process is a secular version of Christianity's view of the soul's progress through hell to purgatory to heaven, which, while the process may not actually occur after death, may symbolize psychological patterns that "lie at the roots of our conduct here and now."

Pollution

We've seen that two consequences of the hierarchy are obedience and communication, but another consequence results as well—guilt or pollution. "Guilt" is Burke's term for the secular equivalent of original sin, an offense that cannot be avoided or a condition in which all people share. It "is intrinsic to the social order . . . 'inherited' by all mankind, being 'prior' to any individual lapse into 'actual sin.'" Other words for guilt might be "anxiety," "social tension," "unresolved tension," or "embarrassment."[55]

Guilt arises inevitably and "in principle" from the nature of hierarchy because it is rooted in our language system. Through the negative, various kinds of hierarchic orders are created, and all of them contain hundreds of "thou shalt nots" or commandments. No person is capable of obeying all of the commandments, and in some way, we all will fail or disobey. This failure or disobedience causes guilt, or what Burke sometimes calls the "hierarchic psychosis." The setting up of any kind of order, then, automatically makes individuals transgressors who experience guilt, a phenomenon summarized by Burke in one of his poems: "Order leads to Guilt/ (for who can keep commandments!)." Wherever an individual is on a hierarchy, then, guilt is inevitable because commandments always are being broken as we strive toward the perfection at the top: "Once you have a laddered society, then, no matter what you are, no matter where you are, you are unsettled. If you are of low status, there is the 'accusation' that you are not higher. If you are at the top, there is your false relation to those at the bottom. You have a basic, unresolved tension." Stated succinctly, "Those 'Up' are guilty of not being 'Down,' those 'Down' are certainly guilty of not being 'Up.'"[56]

In connection with his discussion of pollution, Burke introduces the notion of the fecal motive. The purgation of pollution "readily includes connotations of physical excretion"; just as "only by excretion can the body remain *healthy*," the individual can remain psychologically or spiritually healthy only by getting rid of the guilt or pollution of some aspect of the self. Thus, Burke sees a fecal motive in the redemptive process, driving the rhetor to purge from the self the negatively charged persons, places, things, and ideas.[57]

The fecal motive is indicated in rhetoric, Burke believes, in images of the Demonic Trinity, the "three principles of the erotic, urinary, and excremental." Images in rhetoric that indicate the presence of the fecal motive include the fecal, sexual, and urinal orifices of the body; their products; anything resembling them in size, shape, or color; and the acts themselves. A character who wears a brown suit might suggest feces, for example, while rain might suggest urination. Puns also might reveal such images, as, for example, use of the word "urn" might suggest urine. Such images, Burke asserts, are symbolic of the desire of an individual to be rid of some guilt and attain redemption.

Burke sees the Demonic Trinity as representing the desire for purgation of pollution because he believes "that *all* bodily processes must have their effect upon human imagery." Natural objects or events are "treated as replicas of corresponding mental states." Our sexual and bodily functions are thoroughly infused with negatives, commandments, and taboos that do not allow us to discuss them, so they are discussed in our rhetoric in disguise. In our movement toward change or redemption of any kind, body imagery is likely to surface, enabling us both to signal and purge our guilt and to discuss the unspeakable.[58]

Purification

Guilt is a permanent part of our condition; it is intrinsic in the negative and hierarchy produced by our symbol system. Some means of catharsis, purgation, purification, or cleansing are needed to rid ourselves of this guilt in order to achieve redemption. Just as our language system creates our guilt, it also is the means through which we purge ourselves of it.[59] Symbolic action itself, then, is creative, allowing us to rid ourselves of the language-caused guilt.

The two primary means for relieving our guilt using symbolic action are victimage and mortification. Victimage is the process in which guilt is transferred to a vessel or vessels outside of the rhetor. A transfer is made from the polluted, contaminated person to some other person, place, or thing, so that others are made to suffer for our sins. Victimage is the principle of scapegoating, where a victim is selected to be the representative of unwanted evils and loaded with the guilt of the victimizer.

In this transfer from the self to something else — whether a person, a symbolic figure, a group, an animal, or a place — the victim may be killed (actually or symbolically), driven away, mocked, or defiled. Another option is for the victim simply to absorb or dissolve the evil — the role played by Jesus Christ, for example. Hitler actually killed Jews as scapegoats for the German people; today, American automobile manufacturers attempt to drive away the scapegoat of Japanese imports through the implementation of governmental regulations concerning foreign cars. With victimage through symbolic action, substitution is occurring. The scapegoat in all of these cases is substituted for the victimizer and bears the victimizer's own guilt. A scapegoat thus allows an individual to "battle an external enemy instead of battling an enemy within." The greater the internal inadequacies, the more evils a rhetor is likely to "load upon the back of 'the enemy'" or scapegoat.[60]

Paradoxically, the scapegoat "combines in one figure contrary principles of identification and alienation." An original state of merger or consubstantiality characterizes victimage "in that the iniquities are shared by both the iniquitous and their chosen vessel." In other words, to serve as a scapegoat, something must share some elements with the victimizers. Yet, at the same time, division operates "in that the elements shared in common are being ritualistically alienated," driving the two apart by their differences. Finally, union or identification is once again achieved by those who are purified in the process of victimage as they define themselves in opposition to the scapegoat. Consubstantiality arises from common participation in victimage, so that if the victimizers can agree on nothing else, they "can unite on the basis of a foe shared by all." Is "it not a terrifying fact," Burke asks, "that you can never get people together except when they have a goat in common? That's the terrifying thing that I begin to see as the damnation of the human race. That's how they have to operate; they get congregation by segregation."[61]

In contrast to victimage, where guilt is transferred to someone or something else, mortification is the process in which we make ourselves suffer for our guilt or sins. Mortification is self-inflicted punishment, self-sacrifice, or self-imposed denials and restrictions designed to slay characteristics, impulses, or aspects of the self. For example, a person may feel guilt or pollution arising from a low place on a hierarchy of knowledge or prestige. Thus, she might deny herself free time and pursuit of pleasurable activities to attend classes, write papers, and study for examinations in order to achieve a college degree and the redemption of a higher place on the hierarchical ladder. Similarly, a person dieting denies the body food in an act of mortification in order to be rid of the pollution of fat and gain a new identity as a thin person with perhaps greater psychological confidence.[62]

At the second stage of the movement toward rebirth, then, strategies are employed to attempt to purge the guilt or pollution of the first stage. The two primary means for this purification or catharsis are victimage and mortification.

Redemption

The third stage of the process, redemption, is temporary rest or stasis of some kind that represents symbolic rebirth. At this stage, a change has taken place within the rhetor; the rhetor's self has been purified and redeemed. Redemption could be found in a change of identity, a new perspective, a different view on life, or a feeling "of *moving forward*, towards a *goal*" or better life in general. Thus, the process of pollution-purification-redemption is the drama of the self in quest, the process of building and finding the true self. It represents our attempts to discover and maintain our identities so that we can act purposefully, feel at home in the world, and move toward the perfection we seek. It is a life-long process of growth and change.[63]

Definition of the Human Being

Burke's definition of the human being summarizes the major concepts of his perspective on rhetoric. His concepts of symbolic action, the negative, hierarchy, perfection, and guilt are combined in his definition of the human being:

BEING BODIES THAT LEARN LANGUAGE
THEREBY BECOMING WORDLINGS
HUMANS ARE THE
SYMBOL-MAKING, SYMBOL-USING, SYMBOL-MISUSING ANIMAL
INVENTOR OF THE NEGATIVE
SEPARATED FROM OUR NATURAL CONDITION
BY INSTRUMENTS OF OUR OWN MAKING
GOADED BY THE SPIRIT OF HIERARCHY
ACQUIRING FOREKNOWLEDGE OF DEATH
AND ROTTEN WITH PERFECTION.[64]

In the concept of the symbol-using animal, we see Burke's notion that the possession and use of a symbol system separate human beings from animals and allow them to develop a neurological as well as a biological nature. A symbol system places human beings in the realm of action, where they may engage in symbolic action either wisely or foolishly.

The human being as inventor of the negative is, as we have seen, a crucial concept for Burke. The principle of the negative is inherent in a symbol system; the conception that something can be not something else comes only through language. It does not exist in nature, where things simply are.

Burke's definition of the human being also includes the notion that we are separated or alienated from our natural condition by instruments of our own making. By "nature," Burke means the world of biology, sense perception, and motion. With the tool of language, humans transcend that state of nature, and we never again can be in that purely natural condition. Once language is developed, it "is ever present," and we "must perceive nature through the fog of symbol-ridden social structures." Reality, then, becomes constructed through our symbols — we do not encounter it directly:

> But can we bring ourselves to realize just what that formula implies, just how overwhelmingly much of what we mean by "reality" has been built up for us through nothing but our symbol systems? Take away our books, and what little do we know about history, biography, even some thing so "down to earth" as the relative position of seas and continents? What is our "reality" for today . . . but all this clutter of symbols about the past combined with whatever things we know mainly through maps, magazines, newspapers, and the like about the present?[65]

By "instruments," Burke means language and all of the tools we have invented with our language. These tools, though, are not simply devices for performing physical or mechanical work; rather, he includes in the term all inventions, social structures, systems of governance, and symbolic conceptualizations such as rights, obligations, powers, authorities, awards, technology, and services. In other words, all those things that humans are able to create because they are symbol users are instruments. Words, then, are prior to these tools; only through language use are the tools able to be developed: "Remember always that no modern instrument could have been invented, or could be produced, without the use of a vast linguistic complexity." Burke recognizes that "all animals use tools in the primary sense. But only humans are tool-using in the secondary sense, (as when external agencies are used to produce other external agencies)." Only humans use tools to make tools or use symbols about symbols; only humans can remove themselves many times over from their starting point and are able to be "critics-who-write-critiques-of-critical-criticism."[66]

Burke's definition identifies, in addition to language, an element that separates humans from animals: humans, unlike animals, have a foreknowledge of death. Of course, this foreknowledge of death and our very conception of death are possible only because of our acquisition of language. In its biological state—the state of motion—death is a particular biochemical condition. But as a conception of language, death is an idea capable of, for example, symbolizing the ultimate negative or serving as a motive for action. What humans have done with their foreknowledge of death exemplifies many of Burke's essential characteristics of language.

Finally, Burke's definition includes our motivation by the spirit of perfection that infuses hierarchy. We always are driving toward the perfection embodied in the god terms at the top of the hierarchy, striving to make our lives perfect, despite the fact that such efforts cause us to experience guilt and to carry to resolution even those terminologies detrimental to our well-being.[67] We thus are "rotten with perfection."

Responses to Burke

To attempt to summarize the responses to Burke's works and to assess his contribution to rhetoric is to delve into paradox and antithesis. While a number of critics can be found to praise Burke for a particular contribution or quality, the same number can be found who criticize his work for precisely that contribution or quality. Rueckert has characterized the two opposing camps as apologists who suffer, "in varying degrees of intensity, from Burke-sickness, a disease which produces hysterical enthusiasm and loss of perspective," and adversaries, who "suffer from Burke-nausea, a state which produces hysterical anger and a corresponding loss of perspective."[68] Burke undoubtedly would appreciate the fact that the clash of the opposing sides is seen to produce consubstantiality in their shared loss of perspective, a view similar to that of Slochower, who explains that Burke strives toward "unification, a unification to be won *through* diversification."[69]

The substance of Burke's work has been praised in terms such as "brilliantly original," "penetrating," "fecund," "extraordinarily rich and suggestive," and as representative of "agility of mind," "intellectual virtuosity," and a "systematic intellect."[70] "There is no question that Burke is one of the major critical minds of the 20th century," asserts Rueckert. Others echo this theme; Kazin, for example, asserts that he "is an original. One can't really compare him with other people."[71]

Yet, some hold exactly the opposite opinion concerning the quality of Burke's work. Philosophers, in particular, tend not to see much merit in his work, and among the charges raised is that his work appears incapable of "system-building, which at length it craves." It also has been described as a "vast rambling edifice of quasi-sociological and quasi-psychoanalytical speculation" that rests "on nothing more solid than a set of unexamined and uncriticized metaphysical assumptions." It is seen as "inconclusive" and as characterized by "theoretical limitations" that "prevent him from turning up the deeper ground of the fallacies he means to destroy."[72] Perhaps Hook summarizes the negative view of the substance of Burke's work when he suggests, "I think he's a man devoid of common sense and political judgment. He has no philosophical standing whatsoever."[73]

The breadth of topics with which Burke deals also is the subject of both negative and positive comment. His work is seen by some as characterized by "a dizzying array of subject matters—among them anthropology, linguistics, religion, oratory, fiction, history, economics, philosophy, and politics. . . ."[74] The result of this breadth, says Hyman, is that his work "has had the compensatory virtue of endless fertility, suggestiveness, an inexhaustible throwing off of sparks."[75] It also frees his work, argues Duffey, "from the constraints of aesthetics, ontology, or mere semantics which have provided uneasy bounds for the views of other critics."[76]

Burke's breadth, however, is cause for complaint by critics such as Stauffer, who asserts that his work "is too eclectic. How long can we read with both attention and pleasure when, opening at random, we come on a single page that refers to, or quotes, Horace Gregory, Wallace Stevens, 'another writer,' Descartes, 'the idealist scientist Shelley,' Leibnitz, an editor, Pascal, and Rabelais? Ambition here surpasses discrimination."[77] Much of the material Burke discusses, Wirth says, "may be regarded as extraneous material from poetry, philosophy, and politics."[78] Recognition of the fact that Burke largely is self-taught and has acquired his breadth through his own study leads critics such as DuBois to suggest that Burke's motive for including so many topics in his work is simply an eagerness to display his learning: "And then Kenneth Burke is doubtless a little overproud or ostentatious of his self-made learning."[79]

Not only the content of Burke's thought but his style of writing has been criticized, described variously as "too technical and abstract," "difficult and often confusing," "turbid," "baffling," "obscure," and "not 'inviting.'"[80] "The greatest difficulty that confronts the reader of Burke," Hook goes so far as to assert, "is finding out what he means," a remark echoed in the charge that Burke does not write English.[81] Perhaps these negative reactions best are summarized by Warren, who explains that understanding the point of Burke's writing is difficult: "To discern its drift is another matter; and one has long to wait before the smoke sufficiently clears to let one discover who has won and why."[82]

Two sources of difficulty with Burke's style are mentioned most often. The unusual and specialized terminology he employs creates much of his distinctive style. As Nichols explains, "In part the difficulty arises from the numerous vocabularies he employs. His words in isolation are usually simple enough, but he often uses them in new contexts."[83] Another characteristic of Burke's style is that his discussion of central issues often is drowned amid discussions and references that appear irrelevant to the main line of thought. The result, Stauffer suggests, is "a style where exceptions, illustrations, by-plays, new ideas, and sudden speculations burgeon from the main stem of the thought."[84] As Knox explains, he seems to have a "sense of responsibility to shovel around a growing heap of apparently uncorrelated documentation."[85]

Yet, some argue that Burke "has said something worth saying and said it well."[86] While some describe his style in positive terms such as "incisive eloquence,"[87] more common is to recognize his style as difficult and then justify it. His "style is seen to be," asserts Rosenberg, "by the steady and serene progress of its arguments, remarkably suited to its purpose."[88] Nichols finds justification for the difficulty of his style in the quality of the thought, attributing some of the difficulty of comprehension to "the compactness of his writing, the uniqueness of his organizational patterns, the penetration of his thought, and the breadth of his endeavor."[89] Such an undertaking as Burke's, these arguments suggest, requires the kind of style Burke employs.

Disagreement over the value of Burke's style leads, as Burke might suggest it would, to unity—based on the agreement that the active participation and commitment of the reader are required in reading the work of Burke. He "has never dissolved it into pap for the multitude or codified it into tablets for quick absorption by graduate students. He has never made it with a book club."[90] Thus, only the determined push on: "Let anyone avoid it who is not endowed with some philosophic, linguistic, and esthetic training coupled with some power of taut attentiveness"; it requires that the reader be someone "with a strenuous brain who wishes to go pioneering."[91] If the reader is willing to engage in the adventure, however, the results are "rewarding," "exhilarating," and "extraordinarily enriching."[92] In short, as De Mott explains, Burke's work "is generous to its reader: it tells him he has an active mind, is agile and quick, relishes complication, is scornful of emotional posturing and human enough to enjoy being silly now and then.''[93]

Burke's contributions to rhetoric are less in dispute than is the usefulness of his style. Agreement in this area may be due to recognition of the rhetorical focus of his work. Nichols, for example, asserts that "he has become the most profound student of rhetoric now writing in America," while Melia argues that he is "probably the most significant contributor to rhetorical theory since Cicero." Similarly, Duncan asserts, "As matters now stand, it is unwise to talk about communication without some understanding of Burke.''[94] Three primary contributions Burke makes to rhetorical thought seem to justify such praise.

First, while many earlier rhetoricians intended and attempted to build an entire system, theory, or philosophy to explain how rhetoric operates, Burke has come very close to creating it. His system allows for the discovery of the way the mind works and why in its use of rhetoric. He incorporates into his perspective on rhetoric assumptions about the nature of the human being, the human's relation to rhetoric, the nature of rhetoric, and the part rhetoric plays in the motivations of human beings. While he still is working out some aspects of his perspective and their ramifications, his work represents near completion of a coherent, thoroughly developed system explaining the operation of rhetoric in human life.

Second, Burke makes a major contribution to rhetoric in his reaffirmation of the importance of rhetoric and its study in human life. He sees rhetoric as at the very center of life, as the ground that underlies all human activity and that is one with all human action. Rhetoric is not something apart from life or one component of life; it is life. To understand the operation and nature of rhetoric, for Burke, is to understand a great many other things about human beings as well.

Perhaps more than any other contemporary scholar of rhetoric, Burke's works also have contributed to the practice of rhetorical criticism. His concepts have suggested numerous methods to be used in the analysis of rhetoric. The pentad, strategies of redemption, types of form, and identification, for example, all have been used extensively by rhetorical critics in their studies of specific rhetorical acts. Yet, as Burke explicitly suggests and as he demonstrates in his own criticism, the methods arising from his notions should not and do not limit the critic to these notions alone. They are to be used only as guides for the critic to encourage an exploration of various perspectives and interpretations.[95] His methods, more than many others, allow for expansion and freedom, not reduction and confinement.

The contradictions and paradoxes of Burke's work and the critics who respond to it seem reconciled when his work is viewed from the perspective that its primary concern is with rhetoric. That his work may lack formal philosophical grounding is less important given a goal of the explanation of rhetoric, which deals not with formal logic but with the reasoning of humans in their daily lives. His breadth is less irrelevant excursion than a recognition that the scope of rhetoric is broad, encompassing all of the topics with which he deals and more. His style, too, seems less formidable when it is viewed as a rhetorical strategy designed to invite the reader to active participation with Burke in a process of sharing visions of the world. Blackmur describes well Burke's focus on rhetoric and the appropriateness of the rhetorical perspective by which to judge it, explaining that while some "may object to being called rhetoricians . . . Kenneth Burke must have found it his first cradle-word, and I think he would rather be called Rhetor, as honorific and as description, than anything else."[96]

Notes

[1] Stanley Edgar Hyman, *The Armed Vision: A Study in the Methods of Modern Literary Criticism* (1947; rpt. New York: Vintage, 1955), p. 359.

[2] William H. Rueckert, *Kenneth Burke and the Drama of Human Relations*, 2nd ed. (1963; rpt. Berkeley: University of California Press, 1982), p. 227.

[3] Matthew Josephson, *Life Among the Surrealists: A Memoir* (New York: Holt, Rinehart and Winston, 1962), p. 35.

[4] Biographical information on Burke was obtained from the following sources: John Woodcock, "An Interview with Kenneth Burke," *Sewanee Review*, 85 (October-December 1977), 704-18; Austin Warren, "Kenneth Burke: His Mind and Art," *Sewanee Review*, 41 (1933), 225-36; Ben Yagoda, "Kenneth Burke," *Horizon*, 23 (June 1980), 66-69; Carlin Romano, "A Critic Who Has His Critics—Pro and Con," *Philadelphia Inquirer*, March 6, 1984, sec. D, p. 1; "Critic, Poet Kenneth Burke, 84 Will Receive Literature Medal," *Denver Post* April 20, 1981, p. 32; Armin Paul Frank, *Kenneth Burke* (New York: Twayne, 1969), pp. 19-27; Daniel Aaron, moderator, "Thirty Years Later: Memories of the First American Writers' Congress," *American Scholar*, 35 (Summer 1966), 507; Robert L. Heath, *Realism and Relativism: A Perspective on Kenneth Burke* (Macon, GA: Mercer University Press, 1986); Paul Jay, ed., *The Selected Correspondence of Kenneth Burke and Malcolm Cowley 1915-1981* (New York: Viking, 1988), p. 56; Grant Webster, *The Republic of Letters: A History of Postwar American Literary Opinion* (Baltimore: Johns Hopkins University Press, 1979); and J. Clarke Rountree, III, ed., "Richard Kostelanetz Interviews Kenneth Burke," *Iowa Review*, 17 (Fall 1987), 1-23.

[5] For a description of what purportedly is contained in *The Symbolic of Motives*, see Rueckert, *Kenneth Burke*, pp. 230-35, 288-92.

[6] Kenneth Burke, "Know Thyself," in his *Collected Poems 1915-1967* (Berkeley: University of California Press, 1968), p. 208.

[7] Kenneth Burke, *A Rhetoric of Motives* (1950; rpt. Berkeley: University of California Press, 1969), pp. 41, 43.

[8] Victor J. Vitanza, "A Mal-Lingering Thought (Tragic—Comedic) About KB's Visit," *Pre/Text*, 6 (Fall/Winter 1985), 163-64.

[9] Substance is discussed in Burke, *A Rhetoric of Motives*, pp. 20-21, 24, 64; and Kenneth Burke, *A Grammar of Motives* (1945; rpt. Berkeley: University of California Press, 1969), pp. 21-23, 57.

[10] Identification is discussed in Burke, *A Rhetoric of Motives*, pp. xiv, 21, 24, 46, 55; and Kenneth Burke, *Language as Symbolic Action: Essays on Life, Literature, and Method* (Berkeley: University of California Press, 1966), p. 301.

[11] Burke discusses types of identification in *Dramatism and Development* (Barre, Mass.: Clark University Press, 1972), p. 28; and *A Rhetoric of Motives*, p. 20.

[12] For discussions of division, see Burke, *A Rhetoric of Motives*, pp. 21-22, 130, 150, 211, 326; and Kenneth Burke, *The Philosophy of Literary Form: Studies in Symbolic Action* (1941; rpt. Berkeley: University of California Press, 1973), p. 306.

[13] Unconscious persuasion is discussed in Burke, *Language as Symbolic Action*, p. 301; and Kenneth Burke, "Rhetoric—Old and New," *Journal of General Education*, 5 (1951), 203.

[14] For Burke's discussion of self as audience, see *A Rhetoric of Motives*, pp. 38, 44, 46.

[15] For a discussion of the relationship Burke sees between rhetoric and poetics, see Burke, *Language as Symbolic Action*, pp. 28, 38, 102, 302, 304.

[16] Nonverbal rhetoric is discussed in Burke, *A Rhetoric of Motives*, pp. 161, 171-73, 186; and Burke, *Language as Symbolic Action*, p. 301.

[17] For a discussion of rhetoric as a strategy, see Burke, *The Philosophy of Literary Form*, pp. 1, 6, 109, 283, 298, 304; and Kenneth Burke, *Counter-Statement* (1931; rpt. Berkeley: University of California Press, 1968), pp. xi, 105.

[18] Burke discusses the ways in which rhetoric functions to provide assistance in orientation and adjustment in *Counter-Statement*, pp. 154-56; and *The Philosophy of Literary Form*, pp. 64, 294, 298-99.

[19] Style is discussed in Burke, *The Philosophy of Literary Form*, pp. 1, 126-30, 309-10; and Kenneth Burke, *Permanence and Change: An Anatomy of Purpose* (1935; rpt. Indianapolis: Bobbs-Merrill, 1965), pp. 50-58.

[20] See Burke, *Language as Symbolic Action*, p. 487; and Burke, *A Rhetoric of Motives*, p. 65, for a discussion of the inseparability of form and content.

[21] For discussions of the relationship among form, effects, and expectation, see: Heath, pp. 59-61; and Kenneth Burke, "A Philosophy of Drama," *University of Chicago Magazine*, September, 1961, pp. 7-8, 20.

[22] Burke's definition of form is discussed in Burke, *Counter-Statement*, pp. 31, 124, 138; and Rueckert, *Kenneth Burke*, pp. 26-27.

[23] Types of form are discussed in: Burke, *Counter-Statement*, pp. 124-29; Burke, *Language as Symbolic Action*, p. 486; Burke, *Dramatism and Development*, p. 16; and Kenneth Burke, "Dramatic Form—And: Tracking Down Implications," *Tulane Drama Review*, 10 (Summer 1966), 54.

[24] Burke, *A Rhetoric of Motives*, pp. 58-59.

[25] For a discussion of dramatism, see: Burke, *Language as Symbolic Action*, p. 54; Burke, *The Rhetoric of Religion*, pp. 40-41; Burke, *The Philosophy of Literary Form*, p. 103; Burke, *A Grammar of Motives*, pp. xxii, 60; Kenneth Burke, "The Five Master Terms: Their Place in a 'Dramatistic' Grammar of Motives," *View*, 2 (June 1943), 50-52; Kenneth Burke, "Dramatism," *International Encyclopedia of the Social Sciences*, ed. David L. Sills ([New York]: Macmillan/Free Press, 1968), VII, 445-52; Kenneth Burke, "Rhetoric, Poetics, and Philosophy," in *Rhetoric, Philosophy, and Literature: An Exploration*, ed. Don M. Burks (West Lafayette, IN: Purdue University Press, 1978), pp. 32-33; *Webster's Third New International Dictionary*, 1965, p. 685; Heath, pp. 132-42, 160; and Greig E. Henderson, *Kenneth Burke: Literature and Language as Symbolic Action* (Athens: University of Georgia Press, 1988), p. 101.

[26] The distinction between action and motion is discussed in: Burke, "Dramatism," p. 445; Burke, *Permanence and Change*, pp. 162, 215; Burke, *Language as Symbolic Action*, pp. 28, 53, 63, 67, 482; Kenneth Burke, *The Rhetoric of Religion: Studies in Logology* (Berkeley: University of California Press, 1970), pp. 16, 274; and Woodcock, p. 709.

[27] Burke discusses conditions required for action in: *The Rhetoric of Religion*, pp. 39, 188, 281; *A Grammar of Motives*, pp. 14, 276; *The Philosophy of Literary Form*, p. xvi; and Burke, "Dramatism," p. 447.

[28] For a discussion of dramatism as literal, see: Burke, "Rhetoric, Poetics, and Philosophy," pp. 16, 25, 27-30; Burke, "Dramatism," p. 448; Burke, *A Rhetoric of Motives*, p. 283; Heath, pp. 2, 121, 145, 156, 166, 167; Bernard L. Brock, Kenneth Burke, Parke G. Burgess, and Herbert W. Simons, "Dramatism as Ontology or Epistemology: A Symposium," *Communication Quarterly*, 33 (Winter 1985), 17-33; and Walter R. Fisher and Wayne Brockriede, "Kenneth Burke's Realism," *Central States Speech Journal*, 35 (Spring 1984), 35-42.

29 Burke, *The Philosophy of Literary Form*, p. 20. For more on Burke's notion of motives, see: Burke, *Permanence and Change*, pp. 23-36; and Gerard A. Hauser, *Introduction to Rhetorical Theory* (New York: Harper and Row, 1986), pp. 131-37.

30 The pentad is discussed in: Burke, *A Grammar of Motives*, pp. xv, xvi, xx; Kenneth Burke, "The Tactics of Motivation," *Chimera*, 26 (Spring 1943), 42; Charles Conrad, "Phases, Pentads, and Dramatistic Critical Process," *Central States Speech Journal*, 35 (Summer 1984), 94-104; Timothy W. Crusius, "A Case for Kenneth Burke's Dialectic and Rhetoric," *Philosophy and Rhetoric*, 19 (1986), 23-37; Joseph R. Gusfield, "The Bridge Over Separated Lands: Kenneth Burke's Significance for the Study of Social Action," in *The Legacy of Kenneth Burke*, ed. Herbert W. Simons and Trevor Melia (Madison: University of Wisconsin Press, 1989), pp. 28-54; and Heath, pp. 184-93.

31 Burke discusses act in *A Grammar of Motives*, pp. 14, 227-74.

32 Scene is discussed in: Burke, *A Grammar of Motives*, pp. xvi, 12, 77, 84, 85, 90; Burke, *The Rhetoric of Religion*, p. 26; and Burke, *Language as Symbolic Action*, p. 360. For a discussion of circumference in connection with scene, see: C. Ronald Kimberling, *Kenneth Burke's Dramatism and Popular Arts* (Bowling Green, OH: Bowling Green State University Popular Press, 1982), pp. 17-18.

33 See Burke, *A Grammar of Motives*, pp. 20, 171-226, for a discussion of agent.

34 Agency and purpose are discussed in Burke, *A Grammar of Motives*, pp. 275-320.

35 Burke discusses motive in *Philosophy of Literary Form*, pp. 18, 90; and *Permanence and Change*, pp. 29-36.

36 Attitude is discussed in Burke, *A Grammar of Motives*, pp. 20, 236, 242, 443, 476; and Burke, *Dramatism and Development*, p. 23.

37 For a discussion of Burke's concept of ratio, see Burke, *Dramatism and Development*, p. 22; Burke, *A Grammar of Motives*, pp. xix, 3, 15, 18-19, 53; and Vito Signorile, "Ratios and Causes: The Pentad as an Etiological Scheme in Sociological Explanation," in *The Legacy of Kenneth Burke*, ed. Herbert W. Simons and Trevor Melia (Madison: University of Wisconsin Press, 1989), pp. 81-82.

38 For an example of this use of the pentad, see: Sonja K. Foss, "Constituted by Agency: The Discourse and Practice of Rhetorical Criticism," in *Speech Communication: Essays to Commemorate the 75th Anniversary of The Speech Communication Association*, ed. Gerald M. Phillips and Julia T. Wood (Carbondale: Southern Illinois University Press, 1990), pp. 33-51.

39 A summary of the concept of logology can be found in Rueckert, *Kenneth Burke*, pp. 236, 242,; Frank, p. 141; Fisher and Brockriede, pp. 36-37; Heath, pp. 117-20; David Cratis Williams, "Under the Sign of (an)nihilation: Burke in the Age of Nuclear Destruction and Critical Deconstruction," in *The Legacy of Kenneth Burke*, ed. Herbert W. Simons and Trevor Melia (Madison: University of Wisconsin Press, 1989), p. 212; Rountree, p. 13; and Kenneth Burke, "Dramatism and Logology," *Communication Quarterly*, 33 (Spring 1985), 91.

40 Theology as a model for symbol use is discussed in: Burke, *The Rhetoric of Religion*, pp. v-vi, 33-34; Frank, p. 142; and Rueckert, *Kenneth Burke*, p. 241.

41 Burke discusses the negative in: *The Rhetoric of Religion*, pp. 18-22, 41, 283; *Language as Symbolic Action*, pp. 9, 419-20, 457, 461, 472; and *A Grammar of Motives*, pp. 295-97. A summary of the concept of the negative can be found in Heath, pp. 98-102.

42 Moral action is discussed in Burke, *The Rhetoric of Religion*, pp. 187, 278, 290-91; and Burke, *Language as Symbolic Action*, pp. 421-22.

43 Discussions of hierarchy can be found in: Burke, *A Rhetoric of Motives*, pp. 118, 138-41, 265; Burke, *Language as Symbolic Action*, pp. 15-16, 89; and Rueckert, *Kenneth Burke*, pp. 131, 144.

44 For a discussion of perfection, see: Burke, *A Rhetoric of Motives*, p. 14; Burke, *The Rhetoric of Religion*, pp. 246-47; and Kenneth Burke, "Freedom and Authority in the Realm of the Poetic Imagination," in *Freedom and Authority in Our Time: Twelfth Symposium of the Conference on Science, Philosophy and Religion*, ed. Lyman Bryson, Louis Finkelstein, R.M. MacIver, and Richard McKeon (New York: Conference on Science, Philosophy and Religion, in Their Relation to the Democratic Way of Life, Inc.; dist. New York: Harper, 1953), p. 367.

45 Perfection as derived from language is discussed in: Burke, *Language as Symbolic Action*, pp. 16-17; Burke, *The Rhetoric of Religion*, p. 296; Burke, *Permanence and Change*, pp. 184-85;

Burke, "Rhetoric, Poetics, and Philosophy," p. 25; and Rueckert, *Kenneth Burke*, p. 135.

46 Burke discusses the infusion of the ideal throughout a hierarchy in *A Rhetoric of Motives*, pp. 118, 141, 195.

47 For a discussion of the notion of division, see: Burke, *A Rhetoric of Motives*, pp. 139, 147, 211; Burke, *Language as Symbolic Action*, p. 15; and Burke, *The Rhetoric of Religion*, p. 308.

48 Occupational psychosis is discussed in Burke, *Permanence and Change*, pp. 40-44, 237, 240; and Burke, *The Philosophy of Literary Form*, p. 315.

49 Burke's discussion of the terministic screen can be found in *Language as Symbolic Action*, pp. 44-52; and Burke, *Permanence and Change*, p. 240.

50 Burke discusses trained incapacity in *Permanence and Change*, pp. 7-11.

51 Mystery is discussed in: Burke, *A Rhetoric of Motives*, pp. 122, 174; Burke, *The Rhetoric of Religion*, pp. 308-09; Kenneth Burke, *Attitudes Toward History* (New York: New Republic, 1937), II, 3; and Kenneth Burke, "Mysticism as a Solution to the Poet's Dilemma: II: Appendix," in *Spiritual Problems in Contemporary Literature*, ed. Stanley Romaine Hopper (New York: Institute for Religious and Social Studies, 1952), p. 105.

52 Burke, *The Rhetoric of Religion*, p. 307. Burke also discusses mystery as a source of obedience and cohesion in *A Rhetoric of Motives*, p. 174; and *The Rhetoric of Religion*, p. 309.

53 Burke, "Mysticism as a Solution," p. 105. Burke also discusses mystery as a source of persuasion in *A Rhetoric of Motives*, pp. 276, 278.

54 Burke, *Permanence and Change*, p. 84.

55 Guilt is discussed in: Burke, *The Rhetoric of Religion*, pp. 4-5; Burke, *A Rhetoric of Motives*, p. 148; Burke, *Language as Symbolic Action*, pp. 81, 94, 144; and Burke, *Permanence and Change*, p. 283.

56 Burke discusses the connection between guilt and hierarchy in: *Permanence and Change*, p. 279; *Dramatism and Development*, p. 44; *The Rhetoric of Religion*, pp. 4, 222, 294; *Language as Symbolic Action*, p. 15; and Hiram Haydn, moderator, "American Scholar Forum: The New Criticism," *American Scholar*, 20 (Winter 1950-51), 95.

57 The fecal motive is discussed in Burke, *Language as Symbolic Action*, pp. 308, 341. A summary of the concept is provided in Rueckert, *Kenneth Burke*, p. 104.

58 For Burke's discussion of the Demonic Trinity, see: *A Grammar of Motives*, p. 302; *Language as Symbolic Action*, pp. 340, 345, 477; *The Philosophy of Literary Form*, p. 36; and *A Rhetoric of Motives*, p. 256. A summary of the concept is provided in Rueckert, *Kenneth Burke*, pp. 102, 149, 223.

59 Language as a means of purgation is discussed in Burke, *The Rhetoric of Religion*, p. 231; and Kenneth Burke, *Terms for Order*, ed. Stanley Edgar Hyman and Barbara Karmiller (Bloomington: Indiana University Press, 1964), p. 166.

60 Burke discusses victimage in *Language as Symbolic Action*, pp. 47, 203, 435, 478; and *The Philosophy of Literary Form*, pp. 39, 203. A summary of the concept is provided in Rueckert, *Kenneth Burke*, p. 151.

61 Identification and alienation in victimage are discussed in: Burke, *A Rhetoric of Motives*, pp. 140-41, 265-66; Burke, *A Grammar of Motives*, p. 406; Burke, *The Philosophy of Literary Form*, p. 193; and Aaron, p. 499 [Burke was a participant in the forum].

62 Burke discusses mortification in *The Rhetoric of Religion*, pp. 190, 206.

63 Redemption is discussed in: Burke, *The Philosophy of Literary Form*, p. 203; Burke, *Attitudes Toward History*, II, 46; Kenneth Burke, *Attitudes Toward History* (New York: New Republic, 1937), I, 204-05; and Burke, *Permanence and Change*, p. 78. A summary of the concept is provided in Rueckert, *Kenneth Burke*, pp. 45, 48, 150.

64 Kenneth Burke, "Poem," in *The Legacy of Kenneth Burke*, ed. Herbert W. Simons and Trevor Melia (Madison: University of Wisconsin Press, 1989), p. 263.

65 Burke, *Language as Symbolic Action*, p. 5. Burke also discusses the pervasiveness of symbolicity in *A Rhetoric of Motives*, p. 192; and *Language as Symbolic Action*, pp. 378, 456.

66 Instruments or tools are discussed in: Kenneth Burke, "Creation Myth," in his *Collected Poems 1915-1967*, p. 5; Burke, *The Rhetoric of Religion*, pp. 276, 288; Burke, *A Grammar of Motives*, p. 319; and Burke, *A Rhetoric of Motives*, p. 288.

67 Burke discusses the motivation of perfection in *Language as Symbolic Action*, p. 18; and *A Rhetoric of Motives*, pp. 187, 299-301, 333.

68 Rueckert, *Kenneth Burke*, pp. 4-5.

69 Harry Slochower, in William H. Rueckert, ed., *Critical Responses to Kenneth Burke: 1924-1966* (Minneapolis: University of Minnesota Press, 1969), p. 135. While most of the essays in this book are reprinted from other sources, we have chosen to cite them in Rueckert's book for the ease of the reader.

70 John Crowe Ransom, Charles Morris, Donald A. Stauffer, Abraham Kaplan, Arthur E. DuBois, Joseph Frank, Kermit Lansner, in Rueckert, *Critical Responses*, pp. 158, 163, 187, 170, 83, 403, 261.

71 Rueckert and Alfred Kazin, as quoted in Romano, p. 6.

72 Austin Warren, Abraham Kaplan, Charles Morris, Harold Rosenberg, in Rueckert, *Critical Responses*, pp. 53, 168-69, 163, 29.

73 Sidney Hook, as quoted in Romano, p. 6.

74 Herbert W. Simons, "Introduction: Kenneth Burke and the Rhetoric of the Human Sciences," in *The Legacy of Kenneth Burke*, ed. Herbert W. Simons and Trevor Melia (Madison: University of Wisconsin Press, 1989), p. 4.

75 Hyman, *The Armed Vision*, p. 384.

76 Bernard I. Duffey, in Rueckert, *Critical Responses*, p. 229.

77 Donald A. Stauffer, in Rueckert, *Critical Responses*, p. 184.

78 Louis Wirth, in Rueckert, *Critical Responses*, p. 102.

79 Arthur E. DuBois, in Rueckert, *Critical Responses*, p. 82.

80 Charles I. Glicksburg, Marie Hochmuth Nichols, Max Black, Charles Morris, Sidney Hook, Harry Slochower, in Rueckert, *Critical Responses*, pp. 79, 283, 168, 90, 131.

81 Sidney Hook, in Rueckert, *Critical Responses*, p. 89; and John Simon, as quoted in Romano, p. 6.

82 Austin Warren, in Rueckert, *Critical Responses*, p. 52.

83 Marie Hochmuth Nichols, in Rueckert, *Critical Responses*, p. 283.

84 Donald A. Stauffer, in Rueckert, *Critical Responses*, pp. 183-84.

85 George Knox, in Rueckert, *Critical Responses*, p. 318.

86 Louis Wirth, in Rueckert, *Critical Responses*, p. 102.

87 Margaret Schlauch, in Rueckert, *Critical Responses*, p. 106.

88 Harold Rosenberg, in Rueckert, *Critical Responses*, p. 26.

89 Marie Hochmuth Nichols, in Rueckert, *Critical Responses*, p. 283.

90 Robert M. Adams, Foreword, in Rueckert, *Critical Responses*.

91 Donald A. Stauffer, in Rueckert, *Critical Responses*, pp. 185-86.

92 Charles Morris, Austin Warren, Harry Slochower, in Rueckert, *Critical Responses*, pp. 163, 52, 131.

93 Benjamin De Mott, in Rueckert, *Critical Responses*, p. 361.

94 Marie Hochmuth Nichols, in Rueckert, *Critical Responses*, p. 284; Trevor Melia, as quoted in Romano, p. 6; and Hugh Dalziel Duncan, in Rueckert, *Critical Responses*, p. 259.

95 Burke encourages critical pluralism in *The Philosophy of Literary Form*, p. 21; and *A Rhetoric of Motives*, p. 265.

96 R.P. Blackmur, in Rueckert, *Critical Responses*, p. 245.

8

Michel Foucault

A cursory review of the writings and educational background of Michel Foucault might suggest that his contributions to rhetorical thought were somewhat limited. His educational training was in philosophy, psychology, and psychiatry. The titles of his books include *Discipline and Punish, The History of Sexuality*, and *The Order of Things*, suggesting that he was more concerned with subjects such as the history of institutions or the history of ideas than with rhetoric. Foucault described himself as "a dealer in instruments, an inventor of recipes, a cartographer,"[1] a description that did not encourage a view of his work as concerned with rhetoric. Yet, Foucault discussed several concepts that provide the basis for a coherent perspective on rhetoric, and these will be our focus here.

Born in Poitier, France, in 1926, Foucault began his study in local state schools. When his father, a surgeon, became dissatisfied with his progress, he was transferred to a Catholic school. While he did not yet know what to do with his life, he was attracted to the scholarly environment:

> We did not know when I was ten or eleven years old, whether we would become German or remain French. We did not know whether we would die or not in the bombing and so on. When I was sixteen or seventeen I knew only one thing: school life was an environment protected from exterior menaces, from politics. And I have always been fascinated by living protected in a scholarly environment, in an intellectual milieu. Knowledge is for me that which must function as a protection of individual existence and as a comprehension of the exterior world. I think that's it. Knowledge as a means of surviving by understanding.[2]

Foucault was dissatisfied, however, with his early exposure to the academic environment. He saw his experience in the French educational system as a continual postponement of promised secret knowledge. In primary school, he was told that the most important things would be revealed at the lycée. At the lycée, he was told he would have to wait until his final year, only to be told at that point that the knowledge he wanted was to be found in the study of philosophy, which would be revealed at the university level. So Foucault pursued his interest in philosophy at the École Normale Supérieure in Paris, a school designed for the intellectual elite who wished to become teachers. His professors included Jean Hyppolite, Georges Canguilhem, and Georges Dumézil, and he earned his university degree in philosophy in 1948.

Foucault's study of philosophy, however, simply convinced him that there was no secret knowledge. Disillusioned with philosophy and appalled at the prospect of spending the rest of his life teaching it, he speculated that science — and the science of human behavior or psychology, in particular — might provide the kind of knowledge he sought. Two years after he had earned his philosophy degree, Foucault took a degree in psychology; this was followed in 1952 by another in psychiatry.

During the next three years, Foucault conducted research and observed psychiatric practice in mental hospitals and taught classes in psycho-pathology at the École Normale. In 1954, he published a book on the subject, *Maladie mentale et personnalité* [*Mental Illness and Personality*], which provides definitions of psychiatric terms and traces the origins of mental illness. In the early 1960s, when the book had gone out of print and a new edition was planned, Foucault changed the title to *Maladie mentale et psychologie* [*Mental Illness and Psychology*] and replaced the second part with new material. Instead of tracing mental illness back to conditions of an individual's development, as he had in the first edition, here Foucault sees mental illness as a changing, historically conditioned notion. In later years, Foucault regarded the book as a product of juvenile thinking; yet, it contains the origins of some of the basic ideas Foucault developed in his later works.

Influenced by the discovery that scientific understanding was as illusory as the study of philosophy had been and by his reading of the works of Friedrich Nietzsche, Foucault left France: "Nietzsche was a revelation to me. I felt that there was someone quite different from what I had been taught. I read him with a great passion and broke with my life, left my job in the asylum, left France: I had the feeling I had been trapped. Through Nietzsche, I had become a stranger to all that." [3] He accepted a teaching position in the French department at Uppsala University in Sweden, where he stayed for four years. In 1958, he left Uppsala for Warsaw, Poland, where he served as director of the French Institute; the following year, he accepted a similar post in Hamburg, Germany. Foucault's experiences abroad introduced him to various forms of social and political power; for at

> the moment when I left France, freedom for personal life was very sharply restricted there. At this time Sweden was supposed to be a much freer country. And there I had the experience that a certain kind of freedom may have, not exactly the same effects, but as many restrictive effects as a directly restrictive society. That was an important experience for me. Then I had the opportunity of spending one year in Poland where, of course, the restrictions and oppressive power of the Communist party are really something quite different. In a rather short period of time I had the experience of an old traditional society, as France was in the late 1940s and early 1950s, and the new free society which was Sweden. I won't say I had the total experience of all the political possibilities but I had a sample of what the possibilities of Western societies were at that moment. That was a good experience. [4]

In Germany, Foucault completed his book, *Folie et déraison: Histoire de la folie à l'âge classique* [*Madness and Civilization*]. The work became his doctoral dissertation in the area of history of science; he submitted it to Georges Canguilhem in 1960, and it was published in 1961. In the book, Foucault discusses the relationship between the conception of madness and the notion of reason. Once reason was established as supreme in Western culture, he argues, anything that constituted a threat to it was disregarded and excluded from the culture, including the notion of madness.

In 1961, Foucault returned to France to become head of the philosophy department at the University of Clermont-Ferrand, remaining at the school for six years. In 1963, he published *Naissance de la clinique* [*The Birth of the Clinic*], which focuses on the point in the eighteenth century when medicine based on the classification of diseases gave way to empirical observation that constitutes medicine as we know it today. Different methods of treatment accompanied this shift, each suggesting entirely different principles of discourse.

Foucault's next work was *Raymond Roussel* [*Death and the Labyrinth: The World of Raymond Roussel*], a work in which he engages in the practice of literary criticism as he examines images, themes, word choice, meanings and functions of words, and order in the works of Roussel, a French writer of the early twentieth century. Although different in subject and style from his other books, Foucault's purpose here is similar to the goal that characterizes his larger project—to discover the rules of discursive practice governing texts; here, the text is the work of Roussel.

Foucault accepted a teaching position at the University of Tunis in 1966 at the time his next major work, *Les mots et les choses* [*The Order of Things*], was published. In it, Foucault identifies three great epochs in European thought; examines the continuities and transformations in the study of living beings, language, and political economy in these epochs; and shows how they all were organized according to the same conceptual structure.

While Foucault was teaching in Tunisia, a period of revolt swept France. It began in May, 1968, with student riots at universities in protest of France's system of higher education. The revolt then spread to the workers, resulting in strikes against many manufacturing companies; the train, subway, and airline systems; the postal service; and the police. Although Foucault did not actually witness or participate in these events, he was affected by the questions they generated. His attention was drawn to the many places in which power was exercised and the many forms it assumed—in housing, schools, prisons, asylums, hospitals, and the army. This awareness led him to study the notion of power and to recognize the political implications of his own work.

Foucault's political awareness, however, had nothing to do with electoral preferences and, in fact, to specify Foucault's own ideological position is difficult. Like many intellectuals of his generation, Foucault joined the Communist Party after World War II but quit it in 1951, after only two years; Marxism interested him but left him dissatisfied. He attributed the attraction of Marxism to its emphasis on a "dream of another world," which Foucault said is appealing to anyone who grew up under the Nazi occupation.

Foucault rejected not only Marxism but also liberalism because of its service to the social status quo, conservatism because of its dependence on tradition, and anarchism because of its naive faith in a benign human nature.[5] He remained politically unclassifiable and saw politics and power as involving much more than such ideologies: "whatever the legal system, mechanisms of power constrain the individual and direct his conduct in an effort to normalize him."

When the French government dispersed the concentration of the University of Paris in the Latin Quarter and set up a number of autonomous campuses throughout the city, Foucault was offered the position of chair of the philosophy department at the experimental university at Vincennes. During his tenure there, Foucault published *L'archéologie du savoir* [*The Archaeology of Knowledge*], in which he criticizes the traditional method of dealing with history in terms of periods and unifying themes and suggests that history be viewed instead from the perspective of contradictions and discontinuities.

In 1970, Foucault was elected to a position in the Collège de France in Paris, a coveted academic honor. His obligation in this position was to deliver ten lectures per year that were open to the public. At his election, Foucault was able to provide his own description for his area of study, and he selected "Professor of the History of Systems of Thought." With this title, Foucault suggested that his primary concern was with the situation of human beings within systems of thought and practice that become so much a part of us that we no longer experience them as confinements but view them as the very structure of being human. He saw his work as focused on the question: to what extent might it "be possible to think differently, instead of legitimating what is already known?"[6]

A few weeks after Foucault delivered his inaugural lecture at the college, hunger strikes began among France's leftist political prisoners. They demanded the special treatment required for political prisoners and initiated a movement of solidarity with all other prisoners. In response, Foucault and others started the Group d'Information sur les Prisons [Information on Prisons Group] (GIP), designed to help prisoners speak out about prison conditions. The riots that occurred in a number of French prisons in 1972 attested to the GIP's effectiveness, and at the end of that year, the founders withdrew and handed over the leadership of the struggle to the prisoners themselves. Giving voice to those whose discourse is not valued or generally heard was an important concept for Foucault.

Foucault continued his work on prisons during the 1971-1972 academic year, when he devoted his course at the college to the topic of penal theories. While researching this topic, he discovered the case of Pierre Rivière, a twenty-year-old French peasant who was convicted of murdering his mother, sister, and brother in 1836. While awaiting trial, Rivière wrote a forty-page account of his life, and Foucault organized a seminar to study the case. In 1973, with the collaboration of ten others, he produced *Moi, Pierre Rivière, ayant égorgé ma mère, ma soeur et mon frère . . . : Un cas de parricide au XIXe siècle* [*I, Pierre Rivière, having slaughtered my mother, my sister, and my brother . . . : A Case of Parricide in the 19th Century*], with the title taken from the opening line of Rivière's own story. The book consists of essays analyzing the case; contemporary documents, including statements by doctors, newspaper reports of the trial, and transcripts of the legal proceedings; and a transcription of Rivière's account of his actions. The book is intended to show how Rivière's desire, action, and text were made possible by particular discursive practices. In 1975, a film was made by René Allio (Paris Planfilm) about Rivière based on Foucault's book, and Foucault himself appeared in it as a judge.

Foucault's continuing study of penal theories and institutions resulted in the publication of *Surveiller et punir: Naissance de la prison* [*Discipline and Punish: The Birth of the Prison*] in 1975. The book charts the emergence of the prison and traces the shift from bodily punishment of criminals to reforming them through an investigation of their souls. He also is concerned with the disciplinary systems that exist beneath the surface of middle-class society and control our behavior without our knowledge.

Foucault's own homosexuality and his discovery that sexuality has been an issue of power throughout much of history led him to write a series of works on the history of sexuality. For Foucault, sexuality is an appropriate topic for genealogical investigation because it constitutes "an especially dense transfer point for relations of power,"[7] and he began to explore how the experience of sexuality "came to be constituted in modern Western societies, an experience that caused individuals to recognize themselves as subjects of a 'sexuality,' which was accessible to very diverse fields of knowledge and linked to a system of rules and constraints."[8] The first volume, *Histoire de la sexualité: La volonté de savoir* [*The History of Sexuality: An Introduction*], was published in 1976. In it, Foucault shows how the history of sexuality, beginning in the seventeenth century, was characterized by a continuous increase in the mechanisms of power. He also charts the shift of the locus of power from the confessional to research laboratories and clinics, showing how the various power mechanisms produced, rather than repressed, discourse on sexuality.

As Foucault attempted to map out the experience of sexuality, he realized that to complete his study, he had to analyze the practices by which individuals constitute themselves as subjects — in particular, as subjects of desire. The second and third volumes of the series, published in 1984, deal with this new area of inquiry — with practices and actions by which individuals "not only set themselves rules of conduct, but also seek to transform themselves, to change themselves in their singular being, and to make their life into an *oeuvre* that carries certain aesthetic values and meets certain stylistic criteria."[9] The second volume, *L'usage des plaisirs* [*The Use of Pleasure*] deals with the manner in which sexual activity was problematized in philosophical and medical discourse in classical Greek culture of the fourth century and what this meant for practices of the self. He examines prescriptive texts concerning the areas of dietetics, the individual's relationship with the body; economics, the conduct of the head of the family or household; and erotica, the relations between men and boys. The third volume, *Le souci de soi* [*Care of the Self*], deals with the same problematization in Greek and Latin texts of the first and second centuries, A.D. In a fourth volume, *The Confessions of the Flesh*, unfinished at the time of his death, Foucault had begun to deal with the doctrine and ministry concerning the flesh.

Never feeling as though he were fully "integrated within French social and intellectual life," Foucault traveled widely throughout his life. "As soon as I can," he declared, "I leave France." [10] In 1978, he reported on the Iranian Revolution for the Italian newspaper, *Corriere della Sera*. He also visited Japan, where he lectured on pastoral power and studied Zen as well as Christian and Buddhist mysticism. In 1981, he began a collaboration with the Polish labor union, Solidarity. He often visited and lectured in the United States, appreciating its varied intellectual and cultural life.

Foucault's discomfort with his own culture was revealed, as well, in his rejection of the lifestyle of the stereotypical French, who make an art out of living well. He lived simply and austerely in an almost entirely white apartment, devoid of adornment and ornamentation. He preferred American food to French food: "A good club sandwich with a coke. That's my pleasure. It's true. With ice cream." [11] In his everyday life, Foucault found little pleasure in those objects or experiences he saw others enjoying and felt he had "real difficulty in experiencing pleasure." As he explained in an interview:

> I think that pleasure is a very difficult behavior. It's not as simple as that [*Laughter*] to enjoy one's self. And I must say that's my dream. I would like and I hope I'll die of an overdose [*Laughter*] of pleasure of any kind. Because I think it's really difficult and I always have the feeling that I do not feel *the* pleasure, the complete total pleasure and for me, it's related to death. . . .
>
> Because I think that the kind of pleasure I would consider as *the* real pleasure would be so deep, so intense, so overwhelming that I couldn't survive it. I would die. I'll give you a clearer and simpler example. Once I was struck by a car in the street. I was walking. And for maybe two seconds I had the impression that I was dying and it was really a very, very intense pleasure. The weather was wonderful. It was 7 o'clock during the summer. The sun was descending. The sky was very wonderful and blue and so on. It was, it still is now, one of my best memories. [*Laughter*]
>
> There is also the fact that some drugs are really important for me because they are the mediation to those incredibly intense joys that I am looking for and that I am not able to experience, to afford by myself. . . . A pleasure must be something incredibly intense. . . .
>
> I'm not able to give myself and others those middle range pleasures that make up everyday life. Such pleasures are nothing for me and I am not able to organize my life in order to make place for them. That's the reason why I'm not a social being, why I'm not really a cultural being, why I'm so boring in my everyday life. [*Laughter*][12]

Foucault died of complications resulting from AIDS in Paris on June 25, 1984.[13]

Despite the wide variety of subject areas with which his work dealt, some essentially rhetorical concepts served as the foundation for much of his work. He began by examining "the forms of discursive practices that articulated the human sciences," a project in which he explored the relationship between rhetoric and knowledge. He then turned his attention to the notion of power, examining "the manifold relations, the open strategies, and the rational techniques that articulate the exercise of powers";[14] in this effort, he suggested a relationship between rhetoric and power. In his final works, he saw that his previous emphasis on discursive practices external to individuals needed to be complemented by a consideration of the techniques of the self and so turned to an analysis of ethics and the means by which individuals constitute themselves as subjects, exploring the connection, then, between the self and rhetoric.

Knowledge

Foucault's interest in the construction of knowledge is summarized in his question: "What are the relations we have to truth through scientific knowledge, to those 'truth games' which are so important in civilization and in which we are both subject and object?"[15] In his effort to understand the process by which disciplines such as psychiatry and education create particular truths about their topic areas, he came to see the process centered in an essentially rhetorical concept—the episteme.

Episteme/Discursive Formation

An episteme is "the total set of relations that unite, at a given period, the discursive practices that give rise to epistemological figures, sciences, and possibly formalized systems." It is a grouping of statements that suggests a consistent pattern in how they function as constituents of a system of knowledge; an episteme exists whenever "one can describe, between a number of statements, such a system of dispersion, whenever, between objects, types of statements, concepts, or thematic choices, one can define a regularity (an order, correlations, positions and functionings, transformations), . . ." An episteme, in other words, might be thought of as a cultural code, characteristic system, structure, network, or ground of thought that governs the language, perception, values, and practices of an age. It is a kind of period style for the organization of knowledge that functions automatically in that age.[16]

Only one episteme can dominate at any one time because the structure governing the episteme is so fundamental that in the age of one episteme, to think by means of another is impossible. The uniqueness of each episteme also suggests that no significant relationships exist among different epistemes. They appear in succession, without any evident rationale or reason; they are not built on each other, nor are they created in response to each other. If a particular set of rules is governing a particular episteme, any carry-over from one period to the next can take place only on the surface and thus must be inconsequential. Discontinuity exists between epistemes, then, for each one constitutes a break from the previous episteme and thus creates a radically different intellectual framework with which to view the world. The closure constituted by each episteme means that all concepts have only one "life"; they are born and die in their own episteme and do not survive into a new episteme without undergoing transformation.[17]

With the publication of *The Archaeology of Knowledge*, Foucault replaced the term "episteme" with "discursive formation," and he abandoned his former label. One reason for this change in terminology may have been Foucault's belief that he was not a structuralist and did not use the methods, concepts, or key terms of the structuralist movement.[18] Foucault perhaps hoped that by discarding one of the most obviously structuralist of his concepts, the differences between his notions and those of the structuralists would be more readily apparent.[19]

Whatever Foucault's rationale for the new term, the replacement of "episteme" with "discursive formation" makes clear the central role Foucault sees for discourse in the structure of knowledge. Foucault uses "discourse" as the plural of "statement"; a statement is the basic unit of the discursive formation. The statement is a set of signs or symbols to which a status of knowledge can be ascribed. It is a type of utterance that, because it follows particular rules or has passed the appropriate tests, is understood to be true in a culture. The statement is not the same as a sentence—governed by grammatical rules—or a proposition—governed by the rules of logic; it is governed by epistemological rules.[20]

For Foucault, knowledge and discursive practices are inseparable. Everything about which we can speak in a discursive formation is knowledge; knowledge is generated by discursive practice. At the same time, this knowledge specifies the form the discourse assumes, for the discourse is knowledge and thought in material form. Only a particular kind of knowledge is allowed by particular discursive formations, and nothing else receives support in the discourse. Foucault demonstrates the link between discourse and knowledge in a discussion of children's sexuality in the Victorian Age:

> Everyone knew, for example, that children had no sex, which was why they were forbidden to talk about it, why one closed one's eyes and stopped one's ears whenever they came to show evidence to the contrary, and why a general and studied silence was imposed. . . . [R]epression operated as . . . an admission that there was nothing to say about such things, nothing to see, and nothing to know.[21]

Statements concerning children's sexuality, then, did not meet the criteria to be considered truth and thus were not even heard in this particular discursive formation.

Governing Rules

The nature of a discursive formation can be known through the discovery of the rules or procedures that characterize it. These rules determine that one statement rather than another comes to be uttered. They are not likely to be conscious and often cannot be articulated without difficulty, but these rules determine the possibilities for the content and form of discourse: "the production of discourse is at once controlled, selected, organised, and redistributed according to a certain number of procedures."[22]

Foucault suggests a number of rules that govern various aspects of the discursive formation. One category includes rules that control the fact that something is able to be talked about; these rules are necessary for the appearance of objects of discourse. Rules in this category include, for example, prohibitions against talking about certain things. Such rules silence certain dimensions of experience simply by not recognizing them as objects of discourse.[23] As we saw in Foucault's example from the Victorian Age, children's sexuality was not discussed, repressing that aspect of children's experience. In other words, it simply was not an object of discourse.

Other rules in this category concern the function of institutional bodies in creating objects of discourse. Sometimes, particular institutions are recognized as the ones with the authority to name and thus distinguish one object from another. One such authority was nineteenth-century medicine, which distinguished madness from other things and became the major authority that established madness as an object. In our society, educational experts distinguish learning-disabled children from others, thus making learning disability a concept about which we are able to speak.

A second category of rules concerns not what is talked about but who is allowed to speak and write. Such rules dictate that we listen to certain people and reject as null and void the discourse of others. The discourse of students, children, and prisoners, for example, generally is not "heard" in our culture. The same was true of the insane individual in the Middle Ages:

> His words were considered nul [sic] and void, without truth or
> significance, worthless as evidence, inadmissible in the authentification
> of acts or contracts, . . . [T]he madman's speech did not strictly exist
> . . . . [His words] were neither heard nor remembered. No doctor before
> the end of the eighteenth century had ever thought of listening to the
> content—how it was said and why—of these words; . . . Whatever a
> madman said, it was taken for mere noise.[24]

Other such rules impose conditions on the individuals who speak so that
only those deemed qualified by satisfying these conditions may engage in
discourse on a specific subject. Among these conditions are legal requirements
that give the right to speak in certain ways; lawyers, for example, must pass
the bar examination in order to practice law. Other such rules might involve
criteria of competence and knowledge. For example, we listen to medical
doctors speak about issues involving health because our society attributes
competence to them in this area; midwives' discourse generally is not heard,
however, because they have not fulfilled the conditions for competence
established for speakers of medical discourse.

Another such condition imposed on those who wish to speak is the production
of certain kinds of discourse, formulated in certain ways. Those who wish
to speak in the academic world, for example, must produce certain types of
statements and use certain forms before they are allowed entrance into the
group of those who engage in scholarly discourse. A scholarly paper or article,
for example, must follow the form of an established style manual—such as
the ones published by the Modern Language Association or the American
Psychological Association—which dictates proper form for such things as
reference citation, types of headings, and use of italics.

Other rules define the gestures, behaviors, and circumstances that must
accompany speakers as they talk; these rituals reflect the meaning of the
discourse. Religious discourse, for example, must be accompanied in many
cases by the wearing of particular clothing and behaviors such as genuflection
if the speaker is to be viewed as legitimate in that role. Judicial discourse,
as well, involves rituals that require those participating to engage in certain
behaviors and convey a particular image. Judges, for example, wear robes
in the courtroom and are greeted by the rising of the audience when they
enter. To violate such rituals is to deny doctrine and to be subject to punishment,
ex-communication, banishment, or some other form of silencing.

Still other conditions imposed on speakers concern the sites from which
the discourse must originate. Certain places are seen as appropriate from which
to speak, while others are not. For professors, for example, such sites include
the university classroom; the documentary field of professional journals, books,
and professional conventions; and, if their field of study has application to
the business world, the corporate setting. For professors to announce research

findings in a bowling alley, for example, would not accord them the status necessary to be heard and taken seriously by those who engage in scholarly discourse.

A third category of rules concerns the form that concepts and theories must assume to be accepted as knowledge in the discourse. Some rules, for example, govern the arrangement of statements necessary in order for the discourse to be seen as making a contribution to knowledge, while others dictate the style and form of that discourse. Other rules determine which terms will be recognized as valid, which will be questionable, and which will be invalid. They specify the kind of discourse in which the highest truth resides by indicating which statements are true and which are false.[25] In our culture, for example, non-linear perspectives and ways of writing or speaking are generally not recognized as valid or appropriate; truth does not reside in statements produced from such approaches.

Rules also govern the process of the generation of knowledge in that they allow only certain individuals to be involved in the formulation of concepts and theories. Economic, theological, medical, and judicial discourses, for example, generally are not discourses to which everyone has access and in which everyone can generate new knowledge. For a lay person to propose changes in the policy of the Catholic Church, for example, would be viewed as inappropriate, and the statements made generally would not even reach the individuals actually involved in policy making.

An episteme or discursive formation, then, is the structure governing knowledge in a culture that is established by particular discursive practices. These practices are governed by rules that prescribe certain objects of discourse, particular types of speakers, and the form that theories and concepts assume.

Concomitant with Foucault's view of the discursive formation governed by rules is a particular view of truth. Truth is always dependent on a particular discursive formation; there is no underlying meaning or truth within or imposed on the things of our world. The truth or knowledge we have about something rests entirely within the relations of statements inside a discursive formation.

Role of the Human Being

One notion that has attracted a great deal of attention to Foucault's works is his assertion that the human being soon will disappear. He is not suggesting that human beings no longer will inhabit the planet but that our current conception of the human being soon will disappear. He argues that in the present episteme, the human being has become the unifying element and the center for the organization of knowledge. The human, in other words, constitutes the foundation and origin of knowledge.

Foucault sees this epistemological consciousness of the human being as a relatively recent invention within European culture; the concept did not exist in previous epistemes: "Strangely enough, man—the study of whom is supposed by the näive to be the oldest investigation since Socrates—is probably no more than a kind of rift in the order of things."[26] The human being as the center for the organization of knowledge, then, appeared only recently. This new conception of the human being, Foucault argues, was the result of changes in the nature of language in the epistemes of the recent past.

The episteme of the sixteenth century, the Renaissance, was based on the idea of resemblance or similitude. Plants resembled stars, for example, the intellect of the human being reflected the wisdom of God, and painting imitated space. Because everything resembled something else and in that sense stood for it, words and things were not thought of as being separate: the "names of things were lodged in the things they designated." Knowledge consisted of the finding of resemblances, and language was not so much used by humans but rather experienced as part of a natural order.[27]

In the Classical Age, or the period of the seventeenth and eighteenth centuries, representation was the principle of the episteme. Language served as the signs of the things that made up reality, severing the natural connection between words and things. Once an object was differentiated from others, it could be represented by a sign that, in turn, allowed it to be assigned its proper place in the order of things. Thus, words stopped being real figures in nature; they no longer were integrated—through resemblance—with what they signified. Instead, they became instruments of analysis and principles by which to organize knowledge. In this episteme, then, language enjoyed a privileged status because it was seen as the space in which things were ordered. Reality took on the characteristics of the language in which it was presented.[28]

In the late eighteenth, nineteenth, and twentieth centuries, what might be called the epoch of Modernity, the theory of representation was replaced by an awareness of history such that elements, including language, became intelligible in terms of their growth and history. Once language began to be seen as a phenomenon with a history that thus was subject to change, it became an object to be known. In its demotion from its former status as the orderer of knowledge, language simply became one object of knowledge or one thing we perceive among others; it no longer had privileged status over any other things. Consequently, this episteme was concerned with "the analysis of meaning and signification"; language no longer functioned without question as it had in the Classical Age. It had become a problem, a barrier, and a medium of expression that needed interpretation.[29]

In the current age of Modernity, human beings, in gaining supremacy over language, have replaced it as the organizing principle of knowledge. While the human being in the seventeenth and eighteenth centuries was a function, in this episteme, the human being has become an origin, constituting the foundation and origin of knowledge. Foucault believes, however, that we are on the brink of a new episteme, in which this conception of the human being will disappear: "It is comforting, however, and a source of profound relief to think that man is only a recent invention, a figure not yet two centuries old, a new wrinkle in our knowledge, and that he will disappear again as soon as that knowledge has discovered a new form."

Evidence for the coming disappearance of this concept of the human being derives, in part, Foucault believes, from new trends in the analysis of language that are incompatible with the idea of the human being as a distinct self. These analyses focus not on a theory of the knowing subject but rather on a theory of discursive practices, linguistic structures, and epistemological structures that have no need of the human being as their central presence. In this view, the focus is not on individuals who speak English but on English as a set of formal relationships long antedating our personal identities. Since language is regaining primacy, the human being once again will return to its previous non-existence as a concept around which to organize knowledge. Foucault asks, "is this not the sign that the whole of this configuration is now about to topple, and that man is in the process of perishing as the being of language continues to shine ever brighter upon our horizon?" [30]

Foucault's belief that we must dispense with the constituent subject or current conception of the human being is his primary reason for rejecting the philosophy and methodology of phenomenology: "If there is one approach that I do reject, however, it is that (one might call it, broadly speaking, the phenomenological approach) which gives absolute priority to the observing subject, which attributes a constituent role to an act, which places its own point of view at the origin of all historicity—which, in short, leads to a transcendental consciousness." [31]

In fact, Foucault not only rejects the constitutive or foundational role of the subject, but he reverses the relation envisioned in phenomenology and argues that the subject receives whatever powers and position it has from discursive practices. The human being does not constitute discursive practices; the human being as an object of knowledge is a product of discursive practices. The human being is the creation of our current way of talking about human beings.

Foucault's stance regarding our conception of the human being might be interpreted as anti-humanist and as an abandonment of the human subject. [32] If humanism is viewed, however, as a perspective that focuses on the freedom of the individual agent; has as its goal the liberation of humankind; and advocates intellectual development, study, and contemplation as the means for accomplishing that goal, [33] Foucault's endeavor is a humanist one. As Blair and Cooper explain:

> The bases for the anti-humanist label are without merit. . . . Though
> he turned the unmasking potential of his method on humanism, his work
> was centered in the substance, end, and means of the humanist project.
> His focus departed from the individual human only in that he suspended
> the traditional, unified view in order to subject it to questioning. He turned
> back to the individual as the producer and user of discourse. His goals
> were emancipatory, and his chosen methods were those of intellectual
> reflection and investigation.[34]

Foucault's focus on the human being is particularly clear in his last works, in which he investigates the nature of subjectivity—how the human being has been made a subject; this notion is discussed in connection with ethics later in this chapter.

As a result of his study of knowledge as constituted in discourse and characterized by various governing rules, Foucault came to understand that knowledge and power are inextricably linked; they are two sides of the same process. All knowledge is "interested" in that it is engaged in and subject to the exertion of power. Traditionally, the assumption has been that once we gain power, we no longer have knowledge: "It has been a tradition for humanism to assume that once someone gains power he ceases to know. Power makes men mad, and those who govern are blind; only those who keep their distance from power, who are in no way implicated in tyranny, shut up in their Cartesian *poêle*, their room, their meditations, only they can discover the truth."[35] We need to abandon this tradition, Foucault asserts, because it "allows us to imagine that knowledge can exist only where the power relations are suspended"—outside the injunctions, demands, and interests of power.[36] Foucault advocates instead a view of power in which "the exercise of power itself creates and causes to emerge new objects of knowledge and accumulates new bodies of information."[37] Thus, a knowledge untainted by relations of power cannot exist.

Foucault does not see power and knowledge as identical, however: "I read—and I know it has been attributed to me—the thesis, 'Knowledge is power,' or 'Power is knowledge,' I begin to laugh, since studying their *relation* is precisely my problem. . . . The very fact that I pose the question of their relation proves clearly that I do not *identify* them."[38] The relation he sees between them is one of co-implication and presupposition: Power and knowledge imply, implicate, and presuppose the other. There "is no power relation without the correlative constitution of a field of knowledge, nor any knowledge that does not presuppose and constitute at the same time power relations."[39] Power and knowledge relations are superimposed on each other and make each other possible, without either being reducible or subordinate to the other. This structure Foucault sees between power and knowledge is made possible through discourse. Power and knowledge are articulated within discourse, and they cannot "be established, consolidated nor implemented without the production, accumulation, circulation and functioning of a discourse."[40]

Power

Foucault turned to the study of power when he came to realize that the treatment of knowledge and discourse could not be separated from the operation of power. For Foucault, power is "a more-or-less organised, hierarchical, co-ordinated cluster of relations." He sees "the relationships of power" as a more accurate descriptor than "power" for the phenomenon he studies, for it suggests a power that resides in a network of relationships that are systematically interconnected.[41]

In Foucault's view, power is not a matter of one person, group, or institution exercising control over another, where some give orders and others obey. Rather, it is "exercised from innumerable points. . . . " Power is a characteristic of all relationships and, in fact, constitutes those relationships, whether economic, social, professional, or familial. Forms of domination are built into the very understanding of the common activity or goods sought or whatever forms the substance of a relationship. Thus, the doctor-patient relationship is defined by a supposed common goal, constituted by a willingness to help on the part of the doctor and a recognition of need for help on the part of the patient. This coming together in a common goal is inseparable from a relation of power that is founded on the presumption that one knows and that the other will take the knower's advice. All individuals exercise power, then, and all are subjected to it: "Power is employed and exercised through a net-like organisation . . . individuals circulate between its threads; they are always in a position of simultaneously undergoing and exercising this power."[42]

Foucault's conception of power requires the abandonment of the legal or judicial view that narrowly defines power as based in the enunciation of the law. In classical judicial theory, power is considered a right, which one is able to possess like a commodity and which can be transferred or alienated through a legal transaction involving a contractual type of exchange. In this conception, "the King remains the central personage," and even when the legal system no longer relies on control by a monarch, the system is based on challenge to the prerogatives of the sovereign power and the limits of this power: "When it comes to the general organisation of the legal system in the West, it is essentially with the King, his rights, his power and its eventual limitations, that one is dealing."[43] But we must "break free" of this reduction of power to law, Foucault asserts, "if we wish to analyze power within the concrete and historical framework of its operation." What is needed is "to cut off the King's head: in political theory that has still to be done."[44]

Because power is a phenomenon constituted by discursive practices, the definition of power and the means used to enact it vary across time and cultures. Disciplinary technologies or procedures of various sorts are the means through which power is exercised in the modern political state. The instruments through which this power achieves its hold are such things as continuous surveillance, recording of information about individuals in reports and files, examinations of various kinds used to classify and judge, and normalizing judgments — standards for correct behavior — established in their infinite variety.

The various techniques through which power is enacted are acceptable to us only because most of this power is hidden. The effectiveness of power increases as its visibility decreases. This disciplinary, normalizing power is far more subtle and pervasive than the easily identifiable, spectacular, repressible, and potentially violent types of power, so we acquiesce readily to it in ways we would not to more overt forms. Usually, we are unaware of the extent to which this power affects our lives, an influence Foucault captures in his term, "bio-power" — power over life: It "exerts a positive influence on life, that endeavors to administer, optimize, and multiply it, subjecting it to precise controls and comprehensive regulations."[45]

Foucault sees power not only as pervasive but as productive and creative; it is not only repressive or prohibitive. When Foucault began to study the prison, he found phenomena that a purely repressive conception of power could not accommodate. Thus, he came to believe that repression "is wholly inadequate to the analysis of the mechanisms and effects of power." He explains why:

> [Repression] is poor in resources, sparing of its methods, monotonous in the tactics it utilizes, incapable of invention, and seemingly doomed always to repeat itself. Further, it is a power that only has the force of the negative on its side, a power to say no; in no condition to produce, capable only of posting limits, it is basically anti-energy. This is the paradox of its effectiveness: it is incapable of doing anything, except to render what it dominates incapable of doing anything either, except for what this power allows it to do.[46]

Power, in Foucault's view, operates as a creative force — one that facilitates, produces, and increases qualities and conditions: "If power were never anything but repressive, if it never did anything but to say no, do you really think one would be brought to obey it? What makes power hold good, what makes it accepted, is simply the fact that it doesn't only weigh on us as a force that says no, but that it traverses and produces things, . . . forms knowledge, produces discourse."[47] In the prison, for example, power generally produces an individual subjected to habits, rules, order, and authority; delinquency; a high rate of recidivism; and destitution in the inmate's family.[48] These are the results of a generative, creative power, not a repressive, restraining one.[49]

Foucault's view of power as omnipresent, dispersed, continuous, and creative raises questions about the nature of resistance to it and whether reform is even possible. Fraser raises such questions: "Foucault calls in no uncertain terms for resistance to domination. But why? Why is struggle preferable to submission? Why ought domination to be resisted?"[50] Foucault suggests that the nature of resistance to the power he describes is much like power itself. He defines resistance as a "centrifugal movement, an inverse energy, or discharge"[51] and sees it is omnipresent, dispersed, and productive. Wherever there is power, there is resistance; resistances are "inscribed" in power as an "irreducible opposite."[52]

Resistance is inescapable in Foucault's system, then, but it is not directed toward the achievement of a particular ideal or utopian society. Every society — every discursive formation — is characterized by discourse that both creates and constrains. Thus, to replace one order with another will not bring about greater freedom from discourse, nor is that sort of freedom even desirable: Those who hold a notion of utopia are "blind to the fact that relations of power are not something bad in themselves, from which one must free one's self. I don't believe there can be a society without relations of power, if you understand them as means by which individuals try to conduct, to determine the behavior of others."[53] Furthermore, there is no way of knowing what a "better" discursive formation might be like because each new one produces particular governing rules for discourse, and there is no particular reason to expect these will be any better under a new system than the ones that characterize the old. Foucault opposes the existing order of things, then, but he does not intend to replace what exists. Humans are justified in opposing an order but not in the name of a better order.[54]

Opposition to existing order occurs, according to Foucault, not through assumption of the role of the universal intellectual but through that of the specific intellectual. The universal intellectual is a defender of natural rights; an advocate of humanity; at the forefront of progress and revolution; and bearer of universal moral, theoretical, and political values. Foucault argues instead for resistance performed by specific intellectuals — ordinary people who have knowledge of their circumstances and are able to express themselves independently of the universal theorizing intellectual. Specific intellectuals work "not in the modality of the 'universal', the 'exemplary', the 'just-and-true-for-all', but within specific sectors, at the precise points where their own conditions of life or work situate them (housing, the hospital, the asylum, the laboratory, the university, family and sexual relations)."[55] This is the level, then, at which criminals challenge prison conditions; welfare workers and clients seek to change the bureaucracy; consumers organize against corporations; and inmates, attendants, and therapists disrupt the asylum.

In his description of his own role in various social movements, Foucault summarizes his view of the specific intellectual: "Whenever I have tried to carry out a piece of theoretical work, it has been on the basis of my own experience, always in relation to processes I saw taking place around me. It is because I thought I could recognize in the things I saw, in the institutions with which I dealt, in my relations with others, cracks, silent shocks, malfunctionings . . . that I undertook a particular piece of work. . . . "[56]

The major tool of resistance is critique, which "is not a matter of saying that things are not right as they are. It is a matter of pointing out what kinds of assumptions, what kinds of familiar, unchallenged, unconsidered modes of thought the practices that we accept rest. . . . to see what is accepted as self-evident will no longer be accepted as such."[57] Examination of a discursive formation to discover the rules that undergird it, then, constitutes the act of critique, which "puts into crisis" or disrupts commonly held conceptions. Critique mounts an attack against the existing order of things. Engagement in critique, however, does not give specific intellectuals the right to speak for those who have been disqualified from speaking in the discursive formation. Instead, they help to create conditions in which the disqualified may express themselves and act by pointing out to them some places where their particular battles may need to be fought and inviting them to do something about it.

Foucault is optimistic about the prospects for reform; his optimism consists of "saying that so many things can be changed, fragile as they are, bound up more with circumstances than necessities, more arbitrary than self-evident, more a matter of complex, but temporary, historical circumstances than with inevitable anthropological constants. . . . "[58]

Ethics

In the course of working on his history of sexuality, Foucault became increasingly interested in how the self constitutes or forms itself as a subject. He turned his attention to a third primary area of study—how individuals act "on their own bodies, souls, thoughts, conduct, and way of being in order to transform themselves" into particular kinds of subjects.[59] The practices individuals use for such transformation—like those used to create institutions and particular types of roles within them—are patterns in a "culture and which are proposed, suggested and imposed on" the individual by that culture.[60] Foucault set out, then, to do an analysis or genealogy of these technologies of the self, or the means by which discursive formations incite individuals to use particular means to turn themselves into subjects.

Foucault's exploration of the technologies of the self begins with the idea that our identity is not fixed by nature or rooted in prior knowledge of who we are; being the subject of one's own experience is not a given. He then asks how we come to be constituted as the subject of our own experience and finds in ethics an area in which he can see the process by which this happens. The study of ethics illustrates how individuals constitute themselves as moral subjects; thus, it allows for the explication of the sort of work, attention, knowledge, and techniques that go into self-formation. For Foucault, then, ethics is not a matter of prudence or duty; instead, it concerns who we are said to be and the various means through which we create that notion of being.[61]

For Foucault, ethics is one part of the study of morals, which consists of three elements. The first is the moral code, or the rules that determine "which acts are permitted or forbidden and the code which determines the positive or negative value of the different possible behaviors. . . . " An example of a moral code is the precept that the individual is not supposed to steal. A second element of morals is the actual activity or behavior in which individuals engage, "the real behavior of people in relation to the moral code . . . imposed on them." The third element of Foucault's view of morals is ethics, "the kind of relationship you ought to have with yourself . . . and which determines how the individual is supposed to constitute" the self as a moral subject.[62]

Foucault further divides the realm of ethics into four aspects. The first is *ethical substance*, which is the particular aspect of the self that is seen as the appropriate domain for moral conduct. It is the part of the self that is taken into account or subjected to ethics—the prime material of moral conduct. In some discursive formations, this ethical substance may be feelings; in others, it is intentions or desire.

A second component of ethics is *mode of subjection*. It is the authority or rationale for moral obligations, "the way in which people are invited or incited to recognize their moral obligations.[63] Moral obligations may be imposed from a wide variety of sources; they may be revealed by divine law, imposed by the demands of reason, or rest on convention, for example.

The third aspect of ethics is asceticism or self-discipline, the practical *means* by which individuals become ethical subjects—the techniques to be used or the ethical work to be performed to bring the self into compliance with the moral code. Techniques may range from painstaking, detailed checking of progress to confessions to exercises to deprivations to be endured.

The fourth aspect of ethics is the *telos*, or the image of the right sort of person, life, or soul—what is considered to be the state of perfection or completion according to the moral code. Foucault sees this aspect of the ethical system summarized in the question, "Which is the kind of being to which we aspire when we behave in a moral way? For instance, shall we become pure, or immortal, or free, or masters of ourselves, and so on?"[64] In what Foucault calls "the Californian cult of the self," the *telos* is discovery of "one's true self," which is to be achieved through such modes of subjection as therapy and the reading of self-help books.[65] The ethical subject, then, is constituted through a focus on a particular aspect of the self as the substance of ethics, the mode of subjection or authority for the moral precepts, the means by which the self is brought into compliance in the ethical system, and the ideal state toward which the self aims in ethical conduct.

Archaeology and Genealogy

Foucault initially called his method of investigating epistemes or discursive formations "archaeology," a term that first appeared in *Madness and Civilization*. This method is a means for analyzing the production of discourse in terms of the conditions of possibility that allow it to appear and that govern the system of knowledge and order. It is a way of analyzing systems of thought through a description of the archive—what may be spoken of in discourse, which terms are recognized as valid, and what individuals or groups have access to particular kinds of discourse. The aim of archaeology, then, is to enter the interior of discourse in order to determine the rules that govern it and to describe the various relations among statements in a discursive formation. For Foucault, the connotations of the term "archaeology" were appealing—the notion of depth and getting below the surface, the idea of a science that is neither science nor history, and the notion of the past as a succession of layers with little to suggest transition between them.[66]

In 1972, Foucault introduced the term "genealogy" as a complement to "archaeology" to describe his method of investigation.[67] The new term added Foucault's new awareness of the importance of power relations to his methodology. Specifically, genealogy looks for the rules governing discursive practices, along with the network of power relations of which these rules are a part: "my main concern will be to locate the forms of power, the channels it takes, and the discourses it permeates."[68] While archaeology involves the identification of the rules of production and transformation for discourse, then, genealogy's focus is on the relations of power connected to the discourse. Inherent in both archaeology and genealogy is the examination of discourse, which implies use of the archaeological method. Archaeology did not disappear as an analytic approach for Foucault; it continued to serve as a complement to and starting point for genealogy, an analytic approach with a wider scope than archaeology.[69]

Methodological Principles

A number of methodological principles for investigating bodies of discourse are suggested in Foucault's writings. While he suggested specific methods for both archaeology and genealogy, the two complementary modes of analysis share some tenets.

First, Foucault's methodology of inquiry is characterized by the nature of the data he chooses to study. Rather than studying renowned documents such as texts produced by famous philosophers or the documentation surrounding extraordinary events, he studies common, generally unknown documents— those often considered to be insignificant and of little value in a society. The documents he studies include, for example, records kept by ordinary doctors, teachers, and priests; popular prescriptive manuals; grant proposals; and files kept by various bureaucratic agencies. As he explains, he wants to address "a layer of material which had hitherto had no pertinence for history and which had not been recognised as having any moral, aesthetic, political or historical value."[70] Such documents allow the researcher to uncover the regularity of a discursive practice and to discover the techniques of power that reside not in centralized and legitimate forms of power but in local, regional, and material institutions.

Second, Foucault's methodology rests on the belief that the analysis of discourse should be a descriptive or transcriptive practice more so than an interpretive one. He does not approach discursive analysis by trying to discover latent and invisible elements or "a hidden element, a secret meaning,"[71] in manifest discourse. Rather, he hopes to discover the boundaries of acceptability for claims to truth in the discursive formation.

While Foucault recognizes that to avoid interpretation is impossible—in part because of individual perception and the discursive formation in which the observer exists—he seeks to avoid it because some crucial content always is lost or suppressed in the process. Interpretation, or what he sometimes calls *commentary*, also is a technique of power in that it selects what is to be suppressed and allows only specially qualified individuals to do the interpreting.[72]

A third characteristic of Foucault's methodology is that it provides the means for an *ascending* analysis of power, starting at the micro-level. While Foucault sometimes begins at the macro-level to describe power,[73] he often begins analysis with a discovery of how the mechanisms of power function in terms of the smallest social units such as the family or such agents as doctors, parents, or teachers. From this starting point, he moves to an investigation of how these mechanisms of power have been appropriated, transformed, annexed, and extended by more general or global forms of domination. Such an analysis is very different from one in which the researcher conceptualizes power as located within a centralized institutional structure and then seeks to trace its diffusion and effect in and through the social order.

Foucault's methodology is characterized, as well, by the particular attention paid to contradiction, disparity, and difference. At the same time that he is comparing discursive practices with each other to discover the common structure in which they are grounded, he is alert to differences. Instead of attempting to make disparate views or modes of thought fit into a coherent pattern of discourse, Foucault seeks to discover and investigate these disparities. He views contradictions as "neither appearances to be overcome, nor secret principles to be uncovered. They are objects to be described for themselves."[74] By determining the extent and form of the gap that separates apparently contradictory statements, Foucault aims to determine if they do belong, in fact, to the same discursive formation. For example, in the eighteenth century, the thesis of the animal nature of fossils was contradicted by the thesis of their mineral nature. The attempt to discover how two statements that now seem contradictory could have been held simultaneously reveals information about the nature of the discursive formation that contained them.

Finally, Foucault rejects the practice of relating a piece of discourse or rhetorical act to its specific author or creator. He is not concerned with the specific person who said or wrote something; he does not connect the discourse to the individual who created it. In his writings, no biographical information is presented about the figures he mentions. The names of individuals that do appear in his writings are merely shorthand devices for referring to texts and are cited as, for example, the "individual we term Hobbes." What is important for Foucault is the discovery of the *role* the individual plays and the rules that govern the nature of that role.

Foucault also assumes this position because he views the author as fulfilling a discursive function. In a discursive formation, the author simply plays a role and fills a vacant space that could be filled by many different individuals. Foucault quotes Samuel Beckett from *Texts for Nothing* to make his point: "What matter who's speaking, someone said, what matter who's speaking."[75]

Foucault, then, prefers to approach a document or body of discourse in its "raw, neutral state," focusing on what is actually said. His aim is simply to give "*a pure description of discursive events*"[76] in order to discover relationships among statements, the discursive formation in which the event took place, and the kind of conceptual and power changes that accompanied the events.

Responses to Foucault

The impact of Foucault's work on a number of fields cannot be disputed. His writings are of interest to literary critics, psychologists, health professionals, linguists, and rhetorical theorists, to name a few. *Discipline and Punish* aroused interest among professionals in criminology, while *Madness and Civilization* has significance for psychiatric practice and for our present conceptions of mental illness.[77]

Foucault's work has been acclaimed not only for its breadth but for its originality as well. It "compels," Pratt asserts, "irresistably [sic], illuminating the darkness, not so much a searchlight as a firework display, brilliant, theatrical, bewildering." Morris and Patton attribute this originality to the creation of "a new conception of philosophical work"; Said calls it "a new field of research (or of a new way of conceiving and doing research)"; and Friedrich commends it for its brilliant analysis of power.[78]

In the area of rhetorical scholarship, Foucault's originality lies not in the introduction of totally new concepts for use in rhetorical theory but in how his notions may be used by others to stretch existing conceptualizations or may be applied to new domains. One such contribution Foucault makes is to strengthen support for the concept that rhetoric is epistemic. While the discourse with which he is concerned certainly is at a different level than that with which the speech communication field generally is concerned, one of his central concepts is that discourse is a way of knowing. A particular discursive formation produces particular kinds of knowledge, just as a particular system of knowledge intimately is linked to the discourse in which it materializes. Knowledge or truth is created by the rhetorical process and is not possible apart from this process. His studies of the development of various institutions with their concomitant systems of knowledge provide much historical support for a view of rhetoric as epistemic.

A second area in which Foucault contributes to existing notions of rhetoric is in the area of speech-act theory. Foucault's notion of the statement is roughly equivalent to the notion of the speech act. The primary difference between them, as Blair explains, is that "the statement may be either a written or an oral utterance, and because it includes graphic and tabular symbols as well as linear, verbal articulations, the statement is a more inclusive construction than the speech act." Although they are not identical constructs, however, Foucault's statement and the speech act are both acts: "They are more than linguistic or transcribed patterns of symbols; they are human events." The significance of this view of the statement (or the speech act) lies beyond its effects on an audience or its specific content. It also encourages the study of what the utterance of the statement reveals about the discursive formation in which it is embedded: "That it was uttered at all provides one clue among many as to the epistemological structures, power relations, and ethical stances operative in a society at a given time."[79]

Foucault makes an additional contribution to the study of rhetoric with his conception of power. While some perspectives on rhetoric deal with power, many tend to limit their views of power to the power of discourse to accomplish certain intended effects or to a particular rhetor's personal power or credibility in a situation. Foucault's view of power is decidedly broader. Power is inseparable from knowledge and discourse, producing and induced by them. Except in superficial ways, rhetoric generally has not been concerned with how power relations operate in discursive formations and come to produce knowledge.

Perhaps Foucault's most original contribution to rhetoric lies in how his notion of the discursive formation may add to the current debate as to how rhetoric should be defined. Foucault's archaeological and genealogical method of discovering rules that govern a discursive formation and their embodiment of power relations could be applied to the body of rhetorical knowledge throughout its history. Such an application might suggest what is essential to a definition of rhetoric, evidenced in characteristic, regular ways of talking and writing about rhetoric.

While few dispute the significance of Foucault's contributions in a number of areas, many respond to Foucault's work by complaining of his difficult style of writing. It has been described as "reckless, irritating, and frequently unfathomable" and "tantalizingly obscure."[80] He has been accused of using a style that is "digressive and repetitive"[81] and that is characterized by "interminable sentences, parentheses, repetitions, neologisms, paradoxes, oxymorons, alternation of analytical with lyrical passages"; his style appears "to be consciously designed to render his discourse impenetrable." One writer summarized Foucault's style by asserting, "He cannot *say* anything directly."[82]

Bannet suggests that Foucault's difficult style is a result of his modes of analysis, which "required him to pursue so many threads at the same time and to encorporate so much specific detail that the reader is in constant danger of missing the wood for the trees, branches, twigs and texture of the bark." Foucault tried, she suggests, to deal with the objections to his style in two ways. He increased his methodological signposting, writing articles and giving interviews to try to clarify his project and what he meant by particular terms. He also changed his style in his later works: "The rhetorical and poetical richness of the early books gives way in the later ones to a much more sparse, straightforward and down-to-earth style, in which imagery is used much more sparingly for essential analogical purposes."[83]

Some critics attribute the difficulty with Foucault's style less to his analytic method than to his terminology, which "presents an undeniable obstacle."[84] The problem, most critics agree, is that Foucault "uses some deceptively ordinary words . . . in senses that are highly specialized."[85] Some writers have responded particularly strongly to this characteristic of Foucault's writing, suggesting that he "is like a magician forever popping rabbits out of his hat and calling them bluebirds."[86] Still another asks whether understanding his work is "worth the trouble of assimilating jargon like this?"[87] While his terminology is an obstacle to a clear understanding of Foucault's work, most critics would respond that clearing the obstacle is, indeed, worth the trouble.

A second problem cited by some readers concerns the evidence that Foucault selects to support the claims he makes. Some critics have noted that he fails to take into account relevant bits of evidence to support the existence of a particular episteme or discursive formation—the central importance of Newtonian physics in the eighteenth century in *The Order of Things*, for example.[88] More serious is the accusation that he ignores evidence that contradicts his thesis—ignoring "numerous documents that by sheer number of pages argue vociferously to the contrary."[89] He has been criticized, for example, for ignoring references to the conception of the human being in such pre-nineteenth-century writers as Aristotle, Locke, Pope, Vico, Shakespeare, and Hume when he develops his thesis that such a conception of the human being did not then exist.[90] Laing summarizes the complaint, commenting that "Foucault sometimes whirls words into pirouettes which are more to be admired for their brilliance than trusted for their veracity."[91]

Others have charged that Foucault's ideas seem inconsistent and that a comparison of his works to one another yields differences in terminology, frameworks, and schema of classification that sometimes are conflicting.[92] He devised numerous classification systems for the rules governing discursive formations, for example, with overlaps and discrepancies among them. Poster summarizes this complaint about Foucault's work as Foucault's refusal "to totalize his position. . . . The syncopated, uneven character of his books rubs unpleasantly against the sensibilities of those expecting a text that resolves all the main questions."[93]

Foucault himself was quite aware of this charge of inconsistency but did not see it as a problem; it simply was evidence of the still-evolving nature of his ideas. He often discussed his own inadequacies or confusions in his previous works,[94] and he deliberately sought to leave a "problematic character, voluntarily uncertain, to the assertions advanced."[95] He was described, as a result, as "the reverse of a guru, a teacher, a subject who is supposed to know, . . . For him uncertainty causes no anguish."[96]

Perhaps Foucault himself best summarized the attitude of deliberate uncertainty and tentativeness that characterizes his works: "Do not ask who I am and do not ask me to remain the same: leave it to our bureaucrats and our police to see that our papers are in order."[97] He saw his "main interest in life and work . . . to become someone else that you were not in the beginning";[98] transformation, indeed, was his goal: My "problem is my own transformation. That's the reason also why, when people say, 'Well, you thought this a few years ago and now you say something else,' my answer is, [*Laughter*] 'Well, do you think I have worked like that all those years to say the same thing and not to be changed?'"[99] His transformation continually challenged the existing order both in the content with which he dealt and in his approach to that content as he deliberately set "out to do cartwheels on the banquet table." And as a result, he managed "to splash through just about everyone's soup."[100]

Notes

[1] Michel Foucault, "Entretien," *Nouvelles littéraires,* March 17, 1975, as quoted in Alan Sheridan, *Michel Foucault: The Will to Truth* (New York: Tavistock, 1980), p. 224.

[2] Stephen Riggins, "The Minimalist Self," in *Michel Foucault: Politics, Philosophy, Culture: Interviews and Other Writings: 1977-1984,* trans. Alan Sheridan et al., ed. Lawrence D. Kritzman (New York: Routledge, 1988), p. 7.

[3] Rux Martin, "Truth, Power, Self: An Interview with Michel Foucault: October 25, 1982," in *Technologies of the Self: A Seminar with Michel Foucault,* ed. Luther H. Martin, Huck Gutman, and Patrick H. Hutton (Amherst: University of Massachusetts Press, 1988), p. 13.

[4] Riggins, p. 5.

[5] Leo Bersani argues that Foucault opposes Marxism because of its conception of power. Under Marxism, the state is seen as an excessively privileged power apparatus that tries to control the "leaks" of power that are natural and inevitable. Such a view is incompatible with Foucault's conception of power as omnipresent and involved in the production of knowledge. See "The Subject of Power," *Diacritics,* 7 (September 1977), 4.

[6] Michel Foucault, *The Use of Pleasure,* trans. Robert Hurley (New York: Pantheon, 1985), p. 9

[7] Michel Foucault, *The History of Sexuality,* trans. Robert Hurley (New York: Vintage, 1980), p. 103.

[8] Foucault, *The Use of Pleasure,* p. 4

[9] Foucault, *The Use of Pleasure,* pp. 10-11.

[10] Martin, p. 13.

[11] Riggins, p. 12.

[12] Riggins, pp. 12-13.

[13] Biographical information on Foucault was obtained from the following sources: Sheridan, pp. 4, 8; Michel Foucault, *Power/Knowledge: Selected Interviews and Other Writings 1927-1977,* trans. Colin Gordon et al., ed. Colin Gordon (New York: Pantheon, 1980), p. 231; Otto Friedrich, "France's Philosopher of Power," *Time,* November 16, 1981, p. 148; Hayden White, "Michel Foucault," in *Structuralism and Since: From Lévi-Strauss to Derrida,* ed. John Sturrock (Oxford: Oxford University Press, 1979), p. 81; "Philosopher and Author M. Foucault," *Chicago Tribune,* June 26, 1984, sec. 1, p. 12; Riggins; and Martin.

[14] Foucault, *The Use of Pleasure,* p. 6.

[15] Martin, p. 15.

[16] The episteme is defined in Michel Foucault, *The Archaeology of Knowledge,* trans. A.M. Sheridan Smith (New York: Pantheon, 1972), pp. 38, 191; and Michel Foucault, *The Order of Things: An Archaeology of the Human Sciences* (New York: Pantheon, 1970), p. xx.

[17] The relationship Foucault sees among epistemes is discussed in David Carroll, "The Subject of Archeology or the Sovereignty of the Episteme," *MLN,* 93 (May 1978), 707, 716; Jan Miel, "Ideas or Epistemes: Hazard Versus Foucault," *Yale French Studies,* 49 (1973), 239; E.M. Henning, "Archaeology, Deconstruction, and Intellectual History," in *Modern European Intellectual History: Reappraisals and New Perspectives,* ed. Dominick LaCapra and Steven L. Kaplan (Ithaca, NY: Cornell University Press, 1982), p. 157; David Carroll, *Paraesthetics: Foucault, Lyotard, Derrida* (New York: Methuen, 1987), pp. 61-62; and Pierre Boncenne, "On Power," in *Michel Foucault: Politics, Philosophy, Culture: Interviews and Other Writings: 1977-1984,* trans. Alan Sheridan et al., ed. Lawrence D. Kritzman (New York: Routledge, 1988), pp. 99-100.

[18] Among those associated with structuralism are Ferdinand de Saussure and Roman Jakobson in linguistics, Roland Barthes in literary criticism, Claude Lévi-Strauss in social anthropology, Jacques Lacan in psychiatry, and Louis Althusser in philosophy. Structuralists generally share the conviction that laws exist by which the human world is ordered and that surface events and phenomena are to be explained by structures, data, and phenomena below the surface. Richard T. De George and Fernande M. De George, eds., *The Structuralists: From Marx to Lévi-Strauss* (Garden City, NY: Anchor, 1972), p. xii. Whether or not Foucault is a structuralist has been the subject of a great deal of discussion; he denied that he was. See, for example, Foucault, *The Order of Things*, p. xiv; Foucault, *Power/Knowledge*, p. 114; and Allan Megill, *Prophets of Extremity: Nietzsche, Heidegger, Foucault, Derrida* (Berkeley: University of California Press, 1985), pp. 183-219. For a summary of the arguments on both sides, see Allan Megill, "Foucault, Structuralism, and the Ends of History," *Journal of Modern History*, 51 (September 1979), 451-503.

[19] Jean-Paul Brodeur, "McDonnell on Foucault: Supplementary Remarks," *Canadian Journal of Philosophy*, 7 (September 1977), 558-59; and Dominique Lecourt, *Marxism and Epistemology: Bachelard, Canguilhem and Foucault*, trans. Ben Brewster (London: HLB, 1975), p. 189.

[20] Foucault defines statement in *The Archaeology of Knowledge*, pp. 80, 86. Other discussions of this concept can be found in: Carole Blair, "The Statement: Foundation of Foucault's Historical Criticism," *Western Journal of Speech Communication*, 51 (Fall 1987), 364-83; Carole Blair and Martha Cooper, "The Humanist Turn in Foucault's Rhetoric of Inquiry," *Quarterly Journal of Speech*, 73 (May 1987), 152-64; and Gilles Deleuze, *Foucault*, trans. and ed. Séan Hand (Minneapolis: University of Minnesota Press, 1988), pp. 2-12.

[21] Michel Foucault, *The History of Sexuality: Volume 1: An Introduction*, trans. Robert Hurley (New York: Pantheon, 1978), 4. The link between discourse and knowledge is summarized in Hubert L. Dreyfus and Paul Rabinow, *Michel Foucault: Beyond Structuralism and Hermeneutics* (Chicago: University of Chicago Press, 1982), p. 48.

[22] Michel Foucault, "The Discourse on Language," in *The Archaeology of Knowledge*, p. 216.

[23] Rules concerning objects of discourse are discussed in Foucault, *The Archaeology of Knowledge*, pp. 41-44.

[24] Foucault, "The Discourse on Language," p. 217. See pp. 224-25 for a discussion of rules concerning who is allowed expression.

[25] Rules concerning the formation of concepts and theories are discussed in: Foucault, *The Archaeology of Knowledge*, pp. 56-57, 68; Michel Foucault, "History, Discourse, and Discontinuity," trans. Anthony M. Nazarro, *Salmagundi*, 20 (Summer-Fall 1972), 234; and Foucault, "The Discourse on Language," pp. 218-19.

[26] Foucault, *The Order of Things*, p. xxiii.

[27] For Foucault's discussion of the episteme of the Renaissance, see *The Order of Things*, pp. 17, 19, 20, 36.

[28] Foucault discusses the episteme of the Classical Age in *The Order of Things*, pp. 58-67.

[29] The episteme of Modernity is discussed in Foucault, *The Order of Things*, pp. xxiii, 43.

[30] Evidence for the emergence of a new conception of the human being is discussed in: Roy McMullen, "Michel Foucault," *Horizon*, 11 (Autumn 1969), 37; Foucault, *The Order of Things*, p. 386; and Foucault, *Power/Knowledge*, p. 117.

[31] Foucault, *The Order of Things*, p. xiv. Phenomenology is an investigative approach based on the premise that all knowledge of the world is gained from our own particular points of view or experiences. It attempts to describe the forms of conscious experience that usually are taken for granted. Edmund Husserl and Maurice Merleau-Ponty are associated with outlining the phenomenological approach.

[32] Carole Blair discusses these responses in rev. of *Michel Foucault: Beyond Structuralism and Hermeneutics*, by Hubert L. Dreyfus and Paul Rabinow, and *Michel Foucault: Social Theory and Transgression*, by Charles C. Lemert and Garth Gillian, *Quarterly Journal of Speech*, 70 (February 1984), 103. See also Blair and Cooper, p. 161.

[33] This summary of humanism is provided in Blair and Cooper, p. 153.

[34] Blair and Cooper, p. 161.

[35] Foucault, *Power/Knowledge*, p. 51.

[36] Foucault, *Discipline and Punish*, p. 27.

37 The relationship between power and knowledge is discussed in Foucault, *Power/Knowledge*, pp. 51, 52.

38 Gerard Raulet, "Critical Theory/Intellectual History," trans. Jeremy Harding, in *Michel Foucault: Politics, Philosophy, Culture: Interviews and Other Writings: 1977-1984*, trans. Alan Sheridan et al., ed. Lawrence D. Kritzman (New York: Routledge, 1988), p. 43.

39 Foucault, *Discipline and Punish*, p. 27.

40 Foucault, *Power/Knowledge*, p. 93.

41 Power is defined in Foucault, *Power/Knowledge*, p. 198; and Raúl Fornet-Betancourt, Helmut Becker, and Alfredo Gomez-Müller, "The Ethic of Care for the Self as a Practice of Freedom: An Interview with Michel Foucault on January 20, 1984," trans. J.D. Gauthier, in *The Final Foucault*, ed. James Bernauer and David Rasmussen (Cambridge: MIT Press, 1988), p. 11.

42 The omnipresence of power is discussed in: Foucault, *The History of Sexuality*, pp. 93, 94; Révoltes Logiques Collective, "Power and Strategies," trans. Paul Patton, in *Michel Foucault: Power, Truth, Strategy* (Sydney, Australia: Feral, 1979), p. 55; Lucette Finas, "Interview with Lucette Finas," trans. Paul Foss and Meaghan Morris, in *Michel Foucault: Power, Truth, Strategy* (Sydney, Australia: Feral, 1979), p. 70; and Foucault, *Power/Knowledge*, p. 98.

43 For Foucault's discussion of the traditional legal view of power, see *Power/Knowledge*, pp. 88, 94, 95.

44 The need to break with the legal view of power is discussed in Foucault, *The History of Sexuality*, p. 90; and Foucault, *Power/Knowledge*, p. 121.

45 Foucault, *The History of Sexuality*, p. 137.

46 Foucault, *The History of Sexuality*, p. 85.

47 Foucault, *Power/Knowledge*, p. 119.

48 Foucault, *Discipline and Punish*, pp. 266-68.

49 The inadequacy of a repressive view of power is discussed in Foucault, *Power/Knowledge*, pp. 92, 184.

50 Nancy Fraser, "Foucault on Modern Power: Empirical Insights and Normative Confusions," *Praxis International*, 1 (October 1981), 283. Others who discuss the issue of resistance in Foucault's works are: Tom Keenan, "The 'Paradox' of Knowledge and Power: Reading Foucault on a Bias," *Political Theory*, 15 (February 1987), 5-37; and Barry Smart, "The Politics of Truth and the Problem of Hegemony," in *Foucault: A Critical Reader*, ed. David Couzens Hoy (New York: Basil Blackwell, 1986), pp. 166-69.

51 Foucault, *Power/Knowledge*, p. 138.

52 Foucault, *History of Sexuality*, p. 96.

53 Fornet-Betancourt, Becker, and Gomez-Müller, p. 18.

54 For discussions of Foucault's refusal to envision an ideal society, see: Michael Walzer, "The Politics of Michel Foucault," in *Foucault: A Critical Reader*, ed. David Couzens Hoy (New York: Basil Blackwell, 1986), pp. 51-68; Megill, *Prophets of Extremity*, pp. 195-98; and Nancy Fraser, "Foucault's Body-Language: A Post-Humanist Political Rhetoric?," *Salmagundi*, 61 (Fall 1983), 55-70.

55 Foucault, *Power/Knowledge*, p. 126.

56 Michel Foucault, "Politics and Reason," in *Michel Foucault: Politics, Philosophy, Culture: Interviews and Other Writings: 1977-1984*, trans. Alan Sheridan et al., ed. Lawrence D. Kritzman (New York: Routledge, 1988), p. 156. Differences between universal and specific intellectuals also are discussed in: Eve Tavor Bannet, *Structuralism and the Logic of Dissent: Barthes, Derrida, Foucault, Lacan* (Urbana: University of Illinois Press, 1989), pp. 170-83; and Barry Smart, *Michel Foucault* (New York: Tavistock, 1985), pp. 66-68.

57 Didier Eribon, "Practicing Criticism," in *Michel Foucault: Politics, Philosophy, Culture: Interviews and Other Writings: 1977-1984*, trans. Alan Sheridan et al., ed. Lawrence D. Kritzman (New York: Routledge, 1988), pp. 154-55. Foucault also discusses the notion of criticism in: Francois Ewald, "The Concern for Truth," in *Michel Foucault: Politics, Philosophy, Culture: 1977-1984*, trans. Alan Sheridan et al., ed. Lawrence D. Kritzman (New York: Routledge, 1988), p. 265; and Martin, p. 10.

58 Eribon, p. 156.

59 Martin, p. 4.

[60] Fornet-Betancourt, Becker, and Gomez-Müller, p. 11.

[61] For an excellent summary of Foucault's view of ethics, see: John Rajchman, "Ethics After Foucault," *Social Text*, 13/14 (Winter/Spring 1986), 165-83.

[62] Michel Foucault, "On the Genealogy of Ethics: An Overview of Work in Progress," in *The Foucault Reader*, ed. Paul Rabinow (New York: Pantheon, 1984), p. 352.

[63] Foucault, "On the Genealogy of Ethics," p. 353.

[64] Foucault, "On the Genealogy of Ethics," p. 355.

[65] Foucault, "On the Genealogy of Ethics," p. 362. For other discussions of the four aspects of ethics, see: Foucault, *The Use of Pleasure*, pp. 26-28; and Arnold I. Davidson, "Archaeology, Genealogy, Ethics," in *Foucault: A Critical Reader*, ed. David Couzens Hoy (New York: Basil Blackwell, 1986), pp. 228-29.

[66] Archaeology is discussed in: Michel Foucault, *Madness and Civilization: A History of Insanity in the Age of Reason*, trans. Richard Howard (New York: Vintage, 1973), p. xi; John K. Simon, "A Conversation with Michel Foucault," *Partisan Review*, 38 (1971), 192; Foucault, *The Archaeology of Knowledge*, p. 29; Miel, p. 235; and Smart, pp. 48-54.

[67] "Genealogy" was a term used by Nietzsche, who had a major influence on Foucault's work. Foucault discusses his debt to Nietzsche in *Language, Counter-Memory, Practice: Selected Essays and Interviews*, trans. Donald F. Bouchard and Sherry Simon, ed. Donald F. Bouchard (Ithaca, NY: Cornell University Press, 1977), pp. 139-64. For more on Nietzsche's influence on Foucault, see Megill, "Foucault, Structuralism, and the Ends of History," p. 459; and Sheridan, pp. 114-20.

[68] Foucault, *The History of Sexuality*, p. 11.

[69] For discussions of the differences between "archaeology" and "genealogy," see: Michel Foucault, *Discipline and Punish: The Birth of the Prison*, trans. Alan Sheridan (New York: Pantheon, 1977), p. 31; Simon, p. 192; Michael S. Roth, "Foucault's 'History of the Present,'" *History and Theory*, 20 (1981), 44; Dreyfus and Rabinow, pp. 102-03; and Blair, p. 102. Martha Cooper's interpretation of archaeology and genealogy is different from that of many scholars in that she does not see Foucault as having abandoned archaeology once he developed the notion of genealogy; her interpretation has influenced our discussion here. See Martha Cooper, "The Implications of Foucault's Archaeological Theory of Discourse for Contemporary Rhetorical Theory and Criticism," Diss. Pennsylvania State University 1984.

[70] Foucault, *Power/Knowledge*, pp. 50-57.

[71] Foucault, *The Archaeology of Knowledge*, p. 109.

[72] For a summary of Foucault's position on interpretation, see Blair, rev. of *Michel Foucault*, p. 102.

[73] See, for example, Foucault, "Politics and Reason," pp. 57-85.

[74] Foucault, *The Archaeology of Knowledge*, p. 151.

[75] The author as a discursive function is discussed in: Foucault, "History, Discourse and Discontinuity," p. 235; Foucault, *The Order of Things*, p. 63; and Foucault, *Language, Counter-Memory, Practice*, p. 115.

[76] Foucault, *The Archaeology of Knowledge*, p. 27. Description is also discussed in Michel Foucault, *The Birth of the Clinic: An Archaeology of Medical Perception*, trans. A.M. Sheridan Smith (New York: Pantheon, 1973), p. xvii. Foucault discusses his methodological principles in *The Archaeology of Knowledge*, pp. 141-77. For a good summary, see Blair and Cooper, pp. 165-67.

[77] Brodeur, pp. 565-66.

[78] Vernon Pratt, "Foucault & the History of Classification Theory," *Studies in History and Philosophy of Science*, 8 (1977), 163; Meaghan Morris and Paul Patton, "Preface," in *Michel Foucault: Power, Truth, Strategy*, p. 8; Edward W. Said, *Beginnings: Intention and Method* (New York: Basic, 1975), p. 291; and Friedrich, p. 147.

[79] Blair, "The Statement," pp. 368-69.

[80] McMullen, p. 39; and Pratt, p. 163.

[81] Miel, p. 236.

[82] White, pp. 81, 92.

[83] Bannet, p. 109.

[84] Ronald Hayman, "Cartography of Discourse?" *Encounter*, 47 (December 1976), 72.

[85] Megill, "Foucault, Structuralism, and the Ends of History," p. 486.

86 Rev. of *The Archaeology of Knowledge and the Discourse on Language*, *Kirkus Reviews*, 40 (July 15, 1972), 834.

87 Hayman, p. 74.

88 John Mepham, "The Structuralist Sciences and Philosophy," in *Structuralism: An Introduction*, ed. David Robey (Oxford: Clarendon, 1973), p. 106.

89 Sidonie Clauss, "John Wilkins' Essay Toward a Real Character: Its Place in the Seventeenth-Century Episteme," *Journal of the History of Ideas*, 43 (October-December 1982), 552.

90 McMullen, pp. 38-39; Mepham, p. 106; George Huppert, *"Divinatio et Eruditio:* Thoughts on Foucault," *History and Theory*, 13 (1974), 198; David E. Leary, "Essay Review: Michel Foucault, an Historian of the Sciences Humaines," *Journal of the History of the Behavioral Sciences*, 12 (July 1976), 291-92.

91 R.D. Laing, "'Insanity and Madness': The Invention of Madness," *New Statesman*, 71 (June 16, 1967), 843.

92 Friedrich, p. 148.

93 Mark Poster, *Foucault, Marxism and History: Mode of Production versus Mode of Information* (Cambridge, England: Polity, 1984), pp. 146-47.

94 For example, see Finas, p. 67.

95 Révoltes Logiques Collective, p. 58.

96 Sheridan, p. 222.

97 Foucault, *The Archaeology of Knowledge*, p. 17.

98 Martin, p. 9.

99 Foucault, "The Minimalist Self," p. 14.

100 Robert J. Ellrich, rev. of *Language, Counter-Memory, Practice*, by Michel Foucault, *Modern Language Journal*, 62 (April 1978), 206.

9

Jürgen Habermas

"Scarcely anyone would now challenge what other people have said many times about Habermas, namely that he is one of the most important figures in German intellectual life today and perhaps the most important sociologist since Max Weber."[1] Despite the considerable influence of Habermas, reflected in Michael Pusey's statement, Habermas' works have begun to be integrated into the discipline of communication only in the last decade.

Several factors are responsible for the relatively limited reception Habermas has received by communication scholars. First, his work is interdisciplinary; debates with contemporary thinkers are interspersed with reconstructions of the work of philosophers and theorists of the past—Karl Marx, Max Weber, Wilhelm Dilthey, Georg Lukács, Sigmund Freud, George Herbert Mead, and Talcott Parsons—whom Habermas treats as dialogue partners. Habermas' knowledge is encyclopedic, and he assumes that his readers also are familiar with a range of disciplines, philosophical traditions, and approaches. His dense writing style, combined with the difficulties of translation, also hinders understanding. As Wilby comments: "His writing is about as accessible to the average man (even the average honours graduate) as an engineering textbook in Swahili.''[2] Despite these potential obstacles, however, Habermas' thought is finding its way into a variety of disciplines, including that of speech communication.

Jürgen Habermas is the son of Ernst Habermas and Greta Kottgen Habermas. He was born in Dusseldorf, Germany, on June 18, 1929, but grew up in Gummersbach, where his father was head of the Bureau of Industry and Trade. He was raised in Nazi Germany, and as a child, he was in the Hitler Youth. His parents, however, were neither pro-Nazi nor pro-opposition, a response to the political climate Habermas believes was fairly typical of the times; he calls it "bourgeois adaptation to a political situation with which one did not fully identify, but which one didn't seriously criticize, either." For Habermas, the turning point in his awareness was the end of the war. Fifteen years old at the time, he remembers radio news reports of the Nuremberg trials and documentary films of concentration camps playing in movie theatres. The effect of these experiences was the shattering of normality: "All at once we saw that we had been living in a politically criminal system." Habermas summarizes the impact of these experiences on his political development this way: "For my generation, it was an experience of such magnitude that it affected the rest of our lives. There was no choice but to become more or less politically minded."[3]

Habermas graduated from high school in 1949 and went on to the Universities of Gottingen, Zurich, and Bonn, where he studied philosophy, history, psychology, German literature, and economics. He recalls his alarm at finding that his professors' thinking did not seem to have been altered by the war, nor did they seem to reflect critically on the philosophical views they espoused; his reaction to these observations was formative in Habermas' subsequent enthusiasm for critical theory. He received his doctorate from the University of Bonn in 1954, having written his dissertation on Friedrich Schelling's philosophy of history. He married Ute Wesselhöft in 1955; they have three children.

In 1955, Habermas read Max Horkeimer and Theodor Adorno's *Dialectic of Enlightenment*, which was his first exposure to critical theory. He described its impact on his thinking this way:

> What fascinated me right away with those two was that they weren't engaging in a reception of Marx; they were utilizing him. It was a great experience for me to see that one could relate systematically to the Marxist tradition. . . . At that point philosophical and political things began to come together for the first time.

Habermas' interest in critical theory brought him to the Institute for Social Research in Frankfurt, or the "Frankfurt School," as it is sometimes called, where he served as a research assistant to Adorno from 1955 to 1959. His association with Adorno and the other "critical theorists" at the Institute was a major influence on his thinking, an influence Habermas describes as "absolutely electrifying." Today, Habermas is considered the leading spokesperson for a new generation of critical theorists coming out of the Institute for Social Research. We will return to Habermas' association with the Frankfurt School when we discuss the major influences on his work.

Following his direct association with the Institute, Habermas obtained a professorship in philosophy at the University of Heidelberg. He held this position until 1964, when he became a professor of philosophy and sociology at the University of Frankfurt. Seven years later, he took over the directorship of the Max Planck Institute in Starnberg, West Germany. At the same time, in 1971, Habermas' *Theory and Practice* was published in German; it was translated into English in 1973. Habermas was offered a professorship in philosophy at the University of Frankfurt in 1975, a position he held until 1982. Since then, he has had a regular appointment as a professor of philosophy at the University of Frankfurt.

Interspersed throughout Habermas' career have been several visiting professorships to universities in the United States. In 1967, he was the Theodor Heuss professor at the New School for Social Research in New York, a position followed by service as the Christian Gauss Lecturer at Princeton University in 1971. Habermas became a research fellow at the Center for the Humanities at Wesleyan University in Middletown, Connecticut, in 1972, and in 1974, he moved to the Department of Sociology at the University of California, Santa Barbara, as a visiting professor. He held the position of visiting professor jointly in the department of Sociology at the University of Pennsylvania in Philadelphia and at Haverford College in Haverford, Pennsylvania, in 1976. In that year, too, his book, *Communication and the Evolution of Society*, was published. In 1980, he was visiting professor in both sociology and philosophy at the University of California at Berkeley. He continues to write prolifically, publishing *Philosophical-Political Profiles: Studies in Contemporary German Social Theory* in 1983 and two additional books in 1984—*Observations on the Spiritual Situation of the Age: Contemporary German Perspectives* and *The Theory of Communicative Action, Volume I: Reason and the Rationalization of Society*. The second volume in the series, *The Theory of Communicative Action: Life-world and System: A Critique of Functionalist Reason*, was published in 1987, and *On the Logic of the Social Sciences* followed in 1988.

Habermas has received several distinguished awards throughout his career, including the Hegel Prize in 1974, the Sigmund Freud Prize in 1976, and the Adorno Prize in 1980. He was awarded an honorary doctorate of law from the New School for Social Research in 1980.

In addition to his academic career, Habermas gained considerable renown during the student protests of the 1960s. He was considered one of the intellectual mentors of the *Socialistische Deutsche Studentenbund*, the German equivalent of the Students for a Democratic Society. He served as a spokesperson for the radicalization of society from within the student ranks, arguing that "the only comprehensive conceptions for universities in a democratically constituted industrial society have been worked out by students."[4]

In the late 1960s, however, Habermas fell into disfavor with the student movement. He published *Toward a Rational Society: Student Protest, Science and Politics* in 1968, in which he criticized the student movement for its disintegration into "actionism," a term he uses to mean direct political action as a compulsive and unthinking response to all conflict situations: "The new tactics have the advantage of obtaining rapid publicity. But they also bear dangers, . . . the danger of diversion, either into the privatization of an easily consolable hippie subculture or into the fruitless violent acts of the actionists."[5]

The students, in turn, criticized Habermas' failure to become involved in actual struggles—they claimed he stays in the realm of academic theory although he advocates the unity of theory and practice in the practical arena. His book, *Knowledge and Human Interests*, published in 1968, is a theoretical effort to delimit a social theory and, as such, may have been used as evidence for Habermas' retreat into the theoretical realm. Despite such criticisms, Habermas still sees the protest movement as having significant effects: "It brought about a certain rupture in the normative area, in attitudes, in the cultural value system."[6]

Habermas has emphasized his theoretical interests in the last couple of decades, although he is not unaware of and unconcerned about their practical implications. According to Habermas, theoretical matters "are not simply arguments which are absorbed by the scholarly process and then survive or dissolve within it. On the contrary, as published and spoken words, they have an effect on readers and listeners at the moment of their reception which the author cannot revoke or withdraw as if he or she were dealing with logical propositions."[7] Thus, Habermas sees himself as engaged in several distinct but not separate spheres, including "real" philosophizing; teaching; scientific work; and political *praxis*, or practical application. However, he appreciates— and perhaps even prefers—the opportunities provided by the academic life for examining questions of truth and believes a place for this kind of work is needed in society.

Sources of Habermas' Thought

The overall purpose of Habermas' work is to develop a theory of society that aims at the self-emancipation of people from domination, and a theory of communication lies at its core. He is a prolific writer, and with each new publication, his views continue to be developed and elaborated. Furthermore, Habermas never has been content to rely on a single intellectual tradition. Instead, he is a synthesizer: he makes use of those ideas of a school or individual he finds valuable in order to "open up subjects from the inside out." Habermas comments on his approach: "Even when I quote a good deal and take over other terminologies I am clearly aware that my use of them often has little to do with the authors' original meaning. . . . I take over other theories. Why not? One should accept others according to their strengths and then see how one can go from there."[8]

Our intent here, then, is to sketch Habermas' major themes and the general evolution of his thought, while recognizing the encyclopedic range of his writing and the fact that a final account of his work is impossible. The six major philosophical traditions important to Habermas' work that we will discuss are Marxism, critical theory, hermeneutics, positivism, Freudian psychoanalysis, and language philosophy.

Marxism

Probably the most powerful influence on Habermas' thought was Marx, whose work Habermas first encountered as a young boy. Not until he read Georg Lukács, however, who relies heavily on Marx, did Habermas begin to take Marxism seriously. But even when Habermas began to associate with the critical theorists of the Frankfurt School, for whom Marxism was central, he did not consider himself a Marxist. Adorno recalls that Habermas avoided saying Marx's name: "'Have a look at this withering away of the state stuff, he used to ask me.'"[9] Habermas seems to have been reluctant to commit himself to a single orientation, such as Marxism, but now accepts the label willingly: "I was taken aback when my friend [Karl-Otto] Apel publicly called me a Neo-Marxist for the first time. Then I thought it over and decided he was right. Today I value being considered a Marxist."[10]

Given the Marxist influence on Habermas' work, a discussion of the sources of Habermas' thought would be incomplete without a brief mention of the tenets of Marxism. They can be summarized as follows:

1. Humans' self-realization or growth depends on production or work and on the relationships established around the processes of production.

2. Under capitalism, products are manufactured primarily for value and profit and not to fulfill human needs.

3. In such a society, the products of human labor are objectified; they are seen as having lives of their own apart from those who make

them. As a result, the commodities begin to control the nature of human labor or work rather than the reverse.

4. The control of society by the process of production is not immediately comprehensible to the members of that society because of ideologies or illusionary belief systems which, though false, are taken as adequate by society. Social change occurs when the dogmatic and false character of ideologies is dispelled.[11]

While Marxist thought served as a starting point for Habermas, he does not accept all of Marx's ideas. He offers what he calls a "reconstruction" of Marxism, by which he means "taking a theory apart and putting it back together in a new form in order to attain more fully the goal it has set for itself."[12] The core ideas of Marxism, then, appear less frequently in Habermas' later writing, prompting Wilby to assert that Marx is "only a distant echo [in Habermas' work], like the Book of Genesis in the writings of radical theologians."[13]

Critical Theory

Habermas' first systematic encounter with Marx came from the critical theorists of the Frankfurt School, and they influenced Habermas in ways other than simply introducing him to Marxism. Founded in 1923 by Felix Weil, the Institute's members believe that society itself can be experienced as an arrangement of ideas that invites rational critique. For critical theorists, knowledge inevitably is connected with the situation and interests of those involved; it is not something objective and uncontaminated by the inquirer or researcher. Therefore, rather than objectively removing themselves from society, critical theorists involve themselves in it in order to discern and reveal the contradictions in society. The second step for critical theorists is the critique of society, undertaken in order to create a more rational society in the future. Thus, it aims at both the interpretation and transformation of society.

Carl Grünberg was the first director of the Institute for Social Relations and was responsible for the Marxist underpinnings of the school. Marx's *Critique of Political Economy* served as the starting point for interdisciplinary analyses of a variety of social concerns, ranging from European labor movements to capitalism, authoritarianism, and ideology.[14]

In 1933, with the rise of Nazism, the members of the Institute were forced to flee Germany and emigrated briefly to Geneva, Switzerland. In 1935, the Institute moved to New York City, where it existed under the protective wing of Columbia University until it was re-established in Frankfurt in 1953.

Although the concerns of critical theorists have shifted in focus over time, three tenets have remained fundamental to their thought. First, critical theory includes the desire for society to move in the direction of the rational or to be emancipated from unnecessary domination. The fear that technological rationality will take over all human values is the impetus for this focus. Thus, reason is not seen as a pure and unattainable absolute for the members of the school of critical theory. Rather, it is understood to be a progressive sense of self-consciousness, or the ability to see that the existing world is not inherently rational but can be made so. The term ''self-consciousness'' is crucial here. Inherent to the concept of reason, as articulated by the critical theorists, is the notion that the rational embodies contradictions—that one cannot be rational if one cannot see the evils or irrationality of the world as well as understand that it need not remain that way.[15] The early generation of critical theorists sought to inform the world about the seemingly unconscious acceptance of technological rationality at the expense of more human concerns.

Critical theorists also advocate a need for a unity of theory and practice. In attempting to analyze the shortcomings of society and to aid in the development of practical remedies for them, they seek to relate their research into the various forms of social life to the nature of society as a whole. Thus, current events contribute substantially to the development of critical theory and, in turn, the resulting theoretical knowledge is used in the study of the conditions of existing society. If, as critical theorists, for example, we were to study the rise of the contemporary women's movement in the United States, we would need to make our theoretical knowledge concrete by researching the activities of actual women's groups. At the same time, we would need to place our research in a broader historical framework. In the end, our observations would allow us to offer suggestions to the movement about tactics and strategies. This is precisely Habermas' task in *Toward a Rational Society*, in which he offers a critique of the student protest movement in Germany. In addition to making tactical suggestions to the students, Habermas places their position in a historical context as well by discussing the role of the university and education in German society as a whole.

The emphasis on reason and on the inseparability of theory and practice makes inevitable the next tenet of critical theory—the critique of ideology or false consciousness. An ideology, as defined by the critical theorists, is a system of irrational or distorted beliefs that maintains its legitimacy despite the fact that it could not be validated if subjected to rational discourse.[16] By the analysis and penetration of such ideologies, critical theorists show the irrationality of such systems, thereby contributing to society's move toward reason.

Under the direction of Habermas and his colleagues—the second generation of critical theorists—new concerns have altered the research directions of the Institute. One such element is an interest in interaction. Habermas argues that social life is based on a variety of symbolic exchanges that must be considered if a theory of society is to be grounded in actuality. Thus, the current group of critical theorists devotes considerably more attention to communication, dialogue, and discourse than did the earlier generation, who essentially ignored the effects of discourse and communication systems on society.[17]

Hermeneutics

The next two major sources of influence on Habermas — hermeneutics and positivism — may be thought of as ways to discover or approach knowledge. Hermeneutics influenced Habermas favorably, while much of Habermas' work is a reaction against positivism. Ultimately, however, Habermas sees both approaches as incapable of providing a complete explanation of the world.

"Hermeneutics" means interpretation or "interpretative understanding." Originally, hermeneutics was a method for the interpretation of Biblical texts. It was used for the understanding of texts both in their own context — on their own terms — and for taking their contemporary meanings into account. The German theologian Friedrich Schleiermacher laid the foundations for a general science of interpretation with the publication of his book, *Hermeneutik* [*Hermeneutics*] in 1819. For Schleiermacher, hermeneutics was the study of understanding, an effort at re-experiencing the world and consciousness of the text, action, or object under consideration as the original creator(s) meant it. Martin Heidegger introduced the notion of hermeneutical understanding as a dialogue between the text and the interpreter. The interpreter asks "questions" of the text and receives understanding through the "answers" received.[18]

Wilhelm Dilthey is another major figure in the hermeneutic tradition and one whose works have had a significant impact on Habermas' thinking. For Dilthey, hermeneutics is a universal method by which to know the life-world. For both Schleiermacher and Dilthey, the interpreter's own situation is considered to be negative; it is a source of biases that inevitably distorts understanding. On the other hand, Hans-Georg Gadamer, a contemporary contributor to hermeneutics, argues that the knower's situation, with all its prejudices and interests, is productive to understanding; such filters allow for different meanings to emerge as each new interpreter approaches a text. Habermas criticized Gadamer's view of hermeneutics in 1967, which prompted a continuing exchange between the two on the subject of hermeneutics and its value for critical theory. While Habermas sees much to commend in hermeneutics, he tends to see it as a method or way of knowing for the social sciences. Gadamer, in contrast, emphasizes hermeneutics as a fundamental way of being.[19] Hermeneutics, then, has expanded beyond the analysis of literal texts; it now is considered applicable to all situations, events, and phenomena that can be subjected to interpretation. All of these kinds of phenomena are "texts" that offer clues about how humans give meaning to their world.

Positivism

Hermeneutics exists in direct contrast to positivism, or the purely disinterested scientific interpretation of experience. Thus, positivism is not a constructive influence on Habermas in the same way that Marxism, critical theory, and hermeneutics have been; rather, it is a philosophy against which he generally reacts. While hermeneutics takes into account the responses of the interpreter or knower, the positivist approach attempts to separate the knower from the object of study and to examine it in an objective fashion.

The term "positivism" has become so encompassing and has taken such a variety of forms in different historical contexts that the basic positivist position is not easy to identify. Phrases such as "hypothetical-deductive," "empiricism," "scientism," and "logical positivism" are seen as embodying the basic positivist perspective, although these are by no means synonymous terms. We will not attempt to discuss all of the nuances of positivism and its derivatives here, but because much of Habermas' work is a critique of positivism, an understanding of its basic tenets is necessary.

The origins of positivism as a philosophy are said to lie with Auguste Comte, who wrote *Course de philosophie positive* [*The Course of Positive Philosophy*] in 1864. Comte used the term "positive" to refer to factual and certain knowledge as opposed to the imaginary and inexact.[20] In essence, positivism links knowledge with science. It is based on the assumption that the scientific method provides the key to certain knowledge and that something is not real unless it can be tested empirically. In general, positivism is characterized by the following beliefs:

1. The scientific method is superior for investigating not only the realm of the natural sciences but the human social realm as well.

2. Scientific knowledge is testable. Thus, it deals with those experiences that can be observed and reported, and it denies the significance or validity of subjective states such as feelings, desires, emotions, values, and thoughts that cannot be measured empirically.

3. The aim of positivistic inquiry is the discovery of law-like generalizations that then can be used to explain and predict behavior.

4. Scientific inquiry is value-free; it strives for objectivity and neutrality.[21]

As we will see, Habermas attacks positivism for its singular view of the world. He distinguishes knowledge of the natural world from the knowledge of what is human and believes that when the scientific method is applied to the human realm, dehumanization results. Thus, he faults the exclusive validity of positivism and attempts to develop an approach to knowledge that also takes into account the subjective.

Freudian Psychoanalysis

Habermas found in Freudian psychoanalysis a model to use as a starting point for a critical theory of society that is grounded in both the empirical and hermeneutic sciences and yet allows for self-reflection. A brief description of the process of psychoanalysis will show why Habermas chooses this as his model for a critical theory. In psychoanalysis, analyst and patient engage in dialogue, the purpose of which is to enable the analyst to attempt to get behind the explanations offered by the patient and to reveal the unconscious structure responsible for the dysfunctional pattern of behavior. The patient's responsibility is to confirm or reject the psychoanalyst's interpretations; where the pattern is shown to be disturbed or distorted, the patient can correct it. The analyst reconstructs what has been forgotten from the patient's "faulty texts" — dreams, associations, repetitions, and the like.

Exposing the motivational bases of behavior to critical perusal allows the patient to see self-deceptions. Motivated by the constructions suggested by the analyst, the patient is led through the process of self-reflection: "Only the patient's recollection decides the accuracy of the construction. If it applies, then it must also 'restore' to the patient a portion of lost life history: that is it must be able to elicit a self-reflection."[22]

Habermas sees parallels between psychoanalysis and the critical theory he envisions for society. The effort to get to the unconscious sources of an individual's thought and behavior suggests the efforts of critical thought to uncover the limitations and constraints operating in society. What Freud provided the individual, then, Habermas wants to provide society. At both the individual and cultural levels, systematically distorted or deviant communication must be uncovered, penetrated, and reconstructed rationally. At the individual level, systematically distorted communication is manifest in *neuroses*; the individual is unconsciously self-deceptive in dealing with or talking to self. These neuroses have their counterpart at the societal level in the form of *ideologies*. Thus, just as psychoanalysis is useful when an individual's "texts" are distorted by repressions, so the distorted "texts" of society can benefit from the application and reflexivity of critical thought. Psychoanalysis and critical theory also share a common goal — emancipation — which for Habermas implies self-understanding, autonomy of action, and the achievement of rational control over influences that previously dominated conduct. Finally, the emancipatory aims of psychoanalysis and critical theory can be realized only through language; language is the medium through which personal understanding occurs as well as the basis for Habermas' model of a rational society.

Philosophy of Language

The tradition of the philosophy of language is another major influence on Habermas. He relies heavily on the work of linguistic scholars, who attempt to analyze such features of language as meaning, reference, verification, speech acts, and logical necessity.[23] Two approaches within this tradition have proved particularly important to Habermas.

The first is the "ordinary language" approach of Ludwig Wittgenstein, J.L. Austin, and J.R. Searle. These philosophers believe the way language is used in interaction is a more important source of meaning than its logical structure or the way words stand for the things they represent. Wittgenstein, a German philosopher who is considered the founder of ordinary language philosophy, believes language in use constitutes a language game, in which we use rules to perform verbal acts. Austin and his student, Searle, further elaborated this notion by developing the concept of a speech act. A speech act is the basic unit of language for expressing intention. In other words, when we speak, we perform an intentional act—whether it involves promising, asking, demanding, or simply stating. Usually, a sentence is a speech act, but a word or phrase can be a speech act if it includes intention and is governed by the rules necessary to play the particular language game. A word such as "please" is a speech act, as is the sentence, "It is five o'clock." In each case, however, the exact meaning of the speech act cannot be determined unless the context and intention involved are known. Habermas' notion of the ideal speech situation, as we will see, relies heavily on speech-act theory.

A second approach within the philosophy of language that has been significant in terms of Habermas' work is Noam Chomsky's generative or transformational grammar. Chomsky focuses on the rules we use to generate sentences and on how speakers become competent at constructing sentences.[24] Habermas combines Chomsky's notion of communication competence with the notion of speech acts; together, these serve as the foundation for his theory of communicative competence.

The six sources of influence just discussed are included merely to suggest the breadth of Habermas' thought. He refuses to rely on any single tradition or approach, preferring to choose from among a variety of perspectives those concepts he finds valuable. While he began as a Marxist and still directs his efforts at critical theory—the aim of the Marxists of the Frankfurt School— he finds Marx's economic determinism and the reduction of all culture to an economic base essentially in line with scientific positivism. Habermas also believes Marx ignored the importance of communication and interaction, which best can be understood by drawing upon the traditions of hermeneutics and philosophy of language. But neither does hermeneutics provide all the answers. Habermas is critical of positivism and hermeneutics because they both attempt to accommodate the entire range of human behavior within their conceptual schemes—something Habermas believes is impossible. Habermas' critical theory, then, is a combination of a variety of approaches to knowledge, as he attempts to arrive at a comprehensive model for the analysis of society.

Habermas' Approach to Communication

The various influences on Habermas have been combined in his effort to recast the study of society as a study of communication. He has been engaged in a systematic and ongoing effort to illustrate how a theory of communication is fundamental to and pervades every level of society. The development of Habermas' perspective was evident as early as 1965, in his inaugural lecture at the University of Frankfurt, in which he asserted the fundamental importance of language: "What raises us out of nature is the only thing whose nature we can know: *language.*"[25]

Because a complete discussion of Habermas' work is beyond the scope of this chapter, we will outline four major stages in the development of Habermas' theory of communication, ranging from specific concerns about the nature of knowledge and language to the function of communication at the level of culture and social institutions: (1) the nature of human knowledge; (2) universal pragmatics, or the study of the universal aspects of reason embedded in language; (3) communicative action, or the possibilities for a rational society that stem from the use of language in interaction with others; and (4) critical theory, or the exploration of the ways communication is enhanced or limited by social, institutional, and structural parameters.

At each level, Habermas is interested in the capacity for rationality based in language use and the systematic distortions that impede the realization of rationality. One of Habermas' major contributions to the study of social interaction is his theory that a model of rationality is embedded in every level of society—from the level of the individual to the level of social institutions. Based on an inherent and shared capacity for communication and understanding, Habermas presents an optimistic vision of the possibilities of human society.

Human Knowledge

At the foundation of Habermas' theory of society is his view of human knowledge. Habermas believes humans have three basic orientations or interests that govern all human activity and that essentially constitute the human species — work, interaction, and power. He defines these interests as "specific viewpoints," from which we grasp reality with transcendental necessity. He also uses the phrases, "generalized motives" and "cognitive strategies," to refer to these three interests.[26] Each of these interests stems from our biological nature as humans — we are forced to work, or to deal with our physical environment; to interact with other humans in social groups; and to encounter power relations as a function of these social groups. Habermas labels each of these forms "social media" because they mediate between the natural and human realms. Habermas also calls these three orientations "quasi-transcendental." With the term, "transcendental," he suggests that these represent a *priori* and universal conditions underlying human experience. He explains: "to the extent that we discover the same implicit conceptual structure in any coherent experience whatsoever, we may call this basic conceptual system of possible experience *transcendental*."[27] The "quasi" part of the term suggests that these interests are not completely above any consideration of material existence because they are grounded in fundamental and irreducible necessities of the human condition.

Work, the first domain of human concern, is the basic means by which we provide for the material aspects of existence. To survive, we must build shelter, gather food, clothe ourselves, and the like, which we do by manipulating various aspects of our environment. We fashion tools and develop techniques in order to bring nature under our control. The approach or strategy inherent to the domain of work is the *technical interest*. This is a basic attitude or way of knowing that allows us to exert control over the natural world. When systematized as a mode of cognition, it culminates in the *empirical/ analytic sciences*. These sciences, put another way, are simply the logical outgrowth of our fundamental interest in controlling various features of our world in order to provide for the basics of existence. The particular type of rationality associated with the technical interest is means/ends thinking, or what Habermas calls *instrumental rationality*.

A second domain in which humans operate is the social realm. Fundamentally, humans are social creatures; to survive, we must live and function in groups with other people. Language and other symbolic forms of communication are the means by which we create and maintain such groups. Thus, interaction through symbols is a second domain basic to human life. Habermas calls this the *practical interest*, meaning the human need to interact and work toward mutual understanding. The exchange of messages, the internalization of norms, and the institutionalization of social roles all are governed by this interest. As with the technical interest, this is a basic mode of knowing that arises from a fundamental condition of the human experience. The basic form of rationality operating here is that of *practical reasoning*, or reasoning by which we create shared meanings useful to the conduct of practical or everyday life. It, too, has a systematized counterpart at the theoretical level; when raised to a formal mode of knowing, it is realized in the *historical/hermeneutic sciences* —those that deal with the interpretation of meaning.

The third aspect of life with which all humans must deal is domination or power. Because we must live in social groups, we cannot avoid the organization of these groups into some kind of order, which necessarily implies hierarchy and thus differential power arrangements. Although power or domination is just as unavoidable as work and interaction, all humans have a natural or fundamental interest in freeing themselves from unnecessary forms of power and control. For Habermas, unnecessary power takes the form of distorted communication or ideologies that are embedded in our society to the point that we are unconscious of their existence. By becoming conscious of these ideologies, we can begin to free ourselves from their power and thus move toward greater freedom and autonomy. This desire for greater freedom is what Habermas calls the *emancipatory interest*. Like the other two interests, this one also represents a fundamental way of knowing the world, and a particular mode of rationality is associated with it. This is the rationality of critical reasoning or *self-reflection*. Only through the ability to self-reflect can humans become conscious of the limitations, constraints, and distortions of knowledge. When formalized, the emancipatory interest takes the form of the critical sciences or *critical theory*, which is concerned with the ways in which individuals and societies can liberate themselves from unnecessary forms of control. The following chart summarizes Habermas' conceptualization of the three domains and their various extensions.

Domain	Interest	Form of Rationality	Scientific Embodiment
work	technical	instrumental	empirical/analytic sciences
language	practical	practical	historical/hermeneutic sciences
power	emancipatory	self-reflection	critical theory

By means of this scheme, Habermas suggests that any one-dimensional approach for understanding the world is incomplete. No domain of humanity is value free—not even science, which aims at objectivity. Rather, each interest shapes one realm of human experience and determines how we experience that realm. Furthermore, one interest should not be considered separately from the others in a given situation. For every system of communicative interaction in the practical realm — the realm of language, for example — a corresponding system exists in the domains of power and work.

The domination of society by the technical interest is the subject of one of Habermas' books, *Legitimation Crisis*. He explains how the technical interest has come to dominate advanced capitalism and the impact of this domination for all features of human life. As part of this analysis, Habermas distinguishes the public sphere in early capitalistic societies from advanced ones. In the early societies, the private and public domains were distinct, and a "public sphere" mediated between the two. In the public domain, rational decisions about society were made, a process in which all citizens theoretically could participate. One of the main reasons for the existence of the public domain was to make the political and administrative decisions of the state transparent by subjecting them to the discourse and discussion of the members of that society.

With the coming of advanced capitalism, the state and social systems became intertwined rather than distinct because private interests began to overlap onto the political domain. The public sphere no longer existed as a place and space for rational discussion and consensus because all members of society no longer could participate equally. Those whose private interests were connected directly with political aims sought to influence how those aims fared in the public sphere, rather than allowing for open discussion about them. The problem of the public sphere is compounded by the fact that the technical interest — epitomized by the empirical sciences — has come to be valued above the other domains in such a society.

By examining the interaction of the three domains of work, language, and power in the modern state, Habermas points out possible trouble spots or areas where crisis might occur. Difficulties in the economic system or domain of work appear as legitimation crises; problems in the sociocultural system or the nature of interaction are manifest as crises of motivation; and difficulties in the area of politics or power are constituted as crises of rationality.[28] By identifying possible conflicts or crises in a system, Habermas hopes to reveal alternative approaches as well as the mechanisms that conceal conflict and ideologies. Habermas turns to speech-act theory for the foundations of a model to explain social evolution and to provide direction for how society can and should be changed in order to free its participants from social domination.

Universal Pragmatics

The starting point for Habermas' theory of communication is the notion of "universal pragmatics," or the study of the general or universal aspects of language use. He is not interested in the syntactic dimensions of language, as is Chomsky, who attempts to isolate general rules for generating and understanding sentences. Rather, Habermas seeks to isolate universal rules for *using* such sentences in communication: "The task of universal pragmatics is to identify and reconstruct universal conditions of possible understanding."[29] His universal pragmatics, then, essentially is a theory of speech acts, or how we use utterances to accomplish our intentions.

Habermas distinguishes three fundamental assumptions upon which universal pragmatics is based: (1) speakers are competent to use sentences in speech acts—that is, we know how to communicate our intentions; (2) our competence is based on "intuitive rule consciousness"—universal rules that are known by all communicators regardless of language, culture, or other specifics of situation; and (3) the objective of universal pragmatics is to discover this universal system of rules.[30] From this foundation in speech-act theory, Habermas moves to the notion of communicative competence.

Chomsky uses the term "competence" to refer to a knowledge of the universal rules by which we construct sentences, and Habermas expands this concept. He believes linguistic competence of the kind Chomsky studies is fundamental but that a second level of competence also exists. This is knowledge of the rules for how to use speech acts—how we adapt sentences for use in various contexts. A speaker, in Habermas' scheme, must do more than master linguistic rules to be considered a competent communicator: "By 'communicative competence' I understand the ability of a speaker oriented to mutual understanding to embed a well-formed sentence in relation to reality."[31] More specifically, this level of competence involves the ability to communicate in such a way that: (1) the truth claim of an utterance is shared by both speaker and hearer; (2) the hearer is led to understand and accept the speaker's intention; and (3) the speaker adapts to the hearer's world view. For Habermas, speech-act theory demonstrates the possibilities of communicative competence.

A speech act is an utterance that also accomplishes an act or does something beyond the utterance itself. Habermas explains: "In uttering a promise, an assertion, or a warning, . . . I execute an action—I try to *make* a promise, to *put forward* an assertion, to *issue* a warning—I do things by saying something."[32] A speech act always has two dimensions—propositional content—or the basic factual sense and reference—and illocutionary force—that aspect that makes it a performance. Habermas' intent is to analyze this twofold nature of speech acts: "I consider the task of universal pragmatics to be the rational reconstruction of the double structure of speech."[33]

Habermas turns to Austin's approach to speech acts as his point of departure for the analysis of the double structure of speech. Austin refers to the propositional content of an utterance as its meaning or *locution* and to the level of intention or action as *illocution*. Habermas criticizes Austin for claiming that these two levels of meaning—locutionary and illocutionary—are actually different kinds of speech acts. According to Habermas, all speech acts contain two dimensions or levels—propositional content and illocutionary force. An utterance with a particular propositional content might have various illocutionary functions, depending upon the speaker's intention in uttering the sentence. Because the propositional content and the illocutionary force of the sentence are interdependent, Habermas prefers to conceptualize the two types of meaning as two aspects of the act itself. Having made this point, Habermas goes on to designate specific types of speech acts.

Habermas is concerned with three major types of speech acts: constatives, regulatives, and avowals. *Constatives* are speech acts that serve primarily to assert a truth claim. The propositional content explicitly is stated in a constative speech act, making its meaning or locutionary aspect the focus, as in the utterance, "The grass is green." Habermas is careful to note that constatives are not substantially different in their structure from non-constative speech acts: Constatives "do not differ from other types of speech actions in their performative/propositional double structure, . . . but they do differ from (almost) all other types of speech actions in that they prima facie imply an unmistakable validity claim, a truth claim."[34] Habermas makes clear that even a constative utterance has illocutionary force because it, too, is an act with the force of stating, claiming, or asserting.

Non-constative speech acts include regulatives and avowals. *Regulatives* govern or regulate in some way the relationship between speaker and hearer. Commands, prohibitions, and promises are examples of this type of speech act; the focus is on the illocutionary force or performative aspect of an utterance, and the propositional content may or may not be stated explicitly. *Avowals*, on the other hand, refer to those speech acts that correspond to the function of expression—to the disclosure of feelings, wishes, intentions, and the like.

Habermas is not suggesting that every speech act can be classified into one of these three categories. But he is claiming that "every competent speaker has in principle the possibility of unequivocally selecting one mode because with every speech act he *must* raise three universal validity claims, so that he *can* single out one of them to thematize a component of speech."[35] The following chart summarizes the types of speech acts, the corresponding themes, and the validity claims involved.

Type of Speech Act	Theme	Thematic Validity Claim
constatives	propositional content	truth
regulatives	interpersonal relation	rightness or appropriateness
avowals	speaker's intention	truthfulness or sincerity

Validity Claims

Habermas moves to connect speech acts to rationality by showing how each type of speech act stresses a different validity claim. Validity is a rational notion, for it suggests that a speech act is grounded in a particular reality domain and in particular relationships to the other participant(s) in the interaction. Habermas posits that these validity claims are recognized by all participants as obligations to fulfill when speaking; when we perform a speech act, we do so with the understanding that all parties involved recognize certain validity claims as operative. In other words, speech acts oblige us to provide grounds; these same grounds allow the hearer to decide whether to accept or believe the communication.[36] In this way, our interactions are understood to have a rational basis.

Habermas' discussion of validity claims hinges on the distinction he makes between linguistic competence (mastering linguistic rules necessary to construct sentences) and communicative competence (the capacity to employ sentences in acts) or, as Habermas puts it, *"the conditions for a happy employment of sentences in utterances."*[37] Linguistic competence is measured by comprehensibility; a sentence is considered valid if it conforms to the grammatical rules of a language and is comprehensible to all hearers who have mastered those grammatical rules. Every utterance must fulfill the presupposition of comprehensibility. To be valid as a speech act, however, an utterance also must satisfy at least one of three additional validity claims: truth, rightness or appropriateness, and truthfulness or sincerity.

These validity claims correspond to the three types of speech acts Habermas describes. Constative speech acts focus on the condition of truth—they contain the offer to refer to actual experiences to determine the certainty of a statement. If we say, "the grass is green," and someone doubts the truth of this assertion, theoretically we could go over to the window and look at the color of the grass outside. This type of speech act occurs whenever someone asks for an explanation or clarification of content, as in, "What do you mean by that? How did you arrive at that?" Regulative speech acts are concerned primarily with the appropriateness of the norms operating in a particular context—the socially accepted rules in operation that are binding on all participants. For example, a police officer may have the right to perform the act of *demanding* that a prisoner be shackled; the opposite is not the case, however. If a prisoner says to an officer, "Hold out your hands," the act would be judged invalid given the norms operating in the situation. Finally, avowals raise the validity claim of truthfulness, or the obligation to show that the stated intention behind behavior is the actual motive operating. The statement, "you've hurt my feelings," is an example of an avowal. "Credibility" is another word that could be used to describe this kind of claim; it refers to whether we perceive you mean what is expressed in the statement about hurt feelings. If intentions are judged to be sincere, the validity claim of truthfulness has been fulfilled successfully.

These three types of validity claims, according to Habermas, are taken for granted in everyday discourse. They are implicit in every speech act; communication is a matter of performing speech acts in accordance with systems of rules that we intuitively know and follow. What is more important for Habermas, however, is what happens when the assumptions behind our speech acts are called into question.

When one of the validity claims is questioned, three communicative options are possible: (1) one or both of the participants can withdraw from the interaction—a possibility to which Habermas does not give much attention; (2) the problem can be resolved by means of further communicative action; or (3) the participants can move to what Habermas calls the level of discourse for resolution, which lies beyond everyday communication. If *sincerity* claims are questioned, the participants make use of the second option—they use additional communicative action to achieve resolution of the problematic communication.

In contrast, when someone questions *truth* or *appropriateness* claims, resolution cannot be obtained through further communicative action. The participants must move to the third option—to the level of what Habermas calls "discourse": truth and appropriateness "are claims of validity which can be proven only in discourse. The factual recognition of these claims bases itself in every case, even that of error, on the possibility of the discursive validation of the claims made. Discourses are performances, in which we seek to show the grounds for cognitive utterances."[38]

Discourse, then, is a mode of communication in which nothing is taken for granted. The participants suspend the usual assumptions about communication and move to the level of argumentation to examine and either accept or reject the problematic claim. Habermas relies heavily on Stephen Toulmin's work here to explain how the interactants subject themselves to the force of the better argument at this level. The participants advance conclusions, data, warrants, and backing for warrants in an attempt to make a case for their point of view: "The participants of a discourse no longer seek to exchange information or to convey experiences, but rather to proffer arguments for the justification of problematicised validity claims."[39] In other words, both parties deal with the assumptions behind their validity claims.

Habermas calls discourse that deals with the validity claim of truth "theoretic" discourse. If, for instance, someone asserts that the government has the right to regulate and restrict abortions and another disagrees, both must be willing to suspend judgment and to operate instead as if the statement is a hypothesis and may or may not be valid. Both parties, then, set out to marshal evidence for their respective positions. Throughout the discussion, they are functioning at the level of theoretic discourse.

When the claim of appropriateness is under scrutiny, "discourse" again is operating. Here, we argue that certain norms that guide actions are or are not the appropriate ones. One speaker might argue, for example, that for a man to open a door for a woman is appropriate, while another might insist that whoever gets to a door first should open it, regardless of sex. This discourse must deal with the correctness of social rules and the implications of those rules for male-female relationships, and Habermas terms this level "practical" discourse.

But there also is a level of communication beyond practical discourse—the level of meta-theoretical discourse. At this level, arguers move to question the basic conceptual framework or, in Toulmin's terms, the "field" in which arguments are grounded. The strength of an argument ultimately depends on the system or context in which data and warrants are selected. Habermas calls this the level of "meta-theoretical discourse." Paradigm shifts in science are examples of the questioning and overturning of the basic framework of arguments, exemplified when scientists moved from believing the world was flat to believing it to be round. Or, to return to our earlier example, rather than simply marshaling evidence for the assertion that the government does or does not have the right to regulate abortion, the participants would look at the source of that assertion—including the context in which the statement is made.

A final level exists as well—that of "meta-ethical" discourse. As the most abstract level, this is the realm of critical theory, where the structure of knowledge itself is examined. Here we make choices about how we wish to conceptualize knowledge and the criteria we will use to determine what counts as knowledge.[40] The following chart shows the various levels of communication and the corresponding validity claims.

Level of Communication	Validity Claim
communicative action	sincerity questioned
theoretic discourse	truth questioned
practical discourse	rightness and appropriateness questioned
meta-theoretical discourse	conceptual field questioned
meta-ethical discourse	knowledge itself questioned

For Habermas, the entry into discourse presupposes that the discourse will be conducted in accordance with principles of the ideal speech situation. This situation exists when symmetry is evident in terms of three dimensions among the partners in the interaction. These dimensions comprise what Habermas calls the "general symmetry requirement." First, no constraints must exist in terms of discussion—all those involved in the speaking situation must have the same opportunity to speak. This is the principle of unrestrained discussion. A second principle is unimpaired self-representation. By this, Habermas means that all participants in a speech situation have an equal opportunity to gain individual recognition by expressing their attitudes, feelings, intentions, and motives. A final condition that must be met in an ideal speech situation is that of a full complement of norms and expectations. This means that all participants have the equal right to give commands to others—there are no one-sided obliging norms—and are required to justify their discourse and actions in terms of mutually recognized norms and rules of interaction.

The general symmetry requirement means that all speakers have equal access to and opportunities to use constative, regulative, and avowal speech acts. Each of the dimensions, in other words, is linked to a type of speech act. Unrestrained discussion refers to the capacity to use constatives; unimpaired self-representation is, in essence, the right to use regulative speech acts; and avowal speech acts govern norms and expectations—the third symmetry requirement. This symmetry among the three dimensions of the ideal speech situation represents a linguistic conceptualization of the ideas of truth, freedom, and justice respectively. Put another way, the ideal speech situation consists of rules of discourse that we have no good reasons to want to deny. Habermas' ideal speech situation, then, is conceptualized both as a means of analyzing the nature of a society and as an imaginative model or end in itself of autonomous human activity.[41] It also can suggest standards for ethical communication; communication that meets the tests of comprehensibility, truth, sincerity, and appropriateness and allows for unrestrained discourse can be considered fair and just.

Habermas' ideal speech situation should not be taken as anything but an ideal. He acknowledges that discourse rarely achieves this level of purity, but for him, this is not the issue. Its value lies in its function as an assumption that is made whenever we enter into conversation, thus supplying communication with a rational base. When both participants in an interaction operate as if "free to speak their minds" and to "listen to reason" without fear of constraints, the possibility for a rationally motivated consensus exists. As such, it is a consensus based not on the arbitrary norms of one interest group or another but on norms inherent in language itself:

> The *design* of an ideal speech situation is necessarily implied in the structure of potential speech, since all speech, even of intentional deception, is oriented towards the idea of truth. . . . Insofar as we master the means for the construction of an ideal speech situation, we can conceive the ideas of truth, freedom, and justice, which interpret each other   although

of course only as ideas. On the strength of communicative competence alone, however, . . . we are quite unable to realize the ideal speech situation; we can only anticipate it.[42]

Communicative Action

There is not a clear line separating Habermas' universal pragmatics from communicative action—the third component of his theory—because to talk about the rational features embedded in speech acts is impossible without also discussing communication in action. The characteristics of speech acts that Habermas describes are the fundamental building blocks of his theory of communicative action. Habermas defines communicative action as "the interaction of at least two subjects capable of speech and action who establish interpersonal relations . . . and seek to reach an understanding about the action situation and their plans of action in order to coordinate their actions by way of agreement."[43]

As Habermas moves from speech acts themselves to broader issues of interaction, he adds three dimensions to his model: (1) domains of reality; (2) functions of speech; and (3) attitude of speaker. These three functions are added to Habermas' earlier conceptualization, depicted on page 257.

Type of Speech Act	Theme	Validity Claim	Domain of Reality	Function of Speech	Attitude
constatives	propositional content	truth	"the" external nature	teleological	objectivating
regulatives	interpersonal relation	rightness or appropriateness	"our" world of society	normative	norm-conforming
avowals	speaker's intention	truthfulness or sincerity	"my" world of internal nature	dramaturgical	expressive

Habermas discusses three domains of reality—the external or objective world, the individual's internal or subjective world, and the communally constructed world of social relations. The objective world consists of the totality of facts, "where 'fact' signifies that a statement about the existence of a corresponding state of affairs . . . can count as true."[44] The attitude of the speaker in this situation is objectivating, treating the object of discussion as having an independent existence, external to and apart from self. Communicators operating within this mode relate to other persons as means or obstacles to their aims; this attitude correlates with a teleological type of action — action undertaken to realize some goal. The validity claim at work here is truth — the degree of correspondence between the objective or external world and our statements about that world.

The second domain Habermas describes is the social world of interaction with others. It is the world characterized by those relationships recognized as legitimate by members of a society. Thus, the attitude toward others is norm conformative — how and in what ways communication is established and maintained. The speech acts performed in this domain are directed toward the conforming of behavior to shared norms and values. Rightness or appropriateness is the validity claim to which speakers engaged in this domain appeal.

Finally, Habermas suggests the existence of a subjective world, which consists of "the totality of experiences to which, in each instance, only one individual has privileged access." As the domain in which "*what is not common*" [italics his] is of primary concern, the attitude taken is expressive — a person "makes known a wish, expresses a feeling, . . . exposes a bit of . . . subjectivity before the eyes of others."[45] The principal aim of this kind of communicative action is self-presentation, or the projection of a public image. The dramaturgical aims of this mode suggest free, selective self-expression, combined with a desired response from an audience. Truthfulness or sincerity is the validity claim of concern to speakers operating within this domain. In each of these domains, language serves a particular function. In the objective domain, language involves the indirect communication of those who have only the realization of their own ends in mind; in the normative mode, language serves to actualize already existing agreements; and in the subjective realm, language realizes the presentation of self to others.[46]

There is a fourth domain in Habermas' scheme, but like the realm of meta-ethical discourse in which knowledge per se is questioned, this domain transcends the other three. This is the domain of communicative rationality or communicative action, which occurs when two or more persons use language expressly to reach voluntary agreement for the sake of cooperation. Only in the communicative mode does language function as a medium of uncurtailed communication in which speakers and hearers simultaneously refer to things in the objective, social, and subjective worlds in order to negotiate common definitions of the situation. Communicative action, then, involves a concerted effort to reach agreement on the entire spectrum of validity claims and therefore transcends the other, more limited types. For Habermas, communicative action, like speech acts, has an inherent rationality since it depends on consensus based on the recognition of validity claims that are negotiated and agreed upon by the speakers and hearers themselves.[47] As with Habermas' ideal speech situation, the notion of communicative action is not an everyday occurrence — in fact, it may be simply an ideal. But it exists as a possibility; thus, rationality itself continues as an underlying notion in society.

Critical Theory

With his discussion of the life-world, the focus of his two volumes of *The Theory of Communicative Action*, Habermas transcends the level of individual human actions to attempt to account for the possibilities of rationality at the level of social institutions. At this level, he realizes the intent of critical theory — to assess the status of modern society and to offer recommendations in regard to it.[48] By "life-world," Habermas means the taken-for-granted universe of daily social activity. It consists of the general storehouse of knowledge, traditions, and customs that unconsciously are passed from one generation to the next. Habermas calls it the background consensus of everyday life — those aspects agreed upon by a culture that generally are not questioned or even thought about.

Habermas distinguishes the "life-world" from social "systems." For Habermas, the life-world is the domain of social integration; language is the dominant medium in this realm, and here communicative action is possible. Habermas suggests that in the life-world, against a shared background of taken-for-granted assumptions, opportunities exist for speakers and hearers to "reciprocally raise claims that their utterances fit the world (objective, social, or subjective), and where they can criticize and confirm those validity claims, settle their disagreements, and arrive at agreements."[49] In other words, speakers and hearers come to an understanding from out of their common life-world about something in the objective, social, or subjective world.

In addition to a life-world component, however, societies also consist of systems — the structural features of life — governed by non-linguistic media. Habermas discusses two such media in particular — money and power — which are "speechless" and thus do not feature the comprehension and agreement orientations of the life-world.[50] Both of these media exert considerable control over the nature of society and consequently impinge on the life-world — the world of communication.

Habermas treats the life-world as existing in opposition to the system; the system of a society is imposed from without, while the life-world is viewed from within — from the standpoint of those who live it. In actuality, however, the line between these dimensions of society is blurred. We react symbolically to a drop in prices or a crash of the stock market — economic events that technically are part of the systems realm. Similarly, power is exercised through communicative forms and thus cannot be separated completely from the communicative concerns of the life-world. While Habermas finds useful the separation of system and life-world in order to provide us with a clear view of what is happening in modern societies, the boundaries between the two are, in fact, fuzzy.

Habermas distinguishes life-world from system in order to provide a critique of the state of contemporary society. For him, the process of making the life-world problematic — bringing its existence to a conscious level and problematizing it — allows us to engage in argument and reflection about it. This process promotes rationality — increasingly greater understanding about our actions and world views that we can use to make informed decisions about our communication. For Habermas, the need to become conscious of the life-world within which we operate is critical because, in modern times, the systemic side of life has proved stronger than the life-world side and has "colonized" it.[51] This means that the systemic forces at work in society — institutions, rules, bureaucracies, economics — exert greater influence than language. As a result, members of a culture are less likely to be in agreement about basic assumptions of the life-world. The colonization of the life-world also means that there is less need for achieving consensus by communicative means because disputes can be resolved and decisions made by recourse to formal regulations, laws, and established structures of power. Mutual understanding is less likely, and the possibility of personal autonomy declines as the separation from structures of decision making and regulation increases.[52]

The documentary film, *Roger & Me*, provides an example of the detrimental effects of the separation of the life-world from the systems aspects of society. The film describes the impact of the layoff of workers from the General Motors plants in Flint, Michigan. Those associated with a systems orientation — Roger Smith, the chair of General Motors; the sheriff charged with evicting tenants who had not paid their rent; managers and security guards at the GM factories; and even city officials — were portrayed as making decisions based on the existing bureaucracy and not because of any kind of genuine understanding of the life-world in which the GM workers lived. Consequently, shared decision making and consensus about how to handle the situation were not possible, and the end result was the devastation of the city.

Habermas contrasts traditional societies with modernity in terms of life-world and systems orientations. In traditional societies, a high degree of consensus exists among members, and life-world and system are coherent and virtually unquestioned by all participants. Modernity, on the other hand, is characterized by the differentiation of society into the objective, social, and subjective spheres, which allows for a greater diversity of response to the various dimensions of society. The realization that different world views exist, then, is a dominant feature of modern societies. Any particular cultural tradition is less likely to be dogmatically believed by members of a modern society, and the agreements realized are based on the critical evaluation of facts and negotiated consensus. Thus, critical theory is possible only in a differentiated society in which diverse views simultaneously exist. For Habermas, such societies are inherently more rational than traditional ones, in which consensus is presumed, unexplained, and unquestioned.[53]

The differentiation of modern societies, then, presents Habermas with a dilemma. While the communicative domain is devalued because of the colonization of the life-world, he still believes that modernity exhibits a greater degree of rationality than traditional societies because its complexity and diversity necessitate reflection on and critical evaluation of the basic assumptions of the life-world. While Habermas suggests that modernity is more rational than traditional societies, in which agreed-upon consensus takes the place of critical thought and evaluation, he does not believe that contemporary society has achieved emancipation — the desired outcome of his critical theory. For Habermas, an emancipated society is one in which the life-world is not subjected to the demands of system maintenance but rather one in which the mechanisms of the system are accommodated to the needs of individuals. There is a balance, in other words, of system and life-world.

Habermas suggests that the conflicts at the core of contemporary social movements are, in fact, efforts to remediate the colonization of the life-world and return to an orientation in which communicative action governs the system orientation. Unlike the social movements of the last century, for example, in which the struggles often concerned the means and nature of production — issues in the systems domain — recent social movements primarily are concerned with protecting the life-world from further colonization. The demands of the ecological or feminist movements, for instance, cannot be alleviated through further economic developments or technical improvements in the administrative apparatus of government. They are centered on efforts to defend the natural environment against despoilation — in the case of the ecology movement — and to establish new forms of communal relationships in order to improve the communicative sphere of life for women and men — the goal of the feminist movement.[54] For Habermas, then, modernity is a paradox. While its increasing differentiation has forced greater reflection and rationalization, such differentiation also has allowed the technocratization of the life-world and the devaluing of communicative action as a means of dealing with human problems.

Responses to Habermas

The range of Habermas' thought; the diversity of questions he tackles; the knowledge of classical and contemporary thinkers he brings into his discussions; and his willingness to rethink, elaborate, and expand on his theories continually have stimulated interest in his ideas from scholars in a wide range of disciplines. Habermas is to be commended for penetrating so many fields of inquiry, generating discussion and debate among disciplines, and offering new vantage points by which to examine society. Connolly describes the impact Habermas has on inquiry in the disciplines affected by his ideas: "The exchange typically begins with specialists . . . complaining about certain misunderstandings on the part of Habermas and ends by many of those ranged on each side viewing their own enterprise in a more refined way."[55]

A project so far reaching and comprehensive as that offered by Habermas necessarily generates considerable criticism as well as praise. The breadth of Habermas' project is a source of admiration but also a source of criticism. By taking on the task of explaining the functions of communication at every societal level, how social evolution occurs, and the nature of modernity, to name only a few of his ongoing themes, Habermas does not always provide the degree of detail his readers expect. A frequent complaint in this area concerns his vision of modernity and its possibilities for rationality. Habermas remains vague about what an emancipated society actually would look like. Howard is among those who call for greater specificity on this issue: "My point is not that a theory must at every moment tell us what to do. But theory ought *at least* to be able to discuss more than the merry-go-round of continued enlightenment."[56]

Jay also suggests that Habermas has not described his vision of modernity adequately; he suggests that some critics see Habermas as still dreaming an idealist dream of a "perfectly harmonious and rational totality," while other critics "attack him precisely for having abandoned it."[57] When the range of interpretations of Habermas' ideas is this broad, more clarification is needed. In addition, Jay argues that Habermas has not dealt specifically enough with the outcome of the contradictory aspects of the modernization process—the increasing differentiation of the separate spheres and the desire for the reintegration of the life-world and system. That these two trends in modernity—one toward increasing differentiation and the other toward increasing integration—can be realized simultaneously seems difficult, if not unrealistic; Habermas needs to articulate more fully how he envisions these functions as working. Furthermore, Habermas needs to do more, according to Jay, to discuss what else is needed, in addition to a communicative concept of rational action, in order to realize the good life, or a balanced, rational society in which autonomy, understanding, and cooperation can flourish. As Jay explains: "Not only is modernity an uncompleted project, so, too, is Habermas' enormously ambitious attempt to salvage its still emancipatory potential."[58]

In response to complaints about lack of specificity, Habermas reminds us that his thought still is in the process of development: "That so many competent and distinguished colleagues have dealt so seriously with publications which, as I know only too well, are at best stimulating but by no means present finished thoughts is a source of both embarrassment and pleasure." He suggests that there "are objections to themes and assumptions that I myself have treated only in a programmatic way and regard as being in need of clarification, without yet having found the time to work my way into them with sufficient intensity."[59] A writer as far ranging, prolific, and intense as Habermas invites comment, and the disagreements ultimately can lead to greater understanding.

Another criticism of Habermas' work is that his tendency to threefold classification schemes results in distinctions that, in fact, are quite blurred in reality. His foundational distinction between work and interaction, for example, seems to allow no way to treat interaction itself as a productive enterprise.[60] As another example, Habermas' desire to separate the media of the system—money and power—from the communicative media of the life-world also is easier to do in theory than in fact. The two domains merge as we talk about and use both money and power symbolically. While Habermas intends to separate domains and functions for the purposes of describing and critically evaluating them, he does not do enough to show how they indeed overlap in life and the impact of this overlap on his social theory.

Habermas also has come under attack from feminist scholars, who argue that his approach to social theory and rationality has a distinctively male bias. Habermas' reliance on Jean Piaget's theory of cognitive development and Lawrence Kohlberg's stages of moral development as parallel to the stages of social evolution has drawn particular criticism because it does not take into account differences in how women and men approach the world. Until Habermas takes the feminist critique into account, his view of autonomy and freedom will neglect notions of sensitivity and caring that characterize women's approach to the moral and social world. In addition, Habermas seems to see the family and the state-regulated official economy on opposite sides of the system/life-world line. Feminists suggest that this dichotomy ignores the similarities between the family as Habermas sees it—as a male-headed, nuclear family—and the state:

> We require, rather, a framework sensitive to the similarities between them, one which puts them on the same side of the line as institutions which albeit in different ways, enforce women's subordination, since both family and official economy appropriate our labor, shortcircuit our participation in the interpretation of our needs and shield normatively-secured need interpretations from political contestation.[61]

A major and continuing difficulty with Habermas' writings is not with content but with style. Despite finding Habermas' ideas thought provoking and praiseworthy, his reviewers inevitably comment on the density of his writing. Rieder's response is typical: "Wading through Habermas's prose demands heroic stamina for even the most zealous Frankfurt School devotee."[62] Held and Simon are even more specific in their criticism: "The writing if [sic] often opaque and dense, the language turgid, the ambiguities frequent, the programmatics seemingly endless."[63] Most are not discouraged by the effort, however, and recommend reading Habermas' works because of the depth and forcefulness of his insights about society.

Habermas' work will continue to attract attention, interpretation, acclaim, and criticism. His vision is appealing and worthy of thought. He seeks

> to find forms for living together in which real autonomy and dependency can appear in a satisfactory relation . . .: [His ideas] are always of successful interaction, of reciprocity and distance, of separation and manageable yet not failed nearness, of vulnerability and complementary caution. All of these images of protection, openness, and compassion, of submission and resistance rise out of a . . . "friendly life together". This friendliness does not exclude conflicts, rather it focusses on those human forms by way of which one can survive them.[64]

No matter what aspects of Habermas' theory attract us, there is room to find answers that are challenging and exciting. Pusey summarizes: "All will find an ordered set of concepts and arguments with which to fathom our own social nature and its possibilities. We may not accept what we read, but who dares ask a single scholar to offer more?"[65] For Habermas, he likely will continue the path he has set for himself—to continue to analyze society in order to emancipate it. As Habermas says: "So much fog lies around today everywhere. I am not giving up the hope that this fog can be lifted. It would be nice if I could do my part to help."[66]

Notes

[1] Michael Pusey, *Jürgen Habermas* (New York: Tavistock, 1987), p. 9.

[2] Peter Wilby, "Habermas and the Language of the Modern State," *New Society*, 47 (March 22, 1979), 669.

[3] Biographical information on Habermas was obtained from the following sources: Detlev Horster and Willem van Reijen, "Interview with Jürgen Habermas: Starnberg, March 23, 1979," trans. Ron Smith, *New German Critique*, 18 (Fall 1979), 30; Wilby, p. 668; *1983-84 International Who's Who*, 47th ed. (London: Europa, 1983) , p. 532; Personal resume obtained from Habermas; Axel Honneth, Eberhard Knödler-Bunte, and Arno Widmann, "The Dialectics of Rationalization: An Interview with Jürgen Habermas," *Telos*, 49 (Fall 1981), 5.; and Martin Jay, *Marxism and Totality: The Adventures of a Concept from Lukács to Habermas* (Berkeley: University of California Press, 1984), pp. 464-68.

[4] Jürgen Habermas, *Toward a Rational Society: Student Protest, Science, and Politics*, trans. Jeremy J. Shapiro (Boston: Beacon, 1970), p. 17.

[5] Habermas, *Toward a Rational Society*, p. 26.

[6] Horster and van Reijen, p. 35.

[7] Jürgen Habermas, "A Test for Popular Justice: The Accusations Against the Intellectuals," *New German Critique*, 12 (1977), 12.

[8] Honneth, Knödler-Bunte, and Widmann, pp. 7, 30.

[9] Wilby, p. 668.

[10] Horster and van Reijen, p. 33.

[11] David Held, *Introduction to Critical Theory: Horkheimer to Habermas* (Berkeley: University of California Press, 1980), p. 41.

[12] Jürgen Habermas, *Communication and the Evolution of Society*, trans. Thomas McCarthy (Boston: Beacon, 1979), p. 95. For a discussion of where Habermas and Marx disagree, see John P. Scott, "Critical Social Theory: An Introduction and Critique," *British Journal of Sociology*, 29 (March 1978), 7; and William M. Sullivan, "Two Options in Modern Social Theory: Habermas and Whitehead," *International Philosophical Quarterly*, 15 (March 1975), 88.

[13] Wilby, p. 667.

[14] Held, pp. 13-23. The interdisciplinary nature of the school also is evident in its membership. The best-known members of the school in the 1930s and 1940s included Max Horkheimer, philosopher and sociologist; Theodor Adorno, philosopher, sociologist, and musicologist; Friedrich Pollock, economist and specialist on problems of national planning; Erich Fromm, psychoanalyst; Herbert Marcuse, philosopher and social theorist; Franz Neumann, political scientist; and Leo Lowenthal, student of popular culture and literature. For an overview of the Frankfurt School, see Judith Marcus and Zoltán Tar, eds., *Foundations of the Frankfurt School of Social Research* (New Brunswick, NJ: Transaction, 1984).

[15] Held, pp. 65-67. See also Vojin Milić, "Method of Critical Theory," *Praxis*, 7 (1971), 625-66, for a discussion of rationality and critical theory.

[16] For a definition of ideology as the term was used by the critical theorists, see Trent Schroyer, *The Critique of Domination: The Origins and Development of Critical Theory* (New York: George Braziller, 1973), p. 163.

[17] David Gross, "On Critical Theory," *Humanities in Society*, 4 (Winter 1981), 92.

[18] Hans-Georg Gadamer, *Philosophical Hermeneutics*, trans. and ed. David E. Linge (Berkeley: University of California Press, 1976), p. xxi. For a history and overview of hermeneutics, see: Gadamer, pp. xi-xiv; Anthony Giddens, *New Rules of Sociological Method: A Positive Critique of Interpretative Sociologies* (New York: Basic, 1976), pp. 54-58; John B. Thompson, *Critical Hermeneutics: A Study in the Thought of Paul Ricoeur and Jürgen Habermas* (Cambridge: Cambridge University Press, 1981) pp. 36-38; Janet Wolff, "Hermeneutics and the Critique of Ideology," *Sociological Review*, 23 (November 1975), 813-15; and David Couzens Hoy, *The Critical Circle: Literature, History, and Philosophical Hermeneutics* (Berkeley: University of California Press, 1978).

[19] For discussions of the Habermas-Gadamer debates see: Paul Ricoeur, "Ethics and Culture: Habermas and Gadamer in Dialogue," *Philosophy Today*, 17 (1973), 153-65; Dieter Misgeld, "Discourse and Conversation: The Theory of Communicative Competence and Hermeneutics in the Light of the Debate Between Habermas and Gadamer," *Cultural Hermeneutics*, 4 (December 1977), 321-44; and Jack Mendelson, "The Habermas-Gadamer Debate," *New German Critique*, 18 (1979), 44-73.

[20] Habermas discusses Comte's role in positivism in *Knowledge and Human Interests*, trans. Jeremy J. Shapiro (Boston: Beacon, 1971), p. 74.

[21] Theodor W. Adorno et al., *The Positivist Dispute in German Sociology*, trans. Glyn Adey and David Frisby (New York: Harper & Row, 1976), p. xii; Donald McIntosh; "Habermas on Freud," *Social Research*, 44 (Autumn 1977), 562-65; and McCarthy, *The Critical Theory of Jürgen Habermas*, pp. 138-39.

[22] Habermas, *Knowledge and Human Interests*, p. 230. For a discussion of Habermas on Freud, see McIntosh; T.A. McCarthy, "A Theory of Communicative Competence," *Philosophy of the Social Sciences*, 3 (June, 1973), 147; Donald P. Cushman and David Dietrich, "A Critical Reconstruction of Jürgen Habermas' Holistic Approach to Rhetoric as Social Philosophy," *Journal of the American Forensic Association*, 16 (Fall 1979), 129; and Anthony Giddens, "Habermas' Critique of Hermeneutics," in *Critical Sociology: European Perspectives*, ed. J.W. Freiberg (New York: Irvington, 1979), p. 46.

[23] For an introduction to the philosophy of language, see J.R. Searle, ed., *The Philosophy of Language* (London: Oxford University Press, 1971), pp. 1-12.

[24] Representative works by Noam Chomsky include *Syntactic Structures* (The Hague: Mouton, 1957); *Topics in the Theory of Generative Grammar* (The Hague: Mouton, 1966); *Language and Mind*

(New York: Harcourt Brace Jovanovich, 1968); and *Current Issues in Linguistic Theory* (The Hague: Mouton, 1970)

25 Habermas, *Knowledge and Human Interests*, p. 314. Habermas' inaugural lecture is published as the appendix to this work.

26 Jürgen Habermas, *Theory and Practice*, trans. John Viertel (Boston: Beacon, 1973), pp. 7-40; and A. Brand, "Interests and the Growth of Knowledge — A Comparison of Weber, Popper and Habermas," *Netherlands' Journal of Sociology*, 13 (July 1977), 11. We are especially indebted to Brant R. Burleson for his cogent discussion of Habermas' interests, Letter to Karen A. Foss, February 15, 1984.

27 Habermas, *Communication and the Evolution of Society*, p. 21. For a discussion of the difficulties with Habermas' use of the term, "quasi-transcendentals," see Brand, pp. 11-12.

28 Robert X. Ware, "Habermas's Evolutions," *Canadian Journal of Philosophy*, 12 (September 1982), 618; and Trent Schroyer, "The Re-politicization of the Relations of Production: An Interpretation of Jürgen Habermas' Analytic Theory of Late Capitalist Development," *New German Critique*, 5 (Spring 1975), 116.

29 Habermas, *Communication and the Evolution of Society*, p. 1.

30 Habermas, *Communication and the Evolution of Society*, p. 26.

31 Habermas, *Communication and the Evolution of Society*, p. 29

32 Habermas, *Communication and the Evolution of Society*, p. 34.

33 Habermas, *Communication and the Evolution of Society*, p. 44. For this discussion of Habermas' notion of speech acts, we have drawn primarily from Habermas' "What is Universal Pragmatics?," the first chapter of *Communication and the Evolution of Society*.

34 Habermas, *Communication and the Evolution of Society*, p. 52.

35 Habermas, *Communication and the Evolution of Society*, p. 59.

36 Habermas, *Communication and the Evolution of Society*, p. 63. For a discussion of validity claims, see Brant R. Burleson and Susan L. Kline, "Habermas' Theory of Communication: A Critical Explication," *Quarterly Journal of Speech*, 65 (December 1979), 417.

37 Habermas, *Communication and the Evolution of Society*, p. 26.

38 Habermas, *Theory and Practice*, p. 18. Habermas uses the term "discourse" in a very specialized way, in contrast to most scholars in rhetoric. Generally, the term is used to refer to verbal or written expression.

39 Thompson, p. 87.

40 McCarthy, *The Critical Theory of Jürgen Habermas*, p. 305.

41 Ben Agger, "A Critical Theory of Dialogue," *Humanities in Society*, 4 (Winter 1981), 7. For discussions of the ethical implications of Habermas' work, see Richard L. Johannesen, *Ethics in Human Communication*, 3rd ed. (Prospect Heights, Ill.: Waveland, 1990), pp. 50-51; Stephen K. White, "Habermas' Communicative Ethics and the Development of Moral Consciousness," *Cultural Hermeneutics*, 2 (1984), 25-48; and Agnes Heller, "The Discourse Ethics of Habermas: Critique and Appraisal," *Thesis Eleven*, 10/11 (November/March 1984/85), 5-17.

42 Jürgen Habermas, "Towards a Theory of Communicative Competence," *Inquiry*, 13 (Winter 1970), 372.

43 Jürgen Habermas, *The Theory of Communicative Actions. Life-world and System: A Critique of Functionalist Reason*, vol. II, trans. Thomas McCarthy (Boston: Beacon, 1987), 86. Notice that Habermas is using the label "communicative action" to refer to two different levels: a specific level of discourse, to which the validity claim of sincerity can be taken, and a general category, in which the opportunity for understanding and coordination exists.

44 Jürgen Habermas, *The Theory of Communicative Action: Reason and the Rationalization of Society*, vol. I, trans. Thomas McCarthy (Boston: Beacon, 1984), 52.

45 Habermas, *Communicative Action*, I, 52.

46 Habermas, *Communicative Action*, I, 95.

47 Habermas, *Communicative Action*, I, 100.

48 Habermas does not believe modernity is unique in its demonstration of rational claims in speech acts. Drawing upon the work of Lawrence Kohlberg in terms of the development of moral consciousness and Jean Piaget's notions of cognitive development in society, Habermas argues

that these norms constitute the highest state in a universal moral consciousness. See Habermas, *Communication and the Evolution of Society*, especially chapter 2.

49 Habermas, *Communicative Action*, II, 126.

50 See Klaus Hartmann, "Human Agency Between Life-World and System: Habermas's Latest Version of Critical Theory," *Journal of the British Society for Phenomenology*, 16 (May 1985), 151.

51 Habermas, *Communicative Action*, II, 293, 522.

52 Habermas, *Communicative Action*, II, 311, 317.

53 Habermas, *Communicative Action*, II, 173.

54 Habermas, *Communicative Action*, II, 393-94.

55 William E. Connolly, rev. of *The Critical Theory of Jürgen Habermas*, by Thomas McCarthy, *History and Theory: Studies in the Philosophy of History*, 18 (1979), 398.

56 Dick Howard, "A Politics in Search of the Political," *Theory and Society*, 1 (Fall 1974), 300.

57 Martin Jay, "Habermas and Modernism," *Praxis International*, 4 (April 1984), 10.

58 Jay, "Habermas and Modernism," p. 12.

59 Thompson and Held, pp. 219-20.

60 J.W. Freiberg, ed., *Critical Sociology: European Perspectives* (New York: Irvington, 1979), p. 55.

61 Nancy Fraser, "What's Critical About Critical Theory? The Case of Habermas and Gender," *New German Critique*, 35 (Spring/Summer 1985), 130. Another feminist critique is offered by Isaac D. Balbus, "Habermas and Feminism: (Male) Communication and the Evolution of (Patriarchal) Society," *New Political Science*, 13 (Winter 1984), 27-47.

62 Jonathan Rieder, "Review Symposium," *Contemporary Sociology,* 6 (1977), 416.

63 David Held and Lawrence Simon, "Toward Understanding Habermas," *New German Critique*, 7 (Winter 1976), 136.

64 Honneth, Knödler-Bunte, and Widmann, p. 27.

65 Pusey, p. 122.

66 Honneth, Knödler-Bunte, and Widmann, p. 31.

10

Challenges to the Rhetorical Tradition

The eight perspectives on rhetoric presented in this book are limited in significant ways. As we explained in the first chapter, a perspective is a particular way of interpreting rhetoric—a set of conceptual lenses through which to view rhetoric. In this chapter, we do more than acknowledge that the scholars represented in this book assume particular perspectives; we point out ways in which those perspectives are limited by exploring some of the challenges being offered to them. The limitations of the mainstream rhetorical tradition are suggested in summaries of three sample challenges to that tradition—the feminist, Afrocentric, and Asian challenges. Scholars working from these perspectives note that most theories of rhetoric are inadequate and misleading because they embody the notion of the white male as standard, thereby distorting or omitting the experiences and concerns of groups such as women, African Americans, and Asians.

The scholars who are challenging the rhetorical tradition in these areas do so to accomplish two primary purposes. The first is to develop rhetorical theories that incorporate the perspectives, meanings, and experiences of those other than European or European-American men. The theories they develop, derived from different experiences, unsettle and challenge common assumptions about rhetoric and foster reconsideration of what has been taken for granted in the rhetorical tradition.

An example of such unsettling can be seen in the notion of theory itself, which is problematic for those who challenge traditional rhetorical thought. The names of European-American men frequently are used to label systems of ideas and theoretical frameworks—Aristotelianism, Marxism, or Burkean theory, for example. The work done on rhetorical processes by women, African Americans, and Asians is not similarly labeled and thus not conceptualized as theory. That there is no [Cheris] Kramaraean theory, no [Molefi Kete] Asanteian theory, and no Hsi K'angian theory of rhetoric is no accident. The perspectives assumed on rhetoric by European-American men simply do not encourage us to view alternate explanations of rhetorical processes as theories; these explanations are denied the status of the theory label because they were created by and represent the concerns of people who are seen as aberrant from the norm, already included in the norm, or insignificant in comparison to the norm—European-American men.[1]

The development of theories that incorporate the perspectives of women, African Americans, and Asians does not mean simply grafting the concerns of these groups onto the theories of rhetoric already in place. Under such a plan, as Dale Spender suggests about the fate of knowledge about women, their "meanings, even if initially *positive*, would soon be pejorated and become negative"[2] simply because they do not conform to the male, European-American norm. To integrate concerns such as gender and race into conceptions of knowledge, the way knowledge is constructed must be reconceptualized. Scholars challenging the rhetorical tradition in these categories, then, seek to change the rules for the construction of knowledge so they reflect pluralism—the experiences and values of all people.

Challenges to mainstream rhetorical perspectives tend to develop through a two-step process. Initially, the focus of a challenge is on inclusion. At this stage, scholars seek to gain legitimacy for the rhetoric of women, African Americans, and Asians as data for the investigation of rhetorical processes; the rhetorical activity of the previously muted groups, however, is not used to reconstruct rhetorical theories. This stage of the challenge is important, however, because it expands awareness of the variety and scope of rhetorical activity, makes problematic forms of rhetorical expression assumed to be universal, and provides new data that eventually will not be able to be fit into previously formulated rhetorical constructs. When such a point is reached, the challenge moves to a second level.

The second step in the process of challenge involves the reconceptualization of rhetorical constructs themselves using the knowledge gained from the study of alternate rhetorics. Here, the rhetorical processes of women or people of color no longer can be confined to the boundaries of previously formulated rhetorical notions; scholars begin to re-examine those notions themselves. This process involves both a critique of rhetorical constructs—a questioning of whether the concerns and experiences of individuals other than European-American men were considered when they were formulated—and a reconceptualization of the constructs to take into account the diversity of human experiences.

The three perspectives represented by the challenges described here are not the prerogative of the members of the groups who developed the challenges. Feminist scholarship is not limited to women, European Americans can study the rhetoric of African Americans, and both can look to Asian rhetoric to expand their perspectives on rhetorical processes. Scholars do not have to possess the traits of muted groups in order to incorporate their experiences, accord them positive value, and seek to construct knowledge by taking them into account. Anyone who attempts to integrate women's voices into rhetorical theory, for example, is adopting a feminist stance. Rhetoricians who are members of the culture that generated the challenging perspective, however, are likely to discover different knowledge and formulate different theories than those who are not. The concerns, angle of vision, and tone of the members and non-members of the cultures will be different simply because of their different experiences in the world.

Likewise, simply because scholars are female, African American, or Asian does not mean they use this perspective in their theorizing about rhetoric. The rewards are great for working within the traditional rhetorical paradigm, and individuals who are trained in the frameworks and standards of that paradigm may choose to create and understand knowledge within its confines, regardless of their membership in submerged groups.

In the summaries of the three sample challenges that follow, we introduce you to the major directions the challenges have taken, some of the scholars involved in generating the challenges, and samples of the studies that are raising questions about our current understandings of rhetoric. We encourage you to use these summaries as starting points for greater exploration of these different rhetorical perspectives and of other perspectives not presented here that similarly challenge traditional rhetorical thought.[3]

Feminist Challenge

"'I am a woman'; on this truth must be based all further discussion."[4] These words, from the opening pages of *The Second Sex* by Simone de Beauvoir, suggest the essence of the feminist challenge to the rhetorical tradition. The fact that a woman is involved in the rhetorical process as a rhetor or is studying that process as a theorist affects the view of rhetoric that emerges.[5]

Because of the many negative popular connotations of the term, "feminism," a discussion of the feminist challenge to rhetorical theory perhaps best is begun with a definition of the term. Feminism is the belief that women and men should have equal opportunities for self-expression.[6] From this definition derive three primary assumptions on which a feminist perspective on theory and research in any discipline is based, including the study of rhetoric.

The first assumption is that gender has been constructed so that women's experiences are subordinated to those of men—women are not allowed equal opportunities for self-expression. By "gender," we do not mean "sex." Sex is a biological given; gender is a social and psychological construction that involves the cultural notions of appropriate behavior for women and men. The construction of gender so that women's experiences are subordinated and the implications of this subordination for both women and men constitute one tenet of a feminist perspective.

A second assumption central to a feminist perspective is that women's perceptions, meanings, and experiences are valued. Their unique biological characteristics, the socialization process that establishes particular expectations for women, and their experience of oppression make women's lives very different from those of men. Among the values and qualities suggested as common to women's experiences are interdependence, emotionality, self-questioning or vulnerability, wholeness, egalitarian use of power, focus on process rather than product, an ethic based on care, and paradox.[7] Feminist scholars take into account and seriously consider these qualities of women's experiences in the development of constructs and theories.

A third assumption of a feminist perspective is that research is conducted for the purpose of improving women's lives. Feminist research is done to empower women—to assist them in developing strategies to make sense of and act with confidence in the world in which they live and in which they are denied status and voice. Adoption of a feminist perspective in research is inherently radical not only because it goes "to the root" of the basic constructs of masculinity and femininity but also because it asks that these fundamental concepts be changed. Thus, the ultimate consequence of research informed by a feminist perspective is social change. Feminist scholars see how gender has been constructed to denigrate women, seek to change that construction, and help women discover options for addressing its impact.

Inclusion Stage

The first stage of the feminist challenge is the inclusion stage, in which women's communication is included as data in rhetorical studies. The inclusion stage consists of research in four areas: the study of sexism in language, differences in communication between women and men, great women speakers, and women's communication as a separate culture.

Sexism in Language. One aspect of the feminist challenge to the rhetorical tradition involves the analysis of language itself as closely tied to the patriarchal social structure. Feminists see male dominance as central to language and raise questions about the ways in which language "helps enact and transmit every type of inequality, including that between the sexes . . . ."[8]

The research on sexism in language undertaken by feminist scholars derives from two primary assumptions. The first is that women's experiences and meanings are not incorporated into language. Whenever members of one group are in an asymmetrical power relationship with members of another group, the dominant group engulfs the subordinate group and renders it inarticulate or mute. Such is the case for women and men, as Cheris Kramarae explains: "the words and norms for speaking are not generated from or fitted to women's experiences. Women are thus 'muted.'"[9]

A second assumption on which feminist work on language is based is that language shapes the perceptions of those who use the language. How something is worded makes a difference in how it is understood and encourages or discourages particular kinds of observations and thought. Spender explains the implications of this idea for women and language:

> Given that language is such an influential force in shaping our world, it is obvious that those who have the power to make the symbols and their meanings are in a privileged and highly advantageous position. They have, at least, the potential to order the world to suit their own ends, the potential to construct a language, a reality, a body of knowledge in which they are the central figures, the potential to legitimate their own primacy and to create a system of beliefs which is beyond challenge . . . .
> In the patriarchal order this potential has been realized.[10]

From these starting assumptions about language, feminists have investigated various dimensions of language in relation to women, including a questioning of generic terms ("he," "mankind," "chairman") that are male in form but are supposed to include both women and men. Such terms indicate, feminists suggest, that men are the standard and are associated with the universal or the norm, and women are somehow different. Studies on this topic focus on the effort to discover how people understand generic language. In these studies, women and girls have been found to be understood to be included in such generic terms significantly less often than men and boys; both women and men report that they usually picture males when they read or hear masculine generic terms. Representative of the studies on the understanding of generic language is Virginia Kidd's study of the images produced through the use of the generic male pronoun. The masculine pronoun was overwhelmingly understood as referencing male: in one set of questions, "male" was given as the sex of the person to whom the sentence referred 407 times, while "female" was cited only 31 times.[11]

That men are considered the standard in language, feminist scholars point out, also is reflected in other linguistic conventions. The addition of the suffix "-ess" or "-ette" to neutral occupational terms so they apply to women—as in "poetess," "sculptress," "waitress," and "majorette"—suggests that the neuter language form is male and that women do not ordinarily belong in the category being named.[12] This assumption also is evident in naming conventions that expect women to change their names to their husbands' when they marry.[13]

Yet another area of research into language concerns the semantic derogation of women in language, a description created by Muriel Schulz to describe the tendency for terms designating women or connected with women in English to acquire debased or obscene references.[14] When women are included in language, feminist researchers assert, the words associated with them tend to acquire connotations conveying weakness, inferiority, and triviality. Consequently, women's positive attributes have no way to be visible in language. The numerous words in our language that describe women in non-human terms exemplify this phenomenon; women are talked about as animals ("chick," "lamb," "bitch") and as food ("dish," "tomato," "sugar and spice"), for example. They also are given labels with negative connotations when the same characteristics in men are described with positive terms ("bachelor"/"spinster," "grandfatherly advice"/"old wives' tales," "wizard"/"witch").[15]

Feminists' exploration of sexism in language involves, as well, inquiry into the relationship between language and social change. Some scholars, such as Robin Lakoff, wonder whether linguistic change can result in social change,[16] but most feminist researchers assume that linguistic changes promote societal changes because "[s]peech is a form of action, not simply a reflection of underlying social processes."[17] Much of the work in this area concerns proposals for and experiments with alternative, non-sexist forms of language, particularly inclusive pronouns such as "thon," "co," and "tey."[18]

Another effort in the area of linguistic change involves the writing and distribution of handbooks and manuals designed to provide guidelines for non-sexist language. Such works offer practical ways to avoid exclusive, distorting, ambiguous, and injurious words and phrases. Miller and Swift's *The Handbook of Nonsexist Writing* is one such manual.[19] Bobbye Sorrels Persing's *The Nonsexist Communicator* is another, directed primarily toward business and organizational use.[20]

Other scholars working in the area of language change investigate the processes through which individuals change in their language use. A study by Barbara Bate is representative; she identifies as factors that contribute to such change encouragement from a woman, the presence of sensitive listeners, pronounceability of an alternative, and knowledge of alternatives.[21] Lynne Webb focuses her efforts on the process of elimination of sexist language in the classroom. She suggests ways in which professors may address common arguments used by students against sex-neutral language and ways to teach alternative language choices.[22]

Feminists investigating language also focus on women's efforts to name their experiences and perspectives. Women have experiences and perceptions for which there are no terms in the language. There is no word in the English language, for example, for what women feel when men stare at or comment on them or for the obligation many women feel to wear make-up when they go out in public. In cases like this, where there are no terms for women's perspectives, those perspectives tend not to be considered real or acceptable, often not even by women.

Some feminists have chosen to address the lack of vocabulary in the English language for women's experiences by creating woman-centered meanings and vocabularies. In Mary Daly's work, for example, in such books as *Gyn/Ecology* and *Pure Lust*,[23] she creates new meanings for words or new words to reflect women's experiences. She redefines terms associated with women that have become negative to reclaim them as positive; "spinster," for example, is defined as someone "who participates in the whirling movement of creation . . . . spinning in a new time/space."[24] Daly also creates new language forms using irregular capitalization, spellings, and hyphens; "Sin-articulate," for example, means "to Pronounce Wicked Words, to Be-Speak Sinful Spells."[25] The culmination of Daly's efforts to create a woman-centered language is a dictionary, *Websters' First New Intergalactic Wickedary of the English Language*, developed with Jane Caputi, described as "a 'Metapatriarchal dictionary, written by and for Wicked/Wiccen Websters . . . that Gossips out the Elemental webs of words hidden in patriarchal dictionaries and other re-sources.'"[26]

A similar construction of a women's dictionary is *A Feminist Dictionary* by Cheris Kramarae, Paula A. Treichler, and Ann Russo. Its purpose is "to document words, definitions, and conceptualizations that illustrate women's linguistic contributions" and "to illuminate forms of expression through which women have sought to describe, reflect upon and theorize about women, language, and the world . . . ."[27] Its focus is less on a newly coined vocabulary and more on women's meanings for words, particularly words that are important in women's lives. Among the approximately 2,000 entries are words such as "birth name," "feminist," "marital rape," "night cleaning," "one of the boys," "pots and pans," "talkative," and "witch."

In her effort to capture women's perspectives in language, linguist Suzette Haden Elgin has created an entirely new language, not rooted in English, called Láadan. She describes it as "a language constructed by a woman, for women, for the specific purpose of expressing the perceptions of women."[28] She created the language during the writing of a science-fiction book, *Native Tongue*, about a future America in which a women's language has been constructed and is in use.

A few samples of the vocabulary of Láadan will suggest the vocabulary's focus on women's experiences. "Lewidan" means "to be pregnant for the first time," while "lalewida" is "to be pregnant joyfully." "Radíidin" is "non-holiday, a time allegedly a holiday but actually so much a burden because of work and preparations that it is a dreaded occasion; especially when there are too many guests and none of them help." "Ralorolo" is "non-thunder, much talk and commotion from one (or more) with no real knowledge of what they're talking about or trying to do, something like 'hot air' but more so." "Rarilh" is "to deliberately refrain from recording; for example, the failure throughout history to record the accomplishments of women."[29]

The examination of the medium of language itself as a vehicle that reflects and aids the patriarchy and the creation of languages to reflect women's experiences suggest to rhetorical theorists that language is not neutral in its structure or impact. Rhetorical scholars are used to viewing language as a political and ideological tool, but that notion usually is not extended to its use as a tool in the construction of the subordinate position of women. This, then, is the contribution to new understandings of rhetoric of feminist scholars working in the area of women and language.

Sex Differences in Communication. A second aspect of the challenge posed to the rhetorical tradition by feminists consists of the study of differences in the rhetorical behaviors of women and men. One of the earliest to call for such study was Kramer (now Kramarae), who suggested questions to be addressed:

> We need to ask if there are differences between the sexes in their linguistic competence. Do women control some speech structures or vocabulary that men lack or vice versa? We need to ask if there are differences in linguistic performance. Are there syntactic structures, vocabulary, phonological rules that, say, women might know but not use while men both know and use?[30]

Some of the earliest work in the area of sex differences in communication involved an examination of such differences in other cultures. Representative is Mary Haas' study, "Men's and Women's Speech in Koasati," in which she identifies differences in the speech of women and men in a Muskogean language spoken in southwestern Louisiana. Among the differences she cites are different word endings according to the sex of the speaker. When the women's form ends in a nasalized vowel, for example, the men's form ends in s.[31]

Marjorie Swacker's study of amount of speech is typical of the initial work done in this area in the American culture. She asked women and men to describe pictures and recorded and timed their responses. Her discovery that men talk more than women led to her call for the investigation of sex-linked communication patterns: "This argues strongly for the adoption of speaker sex as a separate sociolinguistic variable—a variable as important, as methodologically necessary, and as valid as education or region or socioeconomic level."[32]

The research into differences in communication between women and men falls into three primary categories, relating to different views of the sources for the differences: scholars who focus on the personality of the rhetor see sex and/or gender as the origin of differences; those who focus on the audience for the communication see varied expectations as the origin; and those who focus on cultural conditions see men's greater power as the origin of communication differences.

Many studies in the area of communication differences between women and men are conducted from a biological perspective, in which the source of such difference is assumed to be the sex of the rhetor. But contradictory findings and inconsistent results in research in which sex was linked to communication patterns led to research based on psychological gender as well. Biological sex may be less important, scholars have speculated, in determining behavior than psychological identities developed as a result of sex assignment.

The shift away from exploring biological sex differences to the exploration of psychological gender orientation necessitated the development of instrumentation to measure this variable. The most widely used is the Bem Sex-Role Inventory, which classifies individuals as feminine, masculine, androgynous, or undifferentiated; other measures developed include the Personal Attributes Questionnaire and the *PRF ANDRO* scale.[33] The study of sex and gender also involves comparison of the two variables to determine whether biological sex or psychological gender is a better predictor of differences in communication.[34]

A second type of research done on differences in communication between women and men concerns differing expectations about appropriate behavior for women and men. This research is audience centered in that its focus is on what the audience for the communication is likely to perceive as appropriate for each sex. Kramarae was among the first to note expectation as a factor in observations of apparent differences in communication between women and men: "I became aware that there seems to be a conflict not only between what women's speech really is like and what people think women's speech really is like, but also between what people think women's speech is like and what they think it should be like."[35]

Representative of the investigation of communication differences from a starting point of audience expectations is a study by Patricia Hayes Bradley of reactions to discussants who used varying linguistic and substantive strategies to express positions of dissent in small groups. She reports that "the same linguistic device is viewed differently, depending upon its source. . . . In this context it may be that qualifying phrases were perceived as indicators of uncertainty and nonassertiveness when used by women but as tools of politeness and other-directedness when employed by men." She concludes: "What needs to be reassessed, then, is the discriminating way that this culture views men and women, leading to the evaluation of communicative acts performed by the former and the devaluation of those performed by the latter."[36]

Other studies on sex differences in communication are based on the assumption that power differences lie at the heart of communication differences. Pamela Fishman's study of interaction patterns in three heterosexual couples is one that assumes power is a critical dimension in sex differences in communication. She concludes that "women do the work necessary for interaction to occur smoothly'' and interprets this work as evidence of ''the maintenance and expression of male-female power relations . . . .''[37]

The notion of men's greater power at the core of differences in communication behavior between women and men has produced two interpretations of such differences. The first assumes that men's communication, rooted in their greater power, is the standard communication form. Within the context of male communication behavior, women's differences are seen as deficiencies. In this view, the power differences reflected in the communication of women and men can be equalized by women's adoption of the behaviors that are associated with men's power.[38] An alternate interpretation is that differences between women's and men's speech are differences in strategies. When women and men speak, they have particular goals in mind and employ different strategies to achieve those goals; given the different positions of the sexes in society, speech strategies are likely to vary by sex. Men exercise and maintain power through certain strategies, such as interrupting and withholding self-disclosure, and women use strategies that allow them to cope with greater male power, such as politeness and greater interaction work.[39]

Research in the area of sex differences in communication, regardless of the presuppositions made about the sources of those differences, constitutes a challenge to traditional thinking about rhetoric. It calls into question the assumption that explanations of rhetorical processes describe the rhetorical behavior of and are relevant to all people. It also suggests *topoi* in which to seek explanations for diversity in rhetorical behavior: rhetors' gender assignments, the expectations of others about appropriate rhetorical behaviors based on gender constructions, and rhetors' positions in relation to power.

Great Women Speakers. A third area of research into rhetorical practices by feminists deals with the study of great women speakers. The women who are the focus of such research are those who influenced socio-political history through their activity in the public domain, and it is designed to secure recognition for the female influence in the public realm. Karlyn Kohrs Campbell summarizes the rationale for such studies: ''Men have an ancient and honorable rhetorical history. Their speeches and writings, from antiquity to the present, are studied and analyzed by historians and rhetoricians. Public persuasion has been a conscious part of the Western male's heritage from ancient Greece to the present. . . . Women have no parallel rhetorical history.''[40]

The studies prompted by such calls for research on women speakers generally are designed to discover the substance and style of the rhetoric of the individual women. Studies in this category often deal with women involved in the women's suffrage or feminist movements. Examples are Elaine McDavitt's study of Susan B. Anthony[41] and Wil A. Linkugel's studies of Anna Howard Shaw.[42] Sonja Foss' study of the movement to secure passage of the Equal

Rights Amendment[43] and Martha Solomon's study of the opposition to the ERA[44] are examples of studies of the contemporary feminist movement. Other women who tend to be studied as great speakers are those active in political and social causes. Barbara Jordan is the subject of several of these studies, including two by Wayne Thompson, who analyzes her keynote address to the Democratic national convention.[45]

The interest in women speakers has led to the compilation of their speeches in anthologies as a means to provide lost texts for analysis and to begin to correct "an impoverished view of women's role in advocating social, moral, cultural, economic and political change."[46] Patricia Scileppi Kennedy and Gloria Hartmann O'Shields' book, *We Shall Be Heard*, includes speeches by women in three periods—pre-Civil War, the Civil War to the turn of the century, and World War I to contemporary times.[47] Judith Anderson's *Outspoken Women* includes speeches by women orators from 1635 to 1935,[48] while Kohrs Campbell's two-volume set, *Man Cannot Speak for Her*, focuses on a more limited time period—the women's rights movement in the United States from its beginnings through 1920.[49]

Another kind of study of women rhetors is designed less to discover information about individual women and more to investigate a research question about rhetorical processes; in these studies, the rhetoric of a woman or women is used as data. In some cases, the research question involves an inquiry into the nature of the woman as rhetor or the characteristics of women's rhetoric. Elizabeth Berry's study of Emma Goldman is an example. In it, she uses Goldman's rhetoric as a case study to investigate the nature of female agitation.[50] Jean Ward's study of Abigail Scott Duniway, a nineteenth-century women's suffrage leader and newspaper publisher, provides another example. Her study of the novels written by Duniway is used to discover communication strategies women use in response to systems of male authority.[51]

Feminist scholars studying women speakers, then, do so in an effort to correct a rhetorical tradition that has muted women's contributions to the public realm as well as to investigate questions about rhetoric using women's rhetoric as data. Their primary contribution to a challenge of the rhetorical tradition is their addition of data from which to develop explanations for rhetorical processes.

Women's Communication as a Separate Culture. Some feminist scholars see women's and men's different communication as the result of the very different cultures into which they are socialized and live their lives. Women's communication is seen to constitute a separate communication system that is as valuable and effective as that of men. The notion of women's culture often is the starting point for work on this topic, and feminist scholars seek to document the systems of communication, artifacts, and principles that characterize this culture. As Fern Johnson explains, "The documentation functions as the 'archaeology' of uncovering what has been kept from view."[52] Barbara Westbrook Eakins and Gene Eakins describe women's culture as one that values techniques that "promote getting along with members in a group and achieving cooperation, interpersonal discovery, and self-expression."[53]

Women Communicating, edited by Barbara Bate and Anita Taylor, is a volume of studies that describes communication in women's culture. It includes essays on mother-daughter storytelling strategies; Judy Chicago's work of cooperative art, *The Dinner Party*; communication among members of a women's basketball team; and women's forms of humor.[54]

Some researchers investigating differences in communication between the sexes see women's communication not simply as different but as often superior to men's. In their study of women and men as managers, John Baird and Patricia Hayes Bradley, for example, conclude not only that women "communicated in ways markedly different from the behaviors exhibited by male managers" but also that "female managers may be more effective supervisors than the male managers seen in this investigation."[55] Audrey Nelson reaches similar conclusions in her summary of the research concerning sex differences in nonverbal communication. She suggests that women's nonverbal behaviors be viewed as skills or gifts and that many of women's behaviors are ones advocated for effective interpersonal communication.[56]

Once women's forms of expression are studied as valuable in their own right and not simply in comparison to men, rhetorical constructs previously developed only from the experiences of men come to seem inappropriate and irrelevant. The way then is open for the next kind of challenge—the reconceptualization of rhetorical theory itself in the revisionist stage of the challenge.

Revisionist Stage

The second stage of the feminist challenge involves use of the information gathered about women's rhetorical practices to revise and reformulate traditional notions of rhetoric. In this reformulation of rhetorical constructs from a feminist perspective, scholars seek to discover if existing rhetorical notions were developed with a consideration of women's perceptions and experiences and to revise those that were not.[57] Feminists' efforts to evaluate and reconceptualize rhetorical constructs include Sally Miller Gearhart's assessment of the definition of rhetoric. She argues that the definition of rhetoric as persuasion—the effort to change people and things—is a conversion or conquest model of human interaction that does not fit women's experiences of interaction or the values women bring to their interactions.[58]

Another example of such revision is the questioning by feminists of the framework in which women's discourse has been treated in rhetorical studies. Scholars in the area of public address long have focused on the speeches of great men; thus, when feminists turn to the study of women, they often do so within the same framework. Their subjects, then, are great women who give speeches in public—women such as Susan B. Anthony and Barbara Jordan. These studies help to complete a rhetorical tradition and history that earlier had omitted women completely. But a questioning of the framework in which women rhetors are studied has led feminist scholars to discover some negative consequences for our understanding of women as communicators.

First, women often are seen as ineffective speakers in this framework because they are judged by criteria developed for the study of men's rhetoric. When their speaking style deviates from the expected and accepted patterns, developed to apply to men, their rhetoric is seen as "chaotic" and "reactive noise, devoid of meaning and significance."[59] Illustrative is a study of Francis Wright's rhetoric by Kathleen Kendall and Jeanne Fisher. Their use of Aristotelian categories to judge Wright's *ethos* leads them to conclude that she was ineffective as a rhetor: "Eloquence without extrinsic ethos produces museum pieces of oratory, not catalytic compositions that influence the course of history."[60] That women are perceived differently by audiences and critics simply because they are women and that their rhetorical strategies are developed in response to a different set of exigences from those of men simply are not considered in making such evaluations.

Second, traditional conceptions of rhetoric and rhetors are exclusionary and elitist as a result of the great-speakers model of rhetoric. Just as only some men are seen as extraordinary speakers, in this view, so only a few great, special women are seen as worthy of study. Only *some* women have the talents and capabilities necessary to produce significant rhetoric. The great-speakers model excludes many male speakers, but it is even more exclusionary for women, since their forms of expression are not those that tend to qualify rhetors for greatness. The abundant and varied forms of women's expression outside of public speaking are not even defined as significant rhetoric.

There is a third consequence of the great-speakers framework for studying women's rhetoric. Significant discourse for women is seen to be formal speeches in the public realm. This is not, however, where most women's rhetoric occurs, and it certainly is not the site of the discourse that most women consider significant in their daily lives. The very framework by which women's rhetoric is studied does not allow scholars even to see as relevant a whole body of rhetoric practiced by women in what has been labeled the "private realm"—rhetoric such as talk between women on the telephone;[61] talk between women and their children; women's perceptions as revealed in journals and diaries; and women's expressions through sewing, gardening, housekeeping, cooking, and child care.[62] When these kinds of rhetorical expressions are used to develop theories about and frameworks within which to understand rhetoric, we arrive at very different knowledge about rhetoric.

The public-private dichotomy that is central to many rhetorical theories is another notion subject to feminist revision. Kramarae, for example, suggests that the construction of this dichotomy renders women's discourse complementary and inferior to that of men. Within this system, she asserts, "Masculine intellect is seen in contrast to and as transcending the feminine character, which is biologically driven and firmly bound to the body and home. Men make the move away from the body and the home to reason and public activities." [63]

Valerie Endress points out some of the consequences of the public-private dichotomy. It results, she explains, in a particular definition of politics that includes only men's activities and rhetoric; what constitutes a legitimate political notion is determined by men. In this view, politics takes place in the public sphere and deals with issues "such as the political economy, international relations, war and peace, and domestic political dissent . . . ." The politics involved in women's lives—power differences and their impacts on women; the feminization of poverty; and issues such as birth control, abortion, motherhood, sexism, and racism are not seen as legitimate political and rhetorical concerns. [64] The realm of the interpersonal, the private—where women's rhetoric achieves its significance—is simply not considered political.

Belle Edson's reformulation of some of our basic notions about social movements as a result of incorporating qualities of women's experiences provides another example of feminist revision. She suggests that traditional ideas about the features of movements—leadership, group membership, progression of movements, and ideology—are masculine in orientation. She uses Anne Wilson Schaef's characteristics of the female system to reformulate these various dimensions, suggesting how they might change if those characteristics were incorporated into movement theory. [65]

Another example of such reconceptualization is Mary Rose Williams' use of quilts as data from which to reformulate traditional conceptions of protest rhetoric. She studies four quilts—including the Women's Christian Temperance Union's *Crusade Quilt*, created by women in Ohio in 1878, and the *Secession Quilt*, made by Jemima Cook of South Carolina in 1860—to construct a theory of the features of protest rhetoric. The alternate vision of protest rhetoric she formulates is characterized by the quiltmakers' establishment of common ground with the dominant system, lack of denigration of the system they challenge, acknowledgment of their own low status, and ambiguity. [66]

Through their examination of language, study of sex differences in communication, attention to women's rhetorical history through the study of women orators, and examination of women's forms of cultural expression, feminist scholars call into question assumptions about various dimensions of the rhetorical process. They raise questions concerning who is served by language, whether our theories explain rhetorical processes characteristic of both women and men, and revise our understanding of how rhetoric has functioned throughout our history to influence policy in the public realm. In their revision of rhetorical constructs and theories to incorporate women's experiences, feminists provide the greatest challenge to the rhetorical tradition as they clarify the masculine orientation of rhetorical theories and construct alternative and more comprehensive ones—theories that acknowledge women's ways of constructing and using rhetoric.

Afrocentric Challenge

Challenges to rhetorical theory potentially exist from every racial and ethnic group, but the African-American world view provides a particularly well-developed and coherent alternative to contemporary conceptions of rhetoric. Based on African cultural practices adapted to life in the United States, this challenge offers a rhetorical framework substantially at odds with the Western rhetorical tradition.

"Afrocentricity" is the term used to describe the study of rhetoric from an African-American framework. The notion first was presented by Arthur Smith (now Molefi Asante) in 1969, although he did not yet use that label. In his book, *The Rhetoric of Black Revolution*, he assessed the protest speeches of African Americans from a black perspective.[67] His first essay to describe unique features of African-American discourse was "Socio-Historical Perspectives of Black Oratory,"[68] followed a year later by a second essay, "Markings of an African Concept of Rhetoric."[69] He has elaborated on the notion of Afrocentricity since in various books and articles; two books that most clearly define the construct are *African Culture: The Rhythms of Unity* and *The Afrocentric Idea*.[70]

Asante defines "Afrocentricity" as "placing African ideas at the center of any analysis that involves African culture and behavior."[71] When the Afrocentric ideal informs an analysis, the result is a radical critique in that "it is about taking the globe and turning it over so that we see all the possibilities in a world where Africa is subject and not object."[72] Rather than imposing Western constructs onto African-American discourse, then, the critic or theorist grounded in Afrocentricity uses the filter of African culture to understand African-American discourse.

A rhetoric grounded in Afrocentricity differs in significant ways from that developed in the European-American tradition. A fundamental tenet of African culture is the high value placed on *nommo*, the word or expressive quality of life;[73] for Africans, *nommo* is action. Africans do not consider a public speech a "thing"—a static text that can be reprinted in anthologies of public address.[74] Rather, it is a dynamic activity that does not exist apart from the attitude of the speaker at the moment of delivery, the responses of the audience, and the transformatory outcomes it accomplishes.

In contrast to Eurocentric discourse, in which the speaker selects a speaking purpose and attempts to persuade the audience to that point of view, the speaker in the African-American tradition does not exert such control over the text and audience. In the African world view, the speaker strives for harmony; important to African cultures is a belief in a harmonious interrelationship and compatibility among peoples, spirits, plants, and animals. Discourse, then, serves to restore stability when conflict exists; it allows for a collective search for harmony in which both speaker and audience participate.[75]

Just as a single end—the opportunity for harmony—is the goal of an African-American speaker, so a limited number of ways are available to manage a topic and situation. The speaker does not invent a rhetorical text but rather calls into existence a pattern from the past that creatively handles the situation at hand.[76] From the African point of view, life is seen cyclically—what happened in the past will recur in the future, although perhaps in a slightly different form. The speaker's task is not the "invention" of a text designed to further individual goals but the presentation of a familiar pattern that is appropriate for the current situation and that helps restore the fundamental harmony of the universe.

The nature of traditional African society also leads to very different notions about the functions of language and delivery. Rather than furthering a persuasive end about which speaker and audience may disagree, language and delivery function to call up images already held and agreed upon by the audience. The speaker uses concrete images that remind audiences of vital themes and myths, such as resistance to slavery and stories about Shine, John Henry, or Harriet Tubman.[77] The words used, however, are not considered separately from the form of their presentation. The term "styling," used to capture this notion, suggests the essential unity of words and rhythm, sound and meaning.[78] The speaker who can style uses words to trigger emotional responses that are fitting and appropriate for the moment and result in harmonious relationships. Style is not something added onto the speech but is an integral part of the speaker's purpose.

The notion of delivery in the African-American context also differs from the Eurocentric view, in which a speaker presents a text to a largely passive audience. African-American audiences participate in the speech itself—through affirmations, interruptions, and the like. These responses do not constitute a mere expression of agreement with the speaker but are joint creations of the text by members of a culture in which collective experience is valued over individual needs. Africans seek to discover and renew energy among people; there is no tradition of withdrawal.[79] In discourse, this translates into an active engagement with speaker and text in which all parties involved work toward the restoration of a harmonious state. The phrase made popular by black entertainers, "put your hands together," then, is not a call for acknowledgment and applause in the Eurocentric sense; rather, it is a call to a "collective, generative experience" that results in the possession of a sense of harmony by performer and audience alike.[80]

Although the characteristics of African-American rhetoric identified here may suggest a context of formal public speaking, the practice of speechmaking, as conceived in traditional Western rhetorical thought, is not a commonplace in the African-American experience. Interpersonal communicative forms often existed as the only ways, in slave culture, to transmit forbidden information — whether about escaping slaves or about the African heritage, beliefs, and practices.[81] The rhetoric of African Americans, then, more accurately is represented by informal speech acts than by public speeches and consists of efforts to "get over" or survive in a Eurocentric world.[82]

Roger Abrahams offers a taxonomy of African-American speech events, ranging from the more spontaneous modes of talk, in which information is the focus, to more stylized forms, in which the patterning of the message is of as much concern as the message itself. "Running it down" refers to information-centered conversations in which a speaker lets another know what is happening in a situation or offers advice about something.[83] Explanation and understanding receive the primary emphasis, although this is not to suggest that there is not a stylistic element to how the information is offered.

"Signifying" is a general term for talk that is more stylized. While signifying is given different nuances within the African-American community,[84] it generally is seen as expressing oneself indirectly. To ask for a piece of cake by saying, "my brother needs a piece of that cake," is an example of the indirection involved in signifying. Signifying can take the form of "rapping," one-on-one talk in public among those who do not know each other well.[85] When interactants engage in talk in order to elicit more talk or some kind of action, they are "talking shit." Making witty remarks in order to get such responses in return is an example.[86] "Putting down" refers to signifying in which the talker seeks to establish dominance through the use of language; "putting on" is talk in which verbal manipulation is used to establish control.[87] "Shucking and jiving" suggests a deviousness not a part of the other forms of signifying. The talker uses words and gestures to create false information; this form of talk covers "telling a lie, to bullshitting, to subtly playing with someone's mind."[88] Finally, "talking smart" and "talking sweet" are two forms of speech that a black woman might use. A woman might "talk smart" with anyone who threatens her self-image but "talk sweet" with her children.[89]

On the surface, these informal modes of talk seem counter to the aim of harmony that is at the center of African-American discourse. But, in fact, these word games diffuse conflict. They function as mock battles that keep conflict from occurring; only when someone fails to observe the rules of the word game does the possibility of real conflict exist. Verbal skill replaces the need for physical battle in these encounters, thus maintaining the harmony of a situation.

Our purpose here is not to offer a full taxonomy of talk from within the African-American community but to suggest some differences between the traditional Western "speech" and the modes of talk that are functional within the black community. Discovery of how the African-American culture is constituted rhetorically poses a challenge to Eurocentric perspectives on rhetoric. Once African-American rhetoric is seriously considered, it calls into question many of the mainstream assumptions about and descriptions of rhetorical processes.

Inclusion Stage

The African-American challenge to the rhetorical tradition began, as did the feminist challenge, with efforts simply to expand the scope of rhetorical studies to include as data the rhetoric of African-Americans. This approach includes the study of racial differences in rhetoric, African-American protest rhetoric, and the relationship between African Americans and the media.

Racial Differences in Communication. One of the earliest essays on African-American rhetoric dealt with differences in communication between black and white Americans. Its author, Fred Tewell, was intrigued by the fact that during a mock atomic attack and practice evacuation of a Southern city, all groups evacuated the city except for blacks. Tewell interviewed 100 blacks to determine the channels of communication used most frequently and patterns in their habits of seeking information. In his study, he points to differences in the communication channels of blacks and whites, noting that the "Negro church" is a primary communication source and outlet for blacks but that there are no clear channels through which blacks can express their desires to white community leaders.[90] Richard Gregg and A. Jackson McCormack also describe differences in communication between whites and blacks, focusing on use of rhetorical training; they chronicle their efforts to "contribute relevant skills and knowledge to hard-core ghetto youths" by teaching a speech course in a black neighborhood.[91]

A more recent discussion of differences between African-American rhetoric and that of whites is Kohrs Campbell's study of three black women speakers, Sojourner Truth, Ida B. Wells, and Mary Church Terrell. She identifies the substantive and stylistic features of their oratory, concentrating on how their speaking was consistent with or divergent from that of white women's rights speakers.[92] Although the notion that white rhetoric is standard often is implicit in such studies, they serve to undermine that standard simply by pointing out an alternative.

African-American Protest. With the advent of the civil rights movement of the 1960s, rhetorical scholars began to study black rhetoric as an example of protest rhetoric. *The Rhetoric of the Civil-Rights Movement*, edited by Haig Bosmajian and Hamida Bosmajian, is a collection of speeches and essays from the civil rights movement; included are traditional forms of rhetorical discourse by, among others, Martin Luther King, Jr.; Malcolm X; Stokely Carmichael; and Floyd McKissick.[93] Robert Scott and Wayne Brockriede, in *The Rhetoric of Black Power*, provide analyses of the rhetoric of the civil rights struggle, seeking to understand the varieties of discourse and actions used in the movement within the frame of the Western rhetorical tradition.[94] Also representative of this approach to the movement is a section on nonviolent resistance in Birmingham, Alabama, in John Bowers and Donovan Ochs' *The Rhetoric of Agitation and Control*. They use their typology of strategies of protest and response—including petition and avoidance, promulgation and solidification, and nonviolent resistance and violent suppression—to explain and assess the civil rights demonstrations in Birmingham in 1963.[95]

Interest in the rhetoric of African Americans to further the civil rights movement generated interest in individual black speakers—those involved in both the contemporary and historical struggles. For example, Pat Jefferson explains Stokely Carmichael's "cool" style as deriving from his humor and his "hip phraseology";[96] Gregory Mowe and W. Scott Nobles examine James Baldwin's rhetorical themes and strategies when addressing white audiences;[97] and Annjennette McFarlin describes the speaking career of Hallie Quinn Brown, a black elocutionist.[98] Through such essays, some basic features of African-American rhetoric emerge, particularly as it is used in response and as a challenge to the white rhetoric of oppression.

African Americans and the Media. One of the most frequent areas of investigation designed to incorporate an understanding of African Americans into the discipline of communication deals with their depiction in and response to the media, especially television. James Carey's examination of viewing preferences of blacks and whites, for example, suggests that blacks identify more strongly with television characters who directly or indirectly relate to their own culture.[99] A similar study by Thomas Donahue focuses on black children's perceptions of favorite television characters.[100] As a result of Judith Lemon's analysis of dominance patterns between blacks and whites in television programs, she concludes that blacks are portrayed more favorably in situation comedies than in crime dramas.[101] Elizabeth Johnson's study involves the variables of physical appearance, message, believability, and performance; these criteria are used by black viewers to rate the credibility of local black and white newscasters. Johnson reports that black viewers prefer the appearance of black newscasters but rate whites as better performers.[102]

Another example of the studies designed to assess the role of blacks in the media and to integrate this knowledge into theories of communication is David Womack's study of black participation in interviews at the 1984 Democratic national convention. He analyzes the number of blacks selected as news sources in live interviews, the status of those black sources compared to white sources, and the number of black, on-camera news reporters at the convention. He reports that blacks were interviewed in greater numbers than their percentage at the convention, especially on the evening that Jesse Jackson spoke.[103]

The study of the communication of African Americans as different from that of European Americans, as representative of protest against a discriminatory system, and as related to media constituted the primary initial efforts to develop an Afrocentric perspective in the communication discipline. Studies in these areas began to point to ways in which traditional rhetorical theories were not relevant to the communication patterns of African Americans.

Revisionist Stage

The purpose of Afrocentrism is not simply to understand black rhetoric but to revise theories taking into account that understanding. In the second stage of the Afrocentric challenge, then, have come the beginnings of a re-configuration of rhetorical notions themselves. One of the earliest studies to recognize the need for a black framework for the study of black rhetoric is Kohrs Campbell's analysis of the speeches of Malcolm X and Stokely Carmichael. She suggests that critics must recognize and make clear the philosophical presumptions of their critical perspectives; otherwise, the critic may condemn unfamiliar rhetoric rather than find ways to "reveal its assumptions and internal workings."[104] She uses Kenneth Burke's dramatism as the perspective from which to approach the two men's speeches—a perspective that allows her to focus on linguistic rather than logical materials and thus to understand the distinctive black linguistic features of the texts.

Another early study of black rhetoric from the perspective of African-American culture is an examination of the call-response of black churches as an organizing principle of African-American reality. In "How I Got Over: Communication Dynamics in the Black Community," Jack Daniel and Geneva Smitherman (now Smitherman-Donaldson) suggest that the call-response strategy reveals what they call the "Traditional African World View," appropriated and transformed to fit the American situation.[105] B. L. Ware and Wil Linkugel make use of the story of Moses, a powerful myth in the African-American community, to demonstrate Marcus Garvey's oratorical effectiveness,[106] and Patricia Harris analyzes the rhetoric of Dick Gregory from a black perspective.[107] Another example is Thurmon Garner's analysis of the African-American speech event, "playing the dozens"; he suggests this game teaches young blacks ways of handling social conflicts.[108]

The study of black rhetoric from a black perspective is exemplified, as well, in an essay on interethnic communication by Michael Hecht, Sidney Ribeau, and J. K. Alberts. They examine how African Americans perceive communication with whites. The underlying purpose of their essay is to "give voice to Afro-American perceptions of interethnic communication"[109] by exploring what African Americans consider the satisfying and dissatisfying features of their interactions with whites.

The role of blacks in the media also has been approached from an Afrocentric perspective that has implications for the revisions of rhetorical theories. Philip Wander, for example, suggests that the significance of the television movie, *Roots*, lies in its treatment of the institution of slavery from the victim's perspective—an unusual vantage point for television.[110] Robert Johnson analyzes the phrase, "blacks and women," used by the media during the Iranian hostage crisis, and suggests that the fact that the phrase "was so comfortably applied by American journalists to a specific group of black men and white women may be symptomatic of a deeply rooted cultural notion that for males race is the crucial factor while for females it is their sex."[111] William Haskins' fantasy-theme analysis of the vision of equality presented by Southern black journalists during Reconstruction to explain the premises of black protest rhetoric is another example of the assumption of an Afrocentric perspective on media phenomena.[112]

The interaction of race and sex has provided the basis for still other significant challenges to rhetorical theory. Drawing on the feminist and the Afrocentric paradigms, some scholars are studying the communication of black women, taking into account the impact of both sex and race in our theories. Frieda High Tesfagiorgis, an African-American artist, coined the term, "Afrofemcentrism" in 1984 to designate a "unique assertive-consciousness in Afro-American women."[113] Dorothy Williamson's study is an example of the assumption of this perspective in communication; she explores the unique aspects of the communication of black women spokespersons for the women's liberation movement.[114] Marsha Houston Stanback's research efforts to document and analyze the talk of middle-class black women also exemplifies the recognition of the intersection of race and sex in the understanding of communication; her essays include "Language and Black Woman's Place: Evidence from the Black Middle Class."[115] Houston Stanback suggests that many aspects of black women's talk are "survival skills" that should not be changed unless the social relationships that create them are changed."[116]

The creation of a journal, *Sage: A Scholarly Journal on Black Women*, begun in 1983, attests to the strength of the Afrofemcentric challenge to traditional understandings of communication and other disciplines.[117] While *Sage* does not focus specifically on the communication of black women, some essays touch on areas relevant to the study of communication, and many others provide important historical and contextual information for understanding communication. An example is a special issue on black women as leaders that includes articles about black women in Southern legislatures, grassroots activists in the civil rights movement in Mississippi, and black women and organized religion.[118] In another issue, Gladys-Marie Frye's "Portrait of a Black Quilter" is a discussion of how the two extant quilts of Harriet Powers, who lived in the nineteenth century, reveal her life experiences and her African heritage. Such data, generated by black women, have the potential to challenge traditional theories of communication in significant ways.[119]

Discourse and Discrimination, edited by Geneva Smitherman-Donaldson and Teun A. van Dijk, provides an overview of the Afrocentric perspective in research in communication. It is a compilation of essays that deal in various ways with the discursive reproduction of racism. Explored are topics such as differences in storytelling strategies between black and white children and the responses generated by the different styles; the effects of derogatory ethnic labels on users, targets, and in-group members; and the use of discourse by social program administrators in Britain to subsume minority concerns.[120] Such studies represent an evolving understanding of African-American communication from within that community itself; principles from an external and foreign rhetorical tradition are not simply applied to black rhetoric but instead are revised to fit the African-American experience of communication.

Afrocentricity offers a rhetorical experience with a history as ancient as that of classical Greece and Rome. While the African experience has been adapted to Western culture in the United States, its grounding in African roots provides an alternative view of the universe, the role of speaker and discourse, the ends of communication, and the forms of talk available to a rhetorical community. As this perspective becomes more visible, it will generate more radical revisions of rhetorical theories so that they come to reflect the values of the African-American community. Asante's summary of these values suggests the very different kind of rhetorical theory that is likely to emerge:

> Nothing is more beautiful to me than the ecstasy that occurs when a group of people have got on the same road to harmony at the same moment; that is the true manifestation of spirituality, the true materiality of life, which can only be determined by the person joining in the collective expression of power. . . . I experience *nommo*, and I know that nothing can save me except the spoken word.[121]

Asian Challenge

By

Mary Garrett

Asian rhetorics offer a rich source of alternative views to the Euro-American tradition. The language arts, both written and spoken, have been self-consciously practiced and continuously studied in Asia for over two thousand years, as evidenced in a body of models and examples, handbooks, and theories on persuasion, argumentation, and literature. Many of these materials differ in substantial and provocative ways from the Western tradition; they assume a different audience psychology, value different modes of reasoning, recommend different strategies of persuasion, are grounded in a different cosmology, and espouse different goals and standards for the rhetor. Students of contemporary rhetoric are just beginning to acknowledge the existence of these independent, well-developed rhetorics and their value to Western rhetoricians in illuminating culture-bound premises and practices.

Any discussion of Asian rhetorics must begin with recognition of the diversity of such rhetorics. As we move through space and time, from medieval Tibet to modern Korea, from early China to contemporary Korea, the intellectual milieux, major religions, political systems, social and family structures, economic organizations, and languages and writing systems vary tremendously. Since rhetoric is shaped by its historical and cultural contexts, we can expect as much diversity in Asian as in Western rhetorics. This discussion of Asian rhetoric will focus on Chinese rhetoric not because the Chinese case is necessarily typical of a monolithic Asian tradition but because it has received somewhat more study from communication scholars.[122]

Aside from a few brief articles,[123] communication scholars virtually ignored the Chinese rhetorical tradition until Robert Oliver's path-breaking *Culture and Communication in Ancient India and China*, in which he provides a comprehensive survey of the classical rhetorics of both cultures.[124] Since its publication in 1971, several studies of Chinese rhetoric have been published, although all are of more modest scope than is Oliver's book. For example, both Oliver and Vernon Jensen examine the rhetorical aspects of Taoism, the most exotic strand of Chinese philosophical thought.[125]

In the past few decades, an awakening of interest in rhetoric among Chinese scholars has produced several particularly useful introductions to the subject. Karl Kao surveys the rhetorical tradition from its beginnings to the present, emphasizing primarily its literary aspects.[126] In Jean-Paul Reding's book-length study, he traces the emergence of rhetoric from the arts of the sophists of both Greece and China; thus, his focus is on the fifth to second centuries B.C.[127] The first chapter of James Crump's *Intrigues: Studies of the Chan-kuo Ts'e* is an excellent introduction to the rhetorical practices and precepts of the same period.[128] Similarly, J. L. Kroll's detailed overview of debate and disputation covers Chinese rhetoric from the fifth century B.C. to the third century A.D.[129] The bias reflected in these works toward the classical period is still strong and is one reason for Kao's lament that "systematic study of Chinese rhetoric has just begun."[130]

Even so, some general observations about Chinese rhetoric can be made. Most schools of Chinese philosophy held that reality could be known and that language could reflect reality faithfully. Because the Chinese world view was of an organic universe, one that was relational rather than substance oriented, the subject/object division was not strongly marked. This led to a persistent tendency to conceive of knowing the world as somehow being one with it. Truth was not transcendent but this worldly, and the "sages" were those individuals who first discovered, tested, and recorded enduring truths of social, moral, and political life; they thus created in antiquity an unequalled golden age. Finally, since the universe incorporated ethical values, a person who knew — who was in contact with reality — was right both factually and morally.

These assumptions discouraged intellectual pluralism; if conflict arose, rhetors assumed they were absolutely right and others entirely wrong. Disagreement among the educated elite and the resulting need for argumentation were regarded as unfortunate and temporary exigencies. The idea of the masses debating and contending over policies and doctrines was viewed entirely negatively; it was seen as both a cause and an effect of social chaos. The notion of a "loyal opposition" was restricted to close advisors to the emperor, and even they often were executed for their criticisms.

The philosophical assumptions of Chinese philosophy shaped the nature of the justifications offered by rhetors. Given the backward-looking orientation, there was a universal move to ground arguments or doctrines in canonical texts, and new ideas were presented as recovery rather than discovery. There was also a forward-looking orientation, insofar as the truth test of any doctrine was its success when applied. But perhaps the most powerful form of persuasion, given the view of knowing as being, was for persuaders to embody their beliefs in their own lives and persons. Being in the right gave them a suasory force that, in theory, should affect any normal audience and, they hoped, end an argument once and for all.

Inclusion Stage

The study of Chinese rhetoric at the inclusion stage has focused primarily on classical Chinese rhetoric; thus, this summary of the Chinese challenge to rhetorical theory will deal with scholarship on this early period. The scholarship in this area tends to be directed to describing the tradition and identifying the components of Chinese rhetoric. In their identification of the constructs of classical Chinese rhetoric, scholars have focused on four dimensions: (1) the definition of rhetoric; (2) rhetorical genres; (3) modes of argumentation; and (4) rhetorical training.

Definition of Rhetoric. Rhetoric in China, in the classical period, was conceptualized as discourse (*wen*), a term that covers all polished writing. It is often translated as "literature," but a review of the genres classified under *wen* reveals that it is much more comprehensive than our modern conception of literature. *Wen* included poetry, rhapsodies or prose-poems, eulogies, dirges, songs, ditties, and epitaphs, but it also included letters, admonitions, proposals, reports to superiors, commissions, memoranda to inferiors, replies to opponents, proclamations and edicts, history, philosophical essays, prefaces, persuasions, marginal jottings, commentaries, and dialectical treatises.

All discourse was seen as having a didactic function: it embodied and reinforced cultural values, provided models for imitation, and encouraged correct attitudes and actions. Discourse that did not serve these functions was criticized and denounced. The attitude that discourse ought to be didactic and persuasive is evident in Yang Xiong's [Yang Hsiung's][131] explanation that he stopped writing rhapsodies (*fu*) because he came to feel the genre did not have the persuasive impact of some other discursive forms. He pointed out that a rhapsody was supposed to have a "rectifying message" but that really it "only encourages and does not restrain . . . . [I]t sustains nothing of proper rules and measures, nor does it rectify behavior like the poems of worthies and gentlemen."[132]

Several Asian scholars, or sinologists, highlight the pervasive rhetorical concern in classical Chinese discourse. Burton Watson describes the many ways in which Chinese historians selected, framed, and commented upon their materials to drive home the lessons that their readers should learn from history.[133] James Hart analyzes the rhetoric of a representative speech from the histories,[134] and Ronald Egan illustrates the suasory use of narrative in historical writing.[135] Rafe de Crespigny explicates the methods of argumentation used in early "memorials," the written proposals directed to officials in the bureaucracy.[136] Both David Knechtges and Hellmut Wilhelm trace the roots of the rhapsodies to the tradition of political persuasion; both regard the rhapsodies as self-consciously rhetorical productions, in which the speaker exploited every resource of style to create an overwhelming aesthetic experience that induced the hearer to agree with the concluding moral.[137]

Rhetorical Genres. The enterprise of uncovering the rhetorical aspect of Chinese discourse barely has begun. Understandably, most of the work concentrates on those genres that most resemble familiar Western rhetorical situations: political debates, dialectical disputations, speeches, and petitions. Dialectical disputation has received particular attention, with scholarship focused on the evolving tradition of systematic, rigorous, and competitive debate over abstract theses to test their truth value. Such debates, which usually took place in front of an audience, first appeared in the fourth and third centuries B.C. During the third to sixth centuries A.D., these disputations were revived by Buddhist teachers and by the "pure talkers," men who refined the art of witty and educated conversation.[138] The practice continues, though in an extremely attenuated form, among the Neo-Confucians, who reformulated Confucianism in response to Buddhism.

The Later Mohists' logical writings, reconstructed and translated by Angus C. Graham, provide a sample of the treatises associated with such disputation.[139] The Later Mohists were a tightly organized philosophical school of the fourth and third centuries B.C. that spoke for the lower class' interests, specialized in defensive warfare, and made rudimentary investigations into optics and physics. In their logical works, they outlined systematic procedures for resolving disputes over terms, abstract theses, and ethical decisions. They also illustrated their definitions and propositions with examples of their actual argumentation, which took the form of rigorous syllogistic reasoning. For example, they refuted the thesis that "study has no benefits" by arguing that those who hold this thesis "assume that people do not know that study is not beneficial, so they tell them. This is causing them to know that study is not beneficial, which is a type of teaching. If they regard study as not beneficial, to teach such a thesis is contradictory."[140]

The intellectual competition of such specialists in dialectic forced other Chinese philosophers to hone their debating skills and to give some attention to the principles of argumentation. The Confucian thinker Xunzi [Hsün-tzu], for example, developed a sophisticated theory of argumentative competence, which has been pieced together and interpreted by Anthony Cua.[141]

Despite the existence of a strand of rhetoric focused on disputation, it had much less influence on rhetoric in China than in the West, where it was placed at the center of intellectual activity. One reason for this was the strong pragmatic bent of Chinese culture; to split hairs over issues that had no obvious relation to the problems of real life was considered foolish and even irresponsible. Debates on economic policies were acceptable; debates on whether "final being" emerged from "fundamental non-being," for example, were not.[142]

Dialectic's lesser impact in China also was due to cross-cultural differences in the paradigm for persuasion between the two cultures. The paradigm for persuasion in the West reflects Greek and Roman social and political conditions — one person speaks to a large audience of equals, whether in law courts, in legislative assemblies, or on ceremonial occasions. In the Chinese imperial bureaucracy, however, power tended to be centered in one person. Thus, the word for persuasion, *shui*, referred primarily to one individual—usually a subordinate—addressing one other person—usually a superior. The address was sometimes face to face but most often was made in writing; it concerned topics related to politics and statecraft. Since almost all power was centered in the imperial bureacracy, anyone wishing to influence it had to engage in such persuasion.

When a rhetor attempted to persuade this sort of one-person audience, the situational, psychological, and interpersonal factors often had much more bearing on success than the logical validity of the inferences. Consequently, rhetoric became much more the counterpart of psychology than of dialectic. This shift can be seen at the level of practice. It led to the creation of rhetorical strategies of indirection such as "hiddens" (*yin*), which were enigmatic opening lines used to gain an audience (such as "a big fish in the sea!"); *feng*, a form of veiled criticism through riddles and allusions; and "progressive analogies," which approached a sensitive conclusion through a series of increasingly close comparisons.[143]

The need to be effective in the rhetorical situation created by the subordinate-superior address resulted in perceptive treatises on interpersonal persuasion. In Han Feizi's essay, "The Difficulties of Persuasion," the persuader was advised to observe the audience closely, create trust, and couch appeals in terms of audience values and goals, all the while remaining sensitive to shifts in power relations.[144] The essayists of *The Annals of Mr. Lu* described skillful persuaders as those who are able to identify completely with their audiences: they "are born with them [their audiences], grow up with them, and when they make speeches to them, echo them. They reach maturity with them and grow old with them in order to take them to their destination."[145] The book, *The Master of Demon Valley [Guiguzi]*, recently translated by Michael Broschat, was entirely devoted to one-to-one persuasion, recommending a number of practical strategies and explicitly grounding its advice in cosmological and psychological principles.[146]

Modes of Argumentation. Sinologists have devoted much attention to the types of arguments that predominate in Chinese discourse, especially in the more overtly persuasive genres, such as speeches, proposals, and philosophical essays. They generally agree that the preferred modes of argumentation used by the classical Chinese were argument from authority; a distinctive form of the sorites; argument from consequences; and argument by comparison (similes, examples, hypothetical examples, historical parallels, and analogies).

Argument from authority involved quoting a text of some antiquity, reflecting the belief that the distilled wisdom of the past could be applied to the present. This practice of citing authoritative texts as evidence, however, did not end argument; it merely moved it to the commentaries on such works, where battles were fought over how to interpret their meaning or over issues of textual corruption. The Confucian thinker Mengzi [Meng-tzu, also known as Mencius], for example, went so far as to accept only a few sentences in one chapter of the canonical *Book of History*, since the rest conflicted with his interpretation of the participants' characters.[147]

The ''Chinese sorites'' was a series of linked statements that resembles a sorites, a chain of incomplete syllogisms arranged so that the conclusion of one syllogism forms a premise of the next. But it functioned differently; rather than representing a chain of deductions, it either recounted a narrative or described a network of more or less simultaneous events and conditions.[148] In the following passage, Confucius used such reasoning to defend ''rectification of names'' as the proper first task for any new state administration:

> When names are not correct, what is said will not sound reasonable; when what is said does not sound reasonable, affairs will not culminate in success; when affairs do not culminate in success, rites and music will not flourish; when rites and music do not flourish, punishments will not fit the crime; when punishments do not fit the crime, the common people will not know where to put hand and foot. Thus when the gentleman names something, the name is sure to be usable in speech, and when he says something this is sure to be practicable. The thing about the gentleman is that he is anything but casual where speech is concerned.[149]

In the last few lines of this passage, Confucius made an implied argument from consequences for his position. Argument from consequences was based on a pragmatic view of truth: if a policy worked, it was considered true. Conversely, if a doctrine could not be applied in real life or if the results of carrying it out would be disastrous, it was thereby proven false. The following excerpt provides another example of argument from consequences. Gaozi [Kao-tzu] launched his argument that human nature is morally neutral, and Mengzi rebutted it by extending Gaozi's analogy through argument from consequences:

> Gaozi said, ''Human nature is like the willow; proper behavior is like cups and bowls. To make people benevolent and well-behaved is like making cups and bowls out of willow.''
>
> Mengzi said, ''Can you make cups and bowls while respecting the willow's nature? In actuality, you can only make cups and bowls after you've harmed the willow. If you're going to make cups and bowls by harming the willow then you're going to make people benevolent and well-behaved by harming them. Your doctrine will certainly lead people to regard benevolence and proper behavior as calamities, won't it?''[150]

Argument by comparison assumed many forms; one of the favored forms was use of historical parallels. Success was seen to determine truth, and history had tremendous value in deciding political and social issues. It was viewed as a vast compendium of case studies of what worked and what did not. By observing and correlating historical instances carefully, reliable parallels and generalizations could be reached. Han Feizi, for example, concluded that "judging from the tales handed down from high antiquity and the incidents recorded in the *Spring and Autumn Annals* (a historical chronicle), those men who violated the laws, committed treason, and carried out major acts of evil always worked through some eminent and highly placed minister."[151] In the course of his argument, he cited such occasions as when "Li Tui, acting as aid to the king of Chao, starved the Father of the Ruler to death" and when "the actor Shih aided Lady Li to bring about the death of Shen-sheng and to set Hsi-ch'i on the throne."[152]

Analogy was another common form of argument by comparison. Although Mengzi attacked Gaozi's analogy in the passage above, he often used analogies to justify his own doctrines. In the following example, he employed an analogy to defend benevolence as a fundamental principle of government (and again, his argument culminated with an argument by consequences):

> Benevolence overcomes cruelty just as water overcomes fire. Those who practice benevolence today are comparable to someone trying to put out a cartload of burning firewood with a cupful of water. When the fire fails to be extinguished, they say water cannot overcome fire. For a man to do this is for him to place himself on the side of those who are cruel to the extreme, and in the end he is sure only to perish.[153]

The appropriateness of such use of argument by comparison as the major or only evidence for a claim has been hotly debated by Western scholars studying Chinese thought. Derk Bodde, in a useful introduction to the forms of Chinese argument by comparison, denigrates their usefulness generally.[154] John Cikoski, in contrast, uses Boolean algebra, a branch of modern mathematical logic, to demonstrate the validity of analogy. Although his conclusions have not been widely accepted, he also details the prevailing practices, precepts, and technical vocabulary of classical Chinese analogic argument.[155] A good introduction to Chinese analogical reasoning and the evaluative issues it raises can be found in articles by D.C. Lau and A.C. Graham; they defend Mengzi against Arthur Waley's charge that he engaged in flimsy, sophistical analogizing.[156]

Westerners reading Chinese texts often have the feeling that they are confronting a fundamentally different mode of reasoning. With the possible exception of the "Chinese sorites," however, these modes of argumentation are not unique to China. What is distinctive in the Chinese case is, first, the constellation of these four particular types of argument. Second, the use of argument by comparison deserves some attention because the Chinese were highly skilled in such reasoning. Careful study of their texts allows us to see what a sophisticated tradition of argument by comparison looks like.

Rhetorical Training. The educational system provided very little specific training in any one genre of rhetoric, although from the eleventh century on, it was increasingly geared toward preparing the student to produce the essays used in the examinations for government service.[157] In part, this lack of training in specific genres was because the language arts were unitary; people mastered "literature" (*wen*) and then were assumed capable of producing whatever type of writing was needed. For example, Ban Chao, in the first century A.D., not only obeyed the Emperor's order to complete her brother's official history of the Han dynasty after his death, but she also wrote "Narrative Poems, Commemorative Writings, Inscriptions, Eulogies, Argumentations, Commentaries, Elegies, Essays, Treatises, Expositions, Memorials, and Final Instructions, in all (enough to fill) sixteen books."[158]

An epistemological justification also existed for the lack of training in particular rhetorical genres. The fundamental acts of knowing were considered to be observation and categorization; through them, underlying patterns could be recognized and change predicted. Given this view, education was conceived as refinement of the student's powers of observation and intuition. The best way to refine these powers was through emulation of models, primarily the model of the teacher; students internalized the teacher's modes of judging, feeling, and responding. Thus, education demanded transformation and not mere acquisition of information and skills, which typically have characterized the Western educational system.

A secondary model for learning rhetorical effectiveness was the written text, which was internalized through memorization and imitation. In response to a query about how to learn to write rhapsodies, Yang Xiong [Yang Hsiung] confidently advised, "If you read a thousand *fu* [rhapsodies], you will be good at writing them."[159] To assist such study, collections of models were compiled. For example, someone interested in model persuasions could turn to the book, *Han Feizi*, which contained two chapters called "Forest of Persuasions" that offered such models.[160] The entire book, *Records of the Warring States*, consisted of nothing but good speeches.[161] Its contemporary, *The Annals of Mr. Lu*, had a section illustrating excellent, depraved, and misleading speeches.[162] Likewise, the *Garden of Speeches* included chapters called "Excellent Speeches" and "Correct Remonstrations."[163] The bibliographies from the dynastic histories list the titles of many other such collections that are now lost, including *Forest of Remonstrations*, *Responses in Conversation*, and *Excellent Persuasions*.

When more explicit information was needed, occasional specialized treatises were available, including *The Master of Demon Valley*[164] as well as works on the language arts in general. Authors of the latter tended to discuss invention, arrangement, and style in a global way and then to consider the virtues and shortcomings of particular genres and writers. The best known example available in translation was written by Liu Xie [Lie Hsieh].[165] Lu Ji's [Lu Chi's] "Rhapsody on Literature," though much shorter, had the advantage of illustrating the principles it presented.[166]

Contemporary Studies. The efforts of scholars to lay out the nature of rhetorical theory of the classical Chinese also are being extended to studies of modern Chinese rhetoric. They seek to discover how much of the classical theories are still in evidence in Chinese rhetorical theory and practice and to characterize the nature of contemporary rhetoric in China. Although China has undergone great changes in the last two centuries, the assumptions and habits of traditional Chinese rhetoric are far from dead. Like the learned of old, the Communists believe that all discourse should be didactic. To this end, they deliberately have exploited — some would say subverted — such traditional forms as folk songs, stories, serial pictures, opera, theatre, and "big character posters," turning them into vehicles for Communist doctrine.[167]

Much of the work on how classical cultural patterns of communication persist has come from researchers in the emerging field of contrastic rhetoric. The ground-breaking work in this area is Robert Kaplan's study of paragraph structure in various languages, in which he argues that the "Oriental" pattern — in both the classical and contemporary periods — is an "approach by indirection," a spiraling inward as opposed to the linear English paragraph.[168] Carolyn Matalene, echoing many of the observations made above about classical Chinese modes of argumentation, concludes that, even now, the appeal of her Mainland Chinese students' rhetoric is "always to history and to tradition and to the authority of the past; its technique is always the repetition of maxims, exampla, and analogies presented in established forms and expressed in well-known phrases."[169] She remarks also on her students' habit of memorizing and imitating written models as a way of internalizing principles of composition and style, another legacy from their rhetorical tradition.

These patterns are not just fossilized remnants preserved in the educational system: government bureaucracies also justify their policy decisions with arguments by authority. They now cite Marx, Mao, or Deng Xiaoping, of course, rather than Confucius, and the life of the model worker Lei Feng is periodically trotted out as an example for emulation. Argument from consequences still is used, as well. Deng Xiaoping, for example, defended his arrest and imprisonment of the dissident Wei Jingsheng with such an argument, pointing out that we "put Wei Jingsheng behind bars, didn't we? Did that damage China's reputation? We haven't released him, but China's reputation has not been tarnished by that; our reputation improves day by day."[170]

In their study of various dimensions of classical and contemporary Chinese rhetoric, including the definition of rhetoric, rhetorical genres, modes of argumentation, and rhetorical training, scholars are discovering differences between the Chinese and Western rhetorical traditions. They have begun to investigate the significance of those differences for current explanations of rhetorical processes, initiating the revisionist stage of the challenge to traditional rhetorical thought.

Revisionist Stage

The understanding of Chinese rhetoric among communication scholars and China scholars is far from complete. But even the sketchy picture that has begun to emerge suggests some ways in which the Western tradition can be re-examined, refined, and enriched through attention to Asian rhetoric. First, rhetoric often has been described as a unique Western invention, an untenable claim in the light of the Chinese theory and literature concerning rhetoric. Through their history, the Chinese, like Westerners, have constructed theories and prescriptive handbooks for persuasion and disputation, have collected materials for speech construction, have compiled models for imitation, and have engaged in disputation. Further research undoubtedly will disclose more commonalities and further temper our judgments about the distinctive achievements of Western rhetoric.

But significant differences do exist between Western and Chinese rhetorics. For instance, Western analyses of the tropes and figures take Western practices as cultural universals. When the group of French scholars who call themselves Group *Mu* wrote what they intended to be a comprehensive survey of the tropes and figures (a "general rhetoric"), they based it on tropes and figures in the French, English, and German languages.[171] According to Kao, Chinese categorizations of the tropes and figures do not correspond to the Western lists, and some Chinese tropes function in rather unfamiliar and intriguing ways.[172] Along similar lines, the kinds of parallelism used in Chinese discourse require that readers learn to infer meaning in different ways.[173]

Discussions of the best modes of argument sometimes generalize certain Western standards or ideals into cultural universals. The enthymeme has held a place of pride in the Aristotelian tradition; it is assumed to be the most natural, effective, and reliable mode of reasoning. Argument by comparison (especially analogy), in contrast, is often devalued as ineffectual and unreliable. Echoes of this tradition remain in some modern treatments of argumentation; Chaim Perelman and Lucie Olbrechts-Tyteca, for example, describe analogy as "an unstable means of argument."[174] This negative judgment is rejected increasingly by contemporary rhetoricians, such as those discussed in this book, but a great lag remains between theory and pedagogical practice. Many argumentation and debate textbooks still concentrate on syllogistic modes of reasoning, and they either slight or ignore argument by comparison as a form of rhetorical proof. Stephen Toulmin, Richard Rieke, and Allan Janik, for example, begin their discussion of analogy by cautioning that "hardly any type of argument exposes us to the risk of fallacy more often than analogy."[175]

Chinese theory and practice of persuasion call these claims into question. Chinese persuaders could and did reason syllogistically, but they generally preferred the use of comparison. In contrast to many Western rhetorics, conclusions were not seen as less reliable because they rested on a comparison. Comparisons were countered but by such methods as better counter-examples or extension of analogies. Even the Later Mohists, who were highly skilled in deductive reasoning and also committed to theory construction, felt no need to describe and dissect the syllogism. Instead, they turned to linguistic analysis, the comparison of sentences to trace shifts in meaning and truth value as syntax and idiom changed — much in the fashion of modern ordinary language philosophers like John Austin and John Searle. Chinese rhetoric, then, suggests the naturalness and value of non-syllogistic forms of reasoning.

Chinese rhetoric also illuminates some preconceptions underlying Western approaches to communication ethics. Western rhetorics, until quite recently, have tended to emphasize the speaker; the speaker acts on the audience, and thus ethical responsibility rests primarily with the speaker, not the audience. The dominant Western view of the emotions, dominant at least until the development of modern theories of persuasion, reinforces this notion of a passive audience; the emotions are irrational, powerful, and extremely difficult to control. The speaker evokes them, and the audience is virtually defenseless against such manipulation. The Chinese audience, in contrast, is regarded as a much more active party in the exchange. Not only does it often control the communication channels, but it has the duty to ensure that good speeches reach it. It also has to prepare itself to be in the proper state to judge persuasions. Since the Chinese viewed both thinking and feeling as highly amenable to control through education and training, the audience has much more moral responsibility for rejecting the bad speech and adopting the good one. Though developed in a context quite foreign to our modern sensibilities, such Chinese rhetorical concepts and tenets certainly have more to offer rhetorical theory than has been appreciated so far.

Conclusion

Scholars who are challenging the rhetorical tradition in the ways described in this chapter are not interested in replacing the mainstream rhetorical tradition with their new theories. They do not ask that all previous rhetorical theories be dismissed. The Western rhetorical tradition that emerged from classical Greece and Rome always will be with us as an inheritance from the past, and this tradition provides a useful perspective on the nature and function of rhetoric. Those who challenge the tradition simply argue that it has given us only one perspective—that of European-American men—and it is not the "correct" or only perspective. These challenges encourage us to examine the rhetorical tradition with a new consciousness of its less attractive features and to create a new body of theory that is more satisfying to and reflects the perspectives of all people.

Thus, these challenges provide an opportunity to celebrate and make use of the diversity of expression in all of its forms to develop more holistic understandings of rhetoric. If the various fragments of our knowledge, our various perspectives, are respected and combined, we can begin to see, in Minnie Pratt's words, "if our fragments match anywhere, if our pieces, together make another large piece of the truth that can be part of the map we are making together to show us the way to get to the longed-for world."[176]

Notes

[1] This view of theory was proposed by Cheris Kramarae, "Feminist Theories of Communication," in *International Encyclopedia of Communications*, II, ed. Erik Barnouw (New York: Oxford University Press, 1989), 157.

[2] Dale Spender, *Man Made Language* (Boston: Routledge and Kegan Paul, 1980), p. 65.

[3] We acknowledge that this chapter can be viewed as an indictment of the rest of the book because we have included no chapters summarizing the perspectives of any women, African-Americans, or Asians. We, too, have been subject to the biases we describe here in selecting the scholars for inclusion.

[4] Simone de Beauvoir, *The Second Sex*, trans. and ed. H. M. Parshley (New York: Vintage/Random, 1952), p. xvii.

[5] We do not mean to suggest that the description of the feminist perspective summarized here is the "official" feminist approach to research. There are many kinds of feminism, and we do not claim to speak for all feminists. This view is feminist, but it is only one of many feminist perspectives possible. For overviews of feminist perspectives on research in communication, see: Kathryn Carter and Carole Spitzack, eds., *Doing Research on Women's Communication: Perspectives on Theory and Method* (Norwood, NJ: Ablex, 1989); Carole Spitzack and Kathryn Carter, "Women in Communication Studies: A Typology for Revision," *Quarterly Journal of Speech*, 73 (November 1987), 401-23; H. Leslie Steeves, "Feminist Theories and Media Studies," *Critical Studies in Mass Communication*, 4 (June 1987), 96-135; Brenda Dervin, "The Potential Contribution of Feminist Scholarship to the Field of Communication," *Journal of Communication*, 37 (Autumn 1987), 107-20; Karen A. Foss and Sonja K. Foss, "The Status of Research on Women and Communication," *Communication Quarterly*, 31 (Summer 1983), 195-204; and *Women's Studies in Communication*, 11 (Spring 1988), which includes essays by Lois S. Self, Karlyn Kohrs Campbell, Celeste Michelle Condit, Sonja K. Foss and Karen A. Foss, H. Leslie Steeves, Marlene Fine, Jan Muto, Julia T. Wood, Marsha Houston Stanback, and Carole Spitzack and Kathryn Carter in a "Forum on Feminist Scholarship."

[6] For other definitions of "feminism," see Cheris Kramarae, Paula A. Treichler, and Ann Russo, *A Feminist Dictionary* (Boston: Pandora, 1985), pp. 158-60.

7 These and other qualities of women's experiences are suggested in sources such as: Mary Field Belenky, Blythe McVicker Clinchy, Nancy Rule Goldberger, and Jill Mattuck Tarule, *Women's Ways of Knowing: The Development of Self, Voice, and Mind* (New York: Basic, 1986); Carol Gilligan, *In a Different Voice: Psychological Theory and Women's Development* (Cambridge: Harvard University Press, 1982); Gayle Kimball, ed., *Women's Culture: The Women's Renaissance of the Seventies* (Metuchen, NJ: Scarecrow, 1981); and Anne Wilson Schaef, *Women's Reality: An Emerging Female System in the White Male Society* (Minneapolis: Winston, 1981).

8 Barrie Thorne and Nancy Henley, "Difference and Dominance: An Overview of Language, Gender, and Society," in *Language and Sex: Difference and Dominance*, ed. Barrie Thorne and Nancy Henley (Rowley, MA: Newbury, 1975), p. 15. Other major works that address the link between sex and language are: Alleen Pace Nilsen, Haig Bosmajian, H. Lee Gershuny, and Julia P. Stanley, *Sexism and Language* (Urbana, IL: National Council of Teachers of English, 1977); Casey Miller and Kate Swift, *Words and Women* (Garden City, NY: Anchor/Doubleday, 1977); Spender; Barrie Thorne, Cheris Kramarae, and Nancy Henley, eds., *Language, Gender and Society* (Rowley, MA: Newbury, 1983); and Cheris Kramarae, Muriel Schulz, and William M. O'Barr, eds., *Language and Power* (Beverly Hills: Sage, 1984).

9 Cheris Kramarae, *Women and Men Speaking: Frameworks for Analysis* (Rowley, MA: Newbury, 1981), p. 1.

10 Spender, pp. 142-43.

11 Virginia Kidd, "A Study of the Images Produced Through the Use of the Male Pronoun as the Generic," *Moments in Contemporary Rhetoric and Communication* [University of Minnesota], 1 (1971), 25-29. For a summary of studies dealing with generic masculine terms, see Jeanette Silveira, "Generic Masculine Words and Thinking," in *The Voices and Words of Women and Men*, ed. Cheris Kramarae (Oxford: Pergamon, 1980), pp. 165-78.

12 See, for example, Jean Faust, "Words That Oppress," *Women Speaking*, April, 1970; rpt. Pittsburgh: KNOW, n.d.; and Mary Ritchie Key, *Male/Female Language* (Metuchen, NJ: Scarecrow, 1975).

13 For an excellent discussion of naming conventions and their history, see Una Stannard, *Mrs. Man* (San Francisco: Germainbooks, 1977).

14 Muriel R. Schulz, "The Semantic Derogation of Woman," in *Language and Sex: Difference and Dominance*, ed. Barrie Thorne and Nancy Henley (Rowley, MA: Newbury, 1975), pp. 64-75.

15 For discussions of the negative connotations around terms connected with women, see: Casey Miller and Kate Swift, "One Small Step for Genkind," *New York Times Magazine*, April 16, 1972, pp. 36, 99-101, 106; and Alleen Pace Nilsen, "Sexism in English: A Feminist View," in *Female Studies VI: Closer to the Ground: Women's Classes, Criticism, Programs—1972*, ed. Nancy Hoffman, Cynthia Secor, and Adrian Tinsley (Old Westbury, NY: Clearinghouse on Women's Studies, 1972), pp. 102-09.

16 Robin Lakoff, "Language and Woman's Place," *Language in Society*, 2 (April 1973), 73.

17 Thorne and Henley, p. 29.

18 Dennis E. Baron has synthesized the work in this area, compiling 35 proposals for alternative personal pronouns from various nineteenth- and twentieth-century sources. See "The Epicene Pronoun: The Word that Failed," *American Speech*, 56 (Summer 1981), 83-97.

19 Casey Miller and Kate Swift, *The Handbook of Nonsexist Writing* (New York: Lippincott and Crowell, 1980).

20 Bobbye Sorrels Persing, *The Nonsexist Communicator* (East Elmhurst, NY: Communication Dynamics, 1978).

21 Barbara Bate, "Nonsexist Language Use in Transition," *Journal of Communication*, 28 (Winter 1978), 139-49.

22 Lynne Webb, "Eliminating Sexist Language in the Classroom," *Women's Studies in Communication*, 9 (Spring 1986), 21-29.

23 Mary Daly, *Gyn/Ecology: The Metaethics of Radical Feminism* (Boston: Beacon, 1987); and Mary Daly, *Pure Lust: Elemental Feminist Philosophy* (Boston: Beacon, 1984).

24 Daly, *Gyn/Ecology*, pp. 3-4.

[25] Mary Daly and Jane Caputi, *Websters' First New Intergalactic Wickedary of the English Language* (Boston: Beacon, 1987), p. 163.

[26] Daly and Caputi, pp. xiii-xiv. For an overview of Mary Daly's rhetorical theory, see Cindy L. Griffin, "Mary Daly's Rhetorical Theory: Hagography as Mistake," Thesis University of Oregon 1989.

[27] Kramarae, Treichler, and Russo, p. 1.

[28] Suzette Haden Elgin, *A First Dictionary and Grammar of Láadan: Second Edition*, ed. Diane Martin (Madison, WI: Society for the Furtherance and Study of Fantasy and Science Fiction, 1988), p. 1.

[29] Elgin, pp. 61-128.

[30] Cheris Kramer [Kramarae], "Women's Speech: Separate But Unequal?" *Quarterly Journal of Speech*, 60 (February 1974), p. 14.

[31] Mary R. Haas, "Men's and Women's Speech in Koasati," *Language*, 20 (July-September 1944), 142-49.

[32] Marjorie Swacker, "The Sex of the Speaker as a Sociolinguistic Variable," in *Language and Sex: Difference and Dominence*, ed. Barrie Thorne and Nancy Henley (Rowley, MA: Newbury, 1975), p. 82.

[33] For discussions and critiques of these various instruments, see: Virginia Eman Wheeless and Kathi Dierks-Stewart, "The Psychometric Properties of the Bem Sex-Role Inventory: Questions Concerning Reliability and Validity," *Communication Quarterly*, 29 (Summer 1981), 173-86; and "A Symposium: The Measurement of Psychological Gender Orientation," containing essays by Andrew S. Rancer and Kathi J. Dierks-Rancer, Gary A. Copeland and R. C. Adams, and Lawrence R. Wheeless and Virginia Eman Wheeless, in *Women's Studies in Communication*, 8 (Fall 1985), 70-93.

[34] Illustrative is a study by Deborah Weider-Hatfield, "Differences in Self-Reported Leadership Behavior as a Function of Biological Sex and Psychological Gender," *Women's Studies in Communication*, 10 (Spring 1987), 1-14.

[35] Kramer [Kramarae], "Women's Speech," p. 17.

[36] Patricia Hayes Bradley, "The Folk-Linguistics of Women's Speech: An Empirical Examination," *Communication Monographs*, 48 (March 1981), 90.

[37] Pamela M. Fishman, "Interaction: The Work Women Do," in *Language, Gender and Society*, ed. Barrie Thorne, Cheris Kramarae, and Nancy Henley (Rowley, MA: Newbury, 1983), p. 100.

[38] See, for example: Robin Lakoff, *Language and Woman's Place* (New York: Harper Colophon, 1975), pp. 8-19; Nancy M. Henley, *Body Politics* (Englewood Cliffs, NJ: Prentice-Hall, 1977), pp. 202-24; and Judith Anderson, Beatrice Schultz, and Constance Courtney Staley, "Training in Argumentativeness: New Hope for Nonassertive Women," *Women's Studies in Communication*, 10 (Fall 1987), 58-66.

[39] See, for example, Don H. Zimmerman and Candace West, "Sex Roles, Interruptions, and Silences in Conversation," in *Language and Sex: Difference and Dominance*, ed. Barrie Thorne and Nancy Henley (Rowley, MA: Newbury, 1975), p. 105.

[40] Karlyn Kohrs Campbell, *Man Cannot Speak for Her: Vol. 1: A Critical Study of Early Feminist Rhetoric* (New York: Praeger, 1989), 1.

[41] Elaine E. McDavitt, "Susan B. Anthony, Reformer and Speaker," *Quarterly Journal of Speech*, 30 (April 1944), 173-80.

[42] Wil A. Linkugel, "The Speech Style of Anna Howard Shaw," *Central States Speech Journal*, 13 (Spring 1962), 171-78; and Wil A. Linkugel, "The Woman Suffrage Argument of Anna Howard Shaw," *Quarterly Journal of Speech*, 49 (April 1963), 165-74.

[43] Sonja K. Foss, "The Equal Rights Amendment: Two Worlds in Conflict," *Quarterly Journal of Speech*, 65 (October 1979), 275-88.

[44] Martha Solomon, "The 'Positive Woman's' Journey: A Mythic Analysis of STOP ERA," *Quarterly Journal of Speech*, 65 (October 1979), 262-74.

[45] Wayne N. Thompson, "Barbara Jordan's Keynote Address: Fulfilling Dual and Conflicting Purposes," *Central States Speech Journal*, 30 (Fall 1979), 272-77; and Wayne N. Thompson, "Barbara Jordan's Keynote Address: The Juxtaposition of Contradictory Values," *Southern Speech Communication Journal*, 44 (1979), 223-32.

[46] Patricia Scileppi Kennedy and Gloria Hartmann O'Shields, *We Shall Be Heard: Women Speakers in America: 1828-Present* (Dubuque: Kendall/Hunt, 1983), p. xvii.

[47] Kennedy and O'Shields.

[48] Judith Anderson, *Outspoken Women: Speeches by American Women Reformers: 1635-1935* (Dubuque: Kendall/Hunt, 1984).

[49] Campbell, *Man Cannot Speak For Her*, Vol. 1. Vol. 2 is *Key Texts of the Early Feminists*.

[50] Elizabeth Berry, "Emma Goldman: A Study in Female Agitation," *Women's Studies in Communication*, 4 (Fall 1981), 32-46.

[51] Jean Mary Guske Ward, "Women's Responses to Systems of Male Authority: Communication Strategies in the Novels of Abigail Scott Duniway," Diss. University of Oregon 1989.

[52] Fern L. Johnson, "Women's Culture and Communication: An Analytical Perspective," in *Beyond Boundaries: Sex & Gender Diversity in Communication*, ed. Cynthia M. Lont and Sheryl A. Friedley (Fairfax, VA: George Mason University Press, 1989), p. 306.

[53] Barbara Westbrook Eakins and R. Gene Eakins, *Sex Differences in Human Communication* (Boston: Houghton Mifflin, 1978), p. 38.

[54] Barbara Bate and Anita Taylor, eds., *Women Communicating: Studies of Women's Talk* (Norwood, NJ: Ablex, 1988).

[55] John E. Baird, Jr. and Patricia Hayes Bradley, "Styles of Management and Communication: A Comparative Study of Men and Women," *Communication Monographs*, 46 (June 1979), 108, 109.

[56] Audrey A. Nelson, "Women's Nonverbal Behavior: The Paradox of Skill and Acquiescence," *Women's Studies in Communication*, 4 (Fall 1981), 18-31.

[57] For samples of feminist critique in a number of fields, see Paula A. Treichler, Cheris Kramarae, and Beth Stafford, eds., *For Alma Mater: Theory and Practice in Feminist Scholarship* (Urbana: University of Illinois Press, 1985).

[58] Sally Miller Gearhart, "The Womanization of Rhetoric," *Women's Studies International Quarterly*, 2 (1979), 195-201.

[59] Jean Bethke Elshtain, "Feminist Discourse and Its Discontents: Language, Power, and Meaning," in *Feminist Theory: A Critique of Ideology*, ed. Nannerl O. Keohane, Michelle Z. Rosaldo, and Barbara C. Gelpi (Chicago: University of Chicago Press, 1982), p. 130.

[60] Kathleen Edgerton Kendall and Jeanne Y. Fisher, "Frances Wright on Women's Rights: Eloquence Versus Ethos," *Quarterly Journal of Speech*, 60 (February 1974), 68.

[61] A study that deals with women's talk on the telephone is Lana F. Rakow, "Gender, Communication, and Technology: A Case Study of Women and the Telephone," Diss. University of Illinois 1987. The study is summarized in Lana F. Rakow, "Looking to the Future: Five Questions for Gender Research," *Women's Studies in Communication*, 10 (Fall 1987), 79-86.

[62] Samples of such forms of expression are compiled in Karen A. Foss and Sonja K. Foss, *Women Speak* (Prospect Heights, IL: Waveland, 1991).

[63] Kramarae, "Feminist Theories of Communication," p. 159.

[64] Valerie A. Endress, "Feminist Theory and the Concept of Power in Public Address," in *Women and Communicative Power: Theory, Research, and Practice*, ed. Carol Ann Valentine and Nancy Hoar (Annandale, VA: Speech Communication Association, 1988), pp. 103-04.

[65] Belle A. Edson, "Bias in Social Movement Theory: A View from a Female-Systems Perspective," *Women's Studies in Communication*, 8 (Spring 1985), 34-45.

[66] Mary Rose Williams, "A Re-Conceptualization of Protest Rhetoric: Characteristics of Quilts as a Protest Form," Diss. University of Oregon 1990.

[67] Arthur Lee Smith, *The Rhetoric of Black Revolution* (Boston: Allyn and Bacon, 1969).

[68] Arthur L. Smith, "Socio-Historical Perspectives of Black Oratory," *Quarterly Journal of Speech*, 56 (October 1970), 264-69.

[69] Arthur L. Smith, "Markings of an African Concept of Rhetoric," *Today's Speech*, 19 (Spring 1971), 13-18.

[70] Molefi Kete Asante and Kariamu Welsh Asante, *African Culture: The Rhythms of Unity* (Westport, CT: Greenwood, 1985); and Molefi Kete Asante, *The Afrocentric Idea* (Philadelphia: Temple University Press, 1987). See also Molefi Kete Asante and Abdulai S. Vandi, eds., *Contemporary Black Thought: Alternative Analyses in Social and Behavioral Science* (Beverly Hills: Sage, 1980).

For a review of dissertations in various fields that employ an Afrocentric perspective, see Victor O. Okafor, "The Afrocentric Paradigm: A Review of Dissertation and Other Studies in the United States," unpublished manuscript (Philadelphia: Temple University, 1989).

[71] Asante, *The Afrocentric Idea*, p. 6.

[72] Asante, *The Afrocentric Idea*, p. 3.

[73] Smith [Asante], "Markings," p. 14; and Jack L. Daniel and Geneva Smitherman, "How I Got Over: Communication Dynamics in the Black Community," *Quarterly Journal of Speech*, 62 (February 1976), 32-33.

[74] Smith [Asante], "Socio-Historical Perspectives," p. 265; and Asante, *The Afrocentric Idea*, p. 51.

[75] Asante, *The Afrocentric Idea*, p. 71.

[76] Smith [Asante], "Markings," p. 14.

[77] These myths are discussed in Asante, *The Afrocentric Idea*, pp. 97-110. African-American folktales are chronicled by topic in Daryl Cumber Dance, *Shuckin' and Jivin': Folklore from Contemporary Black Americans* (Bloomington: Indiana University Press, 1978).

[78] Asante, *The Afrocentric Idea*, p. 39.

[79] Asante, *The Afrocentric Idea*, p. 185.

[80] Asante, *The Afrocentric Idea*, p. 189; and Roger D. Abrahams, *Talking Black* (Rowley, MA: Newbury, 1976), p. 9.

[81] Lawrence W. Levine, *Black Culture and Black Consciousness: Afro-American Folk Thought from Slavery to Freedom* (New York: Oxford University Press, 1977), pp. 97-101; and Dance, *Shuckin' and Jivin'*, p. xvii.

[82] Geneva Smitherman, *Talkin and Testifyin: The Language of Black America* (Boston: Houghton Mifflin, 1977), p. 73.

[83] Abrahams, p. 52.

[84] Abrahams, pp. 50-51.

[85] Abrahams, p. 51.

[86] Abrahams, pp. 52-53.

[87] Abrahams, p. 54.

[88] Thomas Kochman, "Toward an Ethnography of Black American Speech Behavior," in *Afro-American Anthology: Contemporary Perspectives*, ed. Norman E. Whitten, Jr. and John F. Szwed (New York: Free, 1970), p. 154.

[89] Abrahams, p. 63.

[90] Fred Tewell, "How Negroes Communicate in an American Community," *Today's Speech*, 6 (April 1958), 15-17.

[91] Richard B. Gregg and A. Jackson McCormack, "'Whitey' Goes to the Ghetto: A Personal Chronicle," *Today's Speech*, 16 (September 1968), 25.

[92] Karlyn Kohrs Campbell, "Style and Content in the Rhetoric of Early Afro-American Feminists," *Quarterly Journal of Speech*, 72 (November 1986), 434-45.

[93] Haig A. Bosmajian and Hamida Bosmajian, eds., *The Rhetoric of the Civil-Rights Movement* (New York: Random, 1969).

[94] Robert L. Scott and Wayne Brockriede, *The Rhetoric of Black Power* (New York: Harper and Row, 1969).

[95] John Waite Bowers and Donovan J. Ochs, *The Rhetoric of Agitation and Control* (New York: Random, 1971), pp. 119-35.

[96] Pat Jefferson, "'Stokely's Cool': Style," *Today's Speech*, 16 (September 1968), 19-24.

[97] Gregory Mowe and W. Scott Nobles, "James Baldwin's Message for White America," *Quarterly Journal of Speech*, 58 (April 1972), 142-51.

[98] Annjennette S. McFarlin, "Hallie Quinn Brown: Black Woman Elocutionist," *Southern Speech Communication Journal*, 46 (Fall 1980), 72-82.

[99] James W. Carey, "Variations in Negro/White Television Preferences," *Journal of Broadcasting*, 16 (Summer 1966), 199-212.

[100] Thomas R. Donahue, "Black Children's Perceptions of Favorite TV Characters," *Journal of Broadcasting*, 19 (Spring 1975), 152-67.

[101] Judith Lemon, "Women and Blacks on Prime-Time Television," *Journal of Communication*, 27 (Autumn 1977), 70-79.

[102] Elizabeth Johnson, "Credibility of Black and White Newscasters to a Black Audience," *Journal of Broadcasting*, 28 (Summer 1984), 365-68.

[103] David L. Womack, "Black Participation in Live Network Television: Interviews at the 1984 Democratic Convention," *Howard Journal of Communications*, 1 (Winter 1988-89), 211-18.

[104] Karlyn Kohrs Campbell, "The Rhetoric of Radical Black Nationalism: A Case Study in Self-Conscious Criticism," *Central States Speech Journal*, 22 (Fall 1971), 152.

[105] Jack L. Daniel and Geneva Smitherman, "How I Got Over: Communication Dynamics in the Black Community," *Quarterly Journal of Speech*, 62 (February 1976), 26-39.

[106] B. L. Ware and Wil A. Linkugel, "The Rhetorical *Persona*: Marcus Garvey as Black Moses," *Communication Monographs*, 49 (March 1982), 50-62.

[107] Patricia Ethel Harris, "Afrocentric View of the Rhetoric of Dick Gregory," Diss. Ohio State University 1982.

[108] Thurmon Garner, "Playing the Dozens: Folklore as Strategies for Living," *Quarterly Journal of Speech*, 69 (February 1983), 47-57.

[109] Michael L. Hecht, Sidney Ribeau, and J. K. Alberts, "An Afro-American Perspective on Interethnic Communication," *Communication Monographs*, 56 (December 1989), 385-410.

[110] Philip Wander, "On the Meaning of 'Roots,'" *Journal of Communication*, 27 (Autumn 1977), 64-69.

[111] Robert C. Johnson, "'Blacks and Women': Naming American Hostages Released in Iran," *Journal of Communication*, 30 (Summer 1980), 62.

[112] William A. Haskins, "Rhetorical Vision of Equality: Analysis of the Rhetoric of the Southern Black Press During Reconstruction," *Communication Quarterly*, 29 (Spring 1981), 116-22.

[113] Freida High Tesfagiorgis, "Afrofemcentrism and its Fruition in the Art of Elizabeth Catlett and Faith Ringgold (A View of Women by Women), *Sage*, 4 (Spring 1987), 32.

[114] Dorothy Kay Williamson, "Rhetorical Analysis of Selected Black American Spokespersons," Diss. Ohio State University 1980.

[115] Marsha Houston Stanback, "Language and Black Woman's Place: Evidence from the Black Middle Class," in *For Alma Mater: Theory and Practice in Feminist Scholarship*, ed. Paula A. Treichler, Cheris Kramarae, and Beth Stafford (Urbana: University of Illinois Press, 1985), pp. 177-93.

[116] Marsha Houston Stanback, "Feminist Theory and Black Women's Talk," *Howard Journal of Communications*, 1 (Winter 1988-89), 192.

[117] See Patricia Bell-Scott and Beverly Guy-Sheitall, "The First Five Years: Looking Backward and Forward," *Sage*, 5 (Summer 1988), 2.

[118] *Sage*, 5 (Fall 1988). The articles include: Joanne V. Hawks, "A Challenge to Racism and Sexism: Black Women in Southern Legislatures, 1965-1986," 20-23; Vicki Crawford, "Grassroots Activists in the Mississippi Civil Rights Movement," 24-29; and Jualynne E. Dodson, "Power and Surrogate Leadership: Black Women and Organized Religion," 37-42.

[119] Gladys-Marie Frye, "Harriet Powers: Portrait of a Black Quilter," *Sage*, 4 (Spring 1987), 11-16.

[120] Geneva Smitherman-Donaldson and Teun A. van Dijk, eds., *Discourse and Discrimination* (Detroit: Wayne State University Press, 1988).

[121] Asante, *The Afrocentric Idea*, p. 188.

[122] For a bibliography of works by communication scholars on Asian rhetorics, see J. Vernon Jensen, "Rhetoric of East Asia—A Bibliography," *Rhetoric Society Quarterly*, 17 (Spring 1987), 213-31.

[123] See, for example, Robert T. Oliver, "The Rhetorical Tradition in China: Confucius and Mencius," *Today's Speech*, 17 (February 1969), 3-8; Beatrice Reynolds, "Lao Tzu: Persuasion Through Inaction and Non-Speaking," *Today's Speech*, 17 (February 1969), 23-25; James Crump and John Dreher, "Peripatetic Rhetors of the Warring Kingdoms," *Central States Speech Journal*, 2 (March 1951), 15-17; and John Dreher and James Crump, "Pre-Han Persuasion: The Legalist School," *Central States Speech Journal*, 3 (March 1952), 10-14. This article consists almost entirely of D. K. Liao's translation of Han Feizi's essay, "The Difficulties of Persuasion," from the book that bears his name. For a much superior translation, see *Han Fei Tzu: Basic Writings*, trans. Burton Watson (New York: Columbia University Press, 1964), pp. 73-79.

[124] Robert T. Oliver, *Communication and Culture in Ancient India and China* (Syracuse: Syracuse University Press, 1971).

[125] Robert T. Oliver, "The Rhetorical Implications of Taoism," *Quarterly Journal of Speech*, 47 (February 1961), 27-35; and J. Vernon Jensen, "Rhetorical Emphases of Taoism," *Rhetorica*, 5 (Summer 1987), 219-29.

[126] Karl S. Y. Kao, "Rhetoric," in *The Indiana Companion to Traditional Chinese Literature*, ed. William H. Nienhauser (Bloomington: Indiana University Press, 1986), pp. 121-37.

[127] Jean-Paul Reding, *Les fondements philosophiques de la rhétorique chez les Sophistes grecs and chez les Sophistes chinois* (New York: Peter Lang, 1985).

[128] James Crump, *Intrigues: Studies of the Chan-kuo ts'e* (Ann Arbor: University of Michigan Press, 1964).

[129] J. L. Kroll, "Disputation in Ancient Chinese Culture," *Early China*, 11-12 (1985-87), 118-45.

[130] Kao, p. 129.

[131] The *pinyin* romanization system is used in this essay. Since many of the works cited here use the older Wade-Giles romanization, some titles and names are cited in brackets in that system when the Wade-Giles system differs from *pinyin* in a potentially confusing way. For a conversion chart, see A. C. Graham, *Disputers of the Tao: Philosophical Argument in Ancient China* (La Salle, IL: Open Court, 1989), pp. 441-44.

[132] *The Han Shu Biography of Yang Xiong (53 B.C.—A.D. 18)*, trans. and annotated David Knechtges, Paper No. 14 (Tempe: Center for Asian Studies, 1982), p. 53.

[133] Burton Watson, *Early Chinese Literature* (New York: Columbia University Press, 1962), pp. 17-120. Robert Crawford analyzes the process in further detail for one of the dynastic histories in his "The Social and Political Philosophy of the *Shih-chi,*" *Journal of Asian Studies*, 22 (1963), 401-16.

[134] James Hart, "The Speech of Prince Chin: A Study of Early Chinese Cosmology," in *Explorations in Early Chinese Cosmology*, ed. Henry Rosemont (thematic issue of *Journal of the American Academy of Religion Studies*, vol. 50) (Chico, CA: Scholars, 1984), pp. 35-65.

[135] Ronald Egan, "Narratives in *Tso-chuan*," *Harvard Journal of Asian Studies*, 37 (1977), 323-52.

[136] Rafe de Crespigny, *Portents of Protest in the Late Han Dynasty: The Memorials of Hsiang K'ai to Emperor Huan* (Canberra: Australian National University Centre of Oriental Studies, 1976).

[137] David Knechtges, *The Han Rhapsody: A Study of the Fu of Yang Hsiung* (New York: Cambridge University Press, 1976), especially pp. 12-43; and Hellmut Wilhelm, "The Scholar's Frustration: Notes on a Type of 'Fu,'" in *Chinese Thought and Institutions*, ed. John K. Fairbank (Chicago: University of Chicago, 1957), pp. 310-19.

[138] For an introduction to "pure talk," see Richard Mather, "Some Examples of 'Pure Conversation' in the *Shih-shuo hsin-yü,*" *Transactions of the International Conference of Orientalists in Japan*, 9 (1964), 58-70.

[139] Angus C. Graham, *Later Mohist Logic, Ethics and Science* (Hong Kong: Chinese University Press, 1978).

[140] Graham, B77, p. 452; translation by Mary Garrett.

[141] Anthony Cua, "Hsün Tzu's Theory of Argumentation: A Reconstruction," *Review of Metaphysics*, 36 (June 1983), 867-94. For a more extensive treatment, see his *Ethical Argumentation: A Study in Hsün Tzu's Moral Epistemology* (Honolulu: University of Hawaii, 1985).

[142] For a representative example of debates on economic policies, see Huan Kuan [Huan K'uan], *Discourses on Salt and Iron, Chapters 1-28*, trans. Esson M. Gale (1931-34; rpt. Taipei: Ch'eng Wen, 1973).

[143] For a discussion of progressive analogies, see Crump, pp. 50-54.

[144] *Han Fei Tzu*, chpt. 12; trans. Burton Watson, pp. 73-79.

[145] *The Annals of Mr. Lu [Lushi qunqiu]*, chpt. 15.5; translation by Mary Garrett.

[146] Michael Robert Broschat, "Guiguzi: A Textual Study and Translation," Diss. University of Washington 1985.

[147] *Mengzi*, 7B.3; trans. D. C. Lau, *Mencius* (1979; rpt. New York: Penguin, 1986), p. 194.

[148] For further discussion of the "Chinese sorites," see: Janusz Chmielewski, "Notes on Early Chinese Logic II," *Rocznik Orientalistcyzny* 26.2 (1963), 91-105; and Paul Masson-Oursel, "Equisse d'une théorie comparée du sorite," *Revue de métaphysique et de morale*, 20 (1912), 810-24. For an explanation of why the "Chinese sorites" should not be considered a deductive

chain, see Mary Garrett, "The *Mo-tzu* and the *Lü-shih ch'un-ch'iu*: A Case Study of Classical Chinese Theory and Practice of Argument," Diss. University of California, Berkeley 1983.

[149] *Lunyu* 13.3; trans. D. C. Lau, *The Analects* (1979; rpt. New York: Penguin, 1986), p. 118.

[150] *Mengzi* 6A.1; translation by Mary Garrett.

[151] Watson, trans., *Han Fei Tzu*, p. 88.

[152] Watson, trans., *Han Fei Tzu*, p. 84.

[153] *Mengzi* 6A.18; trans. D. C. Lau, *Mencius*, p. 169.

[154] Derk Bodde, "Types of Reasoning in Li Ssu," *China's First Unifier: A Study of the Ch'in Dynasty as Seen in the Life of Li Ssu* (Leiden, The Netherlands: E. J. Brill, 1938), pp. 223-32.

[155] John Cikoski, "On Standards of Analogic Reasoning in the Late Chou," *Journal of Chinese Philosophy*, 2 (June 1975), 325-57. For a summary of the major criticisms of Cikoski's claims, see Janusz Chmielewski, "Concerning the Problem of Analogic Reasoning in Ancient China (Review Article)," *Rocznik Orientalistcyzny*, 40 (1979), 65-78.

[156] D. C. Lau, "On Mencius' Use of the Method of Analogy in Argument," *Asia Major*, 10 [new series] (1963), 173-94, rpt. in his *Mencius*, pp. 235-63; A. C. Graham, "The Mencian Theory of Human Nature," *Tsing Hua Journal of Chinese Studies*, 6 (1967), 215-74, especially pp. 244-50; and Arthur Waley, *Three Ways of Thought in Ancient China* (Garden City, NY: Doubleday, 1953), p. 243.

[157] Some evidence exists for occasional training in argumentation. Crump makes an intriguing case for use of a suasoria system (pp. 101-09). Along the same lines, the sophist Deng Xi was notorious for teaching people to argue their legal cases successfully—and supposedly was executed for doing so.

[158] From the biography of Ban Chao in *The History of the Later Han* [Hou Han Shu], trans. Nancy Lee Swann, *Pan Chao: Foremost Woman Scholar of China First Century A. D.* (1932; rpt. New York: Russell & Russell, 1968), p. 41.

[159] Watson, *Early Chinese Literature*, p. 284.

[160] Unfortunately, these chapters are available in English only in an awkward and sometimes inaccurate translation by D. K. Liao, *The Complete Works of Han Fei Tzu: A Classic of Chinese Political Science* (1928; rpt. London: Arthur Probsthain, 1959), chpts. 22 and 23.

[161] *Zhanguo ce*, attributed to Liu Xiang. James I. Crump, trans., *Chan-kuo ts'e* (Oxford: Clarendon, 1970).

[162] Lu Buwei, *Lushi qunqiu*, chpt. 18.1-8. The only translation into a Western language is that of Richard Wilhelm, *Fruhling und Herbst des Lü Bu Wei* (1928; rpt. Dusseldorf: Eugen Diederichs, 1971). It is a somewhat loose translation; for difficult passages, Wilhelm sometimes translates the commentary instead of the text.

[163] Liu Xiang, *Shuoyuan*; not yet translated into any Western languages.

[164] This text is translated by and included in Broschat's dissertation.

[165] For Liu Xie's work, see *The Literary Mind and the Carving of Dragons* [Wen xin diao long], trans. Vincent Yu-chang Shih (1959; rev. Taipei: Chung Hwa, 1970).

[166] For a translation, see Achilles Fang, "Rhymeprose on Literature: The *Wen-fu* of Lu Chi (A.D. 261-303)," *Harvard Journal of Asian Studies*, 14 (1951), 527-66. For a more extensive introduction to the author and to Chinese theory and criticism of discourse, see the translation of E. R. Hughes, *The Art of Letters: Lu Chi's "Wen Fu," A.D. 302: A Translation and Comparative Study* (New York: Pantheon, 1951).

[167] See Godwin Chu, ed., *Popular Media in China: Shaping New Cultures* (Honolulu: University Press of Hawaii, 1978); and Alan P. L. Liu, *The Use of Traditional Media for Modernization in Communist China* (Cambridge: MIT Press, 1965).

[168] Robert Kaplan, "Cultural Thought Patterns in Intercultural Education," *Language Learning*, 16 (1966), 1-20. Subsequent researchers have criticized Kaplan's conclusions and have broadened his focus. See, for example, Linda Wai Ling Young, "Inscrutability Revisited," in *Handbook of Discourse Analysis*, ed. T. van Dijk (Orlando: Academic, 1985); Robert Kaplan et al., eds., *Annual Review of Applied Linguistics*, III (Rowley, MA: Newbury, 1983); and Ulla Connors and Robert Kaplan, eds., *Writing Across Languages: Analysis of L2 Texts* (Reading, MA: Addison-Wesley, 1987).

169 Carolyn Matalene, "Contrastive Rhetoric: An American Writing Teacher in China," *College English*, 47 (December 1985), 795.

170 Deng Xiaoping, as quoted in Nicholas Kristof, "Democracy's Martyr, Unsung by the Democracies," *New York Times*, March 29, 1989, p. A4.

171 Group *Mu* [J. Dubois et al.], *A General Rhetoric*, trans. Paul Burrell and Edgar Slotkin (Baltimore: Johns Hopkins University Press, 1981).

172 Karl S. Y. Kao, "Rhetorical Devices in the Chinese Literary Tradition," *Tamkang Review*, 14 (1983-84), 325-37.

173 For an analysis of this process, see James Robert Hightower, "Some Characteristics of Parallel Prose," in *Studies in Chinese Literature*, ed. John L. Bishop (Cambridge: Harvard University Press, 1963), pp. 108-39.

174 Chaim Perelman and L. Olbrechts-Tyteca, *The New Rhetoric: A Treatise on Argumentation*, trans. John Wilkinson and Purcell Weaver (Notre Dame: University of Notre Dame Press, 1969), p. 393.

175 Stephen Toulmin, Richard Rieke, and Allan Janik, *An Introduction to Reasoning* (New York: Macmillan, 1984), p. 161.

176 Minnie Bruce Pratt, "Identity: Skin—Blood—Heart," in *Yours in Struggle: Three Feminist Perspectives on Anti-Semitism*, by Elly Bulkin, Minnie Bruce Pratt, and Barbara Smith (Brooklyn, NY: Long Haul, 1984), p. 16.

11

An Unending Conversation

In our opening chapter, we invited you to join with the eight individuals whose ideas are presented here and become part of the ongoing conversation about rhetoric. We hope that the summaries of the works of Richards, Weaver, Toulmin, Perelman, Grassi, Burke, Foucault, and Habermas and the challenges offered to then, have intrigued you, puzzled you, and captivated you. If they stimulated your thinking about rhetoric in some way, we are satisfied, for that is the beginning of your entrance into this conversation. The role we envision for each of us in this conversation is that described by Burke in his discussion of the "unending conversation" of our lives:

> Imagine that you enter a parlor. You come late. When you arrive, others have long preceded you, and they are engaged in a heated discussion, a discussion too heated for them to pause and tell you exactly what it is about. In fact, the discussion had already begun long before any of them got there, so that no one present is qualified to retrace for you all the steps that had gone before. You listen for a while, until you decide that you have caught the tenor of the argument; then you put in your oar. Someone answers; you answer him; another comes to your defense; another aligns himself against you, to either the embarrassment or gratification of your opponent, depending upon the quality of your ally's assistance. However, the discussion is interminable. The hour grows late, you must depart. And you do depart, with the discussion still vigorously in progress.[1]

Our intent in this last chapter, then, is not to terminate the conversation about rhetoric in any way by stating definitive conclusions about the nature of contemporary rhetorical thought or by recommending some perspectives on rhetoric as superior to others. Instead, we hope to suggest some of the directions that seem to characterize the contemporary conversation about rhetoric as they have emerged from the perspectives taken in the previous chapters.

We see six general areas of concern that are topics in the current discussion about rhetoric. We have phrased these in question form to serve as a reminder that answers to them still are being formulated by those involved in the conversation about rhetoric: (1) What is the nature of the rhetorical act? (2) What is the nature of the world created by rhetoric? (3) What is the purpose of rhetoric? (4) What is the nature of the rhetor? (5) What are appropriate methods for gaining understanding of the rhetorical process? and (6) What new perspectives are emerging as a result of our present knowledge about rhetoric?

We will suggest the nature of these conversational themes by offering examples from the responses formulated to them by the eight scholars and the feminist, Afrocentric, and Chinese challenges discussed in this book. Again, we will not attempt to provide comprehensive or concrete answers to these questions or to suggest that any one individual has the best answers to them. We simply offer samples of the discussion about these issues in the spirit of continued inquiry and dialogue, hoping to contribute to a "discussion still vigorously in progress."

What is the Nature of the Rhetorical Act?

Perhaps the basic topic of conversation concerning rhetoric deals with its nature or distinguishing feature. This theme involves discussion of what makes rhetoric what it is or what the substance is that we study when we investigate rhetoric. This substance is named in various ways by our eight rhetoricians. Some see it as a human quality embodied in rhetoric. For Toulmin and Habermas, for example, rationality is the distinguishing feature of the rhetorical act. Toulmin's perspective suggests that at the heart of rhetoric is the evaluation of claims by persons trained in the rational standards appropriate to a particular field of discourse. Habermas also considers such a rational structure to be inherent in every aspect of language, from speech acts to levels of discourse. For Weaver, the distinguishing feature of rhetoric is its axiological grounding. Rhetoric's inherent concern with values and ethics suggests the proper choices to be made by the rhetor and promotes progress toward attainment of the truth at the center of a culture. Those who study rhetoric from the Afrocentric perspective see yet another feature as central—*nommo*, the active, expressive quality of life.

Others see a particular trait of language as the essential feature of rhetoric. For Grassi, the process of *ingenium*—the seeing of similarities—is the essence of rhetoric. Manifest in language as metaphor, *ingenium* is the basic process by which we think, know, and interpret the events of our world. Chinese rhetoric also privileges the process of comparison, especially that of analogy, seeing it as a natural and valuable rhetorical form. Burke contributes to this aspect of the discussion the concept of the negative. The negative, because it is added to our world only through language, is the ultimate test of symbolicity and allows the creation of other important characteristics of a symbol system such as hierarchy, perfection, and mystery. For Foucault, rhetoric's critical characteristic is its set of rules that govern discursive formations; rules make rhetoric what it is and also are created through rhetoric. An asymmetrical distribution of power is seen by feminist scholars as the essential trait of rhetoric. Power differences are reflected in rhetoric in that men are defined as standard and are given voice and women are denigrated and silenced.

The scope of rhetoric also is of concern in this topic of conversation, for in many cases, what is offered as the critical essence of rhetoric dictates how much is seen to fall within its scope. Implicit in Toulmin's position, in which rationality is a distinguishing feature of rhetoric, is that the scope of rhetoric is argumentative discourse. Perelman holds a similar view, and both limit rhetoric to discursive symbols — verbal expression in speech or writing. For others, such as Grassi, the scope of rhetoric is much broader. Rhetoric is the foundation for all human activity. As the basic process by which we know the world, the scope of rhetoric becomes all of human activity. Burke also sees the scope of rhetoric as wide. It includes spoken and written discourse as well as nonverbal elements that have meaning for an audience.

The scope Foucault sees for rhetoric also encompasses a great deal. His focus is on discourse that, because it follows particular rules or has passed appropriate tests, is understood to be true in a culture. His concern with discursive formations that govern the rhetorical acts of our lives is broad because of the wide impact of the discursive formation; at the same time, he has narrowed considerably the discourse with which his perspective of rhetoric is concerned.

Even the nature of the subject matter being discussed in our conversation, then, is in dispute. While many of the features of rhetoric selected by various rhetoricians to serve as the essential feature are not incompatible and certainly could be integrated into one perspective on rhetoric, little agreement currently exists on what distinguishes rhetoric as an object of study and discourse. Consequently, these rhetoricians differ as to what is seen as proper to include under the umbrella of the label, "rhetoric."

What is the Nature of the World Created by Rhetoric?

A second topic of conversation about rhetoric concerns what we know of our world given that rhetoric acts as an intervening variable between us and the phenomena of that world. Rhetoric, to a great extent, creates the world in which we live by encouraging us to focus on certain phenomena and not others and by labeling these phenomena in particular ways. Our experiences of our world derive from the nature of the symbols we use to describe them.

We find that the particular perspectives assumed by our scholars on the nature of rhetoric lead them to see very different worlds resulting from that rhetoric. For Toulmin, for example, the world created by rhetoric is a rational one, although it is not a world that can be measured by *a priori* standards. The nature of the concepts in the world, according to Toulmin, varies from field to field because of the lack of such standards. Grassi also is concerned with the notion of rationality as characteristic of the world, but this concept does not have the positive connotations associated with Toulmin's use of the term. Grassi sees the rational as separated from the rhetorical in the contemporary world when, in fact, rhetoric provides the basis for rational knowledge. Perelman explicitly includes values in the concept of rationality and thus sees the world of values as a rational one.

Other scholars focus less on a singular quality of the world that is a consequence of the operation of rhetoric and instead focus on a world that is multifaceted and diverse in essence, with rhetoric allowing it to be known in its variety. In other words, rhetoric creates the world on a number of different levels or in a number of different realms. The work of Habermas exemplifies such an approach. He sees the human world as composed of technical, practical, and emancipatory knowledge, and all three depend for their existence on communication. Habermas focuses, however, on how to realize an "emancipated" or rational world through language and offers the ideal speech situation as a model for the possibilities of rationality.

Weaver sees the world divided into facts, theories about the facts, and a metaphysical dream. Human beings know the world by imposing these categories on the raw data of the world, a process guided by the metaphysical dream, which embodies the truth of a culture. Rhetoric plays a critical role in maintaining the metaphysical dream and moving individuals toward the truth it embodies. Thus, it is intimately involved in the creation of this "layered" view of the world for the members of a culture.

Burke does not see different realms of knowledge in which the world is made manifest through rhetoric as much as a number of composite parts that are given significance and predominance in the world as a result of rhetoric. For Burke, the world is composed of various hierarchies that represent different ideals or standards of perfection, generate thou shalt nots, and create mystery among individuals on the hierarchies. For him, then, the world is a hierarchically ordered place, where change is the constant denominator as individuals jockey for positions on various hierarchies, seek to rid themselves of the tension they feel as a result of their place on these hierarchies, and use rhetorical strategies to achieve new identities through new positions on them.

Foucault's contribution to the discussion of the nature of the world created through rhetoric is at once more narrow and more encompassing than the view of many others. He sees the nature of the world as whatever is created by the particular discursive formation that characterizes the world. In other words, the world is the way it is because of the rules governing discursive practices. If the rules of a particular discursive formation establish similarity as the characterizing principle of the formation, the world will be one in which its aspects are viewed as similar to each other in significant ways. To say that the world created by rhetoric has a particular nature is impossible; its nature is determined by the particular characteristics of the governing discursive formation at that time.

The three challenges to the rhetorical tradition offer substantially different perspectives on the nature of the world created by rhetoric. Feminist scholars see the construction of gender at the heart of the rhetorical world. As a consequence of the division of the world into masculine and feminine, separate rhetorical cultures emerge for women and men, each with its own symbol system. The world created by Chinese rhetorics is one in which a singular truth can be discovered; those who are in contact with the reality that represents that truth are right factually and morally. Similarly, in the Afrocentric view, the possible worlds to be created through rhetoric are limited. Rhetoric is designed to tap into already existing and familiar world views that restore universal harmony.

Views of the nature of the world created through rhetorical activity differ in the contemporary discussion of rhetoric. Yet, most contemporary discussants would agree that our rhetoric creates our world and that the phenomena of our world are knowable through the lens of rhetorical practice.

What is the Purpose of Rhetoric?

Many scholars involved in the discussion of rhetoric move beyond simply speculating about the nature of the world created by rhetoric and see rhetoric as having a particular function or serving as a tool for the attainment of a particular goal in that world. In many cases, they seem to see rhetoric as an instrument of reformation or as a change agent to remedy some negative condition. In other words, they see rhetoric as having the capacity to make the world a better place.

For some of those involved in the conversation, the world is seen as out of whack in some fundamental way, and rhetoric is seen as having a noble purpose so that the world can be restored to a previous condition. Richards, for example, sees the purpose of rhetoric as promoting understanding; by remedying misunderstanding, rhetoric accomplishes a number of goals in the world, including the improvement of intercultural relations and facilitating the achievement of world peace. Weaver perhaps is the most explicit in his formulation of a noble purpose for rhetoric. He sees many signs that our culture is degenerating and views the restoration of rhetoric as essential for its revitalization. Rhetoric, in Weaver's perspective, can re-establish a culture based on the ideal and the truth. In the Afrocentric world view, rhetoric also is designed to re-establish a cultural condition—in this case, harmony among peoples, spirits, plants, and animals.

Other rhetoricians see rhetoric as an instrument that enables us to gain essential kinds of knowledge or to restore the validity of certain kinds of knowledge in the world. Toulmin's perspective, for example, implies that rhetoric is an instrument that allows us to progress through periods of conceptual change. Thus, we are able to gain new insights and beliefs and are able to create new disciplines because of the function of rhetoric. Grassi, similarly, sees the purpose of rhetoric as the restoration of humanistic values or the balance between rational and rhetorical knowledge. Rational or scientific language is limited because it does not question its starting premises, can deal only with universals and not particulars, and lacks the capacity for the invention of new codes and structures. Rhetorical language, on the other hand, is able to perform these essential functions in the world.

Perelman believes that an aim of rhetoric is to help us reason about values; because of rhetoric, we are not restricted to reasoning about them solely on the basis of passion and prejudice. Similarly, Toulmin believes rhetoric is a method that people can use to work their way through moral dilemmas by comparing their particular situation with similar type cases. A pragmatic purpose also is evident in Chinese rhetoric. Discourse is seen as having a didactic function; it reflects and reinforces cultural values, provides models for imitation, and encourages correct attitudes and actions.

Foucault's contribution to the discussion focuses on a different undesirable characteristic of the world—the exclusion of certain voices from a culture. For him, the investigation of a discursive formation or rhetorical practices enables us to discover the power relations in a culture and to give voice to those who have no power. Rhetoric thus becomes a means for changing the nature of the power relations in a culture. Change also is the purpose of feminist perspectives on rhetoric. Scholars working within this paradigm seek to change society's construction of gender and, as a result, to improve women's lives.

In contrast to these types of purposes for rhetoric, which are related to cultural concerns, Burke's focus is on a purpose for rhetoric that operates more at the individual level. He sees the purpose of rhetoric as presenting strategies to individuals for dealing with situations or for solving problems. It gives instructions to the rhetor and the audience, helping us maneuver through life and providing ways of feeling more at home in the modern world.

In this strand of the discussion, then, various problems of the contemporary world are identified, with rhetoric seen as a tool to remedy these problems. Whatever the imperfection identified and the role rhetoric is expected to play in alleviating the condition, discussants see rhetoric as a positive, productive force for change in the world.

What is the Nature of the Rhetor?

Discussion about the nature of the rhetor also is part of the current conversation about rhetoric. What is regarded as the essential nature of the human being or what is seen to constitute the humanness of the human being provides different views of the relation between individuals and rhetoric.

While most of the scholars involved in the contemporary conversation about rhetoric would see the human being as symbol using, Burke argues that symbol use is *the* characteristic that distinguishes humans from other animals. The possession and use of a symbol system allow us to develop a neurological nature and thus place us in the realm of action. Symbol use, according to Burke, makes the human being human.

Habermas sees communication as at the heart of the human project as well. The human domains are those of work, interaction, and power, and communication is the essence of and integrating force among these domains. Because these domains are specific to humans, Habermas sees communication, as does Burke, as distinguishing humans from other animals.

For Grassi, symbol use also distinguishes humans from other animals, but he focuses on a particular form of symbol use as of primary importance: *ingenium*, or the capacity to see similarities. From this capacity is derived our humanness; it raises us above nature and operates in the human domains of work, imagination, and language. The Afrocentric world view, in contrast, does not use rhetoric to differentiate humans from animals. The distinction between humans and other life forms is blurred; life is seen as an organic whole, and arbitrary categorizations of life forms destroy its wholeness and harmony.

While Perelman and Toulmin do not discuss whether the difference between humans and other animals is relevant to rhetoric or whether this difference is a significant one, they see the human as a necessary condition for the creation of rhetoric. In their perspectives, rhetoric does not exist without people, as seen in their contrast between rhetoric as personal and formal logic as impersonal. Foucault's contribution to the conversation provides a different view of the rhetor. He does not deny that discourse originates with human beings and that the production of discourse is uniquely human. His focus, however, is on the rules human beings assume in speaking and writing and how these are constrained and created by the norms and rules of the discursive formation. He also is interested in how the rhetor is constituted as a subject through discourse. Feminist scholars also are interested in the constitution of a subject through discourse. For them, gender is a critical dimension of humanness that functions as a lens that affects all human perceptions. This lens is rhetorically constructed, creating the categories of masculine and feminine.

With Foucault's addition to the conversation of the rhetor as the product of particular discursive practices, discussion about the nature of the rhetor turns to how free we are as rhetors in our use of symbols. For many of our scholars, freedom to choose is concomitant with symbol use; rhetorical activity is not possible without the element of choice.

Weaver, for example, sees human beings as creatures of choice or as free agents; our dignity as humans, in fact, arises from this power of choice. Similarly, Richards sees choice as involved in human activity, and he investigates the choices we have as we attribute meanings to words. For Perelman, the human is a choice-making animal as well — speakers make choices about which are the most appropriate starting points and techniques of argument; listeners make choices about which claims to accept. Burke makes perhaps the strongest argument for viewing choice as a condition of or prerequisite to symbol use. In order to have symbolic activity, Burke says, freedom of choice must be involved. If an act is not free, it cannot be considered an act.

While the use of symbols is seen as including capacity for choice, many of our scholars consider the choice-making capacity of the human to be limited in some way so that the rhetor never can be completely free. For Weaver, for example, freedom does not mean license to do whatever we please. Rather, it is freedom to act according to criteria for choice making implicit in the notion of truth held by a culture; we are free to actualize the truth. For Richards, limits on our freedom are imposed by past choices, with each choice limiting our future choices. Technically, we are free in our use of symbols; practically, however, we become less so as we continue to attribute particular meanings to symbols that limit our future attributions of meanings. Burke's notion of choice is limited by our inability to know the consequences involved in making a particular choice. Freedom to choose, he asserts, requires adequate knowledge of an act's consequences. To a degree, then, we cannot be completely free because we do not know the full consequences of our acts. For many involved in the discussion of contemporary rhetorical thought, then, choice is an essential aspect of the rhetor and lies at the heart of symbol use, but this freedom to choose is limited and constrained in various ways.

Foucault assumes the strongest stance of our rhetoricians in terms of limitations on freedom of choice. He defines the rhetor in such a way that we appear to have little choice because of the strength of the rules governing the discursive formation in which we live. We are the creation and product of our discursive formations, he explains. While we technically may be able to break out of that formation, such a break leads only into another system with different rules—rules that continue to constrain us. Our use of rhetoric really is not free, then, whether we want our rhetoric to be valued and viewed as significant in our society or whether we attempt to resist the societal formation.

Even on the issue of what we are like as rhetors, then, disagreements arise and alliances form among our discussants. The lively debate continues as they move on to a discussion of appropriate methods for securing knowledge about rhetoric.

What are Appropriate Methods for Gaining Understanding of the Rhetorical Process?

The starting point for discussion on the topic of how we learn about rhetoric often is the rejection of past methods for gaining knowledge about rhetoric. Some scholars take issue with the ways in which classical scholars investigated rhetoric. Richards, for example, rejects past ways of learning about rhetoric in that they simply were a collection of rules about how to speak and write effectively; such a framework for studying the nature of rhetoric said very little about how words actually work. Foucault, in contrast, rejects past ways of learning about discourse through historical methods that involve an emphasis on continuity, the centrality of the human in the organization of knowledge, and an emphasis on interpretation. These approaches, he believes, do not enable us to get at the most important knowledge about our discursive practices.

Others reject absolute, scientific, or purely logical ways of knowing, as Perelman does when he rejects absolutism as a way for attaining such knowledge. Grassi, in a similar fashion, criticizes the scientific tradition, just as Toulmin rejects syllogism-based logic as the way to know about rhetoric.

After rejecting many traditional approaches to understanding the process of rhetoric, the discussants propose what they consider to be better ways for studying rhetoric. Implicit in Perelman's perspective and in line with his focus on rationality and argumentative discourse is that we come to know about rhetoric, as we come to know generally, through the act of a speaker gaining the adherence of an audience to some claim presented for its assent. Toulmin arrives at knowledge, including that about rhetoric, through the criticism of rational enterprises or disciplines; when arguments are subjected to a rhetorical assessment, rational knowledge results.

The feminist, Afrocentric, and Chinese challenges to the rhetorical tradition suggest that traditional approaches to rhetoric are inherently distorted because of their male, Eurocentric biases. To correct these biases, scholars working in these areas seek both the inclusion of the rhetorical activity of previously muted groups and the use of the knowledge gained from these groups to reconceptualize rhetorical constructs themselves.

Others see broader frameworks for attaining knowledge about rhetoric. Richards, for example, believes that we will know about rhetoric once we begin to study it through a systematic, philosophical framework that allows us to discern the fundamental laws of the use of language. In this way of knowing about rhetoric, scholars must question and evaluate the assumptions of rhetoric and not simply accept as valid the assumptions it has inherited from other disciplines.

Burke provides labels for the framework he recommends for studying or knowing about rhetoric; he suggests that dramatism and logology are useful ways for gathering knowledge about rhetoric. While both constitute models for understanding how rhetoric operates, logology—the theological model— now seems to incorporate and encompass dramatism in Burke's perspective.

Foucault also suggests a specific framework for knowing—the complementary methods of archaeology and genealogy. The aim of archaeology is to analyze discourse in order to determine the rules that govern it and to describe the various relations among statements in a discursive formation. With genealogy, Foucault looks for the rules governing discursive practices along with the network of power relations of which these rules are a part.

We see, then, that not only what we know about the nature of rhetoric is in question but so, too, is how we know what we know. Many past methods for investigating and studying rhetoric are rejected by contemporary scholars of rhetoric as inappropriate for understanding how rhetoric operates, and various frameworks are proposed as more useful replacements.

What New Perspectives are Emerging as a Result of Our Present Knowledge About Rhetoric?

The conversation about rhetoric also includes discussion of the ways in which thought about rhetoric is being extended and applied so that new perspectives on rhetoric emerge. The possible extensions and applications of our knowledge about rhetoric that are being generated are unending, and we could not begin to detail all of them here. One area of particular relevance to those of us in speech communication, however, is that of the generation of additional perspectives about rhetoric in our discipline. We will elaborate briefly on six perspectives that have been developed within our field in order to provide a sample of some of the new perspectives being generated on rhetoric: the epistemic, the argumentative, the fantasy-theme, the performative, the narrative, and the rhetorical perspective on visual imagery. We do not believe these are the only important perspectives being developed out of the current thinking about rhetoric, nor do we believe they are the only important perspectives developing within speech communication. We see these as simply representative of the kind of work that is being done on the basis of contemporary rhetorical discussion.

Epistemic Perspective

In an influential article written for the *Central States Speech Journal* in 1967, Robert L. Scott declared that rhetoric "is a way of knowing; it is epistemic."[2] With this statement, Scott declared his intention to outline a perspective on rhetoric in which humans are seen as generating and creating knowledge in the process of using rhetoric—a perspective that departs in important ways from the traditional point of view of rhetoric as persuasion. Ten years later, he reaffirmed this point of view while responding to some of the major criticisms leveled against it.[3]

Scott begins by outlining some of the presuppositions of traditional perspectives on rhetoric—that truth is certain, knowable, and communicable and that rhetoric is a tool to be used by those who know the truth to communicate it to those who do not. These two assumptions combine to form a perspective in which rhetoric is viewed merely as a tool to be used to pass "the truth" from one person to another.

Scott objects to this traditional view of rhetoric for a variety of reasons. First, if rhetoric's only purpose is to transmit truth from one group of persons to another, it serves an almost meaningless role in human affairs. Scott also objects to the traditional view of rhetoric because he believes that, in human affairs, no certain truth exists; the world of human affairs is one of conflicting beliefs, not truth.

In an attempt to escape what he considers a trivial conception of rhetoric, Scott borrows from the work of scholars such as Toulmin to outline a perspective on rhetoric that views rhetoric as a way of knowing. Some of the presuppositions of this view of rhetoric include the fact that rhetoric is a tool people use to enable them to act in situations of uncertainty where important values are in apparent conflict. Another presupposition of this view of rhetoric is that rhetorical knowledge is "socially constructed" by interaction; "truth" for human beings is something to be created moment by moment in the circumstances in which they find themselves and with which they must cope.[4]

In Scott's view, knowledge as it exists in the realm of human affairs "can be the result of a process of interaction at a given moment. Thus, rhetoric may be viewed not as a matter of giving effectiveness to truth but of creating truth."[5] Scott does not claim that all facets of "creating knowledge" are rhetorical ones, but he believes that all knowledge-creating enterprises have rhetorical aspects. Although the creation of knowledge may not always involve attempts to communicate with others, it often does; the potentiality for rhetoric to be epistemic, then, always exists.[6]

The epistemic perspective has generated both controversy and scholarship in the field of rhetoric. In a eulogy for the epistemic perspective on rhetoric, Barry Brummett describes epistemic rhetoric as a star that has "burned itself out." He claims that between 1981 and 1984, twenty articles that drew heavily on the epistemic perspective were published in major communication journals, but only two such articles were published between 1985 and 1988. He argues that the emphasis has shifted to two other perspectives instead: "This same period has seen an increase in work done in two promising, related fields, theory of argument and the rhetoric of science or of inquiry."[7] Richard A. Cherwitz and James Hikins disagree, claiming that stars "never really die, though they may transform themselves, influencing all surrounding thought and inquiry.[8] They claim that the essential philosophical issues central to both epistemology and rhetoric remain inextricably linked and that the epistemic perspective remains alive in much of the current work in rhetoric.

Argumentative Perspective

An argumentative perspective is, of course, no stranger to students of rhetoric. While argument has been associated with the subject of rhetoric since its roots in classical Greece, Douglas Ehninger and Wayne Brockriede, among others, have expanded and revitalized the concept of argument beyond its traditional boundaries. In his keynote address to the Third Summer Conference on Argumentation, Brockriede maintained that the year 1983 was the "twenty-fifth anniversary of the contemporary renaissance in the study of argument."[9] Twenty-five years earlier, in 1958, Perelman and Toulmin were publishing books on argument that later would prove to have an enormous impact on the direction of the study of argumentation in this country.

In an article that has become a classic for those interested in the argumentative perspective on rhetoric, Brockriede explains his bias as a humanistic or person-centered point of view.[10] Such a perspective "denies an interest in logical systems, in messages, in reasoning, in evidence, or in propositions—*unless these things involve human activity rather directly.*" He further explains that argument is not a thing but a perspective; argument is a set of conceptual lenses persons use to examine rhetorical events. For Brockriede, argument is an open concept that potentially is everywhere—in "the aesthetic experience, the interpersonal transaction, and the construction of scientific theory or the reporting of research studies."

Defining argument as *"a process whereby people reason their way from one set of problematic ideas to the choice of another,"* Brockriede sees it as distinguished by six characteristics. These "help a person decide whether argument is a useful perspective to take in studying a communicative act." First, argument involves "an inferential leap from existing beliefs to the adoption of a new belief or to the reinforcement of an old one." In other words, it involves "leaping" from some starting point to some conclusion other than that contained in the original starting point. Second, argument includes "a perceived rationale to support that leap." It includes "reasons" that are perceived as reasons by the arguers. Third, argument involves "a choice among two or more competing claims." Where no choice exists, no argument is possible. Fourth, argument functions to regulate uncertainty. Argument increases uncertainty when decisionmakers need to increase uncertainty in order to generate new alternatives or to get the attention of others. Argument decreases uncertainty as decisionmakers act on one alternative from a list of several. Fifth, argument involves a "willingness to risk confrontation with peers." An arguer willingly risks the possibility that the other person's arguments may justify modification of the arguer's own claim, of the arguer's self-concept, or of their personal relationship. A person unwilling to risk confrontation, Brockriede asserts, is a person unwilling to argue. Finally, argument involves "a frame of reference shared optimally." Arguers must share points of view, or they are unable to argue.

Since Brockriede expanded the view of argument to include many aspects of rhetoric beyond the logical, scholars from the United States, Canada, and Europe have produced significant work on the argumentative perspective. In the United States, Charles Arthur Willard, for example, has written two books that show how argumentation, like other forms of communication, is instrumental in creating social knowledge.[11] For Willard, argumentation is a sociology of knowledge. A group of philosophers interested in informal logic, primarily from Canada, have begun to recognize the importance of rhetoric to their subject matter; among them are J. Anthony Blair and Ralph H. Johnson.[12] One sign of the interest in the argumentative perspective among Europeans is two international conferences on argumentation that have been sponsored by the University of Amsterdam. Growing out of these conferences is a professional association, the International Society for the Study of Argument, devoted to the study of the argumentative perspective. Among the most well known of the Europeans who are interested in the study of argument are Frans H. van Eemeren and Rob Grootendorst,[13] who have formed what has begun to be called the Amsterdam school of argumentation.

Fantasy-Theme Perspective

The fantasy-theme perspective on rhetoric was suggested by Ernest Bormann in 1972.[14] Impetus for the development of this perspective came from the work of Robert Bales and his associates in their study of communication in small groups. Bales discovered the process of *group fantasizing* or dramatizing as a particular type of communication that occurs in small groups.[15] This communication is characterized in this way: "The tempo of the conversation would pick up. People would grow excited, interrupt one another, blush, laugh, forget their self-consciousness. The tone of the meeting, often quiet and tense immediately prior to the dramatizing, would become lively, animated, and boisterous, . . ."[16] Bormann extended the notion of fantasizing discovered by Bales into a theory — symbolic convergence theory — and a companion method of analyzing rhetoric — fantasy-theme criticism.

Symbolic convergence theory is based on two major assumptions. First, it is grounded in the belief that communication creates reality — there is a connection between the symbols we use and the reality we experience or the knowledge we have of the world. Symbols create reality because of their capacity to introduce form into our disordered sensory experience. They allow us to see a substance or an idea, to make it "real" for us, because they halt the constant flux of consciousness by fixing a substance with a linguistic label. A second assumption on which symbolic convergence theory is based is that individuals' meanings for symbols can converge to create a *shared* reality for participants. In Bormann's theory, *convergence* refers "to the way two or more private symbolic worlds incline toward each other, come more closely together, or even overlap during certain processes of communication."[17] It also might be thought of as shared meaning, consensus, or general agreement on subjective meanings. Convergence suggests that individuals have interpreted some aspect of their experiences in the same way.

In symbolic convergence theory and fantasy-theme criticism, the message is seen as dramatistic in form, filled with all the elements that would be found in a drama — settings, characters, and actions. Statements or themes in the message that establish these elements are called fantasy themes. *Fantasy* is not used here in its popular sense — as something imaginary and not grounded in reality. Instead, it is the creative and imaginative interpretation of events, and a *fantasy theme* is the means through which the interpretation is accomplished in communication. Fantasy themes concerning setting tell where the action is seen as taking place in the rhetorical world; character themes name and identify the characteristics and motives of heroes, villains, and supporting players; and action themes, which also might be called plot lines, tell what is being done in the rhetorical world or drama. As people seek to make sense out of their environment and the events around them, these fantasy themes swirl together to provide a credible interpretation of reality. The total dramatistic explanation of reality is called a rhetorical vision. A rhetorical vision, then, is a symbolic drama that contains fantasy themes dealing with scenes, characters, and actions.

Inherent in this perspective is the notion that emotions and motives for action are embedded in the rhetoric or the rhetorical vision itself. An identification of a particular rhetorical vision, then, provides an explanation for why the participants in that vision act as they do and enables a prediction to be made about how they are likely to behave in the future.

The fantasy-theme perspective on rhetoric originally was formulated by Bormann to study social movements. It has been applied as well to the discourse of rhetors such as politicians to determine their personal world views, to small groups to identify their symbolic realities, to media-created images of politicians and political events, and to organizations to discover their predominant rhetorical visions and which employees participate in which visions. In addition, this perspective is being used as a marketing tool to identify the rhetorical visions of potential users of products, to segment markets by attitudes contained in rhetorical visions, and to develop and test advertising and promotional materials based on the rhetorical visions held by the intended audience. While the fantasy-theme approach has been criticized, in particular by G.P. Mohrmann,[18] it continues to serve as an attractive perspective for many interested in analyzing rhetorical phenomena.

Performance Perspective

For many, the term "performance" means playacting or pretense— something divorced from reality. Originally, however, the term meant "to furnish or to carry through to completion." This latter sense—of "making, not faking"—is what is meant when we talk of rhetoric as performance.[19] To study rhetoric as performance is to examine any of the enabling and energizing forms of action through which humans and cultures constitute and reconstitute themselves. Performance is the act of bringing to completion a sense of reality—of bringing out the significance or meaning of some cultural form: "Cultural performances make social life meaningful, they enable actors to interpret themselves to themselves as well as to others, to become at once actor and audience."[20]

The origin of the performance perspective generally is attributed to anthropologist Victor Turner, whose work emphasizes the way in which performance punctuates virtually every aspect of daily life.[21] Other scholars who have contributed to the development of this perspective include anthropologists and folklorists Clifford Geertz,[22] Dell Hymes,[23] Richard Bauman,[24] Barbara Myerhoff,[25] and Erving Goffman.[26] In the communication field, Dwight Conquergood[27] and Elizabeth Fine[28] have done much to develop and demonstrate the richness of the performance perspective.

The starting point for the performance perspective is a definition of the human being as "'*homo performans*,' a culture-inventing and self-making creature."[29] From this conceptual starting point have developed two complementary directions for performance studies: (1) fieldwork studies of performance in various cultures; and (2) performance as a research paradigm.[30]

One approach to performance involves the study of how people reflect and theorize about themselves through their performance practices. This use of performance serves as a point of entry for cultural studies; people are viewed as continuously enacting or transacting culture in their communication. In other words, we throw off, through our communication, expressions of our culture. To learn about various cultures, these publicly accessible expressions are studied through fieldwork or the use of participant-observation methods. The researcher lives in the culture and acts as a co-performer, participating in and studying cultural performances such as rituals, ceremonies, myths, stories, songs, jokes, contests, and games.

A second approach taken to the performance perspective is the development of performance as a lens, method, or paradigm for conducting research. Three primary commitments characterize the research process from a performance perspective. The first is a commitment to process, rather than product. Human reality is viewed not as facts and variables that can be measured and manipulated but as a process constantly under construction—one that is unfolding and resistant to closure. A second commitment is to embodiment—to understanding through lived experience, participatory ways of knowing, and intimate encounter rather than detached observation. Sympathetic understanding, then, replaces explanation as the goal of research. The third commitment of the performance scholar is to dialogue—to the opening up of the self to the voices and viewpoints of others—and to self-questioning as a result of the conversation that occurs.[31]

The performance perspective is demonstrated in Conquergood's fieldwork in refugee camps in Thailand and the Gaza Strip and with street gangs in an inner-city neighborhood in Chicago. He participates in and observes their various communication activities to discover the structures, principles, and functions of these cultures for those who create and live in them. The tenets of the performance paradigm guide his approach to collecting data and reporting his findings.[32] Michael Pacanowsky and Nick O'Donnell-Trujillo's study of organizational culture is another example of work from a performance perspective. They identify and describe five major performances that occur in organizations—performances of ritual, passion, sociality, politics, and enculturation—and seek to understand them and those who construct their cultures through such expressions.[33]

Narrative Perspective

Alasdair MacIntyre has described the human being as "essentially a story-telling animal."[34] The formulation of a narrative perspective on rhetoric, a perspective developed most fully in the speech communication field by Walter Fisher,[35] has emerged from acknowledgment of the human love of stories and the pervasiveness of this mode of discourse throughout human life.

Fisher labels his perspective the "narrative paradigm" and describes five features as characteristic of it: (1) Humans are essentially storytellers; (2) The paradigmatic mode of human decision making and communication is "good reasons," which vary in form among situations, genres, and media of communication; (3) The production and practice of good reasons are ruled by matters of history, biography, culture, and character; (4) Criteria by which we judge stories are narrative probability (coherence) and narrative fidelity (the correspondence of the story with what we know to be true in our lives); and (5) The world offers a set of stories among which we must choose.[36]

Fisher's notion of the narrative paradigm has spawned a great deal of discussion among rhetorical scholars. One issue of debate concerns the definition of narration. For Fisher, narration is "symbolic actions—words and/or deeds—that have sequence and meaning for those who live, create, or interpret them."[37] Thus, it encompasses nearly all discourse. Among those who take issue with Fisher's conception of narrative as a paradigm is Robert Rowland, who argues that all rhetoric is not a story and that Fisher has defined narration so broadly that the term loses much of its explanatory power. Rowland posits a definition of narration as "essentially a chronological account of an event or process involving the formal characteristics of a plot and character development: "Without a plot and characters, the rhetoric cannot serve the functions generally fulfilled by storytelling and thus should not be considered narrative."[38]

John Lucaites and Celeste Condit also argue against Fisher's definition of narration as a paradigm based on three different functions they see for narratives—the poetic function, the expression of beauty; the dialectic function, the discovery, revelation, and presentation of a truth; and the rhetorical or persuasive function. They suggest that these different functions make the discovery of a unified narrative paradigm of human communication unlikely.[39]

A second issue of concern to narrative scholars involves the relationship between rationality and narrativity. Some take issue with Fisher's notion that there are two separate paradigms of human communication—traditional rationality and narrative rationality. Fisher sees traditional rationality as only relevant in specialized fields and narrative rationality as universally relevant. Further, while the rational paradigm has requirements such as knowing how to reason and the acquisition of knowledge and information, the narrative paradigm does not; anyone can tell, understand, and evaluate stories. Yet another difference is that traditional rationality is prescriptive and normative; narrative rationality, in contrast, is descriptive.[40] Michael McGee and John Nelson,[41] as well as Barbara Warnick,[42] are among those who suggest that Fisher's dichotomy between the two paradigms cannot be as clear and concrete as he suggests. Warnick's questioning of the dichotomy exemplifies such responses to Fisher. She argues that, "in attacking rationality, Fisher really attacks only one subform of it—technical rationality—without acknowledging other forms, such as practical reasoning and moral argument, which may be more pervasive in our culture."[43] She also asserts that Fisher has incorporated into his model of narrative rationality notions of traditional rationality—the logic of good reasons and use of standards from formal and informal logic, when relevant, to test the soundness of narratives. Traditional rationality, then, seems to have been included, at least in part, into narrative rationality, thus blurring the distinction Fisher makes between the two.[44]

A third issue over which narrative scholars disagree concerns the criteria used to assess narratives. In response to Fisher's criteria of narrative probability and narrative fidelity, Warnick asserts that Fisher fails to deal with the possibility that an audience might judge a story probable when, in fact, that judgment was made on the basis of self-delusion or rationalization. Similarly, Fisher does not account for a story that may be coherent but advocates harmful values.[45] Rowland's problem with Fisher's criteria for testing narratives is that probability and fidelity

> do not avoid the problems with evaluating public moral argument that led Fisher to develop the narrative paradigm in the first place. In fact, these standards lead directly to traditional tests for argument and evidence. Narrative probability can be seen as the equivalent of consistency, and narrative fidelity can be treated as the equivalent of informal logic tests of evidence and reasoning.[46]

Various criteria for assessing stories have been suggested to replace probability and fidelity, including consistency and brevity,[47] adaptability of the narrative,[48] the ethical standards suggested in the narrative,[49] the ease with which the narrative can be refuted,[50] and the clarity and significance of the narrative's point.[51]

Despite the criticisms of Fisher's work, it represents an important development in the speech communication field. The narrative perspective has been applied to a variety of communicative events in order to understand and assess them. Lance Bennett and Martha Feldman explain criminal trials according to the narrative perspective.[52] William Lewis uses the perspective to explain why Ronald Reagan remained popular as a President when he was "uninformed, irrational, and inconsistent,"[53] and he concludes that "the predominance of the narrative form in Reagan's rhetoric . . . established the climate of interpretation'' within which he was judged.[54] Thomas Hollihan and Patricia Riley identify the features of stories told by parents of delinquent children in ''Toughlove'' groups in order to understand the appeal of stories and to discover how to avoid the creation of stories that might precipitate harmful consequences.[55]

Rhetorical Perspective on Visual Imagery

The recognition that we live in a visual age has led some rhetorical scholars to the study of visual imagery from a rhetorical perspective. Images in the form of advertisements, television, film, signs, dress, architecture, and the interior design of buildings constitute a major part of our rhetorical environment, and such images now have the significance for us and the impact on our culture that speechmaking once did. Scholars who analyze images rhetorically believe that the study of verbal discourse alone is limiting because it includes only a minute portion of the symbols that affect us daily.

Rhetorical scholars who study visual imagery recognize the contributions made to our understanding of images in disciplines such as art history, psychology, and semiotics, but they suggest that a rhetorical perspective is significantly different from approaches to visual imagery in these other disciplines. The focus in such disciplines is not, as it is in rhetorical studies, on the effect of images on an audience—on their capacity to influence. In the discipline of art history, for example, scholars are largely concerned with attribution, and works of art are treated as attributes that allow the identification of the artist or historical period to which they belong. Those who approach the study of images from the viewpoint of psychology focus on the physiological processes by which human beings acquire and process visual information—how the environment is used or how eye movements function in perception, for example. Although semiotics deals with how signs generate meaning, scholars in this area tend to stop short of addressing the question of how the interpretation of meaning becomes persuasive, which is the special contribution to the study of images that can be made by rhetorical scholars.

The impulse for the study of visual imagery as rhetoric can be traced, in part, to definitions of rhetoric that do not limit the scope of rhetoric to discourse but allow for inclusion of non-discursive phenomena, including visual images. Douglas Ehninger, for example, defined rhetoric as the study of all of the ways in which humans ''may influence each other's thinking and behavior through the strategic use of symbols.'' Appropriate subject matter for study by rhetoricians, he asserted, includes such non-discursive phenomena as art, architecture, dance, and dress.[56] At the National Conference on Rhetoric in 1970, the study committee on rhetorical criticism included in its recommendations a call for an expansion of what is considered appropriate subject matter for rhetorical studies, suggesting as their purview "the non-discursive as well as the discursive, the non-verbal as well as the verbal," and including phenomena "ranging from rock music and put ons, to architecture and public forums, to ballet and international politics."[57] Our definition of rhetoric in Chapter One is another example of a definition of rhetoric in which visual images are not excluded from the scope of rhetoric.

The long tradition of study of verbal discourse in the speech communication field and opposition by some scholars to the expansion of the field to include non-discursive phenomena[58] have restrained the study of visual images from a rhetorical perspective; thus, a body of work in this area is only beginning to emerge. The study of images as rhetoric is characterized by two primary approaches.

Some rhetorical scholars use visual imagery as data to investigate research questions related to the nature and function of rhetoric. Visual images constitute artifacts to use in illustrating, explaining, or investigating rhetorical constructs developed from the study of discursive rhetoric. In such work, visual images are assumed to have essentially the same characteristics as discursive symbols. An example is Lawrence W. Rosenfield's analysis of Central Park in New York City, in which he studies the park as an example of epideictic or celebratory rhetoric.[59] Another example is Sonja K. Foss' study of Judy Chicago's work of cooperative art, *The Dinner Party*, in which she uses the art work to identify strategies used by women to empower and accord legitimacy to their own perspective.[60] Other studies in which visual data are used to illustrate or explore rhetorical constructs include: Janice Hocker Rushing's analysis of the mythic evolution of "The New Frontier" using space fiction films;[61] Harry W. Haines' analysis of the Vietnam Veterans Memorial to demonstrate the process of sight sacralization, in which attributes formerly reserved for holy places are ascribed to tourist attractions;[62] Kathleen G. Campbell's study of the strategy of enactment, in which she uses as her data Peter Weir's film, *The Year of Living Dangerously*;[63] and Lester C. Olson's study of the epideictic, deliberative, and apologetic functions of Benjamin Franklin's commemorative medal, *Libertas Americana*.[64]

A second approach to the study of visual imagery from a rhetorical perspective is the investigation of the rhetorical features of visual images themselves. The assumption of scholars who take this approach is that visual images are different, in significant ways, from discursive symbols, and their concern is with the discovery of how the particular nature of visual symbols themselves affect audiences' responses. Images, for example, do not express a thesis or proposition in the way that verbal messages do—the thesis is usually uncertain and ambiguous. Neither can visual images depict the negative—they cannot say something is not something else—as can words. To give another example of the special characteristics of visual images, their elements are presented simultaneously, in contrast to the linear, successive order of words.[65] How such characteristics of visual images affect their impact is the focus of some work in this area, leading to the development of new rhetorical theories that take such characteristics into account.

Examples of this second approach to the study of visual imagery, in which the unique features of visual images are investigated in order to develop richer and more comprehensive explanations of symbol use, include Stuart Jay Kaplan's work on visual metaphors, which resulted in a description of three characteristics that distinguish visual from language-based metaphors.[66] Sonja K. Foss' study of the Vietnam Veterans Memorial is another example; it is an investigation of ambiguity in visual phenomena and the process by which it persuades.[67] Her examination of body art, in which artists use their bodies as their primary means of expression, also constitutes an investigation into the process by which ambiguous visual messages function, with an emphasis on how unconventional referents are interpreted by an audience.[68]

Continued efforts to create rhetorical theories that are articulate about visual symbols are likely to include attention to questions such as these: What are the rhetorical processes involved in the effects achieved by different types of images? What is the relationship between features of images—style, for example—to the process of visual persuasion? What requirements or conditions must be met by an audience in order for particular effects to occur from the viewing of visual images? How do the characteristics of viewers' world views interact with visual images so that viewers formulate particular messages from those images? What ethical standards should apply to visual persuasion?

Continuing the Conversation...

We hope that this chapter will not be the end of the conversation about contemporary rhetorical thought that we have tried to capture, in part, in the previous chapters. Rather, we hope that we have encouraged you to become involved in this conversation by providing you with an entry point—a basis for understanding how perspectives on rhetoric emerge and what some of the suggested perspectives have been. Your involvement undoubtedly will take various forms. Some of you may tackle a particular perspective in depth, hoping to understand it more fully or to apply it to rhetorical phenomena you encounter. Others of you may take issue with some ideas and, in the resulting discussion, attempt to hammer out points of agreement and clarify those on which you disagree. Whatever the form of your involvement, you will be in exciting company as you help to create future conversations about rhetoric.

Notes

[1] Kenneth Burke, *The Philosophy of Literary Form: Studies in Symbolic Action*, 3rd ed. (1941; rpt. Berkeley: University of California Press, 1973), pp. 110-11.

[2] Robert L. Scott, "On Viewing Rhetoric as Epistemic," *Central States Speech Journal*, 18 (February 1967), 17.

[3] Robert L. Scott, "On Viewing Rhetoric as Epistemic: Ten Years Later," *Central States Speech Journal*, 27 (Winter 1976), 258-66. For essays critical of Scott's perspective, see, for example, Earl Croasmun and Richard A. Cherwitz, "Beyond Rhetorical Relativism," *Quarterly Journal of Speech*, 68 (February 1982), 1-16; and Richard A. Cherwitz and James W. Hikins, "Rhetorical Perspectivism," *Quarterly Journal of Speech*, 69 (August 1983), 249-66. Celeste Condit Railsback attempts a rapprochement between critics and supporters of Scott's position in "Beyond Rhetorical Relativism: A Structural-Material Model of Truth and Objective Reality," *Quarterly Journal of Speech*, 69 (November 1983), 351-63.

[4] Scott, "On Viewing Rhetoric as Epistemic: Ten Years Later," p. 261.

[5] Scott, "On Viewing Rhetoric as Epistemic," p. 13.

[6] Scott, "On Viewing Rhetoric as Epistemic," p. 16. For surveys of the various positions on the issue of rhetoric as epistemic, see: Richard L. Johannesen, *Ethics in Human Communication*, 2nd ed. (1975; rpt. Prospect Heights, IL: Waveland, 1983), pp. 39-42; Richard B. Gregg, "Rhetoric and Knowing: The Search for Perspective," *Central States Speech Journal*, 32 (Fall 1981), 133-44; and Michael C. Leff, "In Search of Ariadne's Thread: A Review of the Recent Literature on Rhetorical Theory," *Central States Speech Journal*, 29 (Summer 1978), 73-91.

[7] Barry Brummett, "A Eulogy for Epistemic Rhetoric," *Quarterly Journal of Speech*, 76 (February 1990), 69-72.

[8] Richard A. Cherwitz and James W. Hikins. "Burying the Undertaker: A Eulogy for the Eulogists of Rhetorical Epistemology," *Quarterly Journal of Speech*, 76 (February 1990), 73-77.

[9] Wayne Brockriede, "The Contemporary Renaissance in the Study of Argument," in *Argument in Transition: Proceedings of the Third Summer Conference on Argumentation*, ed. David Zarefsky, Malcolm 0. Sillars, and Jack Rhodes (Annandale, VA: Speech Communication Association, 1983), p. 17.

[10] Wayne Brockriede, "Where is Argument?" *Journal of the American Forensic Association*, 11 (Spring 1975), 179-82. An important earlier essay is Douglas Ehninger, "Argument as Method: Its Nature, Its Limitations and Its Uses," *Speech Monographs*, 37 (June 1970), 101-10.

[11] Charles Arthur Willard, *Argumentation and the Social Grounds of Knowledge* (University, AL: University of Alabama Press, 1983); and Charles Arthur Willard, *A Theory of Argumentation* (University, AL: University of Alabama Press, 1989).

[12] One of the clearest statements of the relationship between rhetoric and informal logic is J. Anthony Blair and Ralph H. Johnson, "Argumentation as Dialectical," *Argumentation*, 1 (1987), 41-56. Although informal logicians tend to see rhetoric and dialectic as separate, our view of rhetoric is broad enough to include dialectic as they see it.

[13] See, for example, Frans H. van Eemeren and Rob Grootendorst, *Speech Acts in Argumentative Discussions* (Dordrecht: Foris, 1983).

[14] Overviews of symbolic convergence theory and fantasy-theme criticism are provided by Bormann in: "Fantasy and Rhetorical Vision: The Rhetorical Criticism of Social Reality," *Quarterly Journal of Speech*, 58 (December 1972), 396-407; "Ernest Bormann and Fantasy Theme Analysis," in James L. Golden et al., *The Rhetoric of Western Thought*, 3rd ed. (1976; rpt. Dubuque, IA: Kendall-Hunt, 1983), pp. 431-49; "Symbolic Convergence: Organizational Communication and Culture," in *Communication and Organizations: An Interpretive Approach*, ed.. Linda L. Putnam and Michael E. Pacanowsky (Beverly Hills, CA: Sage, 1983), pp. 99-122; and "Symbolic Convergence Theory: A Communication Formulation," *Journal of Communication*, 35 (Autumn 1985), 128-38. For other information on and samples of the fantasy-theme perspective, see: Ernest G. Bormann, *The Force of Fantasy: Restoring the American Dream* (Carbondale: Southern Illinois University Press, 1985); John F. Cragan and Donald Shields, *Applied Communication Research: A Dramatistic Approach* (Prospect Heights, IL: Waveland, 1981); and Sonja K. Foss, "Fantasy-

Theme Criticism," in *Rhetorical Criticism: Exploration & Practice* (Prospect Heights, IL: Waveland, 1989), pp. 289-334.

[15] Robert Freed Bales, *Personality and Interpersonal Behavior* (New York: Holt, Rinehart and Winston, 1970), pp. 136-55.

[16] Bormann, "Fantasy and Rhetorical Vision," p. 397.

[17] Bormann, "Symbolic Convergence: Organizational Communication and Culture," p. 102.

[18] For an attack on and a defense of the usefulness of fantasy-theme criticism, see: G. P. Mohrmann, "An Essay on Fantasy Theme Criticism," *Quarterly Journal of Speech*, 68 (May 1982), 109-32; Ernest G. Bormann, "Fantasy and Rhetorical Vision: Ten Years Later," *Quarterly Journal of Speech*, 68 (August 1982), 288-305; and G. P. Mohrmann, "Fantasy Theme Criticism: A Peroration," *Quarterly Journal of Speech*, 68 (August 1982), 306-13. Additional critiques of fantasy-theme analysis include: Stephen E. Lucas, rev. of *The Force of Fantasy: Restoring the American Dream*, by Ernest G. Bormann, *Rhetoric Society Quarterly*, 16 (Summer 1986), 199-205; and Charles E. Williams, "Fantasy Theme Analysis: Theory Vs. Practice," *Rhetoric Society Quarterly*, 17 (Winter 1987), 11-20.

[19] For a discussion of the various meanings of the term "performance," see Dwight Conquergood, "Communication as Performance: Dramaturgical Dimensions of Everyday Life," in *The Jensen Lectures: Contemporary Communication Studies*, ed. John I. Sisco (Tampa: University of South Florida, 1983), p. 25.

[20] Conquergood, "Communication as Performance," p. 34.

[21] See, for example: Victor Turner, *On the Edge of the Bush: Anthropology as Experience*, ed. Edith L. B. Turner (Tucson: University of Arizona Press, 1985); Victor Turner, *The Anthropology of Performance* (New York: PAJ, 1986); Victor W. Turner and Edward M. Bruner, eds., *The Anthropology of Experience* (Urbana: University of Illinois Press, 1986); and Victor Turner, *Drama, Fields, and Metaphors: Symbolic Action in Human Society* (Ithaca, NY: Cornell University Press, 1974).

[22] Clifford Geertz, *Negara: The Theatre State in Nineteenth-Century Bali* (Princeton: Princeton University Press, 1980); and Clifford Geertz, *Local Knowledge: Further Essays in Interpretive Anthropology* (New York: Basic, 1983).

[23] Dell Hymes, "'In Vain I Tried to Tell You': Essays in Native American Ethnopoetics* (Philadelphia: University of Pennsylvania Press, 1981).

[24] Richard Bauman, *Verbal Art as Performance* (Prospect Heights, IL: Waveland, 1984); and Richard Bauman, *Story, Performance, and Event: Contextual Studies of Oral Narrative* (New York: Cambridge University Press, 1986).

[25] Barbara Myerhoff, *Number Our Days: A Triumph of Culture and Continuity Among Jewish Old People in an Urban Ghetto* (New York: Simon and Schuster, 1978).

[26] Erving Goffman, *The Presentation of Self in Everyday Life* (New York: Doubleday Anchor, 1959); Erving Goffman, *Frame Analysis* (New York: Harper & Row, 1974); and Erving Goffman, *Forms of Talk* (New York: Harper & Row, 1981).

[27] See, for example: Dwight Conquergood, "Poetics, Play, Process, and Power: The Performative Turn in Anthropology," *Text and Performance Quarterly*, 9 (January 1989), 82-88; Dwight Conquergood, "Between Experience and Expression: The Performed Myth," in *Essays on the Theory, Practice, and Criticism of Performance: Festschrift for Isabel Crouch*, ed. Wallace A. Bacon (Las Cruces: New Mexico State University, 1988), pp. 33-57; Dwight Conquergood, "Between Experience and Meaning: Performance as a Paradigm for Meaningful Action," in *Renewal and Revision: The Future of Interpretation*, ed. Ted Colson (Denton, TX: Omega, 1986), pp. 26-59; Dwight Conquergood, "Performing Cultures: Ethnography, Epistemology, and Ethics," in *Miteinander Sprechen und Handeln: Festschrift fur Hellmut Geissner*, ed. Edith Slembek (Frankfurt: Scriptor, 1986), pp. 55-66; Dwight Conquergood, "Performance and Dialogical Understanding: In Quest of the Other," in *Communication as Performance*, ed. J. L. Palmer (Tempe: Arizona State University, 1986), 30-37; Dwight Conquergood, "Performing as a Moral Act: Ethical Dimensions of the Ethnography of Performance," *Literature in Performance*, 5 (April 1985), 1-13; and Dwight Conquergood, "Poetics, Play, Process, and Power: The Performative Turn in Anthropology," *Text and Performance Quarterly*, 1 (January 1989), 82-88.

[28] Elizabeth Fine, *The Folklore Text: From Performance to Print* (Bloomington: Indiana University

Press, 1984); and Elizabeth C. Fine and Jean H. Speer, "A New Look at Performance," *Communication Monographs*, 44 (November 1977), 374-89.

[29] Conquergood, "Poetics, Play, Process, and Power," p. 85.

[30] Conquergood suggests these two dimensions in "Poetics, Play, Process, and Power," p. 82. We are indebted to his work for this summary of the performance perspective.

[31] Conquergood, "Between Experience and Meaning," pp. 37-51.

[32] See, for example: Dwight Conquergood, "Health Theatre in a Hmong Refugee Camp: Performance, Communication, and Culture," *Drama Review*, T119 (Fall 1988), 174-208; Dwight Conquergood, "Street Sense as Cultural Communication in Albany Park," unpublished manuscript; and Dwight Conquergood, "Life in Big Red," unpublished manuscript.

[33] Michael E. Pacanowsky and Nick O'Donnell-Trujillo, "Organizational Communication as Cultural Performance," *Communication Monographs*, 50 (June 1983), 126-47.

[34] Alasdair MacIntyre, *After Virtue: A Study in Moral Theory* (1981; rpt. Notre Dame: Notre Dame University Press, 1984), p. 216.

[35] Walter R. Fisher, *Human Communication as Narration: Toward a Philosophy of Reason, Value, and Action* (Columbia: University of South Carolina Press, 1987); and Walter R. Fisher, "Clarifying the Narrative Paradigm," *Communication Monographs*, 56 (March 1989), 55-58.

[36] Fisher, *Human Communication as Narration*, pp. 64-65.

[37] Fisher, *Human Communication as Narration*, p. 58.

[38] Robert C. Rowland, "Narrative: Mode of Discourse or Paradigm?" *Communication Monographs*, 54 (September 1987), 267. See also: Robert C. Rowland, "The Value of the Rational World and Narrative Paradigms," *Central States Speech Journal*, 39 (Fall/Winter 1988), 204-17; and Robert C. Rowland, "On Limiting the Narrative Paradigm: Three Case Studies," *Communication Monographs*, 56 (March 1989), 39-54.

[39] John Louis Lucaites and Celeste Michelle Condit,"Re-constructing Narrative Theory: A Functional Perspective," *Journal of Communication*, 35 (Autumn 1985), 90-108.

[40] This summary is provided by Barbara Warnick, "The Narrative Paradigm: Another Story," *Quarterly Journal of Speech*, 73 (May 1987), 174-75. Fisher's summary of the rational paradigm can be found in *Human Communication as Narration*, pp. 59-62.

[41] Michael Calvin McGee and John S. Nelson, "Narrative Reason in Public Argument," *Journal of Communication*, 35 (Autumn 1985), 139-55.

[42] Warnick, pp. 174-77.

[43] Warnick, p. 177.

[44] Warnick, pp. 175-76.

[45] Warnick, p. 181.

[46] Rowland, "Narrative: Mode of Discourse or Paradigm?" p. 270.

[47] Lucaites and Condit, pp. 95-98.

[48] Linda Putnam, Steve R. Wilson, Michael S. Waltman, and Dudley Turner, "The Evolution of Case Arguments in Teachers' Bargaining," *Journal of the American Forensic Association*, 23 (Fall 1985), 104-14.

[49] Thomas B. Farrell, "Narrative in Natural Discourse: On Conversation and Rhetoric," *Journal of Communication*, 35 (Autumn 1985), 109-27.

[50] William F. Lewis, "Telling America's Story: Narrative Form and the Reagan Presidency," *Quarterly Journal of Speech*, 73 (August 1987), 289, 296.

[51] Gerald Prince, *Narratology: The Form and Functioning of Narrative* (New York: Mouton, 1982), pp. 158-60; and Louis O. Mink, "Narrative Form as a Cognitive Instrument," in *The Writing of History: Literary Form and Historical Understanding*, ed. Robert H. Canary and Henry Kozicki (Madison: University of Wisconsin Press, 1978), pp. 133-34.

[52] W. Lance Bennett, "Storytelling in Criminal Trials: A Model of Social Judgment," *Quarterly Journal of Speech*, 64 (February 1978), 1-22; W. Lance Bennett and Martha Feldman, *Reconstructing Reality in the Courtroom: Justice and Judgment in American Culture* (New Brunswick, NJ: Rutgers University Press, 1981); and W. Lance Bennett, "Political Scenarios and the Nature of Politics," *Philosophy and Rhetoric*, 8 (Winter 1975), 23-42.

[53] Lewis, p. 280.

[54] Lewis, p. 281.

55 Thomas A. Hollihan and Patricia Riley, "The Rhetorical Power of a Compelling Story: A Critique of a 'Toughlove' Parental Support Group," *Communication Quarterly*, 35 (Winter 1987), 13-25. For additional information on the narrative perspective, Robert L. Scott's review essay of key books is useful: "Narrative Theory and Communication Research," *Quarterly Journal of Speech*, 70 (May 1984), 197-204.

56 Douglas Ehninger, *Contemporary Rhetoric: A Reader's Coursebook* (Glenview, IL: Scott, Foresman, 1972), p. 3.

57 Thomas O. Sloan, chair, "Report of the Committee on the Advancement and Refinement of Rhetorical Criticism," in *The Prospect of Rhetoric: Report of the National Developmental Project* (Englewood Cliffs, NJ: Prentice-Hall, 1971), p. 221.

58 Among those in opposition to the expansion of rhetoric to include visual images are: Barnet Baskerville, "Rhetorical Criticism, 1971: Retrospect, Prospect, Introspect," *Southern Speech Communication Journal*, 37 (Winter 1971), 116; Waldo W. Braden, "Rhetorical Criticism: Prognoses for the Seventies — A Symposium: A Prognosis by Waldo W. Braden," *Southern Speech Journal*, 36 (Winter 1970), 105; and Roderick P. Hart, "Forum: Theory-Building and Rhetorical Criticism: An Informal Statement of Opinion," *Central States Speech Journal*, 27 (Spring 1976), 71-72.

59 Lawrence W. Rosenfield, "Central Park and the Celebration of Civic Virtue," in *American Rhetoric: Context and Criticism*, ed. Thomas W. Benson (Carbondale: Southern Illinois University Press, 1989), pp. 221-65.

60 Sonja K. Foss, "Judy Chicago's *The Dinner Party*: Empowering of Women's Voice in Visual Art," in *Women Communicating: Studies of Women's Talk*, ed. Barbara Bate and Anita Taylor (Norwood, NJ: Ablex, 1988), pp. 9-26.

61 Janice Hocker Rushing, "Mythic Evolution of 'The New Frontier' in Mass Mediated Rhetoric," *Critical Studies in Mass Communication*, 3 (September 1986), 265-96.

62 Harry W. Haines, " 'What Kind of War?': An Analysis of the Vietnam Veterans Memorial," *Critical Studies in Mass Communication*, 3 (March 1986), 1-20.

63 Kathleen Campbell, "Enactment as a Rhetorical Strategy in *The Year of Living Dangerously*," *Central States Speech Journal*, 39 (Fall/Winter 1988), 258-68.

64 Lester C. Olson, "Benjamin Franklin's Commemorative Medal, *Libertas Americana: A Study in Rhetorical Iconology*," *Quarterly Journal of Speech*, 76 (February 1990), 23-45.

65 For discussions of differences between visual and verbal symbols, see, for example: Dorothy Walsh, "Some Functions of Pictorial Representation," *British Journal of Aesthetics*, 21 (Winter 1981), 32-38; David Novitz, *Pictures and Their Use in Communication* (The Hague, Netherlands: Martinus Nijhoff, 1977), pp. 92-95; and Susanne K. Langer, *Philosophy in a New Key: A Study in the Symbolism of Reason, Rite, and Art* (1942; rpt. New York: Mentor/New American Library, 1951), pp. 86-89

66 Stuart Jay Kaplan, "Visual Metaphors in the Representation of Communication Technology," *Critical Studies in Mass Communication*, 7 (March 1990), 37-47.

67 Sonja K. Foss, "Ambiguity as Persuasion: The Vietnam Veterans Memorial," *Communication Quarterly*, 34 (Summer 1986), 326-40.

68 Sonja K. Foss, "Body Art: Insanity as Communication," *Central States Speech Journal*, 38 (Summer 1987), 122-31.

Bibliography

The following bibliography does not include all of the works that have been written by and about each scholar. We omitted dissertations, theses, and book reviews by and about these individuals and, in the case of Kenneth Burke, his essays of music criticism. The volume of works published by and about these scholars also makes comprehensiveness impossible.

In instances where an essay originally published in a journal was reprinted in a book, we have cited only the book, believing it is more accessible to most readers than are many of the journals. We have made exceptions to this policy when an essay is considered so significant and is so linked to its original source of publication that to exclude the original version from the bibliography would be seen as a serious omission. We also have made an exception with the works of Grassi; because so few English translations of his works are available, we have included both original and reprinted citations of his published essays.

In addition, although the works of Foucault, Grassi, Habermas, and Perelman, for the most part, were not written or originally published in English, we have included only works written in or translated into English, on the assumption that the majority of our readers will be reading the English versions.

Finally, also omitted are those works cited in previously compiled bibliographies that we were unable to verify.

I.A. Richards

Works by Richards

Books

Basic English and Its Uses. New York: W.W. Norton, 1943.
Basic in Teaching: East and West. London: Kegan Paul, Trench, Trubner, 1935.
Basic Rules of Reason. London: Kegan Paul, Trench, Trubner, 1933.
Coleridge on Imagination. London: Kegan Paul, Trench, Trubner, 1934.

Complementarities: Uncollected Essays. Ed. John Paul Russo. Cambridge: Harvard University Press, 1976.

Design for Escape: World Education Through Modern Media. New York: Harcourt, Brace and World, 1968.

Development of Experimental Audio-Visual Devices and Materials for Beginning Readers. Cooperative Research Project No. 5,0642. Cambridge, MA: Harvard University, 1964-65. (With Christine M. Gibson.)

English Through Pictures, Book I. New York: English Language Research, 1945. (With Christine M. Gibson.)

English Through Pictures, Book II and a Second Workbook of English. New York: Pocket, 1973. (With Christine M. Gibson.)

A First Book of English for Chinese Learners. Peking: Orthological Institute of China, 1938.

First Steps in Reading English: A First Book for Readers to Be. New York: Pocket, 1957. (With Christine M. Gibson.)

First Steps in Reading Hebrew. New York: Language Research, 1955. (With David Weinstein and Christine [M.] Gibson.)

A First Workbook of English. New York: Language Research, 1959. (With Christine M. Gibson.)

A First Workbook of French. New York: Pocket, 1957. (With M. H. Ilsley and Christine M. Gibson.)

A First Workbook of Russian. New York: Pocket, 1963. (With Evelyn Jasiulko Harden and Christine [M.] Gibson.)

A First Workbook of Spanish. New York: Pocket, 1960. (With Ruth C. Metcalf and Christine [M.] Gibson.)

The Foundations of Aesthetics. London: George Allen and Unwin, 1922. (With C.K. Ogden and James Wood.)

French Self-Taught Through Pictures. New York: Pocket, 1950. (With M. H. Ilsley and Christine M. Gibson.)

French Through Pictures. New York: Pocket, 1950. (With M. H. Ilsley and Christine [M.] Gibson.)

General Education in a Free Society: Report of the Harvard Committee. Cambridge: Harvard University Press, 1946. (Collective work by Committee on the Objectives of a General Education in a Free Society, of which Richards was a member.)

German Through Pictures. New York: Pocket, 1953. (With I. Schmidt Mackey, W.F. Mackey, and Christine M. Gibson.)

Hebrew Reader. New York: Pocket, 1955. (With David Weinstein and Christine M. Gibson.)

Hebrew Through Pictures. New York: Pocket, 1954. (With David Weinstein and Christine M. Gibson.)

How to Read a Page: A Course in Efficient Reading with an Introduction to a Hundred Great Words. New York: W.W. Norton, 1942.

Internal Colloquies, Poems and Plays. New York: Harcourt Brace Jovanovich, 1971.

Interpretation in Teaching. New York: Harcourt, Brace, 1938.

Italian Through Pictures, Book I. New York: Pocket, 1955. (With Italo Evangelista and Christine M. Gibson.)

Learning Basic English: A Practical Handbook for English-Speaking People. New York: W.W. Norton, 1945. (With Christine M. Gibson.)

Learning the English Language, Books I-III. Boston: Houghton Mifflin, 1943. (With Christine M. Gibson.)

Learning the English Language, Book IV. Boston: Houghton Mifflin, 1953. (With Christine M. Gibson.)

The Meaning of Meaning: A Study of the Influence of Language Upon Thought and of the Science of Symbolism. London: Kegan Paul, Trench, Trubner, 1923. (With C.K. Ogden.)

Mencius on the Mind: Experiments in Multiple Definition. London: Kegan Paul, Trench, Trubner, 1932.

Nations and Peace. New York: Simon and Schuster, 1947.

The Philosophy of Rhetoric. New York: Oxford University Press, 1936.

Plato's Republic. Cambridge: Cambridge University Press, 1966. (Trans. and ed. Richards.)

Poetries and Sciences. London: Routledge & Kegan Paul, 1970.

Poetries: Their Media and Ends. Ed. Trevor Eaton. The Hague: Mouton, 1974.

The Portable Coleridge. New York: Viking, 1950. (Ed. Richards.)

Practical Criticism: A Study of Literary Judgment. London: Kegan Paul, Trench, Trubner, 1929.

Principles of Literary Criticism. London: Kegan Paul, Trench, Trubner, 1924.

Russian Through Pictures, Book I. New York: Pocket, 1961. (With Evelyn Jasiulko [Harden] and Christine [M.] Gibson.)

Science and Poetry. London: Kegan Paul, Trench, Trubner, 1926.

So Much Nearer: Essays Toward a World English. New York: Harcourt, Brace & World, 1960.

Spanish Self-Taught Through Pictures. New York: Pocket, 1950. (With Ruth C. Metcalf and Christine M. Gibson.)

Spanish Through Pictures, Book II and A Second Workbook of Spanish. New York: Pocket, 1972.

Speculative Instruments. Chicago: University of Chicago Press, 1955.

Why So, Socrates? A Dramatic Version of Plato's Dialogues: Euthyphro Apology Crito Phaedo. Cambridge: Cambridge University Press, 1964.

Words on Paper: First Steps in Reading. Cambridge, MA: Language Research, 1943. (With Christine [M.] Gibson.)

The Wrath of Achilles: The Iliad of Homer, Shortened and in a New Translation. New York: W.W. Norton, 1950.

Articles

"Basic English." *Fortune*, 23 (June 1941), 89-91, 111-12, 114.

"Basic English and Its Applications." *Royal Society of Arts Journal*, 87 (June 1939), 735-55.

"Basic English Can Be Learned Easily by All." *Rotarian*, 63 (December 1943), 30, 56-57.

"Belief." *Symposium*, 1 (1930), 423-39.

"Between Truth and Truth." *Symposium*, 2 (1931), 226-41.

"Can Education Increase Intelligence?: I. But We Can Be Taught to Think." *Forum*, 76 (October 1926), 504-509.

"The Changing American Mind." *Harper's*, 154 (January 1927), 239-45.

"Chinese Personal Nomenclature: The Advantages of an Ambilateral System." *Psyche*, 12 (July 1931), 86-89.

"The Chinese Renaissance." *Scrutiny*, 1 (September 1932), 102-13.

"A Common Language." *Vital Speeches of the Day*, 10 (December 15, 1943), 158-60.

"Communications: Art and Science—I." *Athenaeum*, June 27, 1919, pp. 534-35.

"Communications: Emotion and Art." *Athenaeum*, July 18, 1919, pp. 630-31.

"Communications: The Instruments of Criticism: Expression." *Athenaeum*, October 31, 1919, p. 1131.

"'A Cooking Egg': Final Scramble." *Essays in Criticism*, 4 (January 1954), 103-105.

"Design and Control in Language Teaching." *Harvard Alumni Bulletin*, 59 (June 8, 1957), 673-74.

"Emotive Language Still." *Yale Review*, 39 (September 1949), 108-18.

"The Eye and the Ear." *English Leaflet*, 47 (May 1948), 65-72.

"First Steps in Psychology." *Psyche*, 2 (1921), 67-79. (With C.K. Ogden.)

"The Future of Reading." In *The Written Word*. Ed. Brian L. McDonough. Rowley, MA: Newbury, 1971, pp. 27-59.

"Gerard Hopkins." *Dial*, 81 (1926), 195-203.

"God of Dostoevsky." *Forum*, 78 (1927), 88-97.

"Idle Fears About Basic English." *Atlantic*, 173 (June 1944), 98-100.

"Instructional Engineering." In *The Written Word*. Ed. Brian L. McDonough. Rowley, MA: Newbury, 1971, pp. 61-86.

"Introduction." In *Opposition: A Linguistic and Psychological Analysis*. By C.K. Ogden. 1932; rpt. Bloomington: Indiana University Press, 1967, pp. 7-13.

"Introduction." In *Semantics: The Nature of Words and Their Meanings*. By Hugh R. Walpole. New York: W. W. Norton, 1941, pp. 11-19.

"Language and World Crisis." *Harvard Graduate School Association Bulletin*, 6 (1961), 8-14, 24. (With Christine M. Gibson.)

"Letter from I.A. Richards to Richard Eberhart, from Magdalene College, Cambridge, December 15, 1938." *Furioso*, 1 (Spring 1940), 43.

"The Linguistic Symbolism." *Cambridge Magazine*, 10 (Summer 1920), 31.

"Literature for the Unlettered." In *Uses of Literature*. Ed. Monroe Engel. Cambridge: Harvard University Press, 1973, pp. 207-24.

"The Lure of High Mountaineering." *Atlantic*, 139 (January 1927), 51-57.

"Mechanical Aids *in* Language Teaching." *English Language Teaching*, 12 (October-December 1957), 3-9.

"Mr. Eliot and Notions of Culture: A Discussion." *Partisan Review*, 11 (Summer 1944), 310-12.

"Mr. I.A. Richards Replies." *American Speech*, 18 (1943), 290-96.

"The Mystical Element in Shelley's Poetry." *Aryan Path*, 30 (July 1959), 290-95.

"The Mystical Element in Shelley's Poetry." *Aryan Path*, 30 (June 1959), 250-56.

"Nineteen Hundred and Now." *Atlantic*, 140 (September 1927), 311-17.

"Notes on the Practice of Interpretation." *Criterion*, 10 (April 1931), 412-20.

"On Reading." *Michigan Quarterly*, 9 (1970), 3-7.

"On TSE: Notes for a Talk at the Institute of Contemporary Arts, London, June 29, 1965."

Sewanee Review, 74 (Winter 1966), 21-30.

"Our Lost Leaders." *Saturday Review of Literature*, 9 (April 1, 1933), 509-10.

"Passage to Forster: Reflections on a Novelist." *Forum*, 78 (1927), 914-20.

"Percy Bysshe Shelley." In *Major British Writers*, Vol. 2. Ed. G.B. Harrison. New York: Harcourt, Brace, & World, 1954, 235-50.

"A Philosophy of Education." *Wellesley Alumnae Magazine*, 53 (1969), 21, 41.

"Poetic Process and Literary Analysis." In *Style in Language*. Ed. Thomas A. Sebeok. Cambridge: MIT Press, 1960, pp. 9-24.

"The Poetry of T.S. Eliot." *Living Age*, 329 (April 4, 1926), 112-15.

"Preface to a Dictionary." *Psyche*, 13 (1933), 10-24.

"Psychopolitics." *Fortune*, 26 (September 1942), 108-109, 114.

"Religion and the Intellectuals: A Symposium." *Partisan Review*, 17 (February 1950), 138-42.

"The Secret of 'Feedforward.'" *Saturday Review*, February 3, 1968, pp. 14-17.

"Some Recollections of C.K. Ogden." *Encounter*, 9 (September 1957), 10-11.

"The Spoken and Written Word." *Listener*, October 16, 1947, pp. 669-70.

"The Teaching of English." *New Statesman*, July 23, 1927, p. 478.

"Technology to the Rescue: Elementary Language Teaching by Film and Tape." *Harvard Alumni Bulletin*, 63 (April 15, 1961), 548-50. (With Christine M. Gibson.)

"The Two Rings: A Communication." *Partisan Review*, 10 (1943), 380-81.

"A Valediction: Forbidden Mourning." In *Master Poems of the English Language*. Ed. Oscar Williams. New York: Trident, 1966, pp. 111-13.

"What is Involved in the Interpretation of Meaning?" In *Reading and Pupil Development: Proceedings of the Conference on Reading Held at the University of Chicago, Vol. II.* Supplementary Educational Monographs, No. 51. Ed. Williams S. Gray. Chicago: University of Chicago Press, 1940, 49-55.

"William Empson." *Furioso*, 1 (Spring 1940), Supplement: "A Special Note."

Works About Richards

Abrams, M.H. "Belief and the Suspension of Disbelief." In *Literature and Belief*. English Institute Essays, 1957. Ed. M.H. Abrams. New York: Columbia University Press, 1958, pp. 1-30.

Aiken, Henry David. "A Pluralistic Analysis of Aesthetic Value." *Philosophical Review*, 59 (October 1950), 493-513.

Belgion, Montgomery. "What is Criticism?" *Criterion*, 10 (October 1930), 118-39.

Bentley, Eric Russell. "An Examination of Modern Critics: 1: The Early I.A. Richards, An Autopsy." *Rocky Mountain Review*, 8 (1944), 29-36.

Berthoff, Ann E. *Forming, Thinking, Writing: The Composing Imagination*. Rochelle Park, NJ: Hayden, 1978.

Berthoff, Ann E. "From *Mencius on the Mind* to *Coleridge on Imagination*." *Rhetoric Society Quarterly*, 18 (Spring 1988), 163-66.

Berthoff, Ann E. "I.A. Richards." In *Traditions of Inquiry*. Ed. John Brereton. New York: Oxford University Press, 1985, pp. 50-80.

Berthoff, Ann E. "I.A. Richards and the Audit of Meaning." *New Literary History*, 14 (Autumn 1982), 63-79.

Berthoff, Ann E. *The Making of Meaning: Metaphors, Models, and Maxims for Writing Teachers*. Montclair, NJ: Boynton/Cook, 1981.

Berthoff, Ann E. "I.A. Richards and the Philosophy of Rhetoric." *Rhetoric Society Quarterly*, 10 (Fall 1980), 195-210.

Bethell, S.L. "Suggestions Towards a Theory of Value." *Criterion*, 14 (January 1935), 239-50.

Bilsky, Manuel. "Discussion: I.A. Richards on Belief." *Philosophy and Phenomenological Research*, 12 (September 1951), 105-15.

Bilsky, Manuel. "I.A. Richards' Theory of Metaphor." *Modern Philology*, 50 (November 1952), 130-37.

Bilsky, Manuel. "I.A. Richards' Theory of Value." *Philosophy and Phenomenological Research*, 14 (June 1954), 536-45.

Bizzell, Patricia, and Bruce Herzberg. "Knowledge and Argument: An Example from English Studies." In *Argument in Transition: Proceedings of the Third Summer Conference on Argumentation*. Ed. David Zarefsky, Malcolm O. Sillars, and Jack Rhodes. Annandale, VA: Speech Communication Association, 1983, pp. 127-34.

Black, Max. *Language and Philosophy: Studies in Method*. Ithaca, NY: Cornell University Press, 1949.

Black, Max. "Some Objections to Ogden and Richards' Theory of Interpretation." *Journal of Philosophy*, 39 (May 21, 1942), 281-90.

Black, Max. "A Symposium on Emotive Meaning: Some Questions about Emotive Meaning." *Philosophical Review*, 57 (1948), 111-26.

Blackmur, R.P. *Language as Gesture: Essays in Poetry*. 1935; rpt. New York: Harcourt, Brace, 1952.

Blackmur, R.P. "San Giovanni in Venere: Allen Tate as Man of Letters." *Sewanee Review*, 67 (1959), 614-31.

Blankenship, Jane. "I.A. Richards' 'Context' Theorem." *Rhetoric Society Quarterly*, 18 (Spring 1988), 153-58.

Booth, T.Y. "I.A. Richards and the Composing Process." *College Composition and Communication*, 37 (December 1986), 453-65.

Booth, T.Y. "The Meaning of Language If Any." *Rhetoric Society Quarterly*, 10 (Fall 1980), 211-30.

Bredin, Hugh. "I.A. Richards and the Philosophy of Practical Criticism." *Philosophy and Literature*, 10 (April 1986), 26-36.

Brower, Reuben. "Beginnings and Transitions: I.A. Richards Interviewed by Reuben Brower." In *I.A. Richards: Essays in His Honor*. Ed. Reuben Brower, Helen Vendler, and John Hollander. New York: Oxford University Press, 1973, pp. 17-41.

Chisholm, Roderick M. "Intentionality and the Theory of Signs." *Philosophical Studies*, 3 (1952), 56-63.

Conley, Thomas M. *Rhetoric in the European Tradition*. New York: Longman, 1990.

Corts, Paul R. "I.A. Richards on Rhetoric and Criticism." *Southern Speech Journal*, 36 (Winter 1970), 115-26.

Crane, R.S. "I.A. Richards on the Art of Interpretation." *Ethics*, 59 (January 1949), 112-26.

Cruttwell, Patrick. "Second Thoughts: IV: I.A. Richards' *Practical Criticism.*" *Essays in Criticism*, 8 (January 1958), 1-15.

Daiches, David. "The Principles of Literary Criticism: The Fifth of the 'Books that Changed Our Minds.'" *New Republic*, 98 (1939), 95-98.

Derrick, Thomas J. "I.A. Richards' Rhetorical Theories in the Classroom." *Rhetoric Society Quarterly*, 10 (Fall 1980), 240-53.

Eastman, Max. *The Literary Mind: Its Place in an Age of Science*. New York: Charles Scribner's Sons, 1931.

Eliot, T.S. *The Use of Poetry and the Use of Criticism: Studies in the Relation of Criticism to Poetry in England*. London: Faber & Faber, 1933.

Elton, William. *A Guide to the New Criticism*. Chicago: Modern Poetry Association, 1948.

Empson, William. *The Structure of Complex Words*. Norfolk, CT: New Directions, n.d.

Enholm, Donald K. "The Most Significant Passage for Rhetorical Theory in the Work of I.A. Richards." *Rhetoric Society Quarterly*, 18 (Spring 1988), 181-89.

Enholm, Donald K. "Rhetoric as an Instrument for Understanding and Improving Human Relations." *Southern Speech Communication Journal*, 41 (Spring 1976), 223-36.

Fisher, B. Aubrey. "I.A. Richards' Context of Language: An Overlooked Contribution to Rhetorico-Communication Theory." *Western Speech*, 35 (Spring 1971), 104-11.

Fisher, Walter R. "The Importance of Style in Systems of Rhetoric." *Southern Speech Journal*, 27 (Spring 1962), 173-82.

Fogarty, Daniel. *Roots for a New Rhetoric*. New York: Bureau of Publications, Teachers College, Columbia University, 1959.

Foss, Karen A. "Celluloid Rhetoric: The Use of Documentary Film to Teach Rhetorical Theory." *Communication Education*, 32 (January 1983), 51-61.

Foss, Sonja K. "Rhetoric and the Visual Image: A Resource Unit." *Communication Education*, 31 (January 1982), 55-66.

Foster, Richard. *The New Romantics: A Reappraisal of the New Criticism*. Bloomington: Indiana University Press, 1962.

Gabin, Rosalind J. "The Most Significant Passage from Rhetoric in the Work of I.A. Richards." *Rhetoric Society Quarterly*, 18 (Spring 1988), 167-71.

Garko, Michael G., and Kenneth N. Cissna. "An Axiological Reinterpretation of I.A. Richards's Theory of Communication and its Application to the Study of Compliance-Gaining." *Southern Speech Communication Journal*, 53 (Winter 1988), 121-39.

Gentry, George. "Reference and Relation." *Journal of Philosophy*, 40 (May 13, 1943), 253-61.

Glicksberg, Charles I. "I.A. Richards and the Science of Criticism." *Sewanee Review*, 46 (October-December 1938), 520-33.

Graff, Gerald E. "The Later Richards and the New Criticism." *Criticism*, 9 (Summer 1967), 229-42.

Hamilton, G. Rostrevor. *Poetry & Contemplation: A New Preface to Poetics*. New York: Macmillan, 1937.

Harding, D.W. "Evaluations (I): I.A. Richards." *Scrutiny*, 1 (March 1933), 327-38.

Hardy, William G. *Language, Thought, and Experience: A Tapestry of the Dimensions of Meaning.* Baltimore: University Park Press, 1978.

Heath, Robert L. "Kenneth Burke's Poetics and the Influence of I.A. Richards: A Cornerstone for Dramatism." *Communication Studies*, 40 (Spring 1989), 54-65.

Hotopf, W.H.N. *Language, Thought, and Comprehension: A Case Study of the Writings of I.A. Richards.* Bloomington: Indiana University Press, 1965.

Hyman, Stanley Edgar. *The Armed Vision: A Study in the Methods of Modern Literary Criticism.* New York: Alfred A. Knopf, 1948.

Isenberg, Arnold. "Critical Communication." *Philosophical Review*, 58 (1949), 330-44.

James, D.G. *Scepticism and Poetry: An Essay on the Poetic Imagination.* London: George Allen & Unwin, 1937.

Jensen, Keith. "I.A. Richards and His Models." *Southern Speech Communication Journal*, 37 (Spring 1972), 304-14.

Johannesen, Richard L. "Attitude of Speaker Toward Audience: A Significant Concept for Contemporary Rhetorical Theory and Criticism." *Central States Speech Journal*, 25 (Summer 1974), 95-104.

Jordan, William J., and W. Clifton Adams. "I.A. Richards' Concept of Tenor-Vehicle Interaction." *Central States Speech Journal*, 27 (Summer 1976), 136-43.

King, Andrew. "The Most Significant Passage in I.A. Richards for the Theory and Practice of Rhetoric." *Rhetoric Society Quarterly*, 18 (Spring 1988), 159-62.

Kneupper, Charles W. "The Referential-Emotive Distinction: A Significant Passage for Understanding I.A. Richards." *Rhetoric Society Quarterly*, 18 (Spring 1988), 173-79.

Knight, E. Helen. "Some Aesthetic Theories of Mr. Richards." *Mind*, 36 (1927), 69-76.

Kotler, Janet. "On Reading I.A. Richards — Again and Again." *Rhetoric Society Quarterly*, 10 (Fall 1980), 231-39.

Krieger, Murray. *The New Apologists for Poetry.* Minneapolis: University of Minnesota Press, 1956.

McLuhan, H.M. "Poetic vs. Rhetorical Exegesis: The Case for Leavis Against Richards and Empson." *Sewanee Review*, 52 (1944), 266-76.

[Nichols], Marie Hochmuth. "I.A. Richards and the 'New Rhetoric.'" *Quarterly Journal of Speech*, 44 (February 1958), 1-16.

Nichols, Marie Hochmuth. *Rhetoric and Criticism.* Baton Rouge: Louisiana State University Press, 1963.

Pollock, T[homas] C[lark]. "A Critique of I.A. Richards' Theory of Language and Literature." In *A Theory of Meaning Analyzed.* General Semantics Monographs, 3. Ed. M. Kendig. Lakeville, CT: Institute of General Semantics, 1942, pp. 1-25.

Pollock, Thomas Clark. *The Nature of Literature: Its Relation to Science, Language and Human Experience.* Princeton, NJ: Princeton University Press, 1942, pp. 145-61.

Pottle, Frederick A. *The Idiom of Poetry.* Ithaca, NY: Cornell University Press, 1946.

Ragsdale, J. Donald. "Problems of Some Contemporary Notions of Style." *Southern Speech Journal*, 35 (Summer 1970), 332-41.

Ransom, John Crowe. *The New Criticism.* Norfolk, CT: New Directions, 1941.

Ransom, John Crowe. "A Psychologist Looks at Poetry." *Virginia Quarterly Review*, 11 (October 1935), 575-92.

Righter, William. *Logic and Criticism.* London: Routledge & Kegan Paul, 1963.

Rudolph, G.A. "The Aesthetic Field of I.A. Richards." *Journal of Aesthetics and Art Criticism*, 14 (March 1956), 348-58.

Russo, John Paul. "Belief and Sincerity in I.A. Richards." *Modern Language Quarterly*, 47 (June 1986), 154-91.

Russo, John Paul. *I.A. Richards: His Life and Work*. Baltimore: Johns Hopkins University Press, 1989.

Russo, John Paul. "I.A. Richards in Retrospect." *Critical Inquiry*, 8 (Summer 1982), 743-60.

Schiller, Jerome [P.] "An Alternative to 'Aesthetic Disinterestedness.'" *Journal of Aesthetics and Art Criticism*, 22 (Spring 1964) 295-302.

Schiller, Jerome P. *I.A. Richards' Theory of Literature*. New Haven: Yale University Press, 1969.

Sesonske, Alexander. "Truth in Art." *Journal of Philosophy*, 53 (May 24, 1956), 345-53.

Sibley, Francis M. "How to Read I.A. Richards." *American Scholar*, 42 (Spring 1973), 318-28.

Sondel, Bess. "An Analysis of *The Meaning of Meaning*." In Sondel, *The Humanity of Words*. Cleveland: World, 1958, pp. 43-78.

Spaulding, John Gordon. "Elementalism: The Effect of an Implicit Postulate of Identity on I.A. Richards' Theory of Poetic Value." In *A Theory of Meaning Analyzed*. General Semantics Monographs, 3. Ed. M. Kendig. Lakeville, CT: Institute of General Semantics, 1942, pp. 26-35.

Stevenson, Charles L. *Ethics and Language*. New Haven: Yale University Press, 1944.

Stolnitz, Jerome. *Aesthetics and Philosophy of Art Criticism: A Critical Introduction*. Boston: Houghton Mifflin, 1960.

Talmor, Sascha. "I.A. Richards Revisited." *Durham University Journal*, 80 (1988), 317-20.

Tate, Allen. *On the Limits of Poetry: Selected Essays: 1928-1948*. New York: Swallow Press and William Morrow, 1948.

Twitchett, E.G. "A Vision of Judgment." *London Mercury*, 20 (October 1929), 598-605.

Vivas, Eliseo. "Four Notes on I.A. Richards' Aesthetic Theory." *Philosophical Review*, 44 (July 1935), 354-67.

Wagner, Geoffrey. "American Literary Criticism: The Continuing Heresy." *Southern Review* [Adelaide, Australia], 2 (1968), 82-89.

Welleck, René. "On Rereading I.A. Richards." *Southern Review*, 3 [new series] (Summer 1967), 533-54.

Wells, Susan. "Richards, Burke and the Relation Between Rhetoric and Poetics." *Pre/Text*, 7 (Spring/Summer 1986), 59-75.

West, Alick. *Crisis and Criticism*. London: Lawrence and Wishart, 1937.

Wimsatt, William K., Jr., and Cleanth Brooks. *Literary Criticism: A Short History*. New York: Alfred A. Knopf, 1957.

Wimsatt, W[illiam] K., Jr., and Monroe C. Beardsley. *The Verbal Icon: Studies in the Meaning of Poetry*. University of Kentucky: University of Kentucky Press, 1954.

Richard M. Weaver

Works by Weaver

Books

The Ethics of Rhetoric. Chicago: Henry Regnery, 1953.
Ideas Have Consequences. Chicago: University of Chicago Press, 1948.
Language is Sermonic: Richard M. Weaver on the Nature of Rhetoric. Ed. Richard L.
   Johannesen, Rennard Strickland, and Ralph T. Eubanks. Baton Rouge: Louisiana
   State University Press, 1970.
Life Without Prejudice and Other Essays. Chicago: Henry Regnery, 1965.
Rhetoric and Composition: A Course in Reading and Writing. New York: Holt, Rinehart,
   and Winston, 1957.
A Rhetoric and Handbook [revision of *Rhetoric and Composition*]. New York: Holt,
   Rinehart, and Winston, 1967. (With Richard S. Beal.)
The Southern Essays of Richard M. Weaver. Ed. George M. Curtis, III, and James J.
   Thompson, Jr. Indianapolis: Liberty, 1987.
The Southern Tradition at Bay: A History of Postbellum Thought. Ed. George Core and
   M.E. Bradford. New Rochelle, NY: Arlington, 1968.
Visions of Order: The Cultural Crisis of Our Time. Baton Rouge: Louisiana State University
   Press, 1964.

Articles and Pamphlets

Academic Freedom: The Principle and the Problems. Philadelphia: Intercollegiate Society
   of Individualists, 1963.
"Agrarianism in Exile." *Sewanee Review*, 58 (October-December 1950), 586-606.
"Albert Taylor Bledsoe." *Sewanee Review*, 52 (January-March 1944), 34-45.
"The American as a Regenerate Being." Ed. George Core and M.E. Bradford. *Southern
   Review*, 4 [new series] (July 1968), 633-46.
"Aspects of the Southern Philosophy." *Hopkins Review*, 5 (Summer 1952), 5-21.
"Contemporary Southern Literature." *Texas Quarterly*, 2 (Summer 1959), 126-44.
"Humanism in an Age of Science." Ed. Robert Hamlin. *Intercollegiate Review*, 7 (Fall
   1970), 11-18.
"The Humanities in a Century of the Common Man." *New Individualist Review*, 3 (1964),
   17-24.
"Individuality and Modernity." In *Essays on Individuality*. Ed. Felix Morley. Philadelphia:
   University of Pennsylvania Press, 1958, pp. 63-81.
"Lee the Philosopher." *Georgia Review*, 2 (Fall 1948), 297-303.
Letter. *New York Times Book Review*, March 21, 1948, p. 29.
"Looking for an Argument." *College English*, 14 (January 1953), 210-16. (With Manuel
   Bilsky, McCrea Hazlett, and Robert E. Streeter.)
"Mass Plutocracy." *National Review*, 9 (November 5, 1960), 273-75, 290.

"The Middle of the Road: Where It Leads." *Human Events*, 8 (March 24, 1956), n.p.
"The Middle Way: A Political Meditation." *National Review*, 3 (January 19, 1957), 63-64.
"The Older Religiousness in the South." *Sewanee Review*, 51 (April-June 1943), 237-49.
"On Setting the Clock Right." *National Review*, 4 (October 12, 1957), 321-23.
"The Pattern of a Life." *Southern Partisan*, Fall 1981, p. 13.
"Realism and the Local Color Interlude." Ed. George Core. *Georgia Review*, 22 (Fall 1968), 300-05.
"The Regime of the South." *National Review*, 6 (March 14, 1959), 587-89.
Relativism and the Crisis of Our Time. Philadelphia: Intercollegiate Society of Individualists, 1961.
"A Responsible Rhetoric." Ed. Thomas D. Clark and Richard L. Johannesen. *Intercollegiate Review*, 12 (Winter 1976-77), 81-87.
The Role of Education in Shaping Our Society. Philadelphia: Intercollegiate Studies Institute, n.d.
"Roots of Liberal Complacency." *National Review*, 3 (June 8, 1957), 541-43.
"Scholars or Gentlemen?" *College English*, 7 (November 1945), 72-77.
"The South and the American Union." In *The Lasting South*. Ed. Louis D. Rubin, Jr. and James Jackson Kilpatrick. Chicago: Henry Regnery, 1957, pp. 46-68.
"The South and the Revolution of Nihilism." *South Atlantic Quarterly*, 43 (April 1944), 194-98.
"Southern Chivalry and Total War." *Sewanee Review*, 53 (April-June 1945), 267-78.
"1. The Southern Tradition." *New Individualist Review*, 3 (1964), 7-17.
"The Tennessee Agrarians." *Shenandoah*, 3 (Summer 1952), 3-10.
"Two Orators." Ed. George Core and M.E. Bradford. *Modern Age*, 14 Summer-Fall 1970), 226-42.

Unpublished Works

"Acceptance of the Young Americans for Freedom Award." Beginning notes for a speech delivered at Madison Square Garden, New York, NY, March 7, 1962. In Gerald Thomas Goodnight. "Rhetoric and Culture: A Critical Edition of Richard M. Weaver's Unpublished Works." Diss. University of Kansas 1978, pp. 570-72.
"Address of Dr. Richard M. Weaver, Chicago University to a Family Meeting." In Goodnight, pp. 467-75.
"The Causes of War: An Essay in One Sentence." In Goodnight, pp. 410-22.
"Conservative Versus 'Progressive' Education." Excerpt from a speech delivered at Holy Name College, Washington, DC, October 15, 1960. In Goodnight, pp. 533-40.
"The Division of Churches Over Slavery (General)." In Goodnight, pp. 335-42.
"The Division of Churches Over Slavery." In Goodnight, pp. 344-57.
"English Composition in the College." In Goodnight, pp. 737-44.
"Hawthorne: What Was He?" Lecture Notes. In Goodnight, pp. 718-19.
Lecture Notes on Conrad. In Goodnight, pp. 677-88.
Lecture Notes on "The Tower." In Goodnight, pp. 704-16.
Lecture Notes on Whitman. In Goodnight, pp. 690-702.
Letter of Application to Graduate School, Louisiana State University, [1940]. In Goodnight, pp. 673-75.

"Making the Most of Two Worlds." Commencement Address, Gilmour Academy, June 1956. In Goodnight, pp. 510-31.

"Oliver Wendell Holmes, Jr." In Goodnight, pp. 359-76.

"'Parson' Weems: A Study in Early American Rhetoric." In Goodnight, pp. 270-98.

"The People of the Excluded Middle." In Goodnight, pp. 378-408.

"The Place of Logic in the English Curriculum." Paper presented to the English B Staff, University of Chicago, March 9, [1957]. In Goodnight, pp. 728-35.

Preliminary Letter of Application to Graduate School at Louisiana State University, January 20,1940. In Goodnight, pp. 668-70.

"Rhetorical Strategies of the Conservative Cause." Speech delivered at the University of Wisconsin, Madison, April 26, 1959. In Goodnight, pp. 574-608.

"The Role of Education in Shaping Our Society." Speech delivered at the Metropolitan Area Industrial Conference, Chicago, October 25, 1961. In Goodnight, pp. 610-40.

"The Strategy of Words." Speech delivered at the Lake Bluff Woman's Club, Lake Bluff, IL, February 13, 1962. In Goodnight, pp. 542-68.

"Two Diarists." In Goodnight, pp. 220-68.

"*Uncle Tom's Cabin*." In Goodnight, pp. 300-33.

"What Students are Thinking." Notes for Essay. In Goodnight, pp. 722-25.

Works About Weaver

Ashin, Mark. "The Argument of Madison's 'Federalist,' No. 10." *College English*, 15 (October 1953), 37-45.

Auerbach, M. Morton. *The Conservative Illusion*. New York: Columbia University Press, 1959.

Baker, Virgil L., and Ralph T. Eubanks. *Speech in Personal and Public Affairs*. New York: David McKay, 1965.

Bliese, John R.E. "The Conservative Rhetoric of Richard M. Weaver: Theory and Practice." *Southern Communication Journal*, 54 (Summer 1989), 401-21.

Bliese, John. "Richard M. Weaver and the Rhetoric of a Lost Cause." *Rhetoric Society Quarterly*, 19 (Fall 1989), 313-25.

Bliese, John. "Richard M. Weaver: Conservative Rhetorician." *Modern Age*, 21 (Fall 1977), 377-86.

Bliese, John. "Richard Weaver: Rhetoric and the Tyrannizing Image." *Modern Age*, 28 (Spring/Summer 1984), 208-14.

Bliese, John R. E. "Richard Weaver's Axiology of Argument." *Southern Speech Communication Journal*, 44 (Spring 1979), 275-88.

Bormann, Dennis R. "The 'Uncontested Term' Contested: An Analysis of Weaver on Burke." *Quarterly Journal of Speech*, 57 (October 1971), 298-305.

Bradford, M.E. "The Agrarianism of Richard Weaver: Beginnings and Completions." *Modern Age,* 14 (Summer-Fall 1970), 249-56.

Brady, George K. Letter to Robert Hamlin describing Weaver's undergraduate days, July 23, 1966. In Gerald Thomas Goodnight. "Rhetoric and Culture: A Critical Edition of Richard M. Weaver's Unpublished Works." Diss. University of Kansas 1978, pp. 750-54.

Campbell, John Angus. "Edmund Burke: Argument from Circumstance in Reflections on the Revolution in France." *Studies in Burke and His Time*, 12 (Winter 1970-71), 1764-83.

Clark, Thomas D. "The Ideological Bases of Richard Weaver's Rhetorical Theory." In *In Search of Justice: The Indiana Tradition in Speech Communication*. Ed. Richard J. Jensen and John C. Hammerback. Amsterdam: Rodopi, 1987, pp. 23-35.

Conley, Thomas M. *Rhetoric in the European Tradition*. New York: Longman, 1990.

Corder, Jim W. *Uses of Rhetoric*. Philadelphia: J .B. Lippincott, 1971.

Cushman, Donald P., and Gerard A. Hauser. "Weaver's Rhetorical Theory: Axiology and the Adjustment of Belief, Invention, and Judgment." *Quarterly Journal of Speech*, 59 (October 1973), 319-29.

Davidson, Donald. "Grammar and Rhetoric: The Teacher's Problem." *Quarterly Journal of Speech*, 39 (December 1953), 401-36.

Davidson, Eugene. "Richard Malcolm Weaver — Conservative." *Modern Age*, 7 (Summer 1963), 226-30.

Diamonstein, Barbara D. "A Turn to the Right." *Saturday Review*, 49 (1966), 38-39.

Duffy, Bernard K. "The Platonic Functions of Epideictic Rhetoric." *Philosophy and Rhetoric*, 16 (1983), 79-93.

East, John P. "Richard M. Weaver: The Conservatism of Affirmation." *Modern Age*, 19 (Fall 1975), 338-54.

Ebbitt, Wilma R. "Two Tributes to Richard M. Weaver: Richard M. Weaver, Teacher of Rhetoric." *Georgia Review*, 17 (Winter 1963), 415-18.

Einhorn, Lois J. "The Argumentative Dimensions of Theorizing: Toward a Method for Analyzing Theories of Rhetoric." *Central States Speech Journal*, 36 (Winter 1985), 282-93.

Enholm, Donald K., David Curtis Skaggs, and W. Jeffrey Welsh. "Origins of the Southern Mind: The Parochial Sermons of Thomas Cradock of Maryland, 1744-1770." *Quarterly Journal of Speech*, 73 (May 1987), 200-18.

Eubanks, Ralph T. "Axiological Issues in Rhetorical Inquiry." *Southern Speech Communication Journal*, 44 (Fall 1978), 11-24.

Eubanks, Ralph T. "Nihilism and the Problem of a Worthy Rhetoric." *Southern Speech Journal*, 33 (Spring 1968), 187-99.

Eubanks, Ralph T. "Richard M. Weaver, Friend of Traditional Rhetoric." In *Language is Sermonic: Richard M. Weaver on the Nature of Rhetoric*. Ed. Richard L. Johannesen, Rennard Strickland, and Ralph T. Eubanks. Baton Rouge: Louisiana State University Press, 1970, pp. 3-6.

Eubanks, Ralph T. "Two Tributes to Richard M. Weaver: Richard M. Weaver: In Memoriam." *Georgia Review*, 17 (Winter 1963), 412-15.

Eubanks, Ralph T., and Virgil L. Baker. "Toward an Axiology of Rhetoric." *Quarterly Journal of Speech*, 48 (April 1962), 157-68.

Fisher, Walter R. "Advisory Rhetoric: Implications for Forensic Debate." *Western Speech*, 29 (Spring 1965), 114-19.

Floyd, James M., and W. Clifton Adams. "A Content-Analysis Test of Richard M. Weaver's Critical Methodology." *Southern Speech Communication Journal*, 41 (Summer 1976), 374-87.

Follette, Charles. "Deep Rhetoric: A Substantive Alternative to Consequentialism in Exploring the Ethics of Rhetoric 1." In *Dimensions of Argument: Proceedings of the Second Summer Conference on Argumentation*. Ed. George Ziegelmueller and Jack Rhodes. Annandale, VA: Speech Communication Association, 1981, pp. 989-1002.

Foss, Sonja K. "Abandonment of Genus: The Evolution of Political Rhetoric." *Central States Speech Journal*, 33 (Summer 1982), 367-78.

Foss, Sonja K. "Rhetoric and the Visual Image: A Resource Unit." *Communication Education*, 31 (January 1982), 55-66.

Gayner, Jeffery B. "The Critique of Modernity in the Work of Richard M. Weaver." *Intercollegiate Review*, 14 (Spring 1979), 97-104.

Geiger, George R. "We Note . . . the Consequences of Some Ideas." *Antioch Review*, 8 (June 1948), 251-54.

Golden, James L., Goodwin F. Berquist, and William E. Coleman. *The Rhetoric of Western Thought*. 3rd ed. Dubuque, IA: Kendall/Hunt, 1983.

Hart, Roderick P. "The Functions of Human Communication in the Maintenance of Public Values." In *Handbook of Rhetorical and Communication Theory*. Ed. Carroll C. Arnold and John Waite Bowers. Boston: Allyn and Bacon, 1984, pp. 749-91.

Haskell, Robert E., and Gerard A. Hauser. "Rhetorical Structure: Truth and Method in Weaver's Epistemology." *Quarterly Journal of Speech*, 64 (October 1978), 233-45.

Hayakawa, S.I. *Symbol, Status, and Personality*. 1950; rpt. New York: Harcourt Brace & World, 1963.

"In Memoriam, Richard M. Weaver." *New Individualist Review*, 2 (Spring 1963), 2.

Irwin, Clark T., Jr. "Rhetoric Remembers: Richard Weaver on Memory and Culture." *Today's Speech*, 21 (Spring 1973), 21-26.

Johannesen, Richard L. "Attitude of Speaker Toward Audience: A Significant Concept for Contemporary Rhetorical Theory and Criticism." *Central States Speech Journal*, 25 (Summer 1974), 95-104.

Johannesen, Richard L. "Conflicting Philosophies of Rhetoric/Communication: Richard M. Weaver Versus S. I. Hayakawa." *Communication*, 7 (1983), 289-315.

Johannesen, Richard L. *Ethics in Human Communication*. 3rd ed. Prospect Heights, IL: Waveland, 1990.

Johannesen, Richard L. "Richard M. Weaver on Standards for Ethical Rhetoric." *Central States Speech Journal*, 29 (Summer 1978), 127-37.

Johannesen, Richard L. "Richard M. Weaver's Uses of Kenneth Burke." *Southern Speech Communication Journal*, 52 (Spring 1987), 312-30.

Johannesen, Richard L. "Richard Weaver's View of Rhetoric and Criticism." *Southern Speech Journal*, 32 (Winter 1966), 133-45.

Johannesen, Richard L. "Some Pedagogical Implications of Richard M. Weaver's Views on Rhetoric." *College Composition and Communication*, 29 (October 1978), 272-79.

Johannesen, Richard L., Rennard Strickland, and Ralph T. Eubanks. "Richard M. Weaver on the Nature of Rhetoric: An Interpretation." In *Language is Sermonic: Richard*

M. Weaver on the Nature of Rhetoric. Ed. Richard L. Johannesen, Rennard Strickland, and Ralph T. Eubanks. Baton Rouge: Louisiana State University Press, 1970, pp. 7-30.

Kendall, Willmoore. "How to Read Richard Weaver: Philosopher of 'We the (Virtuous) People.'" *Intercollegiate Review,* 2 (September 1965), 77-86.

Kendall, Willmoore. *The Conservative Affirmation.* Chicago: Henry Regnery, 1963.

Kirk, Russell. *Beyond the Dreams of Avarice.* Chicago: Henry Regnery, 1956.

Kirk, Russell. "Richard Weaver, RIP." *National Review,* 14 (April 23, 1963), 308.

Kirschke, James. "The Ethical Approach: The Literary Philosophy of Richard M. Weaver." *Intercollegiate Review,* 14 (Spring 1979), 87-94.

Larson, Charles U. *Persuasion: Reception and Responsibility.* 3rd ed. Belmont, CA: Wadsworth, 1983.

Lora, Ronald. *Conservative Minds in America.* Chicago: Rand McNally, 1971.

Medhurst, Martin J. "The First Amendment vs. Human Rights: A Case Study in Community Sentiment and Argument from Definition." *Western Journal of Speech Communication,* 46 (Winter 1982), 1-19.

Medhurst, Martin J. "The Sword of Division: A Reply to Brummett and Warnick." *Western Journal of Speech Communication,* 46 (Fall 1982), 383-90.

Meyer, Frank S. "Richard M. Weaver: An Appreciation." *Modern Age,* 14 (Summer-Fall 1970), 243-48.

Milione, E. Victor. "The Uniqueness of Richard M. Weaver." *Intercollegiate Review,* 2 (September 1965), 67-86.

Montgomery, Marion. "Richard M. Weaver, 1948." *Modern Age,* 26 (Summer-Fall 1982), 252-55.

Montgomery, Marion. "Richard Weaver Against the Establishment: An Essay Review." *Georgia Review,* 23 (Winter 1969), 433-59.

Nash, George H. *The Conservative Intellectual Movement in America Since 1945.* New York: Basic, 1976.

Natanson, Maurice. "The Limits of Rhetoric." *Quarterly Journal of Speech,* 41 (April 1955), 133-39.

Payne, Melinda A., Suzanne M. Ratchford, and Lillian N. Wolley, "Richard M. Weaver: A Bibliographic Essay." *Rhetoric Society Quarterly,* 19 (Fall 1989), 327-32.

Powell, James. "The Conservatism of Richard M. Weaver: The Foundations of Weaver's Traditionalism." *New Individualist Review,* 3 (1964), 3-6.

Regnery, Henry. *Memoirs of a Dissident Publisher.* New York: Harcourt Brace Jovanovich, 1979.

Rieke, Richard D., and Malcolm O. Sillars. *Argumentation and the Decision Making Process.* 2nd ed. Glenview, IL: Scott, Foresman, 1984.

Rossiter, Clinton. *Conservatism in America.* New York: Alfred A. Knopf, 1956.

Schliessmann, Mike. "Free Speech and the Rights of Congress: Robert M. Lafollette and the Argument from Principle." In *Free Speech Yearbook 1978.* Falls Church, VA: Speech Communication Association, 1978, pp. 38-44.

Smith, William Raymond. *History as Argument: Three Patriotic Historians of the American Revolution.* The Hague: Mouton, 1966.

Smith, William Raymond. *The Rhetoric of American Politics: A Study of Documents.* Westport, CT: Greenwood, 1969.

Sproule, J. Michael. "An Emerging Rationale for Revolution: Argument from Circumstance and Definition in Polemics Against the Stamp Act, 1765-1766." *Today's Speech*, 23 (Spring 1975), 17-21.

Sproule, J. Michael. "Using Public Rhetoric to Assess Private Philosophy: Richard M. Weaver and Beyond." *Southern Speech Communication Journal*, 44 (Spring 1979), 289-308.

Szasz, Thomas. *The Myth of Psychotherapy: Mental Healing as Religion, Rhetoric, and Repression*. Garden City, NY: Anchor/Doubleday, 1978.

Thorne, Melvin J. *American Conservative Thought Since World War II: The Core Ideas*. New York: Greenwood, 1990.

Weisman, Eric R. "The Good Man Singing Well: Stevie Wonder as Noble Lover." *Critical Studies in Mass Communication*, 2 (June 1985), 136-51.

White, Bruce A. "Richard M. Weaver: Dialectic Rhetorician." *Modern Age*, 26 (Summer-Fall 1982), 256-59.

Winterowd, W. Ross. *Rhetoric: A Synthesis*. New York: Holt, Rinehart and Winston, 1968.

Winterowd, W. Ross. "Richard M. Weaver: Modern Poetry and the Limits of Conservative Criticism." *Western Speech*, 37 (Spring 1973), 129-38.

Wolfe, Gregory. *Right Mind: A Sourcebook of American Conservative Thought*. Chicago: Regnery, 1987.

Stephen Toulmin

Works by Toulmin

Books

The Abuse of Casuistry. Berkeley: University of California Press, 1988. (With Albert R. Jonsen.)

The Architecture of Matter. New York: Harper & Row, 1962. (With June Goodfield.)

Cosmopolis: The Hidden Agenda of Modernity. New York: Free, 1990.

The Discovery of Time. New York: Harper & Row, 1962. (With June Goodfield.)

An Examination of the Place of Reason in Ethics. Cambridge: Cambridge University Press, 1950.

The Fabric of the Heavens: The Development of Astronomy and Dynamics. New York: Harper & Row, 1961.

Foresight and Understanding: An Enquiry Into the Aims of Science. Bloomington: Indiana University Press, 1961. (With June Goodfield.)

Human Understanding, Volume I: The Collective Use and Evolution of Concepts. Princeton, NJ: Princeton University Press, 1972.

An Introduction to Reasoning. New York: Macmillan, 1979. (With Richard Rieke and
    Allan Janik.)
Knowing and Acting: An Invitation to Philosophy. New York: Macmillan, 1976.
Norwood Russel Hanson: What I Do Not Believe and Other Essays. Dordrecht: D. Reidel,
    1972. (With Harry Wolf.)
The Philosophy of Science: An Introduction. London: Hutchinson University Library, 1953.
Physical Reality: Philosophical Essays on 20th Century Physics. New York: Harper &
    Row, 1970.
The Return to Cosmology: Postmodern Science and the Theology of Nature. Berkeley:
    University of California Press, 1982.
The Uses of Argument. Cambridge: Cambridge University Press, 1958.
Wittgenstein's Vienna. New York: Simon and Schuster, 1973. (With Allan Janik.)

Articles

"Alexandra Trap: 'Thoughts on the Eternal Scientist.' " *Encounter*, 42 (January 1974),
    61-72.
"Astrophysics of Berosos the Chaldean." *Isis*, 58 (Spring 1967), 65-76.
"Brain and Language: A Commentary." *Synthese*, 22 (May 1971), 369-95.
"Can Science and Ethics be Connected?" *Hastings Center Report*, 9 June 1979), 27-34.
"The Complexity of Scientific Choice: A Stocktaking." *Minerva*, 3 (Autumn 1964), 343-59.
"The Complexity of Scientific Choice II: Culture, Overheads or Tertiary Industry?"
    Minerva, 4 (Winter 1964), 155-69.
"Concepts and the Explanation of Human Behavior." In *Human Action*. Ed. Theodore
    Mischel. New York: Academic, 1969, pp. 71-104.
"Concept-Formation in Philosophy and Psychology." In *Dimensions of Mind*. Ed. S. Hook.
    New York: New York University Press, 1960, pp. 211-25.
"Conceptual Revolutions in Science." *Synthese*, 17 (March 1967), 75-91.
"The Construal of Reality: Criticism in Modern and Post Modern Science." *Critical
    Inquiry*, 9 (September 1982), 93-111.
"Creativity: Is Science Really a Special Case?" *Comparative Literature Studies*, 17 (June
    1980), 190-201.
"Critical Notice of R. Carnap, 'Logical Foundations of Probability.' " *Mind*, 62 (January
    1952), 86-99.
"Criticism in the History of Science: Newton on Absolute Space, Time and Motion: II."
    Philosophical Review, 68 (April 1959), 203-27.
"Criticism in the History of Science: Newton on Absolute Space, Time and Motion II."
    Philosophical Review, 68 (April 1959), 203-27.
"Crucial Experiments: Priestley and Lavoisier." *Journal of the History of Ideas*, 18 (April
    1957), 205-20.
"Defense of 'Synthetic Necessary Truth.' " *Mind*, 58 (April 1949), 164-77.
"Ethical Safeguards in Research." *Center Magazine*, 9 (July 1976), 23-26.
"The Evolutionary Development of Natural Science." American Scientist, 55 (December
    1967), 456-71.
[Exchange of Letters Between Stephen Toulmin and Ernest Nagel.] *Scientific American*,
    214 (April 1966), 9-11.

"Exploring the Moderate Consensus." *Hastings Center Report*, 5 (June 1975), 31-35.

"Financing the Universities." *Spectator*, 208 (March 1962), 394.

"From Form to Function: Philosophy and History of Science in the 1950s and Now." *Daedalus*, 106 (Summer 1977), 143-62.

"From Logical Analysis to Conceptual History." In *The Legacy of Logical Positivism*. Ed. Peter Achinstein and Stephen F. Barker. Baltimore: Johns Hopkins University Press, 1969, pp. 25-53.

"From Logical Systems to Conceptual Populations." In *Boston Studies in Philosophy of Science, Vol. VIII*. Ed. Robert S. Buck and Roger C. Cohen. Dordrecht: D. Reidel, 1971, pp. 552-64.

"Historical Inference In Science: Geology As A Model For Cosmology." *Monist*, 47 (Fall 1962), 142-58.

"How Can We Reconnect Sciences With Ethics?" In *Knowing and Valuing: The Search for Common Roots*. Ed. H. Tristram Engelhardt. Hastings on the Hudson: Hastings Center, 1980, pp. 44-64.

"How Can We Reconnect the Sciences With the Foundations of Ethics?" *Hastings Center Series on Ethics*, 1981, pp. 403-23.

"How Was the Tunnel of Eupalinus Aligned?" *Isis*, 56 (Spring 1965), 46-55. (With June Goodfield.)

"Human Adaptation." In *The Philosophy of Evolution*. Ed. Uffe J. Jensen. New York: St. Martin's, 1981, pp. 176-95.

"In Vitro Fertilization: Answering the Ethical Objections." *Hastings Center Report*, 8 (October 1978), 9-11.

"Inwardness of Mental Life." *Critical Inquiry*, 6 (Autumn 1979), 1-16.

"Koestler, Arthur Theodicy—On Sin, Science, and Politics." *Encounter*, 52 (February 1979), 46-57.

"Logic and the Criticism of Arguments." In James L. Golden, Goodwin F. Berquist, and William E. Coleman. *The Rhetoric of Western Thought*. 3rd ed. Dubuque, IA: Kendall-Hunt, 1983, pp. 391-401.

"Logic and the Theory of Mind." In *Nebraska Symposium of Motivation*. Ed. W. J. Arnold. Lincoln, NB: University of Nebraska Press, 1975, pp. 409-76. (With C. F. Feldman).

"Ludwig Wittgenstein." *Encounter*, 32 (January 1969), 58-71.

"Ludwig Wittgenstein." *General Semantics Bulletin*, 37 (1970), 19-32.

"Common Law Tradition." *Hastings Center Report*, 11 (August 1981), 12-13.

"The Moral Admissibility or Inadmissibility of Nontherapeutic Fetal Experiment." In *Medical Responsibility*. Ed. Wade L. Robinson. Clifton, NJ: Humanity, 1979), pp. 113-39.

"The Moral Psychology of Science." *Hastings Center Series on Ethics*, 1981, pp. 223-42.

"On the Nature of the Physician's Understanding." *Journal of Medical Philosophy*, 1 (March 1976), 32-50.

"Plausibility of Theories." *Journal of Philosophy*, 63 (October 1966), 624-66.

"Pluralism and Responsibility in Post-Modern Science." *Science, Technology, and Human Values*, 10 (Winter 1985), 28-37.

"Principles of Morality." *Philosophy*, 31 (1956), 142-53.

"Problem Statement and Tentative Agenda." In *Argumentation As a Way of Knowing*.

Ed. David A. Thomas. Annandale, VA: Speech Communication Association, pp. 1-7. (With Richard Rieke.)

"Qattara: A Primitive Distillation and Extraction Apparatus Still in Use." *Isis*, 55 (September 1964), 339-42.

"Reasons and Causes." In *Explanation in the Behavioral Sciences*. Ed. R.E. Borger and F. Cioffi. Cambridge: Cambridge University Press, 1970), pp. 1-41.

"Recovery of Practical Philosophy." *American Scholar*, 57 (Summer 1988), 337-52.

"Rediscovering History." *Encounter*, 36 (January 1971), 53-64.

"Regaining the Ethics of Discretion: The Tyranny of Principles." *Hastings Center Report*, 11 (1981), 31-39.

"Reply." *Synthese*, 23 (March 1972), 487-90.

"Reply, On Prescribing Description." *Synthese*, 18 (October 1968), 462-63.

"Review Essay: A Sociologist Looks at Wittgenstein." *American Journal of Sociology*, 84 (January 1979), 996-99.

"Rules and Their Relevance for Understanding Human Behavior." In *Understanding Other Persons*. Ed. T. Mischel. Totowa, NJ: Littlefield and Rowman, 1974, pp. 25-60.

"Scientific Strategies and Historical Change." In *Philosophical Foundations of Science*. Ed. R.J. Sieger and Robert S. Cohen. Dordrecht: D. Reidel, 1974, pp. 401-14.

"Scientist-Overlord." *Spectator*, 209 (July 1962), 104-05.

"Steering a Way Between Constructivism and Innatism." In *Language and Learning: The Debate Between Jean Piaget and Noam Chomsky*. Ed. Massimo Paitelli-Palmarini. Cambridge, MA: Harvard University Press, 1980, pp. 276-78.

"Teleology in Contemporary Science and Philosophy." *Neuve Hefte fur Philosphie*, 20 (1981), 140-52.

"On Teilhard de Chardin." *Commentary*, 39 (March 1965), 50-55.

"Tyranny of Principles—Regaining the Ethics of Discretion." *Hastings Center Report*, 11 (December 1981), 31-39.

"You Norman, Me Saxon (Hamburg, Corsica, Stratford-Upon-Avon and Vermont)." *Encounter*, 51 (September 1978), 89-93.

"You Norman, Me Saxon: Reply." *Encounter*, 53 (August 1979), 80-81.

Works About Toulmin

Abelson, Raxiel. "In Defense of Formal Logic." *Philosophy and Phenomenological Research*, 21 (March 1961), 333-46.

Adams, Elie Maynard. *Ethical Naturalism and the Modern World-View*. Chapel Hill, NC: University of North Carolina, 1960.

Aiken, Henry David. "Moral Reasoning." *Ethics*, 64 (October 1953), 24-37.

Ambrester, Marcus L., and Glynis Holm Strause. *A Rhetoric of Interpersonal Communication*. Prospect Heights, IL: Waveland, 1984.

Anderson, Ray Lynn, and C. David Mortensen, "Logic and Marketplace Argumentation." *Quarterly Journal of Speech*, 53 (April 1967), 143-50.

Arnold, Carroll C. *Public Speaking as a Liberal Art*. Boston: Allyn and Bacon, 1964.

Benoit, William Lyon. "An Empirical Investigation of Argumentative Strategies Employed in Supreme Court Opinions." In *Dimensions of Argument: Proceedings of the Second Summer Conference on Argumentation*. Ed. George Ziegelmueller and Jack Rhodes. Annandale, VA: Speech Communication Association, 1981, pp. 179-95.

Binkley, Luther J. *Contemporary Ethical Theories*. New York: Philosophical Libraries, 1961.

Bove, Paul A. "The Rationality of Disciplines: The Abstract Understanding of Stephen Toulmin." In *After Foucault: Humanistic Knowledge, Postmodern Challenges*. Ed. Jonathan Arac. New Brunswick: Rutgers University Press, 1988, pp. 42-70.

Brockriede, Wayne, "The Contemporary Renaissance in the Study of Argument." In *Argument In Transition: Proceedings of the Third Summer Conference on Argumentation*. Ed. David Zarefsky, Malcolm O. Sillars and Jack Rhodes. Annandale, VA: Speech Communication Association, 1983, pp. 17-26.

Brockriede, Wayne, and Douglas Ehninger. "Toulmin on Argument: An Interpretation and Application." *Quarterly Journal of Speech*, 26 (February 1960), 44-53.

Burleson, Brant R. "A Cognitive-Developmental Perspective on Social Reasoning Processes," *Western Journal of Speech Communication*, 45 (Spring 1981), 133-47.

Burleson, Brant R. "On the Analysis and Criticism of Arguments: Some Theoretical and Methodological Considerations." *Journal of the American Forensic Association*, 15 (Winter 1979), 137-47.

Burleson, Brant R. "On the Foundations of Rationality: Toulmin, Habermas, and the *a Priori* of Reason." *Journal of the American Forensic Association*, 16 (Fall 1979), 112-27.

Byker, Donald, and Loren J. Anderson. *Communication as Identification*. New York: Harper & Row, 1975.

Carleton, Lawrence Rickard. "Problems, Methodology, and Outlaw Science." *Philosophy and the Social Sciences*, 12 (June 1982), 143-51.

Castaneda, H. N. "On a Proposed Revolution in Logic." *Philosophy of Science*, 27 (July 1960), 279-92.

Cooley, J. C. "On Mr. Toulmin's Revolution in Logic." *Journal of Philosophy*, 56 (March 1959), 297-319.

Cox, J. Robert. "Investigating Policy Argument as a Field." In *Dimensions of Argument: Proceedings of the Second Summer Conference on Argumentation*. Ed. George Ziegelmueller and Jack Rhodes. Annandale, VA: Speech Communication Association, 1981, pp. 126-42.

Crable, Richard E. *Argumentation as Communication: Reasoning with Receivers*. Columbus, OH: Merrill, 1976.

Cronkhite, Gary. *Persuasion: Speech and Behavioral Change*. Indianapolis: Bobbs-Merrill, 1969.

D'Angelo, Gary. "A Schema for the Utilization of Attitude Theory within the Toulmin Model of Argument." *Central States Speech Journal*, 22 (Summer 1971), 100-09.

Dellapenna, Joseph W., and Kathleen M. Farrell. "Modes of Judicial Discourse: The Search for Argument Fields." In *Argumentation: Analysis and Practices*. Ed. Frans H. van Eemeren, Rob Grootendorst, J. Anthony Blair, and Charles A. Willard. Dordrecht: Foris, 1987, pp. 94-101.

Donmoyer, Robert. "The Rescue from Relativism: Two Failed Attempts and an Alternative Strategy." *Educational Researcher*, 14 (December 1985), 13-20.

Dykstra, Vergil H. "The Place of Reason in Ethics." *Review of Metaphysics*, 8 (March 1955), 458-67.

Ehninger, Douglas, and Wayne Brockriede. *Decision by Debate*. New York: Dodd, Mead, 1963.

Fine, Arthur. "Creativity: Is Science Really A Special Case?: Response." *Comparative Literature Studies*, 17 (June 1980), 201-05.

Fine, Arthur I. "Explaining the Behavior of Entities." *Philosophical Review*, 75 (October 1966), 496-509.

Fisher, Frank. "Science and Critique in Political Discourse: Elements of a Postpositivistic Methodology." *New Political Science*, 9/10 (Summer/Fall 1982), 9-32.

Fisher, Walter R. "Good Reasons: Fields and Genre." In *Dimensions of Argument: Proceedings of the Second Summer Conference on Argumentation*. Ed. George Ziegelmueller, and Jack Rhodes. Annandale, VA: Speech Communication Association, 1981, pp. 114-25.

Freeley, Austin J. *Argumentation and Debate: Rational Decision Making*. Belmont, CA: Wadsworth, 1976.

Fulkerson, Richard. "Technical Logic, Comp-Logic, and the Teaching of Writing." *College Composition and Communication*, 39 (December 1988), 436-52.

Goodnight, G. Thomas. "The Personal, Technical, and Public Spheres of Argument: A Speculative Inquiry into the Art of Public Deliberation." *Journal of the American Forensic Association*, 28 (Spring 1982), 214-27.

Graham, Loren R. "The Multiple Connections Between Science and Ethics." *Hastings Center Report*, 9 (June 1979), 35-40.

Gulley, Halbert E. *Discussion, Conference and Group Processes*. New York: Holt, Rinehart and Winston, 1960.

Hample, Dale. "The Functions of Argument." In *Dimensions of Argument: Proceedings of the Third Summer Conference on Argumentation*. Ed. David Zarefsky, Malcolm O. Sillars, and Jack Rhodes. Annandale, VA: Speech Communication Association, 1981, pp. 560-75.

Handler, Ernst W. "The Evolution of Economic Theories: A Formal Approach." *Erkenntnis*, 8 (July 1982), 65-96.

Hayes, James T. "'Creation-Science' Is not 'Science?' — Argument Fields and Public Argument." In *Dimensions of Argument: Proceedings of the Third Summer Conference on Argumentation*. Ed. David Zarefsky, Malcolm O. Sillars, and Jack Rhodes. Annandale, VA: Speech Communication Association, 1981, pp. 416-22.

Hempel, C.G. "What Kind of Discipline is Logic?" *Journal of Symbolic Logic*, 20 (March 1955), 541-45.

Houser, Lloyd. "The Classification of Science Literatures by their 'Hardness.'" *Library and Information Science Research*, 8 (October-December 1986), 357-72.

Kaeser, E. "Physical Laws, Physical Entities, and Ontology." *Dialectica*, 31 (1977), 273-99.

Kaplan, Jorton A. *Justice, Human Nature, and Political Obligation*. New York: Free, 1976.

Karbach, Joan. "Using Toulmin's Model of Argumentation." *Journal of Teaching Writing*, 6 (Spring 1987), 81-91.

Keene, Michael L. "Teaching Toulmin Logic." *Teaching English in the Two-Year College*, 5 (Spring 1979), 193-98.

Keough, Colleen M. "The Nature and Function of Argument in Organizational Bargaining Research." *Southern Speech Communication Journal*, 53 (Fall 1987), 1-17.

Kerner, George C. *The Revolution in Ethical Theory*. New York: Oxford University Press, 1966.

Klumpp, James F. "A Dramatistic Approach to Fields." In *Dimensions of Argument: Proceedings of the Second Summer Conference on Argumentation*. Ed. George Ziegelmueller and Jack Rhodes. Annandale, VA: Speech Communication Association, 1981, pp. 44-55.

Kneupper, Charles. "Teaching Argument: An Introduction to the Toulmin Model." *College Composition and Communication*, 29 (October 1978), 237-241.

Kneupper, Charles W. "The Tyranny of Logic and the Freedom of Argumentation." *Pre/Text*, 5 (Summer 1984), 113-21.

Kordig, Carl R. "Evolutionary Epistemology is Self-Referentially Inconsistent." *Philosophy and Phenomenological Research*, 42 (March 1982), 449-50.

Lawler, Ronald David. *Philosophical Analysis and Ethics*. Milwaukee: Bruce, 1968.

Lewis, Albert L. "Stephen Toulmin: A Reappraisal." *Central States Speech Journal*, 23 (Spring 1972), 48-55.

McCann, Thomas M. "Student Argumentative Writing Knowledge and Ability at Three Grade Levels." *Research in the Teaching of English*, 23 (February 1989), 62-76.

McCroskey, James C. "Toulmin and The Basic Course." *Speech Teacher*, 14 (March 1965), 91-100.

McKerrow, Ray E. "On Fields and Rational Enterprises." In *Dimensions of Argument: Proceedings of the Summer Conference on Argumentation*. Ed. Jack Rhodes and Sara Newell. Annandale, VA: Speech Communication Association, 1981, pp. 401-13.

Miller, Carolyn R. "Fields of Argument and Special Topoi." In *Dimensions of Argument: Proceedings of the Third Summer Conference on Argumentation*. Ed. David Zarefsky, Malcolm O. Sillars and Jack Rhodes. Annandale, VA: Speech Communication Association, 1981, pp. 147-59.

Miller, Gerald R., and Thomas R. Nilsen. *Perspectives on Argumentation*. Chicago: Scott Foresman, 1966.

Mills, Glen E. *Reason in Controversy: On General Argumentation*. Boston: Allyn and Bacon, 1968.

Mitroff, Ian I. "On the Structure of Dialectical Reasoning in the Social and Policy Sciences." *Theory and Decision*, 14 (December 1982), 331-50.

Mitroff, Ian I., Harold Quinton, and Richard O. Mason. "Beyond Contradiction and Consistency: A Design for a Dialectical Policy System." *Theory and Decision*, 15 (June 1983), 107-20.

Ogden, Schubert Miles. *The Reality of God, and Other Essays*. New York: Harper & Row, 1966.

Palmer, L. M. "Stephen Toulmin: Variations on Vichian Themes." *Scientia*, 227 (1982), 89-104.

Perry, David L. "Cultural Relativism in Toulmin's Reason in Ethics." *Personalist*, 47 (Summer 1966), 328-39.

Reinard, John C. "The Role of Toulmin's Categories of Message Development in Persuasive Communication: Two Experimental Studies on Attitude Change." *Journal of the American Forensic Association*, 20 (Spring 1984), 206-23.

Rieke, Richard D., and Malcolm O. Sillars. *Argumentation and the Decision Making Process*, 2nd ed. Glenview, IL: Scott, Foresman, 1984.

Rowland, Robert. "Argument Fields." In *Dimensions of Argument: Proceedings of the Second Summer Conference on Argumentation*. Ed. George Ziegelmueller and Jack Rhodes. Annandale, VA: Speech Communication Association, 1981, pp. 456-79.

Rowland, Robert. "The Influence of Purpose on Fields of Argument." *Journal of the American Forensic Association*, 28 (Spring 1982), 228-46.

Schon, Donald. "Ultimate Rules and the Rational Settlement of Ethical Conflicts." *Philosophy and Phenomenological Research*, 19 (September 1958), 53-64.

Schultz, Lucille M., and Chester H. Laine. "A Primary Trait Scoring Grid with Assessment and Instructional Uses." *Journal of Teaching Writing*, 5 (Spring 1986), 77-89.

Secor, Marie J. "Recent Research in Argumentation Theory." *Technical Writing Teacher*, 14 (Fall 1987), 337-54.

Seibert, Thomas M. "The Arguments of a Judge." In *Argumentation: Analysis and Practices*. Ed. Frans H. van Eemeren, Rob Grootendorst, J. Anthony Blair, and Charles A. Willard. Dordrecht: Foris, 1987, pp. 119-22.

Shapere, Dudley. "Mathematical Ideals and Metaphysical Concepts." *Philosophical Review*, 69 (July 1960), 376-85.

Schuetz, Janice. "The Genesis of Argumentative Forms and Fields." In *Dimensions of Argument: Proceedings of the Second Summer Conference on Argumentation*. Ed. George Ziegelmueller and Jack Rhodes. Annandale, VA: Speech Communication Association, 1981, pp. 279-94.

Shafer, Charles B. "'Think Like a Lawyer': Valid Law School Admonition?" In *Dimensions of Argument: Proceedings of the Second Summer Conference on Argumentation*. Ed. George Ziegelmueller and Jack Rhodes. Annandale, VA: Speech Communication Association, 1981, pp. 242-78.

Siegel, H. "Truth, Problem Solving and the Rationality of Science." Studies in *History and Philosophy of Science*, 14 (June 1983), 89-112.

Stone, Harold. "A Note on Vico Studies Today: Toulmin and the Development of Academic Disciplines." *New Vico Studies*, 1983, pp. 69-76.

Stratman, James F. "Teaching Written Argument: The Significance of Toulmin's Layout for Sentence-Combining." *College English*, 44 (November 1982), 718-34.

Stygall, Gail. "Toulmin and The Ethics of Argument Fields: Teaching Writing and Argument." *Journal of Teaching Writing*, 6 (Spring 1987), 93-107.

Trent, Jimmie D. "Toulmin's Model of An Argument: An Examination and Extension," *Quarterly Journal of Speech*, 54 (October 1968), 252-59.

Wenzel, Joseph W. "On Fields of Argument as Propositional Systems." *Journal of the American Forensic Association*, 28 (Spring 1982), 204-13.

Willard, Charles Arthur. "Argument Fields." In *Advances in Argumentation Theory and*

Research. Ed. J. Robert Cox and Charles Arthur Willard. Carbondale, IL: Southern
    Illinois University, 1982, pp. 24-77.
Willard, Charles Arthur. *Argumentation and the Social Grounds of Knowledge*. University,
    AL: University of Alabama, 1983.
Willard, Charles Arthur. "Field Theory: A Cartesian Meditation." In *Dimensions of
    Argument: Proceedings of the Second Summer Conference on Argumentation*. Ed.
    George Ziegelmueller and Jack Rhodes. Annandale, VA: Speech Communication
    Association, 1981, pp. 21-43.
Willard, Charles Arthur. "Some Questions About Toulmin's View of Argument Fields."
    In *Proceedings of the Summer Conference on Argumentation*. Ed. Jack Rhodes and
    Sara Newell. Annandale, VA: Speech Communication Association, 1980, pp. 348-400.
Willard, Charles Arthur. *A Theory of Argumentation*. University, AL: University of
    Alabama, 1989.
Willard, Charles Arthur. "On the Utility of Descriptive Diagrams for the Analysis and
    Criticism of Arguments." *Communication Monographs*, 43 (November 1976), 308-19.
Wilson, F. "Explanation in Aristotle, Newton, and Toulmin [Part 1]." *Philosophy of
    Science*, 36 (September 1969), 291-310.
Wilson, F. "Explanation in Aristotle, Newton, and Toulmin [Part 2]." *Philosophy of
    Science*, 36 (December 1969), 400-28.
Windes, Russell R., and Arthur Hastings. *Argumentation and Advocacy* A. New York:
    Random, 1965.
Zappel, Kristiane. "Argumentation and Literary Text: Towards an Operational Model."
    In *Argumentation: Analysis and Practices*. Ed. Frans H. van Eemeren, Rob
    Grootendorst, J. Anthony Blair, and Charles A. Willard. Dordrecht: Foris, 1987,
    pp. 217-24.
Zarefsky, David. "Persistent Questions in the Theory of Argument Fields." *Journal of
    the American Forensic Association*, 28 (Spring 1982), 191-203.
Zarefsky, David. "'Reasonableness' in Public Argument: Fields as Institutions." In
    *Dimensions of Argument: Proceedings of the Second Summer Conference on
    Argumentation*. Ed. George Ziegelmueller and Jack Rhodes. Annandale, VA: Speech
    Communication Association, 1981, pp. 88-100.

Chaim Perelman

Works by Perelman

Books

An Historical Introduction to Philosophical Thinking. Trans. Kenneth A. Brown. New
    York: Random, 1965.
The Idea of Justice and the Problem of Argument. Trans. John Petrie. New York:
    Humanities, 1963.

Justice. New York: Random, 1967.

Justice, Law, and Argument: Essays on Moral and Legal Reasoning. Trans. John Petrie, Susan Rubin, Graham Bird, Melvin T. Dalgarno, Heather Relihan and William Kluback. Dordrecht: D. Reidel, 1980.

The New Rhetoric and the Humanities: Essays on Rhetoric and its Applications. Trans. William Kluback. Ed. Jakko Hintikka, Robert S. Cohen, Donald Davidson, Gabriel Nuchelmans, and Wesley Salmon. Boston: D. Reidel, 1979.

The New Rhetoric: A Treatise on Argumentation. Trans. John Wilkinson and Purcell Weaver. Notre Dame, IN: University of Notre Dame Press, 1969. (With L. Olbrechts-Tyteca.)

The Realm of Rhetoric. Trans. William Kluback. Notre Dame, IN: University of Notre Dame Press, 1982.

Articles

"Act and Person in Argumentation." *Ethics*, 61 (July 1951), 251-69. (With L. Olbrechts-Tyteca.)

"Behaviorism's Enlightened Despotism." In *Beyond the Punitive Society*. Ed. Harvey Wheeler. San Francisco: W.H. Freeman, 1973, pp. 13-27.

"The Dialectical Method and the Part Played by the Interlocutor in the Dialogue." *Proceedings of the 30th Indian Philosophical Congress*, 1955, pp. 179-83.

[Essay] 24. In *Democracy in a World of Tensions*. Proc. of a UNESCO Symposium. Ed. Richard McKeon and Stein Rokkan. New York: Greenwood, 1951.

"The Foundations and Limits of Tolerance." *Pacific Philosophy Forum*, 2 (September 1963), 20-27.

"Fuller's The Morality of Law." *Natural Law Forum*, 10 (1965), 242-45.

"How Do We Apply Reason to Values?" *Journal of Philosophy*, 52 (December 1955), 797-802.

"Interventions." In *Danish Yearbook of Philosophy*, Vol. VII. Copenhagen: Munksgaard, 1972, 188-90.

"Judicial Reasoning." *Israel Law Review*, 1 (1966), 373-79.

"Justice and Justification." *Natural Law Forum*, 10 (July 1965), 1-20.

"Justice and Reasoning." In *Law, Reason and Justice*. Ed. G. Hughes. New York: New York University Press, 1969, pp. 207-25.

"Natural Law and Natural Rights." In *Dictionary of the History of Ideas*. New York: Scribner's, 1973, pp. 13-27. (With P. Foriers.)

"A Naturalistic Interpretation of Authority, Ideology and Violence." In *Phenomenology and Natural Existence: Essays in Honor of Marvin Farber*. Ed. Dale Riepe. Albany, NY: State University of New York Press, 1973, pp. 342-51.

"The New Rhetoric." *Philosophy Today*, 1 (1957), 4-10.

"The New Rhetoric." In *The Prospect of Rhetoric*. Ed. Lloyd F. Bitzer and Edwin Black. Englewood Cliffs, NJ: Prentice-Hall, 1971, pp. 115-22.

"The New Rhetoric." In *Pragmatics of Natural Languages*. Ed. Y. Barhillel. Dordrecht: D. Reidel, 1971, pp. 145-49.

"The New Rhetoric and The Rhetoricians: Remembrances and Comments." *Quarterly Journal of Speech*, 70 (May 1984), 188-96.

"The New Rhetoric: A Theory of Practical Reasoning." In *The Great Ideas Today*. Chicago: Encyclopedia Brittanica, 1970, pp. 272-312.

"On Self Evidence in Metaphysics." *International Philosophical Quarterly*, 4 (February 1964), 5-19.

"Philosophical Studies." *Philosophy Today*, 2 (1957), 4-10.

"Philosophy and Rhetoric." In *Advances in Argumentation Theory and Research*. Ed. J. Robert Cox and Charles Arthur Willard. Carbondale, IL: Southern Illinois University Press, pp. 287-97. (With Judy F. Merryman.)

"Philosophy and the Sciences." *Philosophy Today*, 9 (1965), 273-77.

"The Philosophy of Pluralism." *Philosophic Exchange*. Annual Proc. of the Center for Philosophic Exchange. Brockport: Center for Philosophic Exchange, State University of New York, 1978, pp. 49-56.

"Philosophy, Rhetoric, Commonplaces." *Philosophes critiques d'eux-memes*, 1 (1975), 173-211.

"Polanyi's Interpretation of Scientific Inquiry." In *Intellect and Hope: Essays in the Thought of Michael Polanyi*. Ed. Th. A. Langford and W.M. Poteat. Durham, NC: Duke University Press, 1968, pp. 232-41.

"Proof in Philosophy." *Hibbert Journal*, 52 (1954), 354-59.

"Remarks on the Papers of Prof. Wild and Dr. Dunham." In *Dialogues on the Philosophy of Marxism*. Ed. J. Somerville and H. L. Parsons. Westport, CT: Greenwood, 1974, pp. 360-64.

"A Reply to Henry W. Johnstone, Jr." *Philosophy and Phenomenological Research*, 16 (December 1955), 245-47.

"Reply to Mr. Zaner." *Philosophy and Rhetoric*, 1 (Summer 1968), 168-76.

"Reply to Stanley Rosen." *Inquiry*, 2 (1959), 85-88.

"Rhetoric." In *Encyclopedia Britannica: XV*. Chicago: Encyclopedia Britannica, 1973, pp. 803-805.

"The Rhetorical Point of View in Ethics: A Program." *Communication*, 6 (1981), 315-20.

"Rhetoric and Philosophy." Trans. Henry W. Johnstone, Jr. *Philosophy and Rhetoric*, 1 (January 1968), 15-24.

"Rhetoric and Politics." *Philosophy and Rhetoric*, 17 (1984), 129-34. (With James Winchester and Molly Black Verene.)

"Self Evidence and Proof." *Philosophy*, 33 (1958), 289-302.

"Some Reflections on Classification." *Philosophy Today*, 9 (1965), 268-72.

"The Theoretical Relations of Thought and Action." *Inquiry*, 1 (1958), 130-36.

"The Use and Abuse of Confused Notions." *ETC.: A Review of General Semantics*, 36 (1979), 313-324.

"Value Judgments, Justifications and Argumentation." Trans. Francis B. Sullivan. *Philosophy Today*, 6 (1962), 45-51.

"What is Legal Logic?" *Israel Law Review*, 3 (1968), 1-6.

"What the Philosopher May Learn from the Study of Law." *Natural Law Forum*, 11 (1966), 1-12.

Works About Perelman

Abbott, Don. "The Jurisprudential Analogy: Argumentation and the New Rhetoric." *Central States Speech Journal*, 25 (Spring 1974), 50-55.

Anderson, John R. "The Audience as a Concept in the Philosophic Rhetoric of Perelman, Johnstone, and Natanson." *Southern Speech Communication Journal*, 38 (Fall 1972), 39-50.

Apostal, Leo. "What is the Force of an Argument?" *Review of International Philosophy*, 33 (1979), 29-109.

Arnold, Carroll C. "Perelman's New Rhetoric." *Quarterly Journal of Speech*, 56 (February 1970), 87-92.

Bator, Paul G. "The 'Good Reasons Movement': a 'Confounding' of Dialectic and Rhetoric?" *Philosophy and Rhetoric*, 21 (1988), 38-47.

Betz, Joseph. "The Relationship Between Love and Justice: A Survey of the Five Possible Positions." *I Valie Inquiry*, 4 (Fall 1970), 191-203.

Bitzer, Lloyd F., and Edwin Black, eds. *The Prospect of Rhetoric*. Englewood Cliffs, NJ: Prentice-Hall, 1971.

Braet, Antoine. "The Classical Doctrine of 'Status' and the Rhetorical Theory of Argumentation." *Philosophy and Rhetoric*, 20 (1987), 79-93.

Corgan, Verna C. "Perelman's Universal Audience as a Critical Tool." *Journal of the American Forensic Association*, 23 (Winter 1987), 147-57.

Cox, J. Robert. "The Die is Cast: Topical and Ontological Dimensions of the *Locus* of the Irreparable." *Quarterly Journal of Speech*, 68 (August 1982), 227-39.

"Chaim Perelman." *Who's Who in World Jewry: A Biographical Dictionary of Outstanding Jews*. Ed. J. J. Carmin Karpman. New York: Pittman, 1955, p. 681.

Dearin, Ray D. "Perelman's Concept of 'Quasilogical' Argument: A Critical Elaboration." In *Advances in Argumentation Theory and Research*. Ed. J. Robert Cox and Charles Arthur Willard. Carbondale: Southern Illinois University Press, 1982, pp. 78-94.

Dearin, Ray D. "The Philosophical Basis of Chaim Perelman's Theory of Rhetoric." *Quarterly Journal of Speech*, 55 (October 1969), 213-14.

Dearin, Ray D., ed. *The New Rhetoric of Chaim Perelman: Statement and Response*. Lanham, MA: University Press of America, 1989.

DePoe, Stephen. "Arthur Schlesinger, Jr.'s 'Middle' Way Out of Vietnam': The Limits of 'Technocratic Realism' as the Basis for Foreign Policy Dissent." *Western Journal of Speech Communication*, 52 (Spring 1988), 147-66.

Ede, Lisa S. "Rhetoric vs. Philosophy: The Role of the Universal Audience in Chaim Perelman's *The New Rhetoric*." *Central States Speech Journal*, 32 (Summer 1981), 118-25.

Ewin, R.E. "On Justice and Injustice." *Mind*, 79 (April 1970), 200-16.

Fisher, Walter R. *Human Communication as Narration: Toward a Philosophy of Reason, Value, and Action*. Columbia: University of South Carolina Press, 1987.

Golden, James. L., and Joseph J. Pilotta, eds. *Practical Reasoning in Human Affairs: Studies in Honor of Chaim Perelman*. Dordrecht: D. Reidel, 1986.

Goldstick, D. "Methodological Conservatism." *American Philosophy Quarterly*, 8 (April 1971), 186-91.

Griffin-Collart, Evelyne, and Lucie Olbrechts-Tyteca. "Bibliographie de Chaim Perelman." *Review of International Philosophy*, 33 (1979), 325-42.

Johnstone, Henry W., Jr. "New Outlooks on Controversy." *Review of Metaphysics*, 12 (September 1958), 57-67.

Johnstone, Henry W., Jr. "A New Theory of Philosophical Argumentation." *Philosophy and Phenomenological Research*, 15 (December 1954), 244-52.

Johnstone, Henry W., Jr. "Some Reflections on Argumentation." In *La Theorie de l'Argumentation: Perspectives et Applications*. Paris: Beatrice-Nauwelaerts, n.d., pp. 30-39.

Johnstone, Henry W., Jr. *Validity and Rhetoric in Philosophical Argument*. University Park, PA: Dialogue Press of Man & World, 1978, pp. 86-92.

Karon, Louise A. "Presence in *The New Rhetoric*." *Philosophy and Rhetoric*, 9 (Spring 1976), 96-111.

Kluback, William. "The New Rhetoric as a Philosophical System." *Journal of the American Forensic Association*, 17 (Fall 1980), 73-79.

Kluback, William, and Mortimer Becke. "The Significance of Chaim Perelman's Philosophy of Rhetoric." *Review of International Philosophy*, 33 (1979), 33-46.

Kneupper, Charles W. "The Tyranny of Logic and the Freedom of Argumentation." *Pre/Text*, 5 (Summer 1984), 113-21.

Long, Richard. "The Role of Audience in Chaim Perelman's New Rhetoric." *Journal of Advanced Composition*, 4 (1983), 107-17.

Loreau, Max. "Rhetoric as the Logic of Behavioral Science." Trans. Lloyd I. Watkins and Paul D. Brandes. *Quarterly Journal of Speech*, 50 (October 1964), 323-24.

Mader, Thomas F. "On Presence in Rhetoric." *College Composition and Communication*, 24 (December 1973), 375-82.

Meyer, Michel. "The Perelman-Rawls Debate on Justice." *Review of International Philosophy*, 29 (1975), 316-31.

Oliver, Robert T. "Philosophy and/or Persuasion." In *La Theorie de l'Argumentation: Perspectives et Applications*. Paris: Beatrice-Nauwelaerts, n.d., pp. 571-80.

Parker, Douglas H. "Rhetoric, Ethics and Manipulation." *Philosophy and Rhetoric*, 5 (Spring 1972), 69-87.

Raphael, David D. "Perelman on Justice." *Review of International Philosophy*, 33 (1979), 260-76.

Ray, John W. "Perelman's Universal Audience." *Quarterly Journal of Speech*, 64 (December 1978), 361-75.

Rosen, Stanley H. "Thought and Action." *Inquiry*, 2 (1959), 65-84.

Rotenstreich, Nathan. "Argumentation and Philosophical Clarification." *Philosophy and Rhetoric*, 5 (Winter 1972), 12-23.

Rotenstreich, Nathan. "On Constructing a Philosophical System." In *La Theorie de l'Argumentation: Perspectives et Applications*. Paris: Beatrice-Nauwelaerts, n.d., pp. 179-94.

Scott, Robert L. "Chaim Perelman: Persona and Accommodation in the New Rhetoric." *Pre/Text*, 5 (Summer 1984), 89-95.

Scult, Allen. "Perelman's Universal Audience: One Perspective." *Central States Speech Journal*, 27 (Fall 1976), 176-80.

Secor, Marie J. "Perelman's Loci in Literary Argument." *Pre/Text*, 5 (Summer 1984), 97-110.

Secor, Marie J. "Recent Research in Argumentation Theory." *Technical Writing Teacher*, 14 (Fall 1987), 337-54.

Sillars, Malcolm O. "Audiences, Social Values, and the Analysis of Argument." *Speech Teacher*, 22 (November, 1973), 291-303.

Sillars, Malcolm O., and Patricia Ganer. "Values and Beliefs: A Systematic Basis for Argumentation." In *Advances in Argumentation Theory and Research*. Ed. J. Robert Cox and Charles Arthur Willard. Carbondale: Southern Illinois University Press, pp. 184-201.

Tammelo, Ilmar. "The Rule of Law and the Rule of Reason in International Legal Relations." In *La Theorie de l'Argumentation: Perspectives et Applications*. Paris: Beatrice-Nauwelaerts, n.d., pp. 335-68.

Van Noorden, Sally. "Rhetorical Arguments in Aristotle and Perelman." *Review of International Philosophy*, 1979, pp. 178-87.

Waggenspach, Beth M. "Awakening Society to False Perceptions about Women." In *Rhetorical Studies in Honor of James L. Golden*. Ed. Lawrence W. Hugneberg. Dubuque: Kendall/Hunt, 1986, pp. 163-78.

Wallace, Karl R. " 'Topoi' and the Problem of Invention." *Quarterly Journal of Speech*, 58 (December 1972), 387-96.

Wroblewski, Jerzy. "Semantic Basis of the Theory of Legal Interpretation." In *La Theorie de l'Argumentation: Perspectives et Applications*. Paris: Beatrice-Nauwelaerts, n.d., pp. 397-416.

Zaner, Richard M. "Rejoinder to Messrs. Johnstone and Perelman." *Philosophy and Rhetoric*, 1 (Summer 1968), 171-73.

Ernesto Grassi

Works by Grassi

Books

Folly and Insanity in Renaissance Literature. Binghamton, NY: Medieval & Renaissance Texts & Studies, 1986. (With Maristella Lorch.)

Heidegger and the Question of Renaissance Humanism: Four Studies. Trans. Ulrich Hemel and John Michael Krois. Binghamton, NY: Medieval & Renaissance Texts & Studies, 1983.

Rhetoric as Philosophy: The Humanist Tradition. Trans. John Michael Krois and Azizeh Azodi. University Park: Pennsylvania State University Press, 1980.

Vico and Humanism: Essays on Vico, Heidegger, and Rhetoric. New York: Peter Lang, 1990.

Articles

"Can Rhetoric Provide a New Basis for Philosophizing? The Humanist Tradition." [Part I.] Trans. John Michael Krois. *Philosophy and Rhetoric*, 11 (Winter 1978), 1-18. Rpt. in *Rhetoric as Philosophy*, chpt. 4.

"Can Rhetoric Provide a New Basis for Philosophizing? The Humanist Tradition." [Part II.] Trans. John Michael Krois. *Philosophy and Rhetoric*, 11 (Spring 1978), 75-97. Rpt. in *Rhetoric as Philosophy*, chpt. 4.

"The Claim of the Word and the Religious Significance of Poetry: A Humanist Problem." *Dionysius*, 8 (December 1984), 131-54.

"Critical Philosophy or Topical Philosophy? Meditations on the *De nostri temporis studiorum ratione*." Trans. Hayden V. White. In *Giambattista Vico: An International Symposium*. Ed. Giorgio Tagliacozzo and Hayden V. White. Baltimore: Johns Hopkins University Press, 1969, pp. 39-50.

"The Denial of the Rational." Trans. A. Azodi and U. Hemel. *Man and World*, 16 (1983), 91-103.

"Humanistic Rhetorical Philosophizing: Giovanni Pontano's Theory of the Unity of Poetry, Rhetoric, and History." *Philosophy and Rhetoric*, 17 (1984), 135-55.

"Italian Humanism and Heidegger's Thesis of the End of Philosophy." Trans. John Michael Krois. *Philosophy and Rhetoric*, 13 (Spring 1980), 79-98.

"Marxism, Humanism, and the Problem of Imagination in Vico's Works." Trans. Azizeh Azodi. In *Giambattista Vico's Science of Humanity*. Ed. Giorgio Tagliacozzo and Donald Verene. Baltimore: Johns Hopkins University Press, 1976, pp. 275-94.

"The Originary Quality of the Poetic and Rhetorical Word: Heidegger, Ungaretti, and Neruda." Trans. Lavinia Lorch. *Philosophy and Rhetoric*, 20 (1987), 248-60.

"The Philosophical and Rhetorical Significance of Ovid's *Metamorphoses*." *Philosophy and Rhetoric*, 15 (Fall 1982), 257-61.

"The Priority of Common Sense and Imagination: Vico's Philosophical Relevance Today." Trans. Azizeh Azodi. *Social Research*, 43 (1976), 553-75. Rpt. in *Vico and Contemporary Thought*. Ed. Giorgio Tagliacozzo, Michael Mooney, and Donald P. Verene. Atlantic Highlands, NJ: Humanities, 1979, pp. 163-85.

"Remarks on German Idealism, Humanism, and the Philosophical Function of Rhetoric." Trans. John Michael Krois. *Philosophy and Rhetoric*, 19 (1986), 125-33.

"Response by the Author." Trans. Azizeh Azodi. *Social Research*, 43 (1976), 577-80. Rpt. in *Vico and Contemporary Thought*. Ed. Giorgio Tagliacozzo, Michael Mooney, and Donald P. Verene. Atlantic Highlands, NJ: Humanities, 1979, pp.163-85.

"Rhetoric and Philosophy." Trans. Azizeh Azodi. *Philosophy and Rhetoric*, 9 (Fall 1976), 200-16. Rpt. in *Rhetoric as Philosophy*, chapter 2.

"Vico as Epochal Thinker." Trans. Roberta Piazza. *Differentia*, 1 (Autumn 1986), 73-90.

"Vico, Marx, and Heidegger." Trans. Joseph Vincenzo. In *Vico and Marx: Affinities and Contrasts*. Ed. Giorgio Tagliacozzo. Atlantic Highlands, NJ: Humanities, 1983, pp. 233-50.

"Vico *Versus* Freud: Creativity and the Unconscious." Trans. John Michael Krois. In *Vico: Past and Present*. Ed. Giorgio Tagliacozzo. Atlantic Highlands, NJ: Humanities, 1981.

"Why Rhetoric is Philosophy." Trans. Kiaran O'Malley. *Philosophy and Rhetoric*, 20 (1987), 68-78.

Works About Grassi

Anderson, Wayne C. " 'Perpetual Affirmations, Unexplained': The Rhetoric of Reiteration in Coleridge, Carlyle, and Emerson." *Quarterly Journal of Speech*, 71 (February 1985), 37-51.

Farrell, Thomas B. "Rhetorical Resemblance: Paradoxes of a Practical Art." *Quarterly Journal of Speech*, 72 (February 1986), 1-19.

Krois, John Michael. "Comment on Professor Grassi's Paper" ["Common Sense and Imagination"]. In *Vico and Contemporary Thought*. Ed. Giorgio Tagliacozzo, Michael Mooney, and Donald P. Verene. Atlantic Highlands, NJ: Humanities, 1976, pp. 185-87.

Marassi, Massimo. "Rhetoric and Historicity (An Introduction)." Trans. Kiaran O'Malley. *Philosophy and Rhetoric*, 21 (1988), 245-59.

Veit, Walter. "The Potency of Imagery — the Impotence of Rational Language: Ernesto Grassi's Contribution to Modern Epistemology." *Philosophy and Rhetoric*, 17 (1984), 221-39.

Verene, Donald Phillip. "Philosophy, Argument, and Narration." *Philosophy and Rhetoric*, 22 (1989), 141-44.

Verene, Donald Phillip. "Response to Grassi." *Philosophy and Rhetoric*, 19 (1986), 134-37.

Kenneth Burke

Works by Burke

Books

Attitudes Toward History. 2 vols. New York: New Republic, 1937.

Book of Moments: Poems 1915-1954. Los Altos, CA: Hermes, 1955.

Collected Poems: 1915-1967. Berkeley: University of California Press, 1968.

The Complete White Oxen: Collected Short Fiction of Kenneth Burke. Berkeley: University of California Press, 1968.

Counter-Statement. New York: Harcourt, Brace, 1931.

Dramatism and Development. Barre, MA: Clark University Press, 1972.

A Grammar of Motives. New York: Prentice-Hall, 1945.

Language as Symbolic Action: Essays on Life, Literature, and Method. Berkeley: University of California Press, 1966.

On Symbols and Society. Ed. Joseph R. Gusfield. Chicago: University of Chicago Press, 1989.

Permanence and Change: An Anatomy of Purpose. New York: New Republic, 1935. 3rd ed. Berkeley: University of California Press, 1984.
Perspectives by Incongruity. Ed. Stanley Edgar Hyman and Barbara Karmiller. Bloomington: Indiana University Press, 1964.
The Philosophy of Literary Form: Studies in Symbolic Action. Baton Rouge: Louisiana State University Press, 1941.
A Rhetoric of Motives. New York: Prentice-Hall, 1950.
The Rhetoric of Religion: Studies in Logology. Boston: Beacon, 1961.
The Selected Correspondence of Kenneth Burke and Malcolm Cowley 1915-1981. Ed. Paul Jay. New York: Viking, 1988. (With Malcolm Cowley.)
Terms for Order. Ed. Stanley Edgar Hyman and Barbara Karmiller. Bloomington: Indiana University Press, 1964.
Towards a Better Life Being a Series of Epistles, or Declamations. New York: Harcourt, Brace, 1932.
The White Oxen and Other Stories. New York: Albert & Charles Boni, 1924.

Articles

" 'Act' as Many-in-One." *Location*, 1 (Summer 1964), 94-98.
"Addendum on Bateson." In *Rigor & Imagination: Essays from the Legacy of Gregory Bateson*. Ed. C. Wilder-Mott and John H. Weaklund. New York: Praeger, 1981, pp. 341-46.
"The Allies of Humanism Abroad." In *The Critique of Humanism: A Symposium*. Ed. C. Hartley Grattan. New York: Brewer and Warren, 1930, pp. 169-92.
"Americanism: Patriotism in General, Americanism in Particular, Interspersed with Pauses." *Direction*, 4 (February 1941), 2-3.
"André Gide, Bookman." *Freeman*, 5 (April 26, 1922), 155-57.
"Approaches to Remy de Gourmont." *Dial*, 70 (February 1921), 125-38.
"An *Arion* Questionnaire: 'The Classics and the Man of Letters.' " *Arion*, 3 (Winter 1964), 23-26.
"The Armour of Jules Laforge." *Contact*, 3, [new series] (1920-23), 9-10.
"Art—and the First Rough Draft of Living." *Modern Age*, 8 (Spring 1964), 155-65.
"The Art of Carl Sprinchorn." *Arts*, 2 (December 1921), 158-59.
"As I Was Saying." *Michigan Quarterly Review*, 11 (Winter 1972), 9-27.
"As One Thing Leads to Another." *Recherches anglaises et américaines*, 12 (1979), 13-17.
"Bankers Arise." *Americana, Satire and Humor*, May 1933, p. 4.
"The Brain Beautiful." *Bennington College Bulletin*, 29 (November 1960), 4-7.
"Catharsis—Second View." *Centennial Review*, 5 (Spring 1961), 107-32.
"Character of Our Culture." *Southern Review*, 6 (Spring 1941), 675-94.
"Chicago and Our National Gesture." *Bookman*, 57 (July 1923), 497-501.
"Colloquy: I. The Party Line." *Quarterly Journal of Speech*, 62 (February 1976), 62-68.
"A Comment on 'It Takes Capital to Defeat Dracula.' " *College English*, 49 (February 1987), 221-22.
"Comments." *Western Speech*, 32 (Summer 1968), 176-83.
"Comments on Eighteen Poems by Howard Nemerov." *Sewanee Review*, 60 (January-March 1952), 117-31.

"Communication and the Human Condition." *Communication*, 1 (1974), 135-52.
"Communications." Letter. *Hopkins Review*, 4 (Winter 1951), 77-79.
"Communications." Letter. *Kenyon Review*, 11 (1949), 310-11.
"Communications to P/T." *Pre/Text*, 8 (Spring/Summer 1987), 156.
"Correspondence." Letter. *Sewanee Review*, 73 (January-March 1965), 173-75.
"Correspondence: Munsoniana." *New Republic*, 69 (November 25,1931), 46.
"The Correspondence of Flaubert." *Dial*, 72 (February 1922), 147-55.
"Counterblasts on 'Counter-Statement.'" *New Republic*, 69 (December 9, 1931), 101.
"Dada, Dead or Alive." *Aesthete 1925*, 1 (February 1925), 23-26.
"Dancing with Tears in My Eyes." *Critical Inquiry*, 1 (September 1974), 23-31.
"De Beginnibus." *Bennington College Bulletin*, 31 (November 1962), 4-10.
"Doing and Saying: Thoughts on Myth, Cult, and Archetypes." *Salmagundi*, 15 (Winter 1971), 100-19.
"Dramatic Form—And: Tracking Down Implications." *Tulane Drama Review*, 10 (Summer 1966), 54-63.
"Dramatism." In *International Encyclopedia of the Social Sciences*. Ed. David L. Sills. [New York]: Macmillan/Free, 1968, VII, 445-52. Rpt. with additional discussion by Burke in *Communication: Concepts and Perspectives*. Ed. Lee Thayer. Washington, DC: Spartan, 1967, 327-60.
"Dramatism and Logology." *Communication Quarterly*, 33 (Spring 1985), 89-93.
"Dramatism and Logology." *Times Literary Supplement*, 4, 193 (August 12, 1983), 859.
"Dramatism as Ontology or Epistemology: A Symposium." *Communication Quarterly*, 33 (Winter 1985), 17-33. (With Bernard L. Brock, Parke G. Burgess, and Herbert W. Simons.)
"A 'Dramatistic' View of 'Imitation.'" *Accent*, 12 (Autumn 1952), 229-41.
"A Dramatistic View of the Origins of Language: Part One." *Quarterly Journal of Speech*, 38 (October 1952), 251-64.
"A Dramatistic View of the Origins of Language: Part Two." *Quarterly Journal of Speech*, 38 (December 1952), 446-60.
"A Dramatistic View of the Origins of Language: Part Ill." *Quarterly Journal of Speech*, 39 (February 1953), 79-92.
"An Ecological Proposal." *New Republic*, 161 (December 13, 1969), 30-31.
"Embargo." *Direction*, 2 (November 1939), 2.
"'Ethan Brand': A Preparatory Investigation." *Hopkins Review*, 5 (Winter 1952), 45-65.
"An Exchange on Machiavelli." *New York Review of Books*, 18 (April 6, 1972), 35-36.
"An Eye-Poem for the Ear: (With Prose Introduction, Glosses, and After-Words)." In *Directions in Literary Criticism: Contemporary Approaches to Literature*. Ed. Stanley Weintraub and Philip Young. University Park: Pennsylvania State University Press, 1973, pp. 228-51.
"The Five Master Terms: Their Place in a 'Dramatistic' Grammar of Motives." *View*, 2 (June 1943), 50-52. Enlarged version in *Twentieth Century English*. Ed. William S. Knickerbocker. New York: Philosophical Library, 1946, pp. 272-88.
"For Whom Do You Write?" *New Quarterly*, 1 (Summer 1934), 8.
"Freedom and Authority in the Realm of the Poetic Imagination." In *Freedom and Authority in Our Time: Twelfth Symposium of the Conference on Science, Philosophy and*

Religion. Ed. Lyman Bryson, Louis Finkelstein, R.M. MacIver, and Richard McKeon. New York: Conference on Science, Philosophy, and Religion; dist. Harper, 1953, pp. 365-75.

"A Further View: II." Letter. *Four Quarters* [LaSalle College, Philadelphia], 5 (January 1956), 17.

"Government in the Making." *Direction*, 5 (December 1942), 3-4.

"Human Nature and the Bomb." *University of Chicago Round Table*, No. 622 (February 19, 1950), pp. 1-11. (With Harrison S. Brown, Herbert Blumer, Helen V. McLean, and William F. Ogburn.)

"Ideology and Myth." *Accent*, 7 (Summer 1947), 195-205.

"The Imagery of Killing." *Hudson Review*, 1 (1948), 151-67.

"In Haste." *Pre/Text*, 6 (Fall/Winter 1985), 329-77.

"In New Jersey, My Adopted, and I Hope Adoptive, State." *New Jersey Monthly*, November 1981, pp. 67-68, 98.

"The Institutions of Art in America." *Arts in Society*, 2 (Fall-Winter 1962), 52-60.

"The Interactive Bind." In *Rigor & Imagination: Essays from the Legacy of Gregory Bateson*. Ed. C. Wilder-Mott and John H. Weaklund. New York: Praeger, 1981, pp. 331-40.

"Intuitive or Scientific?" *Nation*, 146 (January 29, 1938), 139-40.

"Kenneth Burke and Malcolm Cowley: A Conversation." *Pre/Text*, 6 (Fall/Winter 1985), 181-2000. (With Malcolm Cowley.)

"Kenneth Burke and Sidney Hook: An Exchange: Is Mr. Hook a Socialist?" *Partisan Review*, 4 (January 1938), 40-44.

"Kinds of Criticism." *Poetry*, 68 (August 1946), 272-82.

"Kinds of Sensibility." In *Paul Rosenfeld: Voyager in the Arts*. Ed. Jerome Mellquist and Lucie Wiese. New York: Creative Age, 1948, pp. 100-05.

"*King Lear*: Its Form and Psychosis." *Shenandoah*, 21 (Autumn 1969), 3-18.

"The Language of Poetry, 'Dramatistically' Considered, Part I." *Chicago Review*, 8 (Fall 1954), 88-102.

"The Language of Poetry, 'Dramatistically' Considered, Part II." *Chicago Review*, 9 (Spring 1955), 40-72.

"Last Words on the Ephebe." *Literary Review* [*New York Evening Post*], 2 (August 26, 1922), 897-98.

"Letter from a Gentile." *Dialectical Anthropology*, 8 (October 1983), 161-71.

"A Letter from Andover." *Kenneth Burke Society Newsletter*, 2 (July 1986), 3-5.

"Linguistic Approach to Problems of Education." In *Modern Philosophies and Education. The Fifty-Fourth Yearbook of the National Society for the Study of Education*. Ed. Nelson B. Henry. Chicago: National Society for the Study of Education; dist. University of Chicago Press, 1955, Part 1, pp. 259-303.

"Literary Criticism: The Minds Behind the Written Word." *Times Literary Supplement*, September 17, 1954, pp. viii, x.

"The Meaning of C.K. Ogden." *New Republic*, 78 (May 1934), 328-31.

"Methodological Repression and/or Strategies of Containment." *Critical Inquiry*, 5 (Winter 1978), 401-16.

"Motion, Action, Words." *Teachers College Record*, 62 (December 1960), 244-49.

"My Approach to Communism." *New Masses*, 10 (March 20, 1934), 16, 18-20.

"Mysticism as a Solution to the Poets' Dilemma: Addendum." In *Spiritual Problems in Contemporary Literature: A Series of Addresses and Discussions*. Ed. Stanley Romaine Hopper. New York: Institute for Religious and Social Studies; dist. Harper, 1952, pp. 108-15.

"Negro's Pattern of Life." *Saturday Review of Literature*, 10 (July 29, 1933), 13-14.

"(Nonsymbolic) Motion/(Symbolic) Action." *Critical Inquiry*, 4 (Summer 1978), 809-38.

"Notes on the Lit'ry Life: (Its Quirks and Solemnities)." In *Proceedings of the American Academy of Arts and Letters and the National Institute of Arts and Letters*. Second Series, No. 2. New York: American Academy of Arts and Letters, 1952, pp. 39-50.

"Notes on Walter Pater." *1924*, 2 (1924), 53-58.

"NRT Non-Resident Term." *Bennington College Bulletin*, 28 (November 1959), 16-17.

"On Catharsis, or Resolution." *Kenyon Review*, 21 (Summer 1959), 337-75.

"On 'Creativity'—A Partial Retraction." In *Introspection: The Artist Looks at Himself*. Ed. Donald E. Hayden. University of Tulsa Monograph Series, No. 12. Tulsa, OK: University of Tulsa, 1971, pp. 63-81.

"On Form." *Hudson Review*, 17 (Spring 1964), 103-09.

"On Literary Form." In *The New Criticism and After*. Ed. Thomas Daniel Young. Charlottesville: University Press of Virginia, 1976, pp. 80-90.

"On Motivation in Yeats." *Southern Review*, 7 (1941-42), 547-61.

"On Stress, Its Seeking." *Bennington Review*, 1 (Summer 1967), 32-49.

"On the First Three Chapters of Genesis." *Daedalus*, 87 (Summer 1958), 37-64.

"Order, Action, and Victimage." In *The Concept of Order*. Ed. Paul G. Kuntz. Seattle: University of Washington Press (for Grinnell College), 1968, pp. 167-90.

"Panel Discussion." In *What is a Poet? Essays from The Eleventh Alabama Symposium on English and American Literature*. Ed. Hank Lazer. Tuscaloosa: University of Alabama Press, 1987, pp. 185-225. (With Gerald Stern, Charles Bernstein, Denise Levertov, David Ignatow, Marjorie Perloff, Helen Vendler, Charles Altieri, Louis Simpson, Hank Lazer, and Gregory Jay.)

"A Philosophy of Drama." *University of Chicago Magazine*, September 1961, pp. 7-8, 20.

"A Plea to Join the Fray and Make It Worth Our While." *Kenneth Burke Society Newsletter*, 1 (October 1984), 1.

"The Poetic Motive." *Hudson Review*, 11 (Spring 1958), 54-63.

"Poetics and Communication." In *Perspectives in Education, Religion and the Arts*. Ed. Howard E. Kiefer and Milton K. Munitz. Albany: State University of New York Press, 1970, pp. 401-18.

"Poetry and Communication." In *Contemporary Philosophical Thought: Vol. 3: Perspectives in Education, Religion, and the Arts*. Ed. Howard E. Kiefer and Milton K. Munitz. Albany: State University of New York Press, 1970, pp. 401-18.

"Poetry as Symbolic Action." In *What is a Poet? Essays from The Eleventh Alabama Symposium on English and American Literature*. Ed. Hank Lazer. Tuscaloosa: University of Alabama Press, 1987, pp. 157-73.

"Policy Made Personal: Whitman's Verse and Prose-Salient Traits." In *Leaves of Grass One Hundred Years After*. Ed. Milton Hindus. Stanford: Stanford University Press, 1955, pp. 74-108.

"The Position of the Progressive: II. Boring from Within." *New Republic*, 65 (February 4, 1931), 326-29.

"Post Poesque Derivation of a Terministic Cluster." *Critical Inquiry*, 4 (Winter 1977), 215-20.

"Postscript." In *Criticism and Social Change*. By Frank Lentricchia. Chicago: University of Chicago Press, 1985, pp. 165-66. (Essay appears in paperback edition only.)

"Progress: Promise and Problems." *Nation*, 184 (April 1957), 322-24.

"A (Psychological) Fable, with a (Logological) Moral." *American Imago*, 35 (Spring-Summer 1978), 203-07.

"Questions and Answers About the Pentad." *College Composition and Communication*, 29 (December 1978), 330-35.

"Questions for Critics." *Direction*, 2 (May-June 1939), 12-13.

"The Reader Critic." Letter. *Little Review*, 9 (Winter 1922), 45.

"Reading While You Run: An Exercise in Translation from English into English." *New Republic*, 93 (November 17,1937), 36-37.

"Realisms, Occidental Style." In *Asian and Western Writers in Dialogue: New Cultural Identities*. Ed. Guy Amirthanayagam. London: Macmillan, 1982, pp. 26-47.

"Recipe for Prosperity: 'Borrow. Buy. Waste. Want.'" *Nation*, 183 (September 8, 1956), 191-93.

"Redefinitions." *New Republic*, 67 (July 29, 1931), 286-88.

"Redefinitions: 11." *New Republic*, 68 (August 26,1931), 46-47.

"Redefinitions: III." *New Republic*, 68 (September 2, 1931), 74-75.

"Reflections on the Fate of the Union: Kennedy and After." *New York Review of Books*, 1 (December 26, 1963), 10-11.

"The Relation Between Literature and Science." In *The Writer in a Changing World*. Ed. Henry Hart. New York: Equinox Cooperative, 1937, pp. 158-71.

"Responsibilities of National Greatness." *Nation*, 205 (July 17, 1967), 46-50.

"Revolutionary Symbolism in America." In *American Writers' Congress*. Ed. Henry Hart. New York: International, 1935, pp. 87-94.

"The Rhetorical Situation." In *Communication: Ethical and Moral Issues*. Ed. Lee Thayer. New York: Gordon and Breach Science, 1973, pp. 263-75.

"Rhetoric — Old and New." *Journal of General Education*, 5 (April 1951), 202-09.

"Rhetoric, Poetics, and Philosophy." In *Rhetoric, Philosophy, and Literature: An Exploration*. Ed. Don M. Burks. West Lafayette, IN: Purdue University Press, 1978, pp. 15-33.

"The Seven Offices." *Diogenes*, 21 (Spring 1958), 68-84.

"The Study of Symbolic Action." *Chimera*, 1 (Spring 1942), 7-16.

"Surrealism." In *New Directions in Prose and Poetry*. Ed. James Laughlin. Norfolk, CT: New Directions, 1940, pp. 563-79.

"Symbol and Association." *Hudson Review*, 9 (1956), 212-25.

"Symbolic War." *Southern Review*, 2 (1936-37), 134-47.

"Symbolism as a Realistic Mode: 'De-Psychologizing' Logologized." *Psychocultural Review*, Winter 1979, pp. 25-37.

"The Tactics of Motivation." *Chimera*, 1 (Spring 1943), 21-33.

"The Tactics of Motivation." *Chimera*, 2 (Summer 1943), 37-53.

"Thanatopsis for Critics: A Brief Thesaurus of Deaths and Dyings." *Essays in Criticism*, 2 (October 1952), 369-75.

"Theology and Logology." *Kenyon Review*, 1 [new series] (Winter 1979), 151-85.

"A Theory of Terminology." In *Interpretation: The Poetry of Meaning*. Ed. Stanley Romaine Hopper and David L. Miller. New York: Harcourt, Brace & World, 1967, pp. 83-102.

"Thoughts on the Poet's Corner." In *Poetry Therapy: The Use of Poetry in the Treatment of Emotional Disorders*. Ed. Jack J. Leedy. Philadelphia: J.B. Lippincott, 1969, pp. 104-10.

"The Threat of the Trivial." *Nation*, 182 (April 21, 1956), 333.

"Three Definitions." *Kenyon Review*, 13 (Spring 1951), 173-92.

"Three Frenchmen's Churches." *New Republic*, 63 (1930), 10-14.

"Toward a New Romanticism: Proportion is Better than Efficiency." *Films in Review*, 1 (December 1950), 25-27.

"Towards a Post-Kantian Verbal Music." *Kenyon Review*, 20 (Autumn 1958), 529-46.

"Towards a Total Conformity: A Metaphysical Fantasy." *Literary Review*, 2 (1957-58), 203-07.

"Towards Hellhaven: Three Stages of a Vision." *Sewanee Review*, 79 (Winter 1971), 11-25.

"Towards Looking Back." *Journal of General Education*, 28 (Fall 1976), 167-89.

"The Unburned Bridges of Poetics, or, How Keep Poetry Pure?" *Centennial Review*, 8 (Fall 1964), 391-97.

"Variations on 'Providence.'" *Notre Dame English Journal*, 13 (Summer 1981), 155-83.

"Vegetal Radicalism of Theodore Roethke." *Sewanee Review*, 58 (Winter 1950), 68-108.

"War and Cultural Life." *American Journal of Sociology*, 48 (1942-43), 404-10.

"Waste – The Future of Prosperity." *New Republic*, 63 (July 1930), 228-31.

"What is Americanism? Symposium on Marxism and the American Tradition." *Partisan Review and Anvil*, 3 (April 1936), 9-11.

"What's Good About a Bad First Job." *Mademoiselle*, 53 (June 1961), 70-72, 111.

"What to Do till the Doctor Comes: Thoughts on Conscription." *Direction*, 3 (November 1940), 7, 24.

"When 'Now' Became 'Then.'" *Direction*, 5 (February-March 1942), 5.

"Where Are We Now?" *Direction*, 4 (December 1941), 3-5.

"Why Satire, with a Plan for Writing One." *Michigan Quarterly Review*, 13 (Fall 1974), 307-37.

"William Carlos Williams: A Critical Appreciation." In *William Carlos Williams*. Ed. Charles Angoff. Cranbury, NJ: Associated University Presses, 1974, pp. 15-19.

"William Carlos Williams, The Methods of." *Dial*, 82 (February 1927), 94-98.

"Words Anent Logology." In *Perspectives in Literary Criticism*. Ed. Joseph Strelka. Yearbook of Comparative Criticism, Vol. I. University Park: Pennsylvania State University Press, 1968, 72-82.

"The Writers' Congress." *Nation*, 140 (May 15, 1935), 571.

"Your Letters." Letter. *Direction*, 3 (November 1940), 21.

Poetry and Fiction

"Adam's Song, and Mine." *Others*, 2 (March 1916), 184.

"Adam's Song, and Mine" [not identical to above]. *Sansculotte* [Ohio State University],

1 (April 1917), 10.

"Anthology." *Little Review*, Spring-Summer 1926, p. 33.

"Bathos, Youth, and the Antithetical 'Rather.'" *Sansculotte* [Ohio State University], 1 (February 1917), 7.

"Belated Entrance." *Recherches anglaises et américaines*, 12 (1979), 9.

"But for These Lucky Accidents." *Communication,* 1 (1974), 196.

"Case History." *Nation*, 183 (July 7,1956), 21.

"A Count-In." *Poetry*, 113 (October 1968), 29-30.

"A Critical Load, Beyond That Door; or, Before the Ultimate Confrontation; or, When Thinking of Deconstructionist Structuralists; or, A Hermeneutic Fantasy." *Critical Inquiry*, 5 (Autumn 1978), 199-200.

"Eye-Crossing—From Brooklyn to Manhattan." *Nation*, 208 (June 2, 1969), 700-04.

"Her Will." *New Republic*, 161 (July 5, 1969), 28.

"Hokku." *Sansculotte* [Ohio State University], 1 (January 1917), 4.

"Hymn of Hope." *Slate*, 1 (April 1917), 80.

"Idylls." *Smart Set*, 57 (November 1918), 34.

"In the Margin." *New Republic*, 101 (December 20, 1939), 257.

"Invocation for a Convocation." *Kenyon Review*, 1 [new series] (Winter 1979), 3-4.

"Invocations." *Sansculotte* [Ohio State University], 1 (January 1917), 11.

"A Juxtaposition." *Poetry*, 113 (October 1968), 31.

"La Baudelairienne." *Sansculotte* [Ohio State University], 1 (January 1917), 9.

"Modernism So Far is but Peanuts." *New Republic*, 161 (November 8, 1969), 30.

"Nocturne." *Sansculotte* [Ohio State University], 1 (April 1917), 9.

"The Oftener Trinity." *Sansculotte* [Ohio State University], 1 (February 1917), 7.

"Order, Action, and Victimage." In *The Concept of Order*. Ed. Paul G. Kuntz. Seattle: University of Washington Press (for Grinnell College), 1968, pp. 167-90.

"Out of Backwards Sidewise Towards Fromwards (An Attitudinizing Winter-Solstitially)." *Kenyon Review*, 2 [new series] (Summer 1980), 92-93.

"Parabolic Tale, with Invocation." *Sansculotte* [Ohio State University], 1 (January 1917), 8.

"Poem." In *The Legacy of Kenneth Burke*. Ed. Herbert W. Simons and Trevor Melia. Madison: University of Wisconsin Press, 1989, p. 263.

"Poetry and Communication." In *Contemporary Philosophical Thought*, Vol. 3: *Perspectives in Education, Religion, and the Arts*. Ed. Howard E. Kiefer and Milton K. Munitz. Albany: State University of New York Press, 1970, 401-18.

"Post-Roethkean Translations." *Hopkins Review*, 6 (Winter 1953), 6-7.

"Revolt." *Sansculotte* [Ohio State University], 1 (January 1917), [3].

"Spring Song." *Slate*, 1 (January 1917), 11.

"Two Poems of Abandonment." *New Republic*, May 30, 1970, p. 27.

"Two Portraits." *S₄N*, 4 (December 1922), n.p.

Works About Burke

Aaron, Daniel, mod. "Thirty Years Later: Memories of the First American Writers' Congress." *American Scholar*, 35 (Summer 1966), 495-516. (With Malcolm Cowley,

Granville Hicks, William Phillips, and Kenneth Burke.)

Aaron, Daniel. *Writers on the Left*. 1961; rpt. New York: Avon, 1965.

Abbott, Don. "Marxist Influences on the Rhetorical Theory of Kenneth Burke." *Philosophy and Rhetoric*, 7 (Fall 1974), 217-33.

Abdulla, Adnan K. *Catharsis in Literature*. Bloomington: Indiana University Press, 1985.

Adams, Robert M. *Strains of Discord: Studies in Literary Openness*. Ithaca, NY: Cornell University Press, 1958.

Aeschbacher, Jill. "Kenneth Burke, Samuel Beckett, and Form." *Today's Speech*, 21 (Summer 1973), 43-47.

Ambrester, Marcus L., and Glynis Holm Strause. *A Rhetoric of Interpersonal Communication*. Prospect Heights, IL: Waveland, 1984.

Ambrester, Roy. "Identification Within: Kenneth Burke's View of the Unconscious." *Philosophy and Rhetoric*, 7 (Fall 1974), 205-16.

"Announcement." *Dial*, 86 (January 1929), 90.

Appel, Edward C. "The Perfected Drama of Reverend Jerry Falwell." *Communication Quarterly*, 35 (Winter 1987), 26-38.

Auden, W.H. "A Grammar of Assent." *New Republic*, 105 (July 14,1941), 59.

Babcock, C. Merton. "A Dynamic Theory of Communications." Journal of Communication, 2 (May 1952), 64-68.

Baer, Donald M. "A Comment on Skinner as Boy and on Burke as S^{Δ} ." *Behaviorism*, 4 (Fall 1976), 273-77.

Baird, A. Craig. *Rhetoric: A Philosophical Inquiry*. New York: Ronald, 1965.

Baker, Lewis. "Little Kenny Has His Fits." *Pre/Text*, 6 (Fall/Winter 1985), 379-80.

Baker, Lewis. "Some Manuscript Collections Containing Kenneth Burke Materials." *Pre/Text*, 6 (Fall/Winter 1985), 307-11.

Baker, Scott. "Response to the Film, *Platoon*: An Analysis of the Vietnam Veteran as Journalist-Critic and 'Priest.'" *Southern Communication Journal*, 55 (Winter 1990), 123-43.

Baxter, Gerald D., and Pat M. Taylor. "Burke's Theory of Consubstantiality and Whitehead's Concept of Concrescence." *Communication Monographs*, 45 (June 1978), 173-80.

Bellairs, John, Philip Waldron, and Manfred Mackenzie. "Critical Exchange: Variations on a Vase." *Southern Review* [Adelaide, Australia], 1 (1965), 58-73.

Benne, Kenneth D. "Education for Tragedy: I." *Educational Theory*, 1 (November 1951), 199-210, 217.

Benne, Kenneth D. "Education for Tragedy: II." *Educational Theory*, 1 (December 1951), 274-83.

Bennett, William. "Kenneth Burke: A Philosophy in Defense of Un-reason." In *Philosophers on Rhetoric: Traditional and Emerging Views*. Ed. Donald G. Douglas. Skokie, IL: National Textbook, 1973, pp. 243-51.

Bennett, W. Lance. "Political Scenarios and the Nature of Politics." *Philosophy and Rhetoric*, 8 (Winter 1975), 23-42.

Benoit, William L. "Systems of Explanation: Aristotle and Burke on 'Cause.'" *Rhetoric Society Quarterly*, 13 (Winter 1983), 41-58.

Berlin, Isaiah. "An Exchange on Machiavelli: Isaiah Berlin Replies." *New York Review of Books*, 18 (April 6, 1972), 36-37.

Berthold, Carol A. "Kenneth Burke's Cluster-Agon Method: Its Development and an Application." *Central States Speech Journal*, 27 (Winter 1976), 302-09.

Bewley, Marius. "Kenneth Burke as Literary Critic." *Scrutiny*, 15 (December 1948), 254-77.

Biesecker, Barbara. "Kenneth Burke's *Grammar of Motives:* Speculations on the Politics of Interpretation." In *Rhetoric and Ideology: Compositions and Criticisms of Power*. Ed. Charles W. Kneupper. Arlington, TX: Rhetoric Society of America, 1989, pp. 82-89.

Birdsell, David S. "Ronald Reagan on Lebanon and Grenada: Flexibility and Interpretation in the Application of Kenneth Burke's Pentad." *Quarterly Journal of Speech*, 73 (August 1987), 267-79.

Blackmur, R.P. *The Double Agent: Essays in Craft and Elucidation*. New York: Arrow, 1935.

Blackmur, R.P. *Language as Gesture: Essays in Poetry*. 1935; rpt. New York: Harcourt, Brace, 1952.

Blackmur, R.P. *The Lion and the Honeycomb: Essays in Solicitude and Critique*. 1935; rpt. New York: Harcourt, Brace, 1955.

Blankenship, Jane. *Public Speaking: A Rhetorical Perspective*. 2nd ed. Englewood Cliffs, NJ: Prentice-Hall, 1972.

Blankenship, Jane. *A Sense of Style: An Introduction to Style for the Public Speaker*. Belmont, CA: Dickenson, 1968.

Blankenship, Jane, and Barbara Sweeney. "The 'Energy' of Form." *Central States Speech Journal*, 31 (Fall 1980), 172-83.

Blankenship, Jane, Edwin Murphy, and Marie Rosenwasser. "Pivotal Terms in the Early Works of Kenneth Burke." *Philosophy and Rhetoric*, 7 (Winter 1974), 1-24.

Blankenship, Jane, Marlene G. Fine, and Leslie K. Davis. "The 1980 Republican Primary Debates: The Transformation of Actor to Scene." *Quarterly Journal of Speech*, 69 (February 1983), 25-36.

Blankenship, Jane, and Janette Kenner Muir. "On Imagining the Future: The Secular Search for 'Piety.'" *Communication Quarterly*, 35 (Winter 1987), 1-12.

Blau, Herbert. "Kenneth Burke: Tradition and the Individual Critic." *American Quarterly*, 6 (1954), 323-36.

Bloom, Harold. *The Breaking of the Vessels*. Chicago: University of Chicago Press, 1982.

Bloom, Harold. "A Tribute to Kenneth Burke." *Book World*, May 31, 1981, p. 4.

Booth, Wayne C. *Critical Understanding: The Powers and Limits of Pluralism*. Chicago: University of Chicago Press, 1979.

Booth, Wayne C. "Kenneth Burke's Way of Knowing." *Critical Inquiry*, 1 (September 1974), 1-22.

Bostdorff, Denise M. "Making Light of James Watt: A Burkean Approach to the Form and Attitude of Political Cartoons." *Quarterly Journal of Speech*, 73 (February 1987), 43-59.

Bostdorff, Denise M., and Phillip K. Tompkins. "Musical Form and Rhetorical Form:

Kenneth Burke's *Dial* Reviews as Counterpart to *Counter-Statement.*" *Pre/Text*, 6 (Fall/Winter 1985), 235-52.

Brissett, Dennis, and Charles Edgley, eds. *Life as Theatre: A Dramaturgical Sourcebook.* Chicago: Aldine, 1975.

Brock, Bernard L. "Epistemology and Ontology in Kenneth Burke's Dramatism." *Communication Quarterly*, 33 (Spring 1985), 94-104.

Brock, Bernard. "Political Speaking: A Burkeian Approach." In *Critical Responses to Kenneth Burke: 1924-1966.* Ed. William H. Rueckert. Minneapolis: University of Minnesota Press, 1969, pp. 444-55.

Brock, Bernard. "Rhetorical Criticism: A Burkeian Approach." In *Methods of Rhetorical Criticism.* 2nd ed. Ed. Robert Scott and Bernard Brock. Detroit: Wayne State University Press, 1980, pp. 348-60.

Brock, Bernard L. "The Role of Paradox and Metaphor in Kenneth Burke's Dramatism." *Communication Quarterly*, 33 (Winter 1985), 18-22.

Brown, Janet. "Kenneth Burke and *The Mod Donna*: The Dramatistic Method Applied to Feminist Criticism." *Central States Speech Journal*, 29 (Summer 1978), 138-46.

Brown, Merle E. *Kenneth Burke.* University of Minnesota Pamphlets on American Writers, No. 75. Minneapolis: University of Minnesota Press, 1969.

Brummett, Barry. "Burkean Comedy and Tragedy, Illustrated in Reactions to the Arrest of John DeLorean." *Central States Speech Journal*, 35 (Winter 1984), 217-27.

Brummett, Barry. "Burkean Scapegoating, Mortification, and Transcendence in Presidential Campaign Rhetoric." *Central States Speech Journal*, 32 (Winter 1981), 254-64.

Brummett, Barry. "Burkean Transcendence and Ultimate Terms in Rhetoric by and about James Watt." *Central States Speech Journal*, 33 (Winter 1982), 547-56.

Brummett, Barry. "Burke's Representative Anecdote as a Method in Media Criticism." *Critical Studies in Mass Communication*, 1 (June 1984), 161-76.

Brummett, Barry. "Electric Literature as Equipment for Living: Haunted House Films." *Critical Studies in Mass Communication*, 2 (September 1985), 247-61.

Brummett, Barry. "Gastronomic Reference, Synecdoche, and Political Images." *Quarterly Journal of Speech*, 67 (May 1981), 138-45.

Brummett, Barry. "The Homology Hypothesis: Pornography on the VCR." *Critical Studies in Mass Communication*, 5 (September 1988), 202-16.

Brummett, Barry. "A Pentadic Analysis of Ideologies in Two Gay Rights Controversies." *Central States Speech Journal*, 30 (Fall 1979), 250-61.

Brummett, Barry. "Presidential Substance: The Address of August 15, 1973." *Western Speech Communication*, 39 (Fall 1975), 249-59.

Brummett, Barry. "The Representative Anecdote as a Burkean Method, Applied to Evangelical Rhetoric." *Southern Speech Communication Journal*, 50 (Fall 1984), 1-23.

Brummett, Barry. "Symbolic Form, Burkean Scapegoating, and Rhetorical Exigency in Alioto's Response to the 'Zebra' Murders." *Western Journal of Speech Communication*, 44 (Winter 1980), 64-73.

Burgess, Parke G. "The Dialectic of Substance: Rhetoric vs Poetry." *Communication Quarterly*, 33 (Spring 1985), 105-12.

Burgess, Parke G. "The Forum: Murder Will Out—But as Rhetoric?" *Quarterly Journal of Speech*, 60 (April 1974), 225-31.

"Burke, Kenneth (Duva)." *New Encyclopaedia Britannica*. Chicago: Encyclopaedia Britannica, 1986, II, 653.

Burkholder, Thomas R. "Kansas Populism, Woman Suffrage, and the Agrarian Myth: A Case Study in the Limits of Mythic Transcendence." *Communication Studies*, 40 (Winter 1989), 292-307.

Burks, Don M. "Dramatic Irony, Collaboration, and Kenneth Burke's Theory of Form." *Pre/Text*, 6 (Fall/Winter 1985), 255-73.

Burks, Don [M.] "KB at Home" (photographs). *Pre/Text*, 6 (Fall/Winter 1985), 293-95.

Burks, Virginia. "Sculptured Bust of KB" (photographs). *Pre/Text*, 6 (Fall/Winter 1985), 296-303.

Byker, Donald, and Loren J. Anderson. *Communication as Identification: An Introductory View*. New York: Harper & Row, 1975.

Cain, William E. *The Crisis in Criticism: Theory, Literature, and Reform in English Studies*. Baltimore: Johns Hopkins University Press, 1984.

Campbell, Finley C. "Voices of Thunder, Voices of Rage: A Symbolic Analysis of a Selection from Malcolm X's Speech, 'Message to the Grass Roots.'" *Speech Teacher*, 19 (March 1970), 101-10.

Carlson, A. Cheree. "Gandhi and the Comic Frame: 'Ad Bellum Purificandum.'" *Quarterly Journal of Speech*, 72 (November 1986), 446-55.

Carlson, A. Cheree. "Limitations on the Comic Frame: Some Witty American Women of the Nineteenth Century." *Quarterly Journal of Speech*, 74 (August 1988), 310-22.

Carlson, A. Cheree. "Narrative as the Philosopher's Stone: How Russell H. Conwell Changed Lead into Diamonds." *Western Journal of Speech Communication*, 53 (Fall 1989), 342-55.

Carlson, A. Cheree, and John E. Hocking. "Strategies of Redemption at the Vietnam Veterans' Memorial." *Western Journal of Speech Communication*, 52 (Summer 1988), 203-15.

Carpenter, Ronald H. "A Stylistic Basis of Burkeian Identification." *Today's Speech*, 20 (Winter 1972), 19-24.

Carrier, James G. "Knowledge, Meaning, and Social Inequality in Kenneth Burke." *American Journal of Sociology*, 88 (July 1982), 43-61.

Carrier, James G. "Misrecognition and Knowledge." *Inquiry*, 22 (August 1979), 321-42.

Cathcart, Robert. *Post Communication: Critical Analysis and Evaluation*. Indianapolis: Bobbs-Merrill, 1966.

Chapel, Gage William. "Television Criticism: A Rhetorical Perspective." *Western Speech Communication*, 39 (Spring 1975), 81-91.

Charland, Maurice. "Constitutive Rhetoric: The Case of the *Peuple Québécois*." *Quarterly Journal of Speech*, 73 (May 1987), 133-50.

Chase, Richard. "Rhetoric of Rhetoric." In *The New Partisan Reader, 1945-1953*. Ed. William Phillips and Philip Rahv. New York: Harcourt, Brace, 1953, pp. 590-93.

Cheney, George. "The Rhetoric of Identification and the Study of Organizational Communication." *Quarterly Journal of Speech*, 69 (May 1983), 143-58.

Cheney, George, and Phillip K. Tompkins. "Coming to Terms with Organizational Identification and Commitment." *Central States Speech Journal*, 38 (Spring 1987), 1-15.

Chesebro, James W. "A Construct for Assessing Ethics in Communication." *Central States Speech Journal*, 20 (Summer 1969), 104-14.

Chesebro, James W. "Epistemology and Ontology as Dialectical Modes in the Writings of Kenneth Burke." *Communication Quarterly*, 36 (Summer 1988), 175-91.

Chesebro, James W., Davis A. Foulger, Jay E. Nachman, and Andrew Yannelli. "Popular Music as a Mode of Communication, 1955-1982." *Critical Studies in Mass Communication*, 2 (June 1985), 115-35.

Chesebro, James W., and Caroline D. Hamsher. "Rhetorical Criticism: A Message-Centered Approach." *Speech Teacher*, 22 (November 1973), 282-90.

Clark, Robert D. "Lessons from the Literary Critics." *Western Speech*, 21 (Spring 1957), 83-89.

Coe, Richard M. *Form and Substance: An Advanced Rhetoric*. New York: John Wiley, 1981.

Coe, Richard M. "It Takes Capital to Defeat Dracula: A New Rhetorical Essay." *College English*, 48 (March 1986), 231-42.

Coe, Richard M. "Richard M. Coe Responds." *College English*, 49 (February 1987), 222-23.

Combs, James E. *Dimensions of Political Drama*. Santa Monica: Goodyear, 1980.

Combs, James E., and Michael W. Mansfield. *Drama in Life: The Uses of Communication in Society*. New York: Hastings, 1976.

Comprone, Joseph J. "Burke's Dramatism as a Means of Using Literature to Teach Composition." *Rhetoric Society Quarterly*, 9 (Summer 1979), 142-55.

Comprone, Joseph [J.]. "Kenneth Burke and the Teaching of Writing." *College Composition and Communication*, 29 (December 1978), 336-40.

Condit, Celeste Michelle, and J. Ann Selzer. "The Rhetoric of Objectivity in the Newspaper Coverage of a Murder Trial." *Critical Studies in Mass Communication*, 2 (September 1985), 197-216.

Condon, John C., Jr. *Interpersonal Communication*. New York: Macmillan, 1977.

Conley, Thomas M. *Rhetoric in the European Tradition*. New York: Longman, 1990.

Conrad, Charles. "Agon and Rhetorical Form: The Essence of 'Old Feminist' Rhetoric." *Central States Speech Journal*, 32 (Spring 1981), 45-53.

Corcoran, Farrel. "The Bear in the Back Yard: Myth, Ideology, and Victimage Ritual in Soviet Funerals." *Communication Monographs*, 50 (December 1983), 305-20.

"Counter-Gridlock: An Interview with Kenneth Burke." *All Area*, 2 (1983), 4-32.

Cowley, Malcolm. "A Critic's First Principle." *New Republic*, 129 (September 14, 1953), 16-17.

Cowley, Malcolm. *Exile's Return: A Literary Odyssey of the 1920's*. New York: Viking, 1951.

Cowley, Malcolm. "Prolegomena to Kenneth Burke." *New Republic*, 72 (June 5, 1950), 18-19.

Crable, Richard E. "Ethical Codes, Accountability, and Argumentation." *Quarterly Journal of Speech*, 64 (February 1978), 23-32.

Crable, Richard E., and John J. Makay. "Kenneth Burke's Concept of Motives in Rhetorical Theory." *Today's Speech*, 20 (Winter 1972), 11-18.

Crable, Richard E., and Steven L. Vibbert. "Argumentative Stance and Political Faith Healing: 'The Dream Will Come True.'" *Quarterly Journal of Speech*, 69 (August 1983), 290-301.

Cranston, Maurice. *The Mask of Politics and Other Essays*. London: Allen Lane, 1973.

"Critic, Poet Kenneth Burke, 84 Will Receive Literature Medal." *Denver Post*, April 20, 1981, p. 32.

Crocker, J. Christopher. "The Social Functions of Rhetorical Forms." In *The Social Use of Metaphor: Essays on the Anthropology of Rhetoric*. Ed. J. David Sapir and J. Christopher Crocker. Philadelphia: University of Pennsylvania Press, 1977, pp. 33-66.

Crowell, Laura. "Three Sheers for Kenneth Burke." *Quarterly Journal of Speech*, 63 (April 1977), 150-67.

Day, Dennis [G.] "The Forum: Kenneth Burke and Identification — A Reply." *Quarterly Journal of Speech*, 47 (December 1961), 415-16.

Day, Dennis G. "Persuasion and the Concept of Identification." *Quarterly Journal of Speech*, 46 (October 1960), 270-73.

De Mott, Benjamin. "The Little Red Discount House." *Hudson Review*, 15 (Winter 1962/63), 551-64.

Desilet, Gregory. "Nietzsche Contra Burke: The Melodrama in Dramatism." *Quarterly Journal of Speech*, 75 (February 1989), 65-83.

Dickey, James. *Babel to Byzantium: Poets & Poetry Now*. New York: Farrar, Straus, and Giroux, 1968.

Donoghue, Denis. *Ferocious Alphabets*. New York: Columbia University Press, 1984.

Duerden, Richard Y. "Kenneth Burke's Systemless System: Using Pepper to Pigeonhole an Elusive Thinker." *Journal of Mind and Behavior*, 3 (Autumn 1982), 323-36.

Duffey, Bernard I. "Reality as Language: Kenneth Burke's Theory of Poetry." *Western Review*, 12 (Spring 1948), 132-45.

Duncan, Hugh D[alziel]. *Communication and Social Order*. New York: Bedminster, 1962.

Duncan, Hugh D[alziel]. "Introduction." In *Permanence and Change: An Anatomy of Purpose*. By Kenneth Burke. Indianapolis: Bobbs-Merrill, 1965, pp. xiii-xliv.

Duncan, Hugh Dalziel. *Language and Literature in Society*. Chicago: University of Chicago Press, 1953.

Duncan, Hugh D[alziel]. "Literature as Equipment for Action: Burke's Dramatistic Conception." In *The Sociology of Art and Literature: A Reader*. Ed. Milton C. Albrecht, James H. Barnett, and Mason Griff. New York: Praeger, 1970, pp.713-23.

Duncan, Hugh D[alziel]. "Sociology of Art, Literature and Music: Social Contexts of Symbolic Experience." In *Modern Sociological Theory*. Ed. Howard Becker and Alvin Boskoff. New York: Holt, Rinehart and Winston, 1957, pp. 482-97.

Duncan, Hugh Dalziel. "The Symbolic Act: Basic Propositions on the Relationship Between Symbols and Society — A Theory that How We Communicate Determines How We Relate as Human Beings." In *Communication: Theory and Research*. Ed. Lee Thayer. Springfield, IL: Charles C. Thomas, 1967, pp. 194-227.

Duncan, Hugh D[alziel]. *Symbols and Social Theory*. New York: Oxford University Press, 1969.

Duncan, Hugh D[alziel]. *Symbols in Society*. New York: Oxford University Press, 1968.

Durham, Weldon. "Kenneth Burke's Concept of Substance." *Quarterly Journal of Speech*, 66 (December 1980), 351-64.
Edelman, Murray. *The Symbolic Uses of Politics*. Urbana: University of Illinois Press, 1964.
Elton, William. *A Guide to the New Criticism*. Chicago: Modern Poetry Association, n.d.
Enholm, Donald K. "Rhetoric as an Instrument for Understanding and Improving Human Relations." *Southern Speech Communication Journal*, 41 (Spring 1976), 223-36.
Ericson, Jon M. "Evaluative and Formulative Functions in Speech Criticism. *Western Speech*, 32 (Summer 1968), 173-76.
Feehan, Michael. "Kenneth Burke's Discovery of Dramatism." *Quarterly Journal of Speech*, 65 (December 1979), 405-11.
Feehan, Michael. "Oscillation as Assimilation: Burke's Latest Self-Revisions." *Pre/Text*, 6 (Fall/Winter 1985), 319-27.
Feehan, Michael. "The Role of 'Attitudes' in Dramatism." In *Visions of Rhetoric: History, Theory and Criticism*. Ed. Charles W. Kneupper. Arlington, TX: Rhetoric Society of America, 1987, pp. 68-76.
Feehan, Michael. "3 Days and 3 Terms with KB." *Pre/Text*, 6 (Fall/Winter 1985), 143-61.
Fergusson, Francis. *The Idea of a Theater*. New York: Doubleday Anchor, 1949.
Fiedelson, Charles, Jr. *Symbolism and American Literature*. Chicago: University of Chicago Press, 1953.
Fiordo, Richard. "Kenneth Burke's Semiotic." *Semiotica*, 23 (1978), 53-75.
Fisher, Jeanne Y. "A Burkean Analysis of the Rhetorical Dimensions of a Multiple Murder and Suicide." *Quarterly Journal of Speech*, 60 (April 1974), 175-89.
Fisher, Jeanne Y. "The Forum: Rhetoric as More than Just a Well Man Speaking: A Rejoinder." *Quarterly Journal of Speech*, 60 (April 1974), 231-34.
Fisher, Walter R. "The Importance of Style in Systems of Rhetoric." *Southern Speech Journal*, 27 (Spring 1962), 173-82.
Fisher, Walter R., and Wayne Brockriede. "Kenneth Burke's Realism." *Central States Speech Journal*, 35 (Spring 1984), 35-42.
Fogarty, Daniel. *Roots for a New Rhetoric*. New York: Bureau of Publications, Teachers College, Columbia University, 1959.
Ford, Newell F. "Kenneth Burke and Robert Penn Warren: Criticism by Obsessive Metaphor." *Journal of English and Germanic Philology*, 53 (1954), 172-77.
Foss, Karen A. "Celluloid Rhetoric: The Use of Documentary Film to Teach Rhetorical Theory." *Communication Education*, 32 (January 1983), 51-61.
Foss, Karen A. "John Lennon and the Advisory Function of Eulogies." *Central States Speech Journal*, 34 (Fall 1983), 187-94.
Foss, Karen A. "Singing the Rhythm Blues: An Argumentative Analysis of the Birth-Control Debate in the Catholic Church." *Western Journal of Speech Communication*, 47 (Winter 1983), 29-44.
Foss, Sonja K. "Constituted by Agency: The Discourse and Practice of Rhetorical Criticism." In *Speech Communication: Essays to Commemorate the 75th Anniversary of The Speech Communication Association*. Ed. Gerald M. Phillips and Julia T. Wood. Carbondale: Southern Illinois University Press, 1989, pp. 33-51.
Foss, Sonja K. "Feminism Confronts Catholicism: A Study of the Use of Perspective by Incongruity." *Women's Studies in Communication*, 3 (Summer 1979), 7-15.

Foss, Sonja K. "Retooling an Image: Chrysler Corporation's Rhetoric of Redemption." *Western Journal of Speech Communication*, 48 (Winter 1984), 75-91.

Foss, Sonja K. "Rhetoric and the Visual Image: A Resource Unit." *Communication Education*, 31 (January 1982), 55-66.

Fraiberg, Louis. *Psychoanalysis & American Literary Criticism*. Detroit: Wayne State University Press, 1960.

Frank, Armin Paul. *Kenneth Burke*. New York: Twayne, 1969.

Frank, Armin Paul. "Notes on the Reception of Kenneth Burke in Europe." In *Critical Responses to Kenneth Burke: 1924-1966*. Ed. William H. Rueckert. Minneapolis: University of Minnesota Press, 1969, pp. 424-43.

Frank, Armin Paul, and Mechthild Frank. "The Writings of Kenneth Burke." In *Critical Responses to Kenneth Burke: 1924-1966*. Ed. William H. Rueckert. Minneapolis: University of Minnesota Press, 1969, pp. 495-512.

Fry, Virginia H. "A Juxtaposition of Two Abductions for Studying Communication and Culture." *American Journal of Semiotics*, 5 (1987), 81-93.

Gabin, Rosalind J. "Entitling Kenneth Burke." *Rhetoric Review*, 5 (January 1987), 196-210.

Gaines, Robert N. "Identification and Redemption in Lysias' *Against Eratosthenes*." *Central States Speech Journal*, 30 (Fall 1979), 199-210.

Gallo, Louis. "Kenneth Burke: The Word and the World." *North Dakota Quarterly*, 42 (Winter 1974), 33-45.

Garlitz, Robert E. "The Sacrificial Word in Kenneth Burke's Logology." *Recherches anglaises et américaines*, 12 (1979), 33-44.

Gaske, Paul C. "The Analysis of Demagogic Discourse: Huey Long's 'Every Man a King' Address." In *American Rhetoric from Roosevelt to Reagan: A Collection of Speeches and Critical Essays*. Ed. Halford Ross Ryan. Prospect Heights, IL: Waveland, 1983, pp. 49-67.

Geiger, Don. "A 'Dramatic' Approach to Interpretative Analysis." *Quarterly Journal of Speech*, 38 (April 1952), 189-94.

Geiger, Don. *The Sound, Sense, and Performance of Literature*. Chicago: Scott, Foresman, 1963.

Gibson, Chester. "Eugene Talmadge's Use of Identification During the 1934 Gubernatorial Campaign in Georgia." *Southern Speech Journal*, 35 (Summer 1970), 342-49.

Glicksberg, Charles I. *American Literary Criticism, 1900-1950*. New York: Hendricks, 1951.

Glicksberg, C[harles] I. "Kenneth Burke: The Critic's Critic." *South Atlantic Quarterly*, 36 (1937), 74-84.

Goedkoop, Richard J. "Taking the Sword from the Temple: Walter Flowers and the Rhetoric of Form." *Pennsylvania Speech Communication Annual*, 38 (1982), 25-31.

Gomme, Andor. *Attitudes to Criticism*. Carbondale: Southern Illinois University Press, 1966.

Goodall, Jr., H. Lloyd, Gerald L. Wilson, and Christopher L. Waagen. "The Performance Appraisal Interview: An Interpretive Reassessment." *Quarterly Journal of Speech*, 72 (February 1986), 74-87.

Gregg, Richard B. "Kenneth Burke's Prolegomena to the Study of the Rhetoric of Form." *Communication Quarterly*, 26 (Fall 1978), 3-13.

Greiff, Louis K. "Symbolic Action in Hardy's *The Woodlanders*: An Application of Burkian Theory." *Thomas Hardy Yearbook*, 14 (1987), 52-62.

Griffin, Leland M. "A Dramatistic Theory of the Rhetoric of Movements." In *Critical Responses to Kenneth Burke: 1924-1966*. Ed. William H. Rueckert. Minneapolis: University of Minnesota Press, 1969, pp. 456-78.

Griffin, Leland M. "The Rhetorical Structure of the 'New Left' Movement: Part I." *Quarterly Journal of Speech*, 50 (April 1964), 113-35.

Griffin, Leland M. "When Dreams Collide: Rhetorical Trajectories in the Assassination of President Kennedy." *Quarterly Journal of Speech*, 70 (May 1984), 111-31.

Gronbeck, Bruce E. "Dramaturgical Theory and Criticism: The State of the Art (or Science?)." *Western Journal of Speech Communication*, 44 (Fall 1980), 315-30.

Gronbeck, Bruce E. "John Morley and the Irish Question: Chart-Prayer-Dream." *Speech Monographs*, 40 (November 1973), 287-95.

Gusfield, Joseph R. *The Culture of Public Problems: Drinking-Driving and the Symbolic Order*. Chicago: University of Chicago Press, 1981.

Gusfield, Joseph [R.] "The Literary Rhetoric of Science: Comedy and Pathos in Drinking Driver Research." *American Sociological Review*, 41 (1976), 16-34.

Gusfield, Joseph R. *Symbolic Crusade: Status Politics and the American Temperance Movement*. Urbana: University of Illinois Press, 1963.

Hagan, Michael R. "Kenneth Burke and Generative Criticism of Speeches." *Central States Speech Journal*, 22 (Winter 1971), 252-57.

Hahn, Dan F., and Anne Morlando. "A Burkean Analysis of Lincoln's Second Inaugural Address." *Presidential Studies Quarterly*, 9 (Fall 1979), 376-79.

Hamlin, William J., and Harold J. Nichols. "The Interest Value of Rhetorical Strategies Derived from Kenneth Burke's Pentad." *Western Speech*, 37 (Spring 1973), 97-102.

Harrington, David V., Philip M. Keith, Charles W. Kneupper, Janice A. Tripp, and William F. Woods. "A Critical Survey of Resources for Teaching Rhetorical Invention." *College English*, 40 (February 1979), 641-61.

Harris, Wendell V. "The Critics Who Made Us: Kenneth Burke." *Sewanee Review*, 96 (Summer 1988), 452-63.

Hartman, Geoffrey H. *Criticism in the Wilderness: The Study of Literature Today*. New Haven: Yale University Press, 1980.

Hauser, Gerard A. "An Afternoon with Burke and Cowley." *Pre/Text*, 6 (Fall/Winter 1985), 177-80.

Hawley, Andrew. "Art for Man's Sake: Christopher Caudwell as Communist Aesthetician." *College English*, 30 (October 1968), 1-19.

Hayakawa, S. I. "The Linguistic Approach to Poetry." *Poetry*, 60 (1942), 86-94.

Haydn, Hiram, mod. "American Scholar Forum: The New Criticism." *American Scholar*, 20 (Winter 1950-51), 86-104. (With William Barrett, Malcolm Cowley, Robert Gorham Davis, Allen Tate, and Kenneth Burke.)

Haydn, Hiram, mod. "American Scholar Forum: The New Criticism." *American Scholar*, 20 (Spring 1951), 218-31. (With William Barrett, Malcolm Cowley, Robert Gorham Davis, Allen Tate, and Kenneth Burke.)

Heath, Bob [Robert L.]. "Kenneth Burke's Perspective on Perspectives." *Pre/Text*, 6 (Fall/Winter 1985), 275-89.

Heath, Robert L. "Dialectical Confrontation: A Strategy of Black Radicalism." *Central States Speech Journal*, 24 (Fall 1973), 168-77.

Heath, Robert L. "Kenneth Burke on Form." *Quarterly Journal of Speech*, 65 (December 1979), 392-404.

Heath, Robert L. "Kenneth Burke's Break with Formalism." *Quarterly Journal of Speech*, 70 (May 1984), 132-43.

Heath, Robert L. "Kenneth Burke's Poetics and the Influence of I.A. Richards: A Cornerstone for Dramatism." *Communication Studies*, 40 (Spring 1989), 54-65.

Heath, Robert L. *Realism and Relativism: A Perspective on Kenneth Burke*. Macon, GA: Mercer University Press, 1986.

Heisey, D. Ray, and J. David Trebing. "A Comparison of the Rhetorical Visions and Strategies of the Shah's White Revolution and the Ayatollah's Islamic Revolution." *Communication Monographs*, 50 (June 1983), 158-74.

Henderson, Greig E. *Kenneth Burke: Literature and Language as Symbolic Action*. Athens: University of Georgia Press, 1988.

Hershey, Lewis B. "Burke's Aristotelianism: Burke and Aristotle on Form." *Rhetoric Society Quarterly*, 16 (Summer 1986), 181-85.

Hicks, Granville. "Counterblasts on 'Counter-Statement.'" *New Republic*, 69 (December 9, 1931), 101.

Hickson, Mark, III. "Kenneth Burke's Affirmation of 'No' and the Absence of the Present." *Etc.*, 33 (March 1976), 44-48.

Hoban, James L., Jr. "Rhetorical Rituals of Rebirth." *Quarterly Journal of Speech*, 66 (October 1980), 275-88.

Hoban, James L., Jr. "Solzhenitsyn on Detente: A Study of Perspective by Incongruity." *Southern Speech Communication Journal*, 42 (Winter 1977), 163-77.

Hoffman, Frederick F. *Freudianism and the Literary Mind*. Baton Rouge: Louisiana State University Press, 1945.

Hoffman, Frederick J., Charles Allen, and Carolyn F. Ulrich. *The Little Magazine: A History and a Bibliography*. Princeton, NJ: Princeton University Press, 1946.

Holland, L. Virginia. *Counterpoint: Kenneth Burke and Aristotle's Theories of Rhetoric*. New York: Philosophical Library, 1959.

Holland, L. Virginia. "Kenneth Burke's Dramatistic Approach in Speech Criticism." *Quarterly Journal of Speech*, 41 (December 1955), 352-58.

Holland, L. Virginia. "Kenneth Burke's Theory of Communication." *Journal of Communication*, 10 (December 1960), 174-84.

Holland, [L.] Virginia. "Rhetorical Criticism: A Burkeian Method." *Quarterly Journal of Speech*, 39 (December 1953), 443-50.

Holman, C. Hugh. "The Defense of Art Criticism Since 1930." In *The Development of American Literary Criticism*. Ed. Floyd Stoval. Chapel Hill: University of North Carolina Press, 1955, pp. 199-245.

Hook, Sidney. "Kenneth Burke and Sidney Hook: An Exchange: Is Mr. Burke Serious?" *Partisan Review*, 4 (January 1938), 44-47.

Hopper, Stanley Romaine. *Spiritual Problems in Contemporary Literature: A Series of Addresses and Discussions*. New York: Institute for Religious and Social Studies; dist. Harper, 1952.

Howell, Wilbur Samuel. "Colloquy: II. The Two-Party Line: A Reply to Kenneth Burke." *Quarterly Journal of Speech*, 62 (February 1976), 69-77.

Howell, Wilbur Samuel. "Peter Ramus, Thomas Sheridan, and Kenneth Burke: Three Mavericks in the History of Rhetoric." In *Retrospectives and Perspectives: A Symposium in Rhetoric*. Ed. Turner S. Kobler, William E. Tanner, and J. Dean Bishop. Denton: Texas Women's University Press, 1978, pp. 91-105.

Howell, Wilbur Samuel. *Poetics, Rhetoric, and Logic*. Ithaca, NY: Cornell University Press, 1975.

Howell, Wilbur Samuel. "Rhetoric and Poetics: A Plea for the Recognition of the Two Literatures." In *The Classical Tradition: Literary and Historical Studies in Honor of Harry Caplan*. Ed. Luitpold Wallach. Ithaca, NY: Cornell University Press, 1966, pp. 374-90.

Hubler, Edward. "The Sunken Aesthete." *English Institute Essays, 1950*. Ed. Alan S. Downer. New York: Columbia University Press, 1951, pp. 32-56.

Huyink, Cynthia J. "A Dramatistic Analysis of *Sexual Politics* by Kate Millett." *Women's Studies in Communication*, 3 (Summer 1979), 1-6.

Hyman, Stanley Edgar. *The Armed Vision: A Study in the Methods of Modern Literary Criticism*. 1947; rpt. New York: Vintage, 1955.

Hyman, Stanley Edgar. *The Critic's Credentials*. Ed. Phoebe Pettingell. New York: Atheneum, 1978.

Irmscher, William F. *The Holt Guide to English: A Contemporary Handbook of Rhetoric, Language, and Literature*. 2nd ed. New York: Holt, Rinehart and Winston, 1976.

Irmscher, William F. "Kenneth Burke." In *Traditions of Inquiry*. Ed. John Brereton. New York: Oxford University Press, 1985, pp. 105-35.

Ivie, Robert L. "Presidential Motives for War." *Quarterly Journal of Speech*, 60 (October 1974), 337-45.

Ivie, Robert L. "Progressive Form and Mexican Culpability in Polk's Justification for War." *Central States Speech Journal*, 30 (Winter 1979), 311-20.

Ivie, Robert L., and Joe Ayres. "A Procedure for Investigating Verbal Form." *Southern Speech Communication Journal*, 43 (Winter 1978), 129-45.

Jameson, Frederic R. "Critical Response: Ideology and Symbolic Action." *Critical Inquiry*, 5 (1978), 417-22.

Jameson, Frederic R. "The Symbolic Inference: or, Kenneth Burke and Ideological Analysis." *Critical Inquiry*, 4 (Spring 1978), 507-23.

Jarrell, Randall. "Changes of Attitude and Rhetoric in Auden's Poetry." *Southern Review*, 7 (1941-42), 326-49.

Jay, Gregory S. "Burke Re-Marx." *Pre/Text*, 6 (Fall/Winter 1985), 169-75.

Jay, Paul. "Kenneth Burke: A Man of Letters." *Pre/Text*, 6 (Fall/Winter 1985), 221-33.

Jennermann, Donald L. "Some Freudian Aspects of Burke's Aristotelean Poetics." *Recherches anglaises et américaines*, 12 (1979), 65-81.

Jensen, J. Vernon. "The Rhetorical Strategy of Thomas H. Huxley and Robert G. Ingersoll: Agnostics and Roadblock Removers." *Speech Monographs*, 32 (March 1965), 59-68.

Johannesen, Richard L. "Attitude of Speaker Toward Audience: A Significant Concept for Contemporary Rhetorical Theory and Criticism." *Central States Speech Journal*, 25 (Summer 1974), 95-104.

Johannesen, Richard L. "Richard M. Weaver's Uses of Kenneth Burke." *Southern Speech Communication Journal*, 52 (Spring 1987), 312-30.

Joost, Nicholas. *Scofield Thayer and The Dial*. Carbondale: Southern Illinois University Press, 1964.

Josephson, Matthew. *Life Among the Surrealists: A Memoir*. New York: Holt, Rinehart and Winston, 1962.

Kaelin, Eugene. *An Existentialist Aesthetic: The Theories of Sartre and Merleau-Ponty*. Madison: University of Wisconsin Press, 1962.

Kauffman, Charles. "Names and Weapons." *Communication Monographs*, 56 (September 1989), 271-85.

Keith, Philip M. "Burke for the Composition Class." *College Composition and Communication*, 28 (December 1977), 348-51.

Keith, Philip M. "Burkeian Invention: Two Contrasting Views: Burkeian Invention, from Pentad to Dialectic." *Rhetoric Society Quarterly*, 9 (Summer 1979), 137-41.

Kelley, Colleen E. "The 1984 Campaign Rhetoric of Representative George Hansen: A Pentadic Analysis." *Western Journal of Speech Communication*, 51 (Spring 1987), 204-17.

Kelley, Colleen E. "The Public Rhetoric of Mikhail Gorbachev and the Promise of Peace." *Western Journal of Speech Communication*, 52 (Fall 1988), 321-34.

Kimberling, C. Ronald. *Kenneth Burke's Dramatism and Popular Arts*. Bowling Green, OH: Bowling Green State University Popular Press, 1982.

King, Robert L. "Transforming Scandal into Tragedy: A Rhetoric of Political Apology." *Quarterly Journal of Speech*, 71 (August 1985), 289-301.

Kirk, John W. "The Forum: Kenneth Burke and Identification." *Quarterly Journal of Speech*, 47 (December 1961), 414-15.

Kirk, John W. "Kenneth Burke's Dramatistic Criticism Applied to the Theater." *Southern Speech Journal*, 33 (Spring 1968), 161-77.

Klope, David C. "Defusing a Foreign Policy Crisis: Myth and Victimage in Reagan's 1983 Lebanon/Grenada Address." *Western Journal of Speech Communication*, 50 (Fall 1986), 336-49.

Klumpp, James, and Jeffrey Lukehart. "The Pardoning of Richard Nixon: A Failure in Motivational Strategy." *Western Journal of Speech Communication*, 42 (Spring 1978), 116-23.

Kneupper, Charles. "Burkeian Invention: Two Contrasting Views: Dramatistic Invention: The Pentad as a Heuristic Procedure." *Rhetoric Society Quarterly*, 9 (Summer 1979), 130-36.

Kneupper, Charles W. "Dramatism and Argument." In *Dimensions of Argument: Proceedings of the Second Summer Conference on Argument*. Ed. George Ziegelmueller and Jack Rhodes. Annandale, VA: Speech Communication Association, October 15, 1981, pp. 894-904.

Knox, George. *Critical Moments: Kenneth Burke's Categories and Critiques*. Seattle: University of Washington Press, 1957.

Kostelanetz, Richard. "Richard Kostelanetz Interviews Kenneth Burke." Ed. J. Clarke Rountree, III. *Iowa Review*, 17 (Fall 1987), 1-14.

Kreilkamp, Thomas. *The Corrosion of the Self: Society's Effects on People*. New York: New York University Press, 1976.

Kuseski, Brenda K. "Kenneth Burke's 'Five Dogs' and Mother Teresa's Love." *Quarterly Journal of Speech*, 74 (August 1988), 323-33.

Lake, Randall A. "Order and Disorder in Anti-Abortion Rhetoric: A Logological View." *Quarterly Journal of Speech*, 79 (November 1984), 425-43.

Larson, Charles U. *Persuasion: Reception and Responsibility*. 3rd ed. Belmont, CA: Wadsworth, 1983.

Lazer, Hank. "Thinking of Kenneth Burke." *Pre/Text*, 6 (Fall/Winter 1985), 132-41.

Lazier, Gil. "Burke, Behavior, and Oral Interpretation." *Southern Speech Journal*, 31 (Fall 1965), 10-14.

Lee, Ronald. "The New Populist Campaign for Economic Democracy: A Rhetorical Exploration." *Quarterly Journal of Speech*, 72 (August 1986), 274-89.

Leff, Michael C. "Redemptive Identification: Cicero's Catilinarian Orations." In *Explorations in Rhetorical Criticism*. Ed. G.P. Mohrmann, Charles J. Stewart, and Donovan J. Ochs. University Park: Pennsylvania State University Press, 1973, pp. 158-77.

Lemon, Lee T. *The Partial Critics*. New York: Oxford University Press, 1965.

Lentricchia, Frank. *Criticism and Social Change*. Chicago: University of Chicago Press, 1983.

Lessl, Thomas M. "Science and the Sacred Cosmos: The Ideological Rhetoric of Carl Sagan." *Quarterly Journal of Speech*, 71 (May 1985), 175-87.

Lewis, Clayton W. "Identifications and Divisions: Kenneth Burke and the Yale Critics." *Southern Review*, 22 (Winter 1986), 93-102.

Ling, David A. "A Pentadic Analysis of Senator Edward Kennedy's Address to the People of Massachusetts, July 25, 1969." *Central States Speech Journal*, 21 (Summer 1970), 81-86.

McConachie, Bruce A. "Towards a Postpositivist Theatre History." *Theatre Journal*, 37 (December 1985), 465-86.

McGill, V.J. "Comments on Burke's Propositions." *Science and Society*, 2 (Spring 1938), 253-56.

Macksoud, S. John. "Kenneth Burke on Perspective and Rhetoric." *Western Speech*, 33 (Summer 1969), 167-74.

Macksoud, S. John, and Ross Altman. "Voices in Opposition: A Burkeian Rhetoric of Saint Joan." *Quarterly Journal of Speech*, 57 (April 1971), 140-46.

Mader, Thomas F. "Agitation over Aggiornamento: William Buckley vs. John XXIII." *Today's Speech*, 17 (November 1969), 4-15.

Maimon, Elaine P., Gerald L. Belcher, and Gail W. Hearn. *Writing in the Arts and Sciences*. Cambridge, MA: Winthrop, 1981.

Mann, Charles W. "The KB Collection: The Penn State Library." *Pre/Text*, 6 (Fall/Winter 1985), 313-15.

Meadows, Paul. "The Semiotic of Kenneth Burke." *Philosophy and Phenomenological Research*, 18 (September 1957), 80-87.

Mechling, Elizabeth Walker, and Gale Auletta. "Beyond War: A Socio-Rhetorical Analysis of a New Class Revitalization Movement." *Western Journal of Speech Communication*, 59 (Fall 1986), 388-404.

Mechling, Elizabeth Walker, and Jay Mechling. "Sweet Talk: The Moral Rhetoric Against Sugar." *Central States Speech Journal*, 34 (Spring 1983), 19-32.

Medhurst, Martin J. "McGovern at Wheaton: A Quest for Redemption." *Communication Quarterly*, 25 (Fall 1977), 32-39.

Meisenhelder, Thomas. "Law as Symbolic Action: Kenneth Burke's Sociology of Law." *Symbolic Interaction*, 4 (Spring 1981), 43-57.

Miller, Carolyn R. "Genre as Social Action." *Quarterly Journal of Speech*, 70 (May 1984), 151-67.

Moore, Marianne. *Predilections*. New York: Viking, 1955.

Moore, Mark P. "The Rhetoric of Ideology: Confronting a Critical Dilemma." *Southern Communication Journal*, 54 (Fall 1988), 74-92.

Morris, Barry Alan. "The Communal Constraints on Parody: The Symbolic Death of Joe Bob Briggs." *Quarterly Journal of Speech*, 73 (November 1987), 460-73.

Mouat, L.H. "An Approach to Rhetorical Criticism." In *The Rhetorical Idiom: Essays in Rhetoric, Oratory, Language, and Drama*. Ed. Donald C. Bryant. Ithaca, NY: Cornell University Press, 1958, pp. 170-77.

Muller, Herbert J. *Science and Criticism: The Humanistic Tradition in Contemporary Thought*. New Haven: Yale University Press, 1943.

Mullican, James S. "A Burkean Approach to *Catch-22*." *College Literature*, 8 (Winter 1981), 42-52.

Munson, Gorham B. *Destinations: A Canvass of American Literature Since 1900*. New York: J.H. Sears, 1928.

Munson, Gorham B. "The Fledgling Years, 1916 1924." *Sewanee Review*, 40 (January-March 1932), 24-54.

Murphy, John M. "Comic Strategies and the American Covenant." *Communication Studies*, 40 (Winter 1989), 266-79.

Murphy, Marjorie N. "Silence, the Word, and Indian Rhetoric." *College Composition and Communication*, 21 (December 1970), 356-63.

Murray, Timothy C. "Kenneth Burke's Logology: A Mock Logomachy." In *Glyph 2: Johns Hopkins Textual Studies*. Ed. Samuel Weber and Henry Sussman. Baltimore: Johns Hopkins University Press, 1977, pp. 144-61.

Neild, Elizabeth. "Kenneth Burke and Roland Barthes: Literature, Language, and Society." *Recherches anglaises et américaines*, 12 (1979), 98-108.

Nelson, Jeffrey. "Using the Burkeian Pentad in the Education of the Basic Speech Student." *Communication Education*, 32 (January 1983), 63-68.

Nemerov, Howard. "The Agon of Will as Idea: A Note on the Terms of Kenneth Burke." *Furioso*, 2 (Spring 1947), 29-42.

Nemerov, Howard. "Everything, Preferably All at Once: Coming to Terms with Kenneth Burke." *Sewanee Review*, 79 (Spring 1971), 189-201.

Nemerov, Howard. "Four Poems: Gnomic Variations for Kenneth Burke." *Kenyon Review*, 5 [new series] (Summer 1983), 23-25.

[Nichols], Marie Hochmuth. "Burkeian Criticism." *Western Speech*, 21 (Spring 1957), 89-95.

[Nichols], Marie Hochmuth. "Kenneth Burke and the 'New Rhetoric.'" *Quarterly Journal of Speech*, 38 (April 1952), 133-44.

Nichols, Marie Hochmuth. *Rhetoric and Criticism*. Baton Rouge: Louisiana State University Press, 1963.

Nimmo, Dan [D.] *Political Communication and Public Opinion in America*. Santa Monica, CA: Goodyear, 1978.

Nimmo, Dan D. *Popular Images of Politics: A Taxonomy*. Englewood Cliffs, NJ: Prentice-Hall, 1974.

Nimmo, Dan [D.] *Subliminal Politics: Myths & Mythmakers in America*. Englewood Cliffs, NJ: Prentice-Hall, 1980.

Nimmo, Dan [D.], and James E. Combs. *Mediated Political Realities*. New York: Longman, 1983.

O'Connor, William Van. *An Age of Criticism: 1900-1950*. Chicago: Henry Regnery, 1952.

O'Keefe, Daniel J. "Burke's Dramatism and Action Theory." *Rhetoric Society Quarterly*, 8 (Winter 1978), 8-15.

Osborn, Neal J. "Kenneth Burke's Desdemona: A Courtship of Clio?" *Hudson Review*, 19 (Summer 1966), 267-75.

Osborn, Neal J. "Toward the Quintessential Burke." *Hudson Review*, 21 (Summer 1968), 308-21.

Overington, Michael A. "Kenneth Burke and the Method of Dramatism." *Theory and Society*, 4 (1977), 131-56.

Overington, Michael A. "Kenneth Burke as a Social Theorist." *Sociological Inquiry*, 47 (1977), 133-41.

Pattison, Sheron Dailey. "Rhetoric and Audience Effect: Kenneth Burke on Form and Identification." In *Studies in Interpretation*, II. Ed. Esther M. Doyle and Virginia Hastings Floyd. Amsterdam: Rodopi, 1977, 183-98.

Paul, Sherman. "A Letter on Olson and Burke." *All Area*, 2 (1983), 64-65.

Payne, David. "Adaptation, Mortification, and Social Reform." *Southern Speech Communication Journal*, 51 (Spring 1986), 187-207.

Payne, David. "*The Wizard of Oz*: Therapeutic Rhetoric in a Contemporary Media Ritual." *Quarterly Journal of Speech*, 75 (February 1989), 25-39.

Peterson, Tarla Rai. "The Meek Shall Inherit the Mountains: Dramatistic Criticism of Grand Teton National Park's Interpretive Program." *Central States Speech Journal*, 39 (Summer 1988), 121-33.

Peterson, Tarla Rai. "The Rhetorical Construction of Institutional Authority in a Senate Subcommittee Hearing on Wilderness Legislation." *Western Journal of Speech Communication*, 52 (Fall 1988), 259-76.

Peterson, Tarla Rai. "The Will to Conservation: A Burkeian Analysis of Dust Bowl Rhetoric and American Farming Motives." *Southern Speech Communication Journal*, 52 (Fall 1986), 1-21.

Pettigrew, Loyd S. "Psychoanalytic Theory: A Neglected Rhetorical Dimension." *Philosophy and Rhetoric*, 10 (Winter 1977), 46-59.

Poirier, Richard. "Frost, Winnicott, Burke." *Raritan*, 2 (Fall 1982), 114-27.

Pounds, Wayne. "The Context of No Context: A Burkean Critique or Rogerian Argument." *Rhetoric Society Quarterly*, 17 (Winter 1987), 45-59.

Pritchard, John Paul. *Criticism in America*. Norman: University of Oklahoma Press, 1956.

Procter, David E. "The Rescue Mission: Assigning Guilt to a Chaotic Scene." *Western Journal of Speech Communication*, 51 (Summer 1987), 245-55.

Ragsdale, J. Donald. "Problems of Some Contemporary Notions of Style." *Southern Speech Journal*, 35 (Summer 1970), 332-41.

Ransom, John Crowe. "An Address to Kenneth Burke." *Kenyon Review*, 4 (1942), 218-37.

Rasmussen, Karen, and Sharon D. Downey. "Dialectical Disorientation in *Agnes of God*." *Western Journal of Speech Communication*, 53 (Winter 1989), 66-84.

Raymond, James C. *Writing (Is an Unnatural Act)*. New York: Harper & Row, 1980.

Rod, David K. "Kenneth Burke and Susanne K. Langer on Drama and Its Audience." *Quarterly Journal of Speech*, 72 (August 1986), 306-17.

Rod, David K. "Kenneth Burke's Concept of Entitlement." *Communication Monographs*, 49 (March 1982), 20-32.

Rodriguez, Linda. "The Latticework of Imagery." *Main Currents in Modern Thought*, 32 (September-October 1975), 24-28.

Romano, Carlin. "A Critic Who Has His Critics — Pro and Con." *Philadelphia Inquirer*, March 6, 1984, sec. D., p. 1.

Rosenfeld, Lawrence B. "Set Theory: Key to the Understanding of Kenneth Burke's Use of the Term 'Identification.'" *Western Speech*, 33 (Summer 1969), 175-83.

Rosteck, Thomas. "Irony, Argument, and Reportage in Television Documentary: *See It Now* Versus Senator McCarthy." *Quarterly Journal of Speech*, 75 (August 1989), 277-98.

Rosteck, Thomas, and Michael Leff. "Piety, Propriety, and Perspective: An Interpretation and Application of Key Terms in Kenneth Burke's *Permanence and Change*." *Western Journal of Speech Communication*, 53 (Fall 1989), 327-41.

Rountree, III, J. Clarke. "Kenneth Burke: A Personal Retrospective." *Iowa Review*, 17 (Fall 1987), 15-23.

Rueckert, William H., ed. *Critical Responses to Kenneth Burke: 1924-1966*. Minneapolis: University of Minnesota Press, 1969.

Rueckert, William H. "Kenneth Burke and Structuralism." *Shenandoah*, 21 (Autumn 1969), 19-28.

Rueckert, William H. *Kenneth Burke and the Drama of Human Relations*. 2nd ed. Berkeley: University of California Press, 1982.

Rueckert, William H. "Kenneth Burke's Encounters with Walt Whitman." *Walt Whitman Quarterly Review*, 6 (Fall 1988), 61-90.

Rushing, Janice Hocker. "Mythic Evolution of 'The New Frontier' in Mass Mediated Rhetoric." *Critical Studies in Mass Communication*, 3 (September 1986), 265-96.

Rushing, Janice Hocker. "Ronald Reagan's 'Star Wars' Address: Mythic Containment of Technical Reasoning." *Quarterly Journal of Speech*, 72 (November 1986), 415-33.

Rushing, Janice Hocker, and Thomas S. Frentz. "The Frankenstein Myth in Contemporary Cinema." *Critical Studies in Mass Communication*, 6 (March 1989), 61-80.

Sanbonmatsu, Akira. "Darrow and Rorke's Use of Burkeian Identification Strategies in *New York vs. Gitlow* (1920)." *Speech Monographs*, 38 (March 1971), 36-48.

Sapir, David, and J. Christopher Crocker, eds. *The Social Use of Metaphor: Essays on* the Anthropology of Rhetoric. University of Pennsylvania: University of Pennsylvania Press, 1977.

Schlauch, Margaret. "A Reply to Kenneth Burke." *Science & Society*, 2 (Spring 1938), 250-53.

Schwartz, Joseph. "Kenneth Burke, Aristotle, and the Future of Rhetoric." *College Composition and Communication*, 17 (December 1966), 210-16.

Scodari, Christine. "Contemporary Film and the Representative Anecdote of 'Unmasking': Coping Strategies for a Narcissistic Society." *Central States Speech Journal*, 38 (Summer 1987), 111-21.

Scott, Robert L. "To Burke or Not to Burke: A Brief Note on the Pious Neo-Burkeians with a Glance at True Believerism Generally in the Quest for the Perfect Communicology." *Spectra* [Speech Communication Association], 11 (August 1975), 1-2.

Sharf, Barbara F. "A Rhetorical Analysis of Leadership Emergence in Small Groups." *Communication Monographs*, 45 (June 1978), 156-72.

Shaw, Leroy Robert. *The Playwright & Historical Change: Dramatic Strategies in Brecht, Hauptmann, Kaiser, and Wedekind*. Madison: University of Wisconsin Press, 1970.

Shoemaker, Francis, and Louis Forsdale, eds. *Communication in General Education*. Dubuque, IA: William C. Brown, 1960.

Sillars, Malcolm O. "Rhetoric as Act." *Quarterly Journal of Speech*, 50 (October 1964), 277-84.

Simons, Herbert W., and Trevor Melia, eds. *The Legacy of Kenneth Burke*. Madison: University of Wisconsin Press, 1989.

Sivaramkrishna, M. "Epiphany and History: The Dialectic of Transcendence and *A Passage to India*. In *Approaches to E.M. Forster: A Centenary Volume*. Ed. Vasant A. Shahane. Atlantic Highlands, NJ: Humanities, 1981, pp. 148-61.

Slochower, Harry. *No Voice is Wholly Lost: Writers and Thinkers in War and Peace*. New York: Creative Age, 1945.

Smith, Bernard. *Forces in American Criticism: A Study in the History of American Literary Thought*. New York: Harcourt, Brace, 1939.

Smith, Charles Daniel. "From the Discipline of Literary Criticism." *Today's Speech*, 3 (November 1955), 33-34.

Smith, Janice M. "Erik H. Erikson's Sex Role Theories: A Rhetoric of Hierarchical Mystification." *Today's Speech*, 21 (Spring 1973), 27-31.

Smith, Larry David. "The Nominating Convention as Purveyor of Political Medicine: An Anecdotal Analysis of the Democrats and Republicans of 1984." *Central States Speech Journal*, 38 (Fall/Winter 1987), 252-61.

Smith, Larry David, and James L. Golden. "Electronic Storytelling in Electoral Politics: An Anecdotal Analysis of Television Advertising in the Helms-Hunt Senate Race." *Southern Speech Communication Journal*, 53 (Spring 1988), 244-58.

Solomon, Martha. "Ideology as Rhetorical Constraint: The Anarchistic Agitation of 'Red Emma' Goldman." *Quarterly Journal of Speech*, 74 (May 1988), 184-200.

Solomon, Martha. "Redemptive Rhetoric: The Continuity Motif in the Rhetoric of Right to Life." *Central States Speech Journal*, 31 (Spring 1980), 52-62.

Solomon, Martha. "The Rhetoric of Dehumanization: An Analysis of Medical Reports of the Tuskegee Syphilis Project." *Western Journal of Speech Communication*, 49 (Fall 1985), 233-47.

Southwell, Samuel B. *"Kenneth Burke and Martin Heidegger: With a Note Against Deconstructionism*. Gainesville: University Presses of Florida, 1987.

Starosta, William J. "The United Nations: Agency for Semantic Consubstantiality." *Southern Speech Journal*, 36 (Spring 1971), 243-54.

States, Bert O. *Irony and Drama: A Poetics*. Ithaca, NY: Cornell University Press, 1971.

States, Bert O. "Kenneth Burke and the Syllogism." *South Atlantic Quarterly*, 68 (Summer 1969), 386-98.

Stelzner, Hermann G. " 'War Message,' December 8, 1941: An Approach to Language," *Speech Monographs*, 33 (November 1966), 419-37.

Stuart, Charlotte L. "The Constitution as 'Summational Anecdote.' " *Central States Speech Journal*, 25 (Summer 1974), 111-18.

Sutton, Walter. *Modern American Criticism*. Englewood Cliffs, NJ: Prentice-Hall, 1963.

Tate, Allen. "Mr. Burke and the Historical Environment." *Southern Review*, 2 (1936-37), 363-72.

Tate, Allen. "A Note on Autotelism." *Kenyon Review*, 11 (Winter 1949), 13-16.

Thompson, David W. "Interpretative Reading as Symbolic Action." *Quarterly Journal of Speech*, 42 (December 1956), 389-97.

Thorp, Willard. "American Writers on the Left." In *Socialism and American Life*. Ed. Donald Drew Egbert and Stow Persons. Princeton, NJ: Princeton University Press, 1952, I, 601-20.

Tompkins, Phillip K. *Communication as Action: An Introduction to Rhetoric and Communication*. Belmont, CA: Wadsworth, 1982.

Tompkins, Philip K. "On Hegemony — 'He Gave it no Name' — and Critical Structuralism in the Work of Kenneth Burke." *Quarterly Journal of Speech*, 71 (February 1985), 119-30.

Tompkins, Phillip K., Jeanne Y. Fisher, Dominic A. Infante, and Elaine L. Tompkins. "Kenneth Burke and the Inherent Characteristics of Formal Organizations: A Field Study." *Speech Monographs*, 42 (June 1975), 135-42.

Tracy, David. "Mystics, Prophets, Rhetorics: Religion and Psychoanalysis." In *The Trial(s) of Psychoanalysis*. Ed. Françoise Meltzer. Chicago: University of Chicago Press, 1988, pp. 259-72.

Valesio, Paolo. *Novantiqua: Rhetorics as a Contemporary Theory*. Bloomington: Indiana University Press, 1980.

Vitanza, Victor J. "A Mal-Lingering Thought (Tragic-Comedic) About KB's Visit." *Pre/Text*, 6 (Fall/Winter 1985), 163-67.

Vitanza, Victor J. "Pre/face#8: KB X 2." *Pre/Text*, 6 (Fall/Winter 1985), 121-28.

Wadlington, Warwick, *The Confidence Game in American Literature*. Princeton, NJ: Princeton University Press, 1975.

Wagner, Geoffrey. "American Literary Criticism: The Continuing Heresy." *Southern Review* [Adelaide, Australia], 2 (1968), 82-89.

Walter, Otis M. "Toward an Analysis of Motivation." *Quarterly Journal of Speech*, 41 (October 1955), 271-78.

Warnock, Tilly. "Anecdotes on Accessibility: KB in Wyoming." *Pre/Text*, 6 (Fall/Winter 1985), 203-17.

Warnock, Tilly. "Reading Kenneth Burke: Ways In, Ways Out, Ways Roundabout." *College English*, 48 (January 1986), 62-75.

Warren, Austin. "Kenneth Burke: His Mind and Art." *Sewanee Review*, 41 (1933), 225-36, 344-64.

Warren, Austin. "The Sceptic's Progress." *American Review*, 6 (1936-37), 193-213.

Washburn, Richard Kirk. "Burke on Motives and Rhetoric." *Approach*, 9 (1953), 2-6.

Wasserstrom, William, ed. *A Dial Miscellany*. Syracuse: Syracuse University Press, 1963.

Wasserstrom, William. "Marianne Moore, *The Dial*, and Kenneth Burke." *Western Humanities Review*, 17 (Summer 1963), 249-62.

Wasserstrom, William. *The Time of the Dial*. Syracuse: Syracuse University Press, 1963.

Watson, Edward A. "Incongruity without Laughter: Kenneth Burke's Theory of the Grotesque." *University of Windsor Review*, 4 (Spring 1969), 28-36.

Watson, Karen Ann. "A Rhetorical and Sociolinguistic Model for the Analysis of Narrative." *American Anthropologist*, 75 (February 1973), 243-64.

Webster, Grant. *The Republic of Letters: A History of Postwar American Literary Opinion*. Baltimore: Johns Hopkins University Press, 1979.

Wellek, René. "Kenneth Burke and Literary Criticism." *Sewanee Review*, 79 (Spring 1971), 171-88.

Wellek, René, "The Main Trends of Twentieth-Century Criticism." *Yale Review*, 51 (Autumn 1961), 102-18.

Wells, Susan. "Richards, Burke and the Relation Between Rhetoric and Poetics." *Pre/Text*, 7 (Spring/Summer 1986), 59-75.

Wess, Robert. "Utopian Rhetoric in *The Man of Mode*." *Eighteenth Century: Theory and Interpretation*, 27 (Spring 1986), 141-61.

White, Hayden, and Margaret Brose, eds. *Representing Kenneth Burke*. Baltimore: Johns Hopkins University Press, 1982.

Wilkie, Carol. "The Scapegoating of Bruno Richard Hauptmann: The Rhetorical Process in Prejudicial Publicity." *Central States Speech Journal*, 32 (Summer 1981), 100-10.

Wilkinson, Charles. "The Rhetorical Criticism of Movements: A Process Analysis of the Catonsville Nine Incident." *Journal of the Illinois Speech & Theatre Association*, 31 (1977), 23-36.

Williams, Dale E. "*2001: A Space Odyssey*: A Warning Before Its Time." *Critical Studies in Mass Communication*, 1 (September 1984), 311-22.

Williams, William Carlos. "Kenneth Burke." *Dial*, 86 (January 1929), 6-8.

Winterowd, W. Ross. "Black Holes, Indeterminacy, and Paolo Freire." *Rhetoric Review*, 2 (September 1983), 28-35.

Winterowd, W. Ross. *The Contemporary Writer*. New York: Harcourt, Brace, Jovanovich, 1975.

Winterowd, [W.] Ross. "Dear Peter Elbow." *Pre/Text*, 4 (Spring 1983), 95-101.

Winterowd, W. Ross. "Kenneth Burke: An Annotated Glossary of His Terministic Screen and a 'Statistical' Survey of His Major Concepts." *Rhetoric Society Quarterly*, 15 (Summer-Fall 1985), 245-77.

Winterowd, W. Ross. *Rhetoric and Writing*. Boston: Allyn and Bacon, 1965.

Winterowd, W. Ross. *Rhetoric: A Synthesis*. New York: Holt, Rinehart and Winston, 1968.

Wise, Gene. *American Historical Explanations: A Strategy for Grounded Inquiry*. Minneapolis: University of Minnesota Press, 1980.

Woodcock, John. "An Interview with Kenneth Burke." *Sewanee Review*, 85 (October-December 1977), 704-18.

Woodward, Gary C. "Mystifications in the Rhetoric of Cultural Dominance and Colonial Control." *Central States Speech Journal*, 26 (Winter 1975), 298-303.

Yagoda, Ben. "Kenneth Burke: The Greatest Literary Critic Since Coleridge?" *Horizon*, 23 (June 1980), 66-69.

Yingling, Julie. "Women's Advocacy: Pragmatic Feminism in the YWCA." *Women's Studies in Communication*, 6 (Spring 1983), 1-11.

Young, Richard. "Invention: A Topographical Survey." In *Teaching Composition: 10 Bibliographical Essays*. Ed. Gary Tate. Fort Worth: Texas Christian University Press, 1976.

Zollschan, George K., and Michael A. Overington. "Reasons for Conduct and the Conduct of Reason: The Eightfold Route to Motivational Ascription." In *Social Change: Explorations, Diagnoses, and Conjectures*. Ed. George K. Zollschan and Walter Hirsch. New York: John Wiley, 1976, pp. 270-317.

Michel Foucault

Works by Foucault

Books

The Archaeology of Knowledge. Trans. A.M. Sheridan Smith. New York: Pantheon, 1972.

The Birth of the Clinic: An Archaeology of Medical Perception. Trans. A.M. Sheridan Smith. New York: Pantheon, 1973.

The Care of the Self: The History of Sexuality: Volume 3. Trans. Robert Hurley. New York: Pantheon, 1986.

Death and the Labyrinth: The World of Raymond Roussel. Trans. Charles Ruas. Garden City, NY: Doubleday, 1986.

Discipline and Punish: The Birth of the Prison. Trans. Alan Sheridan. New York: Pantheon, 1977.

The Foucault Reader. Ed. Paul Rabinow. New York: Pantheon, 1984.

Herculine Barbin: Being the Recently Discovered Memoirs of a Nineteenth-Century French Hermaphrodite. Trans. Richard McDougall. New York: Pantheon, 1980. (Collective work by Foucault and others.)

The History of Sexuality: Volume I: An Introduction. Trans. Robert Hurley. New York: Pantheon, 1978.

I, Pierre Revière having slaughtered my mother, my sister and my brother. . . .: A Case of Parricide in the 19th Century. Trans. Frank Jellinek. New York: Pantheon, 1975. (Collective work by Foucault and others.)

Language, Counter-Memory, Practice: Selected Essays and Interviews. Trans. Donald F. Bouchard and Sherry Simon. Ed. Donald F. Bouchard. Ithaca, NY: Cornell University Press, 1977.

Madness and Civilization: A History of Insanity in the Age of Reason. Trans. Richard Howard. New York: Pantheon, 1965.

Mental Illness and Psychology. Trans. A.M. Sheridan Smith. New York: Harper & Row, 1976.

Michel Foucault: Politics, Philosophy, Culture: Interviews and Other Writings: 1977-1984. Trans. Alan Sheridan and others. Ed. Lawrence D. Kritzman. New York: Routledge, 1988.

The Order of Things: An Archaeology of the Human Sciences. New York: Pantheon, 1970.

Power/Knowledge: Selected Interviews and Other Writings 1972-1977. Trans. Colin Gordon, Leo Marshall, John Mepham, and Kate Soper. Ed. Colin Gordon. New York: Pantheon, 1972.

This is Not a Pipe. Trans. and ed. James Harkness. Berkeley: University of California Press, 1982.

The Use of Pleasure: The History of Sexuality: Volume 2. Trans. Robert Hurley. New York: Pantheon, 1985.

Articles

"About the Concept of the 'Dangerous Individual' in 19th-Century Legal Psychiatry." Trans. Alain Baudot and Jane Couchman. *International Journal of Law and Psychiatry*, 1 (January 1978), 1-18.

"Afterward: The Subject and Power." Trans. Leslie Sawyer. In *Michel Foucault: Beyond Structuralism and Hermeneutics*. By Hubert L. Dreyfus and Paul Rabinow. Chicago: University of Chicago Press, 1982, pp. 208-26.

"The Catch-all Strategy." Trans. Neil Duxbury. *International Journal of the Sociology of Law*, 16 (May 1988), 139-62.

"Contemporary Music and the Public." *Perspectives of New Music*, 24 (1985), 6-12. (With Pierre Boulez.)

"The Discourse on Language." Trans. Rupert Swyer. In *The Archaeology of Knowledge*. By Michel Foucault. New York: Pantheon, 1972, pp. 215-37.

"An Exchange with Michel Foucault." *New York Review of Books*, 30 (March 31, 1983), 42.

"The Eye of Power." *Semiotexte*, 3 (1978), 6-19.

"Foucault Responds/2." *Diacritics*, 1 (Winter 1971), 60.

"Georges Canguilhem: Philosopher of Error." Trans. Graham Burchell. *Ideology and Consciousness*, 7 (1980), 51-62.

"Governmentality." *Ideology and Consciousness*, 6 (1979), 5-21.

"History, Discourse and Discontinuity." Trans. Anthony M. Nazzaro. *Salmagundi*, 20 (Summer-Fall 1972), 225-48.

"History of Systems of Thought, 1979." *Philosophy and Social Criticism*, 8 (1981), 353-59.

"Introduction." In *Fromanger: le desir est partout*. By Gérard Fromanger. [Catalogue of an exhibition.] Paris: Galerie Jeanne Bucher, 1975.

"Kant on Enlightenment and Revolution." Trans. Colin Gordon. *Economy and Society*, 15 (February 1986), 88-96.

"Maurice Blanchot: Thought from Outside." In *Foucault/Blanchot*. New York: Zone, 1987, pp. 7-58.

"Monstrosities in Criticism." Trans. Robert J. Matthews. *Diacritics*, 1 (Fall 1971), 57-60.

"My Body, This Paper, This Fire." Trans. Geoff Bennington. *Oxford Literary Review*, 4 (Autumn 1979), 9-28.

"Nineteenth Century Imaginations." Trans. Alex Susteric. *Semiotext(e)*, 4 (1982), 182-90.

"Of Other Spaces." Trans. Jay Miskowiec. *Diacritics*, 16 (Spring 1986), 22-27.

"On the Archaeology of the Sciences." *Theoretical Practice*, 3-4 (Autumn 1971), 108-27.

"On Revolution." *Philosophy and Social Criticism*, 8 (1981), 3-9.

"Other Spaces: The Principles of Heterotopia." *Lotus International*, 48/49 (1986), 9-17.

"The Political Function of the Intellectual." Trans. Colin Gordon. *Radical Philosophy*, 17 (1977), 12-14.

"The Political Technology of Individuals." In *Technologies of the Self: A Seminar with Michel Foucault*. Ed. Luther H. Martin, Huck Gutman, and Patrick H. Hutton. Amherst: University of Massachusetts Press, 1988, pp. 145-62.

"Politics and the Study of Discourse." Trans. Colin Gordon. *Ideology and Consciousness*, 3 (1978), 7-26.

"The Politics of Crime." Trans. Mollie Horwitz. *Partisan Review*, 43 (1976), 453-59.

"Preface." In *Anti-Oedipus*. By Gilles Deleuze and Felix Guattari. Trans. Robert Hurley, Mark Seem, and Helen R. Lane. New York: Viking, 1977.

"Sexuality and Solitude." *London Review of Books*, 3 (May 21-June 3, 1981), 3, 5-7. (With Richard Sennett.)

"The Simplest of Pleasures." Trans. Mike Riegle and Gilles Barbedette. *Fag Rag*, 29 (n.d.), 3.

"The Subject and Power." *Critical Inquiry*, 8 (Summer 1982), 777-95.

"Technologies of the Self." In *Technologies of the Self: A Seminar with Michel Foucault*. Ed. Luther H. Martin, Huck Gutman, and Patrick H. Hutton. Amherst: University of Massachusetts Press, 1988), pp. 16-49.

"War in the Filigree of Peace: Course Summary." Trans. Ian Mcleod. *Oxford Literary Review*, 4 (1980), 15-19.

"The West and the Truth of Sex." Trans. Lawrence E. Winters. *Sub-stance*, 20 (1978), 5-8.

"What is an Author?" Trans. James Venit. *Partisan Review*, 42 (1975), 603-14.

Works About Foucault

Albury, W.R., and D.R. Oldroyd. "From Renaissance Mineral Studies to Historical Geology, in the Light of Michel Foucault's *The Order of Things*." *British Journal for the History of Science*, 10 (November 1977), 187-215.

Allen, Robert van Roden. "Discourse and Sexuality: Toward the Texture of Eros." *Semiotext(e)*, 4 (1981), 249-58.

Almansi, Guido. "Foucault and Magritte." *History of European Ideas*, 3 (1982), 303-09.

Arac, Jonathan, ed. *After Foucault: Humanistic Knowledge, Postmodern Challenges*. New Brunswick: Rutgers University Press, 1988.

Arac, Jonathan. "The Function of Foucault at the Present Time." *Humanities in Society*, 3 (Winter 1980), 73-86.

Archambault, Paul J. "Michel Foucault's Last Discourse on Language." *Papers on Language and Literature*, 21 (Fall 1985), 433-42.

Aron, Harry. "Wittgenstein's Impact on Foucault." In *Wittgenstein and His Impact on Contemporary Thought*. Proceedings of the Second International Wittgenstein Symposium. Ed. Elisabeth Leinfellner, Werner Leinfellner, Hal Berghel, and Adolf Hübner. Vienna: Hölder, Pichler, Tempsky, 1978, pp. 58-60.

Aronowitz, Stanley. "History as Disruption." *Humanities in Society*, 2 (Spring 1979), 125-52.

Bahr, Ehrhard. "In Defense of Enlightenment: Foucault and Habermas." *German Studies Review*, 11 (1988), 97-109.

Balbus, Isaac D. "Disciplining Women: Michel Foucault and the Power of Feminist Discourse." *Praxis International*, 5 (January 4, 1986), 466-83.

Bannet, Eve Tavor. *Structuralism and the Logic of Dissent: Barthes, Derrida, Foucault, Lacan*. Urbana: University of Illinois Press, 1989.

Barbedette, Gilles. "A Conversation with Michel Foucault: The Social Triumph of the Sexual Will." Trans. Brendan Lemon. *Christopher Street*, 64 (May 1982), 36-41.

Barbadette [sic], Gilles, and André Scala. "Final Interview: Michel Foucault." Trans. Thomas Levin and Isabelle Lorenz. *Raritan Review*, 5 (Summer 1985), 1-13.

Barthes, Roland. *Critical Essays*. Trans. Richard Howard. Evanston: Northwestern University Press, 1972.

Baudrillard, Jean. "Forgetting Foucault." Trans. Nicole Dufresne. *Humanities in Society*, 3 (Winter 1980), 87-111.

Bennington, Geoff P. "Cogito Incognito: Foucault's 'My Body, This Paper, This Fire.'" *Oxford Literary Review*, 4 (Autumn 1979), 5-8.

Berlin, James. "Revisionary History: The Dialectical Method." *Pre/Text*, 8 (Spring/ Summer 1987), 47-61.

Bernauer, James. "Feature Review-Article: Foucault's Political Analysis." *IPQ: International Philosophical Quarterly*, 22 (March 1982), 87-95.

Bernauer, James W. "Michel Foucault's Ecstatic Thinking." *Philosophy and Social Criticism*, 12 (1987), 156-93.

Bernauer, James, and David Rasmussen, eds. *The Final Foucault*. Cambridge: MIT Press, 1988.

Bersani, Leo. "The Subject of Power." *Diacritics*, 7 (September 1977), 2-21.

Biemel, Walter. "Philosophy and Art." *Man and World*, 12 (1979), 267-83.

Blair, Carole. "The Statement: Foundation of Foucault's Historical Criticism." *Western Journal of Speech Communication*, 51 (Fall 1987), 364-81.

Blair, Carole, and Martha Cooper. "The Humanist Turn in Foucault's Rhetoric of Inquiry." *Quarterly Journal of Speech*, 73 (May 1987), 151-71.

Blanchot, Maurice. "Michel Foucault as I Imagine Him." In *Foucault/Blanchot*. New York: Zone, 1987, pp. 61-109.

Bouchard, Donald F. "For Life and Action: Foucault, Spectacle, Document." *Oxford Literary Review*, 4 (1980), 20-28.

Bourdieu, Pierre, and Jean-Claude Passeron. "Sociology and Philosophy in France Since 1945: Death and Resurrection of a Philosophy without Subject." *Social Research*, 34 (Spring 1967), 162-212.

Bóve, Paul A. "The End of Humanism: Michel Foucault and the Power of Disciplines." *Humanities in Society*, 3 (Winter 1980), 23-40.

Brodeur, Jean-Paul. "McDonell on Foucault: Supplementary Remarks." *Canadian Journal of Philosophy*, 7 (September 1977), 555-68.

Brown, B., and M. Cousins. "The LInguistic Fault: The Case of Foucault's Archaeology." *Economy and Society*, 9 (August 1980), 251-78.

Brown, P.L. "Epistemology and Method: Althusser, Foucault, Derrida." *Cultural Hermeneutics*, 3 (1975), 147-63.

Bruce, Douglas R. "Silence, Rhetoric, and Freedom: Explicating Foucault Through Augustine." In *Visions of Rhetoric: History, Theory and Criticism*. Ed. Charles W. Kneupper. Arlington, TX: Rhetoric Society of America, 1987, pp. 157-68.

Burrell, Gibson. "Modernism, Post Modernism and Organizational Analysis 2: The Contribution of Michel Foucault." *Organization Studies*, 9 (1988), 221-35.

Butler, Judith. "Variations on Sex and Gender: Beauvoir, Wittig, and Foucault." *Praxis International*, 5 (January 4, 1986), 505-16.

Carroll,David. *Paraesthetics: Foucault, Lyotard, Derrida*. New York: Methuen, 1987.

Carroll, David. "The Subject of Archeology or the Sovereignty of the Episteme." *MLN*, 93 (May 1978), 695-722.

Casey, Edward S. "The Place of Space in *The Birth of the Clinic*. *Journal of Medicine and Philosophy*, 12 (November 1987), 351-56.

Cavallari, Hector Mario. "*Savoir* and *Pouvoir*: Michel Foucault's Theory of Discursive Practice." *Humanities in Society*, 3 (Winter 1980), 55-72.

Chua, Beng-Huat. "The Structure of the Contemporary Sociological Problematic: A Foucaultian View." *American Sociologist*, 15 (May 1980), 82-93.

Clark, E. Culpepper, and Raymie E. McKerrow . "The Historiographical Dilemma in Myrdal's American Creed: Rhetoric's Role in Rescuing a Historical Moment." *Quarterly Journal of Speech*, 73 (August 1987), 303-16.

Clark, Michael. *Michel Foucault, An Annotated Bibliography: Tool Kit for a New Age*. New York: Garland, 1983.

Clauss, Sidonie. "John Wilkins' Essay Toward a Real Character: Its Place in the Seventeenth-Century Episteme." *Journal of the History of Ideas*, 43 (October-December 1982), 531-53.

Clifford, Michael R. "Crossing (out) the Boundary: Foucault and Derrida on Transgressing Transgression." *Philosophy Today*, 31 (Fall 1987), 223-33.

Cobley, Evelyn. "Toward History as Discontinuity: The Russian Formalists and Foucault." *Mosaic*, 20 (Spring 1987), 41-56.

"Cogito Incognito: Foucault's 'My Body, This Paper, This Fire.'" *Oxford Literary Review*, 4 (Autumn 1979), 5-8.

Colburn, Jr., Kenneth. "Desire and Discourse in Foucault: The Sign of the Fig Leaf in Michelangelo's *David*." *Human Studies*, 10 (1987), 61-79.

Cooper, Barry. *Michel Foucault: An Introduction to his Thought*. New York: Edwin Mellen, 1981.

Cooper, Martha. "Reconceptualizing Ideology According to the Relationship Between Rhetoric and Knowledge/Power." In *Rhetoric and Ideology: Compositions and Criticisms of Power*. Ed. Charles W. Kneupper. Arlington, TX: Rhetoric Society of America, 1989, pp. 30-41.

Cooper, Martha. "Rhetorical Criticism and Foucault's Philosophy of Discursive Events." *Central States Speech Journal*, 39 (Spring 1988), 1-17.

Cooper, Martha, and John J. Makay. "Knowledge, Power, and Freud's Clark Conference Lectures." *Quarterly Journal of Speech*, 74 (November 1988), 416-33.

Cousins, Mark, and Athar Hussain. *Michel Foucault*. London: Macmillan, 1984.

Cousins, Mark, and Athar Hussain. "The Question of Ideology—Althusser, Pecheux and Foucault." In *Power, Action and Belief: A New Sociology of Knowledge?* Ed. John Law. Boston: Routledge & Kegan Paul, 1986.

Cranston, Maurice. *The Mask of Politics and Other Essays*. London: Allen Lane, 1973.

Cranston, Maurice. "Michel Foucault." *Encounter*, 30 (June 1968), 34-42.

Cranston, Maurice. *Philosophy and Language*. Toronto: Canadian Broadcasting Corporation, 1969.

Culler, Jonathan. "The Linguistic Basis of Structuralism." In *Structuralism: An Introduction*. Ed. David Robey. Oxford: Clarendon, 1973, pp. 20-36.

Dallmayr, Fred R. *Polis and Praxis: Exercises in Contemporary Political Theory*. Cambridge: MIT Press, 1984.

Dallmayr, Fred R., and Gisela J. Hinkle. "Editors' Preface: Foucault *in memoriam* (1926-1984)." *Human Studies*, 10 (1987), 3-13.

D'Amico, Robert. "The Contours and Coupures of Structuralist Theory." *Telos*, 17 (Fall 1973), 70-97.

D'Amico, Robert. "Desire and the Commodity Form." *Telos*, 35 (Spring 1978), 88-122.

D'Amico, Robert. "Introduction to the Foucault-Deleuze Discussion." *Telos*, 16 (Summer 1973), 101-02.

Defolter, Rolf S. "On the Methodological Foundation of the Abolitionist Approach to the Criminal Justice System: A Comparison of the Ideas of Hulsman, Mathiesen and Foucault." *Contemporary Crises*, 10 (1986), 39-62.

Deleuze, Gilles. *Foucault*. Trans. and ed. Sean Hand. Minneapolis: University of Minnesota Press, 1988.

Derrida, Jacques. *Writing and Difference*. Trans. Alan Bass. Chicago: University of Chicago Press, 1978.

Descombes, Vincent. *Modern French Philosophy*. Trans. L. Scott-Fox and J.M. Harding. New York: Cambridge University Press, 1980.

Dews, Peter. "The Nouvelle Philosophie and Foucault." *Economy and Society*, 8 (May 1979), 127-68.

Dews, Peter. "Power and Subjectivity in Foucault." *New Left Review*, 144 (March/April 1984), 72-95.

Diamond, Irene, and Lee Quinby, eds. *Feminism & Foucault: Reflections on Resistance*. Boston: Northeastern University Press, 1988.

Dillon, Millicent. "Conversation with Michel Foucault." *Three Penney Review*, 1 (Winter-Spring 1980), 4-5.

Doerner, Klaus. *Madmen and the Bourgeoisie: A Social History of Insanity and Psychiatry*. Trans. Joachim Neugroschel and Jean Steinberg. Oxford: Basil Blackwell, 1981.

Donato, Eugenio. "Structuralism: The Aftermath." *Sub-Stance*, 7 (Fall 1973), 9-26.

Donzelot, Jacques. "The Poverty of Political Culture." Trans. Couze Venn. *Ideology and Consciousness*, 5 (Spring 1979), 73-86.

Dreyfus, Hubert L. "Foucault's Critique of Psychiatric Medicine." *Journal of Medicine and Philosophy*, 12 (November 1987), 311-33.

Dreyfus, Hubert L., and Paul Rabinow. *Michel Foucault: Beyond Structuralism and Hermeneutics*. Chicago: University of Chicago Press, 1982.

Eagleton, Terry. "Foucault, Michel." In *International Encyclopedia of Communications*. Vol.II. Ed. Erik Barnouw. New York: Oxford University Press, 1989, 201-02.

Elders, Fons, mod. "Human Nature: Justice versus Power." (Debate between Michel Foucault and Noam Chomsky.) In *Reflexive Water: The Basic Concerns of Mankind*. London: Souvenir, 1974, pp. 136-97.

Emad, Parvis. "Foucault and Biemel on Representation: A Beginning Inquiry." *Man and World*, 12 (1979), 284-97.

Ferguson, Kathy E. *The Feminist Case Against Bureaucracy*. Philadelphia: Temple University Press, 1984.

"Film and Popular Memory: An Interview with Michel Foucault." Trans. Martin Jordin. *Radical Philosophy*, 11 (Summer 1975), 24-29.

Fine, Bob. "The Birth of Bourgeois Punishment." *Crime and Social Justice*, 13 (Summer 1980), 19-26.

Fine, Bob. "Struggles Against Discipline: The Theory and Politics of Michel Foucault." *Capital and Class*, 9 (1979), 75-96.

Flaherty, P. "(Con)textual Contest: Derrida and Foucault on Madness and the Cartesian Subject." *Philosophy of the Social Sciences*, 16 (1986), 157-75.

Flynn, Bernard Charles. "Foucault and the Body Politic." *Man and World*, 20 (1987), 65-84.

Flynn, Bernard Charles. "Michel Foucault and Comparative Civilizational Study." *Philosophy and Social Criticism*, 5 (July 1978), 146-58.

Flynn, Bernard Charles. "Michel Foucault and the Husserlian Problematic of a Transcendental Philosophy of History." *Philosophy Today*, 22 (Fall 1978), 224-38.

Flynn, Bernard. "Sexuality, Knowledge and Power in the Thought of Michel Foucault." *Philosophy and Social Criticism*, 8 (Fall 1981), 329-48.

Flynn, Thomas. "Foucault as Parrhesiast: His Last Course at the Collège de France (1984)." *Philosophy and Social Criticism*, 12 (1987), 213-29.

Fornet-Betancourt, Raúl, Helmut Becker, and Alfredo Gomez-Müller. "The Ethic of Care for the Self as a Practice of Freedom: An Interview with Michel Foucault on January 20, 1984." *Philosophy and Social Criticism*, 12 (1987), 112-31.

Foss, Sonja K., and Ann Gill. "Michel Foucault's Theory of Rhetoric as Epistemic." *Western Journal of Speech Communication*, 51 (Fall 1987), 384-401.

Frank, III, Arthur W. "The Politics of the New Positivity: A Review Essay of Michel Foucault's *Discipline and Punish*." *Human Studies*, 5 (January-March 1982), 61-67.

Fraser, Nancy. "Foucault on Modern Power: Empirical Insights and Normative Confusions." *Praxis International*, 1 (October 1981), 272-87.

Fraser, Nancy. "Foucault's Body Language: A Post-Humanist Political Rhetoric?" *Salmagundi*, 61 (Fall 1983), 55-70.

Fraser, Nancy. "Michel Foucault: A 'Young Conservative'?" *Ethics*, 96 (October 1985), 165-84.

Fraser, Nancy. *Unruly Practices: Power, Discourse and Gender in Contemporary Social Theory*. Minneapolis: University of Minnesota Press, 1989.

Freundlieb, Dieter. "Rationalism *v.* Irrationalism? Habermas's Response to Foucault." *Inquiry*, 31 (June 1988), 171-92.

Friedrich, Otto, and Sandra Burton. "France's Philosopher of Power." *Time*, November 16, 1981, pp. 147-48.

"Friendship as a Lifestyle: An Interview with Michel Foucault." *Gay Information*, 7 (Spring 1981), 4-6.

Funt, David Paul. "The Structuralist Debate." *Hudson Review*, 22 (Winter 1969-70), 623-46.

Gallagher, Bob, and Alexander Wilson. "Michel Foucault: An Interview: Sex, Power and the Politics of Identity." *The Advocate* [San Mateo, CA], 400 (August 7, 1984), 26-30, 58.

Gandelman, Claude. "Foucault as Art Historian." *Hebrew University Studies in Literature and the Arts*, 13 (1985), 266-80.

Gane, Mike, ed. *Towards a Critique of Foucault*. New York: Routledge and Kegan Paul, 1986.

Gaonkar, Dilip Parameshwar. "Foucault on Discourse: Methods and Temptations." *Journal of the American Forensic Association*, 18 (Spring 1982), 246-57.

Giddens, Anthony. *Profiles and Critiques in Social Theory*. Berkeley: University of California Press, 1982.

Gilder, Eric. "The Process of Political *Praxis*: Efforts of the Gay Community to Transform the Social Signification of AIDS." *Communication Quarterly*, 37 (Winter 1989), 27-38.

Gillan, Garth. "Foucault's Philosophy." *Philosophy and Social Criticism*, 12 (1987), 145-55.

Gordon, Colin. "Birth of the Subject." *Radical Philosophy*, 17 (Summer 1977), 15-25.

Gordon, Colin. "Introduction to Pasquino and Procacci." *Ideology and Consciousness*, 4 (Autumn 1978), 37-39.

Gordon, Colin. "Question, Ethos, Event: Foucault on Kant and Enlightenment." *Economy and Society*, 15 (February 1986), 71-87.

Griffioen, Sander. "Changes in the Climate of Thought." Trans. J.A. Peterson. *Philosophia Reformata*, 46 (1981), 103-18.

Grossberg, Lawrence. "Strategies of Marxist Cultural Interpretation." *Critical Studies in Mass Communication*, 1 (December 1984), 392-421.

Guédon, Jean Claude. "Michel Foucault: The Knowledge of Power and the Power of Knowledge." *Bulletin of the History of Medicine*, 51 (1977), 245-77.

Gutting, Gary. "Continental Philosophy of Science." In *Current Research in Philosophy of Science*. Ed. Peter D. Asquith and Henry E. Kyburg, Jr. East Lansing, MI: Philosophy of Science Association, 1979, pp. 94-117.

Habermas, Jürgen. *The Philosophical Discourse of Modernity: Twelve Lectures.* Trans. Frederick Lawrence. Cambridge: MIT Press, 1987.

Hacking, Ian. "Michel Foucault's Immature Science." *Noûs*, 13 (March 1979), 39-51.

Hall, Stuart. "Signification, Representation, Ideology: Althusser and the Post-Structuralist Debates." *Critical Studies in Mass Communication*, 2 (June 1985), 91-114.

Harvard-Watts, John. "Michel Foucault." *Times Literary Supplement*, July 31, 1970, p. 855.

Hattiangadi, J.N. "Language Philosophy: Hacking: Foucault." *Dialogue*, 17 (1978), 513-28.

Hayman, Ronald. "Cartography of Discourse? On Foucault." *Encounter*, 47 (December 1976), 72-75.

Henning, E.M. "Archaeology, Deconstruction, and Intellectual History." In *Modern European Intellectual History: Reappraisals and New Perspectives.* Ed. Dominick LaCapra and Steven L. Kaplan. Ithaca, NY: Cornell University Press, 1982, pp. 153-96.

Hinkle, Gisela J. "Foucault's Power/Knowledge and American Sociological Theorizing." *Human Studies*, 10 (1987), 35-59.

Hodges, Jill, and Athar Hussain. "La police des familles." *Ideology and Consciousness*, 5 (1979), 87-123.

Hooke, Alexander E. "The Order of Others: Is Foucault's Antihumanism Against Human Action?" *Political Theory*, 15 (February 1987), 38-60.

Horowitz, Gad. "The Foucaultian Impasse: No Sex, No Self, No Revolution." *Political Theory*, 15 (February 1987), 61-80.

Hoy, David Couzens, ed. *Foucault: A Critical Reader.* New York: Basil Blackwell, 1986.

Hoy, David Couzens. "Power, Repression, Progress: Foucault, Lukes, and the Frankfurt School." *TriQuarterly*, 52 (Fall 1981), 43-63.

Hoy, David Couzens. "Taking History Seriously: Foucault, Gadamer, Habermas." *Union Seminary Quarterly Review*, 34 (Winter 1979), 85-95.

Huppert, George. *"Divinatio et Eruditio*: Thoughts on Foucault." *History and Theory*, 13 (1974), 191-207.

Hutton, Patrick H. "The History of Mentalities: The New Map of Cultural History." *History and Theory*, 20 (1981), 237-59.

Ijsseling, S. "Foucault with Heidegger." *Man and World*, 19 (1986), 413-24.

Ijsseling, Samuel. *Rhetoric and Philosophy in Conflict: An Historical Survey.* The Hague: Martinus Nijhoff, 1976.

"Is It Really Important to Think? An Interview with Michel Foucault." *Philosophy and Social Criticism*, 9 (1982), 31-40.

Jacoby, Russell. "The Jargon of the Discourse." *Humanities in Society*, 2 (Spring 1979), 149-52.

Jameson, Fredric. *The Prison-House of Language: A Critical Account of Structuralism and Russian Formalism.* Princeton, NJ: Princeton University Press, 1972.

Keenan, Tom. "The 'Paradox' of Knowledge and Power: Reading Foucault on a Bias." *Political Theory*, 15 (February 1987), 5-37.

Kurzweil, Edith. *The Age of Structuralism: Lévi-Strauss to Foucault.* New York: Columbia University Press, 1980.

Kurzweil, Edith. "Michel Foucault: Ending the Era of Man." *Theory and Society*, 4 (1977), 395-420.

Kurzweil, Edith. "Michel Foucault's History of Sexuality as Interpreted by Feminists and Marxists." *Social Research*, 53 (Winter 1986), 647-63.

LaCapra, Dominick, and Steven L. Kaplan, eds. *Modern European Intellectual History*. Ithaca, NY: Cornell University Press, 1982.

LaFountain, Marc J. "Foucault and Dr. Ruth." *Critical Studies in Mass Communication*, 6 (June 1989), 123-37.

Laing, R.D. "Sanity and 'Madness': The Invention of Madness." *New Statesman*, 71 (June 16, 1967), 843.

Lapointe, Francois H. "Michel Foucault: A Bibliographic Essay." *Journal of the British Society for Phenomenology*, 4 (May 1973), 195-97.

Lapointe, Francois H., and Claire Lapointe. "Bibliografia: Essay: Michel Foucault: A Bibliographic." *Dialogos*, 10 (April 1974), 153-57.

Lapointe, Francois [H.], and Claire Lapointe. "Bibliografia: Michel Foucault." *Dialogos*, 11 (November 1977), 245-54.

Lavers, Annette. "Man, Meaning and Subject, A Current Reappraisal." *Journal of the British Society for Phenomenology*, 1 (October 1970), 44-49.

Leary, David E. "Essay Review: Michel Foucault, an Historian of the *Sciences Humaines*." *Journal of the History of the Behavioral Sciences*, 12 (July 1976), 286-93.

Lecourt, Dominique. *Marxism and Epistemology: Bachelard, Canguilhem and Foucault*. London: NLB, 1975.

Leland, Dorothy. "On Reading and Writing the World: Foucault's History of Thought." *Clio*, 4 (February 1975), 225-43.

Lemert, Charles C., and Garth Gillan. *Michel Foucault: Social Theory and Transgression*. New York: Columbia University Press, 1982.

Lemert, Charles, and Garth Gillan. "The New Alternative in Critical Sociology: Foucault's Discursive Analysis." *Cultural Hermeneutics*, 4 (December 1977), 309-20.

Lentricchia, Frank. *Ariel and the Police: Michel Foucault, William James, Wallace Stevens*. Madison: University of Wisconsin Press, 1988.

LeSage, Laurent. *The New French Criticism: An Introduction and a Sampler*. University Park: Pennsylvania State University Press, 1967.

Lévy, Bernard-Henri. "The History of Sexuality: Interview." Trans. Geoff Bennington. *Oxford Literary Review*, 4 (1980), 3-14.

Lévy, Bernard-Henri. "Power and Sex: An Interview with Michel Foucault." Trans. David J. Parent. *Telos*, 32 (Summer 1977), 152-61.

Levy, Zeev. "The Structuralist Epistemology of Michel Foucault" [in Hebrew]. *Iyyun*, 25 (January-April 1974), 39-51; English summary, pp. 133-34.

Lowell, Edmunds. "Foucault and Theories." *Classical and Modern Literature*, 8 (1988), 79-91.

Maass, Peter, and David Brock. "The Power and Politics of Michel Foucault." *Inside* [weekly magazine of the *Daily Californian*, University of Californian, Berkeley], 7 (April 22, 1983), pp. 7, 20-22.

McBride, Maggie. "A Foucauldian Analysis of Mathematical Discourse." *For the Learning of Mathematics*, 9 (February 1989), 40-46.

Macdonell, Diane. *Theories of Discourse: An Introduction.* Oxford: Basil Blackwell, 1986.

McDonell, Donald J. "On Foucault's Philosophical Method." *Canadian Journal of Philosophy*, 7 (September 1977), 537-53.

McKerrow, Raymie E. "Critical Rhetoric: Theory and Praxis." *Communication Monographs*, 56 (June 1989), 91-111.

McMullen, Roy. "Michel Foucault." *Horizon*, 11 (Autumn 1969), 36-39.

Major-Poetzl, Pamela. *Michel Foucault's Archaeology of Western Culture.* Chapel Hill: University of North Carolina Press, 1983.

Mall, James P. "Foucault as Literary Critic." In *French Literary Criticism.* Ed. Philip Crant. Columbia: University of South Carolina, 1977, pp. 197-204.

Martin, Luther H., Huck Gutman, and Patrick H. Hutton. *Technologies of the Self: A Seminar with Michel Foucault.* Amherst: University of Massachusetts Press, 1988.

Maslan, Mark. "Foucault and Pragmatism." *Raritan*, 7 (Winter 1988), 94-114.

Megill, Allan. "Foucault, Structuralism, and the Ends of History." *Journal of Modern History*, 51 (September 1979), 451-503.

Megill, Allan. *Prophets of Extremity: Nietzsche, Heidegger, Foucault, Derrida.* Berkeley: University of California Press, 1985.

Megill, Allan. "The Reception of Foucault by Historians." *Journal of the History of Ideas*, 48 (June-March 1987), 117-41.

Merquior, J.G. *Foucault.* Berkeley: University of California Press, 1987.

Midelfort, H.C. Erik. "Madness and Civilization in Early Modern Europe: A Reappraisal of Michel Foucault." In *After the Reformation: Essays in Honor of J.H. Hexter.* Ed. Barbara C. Malament. n.p.: University of Pennsylvania Press, 1980, pp. 247-65.

Miel, Jan. "Ideas or Epistemes: Hazard Versus Foucault." *Yale French Studies*, 49 (1973), 231-45.

Minson, Jeff. "Strategies for Socialists? Foucault's Conception of Power." *Economy and Society*, 9 (February 1980), 1-43.

Moore, Mary Candace. "Ethical Discourse and Foucault's Conception of Ethics." *Human Studies*, 10 (1987), 81-95.

Morris, Meaghan, and Paul Patton, eds. *Michel Foucault: Power, Truth, Strategy.* Sydney, Australia: Feral, 1979.

Nehamas, Alexander. "What an Author Is." *Journal of Philosophy*, 83 (November 1986), 685-91.

Nye, Robert A. "Crime in Modern Societies: Some Research Strategies for Historians." *Journal of Social History*, 11 (Summer 1978), 491-507.

O'Higgins, James. "Sexual Choice, Sexual Act: An Interview with Michel Foucault." *Salmagundi*, 58-59 (Fall 1982-Winter 1983), 10-24.

O'Neill, John. "The Disciplinary Society: From Weber to Foucault." *British Journal of Sociology*, 37 (March 1986), 42-60.

Ostrander, Greg. "Foucault's Disappearing Body." *Canadian Journal of Political and Social Theory*, 11 (1987), 120-33.

Pace, David. "Structuralism in History and the Social Sciences." *American Quarterly*, 30 (1978), 282-97.

Paden, Roger. "Foucault's Anti-Humanism." *Human Studies*, 10 (1987), 123-41.

Pasquino, Pasquale. "Michel Foucault (1926-84): *The Will to Knowledge*." Trans. Chloe Chard. *Economy and Society*, 15 (February 1986), 97-109.

Paternek, Margaret A. "Norms and Normalization: Michel Foucault's Overextended Panoptic Machine." *Human Studies*, 10 (1987), 97-121.

Payer, Pierre J. "Foucault on Penance and the Shaping of Sexuality." *Studies in Religion*, 14 (Summer 1985), 313-20.

Pettit, Philip. *The Concept of Structuralism: A Critical Analysis*. Berkeley: University of California Press, 1975.

Philp, Mark. "Foucault on Power: A Problem in Radical Translation?" *Political Theory*, 11 (February 1983), 29-52.

Poster, Mark. "Foucault and History." *Social Research*, 49 (Spring 1982), 116-41.

Poster, Mark. *Foucault, Marxism and History: Mode of Production versus Mode of Information*. Cambridge, United Kingdom: Polity, 1984.

Poster, Mark. "Foucault's True Discourses." *Humanities in Society*, 2 (Spring 1979), 153-66.

Poster, Mark. "Foucault, the Present and History." *Cultural Critique*, 8 (1988), 105-21.

Poster, Mark. "The Future According to Foucault: *The Archaeology of Knowledge* and Intellectual History." In *Modern European Intellectual History: Reappraisals and New Perspectives*. Ed. Dominick LaCapra and Steven L. Kaplan. Ithaca, NY: Cornell University Press, 1982, pp. 137-52.

Pratt, Vernon. "Foucault & the History of Classification Theory." *Studies in History and Philosophy of Science*, 8 (1977), 163-71.

"Questions of Method. An Interview with Michel Foucault." Trans. Colin Gordon. *Ideology and Consciousness*, 8 (1981), 3-14.

Rabinow, Paul. "Interview: Michel Foucault: Space, Knowledge, and Power." Trans. Christian Hubert. *Skyline*, March 1982, pp. 16-20.

Racevskis, Karlis. "The Discourse of Michel Foucault: A Case of an Absent and Forgettable Subject." *Humanities in Society*, 3 (Winter 1980), 41-53.

Racevskis, Karlis. *Michel Foucault and the Subversion of Intellect*. Ithaca, NY: Cornell University Press, 1983.

Rajchman, John. "Ethics After Foucault." *Social Text*, 13/14 (Winter/Spring 1986), 165-83.

Rajchman, John. "Foucault's Art of Seeing." *October*, 44 (Spring 1988), 89-117.

Rajchman, John. *Michel Foucault: The Freedom of Philosophy*. New York: Columbia University Press, 1985.

Rajchman, John. "Nietzsche, Foucault and the Anarchism of Power." *Semiotexte*, 3 (1978), 96-107.

Rawlinson, Mary C. "Foucault's Strategy: Knowledge, Power, and the Specificity of Truth." *Journal of Medicine and Philosophy*, 12 (November 1987), 371-95.

Riddel, Joseph N. "Re-Doubling the Commentary." *Contemporary Literature*, 20 (Spring 1979), 237-50.

Riggins, Stephen. "Michel Foucault: An Interview by Stephen Riggins." *Ethos*, 1 (Autumn 1983), 4-9.

Rolleston, James. "The Expressionist Moment: Heym, Trakl, and the Problem of the Modern." *Studies in Twentieth Century Literature*, 1 (Fall 1976), 65-90.

Rorty, Richard. *Consequences of Pragmatism (Essays: 1972-1980)*. Minneapolis: University of Minnesota Press, 1982.

Rorty, Richard. "Method, Social Science, and Social Hope." *Canadian Journal of Philosophy*, 11 (December 1981), 569-88.

Rose, Gillian. *Dialectic of Nihilism: Post-Structuralism and Law*. Oxford: Basil Blackwell, 1984.

Ross, Stephen David. "Belonging to a Philosophic Discourse." *Philosophy and Rhetoric*, 19 (1986), 166-77.

Roth, Michael S. "Foucault's 'History of the Present.'" *History and Theory*, 20 (February 1981), 32-46.

Rousseau, G.S. "Whose Enlightenment? Not Man's: The Case of Michel Foucault." *Eighteenth-Century Studies*, 6 (Winter 1972-73), 238-56.

Said, Edward W. "Abecedarium culturae: Structuralism, Absence, Writing." *Tri-Quarterly*, 20 (Winter 1971), 33-71.

Said, Edward W. *Beginnings: Intention and Method*. New York: Basic, 1975.

Said, Edward W. "Linguistics and the Archeology of Mind." *IPQ: International Philosophical Quarterly*, 11 (March 1971), 104-34.

Said, Edward W. "Michel Foucault as an Intellectual Imagination." *Boundary*, 1 (1972), 1-27.

Said, Edward W. "Michel Foucault, 1926-1984." *Raritan*, 4 (Fall 1984), 1-11.

Said, Edward W. "The Problem of Textuality: Two Exemplary Positions." *Critical Inquiry*, 4 (Summer 1978), 673-714.

Said, Edward W. *The World, the Text, and the Critic*. Cambridge: Harvard University Press, 1983.

Sawicki, Jana. "Heidegger and Foucault: Escaping Technological Nihilism." *Philosophy and Social Criticism*, 13 (1987), 155-73.

Schneck, Stephen Frederick. "Michel Foucault on Power/Discourse, Theory and Practice." *Human Studies*, 10 (1987), 15-33.

Schor, Naomi. "Dreaming Dissymmetry: Barthes, Foucault, and Sexual Difference." In *Men in Feminism*. Ed. Alice Jardine and Paul Smith. New York: Methuen, 1987, pp. 98-110.

Scott, Charles E. "History and Truth." *Man and World*, 15 (1982), 55-66.

Scott, Charles E. "The Power of Medicine, The Power of Ethics." *Journal of Medicine and Philosophy*, 12 (November 1987), 335-50.

Sedgwick, Peter. "Mental Illness *Is* Illness." *Salmagundi*, 20 (Summer-Fall 1972), 196-224.

Sedgwick, Peter. *Psycho Politics*. New York: Harper & Row, 1982.

Seem, Mark D. "Liberation of Difference: Toward a Theory of Antiliterature." *New Literary History*, 5 (Autumn 1973), 119-33.

Shaffer, E.S. "The Archaeology of Michel Foucault." *Studies in History and Philosophy of Science*, 7 (1976), 269-75.

Shapiro, Michael J. *Language and Political Understanding: The Politics of Discursive Practices*. New Haven: Yale University Press, 1981.

Shapiro, Michael J. "The Rhetoric of Social Science: The Political Responsibilities of the Scholar." In *The Rhetoric of the Human Sciences: Language and Argument in*

Scholarship and Public Affairs. Ed. John S. Nelson, Allan Megill, and Donald N. McCloskey. Madison: University of Wisconsin Press, 1987, p. 363-80.

Sharratt, Bernard. "Notes After Foucault." *New Blackfriars*, 53 (June 1972), 251-64.

Sheridan, Alan. *Michel Foucault: The Will to Truth*. New York: Tavistock, 1980.

Shiner, Larry. "Foucault, Phenomenology and the Question of Origins." *Philosophy Today*, 26 (1982), 312-21.

Shiner, Larry. "Reading Foucault: Anti-Method and the Genealogy of Power-Knowledge." *History and Theory*, 21 (November 3, 1982), 382-98.

Sholle, David J. "Critical Studies: From the Theory of Ideology to Power/Knowledge." *Critical Studies in Mass Communication*, 5 (March 1988), 16-41.

Shumway, David R. *Michel Foucault*. Boston: Twayne, 1989.

Silverman, Hugh J. "Jean-Paul Sartre versus Michel Foucault on Civilizational Study." *Philosophy and Social Criticism*, 5 (July 1978), 160-71.

Silverman, Hugh J. "Michel Foucault's Nineteenth-Century System of Thought and the Anthropological Sleep." *Seminar*, 3 (1979), 1-8.

Silverman, Hugh J., ed. *Piaget, Philosophy and the Human Sciences*. Atlantic Highlands, NJ: Humanities, 1980.

Simon, John K. "A Conversation with Michel Foucault." *Partisan Review*, 38 (1971), 192-201.

Simon, John K. "Michel Foucault on Attica: An Interview." *Telos*, 19 (Spring 1974), 154-61.

Sluga, Hans. "Foucault, the Author, and the Discourse." *Inquiry*, 28 (December 1985), 403-15.

Smart, Barry. "Discipline and Social Regulation: On Foucault's Genealogical Analysis." In *The Power to Punish: Contemporary Penalty and Social Analysis*. Ed. David Garland and Peter Young. Atlantic Highlands, NJ: Humanities, 1983, pp. 62-83.

Smart, Barry. *Foucault, Marxism and Critique*. Boston: Routledge and Kegan Paul, 1983.

Smart, Barry. "Foucault, Sociology, and the Problem of Human Agency." *Theory and Society*, 11 (1982), 121-41.

Smart, Barry. *Michel Foucault*. New York: Tavistock, 1985.

Snyder, Carol. "Analyzing Classifications: Foucault for Advanced Writers." *College Composition and Communication*, 35 (May 1984), 209-16.

Spicker, Stuart F. "An Introduction to the Medical Epistemology of Georges Canguilhem: Moving Beyond Michel Foucault." *Journal of Medicine and Philosophy*, 12 (November 1987), 397-411.

Spitzack, Carole. "Confession and Signification: The Systematic Inscription of Body Consciousness." *Journal of Medicine and Philosophy*, 12 (November 1987), 357-69.

Sprinker, Michael. "The Use and Abuse of Foucault." *Humanities in Society*, 3 (Winter 1980), 1-21.

Steiner, George. "Steiner Responds to Foucault." *Diacritics*, 1 (Winter 1971), 59.

Stempel, Daniel. "Blake, Foucault, and the Classical Episteme." *PLMA*, 96 (May 1981), 388-407.

Stewart, David. "Why Foucault?" *Architecture and Urbanism*, 121 (October 1980), 100-06.

Struever, Nancy S. "Vico, Foucault, and the Strategy of Intimate Investigation." In *New*

Vico Studies. Vol. II. Ed. Giorgio Tagliacozzo and Donald Phillip Verene. New York: Institute for Vico Studies, 1984, 41-57.

Tambling, Jeremy. "Prison-bound-Dickens and Foucault." *Essays in Criticism*, 36 (January 1986), 11-31.

Tejera, V. "The Human Sciences in Dewey, Foucault and Buchler." *Southern Journal of Philosophy*, 18 (Summer 1980), 221-35.

Thiele, Leslie Paul. "Foucault's Triple Murder and the Modern Development of Power." *Canadian Journal of Political Science*, 19 (June 1986), 243-60.

Thomas, David. "Sociology and Common Sense." *Inquiry*, 21 (Spring 1978), 1-32.

Turner, Byran S. "The Government of the Body: Medical Regimens and the Rationalization of Diet." *British Journal of Sociology*, 33 (June 1982), 254-69.

Van Den Abbeele, Georges. "Sade, Foucault, and the Scene of Enlightenment Lucidity." *Stanford French Review*, 11 (Spring 1987), 7-16.

Wellbery, David E. "Theory of Events: Foucault and Literary Criticism." *Revue Internationale de Philosophie*, 162-63 (1987), 420-32.

White, Hayden V. "Foucault Decoded: Notes from Underground." *History and Theory*, 12 (1973), 23-54.

White, Hayden [V.] "Michel Foucault." In *Structuralism and Since: From Lévi-Strauss to Derrida*. Ed. John Sturrock. Oxford: Oxford University Press, 1979, pp. 81-115.

White, Hayden [V.] "Power and the Word." *Canto*, 2 (Spring 1978), 164-72.

White, Hayden [V.] *Tropics of Discourse: Essays in Cultural Criticism*. Baltimore: Johns Hopkins University Press, 1978.

White, Stephen K. "Foucault's Challenge to Critical Theory." *American Political Science Review*, 80 (June 1986), 419-32.

Williams, Karel. "Unproblematic Archaeology." *Economy and Society*, 3 (February 1974), 41-68.

Wuthnow, Robert, James Davison Hunter, Albert Bergesen, and Edith Kurzweil. *Cultural Analysis: The Works of Peter L. Berger, Mary Douglas, Michel Foucault, and Jürgen Habermas*. Boston: Routledge and Kegan Paul, 1984.

Jürgen Habermas

Works by Habermas

Books

Autonomy and Solidarity: Interviews. Ed. Peter Dews. London: Verso, 1986.

Communication and the Evolution of Society. Trans. Thomas McCarthy. Boston: Beacon, 1979.

Knowledge and Human Interests. Trans. Jeremy J. Shapiro. Boston: Beacon, 1971.

Legitimation Crisis. Trans. Thomas McCarthy. Boston: Beacon, 1975.

Observations on the Spiritual Situation of the Age: Contemporary German Perspectives. Trans. and intro. Andrew Buchwalter. Cambridge: MIT Press, 1984.

On the Logic of the Social Sciences. Trans. Shierry Weber Nicholsen and Jerry A. Stark. Cambridge: MIT Press, 1988.

The Philosophical Discourse of Modernity: Twelve Lectures. Trans. Frederick Lawrence. Cambridge: MIT Press, 1987.

Philosophical-Political Profiles: Studies in Contemporary German Social Theory. Trans. Frederick G. Lawrence. Cambridge: MIT Press, 1983.

Theory and Practice. Trans. John Viertel. Boston: Beacon, 1973.

The Theory of Communicative Action, Volume I: Reason and the Rationalization of Society. Trans. Thomas McCarthy. Boston: Beacon, 1984.

The Theory of Communicative Action, Volume II: Lifeworld and System: A Critique of Functionalist Reason. Trans. Thomas McCarthy. Boston: Beacon, 1987.

Toward a Rational Society: Student Protest, Science, and Politics. Trans. Jeremy J. Shapiro. Boston: Beacon, 1970.

Articles

"The Analytical Theory of Science and Dialectics: A Postscript to the Controversy Between Popper and Adorno." In *The Positivist Dispute in German Sociology*. Trans. Glyn Adey and David Frisby. Ed. Theodor W. Adorno, Hans Albert, Ralf Dahrendorf, Jürgen Habermas, Harald Pilot, and Karl R. Popper. New York: Harper & Row, 1976, pp. 131-62.

"Aspects of the Rationality of Action." In *Rationality To-Day*. Ed. Theodore F. Geraets. Ottawa: University of Ottawa Press, 1979, pp. 185-212.

"Concerning the Public Use of History." Trans. Jeremy Leaman. *New German Critique*, 44 (1988), 40-50.

"Consciousness-Raising or Redemptive Criticism: The Contemporaneity of Walter Benjamin." Trans. Philip Brewster and Carl Howard Buchner. *New German Critique*, 17 (1979), 30-59.

"Discussion." Rpt. in *Understanding and Social Inquiry*. Ed. Fred R. Dallmayr and Thomas A. McCarthy. Notre Dame: University of Notre Dame Press, 1977, pp. 66-72.

"Discussion on Value-Freedom and Objectivity." In *Max Weber and Sociology Today*. Trans. Kathleen Morris. Ed. Otto Stammer. New York: Harper & Row, 1971, pp. 59-66.

"The Entwinement of Myth and Enlightenment: Re-Reading *Dialectic of Enlightenment*." Trans. Thomas Y. Levin. *New German Critique*, 26 (1982), 13-30.

"Ernst Bloch—A Marxist Romantic." *Salmagundi*, 10-11 (Fall 1969-Winter 1970), 311-25.

"The Frankfurt School in New York." In *Foundations of the Frankfurt School of Social Research*. Ed. Judith Marcus and Zoltán Tar. New Brunswick, NJ: Transaction, 1984, pp. 55-65.

"The French Path to Postmodernity: Bataille between Eroticism and General Economics." Trans Frederick Lawrence. *New German Critique*, 33 (Fall 1984), 79-102.

"The Genealogical Writing of History: On Some Aporias in Foucault's Theory of Power." Trans. Gregory Ostrander. *Canadian Journal of Social and Political Theory*, 10 (1986), 1-9.

"Habermas: Questions and Counter-Questions." *Praxis International*, 4 (October 1984), 229-49.

"Hannah Arendt's Communications Concept of Power." *Social Research*, 44 (Spring 1977), 3-24.

"Herbert Marcuse, Jürgen Habermas and Friends: A Discussion on Democracy and Critical Theory." *New Political Science*, 1 (1979), 19-29.

"Historical Consciousness and Post-Traditional Identity: Remarks on the Federal Republic's Orientation to the West." *Acta Sociologica*, 31 (1988), 3-13.

"History and Evolution." *Telos*, 39 (Spring 1979), 5-44.

"The Idea of the University — Learning Processes." Trans. John R. Blazek. *New German Critique*, 41 (1987), 3-22.

"Interpretive Social Science vs. Hermeneuticism." In *Social Science as Moral Inquiry*. Ed. Norma Haan, Robert N. Bellah, Paul Rabinow, and William M. Sullivan. New York: Columbia University Press, 1983.

"A Kind of Settlement of Damages (Apologetic Tendencies)." Trans. Jeremy Leaman. *New German Critique*, 44 (1988), 25-39.

"Martin Heidegger on the Publication of Lectures from the Year 1935." *Graduate Faculty Philosophy Journal*, 6 (Fall 1977), 155-80.

"Modern and Postmodern Architecture." In *Critical Theory and Public Life*. Ed. John Forester. Cambridge: MIT Press, 1985, pp. 317-29.

"Modernity versus Postmodernity." Trans. Seyla Benhabib. *New German Critique*, 22 (Winter 1981), 3-14.

"Moral Development and Ego Identity." *Telos*, 24 (Summer 1975), 41-55.

"Neoconservative Culture Criticism in the United States and West Germany: An Intellectual Movement in Two Political Cultures." *Telos*, 56 (Summer 1983), 75-89.

"The New Obscurity: The Crisis of the Welfare State and the Exhaustion of Utopian Energies." Trans. Phillip Jacobs. *Philosophy and Social Criticism*, 11 (1986), 1-18.

"New Social Movements." *Telos*, 49 (Fall 1981), 33-37.

"On Social Identity." *Telos*, 19 (Spring 1974), 91-103.

"On Systematically Distorted Communication." *Inquiry*, 13 (Autumn 1970, 205-19.

"A Philosophico-Political Profile." *New Left Review*, 151 (May/June 1985), 75-105.

"The Place of Philosophy in Marxism." *Insurgent Sociologist*, 5 (1975), 41-48.

"A Positivistically Bisected Rationalism." In *The Positivist Dispute in German Sociology*. Trans. Glyn Adey and David Frisby. Ed. Theodor W. Adorno, Hans Albert, Ralf Dahrendorf, Jürgen Habermas, Harald Pilot, and Karl R. Popper. New York: Harper & Row, 1976, pp. 198-225.

"A Postscript to *Knowledge and Human Interests*." *Philosophy of the Social Sciences*, 3 (June 1973), 157-89.

"Psychic Thermidor and the Rebirth of Rebellious Subjectivity." *Praxis International*, 1 (April 1981), 79-86.

"The Public Sphere: An Encyclopedia Article (1964)." Trans. Sara Lennox and Frank Lennox. *New German Critique*, 3 (Fall 1974), 49-55.

"Rationalism Divided in Two: A Reply to Albert." Trans. Glyn Adey and David Frisby. In *Positivism and Sociology*. Ed. Anthony Giddens. London: Heinemann, 1974, pp. 195-223.

"A Reply to my Critics." Trans. Thomas McCarthy. In *Habermas: Critical Debates*. Ed. John B. Thompson and David Held. Cambridge: MIT Press, 1982, pp. 219-83.

"Reply to Skjei." *Inquiry*, 28 (March 1985), 105-113.

"Response to the Commentary of Bernstein and Dove." In *Hegel's Social and Political Thought: The Philosophy of Objective Spirit*. Ed. Donald Phillip Verene. [Atlantic Highlands], NJ: Humanities, 1980, pp. 247-50.

"A Review of Gadamer's *Truth and Method*. In *Understanding and Social Inquiry*. Ed. Fred R. Dallmayr and Thomas A. McCarthy. Notre Dame: University of Notre Dame Press, 1977, pp. 335-63.

"Right and Violence—A German Trauma." Trans. Martha Calhoun. *Cultural Critique*, 1 (Fall 1985), 125-39.

"Some Conditions for Revolutionizing Late Capitalist Societies [1968]." *Canadian Journal of Political and Social Theory*, 7 (Winter/Spring 1983), 32-42.

"Some Distinctions in Universal Pragmatics: A Working Paper." *Theory and Society*, 3 (Summer 1976), 155-67.

"Summation and Response." Trans. Martha Matesich. *Continuum*, 8 (1970), 123-33.

"A Test for Popular Justice: The Accusations Against the Intellectuals." *New German Critique*, 12 (1977), 11-13.

"Theory and Politics: A Discussion with Herbert Marcuse, Jürgen Habermas, Heinz Lubasz and Telman Spengler." *Telos*, 38 (Winter 1978-79), 124-53.

"Toward a Reconstruction of Historical Materialism." *Theory and Society*, 2 (Fall 1975), 287-300.

"Towards a Theory of Communicative Competence." In *Recent Sociology 2*. Ed. Hans Peter Dreitzel. London: Collier-Macmillan, 1970, pp. 114-48.

"What Does a Crisis Mean Today? Legitimation Problems in Late Capitalism." *Social Research*, 40 (Winter 1973), 643-67.

"Why More Philosophy?" *Social Research*, 38 (Winter 1971), 633-54.

Works About Habermas

Adamson, Walter L. "Beyond 'Reform or Revolution': Notes on Political Education in Gramsci, Habermas and Arendt." *Theory and Society*, 6 (November 1978), 429-60.

Agger, Ben. "A Critical Theory of Dialogue." *Humanities in Society*, 4 (Winter 1981), 7-30.

Agger, Ben. "Marcuse & Habermas on New Science." *Polity*, 9 (1976), 158-81.

Agger, Ben. "Work and Authority in Marcuse and Habermas." *Human Studies*, 2 (July 1979), 191-208.

Ahlers, Rolf. "How Critical is Critical Theory? Reflections on Jürgen Habermas." *Cultural Hermeneutics*, 3 (August 1975), 119-32.

Alexander, Jeffrey C. "The Parsons Revival in German Sociology." *Sociological Theory*, 2 (1984), 394-412.

Alford, C. Fred. "Is Jürgen Habermas's Reconstructive Science Really Science?" *Theory and Society*, 14 (May 1985), 321-40.

Alford, C. Fred. "Jürgen Habermas and the Dialectic of Enlightenment: What Is Theoretically Fruitful Knowledge?" *Social Research*, 52 (Spring 1985), 119-49.

Alford, C. Fred. *Science and the Revenge of Nature: Marcuse & Habermas*. Tampa: University of South Florida, 1985.

Allen, Robert van Roden. "Emancipation and Subjectivity: A Projected Kant-Habermas Confrontation." *Philosophy and Social Criticism*, 9 (Fall/Winter 1982), 283-301.

Apel, Karl-Otto. "C. S. Peirce and the Post-Tarskian Problem of an Adequate Explication of the Meaning of Truth: Towards a Transcendental-Pragmatic Theory of Truth, Part II." *Transactions of the Charles S. Peirce Society*, 18 (Winter 1982), 3-17.

Apel, Karl-Otto. "Types of Social Science in the Light of Human Interests of Knowledge." *Social Research*, 44 (Autumn 1977), 425-70.

Arac, Jonathan. "The Function of Foucault at the Present Time." *Humanities in Society*, 3 (Winter 1980), 73-86.

Arato, Andrew, and Eike Gebhardt, eds. *The Essential Frankfurt School Reader*. New York: Continuum, 1982.

Árnason, Jóhann P. "Contemporary Approaches to Marx—Reconstruction and Deconstruction." *Thesis Eleven*, 9 (July 1984), 52-72.

Árnason, Jóhann P. "Universal Pragmatics and Historical Materialism." *Acta Sociologica*, 25 (1982), 219-33.

Aune, James A. "The Contribution of Habermas to Rhetorical Validity." *Journal of the American Forensic Association*, 16 (Fall 1979), 104-11.

Balbus, Isaac D. "Habermas and Feminism: (Male) Communication and the Evolution of (Patriarchal) Society." *New Political Science*, 13 (Winter 1984), 27-47.

Bar-Hillel, Y. "On Habermas' Hermeneutic Philosophy of Language." *Synthese*, 26 (1973), 1-12.

Barnes, Barry. *Interests and the Growth of Knowledge*. Boston: Routledge & Kegan Paul, 1977.

Bauman, Zygmunt. *Hermeneutics and Social Science*. New York: Columbia University Press, 1978.

Bauman, Zygmunt. "Ideology and the *Weltanschauung* of the Intellectuals." *Canadian Journal of Political and Social Theory*, 7 (Winter/Spring 1983), 104-17.

Bauman, Zygmunt. *Towards a Critical Sociology: An Essay on Commonsense and Emancipation*. London: Routledge & Kegan Paul, 1976.

Beatty, Joseph. "'Communicative Competence' and the Skeptic." *Philosophy and Social Criticism*, 6 (1979), 269-87.

Benhabib, Seyla. "Epistemologies of Postmodernism: A Rejoinder to Jean-François Lyotard." *New German Critique*, 33 (Fall 1984), 103-26.

Benhabib, Seyla. "The Methodological Illusions of Modern Political Theory: The Case of Rawls and Habermas." *Neue Hefte für Philosophie*, 21 (1982), 47-74.

Benhabib, Seyla. "The Utopian Dimension in Communicative Ethics." *New German Critique*, 35 (Spring/Summer 1985), 83-96.

Bennett, W. Lance. "Communication and Social Responsibility." *Quarterly Journal of Speech*, 71 (August 1985), 259-88.

Bernsen, Niels Ole. "Elementary Knowledge: Transcendental Pragmatics without Consensus Theory and Ideal Community of Communication." *Acta Sociologica*, 25 (1982), 235-47.

Bernstein, Richard J., ed. *Habermas and Modernity*. Cambridge: MIT Press, 1985.

Bernstein, Richard J. *The Restructuring of Social and Political Theory*. New York: Harcourt Brace Jovanovich, 1976.

Birchall, B.C. "Radicalisation of the Critique of Knowledge: Epistemology Overcome or Reinstatement of an Error?" *Man and World*, 10 (1977), 367-81.

Bixenstine, Edwin. "The Fact-Value Antithesis in Behavioral Science." *Journal of Humanistic Psychology*, 16 (Spring 1976), 35-57.

Blakeley, Thomas J. "Praxis and Labor in Jürgen Habermas." *Studies in Soviet Thought*, 20 (October 1979), 291-94.

Blakeley, Thomas. "Responses to 'Theory and Practice.'" *Cultural Hermeneutics*, 2 (February 1975), 353-54.

Blanchette, Oliva. "Language, the Primordial Labor of History: A Critique of Critical Social Theory in Habermas." *Cultural Hermeneutics*, 1 (February 1974), 325-82.

Bleicher, Josef. *Contemporary Hermeneutics: Hermeneutics as Method, Philosophy and Critique*. London: Routledge & Kegan Paul, 1980.

Bocock, Robert. *Freud and Modern Society: An Outline and Analysis of Freud's Sociology*. New York: Holmes & Meier, 1978.

Bohman, James F. "Emancipation and Rhetoric: The Perlocutions and Illocutions of the Social Critic." *Philosophy and Rhetoric*, 21 (1988), 185-204.

Bolaffi, Angelo. "Notes and Commentary: An Interview with Juergen [sic] Habermas." *Telos*, 39 (Spring 1979), 163-72.

Bologh, Roslyn Wallach. *Dialectical Phenomenology: Marx's Method*. London: Routledge & Kegan Paul, 1979.

Botstein, Leon. "German Terrorism from Afar." *Partisan Review*, 46 (1979), 188-204.

Bottomore, Tom. *The Frankfurt School*. New York: Tavistock, 1984.

Boyne, Roy, and Scott Lash. "Communicative Rationality and Desire." *Telos*, 61 (Fall 1984), 152-58.

Brand, A. "Interests and the Growth of Knowledge — A Comparison of Weber, Popper and Habermas." *Netherlands' Journal of Sociology*, 13 (July 1977), 1-20.

Brand, A. "Truth and Habermas' Paradigm of a Critical Social Science." *Sociologische Gids*, 23 (September-October 1976), 285-95.

Brewster, Philip, and Carl Howard Buchner. "Language and Critique: Jürgen Habermas on Walter Benjamin." *New German Critique*, 17 (Spring 1979), 15-29.

Brown, Michael E. "Sociology as Critical Theory." In *Theoretical Perspectives in Sociology*. Ed. Scott G. McNall. New York: St. Martin's, 1979, pp. 251-75.

Bubner, Rüdiger. "Summation." *Cultural Hermeneutics*, 2 (February 1975), 359-62.

Bubner, Rüdiger. "Theory and Practice in the Light of the Hermeneutic-Criticist Controversy." *Cultural Hermeneutics*, 2 (February 1975), 337-52.

Burleson, Brant R. "On the Foundations of Rationality: Toulmin, Habermas, and the *A Priori* of Reason." *Journal of the American Forensic Association*, 16 (Fall 1979), 112-27.

Burleson, Brant R., and Susan L. Kline. "Habermas' Theory of Communication: A Critical Explication." *Quarterly Journal of Speech*, 65 (December 1979), 412-28.

Campbell, John Angus. "A Rhetorical Interpretation of History." *Rhetorica*, 2 (Autumn 1984), 227-66.

Canovan, Margaret. "A Case of Distorted Communication: A Note on Habermas and Arendt." *Political Theory*, 11 (February 1983), 105-16.

Cerroni, Umberto. "The Problem of Democracy in Mass Society." Trans. Patrizia Heckle. *Praxis International*, 3 (April 1983), 34-53.

Cohen, Jean. "Why More Political Theory?" *Telos*, 40 (Summer 1979), 70-94.

Connerton, Paul, ed. *Critical Sociology: Selected Readings*. New York: Penguin, 1976.

Connerton, Paul. *The Tragedy of Enlightenment: An Essay on the Frankfurt School*. Cambridge: Cambridge University Press, 1980.

Craib, Ian. *Modern Social Theory: From Parsons to Habermas*. New York: St. Martin's, 1984.

Culler, Jonathan. "Communicative Competence and Normative Force." *New German Critique*, 35 (Spring/Summer 1985), 133-44.

Cushman, Donald P., and David Dietrich. "A Critical Reconstruction of Jürgen Habermas' Holistic Approach to Rhetoric as Social Philosophy." *Journal of the American Forensic Association*, 16 (Fall 1979), 128-37.

Dallmayr, Fred R. *Beyond Dogma and Despair: Toward A Critical Phenomenology of Politics*. Notre Dame: University of Notre Dame Press, 1981.

Dallmayr, Fred R. "Critical Theory Criticized: Habermas's *Knowledge and Human Interests* and its Aftermath." *Philosophy of the Social Sciences*, 2 (September 1972), 211-29.

Dallmayr, Fred R. "Reason and Emancipation: Notes on Habermas." *Man and World: An International Philosophical Review*, 5 (1972), 79-109.

Dallmayr, Fred R. *Twilight of Subjectivity: Contributions to a Post-Individualist Theory of Politics*. Amherst: University of Massachusetts Press, 1981.

Davey, Nicholas. "Habermas's Contribution to Hermeneutic Theory." *Journal of the British Society for Phenomenology*, 16 (May 1985), 109-31.

Davis, Charles. *Theology and Political Society: The Hulsean Lectures in the University of Cambridge, 1978*. Cambridge: Cambridge University Press, 1980.

Deetz, Stanley. "Representation of Interests and the New Communication Technologies: Issues in Democracy and Policy." In *Communication and the Culture of Technology*. Ed. Martin J. Medhurst, Alberto Gonzalez, and Tarla Rai Peterson. Pullman: Washington State University Press, 1990.

Depew, David J. "The Habermas-Gadamer Debate in Hegelian Perspective." *Philosophy and Social Criticism*, 8 (Winter 1981), 425-46.

Di Norcia, Vincent. "From Critical Theory to Critical Ecology." *Telos*, 22 (Winter 1974-75), 85-95.

Disco, Cornelis. "Critical Theory as Ideology of the New Class: Rereading Jürgen Habermas." *Theory and Society*, 8 (September 1979), 159-214.

Ealy, Steven D. *Communication, Speech, and Politics*. Washington, D.C.: University Press of America, 1981.

Eyerman, Ron. "Social Movements and Social Theory." *Sociology*, 18 (February 1984), 73-82.

Factor, Regis A., and Stephen P. Turner. "The Critique of Positivist Social Science in Leo Strauss and Jürgen Habermas." *Sociological Analysis and Theory*, 7 (1977), 185-206.

Farganis, James. "A Preface to Critical Theory." *Theory and Society*, 2 (Winter 1975), 483-508.

Farrell, Thomas B. "Habermas on Argumentation Theory: Some Emerging Topics." *Journal of the American Forensic Association*, 16 (Fall 1979), 77-82.

Farrell, Thomas B. "The Ideality of Meaning of Argument: A Revision of Habermas." In *Dimensions of Argument: Proceedings of the Second Summer Conference on Argumentation.* Ed. George Ziegelmueller and Jack Rhodes. Annandale, VA: Speech Communication Association, October 15, 1981, pp. 905-26.

Farrell, Thomas B. "Knowledge, Consensus, and Rhetorical Theory." *Quarterly Journal of Speech*, 62 (February 1976), 1-14.

Farrell, Thomas B., and James Aune. "Critical Theory and Communication: A Selective Literature Review." *Quarterly Journal of Speech*, 65 (February 1979), 93-120.

Faught, Jim. "Objective Reason and the Justification of Norms." *California Sociologist*, 4 (Winter 1981), 33-53.

Feenberg, Andrew. *Lukács, Marx and the Sources of Critical Theory.* Totowa, NJ: Rowman Littlefield, 1981.

Ferrara, Allessandro. "A Critique of Habermas's *Diskursethik.*" In *The Interpretation of Dialogue.* Ed. Tullio Maranhao. Chicago: University of Chicago Press, pp. 303-37.

Fields, A. Belden. "In Defense of Political Economy and Systemic Analysis: A Critique of Prevailing Theoretical Approaches to the New Social Movements." In *Marxism and the Interpretation of Culture.* Ed. Cary Nelson and Lawrence Grossberg. Urbana: University of Illinois Press, 1988, pp. 141-56.

Fischer, Frank. "Science and Critique in Political Discourse: Elements of a Postpositivistic Methodology." *New Political Science*, 9/10 (Summer/Fall 1982), 9-32.

Fisher, Walter R. "The Narrative Paradigm: An Elaboration." *Communication Monographs*, 52 (December 1985), 347-67.

Fitzgerald, Ross, ed. *Human Needs and Politics.* New York: Pergamon, 1977.

Flöistad, Guttorm. "Social Concepts of Action: Notes on Habermas's Proposal for a Social Theory of Knowledge." *Inquiry*, 13 (Summer 1970), 175-98.

Flood, Tony. "Jürgen Habermas's Critique of Marxism." *Science and Society*, 41 (Winter 1977-78), 448-64.

Flynn, Bernard Charles. "Reading Habermas Reading Freud." *Human Studies*, 8 (1985), 57-76.

Forester, John. "A Critical Empirical Framework for the Analysis of Public Policy." *New Political Science*, 3 (Summer-Fall 1982), 33-61.

Forester, John, ed. *Critical Theory and Public Life.* Cambridge: MIT Press, 1985.

Forester, John. "Hannah Arendt and Critical Theory: A Critical Response." *Journal of Politics*, 43 (February 1981), 196-202.

Forester, John. "The Policy Analysis-Critical Theory Affair: Wildavsky and Habermas as Bedfellows?" *Journal of Public Policy*, 2 (May 1982), 145-64.

Foster, William P. "Administration and the Crisis in Legitimacy: A Review of Habermasian Thought." *Harvard Educational Review*, 50 (November 1980), 496-505.

Francesconi, Robert. "The Implications of Habermas's Theory of Legitimation for Rhetorical Criticism." *Communication Monographs*, 53 (March 1986), 16-35.

Frankel, Boris. "Habermas Talking: An Interview." *Theory and Society*, 1 (1974), 37-58.

Frankel, Boris. "The State of the State: Marxist Theories after Leninism." *Theory and Society*, 7 (January-March 1979), 199-42.

Fraser, Nancy. "What's Critical About Critical Theory? The Case of Habermas and Gender." *New German Critique*, 35 (Spring/Summer 1985), 97-131.

Freiberg, J.W., ed. *Critical Sociology: European Perspectives*. New York: Irvington, 1979.

Frisby, David. "The Frankfurt School: Critical Theory and Positivism." In *Approaches to Sociology: An Introduction to Major Trends in British Sociology*. Ed. John Rex. London: Routledge & Kegan Paul, 1974, pp. 205-29.

Gadamer, Hans-Georg. *Philosophical Hermeneutics*. Trans. and ed. David E. Linge. Berkeley: University of California Press, 1976.

Gadamer, Hans-Georg. "Responses to 'Theory and Practice.'" *Cultural Hermeneutics*, 2 (February 1975), 357.

Gall, Robert S. "Between Tradition and Critique." *Auslegung*, 8 (Winter 1981), 5-18.

Gay, William. "Justification of Legal Authority: Phenomenology vs Critical Theory." *Journal of Social Philosophy*, 11 (May 1980), 1-8.

Geuss, Raymond. *The Idea of a Critical Theory: Habermas and the Frankfurt School*. New York: Cambridge University Press, 1981.

Giddens, Anthony. *Central Problems in Social Theory: Action, Structure and Contradiction in Social Analysis*. Berkeley: University of California Press, 1979.

Giddens, Anthony. *New Rules of Sociological Method: A Positive Critique of Interpretative Sociologies*. New York: Basic, 1976.

Giddens, Anthony. *Profiles and Critiques in Social Theory*. Berkeley: University of California Press, 1982.

Giddens, Anthony. "Reason Without Revolution? Habermas's *Theorie Des Kommunikativen Handelns*." *Praxis International*, 2 (October 1982), 318-38.

Giddens, Anthony. *Studies in Social and Political Theory*. London: Hutchinson, 1977.

Görtzen, René, and Frederik Van Gelder. "Jürgen Habermas: The Complete Oeuvre. A Bibliography of Primary Literature, Translations and Reviews." *Human Studies*, 2 (October 1979), 285-300.

Gottlieb, Roger S. "The Contemporary Critical Theory of Jürgen Habermas." *Ethics*, 91 (January 1981), 280-95.

Gottlieb, Roger S. "Habermas and Critical-Reflective Emancipation." In *Rationality To-Day*. Ed. Theodore F. Geraets. Ottawa: University of Ottawa Press, 1979, pp. 434-40.

Gouldner, Alvin W. *The Dialectic of Ideology and Technology: The Origins, Grammar and Future of Ideology*. New York: Seabury, 1976.

Gouldner, Alvin W. *The Future of Intellectuals and the Rise of the New Class: A Frame of Reference, Theses, Conjectures, Arguments, and an Historical Perspective on the Role of Intellectuals and Intelligentsia in the International Class Contest of the Modern Era*. New York: Seabury, 1979.

Gross, David. "On Critical Theory." *Humanities in Society*, 4 (Winter 1981), 89-100.

Gutting, Gary. "Continental Philosophy of Science." In *Current Research in Philosophy of Science*. Ed. Peter D. Asquith and Henry E. Kyburg, Jr. East Lansing, MI: Philosophy of Science Association, 1979.

Haes, Julian. "The Problem of Cultural Relativism: Habermas and the Curriculum." *Sociological Review*, 28 (November 1980), 717-43.

Hall, J. A. "Gellner and Habermas on Epistemology and Politics or Need We Feel Disenchanted?" *Philosophy of the Social Sciences*, 12 (December 1982), 387-407.

Hall, John A. Diagnoses of Our Time: Six Views on Our Social Condition. London: Heinemann Educational, 1981.

Hamilton, Peter. *Knowledge and Social Structure: An Introduction to the Classical Argument in the Sociology of Knowledge.* Boston: Routledge & Kegan Paul, 1974.

Hartmann, Klaus. "Human Agency Between Life-World and System: Habermas's Latest Version of Critical Theory." *Journal of the British Society for Phenomenology*, 16 (May 1985), 145-55.

Hearn, Francis. "Toward a Critical Theory of Play." *Telos*, 30 (Winter 1976-77), 145-60.

Heather, Gerald P., and Matthew Stolz. "Hannah Arendt and the Problem of Critical Theory." *Journal of Politics*, 41 (February 1979), 2-22.

Heather, Gerald P., and Matthew F. Stolz. "Reply to Professor Forester." *Journal of Politics*, 43 (February 1981), 203-07.

Hekman, Susan. "Some Notes on the Universal and Conventional in Social Theory: Wittgenstein and Habermas." *Social Science Journal*, 20 (April 1983), 1-15.

Held, David. "The Battle Over Critical Theory." *Sociology*, 12 (September 1978), 553-60.

Held, David. *Introduction to Critical Theory: Horkheimer to Habermas.* Berkeley: University of California Press, 1980.

Held, David, and Larry Simon. "Habermas' Theory of Crisis in Late Capitalism." *Radical Philosophers' Newsjournal*, 6 (1976), 1-19.

Held, David, and Lawrence Simon. "Toward Understanding Habermas." *New German Critique*, 7 (Winter 1976), 136-45.

Heller, Agnes. "The Discourse Ethics of Habermas: Critique and Appraisal." *Thesis Eleven*, 10/11 (November/March 1984-85), 5-17.

Heller, Agnes. "Marxist Ethics and the Future of Eastern Europe: An Interview with Agnes Heller." Trans. David J. Parent. *Telos*, 38 (Winter 1978-79), 153-74.

Hesse, Mary. "In Defence of Objectivity." *British Academy*, 58 (1972), 275-92.

Hesse, Mary. *Revolutions and Reconstructions in the Philosophy of Science.* Bloomington: Indiana University Press, 1980.

Hill, Melvyn Alan. "Jürgen Habermas: A Social Science of the Mind." *Philosophy of the Social Sciences*, 2 (September 1972), 247-59.

Hohendahl, Peter [Uwe]. "Critical Theory, Public Sphere and Culture. Jürgen Habermas and his Critics." Trans. Marc Silberman. *New German Critique*, 16 (Winter 1979), 89-118.

Hohendahl, Peter [Uwe]. "The Dialectic of Enlightenment Revisited: Habermas' Critique of the Frankfurt School." *New German Critique*, 35 (Spring/Summer 1985), 3-26.

Hohendahl, Peter [Uwe]. *The Institution of Criticism.* Ithaca, NY: Cornell University Press, 1982, pp. 242-80.

Hohendahl, Peter [Uwe]. "Jürgen Habermas: 'The Public Sphere' (1964)." Trans. Patricia Russian. *New German Critique*, 3 (Fall 1974), 45-48.

Hollinger, Robert. "Practical Reason and Hermeneutics." *Philosophy and Rhetoric*, 18 (1985), 113-22.

Honneth, Axel. "Communication and Reconciliation: Habermas' Critique of Adorno." *Telos*, 39 (Spring 1979), 45-61.

Honneth, Axel. "Moral Consciousness and Class Domination: Some Problems in the Analysis of Hidden Morality." Trans. Mitchell G. Ash. *Praxis International*, 2 (April 1982), 12-25.

Honneth, Axel. "Work and Instrumental Action." Trans. Mitchell G. Ash. *New German Critique*, 26 (Spring 1982), 31-54.

Honneth, Axel. "Work and Instrumental Action: On the Normative Basis of Critical Theory." Trans. Mitchell G. Ash. *Thesis Eleven*, 5/6 (1982), 162-84.

Honneth, Axel, Eberhard Knödler-Bunte, and Arno Widman. "The Dialectics of Rationalization: An Interview with Jürgen Habermas." *Telos*, 49 (Fall 1981), 5-31.

Horster, Detlev, and Willem van Reijen. "Interview with Jürgen Habermas: Starnberg, March, 23, 1979." Trans. Ron Smith. *New German Critique*, 18 (Fall 1979), 29-43.

How, Alan R. "A Case of Creative Misreading: Habermas's Evaluation of Gadamer's Hermeneutics." *Journal of the British Society for Phenomenology*, 16 (May 1985), 132-44.

How, Alan R. "Dialogue as Productive Limitation in Social Theory: The Habermas-Gadamer Debate." *Journal of the British Society for Phenomenology*, 11 (May 1980), 131-43.

Howard, Dick. *The Marxian Legacy*, 2nd ed. Minneapolis: University of Minnesota Press, 1988.

Howard, Dick. "Moral Development and Ego Identity: A Clarification." *Telos*, 27 (Spring 1976), 176-82.

Howard, Dick. "A Politics in Search of the Political." Theory and Society, 1 (Fall 1974), 271-306.

Hoy, David Couzens. *The Critical Circle: Literature, History, and Philosophical Hermeneutics*. Berkeley: University of California Press, 1978.

Hummel, Ralph P. *The Bureaucratic Experience*, 2nd ed. New York: St. Martin's 1982.

Huyssen, Andreas. "Mapping the Postmodern." *New German Critique*, 33 (Fall 1984), 5-52.

Inglis, Fred. "Good and Bad Habitus: Bourdieu, Habermas and the Condition of England." *Sociological Review*, 27 (May 1979), 353-69.

Ingram, David. *Habermas and the Dialectic of Reason*. New Haven: Yale University Press, 1987.

Ingram, Daavid. "The Historical Genesis of the Gadamer/Habermas Controversy." *Auslegung*, 10 (Spring/Summer 1983), 86-151.

Ingram, David. "The Possibility of a Communication Ethic Reconsidered: Habermas, Gadamer, and Bourdieu on Discourse." *Man and World*, 15 (1982), 149-61.

Jacobson, David C. "Rationalization and Emancipation in Weber and Habermas." *Graduate Faculty Journal of Sociology*, 1 (Winter 1976), 18-31.

James, David. "From Marx to Incoherence: A Critique of Habermas." *Journal of Social Philosophy*, 12 (January 1981), 10-16.

Jansen, Sue Curry. "Power and Knowledge: Toward a New Critical Synthesis." *Journal of Communication*, 33 (Summer 1983), 342-54.

Jay, Martin. *The Dialectical Imagination: A History of the Frankfurt School and the Institute of Social Research*, 1923-1950. Boston: Little, Brown, 1973.

Jay, Martin. "Habermas and Modernism." *Praxis International*, 4 (April 1984), 1-15.

Jay, Martin. *Marxism and Totality: The Adventures of a Concept from Lukács to Habermas*. Berkeley: University of California Press, 1984.

Jay, Martin. "Should Intellectual History Take a Linguistic Turn? Reflections on the Habermas-Gadamer Debate." In *Modern European Intellectual History: Reappraisals and New Perspectives*. Ed. Dominick LaCapra and Steven L. Kaplan. Ithaca: Cornell University Press, 1982.

Keane, John. "Elements of a Radical Theory of Public Life: From Tönnies to Habermas and Beyond." *Canadian Journal of Political and Social Theory*, 6 (Fall 1982), 11-49.

Keane, John. "Notes: On Belaboring the Theory of Economic Crisis: A Replay to Laska." *New German Critique*, 4 (Winter 1975), 125-30.

Keane, John. "On Tools and Language: Habermas on Work and Interaction." *New German Critique*, 6 (Fall 1975), 82-100.

Keat, Russell. *The Politics of Social Theory: Habermas, Freud and the Critique of Positivism*. Chicago: University of Chicago Press, 1981.

Kellner, Douglas. "Critical Theory, Democracy and Human Rights." *New Political Science*, 1 (1979), 12-18.

Kelly, Michael. "The Dialectical/Dialogical Structure of Ethical Reflection." *Philosophy and Rhetoric*, 22 (1989), 174-93.

Kemp, Ray, and Philip Cooke. "Repoliticising the 'Public Sphere': A Reconsideration of Habermas." *Social Praxis: International and Interdisciplinary Quarterly of Social Sciences*, 8 (1981), 125-42.

Kisiel, Theodore. "Habermas' Purge of Pure Theory: Critical Theory Without Ontology?" *Human Studies*, 1 (April 1978), 167-83.

Kisiel, Theodore. "Ideology Critique and Phenomenology: The Current Debate in German Philosophy." *Philosophy Today*, 14 (1971), 151-60.

Kline, Susan L. "The Ideal Speech Situation: A Discussion of its Presuppositions." In *Dimensions of Argument: Proceedings of the Second Summer Conference on Argumentation*. Ed. George Ziegelmueller and Jack Rhodes. Annandale, VA: Speech Communication Association, October 15, 1981, pp. 927-39.

Kline, Susan L. "Toward a Contemporary Linguistic Interpretation of the Concept of Stasis." *Journal of the American Forensic Association*, 16 (Fall 1979), 95-103.

Kolakowski, Leszek. *Main Currents of Marxism: Its Origin, Growth, and Dissolution*. Vol. III. Trans. P. S. Falla. Oxford: Clarendon, 1978.

Kolakowski, Leszek. *Main Currents of Marxism: Its Rise, Growth, and Dissolution*. Vol. I. Trans. P. S. Falla. Oxford: Clarendon, 1978.

Kortian, Garbis. *Metacritique: The Philosophical Argument of Jürgen Habermas*. Trans. John Raffan. Cambridge: Cambridge University Press, 1980.

Krueger, Marlis. "Notes on a Materialistic Theory of Interaction." *Cornell Journal of Social Relations*, 11 (Spring 1976), 97-104.

LaCapra, Dominick. "Habermas and the Grounding of Critical Theory." *History and Theory*, 16 (1977), 237-64.

Lash, Scott. "Postmodernity and Desire." *Theory and Society*, 14 (January 1985), 1-33.

Laska, Peter. "Notes: A Note on Habermas and the Labor Theory of Value." *New German Critique*, 3 (Fall 1974), 154-62.

Leiss, William. *The Domination of Nature*. New York: George Braziller, 1972.

Leiss, William. ''The Problem of Man and Nature in the Work of the Frankfurt School.''
Philosophy of the Social Sciences, 5 (1975), 163-72.

Lemert, Charles C. *Sociology and the Twilight of Man: Homocentrism and Discourse in Sociological Theory*. Carbondale: Southern Illinois University Press, 1979.

Lenhardt, Christian K. ''Rise and Fall of Transcendental Anthropology.'' *Philosophy of the Social Sciences*, 2 (September 1972), 231-46.

Lepenies, Wolf. ''Anthropology and Social Criticism: A View of the Controversy Between Arnold Gehlen and Jürgen Habermas.'' *Human Context*, 3 (July 1971), 205-25.

Lessnoff, Michael. ''Technique, Critique and Social Science.'' In *Philosophical Disputes in the Social Sciences*. Ed. S. C. Brown. [Atlantic Highlands], NJ: Humanities, 1979, pp. 89-116.

Lobkowicz, Nicolaus. ''Interest and Objectivity.'' *Philosophy of the Social Sciences*, 2 (September 1972), 193-210.

Luban, David. ''On Habermas On Arendt On Power.'' *Philosophy and Social Criticism*, 6 (Spring 1979), 79-95.

Lucaites, John Louis. ''Rhetoric and the Problem of Legitimacy.'' In *Dimensions of Argument: Proceedings of the Second Summer Conference on Argumentation*. Ed. George Ziegelmueller and Jack Rhodes. Annandale, VA: Speech Communication Association, October 15, 1981, pp. 799-811.

McCarthy, Thomas [A.] ''Complexity and Democracy, or The Seducements of Systems Theory.'' *New German Critique*, 35 (Spring/Summer 1985), 27-53.

McCarthy, Thomas [A.]. *The Critical Theory of Jürgen Habermas*. Cambridge: MIT Press, 1978.

McCarthy, Thomas [A.] ''Rationality and Discourse.'' In *Rationality To-Day*. Ed. Theodore F. Geraets. Ottawa: University of Ottawa, 1979, pp. 441-47.

McCarthy, Thomas [A.]. ''Rationality and Relativism in Habermas' Critical Theory.'' *Noûs*, 14 (March 1980), 75-76.

McCarthy, Thomas [A.]. ''Reflections on Rationalization in the Theory of Communicative Action.'' *Praxis International*, 4 (July 1984), 177-91.

McCarthy, Thomas A. ''Responses to 'Theory and Practice.''' *Cultural Hermeneutics*, 2 (1975), 357.

McCarthy, T[homas] A. ''A Theory of Communicative Competence.'' *Philosophy of the Social Sciences*, 3 (June 1973), 135-56.

McCumber, John. ''Critical Theory and Poetic Interaction.'' *Praxis International*, 5 (October 1985), 268-82.

McGuire, R. R. ''Speech Acts, Communicative Competence and the Paradox of Authority.'' *Philosophy and Rhetoric*, 10 (Winter 1977), 30-45.

McIntosh, Donald. ''Habermas on Freud.'' *Social Research*, 44 (Autumn 1977), 562-98.

McKerrow, Raymie E. ''Critical Rhetoric: Theory and Praxis.'' *Communication Monographs*, 56 (June 1989), 91-111.

McNall, Scott G., ed. *Theoretical Perspectives in Sociology*. New York: St. Martin's, 1979.

Maddox, Randy L. ''Hermeneutic Circle — Vicious or Victorious.'' *Philosophy Today*, 27 (Spring 1983), 66-76.

Madsen, Peter. ''History and Consciousness: Cultural Studies Between Reification and Hegemony.'' *Thesis Eleven*, 5/6 (1982), 204-14.

Mariante, Benjamin R. "The Frankfurt School and the Sociology of Religion: Religion a la Marx and Freud." *Humboldt Journal of Social Relations*, 9 (Fall-Winter 1981/82), 75-89.

Marković, Mihailo. "The Idea of Critique in Social Theory." *Praxis International*, 3 (July 1983), 108-20.

Marx, Werner. "Habermas' Philosophical Conception of History." *Cultural Hermeneutics*, 3 (July 1976), 335-47.

Mellos, Koula. "The Habermasian Perspective in the Critique of Technocratic Consciousness." *Revue de l'Université d'Ottawa*, 47 (October-December 1977), 427-51.

Mendelson, Jack. "The Habermas-Gadamer Debate." *New German Critique*, 18 (1979), 44-73.

Milić, Vojin. "Method of Critical Theory." *Praxis*, 7 (1971), 625-56.

Miller, James. "Some Implications of Nietzsche's Thought for Marxism." *Telos*, 37 (Fall 1978), 22-41.

Misgeld, Dieter. "Between Philosophy and Science: The Critical Theory of the Frankfurt School of Social Research." *Laurentian University Review*, 4 (1972), 22-34.

Misgeld, Dieter. "Critical Hermeneutics Versus Neoparsonianism?" *New German Critique*, 35 (Spring/Summer 1985), 55-82.

Misgeld, Dieter. "Discourse and Conversation: The Theory of Communicative Competence and Hermeneutics in the Light of the Debate Between Habermas and Gadamer." *Cultural Hermeneutics*, 4 (December 1977), 321-44.

Misgeld, Dieter. "Habermas's Retreat from Hermeneutics: Systems Integration, Social Integration and the Crisis of Legitimation." *Canadian Journal of Political and Social Theory*, 5 (Winter/Spring 1981), 8-44.

Misgeld, Dieter. "Ultimate Self-Responsibility, Practical Reasoning, and Practical Action: Habermas, Husserl, and Ethnomethodology on Discourse and Action." *Human Studies*, 3 (July 1980), 255-78.

Mueller, Claus. *The Politics of Communication: A Study in the Political Sociology of Language, Socialization, and Legitimation.* New York: Oxford University Press, 1973.

Murray, John Patrick. "Enlightenment Roots of Habermas' Critique of Marx." *Modern Schoolman*, 57 (November 1979), 1-24.

Newman, Jay. "Some Tensions in Spinoza's Ethical Theory." *Indian Philosophical Quarterly*, 7 (April 1980), 357-74.

Nichols, Christopher. "Science or Reflection: Habermas on Freud." *Philosophy of the Social Sciences*, 2 (September 1972), 261-70.

Nielsen, Kai. "Enlightenment and Amoralism." *Agora*, 4 (1979-80), 85-89.

Nielsen, Kai. "The Political Relevance of Habermas." *Radical Philosophers' News-Journal*, 7 (1977), 1-11.

Nielsen, Kai. "Rationality as Emancipation and Enlightenment." *International Studies in Philosophy*, 10 (1978), 33-50.

Nielsen, Kai. "Rationality, Needs and Politics: Remarks on Rationality as Emancipation and Enlightenment." *Cultural Hermeneutics*, 4 (July 1977), 281-308.

Nielsen, Kai. "Technology as Ideology." In *Research In Philosophy & Technology: An Annual Compilation of Research.* Vol. 1. Ed. Paul T. Durbin. Greenwich, CT: Jai, 1978), 131-47.

Nielsen, Kai. "True Needs, Rationality and Emancipation." In *Human Needs and Politics*. Ed. Ross Fitzgerald. Elmsford, NY: Pergamon, 1977, pp. 142-56.

Nordquist, Joan. *Jürgen Habermas: A Bibliography*. Santa Cruz: Reference and Research Services, 1986.

O'Neill, John, ed. *On Critical Theory*. New York: Seabury, 1976.

Overend, Tronn. "Enquiry and Ideology: Habermas' Trichotomous Conception of Science." *Philosophy of the Social Sciences*, 8 (March 1978), 1-13.

Overend, Tronn. "Interests, Objectivity and 'The Positivist Dispute' in Social Theory." *Social Praxis: International and Interdisciplinary Quarterly of Social Sciences*, 6 (1979), 69-91.

Overend, Tronn. "The Socialization of Philosophy: Two Monistic Fallacies in Habermas' Critique of Knowledge." *Philosophical and Phenomenological Research*, 38 (1977), 119-24.

Overend, Tronn. "Social Realism and Social Idealism: Two Competing Orientations on the Relation Between Theory, Praxis, and Objectivity." *Inquiry*, 21 (Autumn 1978), 271-311.

Palermo, James. "Pedagogy as a Critical Hermeneutic." *Cultural Hermeneutics*, 3 (August 1975), 137-46.

Parkinson, G.H.R., ed. *Marx and Marxisms*. Cambridge: Cambridge University Press, 1982.

Petryszak, Nicholas. "The Frankfurt School's Theory of Manipulation." *Journal of Communication*, 27 (Summer 1977), 32-40.

Pilotta, Joseph J. "Pilotta on Habermas." *Quarterly Journal of Speech*, 67 (February 1981), 105-08.

Plaut, Martin. "The Problem of Positivism in the Work of Nicos Poulantzas." *Telos*, 36 (Summer 1978), 159-67.

Plant, Raymond. "Jürgen Habermas and the Idea of Legitimation Crisis." *European Journal of Political Research*, 10 (1982), 341-52.

Posner, Roland. "Discourse as a Means to Enlightenment: On the Theories of Rational Communication of Habermas and Albert." In *Language in Focus: Foundations, Methods and Systems*. Ed. Asa Kasher. Boston: D. Reidel, 1976, pp. 641-60.

Pryor, Bob. "Saving the Public Sphere Through Rational Discourse." In *Dimensions of Argument: Proceedings of the Second Summer Conference on Argumentation*. Ed. George Ziegelmueller and Jack Rhodes. Annandale, VA: Speech Communication Association, October 15, 1981, pp. 848-64.

Pusey, Michael. *Jürgen Habermas*. London: Tavistock, 1987.

Radnitzky, Gerard. *Contemporary Schools of Metascience*. New York: Humanities, 1970.

Rasmussen, David M. "Advanced Capitalism and Social Theory: Habermas on the Problem of Legitimation." *Cultural Hermeneutics*, 3 (July 1976), 349-66.

Raulet, Gerard. "The Agony of Marxism and the Victory of the Left." *Telos*, 55 (Spring 1983), 163-78.

Ray, L.J. "Habermas, Legitimation, and the State." *Journal for the Theory of Social Behavior*, 8 (July 1978), 149-63.

Reid, Herbert G., and Ernest J. Yanarella. "Critical Political Theory and Moral

Development: On Kohlberg, Hampden-Turner, and Habermas." *Theory and Society*, 4 (Winter 1977), 505-41.

Ricoeur, Paul. "Ethics and Culture: Habermas and Gadamer in Dialogue." *Philosophy Today*, 17 (1973), 153-65.

Ricoeur, Paul. *Hermeneutics and the Human Sciences: Essays on Language, Action and Interpretation*. Trans. and ed. Iohn B. Thompson. Cambridge: Cambridge University Press, 1981.

Riedmüller, Barbara. "Crisis as Crisis of Legitimation: A Critique of J. Habermas's Concept of a Political Crisis Theory." *International Journal of Politics*, 7 (1977), 83-117.

Rockmore, Tom. "Habermas and the Reconstruction of Historical Materialism." *Journal of Value Inquiry*, 13 (Fall 1979), 195-206.

Rockmore, Tom. *Habermas on Historical Materialism*. Bloomington: Indiana University Press, 1989.

Rockmore, Tom. "Marxian Man." *Monist*, 61 (January 1978), 56-71.

Roderick, Rick. *Habermas and the Foundations of Critical Theory*. New York: St. Martin's, 1986.

Roderick, Rick. "Habermas on Rationality." *Man and World*, 18 (1985), 203-18.

Rodger, John J. "On the Degeneration of the Public Sphere." *Political Studies*, 33 (June 1985), 203-17.

Rorty, Richard. "Epistemological Behaviorism and the De-Transcendentalization of Analytic Philosophy." *Neue Hefte für Philosophie*, 14 (1978), 115-42.

Rossvaer, Viggo. *Kant's Moral Philosophy: An Interpretation of the Categorical Imperative*. Oslo: Universiteforlag, 1979.

Rotenstreich, Nathan. "Conservatism and Traditionalism." *Praxis International*, 3 (January 1984), 412-22.

Roth, Mike. "With Marx Against Marx? Histomat$_1$ and Histomat$_2$: An Alternative to Juergen [sic] Habermas' Theses Towards the Reconstruction of Historical Materialism." Trans. Michael Eldred. *Thesis Eleven*, 3 (1982), 135-47.

Rule, James B. *Insight and Social Betterment: A Preface to Applied Social Science*. New York: Oxford University Press, 1978.

Rumberg, Dirk. "Literature on the German 'Historikerstreit.'" *Millennium: Journal of International Studies*, 17 (1988), 351-56.

Sabia, Daniel R., Jr., and Jerald Wallulis, eds. *Changing Social Science: Critical Theory and Other Critical Perspectives*. Albany: State University of New York Press, 1983.

Schmidt, James. "Jürgen Habermas and the Difficulties of Enlightenment." *Social Research*, 49 (Spring 1982), 181-208.

Schmidt, James. "Offensive Critical Theory? Reply to Honneth." *Telos*, 39 (Spring 1979), 62-70.

Schmidt, James. "Praxis and Temporality: Karel Kosik's Political Theory." *Telos*, 33 (Fall 1977), 71-84.

Schrag, Calvin O. *Communicative Rhetoric and the Claims of Reason*. Evanston, IL: School of Speech, Northwestern University, 1989.

Schroyer, Trent. *The Critique of Domination: The Origins and Development of Critical Theory*. New York: George Braziller, 1973.

Schroyer, Trent. "Critique of the Instrumental Interest in Nature." *Social Research*, 50 (Spring 1983), 158-84.

Schroyer, Trent. "The Dialectical Foundations of Critical Theory: Jürgen Habermas' Metatheoretical Investigations." *Telos*, 12 (Summer 1972), 93-114.

Schroyer, Trent. "Marx and Habermas." *Continuum*, 8 (1970), 52-64.

Schroyer, Trent. "Methodological Grounds for a Reflexive Science." *Contemporary Crises*, 8 (January 1984), 19-32.

Schroyer, Trent. "The Re-politicization of the Relations of Production: An Interpretation of Jürgen Habermas' Analytic Theory of Late Capitalist Development." *New German Critique*, 5 (Spring 1975), 107-28.

Schwartz, Ronald David. "Habermas and the Politics of Discourse." *Canadian Journal of Political and Social Theory*, 5 (Winter/Spring 1981), 45-68.

Schweickart, Patrocinio. " 'What Are We Doing, Really?—Feminist Criticism and the Problem of Theory.' " *Canadian Journal of Political and Social Theory*, 9 (Winter 1985), 148-64.

Scott, John. "On the Classification and Synthesis of Sociological Knowledge." *Jewish Journal of Sociology*, 18 (December 1976), 155-64.

Scott, John P. "Critical Social Theory: An Introduction and Critique." *British Journal of Sociology*, 29 (March 1978), 1-21.

Seidman, Steven, ed. *Jürgen Habermas on Society and Politics: A Reader*. Boston: Beacon, 1989.

Sennat, Julius. *Habermas and Marxism: An Appraisal*. Beverly Hills: Sage, 1979.

Sewart, John J. "Critical Theory and the Critique of Conservative Method." *American Sociologist*, 13 (February 1978), 15-22.

Shapiro, H. Svi. "Habermas, O'Connor, and Wolfe, and the Crisis of the Welfare-Capitalist State: Conservative Politics and the Roots of Educational Policy in the 1980s." *Educational Theory*, 33 (Summer-Fall 1983), 135-47.

Shapiro, Jeremy J. "The Dialectic of Theory and Practice in the Age of Technological Rationality: Herbert Marcuse and Jürgen Habermas." In *Unknown Dimension: European Marxism since Lenin*. Ed. Dick Howard and Karl E. Klare. New York: Basic, 1972, pp. 276-303.

Shapiro, Jeremy J. "From Marcuse to Habermas." *Continuum*, 8 (1970), 65-76.

Shapiro, Jeremy J. "Reply to Miller's Review of Habermas' Legitimation Crisis." *Telos*, 27 (Spring 1976), 170-76.

Siebert, Rudolf. "Communication Without Domination." In *Communication in the Church*. Ed. Gregory Baum and Andrew Greeley. New York: Seabury, 1978, pp. 81-94.

Siebert, Rudolf J. *The Critical Theory of Religion; The Frankfurt School: From Universal Pragmatic to Political Theology*. New York: Mouton, 1985.

Siebert, Rudolf J. *From Critical Theory of Society to Theology of Communicative Praxis*. Washington, D.C.: University Press of America, 1979.

Silvers, Stuart. "The Critical Theory of Science." *Zeitschrift für Allgemein Wissenschafts Theorie*, 4 (1973), 108-32.

Skjei, Erling. "A Comment on Performative, Subject, and Proposition in Habermas's Theory of Communication." *Inquiry*, 28 (March 1985), 87-122.

Smart, Barry. *Sociology, Phenomenology and Marxian Analysis: A Critical Discussion* of the Theory and Practice of a Science of Society. London: Routledge & Kegan Paul, 1976.

Smith, A. Anthony. "Two Theories of Historical Materiallism: G. A. Cohen and Jürgen Habermas." *Theory and Society*, 13 (July 1984), 513-40.

Smith, M. B. "Dialectical Social-Psychology: Comments on a Symposium." *Personality and Social Psychology Bulletin*, 3 (Fall 1977), 719-24.

Smith, Tony. "The Scope of the Social Sciences in Weber and Habermas." *Philosophy and Social Criticism*, 8 (Spring 1981), 69-83.

Snedeker, George. "Western Marxism and the Problem of History." *Psychology and Social Theory*, 4 (1984), 41-50.

Sollner, Alfons. "Anxiety and Politics: Neo-Conservatism and Critical Theory." *Telos*, 60 (Summer 1984), 129-31.

Stockman, Norman. "Habermas, Marcuse and the *Aufhebung* of Science and Technology." *Philosophy of the Social Sciences*, 8 (March 1978), 15-35.

Sullivan, William M. "Communication and the Recovery of Meaning: An Interpretation of Habermas." *International Philosophical Quarterly*, 18 (March 1978), 69-86.

Sullivan, William M. "Two Options in Modern Social Theory: Habermas and Whitehead." *International Philosophical Quarterly*, 15 (March 1975), 83-98.

Sumner, Colin. "The Rule of Law and Civil Rights in Contemporary Marxist Theory." *Kapitalistate*, 9 (1981), 63-91.

Taylor, Laurie. "Freud." *New Society*, 42 (December 8, 1977), 515-18.

Therborn, Goran. "Jürgen Habermas: A New Eclecticism." *New Left Review*, 67 (May-June 1971), 69-83.

Thompson, John B. *Critical Hermeneutics: A Study in the Thought of Paul Ricoeur and Jürgen Habermas*. Cambridge: Cambridge University Press, 1981.

Thompson, John B. "Ideology and the Critique of Domination II." *Canadian Journal of Political and Social Theory*, 8 (Winter/Spring 1984), 179-96.

Thompson, John B., and David Held. *Habermas: Critical Debates*. Cambridge: MIT Press, 1982.

Torpey, J. "Ethics and Critical Theory: From Horkheimer to Habermas." *Telos*, 69 (Fall 1986), 68-84.

Tranöy, Kurt Erik. "The Foundations of Cognitive Activity: An Historical and Systematic Sketch." *Inquiry*, 19 (Summer 1976), 131-50.

Turski, George. "Some Considerations on Intersubjectivity and Language." *Gnosis*, 1 (Spring 1979), 29-44.

Tymieniecka, Anna-Teresa, and Calvin O. Schrag, eds. *Foundations of Morality, Human Rights, and the Human Sciences: Phenomenology in a Foundational Dialogue with the Human Sciences*. London: D. Reidel, 1983.

van den Berg, Axel. "Critical Theory: Is There Still Hope?" *American Journal of Sociology*, 86 (November 1980), 449-78.

Van Hooft, Stan. "Habermas' Communicative Ethics." *Social Praxis: International and Interdisciplinary Quarterly of Social Sciences*, 4 (1976-77), 147-75.

Verene, Donald Phillip, ed. *Hegel's Social and Political Thought: The Philosophy of Objective Spirit*. [Atlantic Highlands], NJ: Humanities, 1980.

Ware, Robert X. "Habermas's Evolutions." *Canadian Journal of Philosophy*, 12 (September 1982), 591-620.

Wellmer, Albrecht. *Critical Theory of Society*. New York: Herder and Herder, 1971.

Wellmer, Albrecht. "Reason, Utopia, and the Dialectic of Enlightenment." *Praxis International*, 3 (July 1983), 83-107.

Wenzel, Joseph W. "Habermas' Ideal Speech Situation: Some Critical Questions." In *Dimensions of Argument: Proceedings of the Second Summer Conference on Argumentation*. Ed. George Ziegelmueller and Jack Rhodes. Annandale, VA: Speech Communication Association, October 15, 1981, pp. 940-54.

Wenzel, Joseph W. "Jürgen Habermas and the Dialectical Perspective on Argumentation." *Journal of the American Forensic Association*, 16 (Fall 1979), 83-94.

White, Stephen K. "Habermas' Communicative Ethics and the Development of Moral Consciousness." *Cultural Hermeneutics*, 2 (1984), 25-47.

White, Stephen K. "On the Normative Structure of Action: Gewirth and Habermas." *Review of Politics*, 44 (April 1982), 282-301.

White, Stephen K. "Reason and Authority in Habermas: A Critique of the Critics." *American Political Science Review*, 74 (December 1980), 1007-17.

White, Stephen K. *The Recent Work of Jürgen Habermas: Reason, Justice and Modernity*. Cambridge: Cambridge University Press, 1988.

Whitebook, Joel. "The Problem of Nature in Habermas." *Telos*, 40 (Summer 1979), 41-69.

Wilbur, Ken. *A Sociable God: A Brief Introduction to a Transcendental Sociology*. San Francisco: McGraw-Hill, 1983.

Wilby, Peter. "Habermas and the Language of the Modern State." *New Society*, 47 (March 22, 1979), 667-69.

Wilson, H.T. "The Meaning and Significance of 'Empirical Method' for the Critical Theory of Society." *Canadian Journal of Political and Social Theory*, 3 (Fall 1979), 57-68.

Wilson, H.T. "The Poverty of Sociology: 'Society' as Concept and Object in Sociological Theory." *Philosophy of the Social Sciences*, 8 (June 1978), 187-204.

Wilson, H.T. "Response to Ray." *Philosophy of the Social Sciences*, 11 (March 1981), 45-48.

Winfield, Richard. "The Dilemma of Labor." *Telos*, 24 (Summer 1975), 115-28.

Winters, Lawrence E. "Habermas' Theory of Truth and Its Centrality in His Critical Project." *Graduate Faculty Philosophical Journal*, 3 (Fall-Winter 1973), 1-21.

Wisman, Jon D. "Toward a Humanist Reconstruction of Economic Science." *Journal of Economic Issues*, 13 (March 1979), 19-48.

Wolff, Ianet. "Hermeneutics and the Critique of Ideology." *Sociological Review*, 23 (November 1975), 811-28.

Wood, Allen W. "Habermas' Defense of Rationalism." *New German Critique*, 35 (Spring/Summer 1985), 145-64.

Wuthnow, Robert, James Davison Hunter, Albert Bergesen, and Edith Kurzweil. *Cultural Analysis: The Work of Peter L. Berger, Mary Douglas, Michel Foucault, and Jürgen Habermas*. Boston: Routledge & Kegan Paul, 1984.

Young, Iris M. "Toward a Critical Theory of Justice." *Social Theory and Practice*, 7 (Fall 1981), 279-302.

Zimmerman, Rolf. "Emancipation and Rationality: Foundational Problems in the Theories of Marx and Habermas." *Ratio*, 26 (December 1984), 143-65.

Subject Index

Name Index

435